LAW, MIND AND BRAIN

Medical Law and Ethics

Series Editor
Sheila McLean, Director of the Institute of Law and Ethics in Medicine, School of Law, University of Glasgow

The 21st century seems likely to witness some of the most major developments in medicine and healthcare ever seen. At the same time, the debate about the extent to which science and/or medicine should lead the moral agenda continues, as do questions about the appropriate role for law.

This series brings together some of the best contemporary academic commentators to tackle these dilemmas in a challenging, informed and inquiring manner. The scope of the series is purposely wide, including contributions from a variety of disciplines such as law, philosophy and social sciences.

Other titles in the series

Biotechnology and the Challenge of Property
Property Rights in Dead Bodies, Body Parts, and Genetic Information
Remigius N. Nwabueze
ISBN 978-0-7546-7168-8

Medical Self-Regulation
Crisis and Change
Mark Davies
ISBN 978-0-7546-4459-0

The Jurisdiction of Medical Law
Kenneth Veitch
ISBN 978-0-7546-4944-1

Altruism Reconsidered
Exploring New Approaches to Property in Human Tissue
Edited by Michael Steinmann, Peter Sykora, and Urban Wiesing
ISBN 978-0-7546-7270-8 (forthcoming)

Disclosure Dilemmas
Ethics of Genetic Prognosis After the 'Right to Know/Not to Know' Debate
Edited by Christoph Rehmann-Sutter and Hansjakob Müller
ISBN 978-0-7546-7451-1 (forthcoming)

Law, Mind and Brain

Edited by

MICHAEL FREEMAN
University College London, UK

and

OLIVER R. GOODENOUGH
Vermont Law School, USA

Routledge
Taylor & Francis Group
LONDON AND NEW YORK

First published 2009 by Ashgate Publishing

2 Park Square, Milton Park, Abingdon, Oxfordshire OX14 4RN
52 Vanderbilt Avenue, New York, NY 10017

Routledge is an imprint of the Taylor & Francis Group, an informa business

First issued in paperback 2020

British Library Cataloguing in Publication Data
Law, mind and brain. - (Medical law and ethics)
1. Medical laws and legislation 2. Brain - Research
3. Medical ethics
I. Freeman, Michael D. A. II. Goodenough, Oliver R.
344'.041

Library of Congress Cataloging-in-Publication Data
Law, mind and brain / edited by Michael Freeman and Oliver R. Goodenough.
p. cm. -- (Medical law and ethics)
Includes index.
ISBN 978-0-7546-7013-1 (hardback) 1. Law--Psychological aspects. 2. Forensic psychology. I. Freeman, Michael D. A. II. Goodenough, Oliver R.

K346.L394 2008
340'.19--dc22

2008030034

ISBN 13: 978-0-7546-7013-1 (hbk)
ISBN 13: 978-0-367-60562-9 (pbk)

Contents

List of Figures

List of Tables

List of Contributors

Professor Theodore Y. Blumoff, Mercer University School of Law, USA

Cheryl Boudreau, Assistant Professor, University of California Davis, USA

Naomi Cahn, Professor of Law, George Washington University, USA

June Carbone, Edward A. Smith/Missouri Professor of Law, the Constitution and Society, University of Missouri-Kansas City, USA

Lisa Claydon, Senior Lecturer, Head of Criminal Justice Unit, University of West of England, UK

Professor John Dawson, Faculty of Law, University of Otago, Dunedin, New Zealand

Gregory Decker, J.D.

Katherine Hunt Federle, Professor of Law and Director of Justice for Children Project, Moritz College of Law, Ohio State University, Columbus, Ohio, USA

Neal Feigenson, Professor of Law, Quinnipiac University School of Law, USA

Michael Freeman, Professor of English Law, University College London, UK

Christopher D. Frith, Professor at the Wellcome Trust Centre for Neuroimaging, University College London, UK

Oliver R. Goodenough, Professor of Law, Vermont Law School, USA

Owen D. Jones, Professor in the School of Law and Department of Biological Sciences at Vanderbilt University, Nashville, Tennessee, USA

Adam Kolber, Professor of Law, University of San Diego, School of Law, USA

Bart du Laing, Postdoctoral Fellow of the Research Foundation, Flanders (FWO), Ghent University, Ghent, Belgium

Hakwan C. Lau, Assistant Professor, Department of Psychology, Columbia University, USA

Robin Mackenzie, Director of Medical Law, School of Law, University of Kent, UK

Dr Dean Mobbs, Post-doctoral scientist at Cambridge Neuroscience, University of Cambridge, UK

Catherine J. Ross, Professor of Law, George Washington University Law School, USA

Paul Skendelas, Assistant Public Defender, Franklin County, Ohio, USA

Christina Spiesel, Senior Research Scholar in Law, Yale Law School, USA

Professor Jeffrey Evans Stake, Indiana University, School of Law, USA

Dr George Szmukler, Dean, Institute of Psychiatry, King's College London, and consultant psychiatrist, South London and Maudsley NHS Trust, UK

Dr Florian Wagner-von Papp, Lecturer in Laws, University College London, UK

Preface

Law, Mind and Brain has grown out of an international interdisciplinary colloquium held in the Law Faculty of University College London (UCL) in 2006. The interdisciplinary approach to the study of law is well-rooted at UCL.

Interdisciplinary colloquia have been held there since 1997 on subjects as varied as law and science, law and history, law and sociology, and law and popular culture. The other sponsor of the event, the Gruter Institute for Law and Behavioral Research in the US, is expressly devoted to interdisciplinary approaches and has been a leader in bringing the insights of neuroscience to the study of law.

The colloquium was jointly convened by Michael Freeman of UCL and Oliver Goodenough of Vermont Law School. Three of the papers were previously published in the *International Journal of Law in Context*. We are most grateful to Cambridge University Press for permitting republication in this volume.

Our gratitude is due also to Lisa Penfold, who, as ever, assisted with the administration of the colloquium, and to Linda Thomas, whose secretarial assistance was invaluable. Alison Kirk, our editor at Ashgate, encouraged the project – we are also most grateful to her.

Michael Freeman

Chapter 1
Introduction

Michael Freeman and Oliver R. Goodenough

The human brain has been a focus of medico-legal debates since the late 1960s. It was then that efforts were made to formulate an alternative definition of death, one centred on brain function rather than heart-and-lung function.[1] It was the development of mechanical ventilation and the emergence of heart transplantation which necessitated this new definition of death. The focus is now rather on the brain in the living human, and it is this that this volume concentrates on.

We are seeing the emergence of 'neurolaw'. In a sense this is only what we have wanted to be able to do since ancient times. As long ago as Hippocrates[2] scientists were searching for the source of our behaviour. With the Renaissance there emerged a new understanding of the brain. In the seventeenth century, the French philosopher Descartes wrote of the brain as a machine: he understood it as based on the principles of hydraulics. He accepted that even with a complete understanding of the brain we would still not completely understand behaviour.[3]

In the eighteenth and nineteenth centuries, the pseudo-sciences of physiognomy and phrenology developed. The former tends to be associated today with Lombroso, an Italian proto-criminologist who tried to explain criminal behaviour in biological terms.[4] Phrenology began with the studies of Gall and Spurzheim: their work related brain functions (and character traits) to protuberances on the skull. It provoked considerable interest at the time.[5] Like Lombroso, Gall studied criminals.[6] Cranioscopy was to become standard within criminology. Carl Wernicke, the nineteenth-century German neurologist, was the first to advance the theory that there are 'centres' in the brain. Though not without his critics,

---

1 See Special Issue of *Bioethics*, vol. 4(3), 1990. See further J.L. Bernat, 'The Biophilosophical Basis of Whole-Brain Death' 19(2) *Social Philosophy and Policy* 324–342 (2004).

2 See L.G. Panourias et al., 'Hippocrates: A Pioneer in the Treatment of Head Injuries' 57 *Neurosurgery* 181 (2005).

3 See R. Mazzolini, 'Schemes and Models of the Thinking Machine' in (ed.) P. Corsi, *The Enchanted Loom: Chapters in the History of Neuroscience* (1991).

4 See M. Gibson, *Born to Crime: Cesare Lombroso and the Origins of Biological Criminology* (Westport, CT: Praeger, 2002).

5 It is completely discredited by the findings of neuropsychology.

6 See C. Pogliano, 'Between Form and Function: A New Science of Man' in op cit. note 3, 144–203.

Wernicke's concept of localization is at the root of brain imaging techniques such as fMRI still today.[7]

The discovery of the X-ray in 1895 (by Roentgen) is a watershed event. For the first time it was possible to see into the body without undertaking surgery. The first arteriogram/angiogram in the brain was performed in 1927; the first recording of electrical brain activity (electroencephalography, or EEG) was made in Germany just after the end of the First World War.[8] By the 1970s computers enabled us to make topograhic maps of brain electrical activity. Quantitative EEG (QEEG) became possible and we had brain maps comparing a patient with groups of patients.

Neuroimaging began with the discovery of computerized axial tomography by Hounsfield and Cormack in 1972 (they were awarded the Nobel Prize for this discovery in 1979).[9] As Hounsfield explained in his Nobel lecture:

> Computer tomography ... measures the attenuation of x-ray beams passing through sections of the body from hundreds of different angles, and then, from the evidence of these measurements, a computer is able to reconstruct pictures of the body's interior. Pictures are based on the separate examination of a series of contiguous cross sections, as though we looked at the body separated into a series of thin 'slices'. By doing so, we virtually obtained total three-dimensional information about the body.[10]

Hounsfield's initial focus was the detection of small tumours in the body, but he found he was able to perform a brain scan on a patient who had a frontal lobe brain tumour. Swiftly, technology enabled the development of CT scanning machines. Though initially criticized – there was concern about their cost – they have come to revolutionize neuroscience and, of course, medicine. It has also had an impact on law, and this will increase. Ten years ago Jennifer Kulynych noted:[11] 'It is now common for a psychiatrist to refer to the physiological state of an individual's brain when evaluating a mental disorder. Moreover, such evaluation increasingly includes a reference to neuroimages. In a legal proceeding, the visual impact of such neuroimages is hard to overstate.' How much more so now! And this is not to underestimate its dangers: that it will, for example, license abuse of detainees in the war against terrorism.[12]

7 See G. Fernandez et al., 'Intrasubject Reproductibility of Resurgical Language Lateralization and Mapping Using fMRI' 60 *Neurology* 969 (2003).

8 By Hans Berger, a psychiatrist in Jena.

9 See R.L. Eisenberg, *Radiology: An Illustrated History* (1992), 467.

10 Ibid.

11 'Psychiatric Neurimaging Evidence: A High-Tech Crystal Ball?' 29 *Stanford Law Review* 1249, 1251 (1997).

12 See J.H. Marks, 'Interrogational Neuroimaging in Counterterrorism: A "No-Brainer" or a Human Rights Hazard?' 33 *American Journal of Law and Medicine* 483–500 (2007).

It is not surprising that the study of law has begun to draw insights from this gushing fountain of new knowledge. It was less than a decade ago that the combination of neuroscience with law first began to be mooted in academic circles at meetings[13] and in writings.[14] The Neuroethics Society was founded as recently as 2006. And now the field is bursting open. Some have rightly raised cautionary warnings that we should not get too carried away and lose our intellectual footing in the flood of discovery.[15] But a flood it is becoming. A major piece of validation occurred in recent months when the MacArthur Foundation, a highly visible American philanthropy best known for its 'genius awards', announced a major programme of law and neuroscience research, focused primarily on questions of criminal law.[16] UCL's Law, Mind and Brain colloquium, and the papers in this volume, are examples of this growing ferment and important contributions to it.

The chapters that follow are a good reflection of the state of the field itself. The greatest concentration of attention is on criminal law and justice. Questions of criminal blame and responsibility are addressed in the work of Mobbs, Lau and Jones, Federle and Skendelas, Ross, Blumoff, and Claydon. Federle and Skendelas, and Ross focus on juveniles, in particular on the death penalty issue. It is a rich discussion and a topic where the potential of neuroscience to contribute to our understanding is particularly salient. But this is only the starting point. As both Feigenson and Boudreau remind us, bringing neuroscience into legal deliberations raises both questions of evidence and procedure, and provides tools for studying them. Neurological enhancement and treatment also pose problems for the law. These are analysed here by Dawson and Szmukler, and by Kolber. Stake, and Goodenough and Decker have contributed papers examining how people think about property. Mackenzie explores end-of-life choices; Du Laing contracting, and Spiesel the effect of words and pictures in law.

---

13 See L.A. Frolik, Report: Seventh Annual Teaching Seminar: 'Neurobiology, Human Behavior, and the Law' Squaw Valley, CA June 17–21 (1998); K. Wermke and O. Goodenough Report: Workshop: 'Law and Neuroscience' Humboldt University, Berlin, February 19, 2001. Available at http://www.gruter.org/index.php?option=com_content&task=view&id=145&Itemid=88888947.

S. Taha and K. Nagel, Report: Workshop: 'Neurological Basis for Justice' University of California at San Francisco, CA. November 16, 2001. Available at http://www.gruter.org/index.php?option=com_coutent&task=view&id=154&Itemid=88888947.

S.E. Hyman, Neuroethics: At age 5, field continues to evolve. Available at http://www.dana.org/news/publications/detail.aspx?id=5850.

14 See O.R. Goodenough, 'Mappping Cortical Areas Associated with Legal Reasoning and with Moral Intuition' 41 *Jurimetrics* 429–442. (2001); B. Garland (ed.) *Neuroscience and the Law, Brain, Mind and the Scales of Justice* (Washington, D.C.: Dana Press) (2004); S. Zeki and O.R. Goodenough (eds) Theme Issue 'Law and the Brain' 359 Phil. Trans. R. Soc. Lond 1661–1890 (2004).

15 See S.J. Morse, 'New Neuroscience, Old Problems: Legal Implications of Brain Science' 6 *Cerebrum* 81–90 (2004).

16 See http://www.lawandneuroscienceproject.org/.

Taken individually, each of these is a significant contribution to its targeted field of study. Taken as a body, they make a clear statement that legal scholarship and practice will be increasingly enriched by an interdisciplinary study of law, mind and brain. We have come a long way since Hippocrates.

Chapter 2
Law, Responsibility, and the Brain[1]

Dean Mobbs,[2,3] Hakwan C. Lau,[3,4] Owen D. Jones,[5]
and Christopher D. Frith[3]

Archaeological discoveries of traumatic injuries in primitive hominid skulls strongly hint that our species has a long history of violence.[6] Despite repeated attempts throughout history, including efforts to eliminate violence through the imposition of criminal sanctions, we have yet to dispel our violent nature. Consequently, criminal violence remains a common feature of most societies. As policy-makers seek deeper understandings of criminally violent and anti-social behaviour, many contemporary neuroscientists assume that the essential ingredients of the human condition, including free will, empathy, and morality, are the calculable consequences of an immense assembly of neurons firing. Intuitively, this view opposes Cartesian dualism (i.e., the brain and mind are separate, but interacting, entities) and assumes that violence and anti-social behaviour emanate from a mechanistically determined brain (see Box 2.1).

From this standpoint, the exciting discoveries of neuroscience resonate far beyond mere philosophical banter and may have important implications for the way government institutions, including education and legal systems, operate. For example, to the extent that legal systems attempt both to move behaviour in socially desirable directions and also to adjudicate transgressions fairly, the legal system's effectiveness can be improved by deepening our understandings about why people behave as they do and both how and why people respond to various changes in legal incentives. Specifically, neuroscience may have important implications for both how we understand the multiple influences on violent behaviour and how the legal system may better engage with violent criminals.

---

1 Republished from: Mobbs D, Lau HC, Jones OD, Frith CD (2007) Law, Responsibility, and the Brain. PLoS Biol 5(4): e103.

2 To whom correspondence should be addressed. Email: d.mobbs@mrc-cbu.cam.ac.uk

3 Wellcome Trust Centre for Neuroimaging, University College London, London, UK.

4 Department of Experimental Psychology, University of Oxford, Oxford, UK.

5 School of Law and Department of Biological Sciences at Vanderbilt University, Nashville, Tennessee, USA.

6 Walker PL (2001) A bioarchaeological perspective on the history of violence. Annu Rev Anthropol 30: 573–596.

Box 2.1 Should We Rethink Free Will?

Research linking the brain to anti-social and criminal behaviour also raises neurophilosophical questions concerning our liberty. Most neuroscientists hold that "minds are simply what brains do".[7] Indeed, with the omission of metaphysical constructs like the "mind", many take the view that we are tied to the physical brain and, as a consequence, have little personal choice. A series of classic, yet controversial, studies by Benjamin Libet and colleagues showed that brain activity associated with deliberate decisions can be detected shortly before we are conscious of making the decision.[8] In these studies, participants reported when they first felt the intention to make a spontaneous movement by noting the position of a dot moving on a computer screen. They apparently first became aware of their intentions about 200 milliseconds before action execution, which is later than the onset of the so-called readiness potential (or "bereitschaftspotential") recorded from the scalp prior to movement. Despite criticisms about the accuracy of this timing method, recent research[9, 10] has shown that if anything, the actual onset of conscious intention is likely to be even later. Moreover, psychologists report that our attributions of agency to actions are often illusory.[11]

Despite these claims, free will as a concept is still unlikely to be eliminated. Clearly free will is a prerequisite for moral agency, and for society to run smoothly, we all need to believe that we are in full control of our actions. Not surprisingly, some have tried to find a middle ground in this argument. For example, Raine has entertained the idea that free will should be viewed along a "dimension rather than a dichotomy",[12] while Gazzaniga has argued that "brains are automatic, but people are free".[13] Is it reasonable, however, to posit that some people are more free than others? For example, few can dispute the fact that brain diseases such as schizophrenia and Huntington's disease reduce the ability to act freely. Nonetheless, most juries may never have explicitly discussed the concept of free will.[14] Neurophilosophy may play an important role in understanding and updating the intuitions concerning free will and responsibility that may implicitly underlie juror deliberations.

7 Minsky M (1986) The society of mind. (New York: Simon and Schuster). 339 p.

8 Libet B, Gleason CA, Wright EW, Pearl DK (1983) Time of conscious intention to act in relation to onset of cerebral activity (readiness potential): The unconscious initiation of a freely voluntary act. Brain 106: 623–642.

9 Lau HC, Rogers RD, Passingham RE (2006) On measuring the perceived onsets of spontaneous actions. J Neurosci 26: 7265–7271.

10 Lau HC, Rogers RD, Passingham RE (2007) Manipulating the experienced onset of intention after action execution. J Cogn Neurosci 19: 81–90

11 Wegner DM (2002) The illusion of conscious will. (Cambridge (Massachusetts): MIT Press). 405 p.

12 Raine A (1993) The psychopathology of crime: Criminal behavior as a clinical disorder (San Diego: Academic Press). note 38 (p320).

13 Gazzaniga MS (2005) The ethical brain. (New York: Dana Press), note 63 (p98).

14 Op. cit. note 63.

Table 2.1 Examples of Prefrontal Brain Regions Associated with Pro-social Behaviour

Brain Region	Pro-social Behaviour
Anterior cingulate cortex	Empathy[15, 16]
Orbital PFC	Regret[17]
Ventromedial PFC	Ethical decisions[18, 19]
Ventrolateral PFC	Inhibition of behaviour[20]
Dorsolateral PFC	Reasoning[21, 22]

doi:10.1371/journal.pbio.0050103.t001

Studies of the Prefrontal Cortex in Anti-Social and Violent Populations

The birth of what may be coined modern "forensic neurology" lies in John Harlow's 19th century observations of Phineas P. Gage.[23] Gage, a railroad worker, suffered the unfortunate experience of having an iron bar blasted through the front of his brain, which resulted in extensive damage to the prefrontal cortex (PFC). Despite Gage's miraculous physical and intellectual recovery, conspicuous changes in his personality were reported. Briefly, the once courteous and diligent man became explicitly anti-social. As Gage's friends famously articulated, "Gage is no longer Gage." Since Harlow's lurid description, computerized reconstructions based on Gage's skull fractures have determined more precisely the damaged PFC regions, which current evidence associates with autonomic, social, and affect

15 Amodio DM, Frith CD (2006) Meeting of minds: The medial frontal cortex and social cognition. Nat Rev Neurosci 7: 268–277.

16 Singer T, Seymour B, O'Doherty J, Kaube H, Dolan RJ, et al. (2004) Empathy for pain involves the affective but not sensory components of pain. Science 303: 1157–1162.

17 Coricelli G, Critchley HD, Joffily M, O'Doherty JP, Sirigu A, et al. (2005) Regret and its avoidance: A neuroimaging study of choice behavior. Nat Neurosci 8: 1255–1262.

18 Heekeren HR, Wartenburger I, Schmidt H, Schwintowski HP, Villringer A (2003) An fMRI study of simple ethical decision-making. Neuroreport 14: 1215–1219.

19 King JA, Blair RJR, Mitchell DGV, Dolan RJ, Burgess N (2006) Doing the right thing: A common neural circuit for appropriate violent or compassionate behavior. Neuroimage 30: 1069–1076.

20 Aron AR, Fletcher PC, Bullmore ET, Sahakian BJ, Robbins TW (2003) Stop-signal inhibition disrupted by damage to right inferior frontal gyrus in humans. Nat Neurosci 6: 115–116.

21 Baird AA, Fugelsang JA (2004) The emergence of consequential thought: Evidence from neuroscience. Philos Trans R Soc Lond B Biol Sci 359: 1797–1804.

22 Bechara A, Van Der Linden M (2005) Decision-making and impulse control after frontal lobe injuries. Curr Opin Neurol 18: 734–739.

23 Harlow J (1848) Passage of an iron bar through the head. Boston Med Surg J 13: 389–393.

regulation.[24] The case of Phineas Gage is compelling to both neuroscientists and legal thinkers because it provided the first indication that reasoning and regard for others can be compromised by frontal lobe injury. Harlow's observations have led many experts to speculate that neurological insult may be a prominent factor in recidivistic and violent criminal transgressions.

Modern empirical endeavours support the claim that the human PFC, a latecomer in the brain's phylogenic history, is what makes us rational, intellectual, and moral entities (Table 2.1). For example, several studies on patients with focal frontal lobe injuries have supported Harlow's case.[25, 26] In one of the largest studies of patients with brain damage to date, Grafman and colleagues found that increased aggressive/violent scale scores were most strongly associated with similarly localized PFC lesions in a sample of 279 veterans of the Vietnam War.[27] Higher scores were, however, mostly associated with verbal aggression and less so with physical aggression, again fitting with Harlow's observations of Gage.[28] These studies, along with clinical observations, have led many to suggest that damage to the PFC results in "acquired sociopathy" or "pseudopsychopathy".

Given the PFC's historical and theoretical relevance to adaptive social behaviour, it is not surprising that this region was among the first to be examined in anti-social and violent populations. Raine and colleagues used non-invasive structural brain imaging to show an 11% reduction in PFC grey matter in patients with anti-social personality disorder (APD).[29] These decreases in grey matter were also associated with decreased autonomic arousal to a social stressor (i.e., videotaped speech about an individual's faults). Similar reductions have been observed in a study of aggressive patients[30] and of pathological liars.[31] Nonetheless, such morphological and volumetric abnormalities may not necessarily relate to behaviour.

---

24 Damasio AR (1994) Descartes' error: Emotion, rationality and the human brain (New York: Putnam). 352 p.

25 Meyers CA, Berman SA, Scheibel RS, Hayman A (1992) Case report: Acquired anti-social personality disorder associated with unilateral left orbital frontal lobe damage. J Psychiatry Neurosci 3: 121–125.

26 Blair RJ, Cipolotti L (2000) Impaired social response reversal. A case of 'acquired sociopathy'. Brain 123: 1122–1141.

27 Grafman J, Schwab K, Warden D, Pridgen A, Brown HR, et al. (1996) Frontal lobe injuries, violence, and aggression: A report of the Vietnam Head Injury Study. Neurology 46: 1231–1238.

28 Op. cit. note 7.

29 Raine A, Lencz T, Bihrle S, LaCasse L, Colletti P (2000) Reduced prefrontal gray matter volume and reduced autonomic activity in anti-social personality disorder. Arch Gen Psychiatry 57: 119–127.

30 Woermann FG, Tebartz van Elst L, Keopp MJ, Free SL, Thompson PJ, et al. (2000) Reduction of frontal neocortical grey matter associated with affective aggression in patients with temporal lobe epilepsy: An objective voxel by voxel analysis of automatically segmented MRI. J Neurol Neurosurg Psychiatry 68: 162–169.

31 Yang YL, Raine A, Lencz T, Bihrle S, Lacasse L, et al. (2005) Prefrontal structural abnormalities in liars. Br J Psychiatry 187: 320–325.

In principle, using brain imaging to look at function rather than structure should reveal stronger relationships between brain and behaviour. Using positron emission tomography scanning, neuroscientists have found attenuated resting regional cerebral blood flow in the frontal lobes of violent individuals[32] and convicted criminals.[33] In healthy volunteers, evoked anger and imagined aggressive transgressions are associated with reduced modulation of the orbital and medial PFC.[34] Collectively, these studies suggest that impulsive violent acts stem from diminished recruitment of the PFC's "inhibition" systems.

Beyond the PFC

The PFC is not, however, the only area where damage may increase propensity toward behaviours deemed criminal or anti-social. It has long been known that ablation of the monkey temporal lobe, including the amygdala, results in blunted emotional responses[35] (Figure 2.1C). In humans, brain-imaging and lesion studies have suggested a role of the amygdala in theory of mind, aggression,[36] and the ability to register fear and sadness in faces.[37] According to the violence inhibition model, both sad and fearful facial cues act as important inhibitors if we are violent towards others. In support of this model, recent investigations have shown that individuals with a history of aggressive behaviour have poorer recognition of facial expressions,[38] which might be due to amygdala dysfunction.[39] Others have recently demonstrated how the low expression of X-linked monoamine oxidase A (MAOA) – which is an important enzyme in the catabolism of monoamines, most notably serotonin (5-HT), and has been associated with an increased propensity

32 Volkow ND, Tancredi L (1987) Neural substrates of violent behaviour. A preliminary study with positron emission tomography. Br J Psychiatry 151: 668–673.

33 Raine A, Buchsbaum MS, Stanley J, Lottenberg S, Abel L, et al. (1994) Selective reductions in prefrontal glucose metabolism in murderers. Biol Psychiatry 36: 365–373.

34 Gordon HL, Baird AA, End AE (2004) Functional differences among those high and low on a trait measure of psychopathy. Biol Psychiatry 56: 516–521.

35 Bucy PC, Kluver H (1955) An anatomical investigation of the temporal lobe in the monkey (*Macaca mulatta*). J Comp Neurol 103: 151–251.

36 van Elst LT, Trimble MR, Ebert D, van Elst LT (2001) Dual brain pathology in patients with affective aggressive episodes. Arch Gen Psychiatry 58: 1187–1188.

37 Blair RJ, Morris RS, Frith CD, Perrett DI, Dolan RJ (1999) Dissociable neural responses to facial expressions of sadness and anger. Brain 122: 883–893.

38 Weiss EM, Kohler CG, Nolan KA, Czobor P, Volavka J, et al. (2006) The relationship between history of violent and criminal behavior and recognition of facial expression of emotions in men with schizophrenia and socioaffective disorder. Aggress Behav 32: 1–8.

39 Adolphs R, Gosselin F, Buchanan TW, Tranel D, Schyns P, et al. (2005) A mechanism for impaired fear recognition after amygdala damage. Nature 433: 68–72.

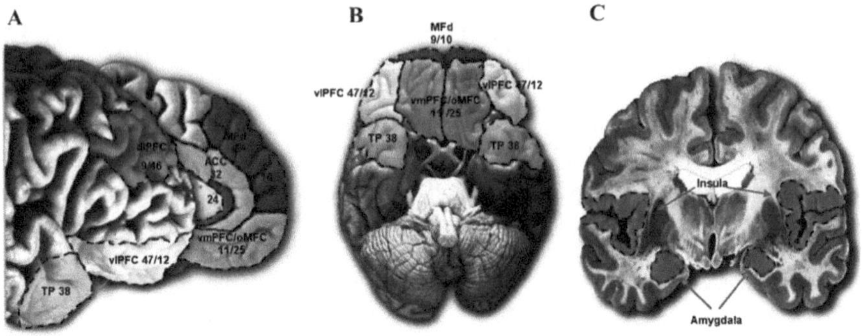

Figure 2.1 Regions Associated with Normal and Atypical Social Behaviour
(A) Medial and lateral view of the PFC.
(B) View of the ventral surface of the PFC and temporal poles.
(C) Coronal slice illustrating the amygdalar and insular cortex.
See also Table 2.1.
ACC, anterior cingulate cortex; dlPFC, dorsolateral PFC; MFd, medial PFC; oMFC, orbitomedial PFC; TP, temporal pole; vlPFC, ventrolateral PFC; vmPFC, ventromedial PFC.
doi:10.1371/journal.pbio.0050103.g001

towards reactive violence in abused children[40] – is associated with volume changes and hyperactivity in the amygdala.[41]

The amygdala has been a major focus of attempts to understand the poor empathy and fear responses observed in psychopathic criminals. Using functional magnetic resonance imaging (fMRI), Birbaumer and coworkers[42] presented individuals with a paradigm in which the appearance of a face on a screen was followed by a painful shock in one condition but not in a second condition. Analysis showed normal volunteers to have increased activity in the amygdala (see Figure 2.1) in response to faces associated with shock, whereas psychopathic individuals showed no significant change in activity in this region. In addition, psychopaths also failed to show normal increases in skin conductance responses. Importantly, Birbaumer et al.'s findings are supported by studies showing that the limbic structures (i.e., amygdala and hippocampus) are functionally abnormal in psychopathic criminals

40 Caspi A, McClay J, Moffitt TE, Mill J, Martin J, et al. (2002) Role of genotype in the cycle of violence in maltreated children. Science 297: 851–854.

41 Meyer-Lindenberg A, Buckholtz JW, Kolachana B, Hariri AR, Pezawas L, et al. (2006) Neural mechanisms of genetic risk for impulsivity and violence in humans. Proc Natl Acad Sci USA 103: 6269–6274.

42 Birbaumer N, Veit R, Lotze M, Erb M, Hermann C, et al. (2005) Deficient fear conditioning in psychopathy: A functional magnetic resonance imaging study. Arch Gen Psychiatry 62: 799–805.

during emotional memory[43] and by studies showing how activity in the amygdala decreases with increased scores on the Psychopathy Personality Inventory.[44, 45] A prevailing hypothesis is that in psychopathic criminals the prefrontal–amygdala connections are disrupted, leading to deficits in contextual fear conditioning,[46] regret,[47] guilt[48] and affect regulation.[49]

Does the Crime Fit the Brain?

While many behaviours can be unambiguously defined, labelling a behaviour as "criminal" is to define how the behaviour will be considered socially. That is, the very same behaviour that might not be deemed criminal in one social context (say, shooting a gun at a target at a shooting range) may be deemed criminal in another (such as shooting a gun in the direction of a crowd of people). Such definitional ambiguities are at their least frequent, however, with respect to interpersonal violence, which is broadly proscribed.

It is clear in at least some contexts that different violent anti-social behaviours can arise from different etiologies. Animal studies have shown that distinct networks underlie different types of aggression (e.g., predatory attack and defensive rage[50]). From these studies, one might expect that in humans, distinct neural topographies exist in, for example, the sexual criminal, the sadistic murderer, and the political terrorist. At first glance, such reasoning looks like phrenological folly; however, evidence does suggest that violent behaviour can be placed into two broad, yet distinct, categories: affective aggression (i.e., impulsive, autonomic arousing, and emotional) and predatory aggression (i.e., premeditated, goal-directed, and emotionless).[51]

---

43 Kiehl KA, Smith AM, Hare RD, Mendrek A, Forster BB, et al. (2001) Limbic abnormalities in affective processing by criminal psychopaths as revealed by functional magnetic resonance imaging. Biol Psychiatry 50: 677–684.

44 Gordon HL, et al (2004). note 18.

45 Tiihonen J, Hodgins S, Vaurio O, Laakso M, Repo E, et al. (2000) Amygdaloid volume loss in psychopathy. Abstr Soc Neurosci 26: 2017

46 LeDoux JE (1996) The emotional brain: The mysterious underpinnings of emotional life (New York: Simon and Schuster). 384 p.

47 Coricelli G, et al. (2005).

48 Takahashi H, Yahata N, Koeda M, Matsuda T, Asai K, et al. (2004) Brain activation associated with evaluative processes of guilt and embarrassment: An fMRI study. Neuroimage 23: 967–974.

49 Dolan RJ (2002) Emotion, cognition and behavior. Science 298: 1191–1194.

50 Gregg TR, Siegel A (2001) Brain structures and neurotransmitters regulating aggression in cats: Implication for human aggression. Prog Neuropsychopharmacol Biol Psychiatry 25: 91–140.

51 Vitiello B, Behar D, Hunt J, Stoff D, Ricciuti A (1990) Subtype aggression in children and adolescents. J Neuropsychiatry Clin Neurosci 2: 189–192.

With this dichotomy in mind, Raine and colleagues[52] reanalyzed positron emission tomography data to tease apart functional differences between premeditated psychopaths and impulsive affective murderers. Compared to controls, the impulsive murderers had reduced activation in the bilateral PFC, while activity in the limbic structures was enhanced. Conversely, the predatory psychopaths had relatively normal prefrontal functioning, but increased right subcortical activity, which included the amygdala and hippocampus. These results suggest that predatory psychopaths are able to regulate their impulses, in contrast to impulsive murderers, who lack the prefrontal "inhibitory" machinery that stop them from committing violent transgressions. Although more work is necessary, these studies strongly suggest that some kinds of criminal behaviour are associated with dysfunction of different regions of the brain.

Does Some Criminal Behaviour Result from Mental Disorder?

A great deal of empirical research demonstrates that mental illness is higher in incarcerated populations and estimates that as many as 25% of defendants evaluated for competency are medically and legally incompetent to stand trial.[53] Moreover, only 36% of the public perceive recidivistic crime as an organic disorder.[54] Consequently, weighing discrepancies between intuitions, expert views, and empirical findings is of fundamental importance to a legal system.

Both the *Diagnostic and Statistical Manual of Mental Disorders* and *International Classification of Diseases 10* classifications of mental and behavioural disorders include APD, which is defined respectively in the two classifications as a lack of regard for the feelings of others and a failure to abide by society's rules. While it can be said that any given population of incarcerated criminals may not be a representative sample of all criminals, or even of all criminals who pass through the prison system, a systematic review of studies examining mental illness in 23,000 prisoners showed that these prisoners were several times more likely to have some form of psychosis or major depression, and ten times more likely to exhibit APD than the general population.[55] The authors suggest that, worldwide, several million prisoners have serious mental illness.[56] Several studies also show

---

52 Raine A, Meloy JR, Bihrle S, Stoddard J, LaCasse L, et al. (1998) Reduced prefrontal and increased subcortical brain functioning assessed using positron emission tomography in predatory and affective murderers. Behav Sci Law 16: 319–332.

53 Golding SL, Roesch R, Schreiber J (1984) Assessment and conceptualization of competency to stand trial: Preliminary data on the Interdisciplinary Fitness Interview. Law Hum Behav 8: 321–334.

54 Raine A (1993).

55 Fazel S, Danesh J (2002) Serious mental disorder in 23000 prisoners: A systematic review of 62 surveys. Lancet 359: 545–550.

56 Ibid.

levels of head injury to be higher in violent and death-row criminals,[57] while birth complications, which can often result in neurological damage (e.g., hypoxic-ischemic encephalopathy) and parental mental illness, are higher in anti-social populations.[58] More often than not, people with APD and violent behaviour have a history of childhood maltreatment or trauma;[59] having such a history has been linked to anomalous development of regions associated with anti-social behaviour, including the PFC, hippocampus, amygdala, corpus callosum, and hypothalamic–pituitary–adrenal axis.[60] Early damage to the orbitofrontal cortex in particular appears to result in poor acquisition of moral and social rules,[61] thus showing the importance of the interaction between environment and brain development.

Discussing the possibility of meaningful links between some anti-social and violent behaviour and various brain disorders can, however, enrage retributivists, who point out that moral responsibility lies in the social rules by which acts are judged – not in the brain itself.[62] Nonetheless, there are many instances where brain disease can lead to anti-social behaviour, and these inevitably pose important complications for moral and legal systems that tend to divide responsibility for actions into dichotomous alternatives – guilty versus not guilty – instead of seeing responsibility as existing along a continuum. For example, compared to the general population, individuals with frontotemporal dementia, Huntington's disease, and attention deficit/hyperactive disorder have a higher prevalence of episodic aggression or anti-social conduct. One disturbing example cited by Goldberg[63] is the case of a New York surgeon who, after finishing surgery, carved his signature in the patient's stomach. The surgeon was later diagnosed with Pick disease (a form of dementia associated with personality changes that presumably result from progressive degeneration of frontal and anterior temporal cortices). He was not considered responsible for his actions by experts, the jury, or even the victim. Beyond these examples lies the possibility that some forms of anti-social or violent behaviour are of unspecified origin, which could place them in the same category as many other neuropsychiatric disorders. Presumably, such unrecognized brain abnormalities might cause acts of gratuitous violence, but the individuals concerned would be considered to be criminally responsible.

---

57 Volavka J, Mohammad Y, Vitrai J, Connolly M, Stefanovic M, et al. (1995) Characteristics of state hospital patients arrested for offenses committed during hospitalization. Psychiatr Serv 46: 796–800.

58 Raine A (1993), note 38.

59 Widom CS (1989) The cycle of violence. Science 244: 160–166.

60 Bremner JD (2005) Effects of traumatic stress on brain structure and function: Relevance to early responses to trauma. J Trauma Dissociation 6: 51–68.

61 Anderson SW, Bechara A, Damasio H, Tranel D, Damasio AR (1999) Impairment of social and moral behavior related to early damage in human prefrontal cortex. Nat Neurosci 2: 1032–1037.

62 Abbott A (2001) Into the mind of a killer. Nature 410: 296–298.

63 Goldberg E (2001) The executive brain: Frontal lobes and the civilized mind (Oxford: Oxford University Press). 251 p.

To be clear, there is at present no reason to believe that all criminal behaviours, or indeed even all violent criminal behaviours, are the result of organically dysfunctional brains. However, there is ample evidence to suggest that some kinds of dysfunction are likely to increase the probability of some kinds of behaviours that society labels as criminal. This suggests that research is urgently needed to elucidate the links between mental illness, neurological disorder, and criminal conduct. And modern and rapidly improving brain-imaging techniques may contribute significantly.

Possible Legal Implications

Advances in neuroscience could have several implications for the legal system. At the broadest level, these include: (i) understanding how cognitive processes of key legal participants (such as judges and jurors) influence trial outcomes; (ii) discovering whether various assumptions underlying the evidentiary rules (such as one suggesting that "excited utterances" are less likely than average to be falsehoods) have any basis in fact; (iii) learning more about how people determine "just" punishments; (iv) anticipating how jurors may over-react to certain kinds of character evidence; (v) determining the extent of injuries from accidents; (vi) improving our abilities to detect mental biases and prejudices that may affect the proper function of legal fact-finding and decision-making; and (vii) learning more about the limits of witness memories. Yet even against this broad background, few implications for the legal system are more important than trying to gain a better understanding of important influences on criminal behaviour.

However, that very significance brings its own important challenges. On one hand, a better understanding may lead to more effective deterrence, to more effective treatment, and to more just and morally sound sentencing. On the other hand, determining criminal responsibility is a normative legal conclusion, not an empirical factual one, made in the context of a variety of often conflicting aspirations.[64] Therefore, even the best neuroscientific study can only afford factual evidence to be weighed alongside other behavioural evidence and normative considerations, rather than actually resolve the legal question as to which the factual evidence is relevant.

Generally speaking, in the Anglo-American criminal justice system, a person can be held criminally responsible if he performs a prohibited act intentionally and with a statutorily specified mental state (which may span such things as "purpose", "knowledge", "recklessness", or "negligence").[65] Yet even if these criteria are satisfied, the defendant can be excused from liability if legally insane. That is, he may have intentionally and knowingly committed a proscribed act, but be found

64 Morse S (2006) Brain overclaim syndrome and criminal responsibility: A diagnostic note. Ohio State J Crim Law 3: 397–412.

65 Ibid.

Box 2.2 Brain Fingerprinting and Lie Detection

Lie detection technology is one of the most obvious legal uses of brain imaging, and several new companies (e.g., No Lie MRI) are beginning to commercialize their services to lawyers and prosecutors. However, despite there being several published empirical studies on lie detection, results seem to be far from conclusive. Early brain-imaging studies of how the brain responds when we willfully lie showed that specific zones of the PFC increase in activity when individuals lie – the same regions known to come online when tasks become more difficult and when we need to control or inhibit responses.[60] However, one problem with most studies of lie detection is that they use group averages, which make firm conclusions about individual cases impossible. Although more work is needed, recent studies on single individuals have shown promise, with lie detection accuracy in the range of 80–90%.[61] Proponents argue that the use of brain imaging to detect deception is less prone to countermeasures, making it more reliable than the polygraph test.[62] Not surprisingly, government institutions have become increasingly interested (e.g., US Department of Defense) and have been criticized as being "Orwellian". However, like the polygraph, brain imaging is unlikely to be universally admissible in court until it is shown to be valid, reliable, and relevant.

Another technique – brain fingerprinting – uses electroencephalography to examine the memory and encoding related multifaceted electroencephalographic response (MERMER). To measure this, an individual is shown crime scene pictures (i.e., the murder weapon), and changes in brain activity (specifically the P300 component) are monitored. The brain reacts differently to images it recognizes versus ones that it does not recognize, so, for example, if an individual did use a specific weapon to kill a person, the brain will react differently to images of the murder weapon than to images of other weapons not used in the crime. Brain fingerprinting evidence has been admitted in some cases, such as in the Iowa murder trial of Terry Harrington. However, despite its claimed potential, brain fingerprinting has been criticized for problems with developing adequate test stimuli, vulnerability to countermeasures, and – because it's patented – a failure to be appropriately verified by peer review.[63]

not blameworthy nonetheless, because a mental condition meeting a specified legal (as distinct from medical) threshold prevented him either from knowing the nature and quality of his act, or from understanding the wrongfulness of the act.[70]

---

66 Spence SA, Farrow TF, Herford AE, Wilkinson ID, Zheng Y, et al. (2001) Behavioural and functional anatomical correlates of deception in humans. Neuroreport 12: 2849–2853.

67 Kozel FA (2005) Detecting deception using functional magnetic resonance imaging. Biol Psychiatry 58: 605–613.

68 Honts CR, Raskin DC, Kircher JC (1994) Mental and physical countermeasures reduce the accuracy of polygraph tests. J Appl Psychol 79: 252–259.

69 Rosenfeld JP (2007) Brain fingerprinting: A critical analysis. Sci Rev Ment Health Pract In press.

70 LaFave WR (2003) Criminal law 4th edition (Hornbook series student edition). (St. Paul (Minnesota): West Group Publishing). 1,223 p.

The possibility of being "not guilty by reason of insanity" can be traced back to the well-known M'Naghten case in 1843. While attempting to kill the British Prime Minister, Daniel M'Naghten mistakenly killed the Prime Minister's secretary. Experts maintained that M'Naghten exhibited such a vast deterioration in his reasoning abilities (believing the Prime Minister to be heading a murderous conspiracy) that he had no comprehension of the act he committed. The modern standards for determining legal insanity, in the long wake of M'Naghten, vary markedly across jurisdictions, with results that have prompted many calls for reform. For example, psychiatrists have been plagued by the need to answer dichotomously whether a defendant is "mad" or "bad" or to opine that "it is not him, it is his disease".[71] Furthermore, medical research indicates that patients with selective damage to the PFC can often know right from wrong, but still be unable to act on such knowledge. This has naturally led defence attorneys and prosecutors to pursue more objective ways of determining whether a defendant is competent to stand trial, and, if so, whether he can be held legally responsible for his actions. This, in turn, has generated significant interest in brain-imaging evidence concerning a defendant's mental functioning (Box 2.2).

Several examples illustrate the kinds of contexts in which many believe that brain imaging may aid the law's ability to accurately assess a defendant's mental functioning. Consider the case of a 40-year-old man who inexplicably became a sexual impulsive with paedophilia. The patient had no prior history of sexual misconduct, but it was soon noted that he was frequenting prostitutes and that he attempted to molest his 12-year-old step-daughter. He was quickly reported to the local authorities, was found guilty of child molestation and was sentenced to either attend a 12-step sexual addiction program or face jail. Despite a strong yearning not to go to prison, the patient could not inhibit his sexual impulses. It was soon discovered that the defendant had a large tumour pressing on his right orbitofrontal cortex (Figure 2.2). Upon the resection of the tumour, the patient's sexual impulsiveness diminished. When the sexual impulsiveness later reappeared, a brain scan revealed that the tumour had grown back. A second resection of tumour again diminished the patient's sexual impulsiveness.[72] Another illustration is the 1998 case of 15-year-old Kip Kinkel, who shot and killed his parents and two high-school colleagues in the state of Oregon. Brain imaging was used as evidence in court to support Kinkel's "not guilty by reason of insanity" plea. The trial defence provided evidence of small cavities in Kinkel's frontal lobe. Although there was no evidence that this abnormality caused his behaviour (Kinkel was ultimately convicted as an adult and sentenced to 111 years in prison[73]), future developments in neuroscience may again aid courts in these kinds of inquiries.

---

71 Sapolsky RM (2004) The frontal cortex and the criminal justice system. Philos Trans R Soc Lond B Biol Sci 359: 1787–1796.

72 Burns JM, Swerdlow RH (2003) Right orbitofrontal tumor with pedophilia symptom and constructional apraxia sign. Arch Neurol 60: 437–440.

73 Frontline (2000) The killer at Thurston High Arlington (Virginia): Public Broadcasting Service. Available: http://www.pbs.org/wgbh/pages/frontline/shows/kinkel. Accessed 18 February 2007.

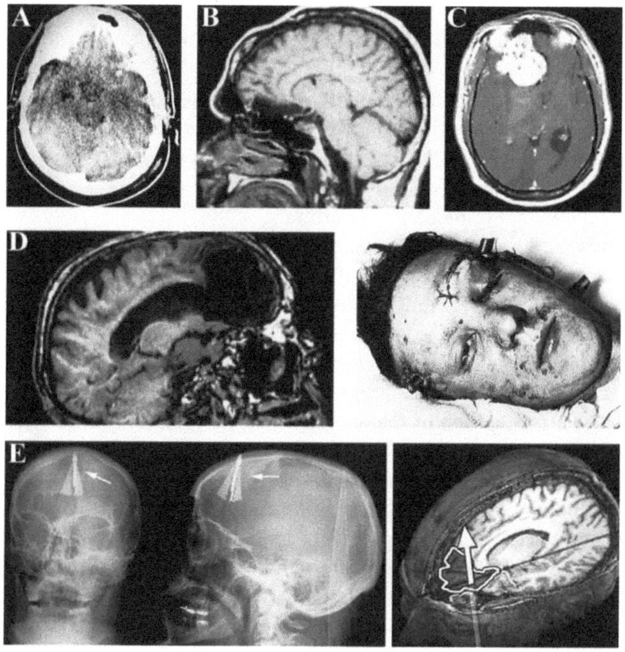

Figure 2.2 Cases Where Brain Anomalies have, or have not, been Linked to Anti-social Behaviour

(A) Brain scan of patient J.S., who exhibited sociopathic behaviour.[64] The image shows a lesion in the orbital frontal cortex.
(B) fMRI sagittal slice of the brain of patient J.Z., showing a lesion that was caused by the resection of pituitary tumour.[65] This lesion led to anti-social conduct, which was not exhibited before the surgery.
(C) Orbitofrontal damage associated with symptoms of paedophilia and sexual misconduct in the case of a 40-year-old male patient.
(D) Photograph of a patient after head injury (right) and fMRI scan 60 years later showing PFC damage (left).[66] This patient showed personality changes, but no signs of anti-social conduct.
(E) Cranial X-ray of a man who attempted suicide with a crossbow. Although the individual exhibited premorbid APD, the PFC damage caused by the crossbow arrow resulted in reversal of anti-social conduct.[67]
doi:10.1371/journal.pbio.0050103.g002

---

74 Blair RJ, Cipolotti L (2000), note 10.

75 Meyers CA, et al. (1992), note 9.

76 Mataró M, Jurado MA, García-Sánchez C, Barraquer L, Costa-Jussà FR, et al. (2001) Long-term effects of bilateral frontal brain lesion: 60 years after injury with an iron bar. Arch Neurol 58: 1139–1142, note 64.

77 Ellenbogen JM, Hurford MO, Liebeskind DS, Neimark GB, Weiss D (2005) Ventromedial frontal lobe trauma. Neurology 64: 757, note 65.

Box 2.3 Plausible Uses of Brain Imaging and Questions for Future Research

Questions for which brain imaging might provide useful answers:

- Does the defendant exhibit any neurological damage?
- Do the brain abnormalities fit with the nature of the crime?
- Is the defendant faking an illness?
- Is the defendant lying about the crime?
- What is the likelihood of future transgressions?

To begin to answer such questions, society needs the following:

- More neurobiological research on anti-social and criminal populations (e.g., post-mortem histology, diffusion tensor imaging, and brain morphometry)
- A better classification of the neural activity associated with different types of criminal activity
- A set of criteria and parameters for using imaging on single individuals with and without neurological abnormalities
- Better understanding of the effects of intrinsic and extrinsic factors on the brain (e.g., interplay between environment, development, and genetics)
- Agreed criteria concerning validity and reliability of brain images
- Agreed procedures for presenting imaging evidence in the courtroom.

These examples raise important questions not only about the extent to which neuroimaging may affect particular trial outcomes, but also about the ways in which the legal system can come to understand changing views of the brain, assess when those views are relevant, and determine how, in appropriate circumstances, to integrate that knowledge into legal decision-making[78] (see Boxes 2.2 and 2.3). For example, recent evidence suggests that the PFC continues to mature until the age of 25[79] and that this maturation correlates with ability in counterfactual (if–then) thinking.[80] An underdeveloped ventrolateral PFC can be directly associated with poorer cognitive control,[81] which some consider a core variable in criminal activity.[82] Such research and theory likely warrants serious consideration, given the robust relationship between

78 Feigenson N (2007) Brain imaging and courtroom evidence: On the admissibility and persuasiveness of fMRI. See this volume, p. 23.

79 Giedd J, Blumenthal J, Jeffries NO, Castellanos FX, Liu H, et al. (1999) Brain development during childhood and adolescence: A longitudinal MRI study. Nat Neurosci 2: 861–863.

80 Baird AA, Fugelsang JA (2004) The emergence of consequential thought: Evidence from neuroscience. Philos Trans R Soc Lond B Biol Sci 359: 1797–1804.

81 Bunge SA, Dudukovic NM, Thomason ME, Vaidya CJ, Gabrieli JD (2002) Immature frontal lobe contributions to cognitive control in children: Evidence from fMRI. Neuron 33: 301–311.

82 Gottfredson MR, Hirschi T (1990) A general theory of crime. (Stanford (California): Stanford University Press). 297 p.

age and violent criminal offences. For example, British Crime Survey statistics show that individuals between the ages of 16 and 24 commit more violent acts than all other age groups combined.

Such statistics have a special relevance in countries such as the United States where the death penalty is applied. For example, many lawyers who oppose capital punishment of juveniles hold the view that the legal system should take such neuroscientific evidence into account (e.g., the Justice for Children Project; http://moritzlaw.osu.edu/jfc).[83] It is possible that the 2005 decision of the Supreme Court of the United States (*Roper v. Simmons*) that made it illegal to use capital punishment for any offender who was under the age of 18 when he committed his crime was influenced in part by evidence presented in *amicus* (so-called "friends of the court") briefs, which included neuroscientific evidence.[84]

The Limits of Brain Imaging as Evidence

There are many exciting possibilities for how law and neuroscience may eventually partner – with neuroscientists discovering new things about the brain potentially relevant to law, and law asking questions that new neuroscientific research may help address. However, it is important to keep in mind a variety of limitations of brain-imaging technology. We highlight six.

First, functional brain imaging is not mind reading. Not only can it not tell us what or how a person was thinking at the time of a legally relevant act, it also cannot tell us with reliable accuracy what a person is thinking while being scanned. In this respect, brain imaging can only provide *post hoc* explanations.[85] The challenge of functional brain imaging has been likened to looking from an airplane window at night: when we look down from the plane we see complex patterns of lights, which we can demarcate into towns and cities and we can gaze at their connections through linking road lights. However, from the plane we achieve little understanding of the different, social, cultural, and political differences that exist in these blobs of light.[86] With respect to fMRI, this analogy is supported on a

---

83 Scott CL (2005) Roper v. Simmons: Can juvenile offenders be executed? J Am Acad Psychiatry Law 33: 547–552. See also this volume, p. 183 and p. 199.

84 McLaughlin JT, Rosenkranz EJ, Wei TP, Clare SM, Haider A, et al. (2004) Brief of the American Medical Association, American Psychiatric Association, American Society for Adolescent Psychiatry, American Academy of Child and Adolescent Psychiatry, American Academy of Psychiatry and the Law, National Association of Social Workers, and National Mental Health Association as *amici curiae* in support of the respondent. Roper v. Simmons, US Supreme Court, no. 03-633. Available: http://www.abanet.org/crimjust/juvjus/simmons/ama.pdf. Accessed 22 February 2007.

85 Raine A (1993), note 38.

86 Nichols MJ, Newsome WT (1999) The neurobiology of cognition. Nature 402: C35–C38.

technical level, as the details of the relationships between metabolic demand and increased neuronal activity are poorly understood.

Second, as important as brain functioning is, brain imaging provides only one window of many into the multiple influences on behaviour that can be relevant to understanding why a person acted in an anti-social manner. Such influences include the intricate interaction between genetic, prenatal, endocrinological, social, cultural, and economic factors: "No pixel in a brain will ever be able to show culpability or nonculpability".[87]

Third, despite showing remarkable consistency with lesion, animal model, and electrophysiological data, brain imaging is not yet in Kuhnian terms a "pure science". Interpretation of brain scans is admittedly somewhat subjective. Anatomical landmarks in the form of gyri and sulci differ very much from individual to individual, and even in adulthood the brain is not fixed, but shows plasticity and change in response to injury that also varies from individual to individual. Moreover, in the case of fMRI, differences in haemodynamic response may not necessarily relate to neuropathology, but to vascular and endocrinological pathology. Thus, even if brain abnormalities are found, individual differences in the extent and location of the injury, and in recovery and plasticity, present major problems for the interpretation of brain images in the legal setting.

While these problems can be reduced in research through averaging across many individuals, these are critical issues when examining a single individual. For example, all the brain-imaging studies conducted on violent and anti-social populations have studied group effects. Moreover, most studies have examined adult males, and the results cannot be generalized to females and children. Accordingly, if brain imaging is to be applied to the forensic evaluation of the single patient, a standardized set of tests, procedures, and imaging parameters are needed to achieve more valid conclusions (see Box 2.3).

Fourth, correlations between brain function and criminal behaviour are imperfect, calling into question both the diagnostic and predictive validity of brain-imaging evidence. That is, brain defects are not observed in all violent criminals, and conversely, not all people with PFC damage exhibit anti-social behaviour. For example, one longitudinal case study showed PFC damage to result in personality changes, but without signs of anti-social behaviour.[88] Some studies have shown how prefrontal damage can even decrease anti-social behaviour.[89] Differences in the PFC may also be caused by other variables, including levels of education and alcoholism.[90] A similar pattern emerges for the amygdala, where damage can result

87 Gazzaniga MS (2005) (p100).

88 Mataró M, et al. (2001).

89 Ellenbogen JM, et al. (2005), 757.

90 Laakso MP, Gunning-Dixon F, Vaurio O, Repo-Tiihonen E, Soininen H, et al. (2002) Prefrontal volumes in habitually violent subjects with anti-social personality disorder and type 2 alcoholism. Psychiatry Res 114: 95–102.

in increased or decreased aggression.[91, 92] Moreover, in court proceedings, many experts have argued against the use of ambitious speculations concerning the brain (e.g., *State of Tennessee v. Paul Dennis Reid Jr.*, 2002, No. 38887), particularly where the link between the criminal act and the neurological damage is based solely on brain-imaging data.

Fifth, just as it would be inappropriate to expect full localization of criminality genetically,[93] it would be inappropriate to expect full localization of criminality neurologically.[94] Indeed, sociologists have long provided explanations for crime and deviance without the slightest reference to the brain.

Sixth, brain images are not only powerful, they can potentially be too powerful – an effect we have referred to as the "Christmas tree phenomenon". For example, in much the same way that a prosecutor may sway jurors with sympathetic pictures of the innocent victim, the defence may show brightly coloured images of the perpetrator's allegedly dysfunctional brain. The vividness and technological sophistication of the images may be over-weighted by the jurors, which can warp justice just as surely as can under-weighting of relevant evidence. Brain imaging can be admissible in courts of different jurisdictions (e.g., under the Federal Rules of Evidence in the United States). However, given the increasing public interest in brain imaging[95] and the misinterpretations of what brain imaging is and can do,[96] it is crucial for proper legal decision-making that judges and jurors understand the limitations of brain imaging.

Concluding Remarks

The goals of science and of law are different. However, important legal questions such as moral blameworthiness, culpability, responsibility, and the likelihood of recidivism depend to some degree on improved understandings of human behaviour. Therefore, biological advances in understanding human brain architecture and function may overlap in important ways with legal inquiries. New studies of the criminal brain are likely to shape moral views on responsibility and free will, with possible impacts on how legal systems punish and treat criminals.[97]

---

91 Le Doux (1996), note 30.

92 Blair RJ (2004) The roles of orbital frontal cortex in the modulation of anti-social behavior. Brain Cogn 55: 198–208.

93 Jones OD (2006) Behavioral genetics and criminal law. J Law Contemp Probl 69: 81–100.

94 Abbot A (2001), note 46.

95 Racine E (2005) fMRI in the public eye. Nat Rev Neurosci 6: 159–164.

96 Illes J, Kirschen MP, Gabrieli JD (2003) From neuroimaging to neuroethics. Nat Neurosci 6: 205.

97 Greene JD, Cohen JD (2004) For the law, neuroscience changes nothing and everything. Philos Trans R Soc Lond B Biol Sci 359: 1775–17785.

A growing body of research gives us good reason to believe that some kinds of brain dysfunction can affect the probability of different kinds of criminal behaviours. However, despite our growing knowledge of the brain abnormalities associated with anti-social and psychopathic behaviour, there are as yet no concrete biological markers – genetic or physiological – that can predict such behaviours. Violent and anti-social behaviours undoubtedly arise from a symphony of factors. Optimal understanding will require cooperation among many disciplines such as economics, sociology, psychology, evolutionary biology, cellular physiology, and neuroscience.[98]

Acknowledgments

We thank Cindy C. Hagan, John Monaghan, and Joshua Buckholtz for their helpful comments.

98 Jones OD, Goldsmith TH (2005) Law and behavioral biology. Columbia Law Rev 105: 405–502.

Chapter 3

Brain Imaging and Courtroom Evidence: On the Admissibility and Persuasiveness of fMRI

Neal Feigenson

Functional magnetic resonance imaging (fMRI) is increasingly favoured as an investigative and diagnostic technique in neuroscience, psychology and psychiatry. Yet the imminent use of expert testimony based on fMRI and the courtroom display of fMRI images pose numerous concerns for the law. (Expert testimony based on other methods of functional neuroimaging, such as PET (positron emission tomography) and SPECT (single photon emission computed tomography) has been offered in many cases, but as of this writing there are only two reported American cases in which fMRI evidence has been mentioned.) These concerns need to be taken very seriously, perhaps more so than some enthusiasts of advanced neuroimaging have done so far.

This chapter consists of three sections. First, I very briefly describe fMRI, outline its likely legal uses, and survey the framework of evidence rules that will govern the admissibility of fMRI testimony and images in American courts. Second, I analyse the admissibility of fMRI evidence in general. One approach to this is based on precedent: the cases dealing with PET and SPECT evidence may tell us something about how courts are likely to treat fMRI evidence. Another approach addresses the conceptual and methodological underpinnings of fMRI. Each link in the chain of inferences from fMRI data to conclusions about the psychological significance of those data suggests basic questions about the reliability of the results and their applicability to law. I conclude this section by discussing the first reported case in which fMRI evidence was used in court, which exemplifies several of these basic concerns.

Third, I explore the admissibility and probative value of the fMRI images themselves. Assuming that the expert testimony that the pictures are offered to illustrate is admissible in the first place, I argue, as against Joseph Dumit (2004) and others, that the best way to respond to jurors' and judges' possible misconstruals of fMRIs is not to exclude the pictures, but instead to admit them and for expert witnesses and lawyers to educate judges and jurors as to how the pictures should be interpreted.

fMRI and Its Legal Applications: Evidentiary Framework

What is fMRI?

Functional neuroimaging (as opposed to structural imaging, as in CT scans or structural MRIs) can track the workings of the brain in real time. Functional MRI does this by tracking changes in local blood flow and blood oxygenation level (BOLD) that are associated with neuronal activity. When neurons are active, they demand energy, which is supplied by adenosine triphosphate (ATP), which in turn is produced by oxygen and glucose in the blood. Because more oxygen is supplied to the active brain region than is consumed (since most glucose is metabolized into ATP nonoxidatively), the ratio of oxygenated to deoxygenated blood in the active region increases. This results in changes in magnetic resonance (MR) signal intensity, as measured by an MR scanner, because oxygenated and deoxygenated blood have different magnetic susceptibilities (e.g., Huettel, Song, & McCarthy, 2004).

Functional MRI has two major advantages over PET and SPECT. First, fMRI is capable of greater spatial and temporal resolution, on the order of millimetres and seconds, respectively (Huettel et al., 2004; Illes & Racine, 2005).[1] Second, fMRI is non-invasive, unlike PET and SPECT, which require the injection of a radioactive tracer. This enables fMRI researchers to include participants who might not want to undergo the injection and to test for people's performances more often and under many more tasks or conditions (because fMRI does not involve injections of radioactive substances, it is not subject to limits on the number of injections that may be given to any given person within a given time frame), thus enhancing the potential reliability and validity of the results (Constable, 2006; Parry & Matthews, 2002).

Many thousands of investigative and exploratory studies indicate that fMRI has great promise in a wide range of in neuroscientific, medical and psychological applications. Its more precise functional brain mapping may facilitate planning for neurosurgery and allow for more effective development and administration of pain therapies (Columbia University functional MRI, 2005). Functional MRI can detect abnormalities in brain function in persons at risk for Alzheimer's before the clinical presentation of symptoms characteristic of the disease (Parry & Matthews, 2002). And fMRI has already yielded unprecedented insights into the physiological bases for human cognitions, perceptions and judgments (e.g., Cabeza & Kingstone, 2006; Greene, 2003; Greene et al., 2001).

Possible Legal Applications of fMRI

The wide range of possible legal applications of fMRI is suggested in part by the previous and ongoing uses of PET, SPECT and other neuroimaging technologies

1 According to Robinson (2004), voxel size is about 1.5 x 1.5 x 4 mm, but according to Constable (2006), the process of registering individual brains to a reference brain (see below) introduces about 1 cm "slop".

in various legal proceedings. First, fMRI evidence may be offered to prove *adjudicative* facts (Davis, 1942), i.e., facts that are germane and limited to the particular case at hand. These include:

- determining the presence of brain injury due to trauma (e.g., *Green v. K-Mart*, 2003; cf. *Penney v. Praxair*, 1997)
- determining possible causes of brain injury (e.g., *Elam v. Lincoln Electric Co.*, 2005; *Hose v. Chicago Northwestern Transp. Co.*, 1995; *Rhilinger v. Jancsics*, 1998)
- determining mental capacity for various purposes, including (a) the insanity defense (e.g., *United States v. Hinckley*, 1981; *People v. Weinstein*, 1992; see also President's Council on Bioethics, 2004), (b) *mens rea*, i.e., the specific intent required for proof of most crimes (e.g., *People v. Williams*, 2004; cf. *Jackson v. Calderon*, 2000) and (c) competency, whether to stand trial (e.g., *United States v. Gigante*, 1997), to receive the death penalty or to be put to death (e.g., *State of Delaware v. Red Dog*, 1993), or to execute a contract or a will or to give informed consent (Greely, 2004; Tancredi, 2004)
- declaring brain death, especially in cases where non-functional testing, such as CAT scans, yield ambiguous results (*In re Guardianship of Schiavo*, 2005; Tancredi, 2004)
- determining racial or other bias (Greely, 2004; see Eberhardt, 2005), and
- detecting deception by witnesses (see, e.g., Kozel et al., 2005; Langleben et al., 2002; Lee et al., 2002, Spence et al., 2004).[2]

Second, fMRI may also be offered to prove *legislative* facts (Davis, 1942), i.e., general facts relevant to legal reasoning and the lawmaking process, including the formulation of legal rules or principles by judges. For instance, fMRI studies showing differences between adolescents' and adults' brain activity while participants were engaged in moral appraisal and reasoning tasks were cited in the briefs to the United States Supreme Court that successfully argued that executing juveniles is unconstitutional (*Roper v. Simmons*, 2005; *Roper v. Simmons*, Briefs for Respondent and Amicus Curiae ABA, 2004; for a review

2 Experimental research has already used fMRI to identify lying or concealed knowledge, using a variety of research designs (e.g., Kozel et al., 2005; Langleben et al., 2002; Lee et al., 2002; for reviews, see Keckler, 2002; Wolpe, Foster, & Langleben, 2005). Other technologies, however, may well be superior to fMRI in detecting lies or concealed knowledge; e.g., EEG used in "brain fingerprinting" (*Harrington v. State of Iowa*, 2003; see, e.g., Iacono & Lykken, 2002) (discussing Lawrence Farwell's ERP (event-related potential) measure (also known as the "P300 wave", the signal being measured) of the GKT (Guilty Knowledge Test)), or electrodermal measures (Ben-Shakhar & Elaad, 2003). For a discussion of the possible admissibility of fMRI lie detection evidence, see Kittay, 2007 (arguing that leading fMRI lie detection technologies may well satisfy basic doctrinal standards for admissibility but may nevertheless be excluded due to cultural suspicion of "mind-reading devices").

of the research, see Beckman, 2004).[3] And in the cases alluded to earlier, fMRI (and other) studies purporting to show connections between exposure to media violence and aggressive ideation and behaviour have been introduced in defence of state laws restricting children's access to violent video games (*Entertainment Software Association v. Blagojevich*, 2005a; *Entertainment Software Association v. Granholm*, 2005b, 2006).[4]

Evidentiary Framework

Testimony based on fMRI studies is, of course, scientific evidence, and is therefore subject to the special rules governing that kind of evidence. In American federal courts and a majority of state courts, the law governing this subject derives from Federal Rule of Evidence 702 (or the state law versions thereof) and the leading Supreme Court decision, *Daubert v. Merrell Dow Pharmaceuticals* (1993). Under Rule 702, if "scientific, technical, or other specialized knowledge will help the trier of fact …, a witness qualified as an expert … may testify thereto in the form of an opinion or otherwise, if[:] (1) the testimony is based upon sufficient facts or data, (2) the testimony is the product of reliable principles and methods, and (3) the witness has applied the principles and methods reliably to the facts of the case" (Federal Rules of Evidence, 2007). Both Rule 702 and *Daubert* require the proponent of the evidence to persuade the court that the evidence is sufficiently reliable and relevant to the matter to be proven for the trier of fact to consider it. *Daubert* proposes four factors for trial judges to use in gauging the reliability of proffered scientific evidence: whether the theory or technique on which the testimony rests can be or has been tested; whether the theory or technique has been subjected to peer review and publication; the known or potential error rate of the theory or technique when applied; and whether the theory or technique has been generally accepted in the relevant scientific community (*Daubert*, 1993, pp. 593–595). Many courts apply these factors with varying degrees of rigour (Merlino, Murray, & Richardson, in press), while other courts have turned to additional or alternative tests (see Advisory Committee Note to Rule 702 (Federal Rules of Evidence, 2007; *Daubert v. Merrell Dow Pharmaceuticals*, 1995). In states that do not follow *Daubert*, the admissibility of scientific evidence continues to

3 The Supreme Court alluded to "scientific and sociological studies" in finding that juveniles are in general less able than adults to control their behaviour in a socially responsible fashion, and therefore, that juveniles cannot be among the "worst offenders" for whom the ultimate punishment of death alone is warranted (*Roper v. Simmons*, 2005, pp. 569–570). The Court did not, however, specifically refer to neuroscientific research. In any event, the Court's prior finding of a "national consensus against the death penalty for juveniles" (p. 564) appears to have been a more important ground for its holding that executing juveniles is unconstitutional.

4 Anti-pornography groups similarly hope to use fMRI research to show a causal link between viewing pornography and anti-social behavior (Jarvik, 2004).

be governed by the older *Frye* test, which asks whether the proffered evidence is based on a theory or technique that is "generally accepted" in the relevant scientific community (*Frye v. United States*, 1923). In any event, the decision whether to admit scientific evidence (like any other evidence) is within the trial judge's discretion and may be overturned only if the appellate court finds that the trial judge abused that discretion (see *Joiner v. General Electric*, 1997).

The admissibility of the fMRI images implicates a few additional rules, although here too, the focus is on the reliability of the (visual) evidence. Most importantly, admissibility may depend on whether the images are considered *substantive* or *demonstrative* evidence. Substantive evidence is evidence offered to prove a fact in the case; demonstrative evidence is offered merely to illustrate testimony rather than as independent proof (Mauet & Wolfson, 2005).[5] Substantive evidence is generally held to a more rigorous standard. In particular, machine-generated images (such as radiographs produced by X-rays) that depict what otherwise could not be seen must, if offered as substantive evidence, be authenticated (under Federal Rule 901(b)(9) or the state law equivalent) by testimony "describing [the] process or system used to produce [the image] and showing that the process or system produces an accurate result" (Federal Rules of Evidence, 2007). Merely illustrative evidence, by contrast, is ordinarily admissible if, in the opinion of the trial court, it will help the jury to understand some fact of consequence in the case (Mauet & Wolfson, 2005). On the other hand, many courts subject computer-generated images (such as computer simulations) to the more demanding authentication standard regardless of whether those images are considered substantive or illustrative.[6]

Finally, all evidence, oral testimony or tangible (real or demonstrative) evidence, is subject to Federal Rule of Evidence 403 (or the state law equivalent), which provides that even relevant evidence "may be excluded if its probative value is substantially outweighed by the danger of unfair prejudice, confusion of the issues, or misleading the jury" (Federal Rules of Evidence, 2007).

---

5 There is considerable controversy and confusion regarding the category of demonstrative evidence and the practical implications of classifying evidence as demonstrative rather than substantive (see, e.g., Mueller & Kirkpatrick, 2003). One such practical implication is that substantive but not demonstrative evidence generally goes to the jury room during deliberations (see Mauet & Wolfson, 2005; cf. Mueller & Kirkpatrick, 2003).

6 The Supreme Court of Connecticut, for instance, recognizing both the difficulty of categorically distinguishing substantive from demonstrative uses of visual evidence (in this case, images enhanced or created by digital image processing software) and the persuasive potential of visual displays regardless of how they are characterized, has recently instituted a single, demanding authentication standard for all computer-generated visual evidence, based on Federal Rule 901(b)(9) and scholarly interpretations thereof (*State of Connecticut v. Swinton*, 2004; see Podolski & Feigenson, 2007). Other rules that may affect the admissibility of fMRI images include Federal Rules 703 and 705, which concern the disclosure of facts or data on which the expert relies in giving an opinion but which are otherwise inadmissible due to hearsay or other restrictions.

The Admissibility of fMRI Expert Evidence

In this section I analyse the potential admissibility of fMRI evidence in two ways. First, I provide an overview of case law regarding the admissibility of expert testimony based on other functional neuroimaging technologies (PET and SPECT). These cases may offer some guidance (all things being equal) for predicting how courts will be inclined, at least initially, to treat fMRI-based testimony.[7] Second, I explore in more detail the conceptual and methodological underpinnings of fMRI research conducted by cognitive scientists and psychologists to learn about human behaviors that may be relevant to law. These concepts and methodologies raise questions about the reliability of fMRI for legal purposes, at least given the current state of the science. I conclude by briefly describing the first reported case in which fMRI-based expert testimony was introduced in court and show how that fMRI evidence implicated a number of these basic reliability concerns.

Legal Treatment of PET and SPECT

To date there have been roughly 130 reported opinions involving PET and/or SPECT evidence.[8] Several general observations are worth making. First, on more than two-fifths (85 of 133, 63.9%) of the occasions on which this expert evidence has been at issue, its proponents have presented or sought to present it not to juries but to judges alone (e.g., proceedings before administrative law judges or relating to non-jury issues such as requests for injunctive relief or determinations of competency to stand trial). This is noteworthy because concerns about the use of fMRI data (and perhaps especially fMRI images; see below) in court usually focus on their use by jurors; more often than not, however, judges, not jurors, will be the decision-makers on the issues for which neuroimaging evidence is offered. Second, PET and/or SPECT evidence has been admitted in more than four-fifths (73 of 89, 82.0%) of cases in which it has either been admitted or excluded.[9] This perhaps surprisingly high admissibility rate may be due in part to the large

7 It has been (successfully) argued that judicial opinions should have limited if any precedential value regarding scientific or medical propositions (*Siebert v. Standard Ins. Co.*, 2002). Certainly, if scientific knowledge changes, courts should not be locked into factual determinations shown to have been mistaken. Nevertheless, the courts' general approaches to PET and SPECT evidence may presage their receptivity (or lack thereof) to fMRI evidence.

8 Cases were identified using LEXIS, US federal and state court cases library, and the following search string: (PET or SPECT) w/15 (scan! or image!). This search was last updated on 4/24/06.

9 The discrepancy between the number of cases in which PET and/or SPECT evidence has been admitted or excluded (89) and the total number of cases in which that evidence has been "involved" (133) is accounted for by cases in which that evidence was sought but not obtained (especially by criminal defendants making post-conviction arguments alleging, e.g., ineffective assistance of counsel) or mentioned in passing.

proportion of bench proceedings: when a judge sits without a jury, there is no jury to protect from evidence deemed insufficiently reliable; instead, the judge typically hears the evidence and then decides how much weight to give it. Indeed, in cases in which PET and/or SPECT evidence has been admitted or excluded, it has been admitted at a significantly higher rate in proceedings before judges (44 of 46, 95.7%) than in those before juries (29 of 43, 67.5%), $X^2 = 15.95$, $\underline{p} < .01$.

Third, there do not (yet) appear to be any clear patterns in the PET and SPECT case law regarding the admissibility of this evidence to prove particular kinds of facts (e.g., to prove brain injury due to workplace exposure to toxins). To a limited extent the decisions may break down by state: for instance, California seems to have been relatively unreceptive to both PET and SPECT evidence to diagnose brain trauma and other conditions (see, e.g., *People v. Protsman*, 2001 (affirming exclusion of PET-based testimony to diagnose prior brain trauma); *People v. Yum*, 2003 (affirming exclusion of SPECT-based evidence to prove defendant's post-traumatic stress disorder (PTSD))), whereas Louisiana has tended to admit neuroimaging evidence for similar purposes (e.g., *Green v. K-Mart Corp.*, 2003 (PET scan evidence admitted to prove traumatic brain injury)). There have been too few cases, however, to support valid inferences about this or any other sort of pattern or trend in the PET and SPECT cases.

If there are indeed no such general patterns, the explanation may well be traced to the fourth (and in some ways the most important) observation: the admissibility and persuasiveness of PET and SPECT evidence very much depend on the case-specific context. Courts do occasionally speak broadly about the general reliability or relevance of functional neuroimaging. For example, a California appellate court in a 2001 case approvingly referred to expert testimony indicating that PET scans were generally accepted for use only in cases of stroke, Alzheimer's and epilepsy, and were not generally used to diagnose or evaluate head trauma; consequently, the court, applying California's *Frye*-like standard for admissibility of scientific evidence, affirmed the trial court's exclusion of the defendant's scans to prove head trauma (*People v. Protsman*, 2001).[10] Similarly, a New York trial court recently ruled that PET scan studies did not meet the *Frye* standard when offered to prove traumatic brain injury, but that neither was such evidence "junk

10 Similarly, in *Jackson v. Calderon* (2000), a federal appellate court upheld the trial court's exclusion (under *Daubert*) of the defendant's proffered PET scans to prove PCP abuse where that use of PET was not generally accepted in the scientific community. Another interesting example of California's attitude towards neuroimaging evidence is provided by *Siebert v. Standard Ins. Co.* (2002), in which a federal court applying California law rejected an insured's claim for extended disability benefits. The court upheld the determination by the insurer that the plaintiff's claimed chronic fatigue syndrome (CFS) could not be verified by laboratory tests, including SPECT. The plaintiff argued that an earlier case, *Friedrich v. Intel Corp.* (1999), had found that SPECT scans and other "objective tests" were "a characteristic finding in patients with CFS". The defendant, however, urged the court "not to rely on judicial opinions that state scientific or medical propositions as precedent". The court agreed with the defendant.

science" justifying an award of costs and attorneys' fees to the adversary (*LaMasa v. Bachman*, 2005).[11]

More often, however, courts make finer-grained determinations, taking into account the claimed relevance and probative value of the evidence, the strength of the testimony supporting or opposing admission, the strength of other evidence going to the same point and, occasionally, the qualifications of the expert. Thus, where proponents of neuroimaging expert evidence are careful to offer that evidence not to "prove" a diagnosis of, say, toxic encephalopathy, but rather as merely "consistent" with such a diagnosis, courts have admitted the evidence (e.g., *Elam v. Lincoln Electric Co.*, 2005; *Hose v. Chicago Northwestern Transp. Co.*, 1995). More generally, PET and/or SPECT evidence has most often been admitted (when it is admitted) along with other neurological and clinical evidence of the party's mental condition. As a consequence, neuroimaging expert evidence rarely seems in itself to be dispositive (in contrast, say, to the well-known CT scans in the *Hinckley* (1981) case); typically, it is admitted but does not seem to affect the outcome (although in the absence of controlled experimental data, this observation is necessarily speculative).

When courts have excluded PET and/or SPECT evidence, they have done so for several kinds of reasons. Proffers may be rejected where the evidence is not shown to be relevant (e.g., *Feria v. Dynagraphics Co.*, 2004 (SPECT offered to prove plaintiff's toxic encephalopathy, but insufficient evidence that condition could have been caused by exposure to the defendant's chemicals); *United States v. Mezvinksy*, 2002 (PET scan evidence offered to prove defendant's diminished frontal lobe activity ruled inadmissible because irrelevant to legal point of dispute, which was whether defendant could have formed an intent to deceive, the *mens rea* required to commit the charged crime of fraud)).[12] Alternatively, the evidence in the particular case may not be sufficiently reliable to be heard by jurors. Under Federal Rule of Evidence 702(3) and *Daubert*, the expert must have reliably applied neuroimaging science to the facts of the case; if, however, the subject and control group in a neuroimaging study are not properly matched, so that a significant possibility of confounds remains, testimony based on the study is properly excluded (e.g., *Penney v. Praxair*, 1997 (PET) (subject and controls

---

11 These cases raise the question whether PET and SPECT (and, by inference, fMRI) evidence is likelier to be admitted in jurisdictions applying the *Daubert* multifactor reliability test instead of the *Frye* "general acceptance" test. While *Daubert* may in general suggest a more restrictive view toward putatively scientific evidence (see, e.g., Saks & Koehler, 2005), some methodologies that have not yet achieved general acceptance (and so would be inadmissible under *Frye*) but that can be shown to be sufficiently reliable may be admissible under *Daubert* (see, e.g., Mueller & Kirkpatrick, 2003).

12 *Mezvinsky* also illustrates another limitation on the admissibility of neuroimaging evidence: a scan performed during pretrial examination of a party may tell the trier of fact little or nothing about the state of the party's brain at the time of the events in question, which may have occurred many years previously.

not adequately matched for age and subject but not controls under medication that might have affected scan results); *United States v. Gigante*, 1997 (same)). When the judge sits as trier of fact, expert testimony based on PET and/or SPECT evidence may be admitted but given very little weight because it is unsupported or even contradicted by other evidence (e.g., *Falksen v. Sec'y of Dept. of Health and Human Servs.*, 2004 (in Vaccine Act case, court finds that claimant did not suffer encephalitis where SPECT scan showed abnormalities but no board-certified neurologist diagnosed encephalitis and the use of SPECT to make such a diagnosis was not generally accepted); *Prince v. Thomas*, 1997 (in admiralty case, PET scan may have indicated that plaintiff suffered permanent brain damage from boating accident but court "d[id] not believe that [this evidence] offset the essentially negative MRI and the absence of objective neurological symptoms"). And some proffers of PET or SPECT evidence have been rejected because the witnesses who sought to introduce that evidence were found unqualified to do so (e.g., *Commonwealth v. Frangipane*, 2001 (PET); *Craig v. Orkin Exterminating Co.*, 2000 (SPECT)).[13]

Fifth and finally, in only two cases have the initial decisions to admit or exclude the evidence been reversed on appeal (*Commonwealth v. Frangipane*, 2001 (admission of PET evidence reversed); *Berry v. CSX Transportation, Inc.*, 1998 (exclusion of SPECT evidence reversed)). This is consistent with the law requiring deference to trial judges' determinations regarding the admission or exclusion of scientific evidence (*Joiner v. General Electric*, 1997)[14] and with the low rate of reversal of evidentiary rulings generally (Berger, 1992).

In short, the courts' treatment of PET and SPECT evidence offers some clues about how fMRI evidence is likely to be received. Broad declarations regarding the reliability of the underlying science may be infrequent and, in any event, of limited precedential value as fMRI science and its applications, especially in non-legal settings, develop. Admissibility and probative value are likely to depend instead on relevant features of the particular case in which the evidence is offered. Finally, trial judges' decisions to admit or exclude fMRI evidence will rarely be overturned.

---

13 Kulynych (1997) argues that it might be difficult to qualify witnesses as experts with regard to functional neuroimaging evidence (including fMRI) because the imaging technologies draw on so many kinds of expertise that no one person may be in a position to explain the process (e.g., as required by Federal Rule of Evidence 901(b)(9)) and to interpret the findings. This, however, has not turned out to be the case with regard to PET scan evidence, nor has it been the case so far with regard to fMRI (see below).

14 For a good illustration of this deferential standard as applied to a non-jury proceeding, see *Blodgett-McDeavitt v. University of Nebraska*, 2004 (appellate court affirms trial court's ruling on medical causation based in part on PET scan evidence, explaining that the trial court's findings of fact were not "clearly wrong").

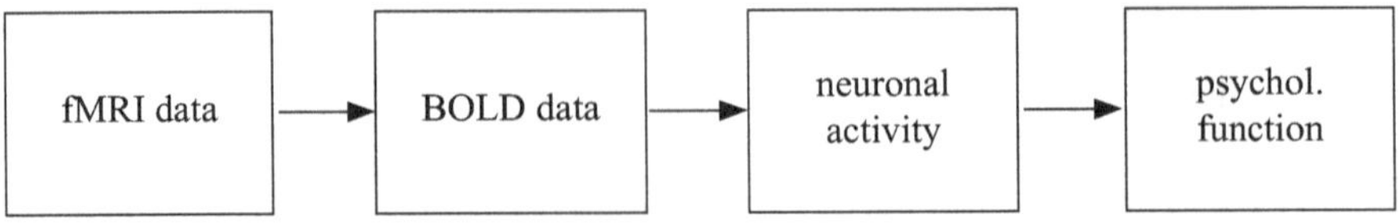

1. fMRI data → BOLD (blood-oxygenation level dependent) signals in regions of interest in brain(s) of subject(s) in task condition
2. BOLD signals → neuronal activity in regions of interest in brain(s) of subject(s) in task condition
3. Neuronal activity → psychological function of interest

Figure 3.1 fMRI Data to BOLD Data

fMRI: Conceptual and Methodological Issues

The analysis and interpretation of fMRIs for purposes of neuroscience and psychology, and hence for law, can be understood as based on a chain of inferences running from the data to the psychological function or construct of interest[15] (see Figure 3.1).

Each step of this model raises potential questions about the reliability (and, in the case of inference (3), the applicability or relevance) of fMRI evidence for law, both of which are crucial considerations, as explained above, under either Federal Rule of Evidence 702 and *Daubert* or the alternative *Frye* test. Inference (1), from the fMRI data to the BOLD data in the regions of interest in the brain(s) of subject(s) in the task or experimental condition, is affected by researchers' decisions regarding and assumptions underlying data processing methods, most of which have not yet converged on the kind of consensus that would allow the basic technology to be "black boxed" (Halfon, 1998; Latour & Woolgar, 1986), thus obviating further doubts about reliability. Inference (2), from the BOLD data to neuronal activity, is less problematic but still fraught with difficulty; although most researchers believe that local blood flow in the brain is related to neural activity, the precise relationship is not yet completely understood (Wolpe, Foster & Langleben, 2005). And inference (3), from neuronal activity to psychological function, raises fundamental questions about the theories and concepts relied upon in the design of fMRI studies and the associations drawn between fMRI data and the cognitive or emotional function of interest, and hence about the application of the data to the legal issue at hand.

15 The sequence of inferences made or projected by scientists designing, conducting and analysing fMRI studies is, of course, different: most likely it begins, not ends, with the psychological phenomenon of interest ("what are the neural correlates of function x?"), and may be recursive (in that patterns of fMRI data prompt further rounds of experiments, with study designs revised as appropriate).

Severally or cumulatively, these issues may affect the perceived reliability and hence admissibility of fMRI research on two levels. First, any aspect of fMRI methods or principles that makes any given finding less robust, less replicable, may make it harder for that finding to acquire general support and acceptance in the relevant scientific community, and this in turn will make courts less likely to regard that finding as a reliable enough basis for legal decision-making. Second, in the aggregate, the various concerns raised by fMRI methods and principles may lead courts to find more generally that fMRI studies do not (yet) provide a sufficiently reliable basis for legal decision-making.

From fMRI Data → BOLD Data in Brain(s) of Subject(s) in Task Condition Whether represented in numbers or the well-known "pretty coloured brain pictures", fMRI data are the outputs of an exceptionally complex technology. The nature and meaning of those data are shaped by a series of methodological and conceptual choices by the fMRI scientists. While the same could be said of many if not all types of scientific data, the decisions implicit in the fMRI data may be especially problematic for law: functional MRI technology is still relatively new, so the experts themselves have not yet reached consensus on methods for producing and interpreting data, and laypeople (including judges and jurors) are less likely to be or to feel that they are familiar with the ramifications of those methodological and conceptual choices, possibly undermining the perceived reliability of the data. The inference from the fMRI data obtained in properly conducted brain studies to BOLD levels in brain regions of interest – the foundation for all subsequent inferences to neuronal activity and hence to psychological function – raises at least half a dozen potential reliability issues.

First, fMRI scans present *differences* in brain activation between control (or rest) and experimental (or task) states, obtained by *subtracting* the BOLD signal of one from the other. That is, fMRI yields a relative, not an absolute, measure of brain activity. What follows from this? Typically, most brain regions are active in both the control and experimental conditions, but the differences in BOLD levels between the conditions (which is what the scans show) may be very small – in the typical reported fMRI study, only a few per cent – or nonexistent (Wexler, 2004). If the brain region is more or less equally active in the two conditions, the fMRI will not show anything. The presentation of only these small differences (what appears depends in part on the thresholding level; this is discussed next) thus ignores the majority of brain activity that is occurring in both conditions. The fMRI data, therefore, may not provide a very firm basis for inferences about "active" versus "inactive" brain regions during a given task – which is how fMRI findings often tend to be described (especially to lay audiences) – and the supposed psychological implications of those different brain activity levels.[16]

---

16 As Wexler (2004, p. 8) puts it, "[i]f we march around the brain associating different cognitive operations each with 2% of neuronal activity at different brain locations, what are

Second, fMRI data are *thresholded* for display at an *arbitrary level* of significance (often but not always $p < .05$) (Wolpe et al., 2005). The lower the bar for statistical significance of reported differences in brain activity between baseline and experimental conditions, the more "active" regions appear and the more widely distributed in the brain they appear to be. Because at present there seems to be no consensus among fMRI researchers about the proper significance cut-off, researchers can obtain different brain activity patterns, and hence find support for different inferences about the structural distribution of psychological functions of interest, based on the identical underlying data.

Third, most fMRI images reported in the literature represent an *average* of data derived by subtracting an average of experimental scans from an average of control scans (e.g., Huettel et al., 2004; Illes & Racine, 2005). "Averaging images across brains can … produce apparent patterns of data that are spatially misleading, with group activity appearing in regions not found in any individual or eliminating aggregate patterns because of structural differences across individuals" (Cacioppo et al., 2003, p. 652).[17]

Fourth, and relatedly, *variability* in *brain anatomy* between individuals creates uncertainty in localization (Brett et al., 2002). In any multi-person study, many steps are involved in *normalizing* the data by reconciling individual anatomical variation to some standardized reference brain map (Brett et al., 2002; Huettel et al., 2004). And every brain registration algorithm embeds assumptions that may not be shared by all or most other researchers (Constable, 2006). These differences and uncertainties may not matter if the brain region of interest is as large as, say, the dorso-lateral prefrontal cortex, but the smaller the structural unit(s) of interest, the more important the decisions regarding the reconciliation of anatomical variability become.[18]

Fifth, although it might seem that the preceding two concerns would be avoided in a single-subject study, fMRI data and hence the inference to BOLD signals

---

we going to do with the unassigned majority of activity? And how are we going to study it with a paradigm that eliminates it?"

17 One psychologist has explained the problem as follows: "[I]magine that each subject had activity on the circumference of a circle, and then if you spatially averaged all those spatial locations, you'd get the center of the circle. So it would appear like there's activity in the middle of the circle when nobody ever had activity there" (*Entertainment Software v. Blagojevich*, 2005b, pp. 371–72).

18 Relatedly, limits on the spatial and temporal resolution of the fMRI may or may not restrict the legally relevant inferences to be validly drawn from the images. Although fMRI offers superior spatial resolution to that provided by other forms of functional neuroimaging (see above), it is unable to detect the activity of individual or small groups of neurons; the BOLD signal in each several cubic milliliter of blood represents the activity of tens of thousands (Robinson, 2004) or even millions (Henson, 2005) of neurons. Whether this matters depends on the spatial scale of functional organization in the brain. If it is sufficiently gross, then resolution at the level of individual neurons may not be required to make meaningful discriminations between brain regions (see Henson, 2005).

for even a single person may be affected by all sorts of *intrasubject variables* that may muddy the data. These include the subject's level of expertise in the experimental task (which may raise or lower BOLD signals and hence inferred brain activity levels; see below), the amount of attention the subject devotes to the task and physiological variations in brain blood flow (on which the BOLD levels depend) due to the subject's absorption of caffeine, nicotine and other substances that may affect baseline (resting) brain activation patterns and hence the measured differences in brain activity between baseline and experimental conditions (Constable, 2006; Huettel et al., 2004).[19] At least one leading brain researcher has gone so far as to state that at present "[t]here is no single-subject reliability" (Robinson, 2004). Since many if not most likely courtroom uses of fMRI data will be to help prove adjudicative facts about individuals – mental impairment as evidence of injury, incompetence to stand trial, reduced brain function as a mitigating factor in sentencing, and so on (see above) – these caveats regarding single-subject data are of great practical importance.

Sixth, the complexity and variability of the experimental designs and methods used in fMRI research, and especially the variability from one lab to another, may undermine the generalizability of results (see, e.g., Illes & Racine, 2005). For instance, MR signal changes increase with increasing magnetic field strength. But clinical fMRI scanners vary in strength – many are 1.5 Tesla, but an increasing number are 3.0 Tesla or greater – so the brain activation patterns detected may vary from lab to lab, even holding everything else constant, making it more difficult for specific findings to be replicated.

None of these issues have prevented the tremendous growth and widespread acceptance of fMRI as a brain research tool, as attested to by the thousands of fMRI studies now appearing annually in dozens of specialized and general scientific journals (Illes & Racine, 2005). Even though peer reviewers routinely recognize (properly conducted) fMRI research as "good enough" science, courts may well hesitate before admitting expert testimony based on fMRI. The inference from fMRI data to BOLD data may well be strong enough to support the always provisional findings of experimental science when addressed to audiences of fellow scientists, but not the conclusive determination of legal facts by non-scientists. Authors of peer-reviewed fMRI studies can satisfy their professional obligations in this regard simply by reporting their methodological and interpretive choices, trusting that their readers will understand the theoretical and practical contexts for those choices and appreciate the limitations on what may be validly inferred by their findings. Judges applying rules of evidence to proffers of fMRI data, in contrast, ought not to be as sanguine, and might well decline to consider (or to allow jurors to consider) that data (or the expert opinions based on it) unless

19 In addition, if the subject moves in the scanner, that motion corrupts the data (motion correction algorithms are used but there is no consensus about these) or, at least increases the variance in the data, making it harder to see significant differences and hence "activity" (Constable, 2006).

persuaded that the data are trustworthy enough to be relied upon by a decision-maker whose judgment might deprive a party of property, liberty or even life.

Although astounding progress has been made in functional brain imaging over the last decade, fMRI science is still in its infancy. Some if not all of the concerns raised above regarding the reliability with which any given fMRI data indicate relative BOLD levels in brain regions of interest may be minimized or eliminated as fMRI technology advances and brain researchers converge on protocols and methods for the processing and interpretation of data. Until enough of these and other conceptual and technological issues are resolved, however, the reliability of the fMRI data (even from properly designed and conducted studies) on which courtroom experts will rely in providing opinions should remain open to question.

From BOLD Data in Regions of Interest in Brain(s) of Subject(s) in Task Condition → Neuronal Activity in Those Regions in Brain(s) of Subject(s) in Task Condition The assumption underlying all fMRI work is that the measured BOLD signal is strongly correlated with neuronal activity; that is, that increases in the MR signal due to increases in the ratio of oxygenated to deoxygenated haemoglobin in particular brain areas reflects increases in neuronal activity (spiking or local field potentials or both) in those areas (Heeger et al., 2000). But while neuroscientists generally agree that local blood flow in the brain is related to neuronal activity, and recent research has shown a strong correlation between neuronal spiking, local field potentials and BOLD signals (Mukamel et al., 2005), "the relationship remains incompletely understood" (Wolpe et al., 2005, p. 5). The BOLD signal "is a complex function of blood flow, oxygenation level, and volume" (Henson, 2005, p. 5), and other physiological events besides neuronal spiking rates, such as the transitory supply of the neurotransmitter dopamine (Huettel et al., 2004), may independently affect local blood flow and hence the BOLD signal. The inference from BOLD signals to neuronal activity levels may well be the least problematic step in the inferential chain and the most likely step to be black-boxed (cf. Halfon, 1998; Latour & Woolgar, 1986) in the foreseeable future. Even so, the science is not yet settled, and therefore, even if this inference is generally accepted in the scientific community for purposes of the *Frye* standard, expert testimony based on fMRI may still be susceptible to objection and exclusion on this ground by judges taking a sufficiently strict view under *Daubert*.

From Neuronal Activity in Brain(s) of Subject(s) in Task Condition → Psychological Function of Interest All brain researchers (and many, but not all, psychologists) presume that there must be some kind of systematic mapping of psychological function onto brain structure; otherwise, measuring brain activity wouldn't tell us anything about the mind (Henson, 2005). But the nature and conceptual precision of this mapping, which should be critical to almost any reliance on fMRI studies in courts, raise a number of questions.

First, many brain-imaging studies simply assume that the differential activation of a particular region of the brain during a specific mental operation means that that region is the neural substrate for that operation, and conversely, that the absence of (relative) activity in a region during a specific operation means that that region is not a neural substrate for that operation (i.e., a *one-to-one* mapping). But neither assumption is necessarily true (Cacioppo et al., 2003; Sarter, Bernston & Cacioppo, 1996). The degree to which the neural correlates of cognitive and emotional functions are localized versus distributed in the brain is a topic of ongoing (and maybe irresolvable) debate, but there is at least substantial support for a *many-to-many* relationship between regions of (relative) brain activity and cognitive function or behaviour.[20] So "activation [in a localized brain region] may reflect not the locus in which a particular function originates but rather may reflect a region that is part of a more distributed network of processing mechanisms that work together to perform the task" (Cacioppo et al., 2003, p. 654). In addition, it could well be that "in a different context or when using a different comparison task, what appears to be the same information-processing operation could be related to activation in a different region of the cortex" (Cacioppo et al., 2003, p. 654). Moreover, the more complex the mental function of interest, the more widely distributed the structural activity patterns, because "more complex" when used to describe functions means (among other things) that more discrete processes are involved (Cacioppo et al., 2003). The complexities of widely distributed structure–function relationships should make it harder to establish sufficiently reliable support for generalizable associations between brain region activation and cognitive functions of interest, because the more multifarious the findings, the more difficult it will be (all things being equal) to replicate the results adequately.

Second, the interpretation of the psychological significance of fMRI data (i.e., significant differences in measured brain activity between experimental and control conditions) always depends on the specification of the psychological construct of interest and the care with which the experimental manipulations are designed. "Unless the information-processing operations that differ between comparison tasks are clearly and narrowly specified, the fact that the data were collected using fMRI and can be rendered in dramatic fashion on anatomically precise [images] may not help address the psychological or theoretical significance of the data" (Cacioppo et al., 2003, p. 658; see also Willingham & Dunn, 2003). Thus, a psychologist may want to do an fMRI study to learn more about memory, but what is memory? If (as most psychologists believe) memory consists of many distinct but sometimes interrelated functions, what are those functions, and how are they related? One must have some theory about this to draw any inferences about what is happening in the mind when certain patterns of activation appear in the brain. So any inferences from brain to mind are necessarily provisional

---

20 One-to-one mapping between localized brain activity and function is better supported with regard to some basic sensory and motor responses, such as the role of the primary visual cortex in elementary visual perception (e.g., Kosslyn, 1994; Palmer, 1999), but much less so with regard to the kinds of more complex cognitive and emotional functions most of interest to law (Constable, 2006).

because they depend on the existing (and often contested) state of psychological theory. Relatedly, the experimental and baseline tasks must also be matched for all dimensions not being deliberately varied, including difficulty and interest, to minimize confounds (Phelps, 1999), and this is more difficult to do the less well defined the psychological function or construct of interest (see Wexler, 2004).

It could be argued that the validity of any experimental psychological research depends on the clarity and coherence of the underlying theoretical constructs and the precision of the experimental design, and that fMRI research is no different in these respects, but merely uses a different dependent variable (see Henson, 2005; Phelps, 1999). The exceptional sensitivity and complexity of that dependent variable (see generally Huettel et al., 2004), however, makes any flaws resulting from imperfections in conceptualization and design (not to mention other factors like individual variability in response; see above) that much more salient.

Third, even to the extent that scientists generally support an inference from relative activity levels in the brain region(s) of interest to psychological function, there may still be a gap between that function and the concept that is material to *legal judgments* of responsibility or guilt, raising concerns under Rule 702(3) (Federal Rules of Evidence, 2007 and *Daubert* (1993). For instance, a criminal defendant who wants to use neuroimaging evidence to support an argument that he was incapable of having the *mens rea* required to commit the crime must do more than show a brain abnormality or even a decrease in cognitive function. He "must introduce evidence of a cognitive or behavioral impairment that directly relates to his capacity to form criminal intent or to control his own behavior" (Kulynych, 1997, p. 1257; see also Dumit, 2004; Kevles, 1997). It was on just this ground that the Ninth Circuit Court of Appeals in *Jackson v. Calderon* (2000), for instance, rejected the defendant's proffer of PET scan evidence to diagnose his PCP abuse. The court reasoned that the PET scan evidence could at most establish only some PCP-induced brain abnormality but not the effect of that abnormality on the defendant's capacity for higher-level thought, including the specific intent required for conviction for the crime charged.[21] Given the current state of forensic psychological neuroimaging, fMRI evidence offered to prove similar matters may face the same sort of challenge.[22]

fMRI Goes to Court: The Entertainment Software Association Litigation

How much any of the issues discussed above will affect the admissibility or perceived probative value of fMRI evidence will depend on the circumstances

---

21 See also, e.g., *United States v. Mezvinsky* (2002) (PET scan evidence indicating cognitive impairment irrelevant to dispositive legal issue of whether the defendant lacked the ability to form an intent to deceive, the required *mens rea* in the charged crime of fraud).

22 For the broader argument that developments in neuroscience such as fMRI should not affect criminal law doctrines of responsibility or their applications, except in very limited circumstances, see Morse (2004, 2006).

of the particular case in which the evidence is offered. The very first reported cases, however, illustrate some of the difficulties that proponents of fMRI evidence may face (*Entertainment Software Association v. Blagojevich*, 2005a; *Entertainment Software v. Granholm*, 2005, 2006). The plaintiffs in both cases are Entertainment Software Association, a trade organization consisting of video game publishers and console manufacturers, and others who sued in federal court to enjoin enforcement of anti-violent video game legislation in Illinois, Michigan, and other states.[23] The most important fact at issue is the legislative finding that (in the words of the Illinois legislature) minors who play violent video games are more likely to "experience a reduction of activity in the frontal lobes of the brain which is responsible for controlling behavior" (*Entertainment Software Association v. Blagojevich*, 2005a, p. 1073). To support this finding at the hearing on the plaintiffs' motion for a preliminary and permanent injunction in the Illinois case, the state offered the testimony of several expert witnesses, including William Kronenberger, a clinical psychologist who, relying in part on fMRI data, sought to show that adolescents exposed to a substantial amount of media violence exhibited deficits (lower activity levels) in particular brain locations (dorso-lateral prefrontal cortex and anterior cingulate cortex), and that these patterns resembled those of the brains of other adolescents clinically diagnosed as aggressive or violent.

In response, the plaintiffs offered the testimony of Howard Nusbaum, a cognitive psychologist. Nusbaum criticized the defendant's fMRI studies and their proposed use in court on many grounds, three of which are particularly noteworthy here because they clearly illustrate concerns raised by the third link in the inferential chain discussed above. First, Nusbaum called attention to a problem of experimental design. In one of the defendant's studies, researchers used fMRI to measure the effects of violent versus non-violent video game play. Since participants could not actually play the games while in the scanner, however, they were instead shown videotapes of game play and asked to press a fake joystick button whenever they would have done so during actual play. But, as Nusbaum pointed out, brain activity would very likely be different during actual play, which requires interacting with the (mediated) world, as opposed to mere viewing. So the study was not a valid measure of the effects of violent versus non-violent game play (*Entertainment Software Association v. Blagojevich*, 2005b, pp. 384–385).

A second and more fundamental criticism attacked the inference that Kronenberger drew from the observed difference in brain activity (in the task versus rest condition) to the claimed difference in mental function. The fMRI study just described showed reduced activity in participants' frontal lobes during (simulated) game play. Kronenberger testified that this reduced level of activity

---

23 The same parties have also (to this point successfully) challenged similar legislation in *Video Software Dealers Ass'n v. Maleng* (2004), *Video Software Dealers Ass'n v. Schwarzenegger* (2005), *Entertainment Software Ass'n v. Foti* (2006), and *Entertainment Software Ass'n v. Hatch* (2006), but the reported opinions in those cases to date have not mentioned fMRI evidence.

meant a reduced capacity for impulse control, self-regulation, and so on, and thus a greater susceptibility to aggressive or violent behaviour. Nusbaum, however, explained that the frontal lobes are involved in many brain functions, and that many areas besides the frontal lobes (e.g., parietal lobes, thalamus, etc.) are also involved in attention (and hence self-regulation), so that it is not possible to draw the kind of one-to-one connection between frontal lobe activity and level of self-regulation on which the defendant's expert's testimony relied. In addition, reduced activity in the frontal lobes may indicate not a mental deficit, but rather greater *expertise* in some task-relevant function(s), because the more expert one is at a task, the less attention one needs to devote to it (*Entertainment Software Association v. Blagojevich*, 2005b, pp. 361–365). Thus, the fMRIs of adolescents who play violent (or any) video games may show less frontal lobe activity not because those adolescents are aggressive or violent but because they are experts at playing those sorts of games.

Third, during his cross-examination, Nusbaum indicated the gap between the psychological constructs measured by well-designed fMRI studies and those on which legal judgments depend. For example, the legislative finding supporting the Illinois statute speaks of behavioral "control", and the defendant's attorney asked Nusbaum whether certain brain functions were associated with "self-control" and "concentration". Nusbaum responded that fMRI cognitive research might (for instance) associate a given part of the brain with "task-switching", but would not purport to reach findings about functions as broadly (and colloquially) labeled as "self-control" (*Entertainment Software Association v. Blagojevich*, 2005b, pp. 406–407).

The federal trial courts in both Illinois and Michigan found these and other criticisms[24] of the fMRI research on which the defendant relied to be convincing, and enjoined enforcement of the anti-violent video game laws (*Entertainment Software Association v. Blagojevich*, 2005a; *Entertainment Software Association v. Granholm*, 2005, 2006).[25] It is possible that in contrast to the very ambitious offer of fMRI (and other) evidence in the *Entertainment Software Association* cases to

24 For instance, Nusbaum also brought to the Illinois federal district court's attention concerns raised by the first link in the inferential chain discussed above, such as the risks of false positives and negatives posed by the averaging of fMRI data across subjects (see above). In its opinion, however, the court seems to have been particularly impressed with the criticisms going to inference (3), from measured brain activity to psychological function of interest (*Entertainment Software Ass'n v. Blagojevich*, 2005a, p. 1074) ("Dr. Nusbaum's testimony persuasively shows the legislature was simply incorrect in concluding that the frontal lobes of the brain are responsible for controlling behavior; no such one-to-one relationship exists. And as Dr. Nusbaum persuasively testified, decreased activity does not necessarily indicate diminished capacity; it can signify expertise or use of an alternative mental method of achieving the same goal.")

25 The court in the Illinois case (*Blagojevich*) consolidated the plaintiffs' motion for a preliminary injunction with the trial on the merits and permanently enjoined enforcement of the statute. The court in the Michigan case has recently granted a permanent injunction

establish an association between ill-defined stimuli ("violent video games") and a complex set of higher-order cognitive/emotional functions (e.g., self-control) to prove a broad legislative fact, other potential uses of fMRI may be less prone to at least some of the basic conceptual and methodological concerns outlined above. For instance, reliability and relevance problems posed by averaging and normalizing multi-person data, specifying the psychological construct of interest, and translating neuroimaging findings into concepts both relevant and material to legal judgments may be mitigated or avoided when fMRI evidence is used to prove case-specific adjudicative facts such as whether a defendant displays mental function *x* that is characteristic of, say, toxic solvent encephalopathy (see, e.g., *Hose v. Chicago Northwestern Transp. Co.*, 1995).[26] On the other hand, the opposite may also be true: Precisely because of difficulties in interpreting individual scans (due to insufficient single-subject reliability; Robinson, 2004), inferences from a scan to the classification of legal interest may be *less* reliable for individuals than for the aggregates that legislative facts purport to describe. In sum, the extent to which proffers of fMRI evidence will be successfully challenged on the basis of the fundamental methodological and conceptual questions discussed above is simply not yet clear.[27]

---

against enforcement of that state's similar statute (see *Entertainment Software Ass'n v. Granholm*, 2006).

26 Another example: the difficulties in drawing structure-to-function inferences given the typical "many–many" relationship between brain activity in regions of interest and psychological function may be beside the point where the relevant legal question is simply establishing a reliable marker of difference between the presence and absence of a given mental state. Thus, if some brain region is significantly and reliably more active when a person recognizes a stimulus fact than when he or she does not (under the GKT [guilty knowledge test] lie detection paradigm; see, e.g., Honts, Raskin & Kircher, 2002; Iacono & Lykken, 2002; Langleben et al., 2002), then that is all that should matter to the trier of fact; it should make no difference what particular brain region is involved.

27 The discussion in the text suggests two other issues. First, however problematic the use of fMRI evidence for a given legal purpose, we might ask: compared to what? The other kinds of expert evidence typically introduced in the PET and SPECT cases include clinical psychiatric or psychological testimony based on various sorts of diagnostic testing and the clinician's observations. Each of these kinds of evidence has its own, in some instances well-recognized, limitations.

Second, to the extent that the methodological and conceptual concerns outlined above apply to the courtroom use of fMRI evidence generally, they would also seem to apply to PET and SPECT evidence. Yet these sorts of concerns do not appear to have generally prevented PET and SPECT data from being used in court, and for the most part they have not even been discussed in the reported opinions. This may suggest that many proffers of fMRI-based testimony will be similarly successful despite these concerns. On the other hand, perhaps the sorts of challenges successfully made to the fMRI evidence in the *Entertainment Software Association* cases will also call into question previously accepted uses of other neuroimaging techniques, just as changes in law and science prompted by *Daubert* may

Should fMRIs Be Shown to Jurors?

If judges admit expert testimony based on fMRI, they must then decide whether to admit the neuroimages themselves if offered to illustrate that testimony. In his leading study of the scientific, cultural and legal significance of PET scans, Joseph Dumit (2004) argues that the images should *not* be used in court, at least not in jury trials. Dumit posits that PET scans are *expert images* and, as such, pose a paradox: "If [the images] are legible, then they should not need interpretation [by an expert], but if they need interpretation, then they probably should not be shown to juries" (Dumit, 2004, p. 112). The problem, Dumit asserts, is that the cultural familiarity of brain images to jurors will lead them to misinterpret the images and draw from them dispositive inferences that the images, as understood by experts, do not support. A related problem is what Mobbs and his colleagues (2007) have referred to as the "Christmas tree phenomenon" – jurors will be dazzled by the "pretty lights" in the fMRI image and will not pay sufficient attention to the expert's interpretation of the image.[28]

Functional MRIs, like PET scans, are unquestionably expert images. The fMRI picture is decidedly not a "snapshot of the brain", readily (and correctly) interpretable by the untrained or uninformed. It is instead a *statistical map* in the guise of an iconic representation (see Illes & Racine, 2005). An expert is needed to explain to a non-expert audience (judge or juror) the array of complex methodological and interpretive techniques and assumptions that contribute to the creation of the image, as outlined above. Moreover, much of what Dumit (2004) writes about the persuasive effects of PET scans applies equally to fMRIs. I disagree with Dumit, however, about the implications for the courtroom use of fMRIs (and by extension, other brain images). If the fMRI science on which proffered expert testimony is good enough, then courts should deal with the potential problems that fMRI images pose not by excluding those images, but rather by admitting them and by educating jurors about the range of appropriate interpretations.

I first sketch some of the ways in which fMRIs, like PET scans, may be misconstrued by lay viewers. I then offer four arguments to support my position that the images should be admitted despite their judgemental risks.

---

be leading to a more thorough re-evaluation of the admissibility of traditionally accepted forensic identification techniques (cf. Mnookin, 2003; Saks & Koehler, 2005).

28 Unless otherwise specified, references to fMRI images are to the most common mode of visualization in the scientific literature, the axial view of the "brain slice", produced by mapping the functional image onto a structural image and highlighting (colouring) voxels that meet the chosen significance threshold (see Brett et al., 2002). Even a cursory review of the literature, however, reveals a variety of ways of presenting fMRI data (see below), and there are no generally accepted standards (Constable, 2006). The observations in this section of the paper apply (all things being equal) to all types of fMRI pictures.

Functional MRI Images may be Inappropriately Persuasive

Functional neuroimages may indeed be highly persuasive evidence of the facts they are offered to prove, but for reasons that go beyond the reasons why brain scientists and other experts might consider them persuasive. First, as one critic of the courtroom use of neuroimages has written, fMRIs "may appear to be deceptively similar to photographs of a person's brain" (Kulynych, 1997, p. 1249). This remark nicely captures two facets of what media theorists call the appeal of *transparency* (Bolter & Grusin, 1999), or what cognitive and social psychologists call *naïve realism*: the convincing notion that one has unmediated access to objective reality (Robinson et al., 1995). First, fMRIs may offer convincing evidence because they seem to allow viewers to *look directly at the brain*. Writing of (and to) professional experimental psychologists, i.e., the experts themselves, Henson (2005, p. 42) states that "[t]here is a real danger that pictures of blobs on brains seduce one into thinking that we can now directly observe psychological constructs." The risk that non-scientists (including jurors and judges) will be prone to similar epistemic confusion must be even greater.[29] At the same time, fMRIs may offer convincing evidence because they look like what people *expect* images of the brain to look like, because they have seen brain images in magazines, on television and on the Internet. That is to say, these images have been assimilated (or *remediated*, to use Bolter and Grusin's (1999) terminology) to a familiar medium (photography) which people are already habituated to "see through" directly onto reality.

Second, fMRI pictures are likely to be especially credible to lay audiences because of their status as prototypical *scientific* images. The fMRI visualizes brain function for the non-scientist audience as an instance of mechanized, computerized and, therefore *objective* (and, consequently, highly reliable), scientific knowledge (see Daston & Galison, 1992). In addition, the fMRI is a *mathematized* object, the visual representation of a series of (computerized) measurements and computations

29 For instance, the defence attorney in *People v. Weinstein* (1992) was quoted as saying that PET "permits the defense to present to the jury, in highly effective color slide form, actual images of the defendant's brain" ('PET Scans Advance as Tool in Insanity Defense,' 1993). Compare the title of a recent *New York Times* feature story: "Can Brain Scans See Depression?" (Carey, 2005). And as one of the plaintiffs' lawyers in the *Entertainment Software Association* case has observed: "Where do Illinois, California, and other states that have recently enacted this sort of anti-violent video game legislation get their findings that exposure to video games damages the frontal lobes? From 'new evidence' from Kronenberger, which [may lead some to believe that] you can look at the brain" (Fallow, 2005). Although "[the defendants] have argued that this 'new evidence' is stronger [than the evidence offered in support of previously rejected anti-violent video game legislation] because it 'appears more scientific'" (Fallow, 2005), the courts thus far, agreeing with the plaintiffs, have found it to be so methodologically and conceptually flawed (see above) that they regard it as even weaker than the social science evidence also submitted by defendants and found inadequate to support the legislation (*Entertainment Software Ass'n v. Blagojevich*, 2005a).

(see Lynch & Woolgar, 1988). In both respects, the persuasiveness of fMRI images derives from their resonance with other representations of scientific truth in the culture at large.

Third, the presumptive credibility of fMRIs may trigger in lay viewers' minds networks of folk psychological inferences that have consequences for legal judgments. Brain images tend to *naturalize* the psychological construct of interest (e.g., mental competence) by appearing to ground them in visible reality and to locate them in the person – specifically, in the brain (Dumit, 2004). This *reduces psychosocial complexity* to supposed features of the brain; it confuses the part (brain) for the whole (person-in-situation) (cf. Bennett & Hacker, 2003). This could exacerbate people's general tendency to commit the fundamental attribution error – to overattribute others' behaviour to the kinds of people they are rather than to the circumstances in which they find themselves (Nisbett & Ross, 1980).[30] Moreover, neuroimages tend to convert (sometimes subtle) differences of degree into differences in kind. Statistically significant but still relatively small distinctions in BOLD levels between two sets of data become contrasts of bright colour versus no colour. The juxtaposed images "just look different", and therefore may be thought to *be* different in psychologically and legally relevant ways (cf. Eberhardt, 2005). This may encourage in triers of fact a false sense of ease in making legally required classifications (e.g., whether the defendant was or was not mentally impaired so as to diminish or avoid legal responsibility for his or her actions). More invidiously, neuroimages of difference may exacerbate the effects of unconscious prejudice against outgroups (although they may also mitigate prejudice by showing people how their race-based perceptions are situation-dependent and amenable to change; Eberhardt, 2005).

The Probative Value of fMRI Images Should Outweigh Their Judgemental Risks

Even though fMRI images may be unduly or improperly persuasive for the reasons just discussed, the dangers they may pose to good legal judgment do not warrant their *per se* exclusion from the courtroom. In the language of Federal Rule of Evidence 403 (Federal Rules of Evidence, 2007) and similar state law rules, the risks of unfair prejudice, confusion or misleading the jury that fMRIs pose need not (substantially) outweigh their probative value in illustrating and clarifying expert testimony. Reliable legal knowledge about matters to which fMRI-based expert testimony is relevant is best sought, not by excluding fMRIs, but rather by admitting them and allowing expert witnesses and lawyers to *educate* jurors (and judges) about scientists' own interpretations of the images.

30 Note that in many situations in which fMRI evidence is likely to be offered, the proponent may want to invite attributions of behavior to personal rather than situational factors – specifically, to aspects of the person (physiological brain impairments) for which they should not be held legally responsible as opposed to aspects of the person (will) for which they should.

Four arguments support this position: (1) *Contra* Dumit (2004), there is no "paradox" of expert images. That judges and jurors need expert testimony to help them interpret fMRIs is not a reason to exclude the pictures; rather, in court as in the everyday practice of science, the scientist's words and images can *explain each other*, increasing the likelihood that legal judgments will be grounded in acceptable science. (2) fMRIs may indeed resonate with jurors' familiarity with other brain images and thus produce "unauthorized" meanings – but *all* images are capable of doing this, yet the law does not for this reason exclude all demonstrative (or real) evidence, and fMRIs are no different from other images in this respect. (3) Although excluding fMRI images may avoid some kinds of potential bias, showing the pictures may help to *correct* for (or at least not exacerbate) *other* biases. (4) Finally, in addition to hearing expert witnesses' explanations of how fMRI images are produced and what they mean, the best way for lay audiences to understand how fMRIs (or any images) represent knowledge is *to be shown more pictures*.

fMRIs and expert testimony can explain each other The first argument is that Dumit's "paradox" of expert images is illusory. Judges and jurors can be taught to know what scientists already know: that fMRIs are not "snapshots" of the brain, not direct read-offs from reality, but rather highly mediated outputs of scientific investigation, and that their probative value depends on the nature of the mediations – the validity of the underlying theories and concepts and of the principles that guide the multiple translations from experimental intervention to final visual representation (see, e.g., Galison, 1997; Hacking, 1983; Latour, 1987, 1999). Judges and jurors can also be instructed to interpret fMRIs in light of their context within relevant scientific discourse. In routine scientific practice, including conference presentations and publications, scientists use images along with words and notations to construct arguments about the reliability, validity and importance of their work. Words and illustrations *back each other up* (Bastide, 1988); each explains the other. The same should be true in court. Here, the relative opacity of the fMRI – "If it's not a snapshot of the brain, then just what are we looking at?" – *enlists the expert* as the interpreter of the image and (as Goodwin (1994) has explained) provides an opportunity for the expert to *perform science* by modelling informed looking at the image. Thus, when an expert's words explain the image in court, each makes the other more intelligible and persuasive. Allowing jurors (and judges) to hear expert testimony and see expert images would therefore actually bring courtroom scientific discourse into closer alignment with scientific practice.[31]

There are reasons to believe that the fMRI pictures will not necessarily trump the testimony (as Dumit (2004), Mobbs et al. (2007), and others have suggested they might). First, expert testimony will frame the fMRI, from the authentication to the description to the interpretation of the image. The foundation needed to

31 Whether this sort of conformity or "strong link" between scientific knowledge and legal knowledge is the preferred relationship between law and science after *Daubert* is itself a matter of dispute (see Caudill, 2001; Jasanoff, 1993).

authenticate (see Federal Rule of Evidence 901(b)(9)), for instance, will prompt jurors to focus on the image's mediated aspects, and competent cross-examination should help to ferret out the limitations of the data to prove the fact at issue. (Of course there remains the possibility that cross-examination in any given case may not be sufficiently competent.) Second, expert witnesses are capable of setting forth the science clearly enough for laypeople to understand (as exemplified by Nusbaum's testimony in the *Entertainment Software* hearing, discussed above). Research shows that when expert scientific evidence is clearly presented, jurors generally do a satisfactory job of understanding it and using it properly to inform their judgments (e.g., Vidmar & Diamond, 2001). More specifically, although jurors of course come to court with preconceived notions of every sort which may sometimes diverge from legal norms, when those preconceptions are explicitly identified and addressed, jurors are likelier to decide in accordance with the law rather than with the preconceptions (see, e.g., Diamond & Casper, 1992; Smith, 1991, 1993). Similarly, we might expect that if jurors' naïve notions about the "pretty coloured brain pictures" are acknowledged and then addressed through expert testimony, jurors' judgments are less likely to be driven by their preconceptions about what the pictures mean.

The problem of polysemy is not confined to brain images Although it is true that the polysemy of fMRIs may prompt "unauthorized" readings, this is true of *all* images, expert or non-expert, displayed in court. Recognizing that visual displays may prompt decision-makers to reach judgments on inappropriate grounds (e.g., animosity towards a party), the law of evidence subjects them (as it does all other evidence) to a balancing test, admitting them unless any risk of undue prejudice or confusion they pose substantially outweighs their probative value (Federal Rule of Evidence 403). Some visual displays pass this test; others do not. There is no reason to treat neuroimages in general any differently.[32]

fMRIs may on balance reduce, not aggravate, judgemental biases Even if not showing the fMRI scans in court would avoid certain judgemental biases (as described above), showing the scans could help to avoid others. For example, many lawyers and commentators claim to have observed what has been called "the *CSI* effect" (Baar, 2006; Stockwell, 2005; but cf. Podlas, 2006; Tyler, 2006): jurors expect prosecutors to produce forensic DNA evidence in every case, and tend to judge the prosecution more harshly when the proof disappoints these expectations.[33]

---

32 More broadly, the proliferation of implicit meaning is not something that the law should strive to banish in order to conform to some naïve ideal of science as "free from rhetoric". Rather, it is inherent in all visual representation (see, e.g., Sherwin, Feigenson & Spiesel, 2007), and it presents the law, like science, with occasions for elucidating those meanings and subjecting them to critical scrutiny.

33 Podlas (2006) and Tyler (2006) explain how the effect of *CSI* viewing on juror decision-making may well differ from what is popularly supposed. For instance, contrary

More generally, exposure to television programs like *CSI* has shaped jurors' ideas of what scientific truth looks like. In the case of *Old Chief v. United States* (1997), the United States Supreme Court recognized that parties have a right to present evidence in the form that they deem best suited to meet jurors' expectations of what convincing proof should be, even if that evidence is not logically necessary to the determination of guilt or innocence. Thus, if the fMRI-based expert testimony itself is admissible, the proponent of the fMRI evidence ought to be permitted to show the pictures in order to avoid being unfairly prejudiced by having disappointed the jurors' expectations about what scientific proof looks like.[34]

The cure for naïve realism is more, not fewer, images To the extent that those opposing the courtroom display of fMRIs are concerned that judges and jurors will mistakenly believe that the images offer direct, infallible access to objective reality (and thus accord the fMRIs too much weight), the solution is not to keep the images out. Instead, the law should confront decision-makers' possible naïve realism head on and refocus the search for legal truth where it should be, on the ways in which legal knowledge is mediated. And the way to do that is to *show more images* – to *multiply* the styles of representation. As Hacking (1983) argued, when representations are undifferentiated, the problem of realism does not arise; in other words, we are all naïve realists. "But as soon as representations begin to compete, we ha[ve] to wonder what is real" (p. 139). A variety of modes of representation makes it possible to ask how each mode mediates reality, and with what consequences.

If all viewers see are the standard axial views of the functional data superimposed on the structural brain image, highlighted in the usual fashion, they may well remain captivated by the notion that they are "looking at the brain". But if they also see fMRI data represented on rotated 3-D views of a highly articulated cortex (e.g., Brett et al., 2002, figure 2), on "smoothed" brain images (e.g., Spence et al., 2004, figure 4), and/or "glass brain" views, outlines of brains mapped onto grids and shown from three views (axial, coronal [from behind], and sagittal [from the side]) (e.g., Huettel et al., 2004, figure 12.11; Spence et al., 2004, figure 3), they are much likelier to understand that none of these are "snapshots" of the

to the presumed pro-criminal defendant effect, viewing the show may incline jurors to give greater credence and weight to the prosecution's forensic evidence generally, which would lead to a pro-prosecution effect; and other basic social psychological principles (such as the need to see justice done; Tyler, 2006) may incline jurors to convict the defendant despite any *CSI*-induced pro-defendant bias.

34 Judges, too, may be prone to biases that displaying the fMRI images may help to counter. Recent research on trial court judges' efforts to implement *Daubert*, and in particular the degree of scrutiny they give to different kinds of proffered evidence, indicates that the more quantitative the expert evidence, the more likely that judges applying *Daubert* are to exclude it (Merlino, Murray & Richardson, in press). It could well be that presenting the essentially quantitative data generated by fMRI technology in the non-quantitative form of a brain picture could help to counter this bias.

brain, and that each is no more (and no less) than a particular visual representation of the scientific data, the product of deliberate and often debatable choices by the research team (see Constable, 2006).[35] It is the variety of representational styles itself that makes the point that different modes of imaging can convey the "same" information in very different ways, offering different signal-to-noise ratios, methods of visualizing statistical significance, and implications regarding neuronal activity in areas other than the regions of interest quantification,[36] as well as other explicit and implicit differences in visual meaning.[37] Finally, images can help explain how fMRIs mediate scientific knowledge of the brain in yet another way: by explicitly diagramming the stages of data generation (e.g., Huettel et al., 2004, box 8.1) and/or image processing (e.g., Brett et al., 2002, figure 1). The courtroom display of such images should not only greatly assist triers of fact in understanding the fMRI expert testimony but also disabuse them of the tendency to view the data representations naïvely and hence uncritically.

Conclusion

In any given legal proceeding there may be real concerns about the reliability and relevance of fMRI-based expert testimony. Some of the fundamental questions raised by the contestable assumptions and varying methods underlying the creation and interpretation of fMRI data recommend a highly cautious approach to this evidence in general, at least given the present state of the science. Assuming, however, that the experts are qualified and that the testimony satisfies the basic criteria for admissibility, the law should not respond to the problems that the courtroom display of fMRIs may pose for good legal judgment by barring the images. Instead, the judges should admit the images (as appropriate) and seek to enhance everyone's visual literacy – that of the jurors, the lawyers and the judges themselves – so that legal judgments can, insofar as possible, be rendered consistently with the best available scientific knowledge.

35 And just as NIH has created an fMRI data centre in which researchers who want to publish fMRI studies must deposit their raw data so that other researchers can reprocess that data (if they desire) using their own methodologies, it might be advisable to require parties who seek to introduce fMRI images into evidence to submit the raw data to their opponents (and to the court) so that the opponents can have their experts reprocess the data and show the court how different methodological choices and assumptions can yield different visual representations of the data. (I would like to thank Patrick LaRiviere of the University of Chicago for suggesting this.)

36 See Constable (2006).

37 The next task is to examine more closely the variety of fMRI images, along the lines of studies such as those by Lynch & Woolgar (1988) of illustrations in the life sciences, Hoffmann and Laszlo (1989) of diagrams of chemical structures, and Latour (1999) of representation and reference in soil science in the Amazon, in order to explore how methods of representation make meaning.

References

Baar, Karen (2006) 'Jurors, Spoiled by TV Dramas, Are Saying, "Show Me the DNA Evidence"', *Quinnipiac Law*, 12(1): 17–21.

Bastide, Françoise (1988) 'The Iconography of Scientific Texts: Principles of Analysis' in Michael Lynch and Steve Woolgar (eds) *Representation in Scientific Practice*. Cambridge, MA: Cambridge University Press, 187–229.

Beckman, Mary (2004) 'Crime, Culpability, and the Adolescent Brain', *Science*, 305: 596–599.

Bennett, M.R. & Hacker, P.M.S. (2003) *Philosophical Foundations of Neuroscience*. Oxford: Blackwell.

Ben-Shakhar, Gershon & Elaad, Eitan (2003) 'The Validity of Psychophysiological Detection of Information with the Guilty Knowledge Test: A Meta-analytic Review', *Journal of Applied Psychology*, 88: 131–151.

Berger, Margaret A. (1992) 'When, If Ever, Does Evidentiary Error Constitute Reversible Error?', *Loyola of Los Angeles Law Review*, 25: 893–908.

Berry v. CSX Transportation, Inc., 709 So. 2d 552 (Fla. App. 1998).

Blodgett-McDeavitt v. University of Nebraska, 2004 Neb. App. LEXIS 329.

Bolter, Jay David & Grusin, Richard (1999) *Remediation*. Cambridge, MA: MIT Press.

Brett, Matthew, Johnsrude, Ingrid S. & Owen, Adrian M. (2002) 'The Problem of Functional Localization in the Human Brain', *Nature Reviews: Neuroscience*, 3: 243–249.

Cabeza, Roberto & Kingstone, Alan (eds) (2006) *Handbook of Functional Neuroimaging of Cognition*. Cambridge, MA: MIT Press (2nd ed.).

Cacioppo, John T., Bernston, Gary G., Lorig, Tyler S., Norris, Catherine J., Rickett, Edith & Nusbaum, Howard (2003) 'Just Because You're Imaging the Brain Doesn't Mean You Can Stop Using Your Head: A Primer and Set of First Principles', *Journal of Personality and Social Psychology*, 85: 650–661.

Carey, Benedict (2005) 'Can Brain Scans See Depression?', *The New York Times*, sec. F: 1, 6 (October 18).

Caudill, David S. (2001) 'Law and Science: An Essay on Links and Socio-Natural Hybrids', *Syracuse Law Review*, 51: 841–862.

Columbia University functional MRI (2005) 'About functional MRI: The future role of functional MRI in medical applications', http://www.fmri.org/fmri.htm (accessed 25 April 2006).

Commonwealth v. Frangipane, 433 Mass. 527 (2001).

Constable, R. Todd (2006) Private communications between co-Director, Yale Magnetic Resonance Research Center and author (3 February, 13 April).

Craig v. Orkin Exterminating Co., 2000 U.S. Dist. LEXIS 19240.

Daston, Lorraine & Galison, Peter (1992) 'The Image of Objectivity', *Representations*, 40: 81–128.

Daubert v. Merrell Dow Pharmaceuticals, 509 U.S. 579 (1993), *on remand*, 43 F.3d 1311 (9th Cir. 1995).

Davis, Kenneth (1942) 'An Approach to Problems of Evidence in the Administrative Process', *Harvard Law Review*, 55: 364–425.

Diamond, Shari & Casper, Jonathan (1992) 'Blindfolding the Jury to Verdict Consequences: Damages, Experts, and the Civil Jury', *Law and Society Review*, 26: 513–563.

Dumit, Joseph (2004) *Picturing Personhood*. Princeton, NJ: Princeton University Press.

Eberhardt, Jennifer L. (2005) 'Imaging Race', *American Psychologist*, 60: 181–190.

Elam v. Lincoln Electric Co., 362 Ill. App. 3d 884 (2005).

Entertainment Software Association et al. v. Blagojevich (2005a), 404 F. Supp. 2d 1051 (N.D. Ill.), affirmed 469 F.3d 641 (7th Cir. 2006).

Entertainment Software Association et al. v. Blagojevich (2005b), case no. 05 C 4265 (N.D. Ill.) (transcript of hearing on preliminary injunction (November 14–15).

Entertainment Software Association et al. v. Foti (2006), 451 F. Supp. 2d 823 (M.D. La.).

Entertainment Software Association et al. v. Granholm, 404 F. Supp. 2d 978 (E.D. Mich. 2005) (preliminary injunction), 426 F. Supp. 2d 626 (E.D. Mich. 2006) (permanent injunction).

Entertainment Software Association et al. v. Hatch (2006), 443 F.Supp.2d 1065 (D. Minn.).

Falksen v. Secretary of Department of Health and Human Services, 2004 U.S. Claims LEXIS 74.

Fallow, Katherine (2005) Private communication between attorney for plaintiffs in *Entertainment Software Association* cases and author (23 December).

Federal Rules of Evidence (2007). St. Paul, MN: West Publishing.

Feria v. Dynagraphics Co., 2004 Tex. App. LEXIS 2366.

Friedrich v. Intel Corp., 181 F.3d 1105 (9th Cir. 1999).

Frye v. United States, 293 F. 1013 (D.C. Cir. 1923).

Galison, Peter (1997) *Image and Logic*. Cambridge, MA: Harvard University Press.

Goodwin, Charles (1994) 'Professional Vision', *American Anthropologist*, 96: 606–633.

Greely, Henry (2004) 'Prediction, Litigation, Privacy, and Property: Some Possible Legal and Social Implications of Advances in Neuroscience' in Brent Garland (ed.) *Neuroscience and the Law*. New York: Dana Press, 114–156.

Green v. K-Mart Corp., 849 So. 2d 814 (La. App. 2003).

Greene, Joshua (2003) 'From Neural "Is" to Moral "Ought": What Are the Moral Implications of Neuroscientific Moral Psychology?', *Nature Reviews: Neuroscience*, 4: 847–850.

Greene, Joshua, Sommerville, R. Brian, Nystrom, Leigh E., Darley, John M. & Cohen, Jonathan D. (2001) 'An fMRI Investigation of Emotional Engagement in Moral Judgment', *Science*, 293: 2105–2108.

Hacking, Ian (1983) *Representing and Intervening*. Cambridge: Cambridge University Press.

Halfon, Saul (1988) 'Collecting, Testing and Convincing: Forensic DNA Experts in the Courts', *Social Studies of Science*, 28: 801–828.

Harrington v. State of Iowa, 659 N.W.2d 509 (Iowa Sup. Ct. 2003).

Heeger, David J., Huk, Alex C., Geisler, Wilson S. & Albrecht, Duane G. (2000) 'Spikes Versus BOLD: What Does Neuroimaging Tell Us About Neuronal Activity?', *Nature Neuroscience*, 3: 631–633.

Heeger, David J. & Ress, David (2002) 'What Does fMRI Tell Us About Neuronal Activity?', *Nature Reviews: Neuroscience*, 3:142–151.

Henson, R. (2005) 'What Can Functional Neuroimaging Tell the Experimental Psychologist?', *Quarterly Journal of Experimental Psychology*, A 58: 193–233.

Hoffmann, Roald & Laszlo, Pierre (1989) 'Representation in Chemistry', *Diogenes* 147: 23–51.

Honts, Charles R., Raskin, David C. & Kircher, John C. (2002) 'The Scientific Status of Research on Polygraph Techniques: The Case For Polygraph Tests' in David Faigman et al. (eds), *Science in the Law: Forensic Science Issues*. St. Paul, MN: West Publishing, 573–609.

Hose v. Chicago Northwestern Transp. Co., 70 F.3d 698 (8th Cir. 1995).

Huettel, Scott A., Song, Allen W. & McCarthy, Gregory (2004) *Functional Magnetic Resonance Imaging*. Sunderland, MA: Sinauer Associates, Inc.

Iacono, William G. & Lykken, David T. (2002) 'The Scientific Status of Research on Polygraph Techniques: The Case Against Polygraph Tests' in David Faigman et al. (eds), *Science in the Law: Forensic Science Issues*. St. Paul, MN: West Publishing, 609–663.

Illes, Judy & Racine, Eric (2005) Imaging or Imagining? A Neuroethics Challenge Informed by Genetics', *The American Journal of Bioethics*, 5(2): 1–14.

In re: Guardianship of Schiavo, 2005 WL 465405 (Fla. Cir. Ct.).

Jarvik, Elaine (2004) 'Group Fighting Porn – Via MRIs', *Deseret Morning News*, p. xx (May 5).

Jackson v. Calderon, 211 F.3d 1148 (9th Cir. 2000).

Jasanoff, Sheila (1993) 'What Judges Should Know About the Sociology of Science', *Judicature*, 77: 77–82.

Joiner v. General Electric, 522 U.S. 136 (1997).

Keckler, Charles (2002) 'Cross-examining the Brain: Legal Analysis of Neural Imaging for Credibility Impeachment', George Mason University School of Law, Law and Economics Working Paper Series (available SSRN).

Kevles, Bettyann (1997) *Naked to the Bone*. Reading, MA: Addison-Wesley.

Kittay, Leo (2007) 'Admissibility of fMRI Lie Detection', *Brooklyn Law Review*, 72: 1351–1399.

Kosslyn, Stephen M. (1994) *Image and Brain*. Cambridge, MA: MIT Press.

Kozel, F. Andrew, Johnson, Kevin A., Mu, Qiwen, Grenesko, Emily L., Laken, Steven J. & George, Mark S. (2005) 'Detecting Deception Using Functional Magnetic Resonance Imaging', *Biological Psychiatry*, 58: 605–613.

Kulynych, Jennifer (1997) 'Psychiatric Neuroimaging Evidence: A High-tech Crystal Ball?', *Stanford Law Review*, 49: 1249–1270.

LaMasa v. Bachman, 2005 N.Y. Misc. LEXIS 1164.

Langleben, D.D., Schroeder, L., Maldjian, A., Gur, R., McDonald, S., Ragland, J.D., O'Brien, C.P. & Childress, A.R. (2002) 'Brain Activity During Simulated Deception: An Event-related Functional Magnetic Resonance Study', *Neuroimage*, 15: 727–732.

Latour, Bruno (1987) *Science in Action*. Cambridge, MA: Harvard University Press.

Latour, Bruno (1999) *Pandora's Hope*. Cambridge, MA: Harvard University Press.

Latour, Bruno & Woolgar, Steve (1986) *Laboratory Life*. Princeton, NJ: Princeton University Press.

Lee, Tatia M.C., Liu, Ho-Ling, Tan, Li-Hai, Chan, Chetwyn C.H., Mahankali, Srikanth, Feng, Ching-Mei, Hou, Jinwen, Fox, Peter T. & Gao, Jia-Hong (2002) 'Lie Detection by Functional Magnetic Resonance Imaging', *Human Brain Mapping*, 15: 157–164.

Lynch, Michael & Woolgar, Steve (eds) (1988) *Representation in Scientific Practice*. Cambridge, MA: Cambridge University Press.

Mauet, Thomas A. & Wolfson, Warren D. (2005) *Trial Evidence*. New York: Aspen (3rd ed.).

Merlino, Mara L., Murray, Colleen I. & Richardson, James T. (in press) 'Judicial Gatekeeping and the Social Construction of the Admissibility of Expert Testimony', *Behavioral Sciences and the Law.*

Mnookin, Jennifer (2003) 'Fingerprints: Not a Gold Standard', *Issues in Science and Technology*, 20: 47–54.

Mobbs, Dean, Lau, Hakwan C., Jones, Owen D. & Frith, Christopher D. (2007) 'Law, Responsibility, and the Brain', *PLOS Biology, Public Library of Science*, 5(4), http://biology.plosjournals.org/perlserv/ (accessed 23 August 2007).

Morse, Stephen (2004) 'New Neuroscience, Old Problems' in Brent Garland (ed.) *Neuroscience and the Law*. New York: Dana Press, 157–198.

Morse, Stephen (2006) 'Brain Overclaim Syndrome and Criminal Responsibility: A Diagnostic Note', *Ohio State Journal of Criminal Law*, 3:397–412.

Mueller, Christopher B. & Kirkpatrick, Laird C. (2003) *Evidence*. New York: Aspen (3rd ed.).

Mukamel, Roy, Gelbard, Hagar, Arieli, Amos, Hasson, Uri, Fried, Itzhak & Malach, Rafael (2005) 'Coupling Between Neuronal Firing, Field Potentials, and fMRI in Human Auditory Cortex', *Science*, 309: 951–954.

Nisbett, Richard & Ross, Lee (1980) *Human Inference: Strategies and Shortcomings of Social Judgment*. Englewood Cliffs, NJ: Prentice Hall.

Old Chief v. United States, 519 U.S. 172 (1997).

Palmer, Stephen E. (1999) *Vision Science*. Cambridge, MA: MIT Press.

Parry, A. & Matthews, P.M. (2002) 'Functional Magnetic Resonance Imaging (fMRI): A "Window" Into the Brain', http://www.fmrib.ox.ac.uk/fmri_intro/fmri_intro.php (accessed 25 April 2006).

Penney v. Praxair, Inc., 116 F.3d 330 (8th Cir. 1997).

People v. Protsman, 88 Cal. App. 4th 509 (2001).
People v. Weinstein, 591 N.Y.S.2d 715 (Sup. Ct. 1992).
People v. Williams, 2004 Cal. App. Unpub. LEXIS 3213 (Ct. App. 2004).
People v. Yum, 111 Cal. App. 4th 635 (2003).
PET Scans Advance As Tool in Insanity Defense (1993), *Journal of Nuclear Medicine*, 34(1): 13N-16N, 25N-26N.
Phelps, Elizabeth A. (1999) 'Brain Versus Behavioral Studies of Cognition' in Robert Sternberg (ed.) *The Nature of Cognition*. Cambridge, MA: MIT Press, 297–322.
Podlas, Kimberlane (2006) '"The CSI Effect": Exposing the Media Myth', *Fordham Intellectual Property, Media, and Entertainment Law Journal*, 16: 429–465.
Podolski, Lisa & Feigenson, Neal (2007) 'Digitally Processed Images in Connecticut After *Swinton*', *Connecticut Trial Lawyers Association Forum*, 25(1): 32–40.
President's Council on Bioethics (2004) 'An Overview of the Impact of Neuroscience Evidence in Criminal Law', http://www.bioethics.gov/background/neuroscience_evidence.html (accessed 26 April 2006).
Prince v. Thomas, 25 F. Supp. 2d 1045 (N.D. Cal. 1997).
Rhilinger v. Jancsics, 8 Mass. L. Rep. 373 (Super. Ct. 1998).
Robinson, Richard (2004) 'fMRI Beyond the Clinic: Will It Ever Be Ready for Prime Time?', *PLOS Biology, Public Library of Science*, 2(6), http://biology.plosjournals.org/perlserv/ (accessed 26 April 2006).
Robinson, Robert J., Keltner, Dacher, Ward, Andrew & Ross, Lee (1995) 'Actual Versus Assumed Differences in Construal: "Naïve Realism" in Intergroup Perception and Conflict', *Journal of Personality and Social Psychology*, 68: 404–417.
Roper v. Simmons, 543 U.S. 551 (2005); Brief for Respondent, 2004 U.S. Supreme Court Briefs LEXIS 559; Brief Amicus Curiae of the American Bar Association, 2004 U.S. Supreme Court Briefs LEXIS 425.
Saks, Michael J. & Koehler, Jonathan J. (2005) 'The Coming Paradigm Shift in Forensic Identification Science', *Science* 309: 892–895.
Sarter, Martin, Bernston, Gary G. & Cacioppo, John T. (1996) 'Brain Imaging and Cognitive Neuroscience: Toward Strong Inference in Attributing Function to Structure', *American Psychologist*, 51: 13–21.
Sherwin, Richard, Feigenson, Neal & Spiesel, Christina (2006) 'Law in the Digital Age: How Visual Communication Technologies are Transforming the Practice, Theory, and Teaching of Law', *Boston University Journal of Science and Technology Law*, 12: 227–270.
Siebert v. Standard Insurance Co., 220 F. Supp. 2d 1128 (C.D. Cal. 2002).
Smith, Vicki (1991) 'Prototypes in the Courtroom: Lay Representations of Legal Concepts', *Journal of Personality and Social Psychology*, 61: 857–872.
Smith, Vicki (1993) 'When Prior Knowledge and Law Collide: Helping Jurors Use the Law', *Law and Human Behavior*, 17: 507–535.

Spence, Sean A., Hunter, Mike D., Farrow, Tom T.D., Green, Russell D., Leung, David H., Hughes, Catherine J. & Ganesan, Venkatasubramanian (2004) 'A Cognitive Neurobiological Account of Deception: Evidence from Functional Neuroimaging', *Philosophical Transactions of the Royal Society of London*, B 359: 1755–1762.

State of Delaware v. Red Dog, 1993 Del. Super. LEXIS 93.

State of Connecticut v. Swinton, 268 Conn. 781 (2004).

Stockwell, Jamie (2005) 'Defense, Prosecution Play to New "CSI" Savvy', *The Washington Post*, p.A1 (May 22).

Tancredi, Laurence (2004) 'Neuroscience Developments and the Law' in Brent Garland (ed.) *Neuroscience and the Law*. New York: Dana Press, 71–113.

Tyler, Tom (2006) 'Viewing CSI and the Threshold of Guilt: Managing Truth and Justice in Reality and Fiction', *Yale Law Journal*, 115: 1050–1083.

United States v. Gigante, 982 F. Supp. 140 (E.D.N.Y. 1997).

United States v. Hinckley, 525 F. Supp. 1324 (D.D.C. 1981).

United States v. Mezvinsky, 206 F. Supp. 2d 661 (E.D. Pa. 2002).

United States v. Seifert, 351 F. Supp. 2d 926 (D. Minn. 2005).

Vidmar, Neil & Diamond, Shari (2001) 'Juries and Expert Evidence', *Brooklyn Law Review*, 66: 1121–1180.

Video Software Dealers Association et al. v. Maleng, 325 F. Supp. 2d 1180 (W.D. Wash. 2004).

Video Software Dealers Association et al. v. Schwarzenegger, 401 F. Supp. 2d 1034 (N.D. Cal. 2005) (preliminary injunction), 2007 WL 2261546 (N.D. Cal. 2007) (permanent injunction).

Wexler, Bruce (2004) 'Using fMRI to Study the Mind and Brain' in Robert G. Shulman & Douglas L. Rothman (eds), *Brain Energetics and Neuronal Activity: Applications to fMRI and Medicine*. New York: Wiley.

Willingham, Daniel T. & Dunn, Elizabeth W. (2003) 'What Neuroimaging and Brain Localization Can Do, Cannot Do, and Should Not Do for Social Psychology', *Journal of Personality and Social Psychology*, 85: 662–671

Wolpe, Paul, Foster, Kenneth R. & Langleben, Daniel D. (2005) 'Emerging Neurotechnologies for Lie-detection: Promises and Perils', *The American Journal of Bioethics*, 5(2), 1–11.

Chapter 4
Mind the Gap: Problems of Mind, Body and Brain in the Criminal Law

Lisa Claydon

The normative structures of the criminal law are problematic. There is an implicit assumption which underpins the criminal law that mind and body are separate. This assumption is by its nature dualist. The mind is represented by mental states (*mens rea*) and bodily movement by the results of actions (*actus reus*). The acts or actions are thus separated from the mental states which brought about the prohibited result. Furthermore, in mental condition defences it adopts a materialist stance. The mind is abnormal or diseased – a malfunction of the brain is defined as a disease of the mind.

However, it may be possible to construct a model of human behaviour utilizing modern philosophical arguments based on scientific advances, which permit a greater understanding of the structure of consciousness and thereby develop a more consistent model of criminal responsibility.

Acknowledging the Problem

The starting point for this chapter is that the criminal law is a body of law which has as one of its purposes a need to promulgate the desirability or undesirability of certain types of behaviour. This need has contributed to the adoption and statement within the criminal law of a set of normative values. For the purposes of this chapter the following description given to the working of normative judgment in law will suffice:

> as an inclusive description of the many flavours humans find among those things that ought to be done and those that ought not to be done, particularly in the social context of interaction with other humans. In this sense, normative judgment first involves the construction of a system (or systems) of norms, values and expectations, and, second, the evaluation of the actions of another agent, or of our own actions, made with respect to these norms, values and expectations (Goodenough and Prehn 2006, 78).

These legal norms pervade the description of the fault elements within the criminal law and also permeate the requirements of criminal law defences. However, there is a difficulty because legal and factual judgments in court are often reached on the basis of evidence supplied to the judge and jury drawn from a variety of moral, emotional and scientific positions which do not acknowledge or share the same normative perspectives as the criminal law.

This difference of approach can be traced, in part, to the stance taken by the criminal law to claims that someone's actions are involuntary. In a very basic sense, the criminal law recognizes individual autonomy by insisting that the criminal act be voluntary. However, this has a very minimalist meaning in the criminal law. This is best demonstrated by an examination of the criminal law defence of automatism. Pleas of automatism, where claims are made that the defendant was not conscious of her actions, have contributed to the development of the current definition of insanity in English criminal law.

However, to consider the criminal law simply on the basis of defence requirements would be confusing and would fail to illustrate the more complex manner in which the criminal law is implicitly dualist in its construction of a model of criminal responsibility. In the main, criminal responsibility requires an element of *mens rea*; this is sometimes described as the "the defendant's mental state" (see for example Simester and Sullivan 2003, 126). This *mens rea* element in the traditionally formulated serious offences is described in such a way as to give some acknowledgement to the ideal of individual autonomy.[1] For example in the offence of murder, as defined in English law, part of the fault requirements are that the defendant should have an intention to kill or cause grievous bodily harm at the time of the killing. This intention[2] may be expressed as an aim or purpose to kill or cause grievous bodily harm. If this type of intention is not established the criminal law still allows a jury to find intention where they conclude that, *inter alia*, at the time of acting the defendant had foresight of virtual certainty that their actions would result in death or serious harm.[3] To say the least this introduces into the equation an odd view of human action that is implicitly dualist; in the sense that mental activities are separated from the actions which result from them. Clearly in some instances of murder there will be an element of prior planning; this may suggest that premeditation and considerable mental deliberation took place before the commission of the crime. However, this will not be true of killings which are an act of spontaneous violence, for example, due to extreme loss of temper.

At issue here is whether an individual may be viewed as having access to interior decision-making processes in cases where action is spontaneous. Scientifically, what is known of conscious preplanning casts doubt upon whether a defendant

1 See footnote 7 and accompanying text for a discussion of the meaning attributed to individual autonomy in the criminal law.

2 The word intention has a quite different meaning in the criminal law from the philosophical meaning of intention.

3 See the discussion of the meaning of intention in murder by Lord Steyn in *R v Woollin* [1999] 1 AC 82 and the discussion of the meaning of serious harm, grievous bodily harm, in *DPP v Smith* [1961] AC 290.

can accurately report all of the mental events which caused them to behave as they did.[4] Normally, this would not require the use of scientific evidence in court but, when it does, the dualism apparent in legal thinking becomes problematic.

To explain for a moment why the law takes this stance it must be accepted that in the eyes of the law there is a considerable difference between behaviour that is reckless and behaviour that is intentional in the legal sense. As has already been stated, intention has a specific meaning within English law in relation to murder – an act is intended if it is the actor's aim or purpose or if the actor may be found to have foresight of virtual certainty that their actions will bring about unlawful killing whether they desire it or not. The reason for this is that the criminal law links its evaluations of culpability to sentencing and some types of killings are seen by the law as more culpable than others.[5] Because of a further legal principle, that of fair labelling, the manner in which criminal culpability is constructed is deeply interrelated with the legal descriptions of *mens rea* states. This is particularly true of the homicide offences.[6]

Additionally somewhere in the equation of criminal culpability sits the requirement that the defendant's actions be voluntary and, interestingly, where it should sit and how it should be described is highly controversial. At its most basic level the criminal law protects individual autonomy[7] by insisting that the criminal act be voluntary. But how the law does this has raised profound moral and policy difficulties because defendants in criminal cases sometimes claim that their actions are involuntary when they have committed an action which, even if it does not endanger life, puts people at risk of serious personal injury.[8]

---

4 See footnote 21 and the subsequent text.

5 See Law Commission (2005) for a detailed discussion of the ladder of criminal responsibility in homicide.

6 For a thorough discussion of culpability in relation to homicide (see Ashworth 2006, Chapter 7).

7 Raz has suggested that this ideal of autonomy takes three forms:

> Three main features characterize the autonomy-based doctrine of freedom. *First* its primary concern is the promotion and protection of positive freedom which is understood as the capacity for autonomy, consisting of the availability of an adequate range of options, and of mental abilities necessary for an autonomous life. *Second*, the state has a duty not merely to prevent the denial of freedom, but also to promote it by creating the conditions of autonomy. *Third*, one may not pursue any goal by means which infringe people's autonomy unless such action is justified by the need to protect or promote the autonomy of those people or of others (1986, 425, emphasis in original).

8 There are therefore obvious policy issues related to the development of the insanity defence which have been clearly articulated by the courts. As Lord Diplock stated in *R v Sullivan* [1983] 2 All ER 673, 677–8:

> The purpose of the legislation relating to the defence of insanity … has been to protect society against recurrence of the dangerous conduct. The duration of a temporary suspension of the mental faculties of reason, memory and understanding, particularly if, … it is recurrent, cannot on any rational ground be relevant to the application by the courts of the M'Naghten Rules.

The "principle of individual autonomy"[9] is described by Ashworth as having normative and factual elements. The factual he describes as "individuals in general have the capacity and sufficient free will to make meaningful choices" (2006, 25). Whereas he describes the normative element as "individuals should be respected and treated as agents capable of choosing their acts and omissions, and that without recognizing individuals as capable of independent agency they could hardly be recognized as moral persons" (2006, 26).Whether the division of fact and norms is as Ashworth describes them is a moot point, but what is not disputable is that this is, on the whole, the way the criminal law functions. Similarly, Ashworth's other argument that the way that individual autonomy is viewed is linked to a hotly contested area of philosophical and scientific debate – that of freedom of will – is well evidenced.[10]

One method of avoiding the issues arising from the difficulties in attempting to address the different approaches to individual autonomy, particularly in addressing the more determinist thesis, is that taken by Halpin, who writes that some approaches to the issue of individual autonomy challenge the whole foundations of the criminal law. Halpin writes: "Concern that the legitimacy of the criminal law is founded on an assumption of free will which cannot be sustained, does not challenge particular points of the substantive criminal law. It challenges the whole enterprise of the criminal law" (2004, 62–3). Halpin's response is to avoid the issue because, according to him, it questions the very foundations of criminal responsibility. However arguably, in law as in science, ignoring hard questions does not yield satisfying results. One response, the response adopted by Halpin, is simply to say: "Such an extreme disagreement with the legitimacy of the criminal law cannot sensibly be regarded as relating to disagreement over the substantive values of the criminal law." His reason for this conclusion is "it denies any room to such values" (2004, 63). Halpin quotes, seemingly with approval, Horder when Horder writes of the construction of criminal liability: "Questions about whether she 'really' had a choice are irrelevant, or subordinated to this ethical evaluation of the conduct in which she engaged" (Horder 1996, 164).[11] In adopting this approach Halpin is avoiding addressing the root of the philosophical problem. If she did not have a choice on what basis could responsibility for her action be assessed?

9 Ashworth describes this principle as encapsulated within the claim that "each individual should be treated as responsible for his or her own behaviour" (2006, 25).

10 The area of this debate has a long history in both criminal law and within philosophy and takes a variety of forms. There are semantic arguments concerning the meaning of act and action. See for example White (1968). There also the reductionist arguments of philosophers such as Ryle (1963) and Dennett (1991). For an interesting essay deconstructing legal interpretations of freedom see Norrie (2005, chapter 9).

11 Many lawyers write of philosophical constructions of responsibility in a similar manner. Cane argues that care needs to be taken when examining philosophical explanations of human behaviour which decontextualize human acts. He writes: "According to this account, responsibility is a matter of fact, not of social construction." And that "understanding responsibility, on this view, is an empirical, not an evaluative, exercise" (2002, 23).

How can an ethical judgment as to how someone acted be achieved if you do not know whether they had the capacity to choose how to act? Arguably the failure to directly address this issue is a fundamental flaw in the criminal law. Halpin is right to state that the criminal law cannot accept the determinist thesis. The means of remedying this problem is not to refuse to engage in the debate. Rather it is to seek a justifiable basis for the law's conception of individual autonomy. The principles of the criminal law are based, in large part, on the work of traditional philosophers. But does this philosophy need to be reviewed? Does the criminal law employ the correct framework to assess individual responsibility?

What Can Science Bring to the Table?

From the traditional legal viewpoint, law is materially different from scientific disciplines. Law may therefore choose to view scientific discussion of causality through its own normative framework. The standard conclusion reached in these circumstances by lawyers is exemplified by Cane, who writes: "Regardless of the truth or falsity of determinism, we hold ourselves and others responsible, and we accept responsibility, for at least some (of their and our) conduct and some of its consequences" (2002, 66). Cane makes it clear that what counts in terms of criminal responsibility in his view is the capacity to make choices and to control our actions.[12] But in adopting such an approach, Cane does not explain how the relevant connections are to be made between capacity for choice and responsibility utilizing empirical, often scientific evidence; and how the use of empirical observations of events and medical or scientific data and evidence may relate to criminal responsibility. One method would of course be to deal with such evidence as a factual demonstration unrelated to any normative legal judgment. Indeed this approach is adopted by Hart, who writes: "It is clear that not only lawyers but scientists and plain men differ as to the relevance of some excusing conditions, and this lack of agreement is usually expressed as a difference of view regarding what kind of factor limits the human *capacity* to control behaviour" (Hart 1992, 32, emphasis in original). Though, as Hart admits: "Views so expressed have indeed changed with the advance of knowledge about the human mind" (Hart 1992, 32).

---

12 More fully Cane writes of the determinist thesis:

> … it was suggested that for the purposes of analysing responsibility practices, the truth or falsity of causal determinism can be ignored. Even if causal determinism is true, the facts remain that although we feel our conduct to be subject to varying degrees of external and internal limitation and constraint, we experience freedom of choice and a fair degree of control over our conduct and the world around us; that people differ in terms of their capacities and abilities to achieve good outcomes and avoid bad outcomes; that people can change their behaviour patterns; and so on. Regardless of the truth or falsity of determinism, we hold ourselves and others responsible, and we accept responsibility, for at least some (of their and our) conduct and some of its consequences (2002, 66).

To summarize then, the gap which is being considered is that created by differences in approaches as to what may "count as causes" for which a defendant may be held responsible. This is an area on which much effort and energy has been expended both scientifically and philosophically and much of the debate may be traced back to the enlightenment and the work of the philosopher David Hume.[13] Hume, when considering the relationship of cause and effect in the context of religious doctrine, writes: "I much doubt whether it be possible for a cause to be known only by its effect." This is because if such a statement were to be accepted it would in his view mean that "both the effect and cause must bear a similarity and resemblance to other effects and causes, which we know, and which we have found, in many instances, to be conjoined with each other" (Hume 1963, 148, both quotations). Hume's scepticism is perhaps at its most vehement in relation to the use of human testimony to support religious doctrine. He writes of narratives which seek to explain miracles that such confused evidence as there is suggests that miracles "may be derived from several different causes from the opposition of contrary testimony". This leads him to the view that such human explanations of causes in relation to effects are unreliable. In his view such disagreement in relation to the cause of known "effects" diminishes or destroys "the force of any argument, derived from human testimony" (Hume 1963, 148, all quotations). According to Hume, knowledge of an effect is not sufficient, of itself, to establish causality. Though causes may be associated with their effects via the medium of what he describes as natural laws, this we might describe as empirical observation. Mackie writes: "Under this interpretation, the necessity for the second billiard-ball to move when the first hits it is only a *hypothetical* or *conditional* necessity: necessity 'given the laws of nature'" (1995, 127).

Some modern philosophers of the mind take a similarly reductionist view of the relation of cause and effect and explain mental causation in terms of purely physical laws.[14] But clearly in the criminal law much of the discussion of causality

13 Hume famously wrote: "All reasonings concerning matter of fact seem to be founded on the relation of *Cause and Effect*. By means of that relation alone we can go beyond the evidence of our memory and senses" (Hume 1963, 26–7, emphasis in the original). He defines cause as "an object precedent and contiguous to another, and so united with it, that the idea, of the one determines the mind to form the idea of the other, and the impression of the one to form a more lively idea of the other" (Hume 1888, 170). Hume argues that the relationship between cause and effect in relation to reasoning is wrongly interpreted. Hume further argues that "reason alone can never produce any action, or give rise to volition … Reason is and ought only to be the slave of the passions, and can never pretend to any other office than to serve and obey them" (Ibid. 414–5).

14 Dennett, when exploring the flaws of the dualist approach to human reasoning, explains the giving of directives within the brain as related to and governed by the laws of physics:

> These [the directives] … are not physical; they are not light waves or sound waves or cosmic rays or streams of subatomic particles. No physical energy or mass is associated

is practically related to issues of criminal culpability and particularly in homicide to policy issues[15] rather than pure scientific proof of causal power. For lawyers, like Cane and Hart, the answer to the differences between scientific empirical observations of behaviour is to accept the facts as medical evidence but to evaluate the question of guilt or innocence against a broader legally constructed framework.

However, there are those who challenge the traditional viewpoint as expressed in the works of Hume. Horder, in his more recent published work, adopts a slightly different approach to the questions of causation and control of actions (Horder 2004). He argues that "one can be morally active either through one's 'causal' contribution to events, or through one's 'control' relationship to events". This of itself is not novel. However, in looking for what might count as an excuse for criminal conduct, Horder has to consider the nature of the "emotional responses" that trigger actions (Horder 2004, 81, both quotations). Here, Horder seems to be investigating what it means to make a decision to act for which one should be held responsible. In basing responsibility upon control Horder, to some extent, sidesteps the Humean objection, that reasons cannot of themselves be direct causes of events. The missing link as to how this might be achieved philosophically will be discussed later when evaluating the work of the philosopher John Searle and its relevance to the criminal law.

This is the background to the debate about criminal responsibility. However, as Hart argued as long ago as 1968,[16] there have been great advances in knowledge of the brain[17] and it could now be argued that the study of the brain and its working through the study of consciousness poses new challenges to our understanding of what it means to be an agent acting in a manner for which one should be held accountable. Inevitably scientific research into conscious states and the work which parallels it in the philosophy of the mind have changed some scientists' and some philosophers' conceptions of mental causation in relation to action.[18] This provides a further and important perspective on the debate about voluntariness,

with them. How, then, do they get to make a difference to what happens in the brain cells they must affect, if the mind is to have any influence over the body? A fundamental principle of physics is that any change in the trajectory of any physical entity is an acceleration requiring the expenditure of energy, and where is this energy to come from? It is this principle of the conservation of energy that accounts for the physical impossibility of "perpetual motion machines," and the same principle is apparently violated by dualism. This confrontation between quite standard physics and dualism has been endlessly discussed since Descartes's own day, and is widely regarded as the inescapable and fatal flaw of dualism (Dennett 1991, 34–5).

15 To see evidence of some of the forces at play in the determination of criminal culpability see Law Commission (2005) and Ormerod and Fortson (2005).

16 Reprinted with revisions (Hart 1992).

17 For a general review of scientific knowledge of conscious states see Greenfield (1995 and 1997). For an interesting explanation of consciousness see Penrose (1995).

18 For a flavour of this debate, particularly in terms of the relationship between consciousness and mind/brain states and free will, see Chalmers (1996); Churchland (1995); Dennett (1991); Hornsby (1997); Libet (2004) and Searle (2001).

choice and individual autonomy. This viewpoint is very relevant when scientific evidence concerning mental condition defences is being considered in court. Here the differences in scientific and legal opinion are perhaps at their most marked in terms of the differing viewpoints as to how to explain mental causes of physical actions. This has a direct impact upon arguments in court which aim to establish criminal culpability for the results of human actions.

How is Knowledge about the Brain Relevant to Criminal Culpability?

Where some philosophical and scientific approaches provide the law with a difficulty is in relation to first person narratives explaining, excusing or justifying behaviour. The challenge is most acute when viewed from the perspective of neuroscientific explanations of behaviour; and more pertinently conscious access to the mental antecedents of such behaviour. In the case of attributing responsibility the law is seeking a cognitive centre of conscious control. The law seeks an identifiable actor, a narrator, within the brain who will, for the individual actor, make clear the precise basis for their decisions and actions.[19] Whether such a centre exists is hotly debated. For many scientists the idea of such a continuous narrative explanation for actions existing within an individual's mind is deeply problematic.[20]

To return to the issue that arose earlier in the chapter when discussing the meaning of intention in the criminal law. It is this concept, of a narrator, that is to many scientists the ghost in the machine. It is necessary to realize and accept that many scientists would only accept third-party observations of behaviour as establishing a scientifically meaningful explanation of behaviour. The idea of mental causation being linked to criminal responsibility in the manner discussed above would not be accepted as part of physically determined laws.[21] This difference of approach to defining causation may have an impact on scientific evidence produced in court. To understand the gap, it is necessary to consider the idea of the ghost in the machine. This concept is not new. Gilbert Ryle, in his book, *The Concept of the Mind*, first published in 1949, wrote dismissively of the idea of

19 This is perhaps most clearly illustrated by the statement of Lord Bingham giving his opinion in the House of Lords when he said "conviction of a serious crime should depend on proof not simply that the defendant caused (by act or omission) an injurious result to another but that his state of mind when so acting was culpable" (*R v G and another (Appellants)* [2003] UKHL 50, [32]).

20 See Dennett (1991) for a full exposition of this argument.

21 For a discussion of this see Penrose (1995), where he writes: "The legal issue of 'responsibility' *seems* to imply that there is indeed, within each one of us, some kind of an independent 'self' with its *own* responsibilities – and, by implication, rights – whose actions are *not* attributable, to inheritance, environment or chance." He goes on to conclude that if such a self were to exist it would mean that "there must be an ingredient missing from our presentday physical understandings." He adds: "The discovery of such an ingredient would surely profoundly alter our scientific outlook" (1995, 36, emphasis in original).

the "anterior internal operation of planning what to do". Ryle was of the opinion that thinking and physical doing were one, not two, physical processes. He posed the question: "Why are people so strongly drawn to believe, in the face of their own daily experience, that the intelligent execution of an operation must embody two processes, one of doing and another of theorizing?" (Ryle 1980, 32).

The answer he proposes is that people are "wedded to the dogma of the ghost in the machine" (Ryle 1980, 32–3).[22] Ryle doubts that we could ever adequately explain our actions by reference to our own intellectual explanations of such actions. These internal musings are the ghost in the machine, according to Ryle; intellectual activity of this sort is genuinely unwitnessable and indeed mythical. Ryle's evaluation of the usefulness of action explanations is to say the least controversial and reductionist. If the only reliable data to explain human action was derived from third-party scientific observations of events, then Horder's argument in relation to excuses would be somewhat hard to establish. There would be at least two difficulties for Horder's analysis. The first is that there may not be a third-party observer to a criminal act. Even if there were, the question arises as to how a third-party observer would note the subjective reasons which caused the actions? Some subjective first person testimony would be essential in gaining insight into reasons for the action. However, it is overstating the case to argue that the legal view of guilt or innocence is separate and removed from the scientific viewpoint. It is far better to admit that there is a gap and then look at the means of bridging the gap so that scientific evidence in court is adequately incorporated into the legal framework.

The clearest example of the gap between legal, medical and scientific views of the brain occurs when either of the defences of insanity or sane automatism are raised in court. On the one side there is the desire of the law to reach an apparently rational judgment about culpability and blame. On the other the judgment of medical experts as to the diagnosed causes of behaviour, usually the existence of a mental or sometimes a physical disorder. What makes the gap between the two explanations more difficult to bridge is that the basis of the law's description of excusing mental condition defences is based upon late nineteenth century and early twentieth century views of insanity and criminal culpability. As stated earlier, for criminal lawyers it is the mind which is diseased, not the brain.

The gap may be further examined with the assistance of some black letter law. Legally the subjective state of mind of the defendant is relevant to liability in insanity cases. The reason for this is that a claim of insanity is seen as a denial of *mens rea*. In *M'Naghten's case*[23] Daniel M'Naghten was found by the court to be insane when, as a result of a delusion that he was being persecuted by the Tory Party, he mistakenly shot and killed the Prime Minister's secretary. He intended to kill the Prime Minister, Robert Peel.

22 This approach of viewing third-party explanations as the most satisfactory basis for assessing human behaviour is still held by many prominent researchers and philosophers (see for example Churchland 1995; Dennett 1991).

23 [1843–60] All ER Rep 229.

Needless to say the case caused considerable uproar and the 13 puisne judges were summoned to the House of Lords to hear the views of their Lordships on the decision of Tindall LCJ to recognize M'Naghten's plea of insanity; and incidentally, to justify their reasoning through a declaration of the relevant legal basis of the law of insanity. It has to be remembered that psychiatry and psychology were very much in their infancy. However the M'Naghten rules remain the definition of legal insanity to this day. They state that to be insane the defendant must be: "labouring under such a defect of reason, from disease of the mind, as not to know the nature and quality of the act he was doing, or, if he did know it, that he did not know he was doing what was wrong."[24]

In order to establish that the defendant was suffering from a disease of the mind at the time of the act, objective evidence will be required.[25] This requirement has come to be interpreted to mean relevant medical and scientific evidence. Here the gulf between law with its normative values and the scientific enterprise becomes most apparent. Insanity as a legal definition does not coincide with medically recognized mental disorders. The situation is further complicated because the definition of insanity has become a means of controlling the dangerous defendant, particularly dangerous defendants who have killed.[26] This is partly because of the historical development of the law. Before the abolition of the death penalty, a defence of insanity was one of the few defences which protected an alleged murderer from the hangman's noose. So the pre-1965[27] case authorities were careful to control the availability of the insanity defence. Thus the definition was framed to ensure that whilst it was available to those who were legally seen as

---

24 [1843–60] All ER Rep 229, 233.

25 This conclusion follows from the application of Article 5 of the European Convention for the Protection of Human Rights and Fundamental Freedoms. This Article concerns the right to liberty of the person and it is important in this context to understand the effect of an insanity verdict. Once the jury finds a defendant not guilty by reason of insanity she is deemed not criminally responsible and is therefore technically not convicted of a crime – but remains subject to disposal by the court. In the case of murder the sentence is mandatory – see footnote 33 for disposal options open to a court.

Article 5(e) makes it clear that someone may only be deprived of their liberty when the detention is lawful and they are a person of unsound mind. Crucially the meaning of unsound mind given by the case law of the European Court of Human Rights is different from that given by the English courts to disease of the mind. The principles are set out in the case of *Winterwerp v The Netherlands* (1979) 2 EHRR 387 [39]

> In the Court's opinion, except in emergency cases, the individual concerned should not be deprived of his liberty unless he has been reliably shown to be of unsound mind. The very nature of what has to be established before the competent national authority – that is, a true mental disorder – calls for objective medical expertise. Further, the mental disorder must be of a kind or degree warranting compulsory confinement. What is more, the validity of continued confinement depends upon the persistence of such a disorder.

26 See footnote 8 and accompanying text.

27 The death penalty was abolished in England and Wales in 1965. Murder (Abolition of Death Penalty) Act 1965.

having a disease of the mind which was broadly defined, the disease of the mind would only excuse if it affected cognitive function. Thus only defendants who could establish that they did not know the nature and quality of their act or who did not know that it was legally wrong fell within the ambit of the defence.[28] This has had the effect that certain well-known defendants have been unable to plead insanity. For example Peter Sutcliffe, the "Yorkshire Ripper", knew both the nature and quality of the act he was committing and that it was legally wrong.[29]

There is a further problem with mental disorder defences in the criminal law. Normally when looking at criminal responsibility, issues of causation have some relevance as to how culpability is established. Yet when the insanity defence is raised there is no test as to whether insanity of the type suffered by the defendant actually reduces the defendant's responsibility for their criminal behaviour.

Perhaps this is because insanity is said to be a denial of *mens rea*.[30] However, the related partial defence of diminished responsibility does require that the jury be satisfied that the defendant's "mental responsibility" was "substantially impaired" by their "abnormality of mind".[31] The blanket exemption for those who succeed in pleading the insanity defence may seem odd in a world that increasingly accepts mental disorder as a type of disorder which may be suffered in varying degrees, but nonetheless many legal textbooks repeat the phrase that a successful insanity plea is a denial of *mens rea*.[32] So in court, provided that the defendant can establish cognitive impairment in the sense that they do not know the nature and quality of their act or that it is legally wrong, then they may be found M'Naghten insane.

Policy has played a substantial part in the development of the normative structures of the insanity defence. A finding of insanity does not automatically mean that the defendant is removed from the ambit of detention. The defendant who is found insane may still be detained, may receive an absolute discharge, or alternatively may be subject to a disposal order of some kind.[33] Indeed it is this

28 *R v Windle* [1952] 2 QB 826 this case is authority for the proposition that the meaning to be given to the second limb of the M'Naghten Rules is that wrong means legally, not morally, wrong.

29 For a review of the operation of the insanity defence see Mackay and Kearns (1999).

30 Ormerod writes that to require the prosecution to prove *mens rea* would be "inconsistent with the rule that the onus is on D to prove that he did not know the nature and quality of his act" (2005, 268).

31 Homicide Act 1957 section 2(1) and *Sanders* (1991) 93 Cr App R 245, where the decision as to whether there was substantial impairment was said to require consideration of all the relevant facts, not simply the medical evidence.

32 Ashworth discusses this issue in relation to the reform of the law in relation to insanity (2006, 209–10).

33 The court has a range of disposal options open to them under the provisions of The Criminal Procedure (Insanity) Act 1964 section 5 (as amended by the Criminal Procedure (Insanity and Unfitness to Plead) Act 1991 and the Domestic Violence, Crime and Victims Act 2004). This provides that where an insanity verdict is returned by the jury, the court may make a hospital order, a supervision order or an order for an absolute discharge. In

perception by the law that retaining the options in relation to sentencing is of major importance in such cases, which explains some of the disjuncture between legal and scientific approaches to mentally disordered offenders.

Perhaps the most problematic area of law central to the melding of philosophical, scientific and legal conceptions of mental disorder and consciousness is the legal plea of automatism. This plea covers two forms of lack of conscious control over actions. The standard definition of automatism is that given by Lord Denning in *Attorney General for Northern Ireland v Bratty*:

> No act is punishable if it is done involuntarily: and an involuntary act in this context … means an act which is done by the muscles without any control by the mind, such as a spasm, a reflex action or a convulsion; or an act done by a person who is not conscious of what he is doing … [34]

Legally a claim that the action was not the voluntary act of the defendant is a claim that the defendant was an automaton. Such a claim if recognized leads to a legal defence based on the fact that the individual did not commit the criminal act, the *actus reus* of the offence, and as such is a claim of lack of responsible agency. The criminal law has been deeply suspicious of such claims and has sought to restrict their legal efficacy by broadening the definition of disease of the mind under the M'Naghten Rules. The diabetic or sleepwalker who commits a crime whilst not fully conscious may, legally speaking, suffer from a "disease of the mind". Claims that a defendant's actions are involuntary have broadened the ambit of the insanity defence by broadening the definition of disease of the mind to include those who are said to be insane automatons.[35]

It has been made clear that disease of the mind is very broadly defined for policy reasons. The case law[36] makes it clear that where the defect of reason results from disease of the mind, if the cause is internal, then the defendant is an insane automaton. If the cause is external, the plea is sane automatism. This decision is to say the least arbitrary and has some rather odd effects. But here the difficulty of defining what it means to be held responsible for consciously choosing to act

---

cases where the verdict leads to the imposition of a mandatory sentence, the disposal has to be a hospital order together with a restriction order.

34 [1963] AC 386, 409.

35 Lord Diplock rejected a submission that "'disease of the mind' or 'mental illness' … must be prolonged for a period of time usually more than a day …" And defined mind as follows:

> … "mind" in the M'Naghten Rules is used in the ordinary sense of mental faculties of reason, memory and understanding. If the effect of a disease is to impair those faculties so severely … it matters not whether the aetiology of the impairment is organic, as in epilepsy, or functional, or whether the impairment itself is permanent or transient and intermittent, provided that it subsisted at the time of the commission of the act (Extracted from *R v Sullivan* [1983] 2 All ER 673, 677).

36 *R v Quick* [1973] 3 WLR 26.

is central to the confusion. It is precisely because there is no general consensus in medical, philosophical or legal circles as to what should count as free choice that the whole issue is fraught with difficulty. If one then adds in the further difficulty that those who claim automatism may have committed violent acts, then it is no wonder that there is little political appetite for reform of this area of law.

So the sleepwalker[37] has contentiously[38] been labelled as insane by the courts in England and Wales, as has the epileptic[39] and the hyperglycaemic diabetic.[40] This has led to real difficulties for the law since the passage of the Human Rights Act 1998, with its accompanying requirement that note be taken by the courts of the European Convention for the Protection of Human Rights and Fundamental Freedoms and its accompanying case law.[41] This has placed the courts in England and Wales in the position that, whilst the insanity defence with all its contradictions has been retained, the sentencing regime now offers far greater discretion and is more suitable in its application to a wider range of mental disorders. This solution has enabled the Government to sidestep the need for amending legislation which might have created a defence which had greater links to medical and/or scientific descriptions of mental disorder. Arguably, in taking this route, the Government preferred administrative reform of sentencing to addressing the issue of responsibility in the criminal law with its wider policy issues.

It is the gap between medical, scientific and philosophical approaches and the legal construction of responsibility in the area of both sane and insane automatism that is one of the areas that is the focus in the rest of this chapter. Arguably this is one of the coalfaces between scientific, philosophical and legal constructions of responsibility. The legal meaning of consciousness in the defence of sane automatism is often very narrowly construed.[42] However, consciousness is a word which is in common usage and it would be reasonable to expect that at least in terms of explanations to juries there should be some comparison between legal, scientific and popular conceptions of consciousness. But if other explanations of lack of consciousness are examined then a different explanation of human behaviour emerges from the concept employed by the criminal law and the interesting question is how informed opinion from other disciplines may fit within the legal debate.

---

37 *R v Burgess* [1991] 2 All ER 769.

38 For a discussion of the issues see Ebrahim et al. 2005; McCall Smith and Shapiro 1997; Wilson et al. 2005.

39 *R v Sullivan* [1983] 2 All ER 673.

40 *R v Hennessy* [1989] 1 WLR 287.

41 See footnote 24.

42 *Attorney General's Reference (No 2 of 1992)* [1993] 4 All ER 683, 689 the appeal fell at the first hurdle because:

> the "proper evidential foundation" was not laid in this case by Professor Brown's evidence of "driving without awareness". As the authorities cited above show, the defence of automatism requires that there was a total destruction of voluntary control on the defendant's part. Impaired, reduced or partial control is not enough. Lord Taylor.

The law through its requirement that actions be voluntary before criminal responsibility may be attributed to the actor is placing an emphasis on the need for agency in evaluations of culpability. Case law reveals some interesting examples of claims that actions were involuntary and therefore not deserving of criminal liability.

Two examples immediately spring to mind from different jurisdictions: one from Australia and one from England. Each case was dealt with differently by the appeal courts in their jurisdiction. If examined in detail they suggest that greater attention to the modern philosophy of the mind and to modern empirical descriptions of conscious states might assist the legal analysis.

What the Case Law Tells Us

The first case concerns a plea of automatism by a bus driver who killed two people when driving his bus out of a bus station.[43] It was claimed in court that what had happened was that the driver had confused the accelerator pedal with the brake pedal. He had therefore continued to apply pressure to the accelerator as the bus went out of control. He was charged with the offence of dangerous driving and at his trial the judge withdrew the case from the jury ruling that the Crown could not prove that the driver's actions were a deliberate act done by the defendant. The actions were not directed by a mind which was conscious of what his body was doing. This decision was the subject of an appeal by the Attorney General to the Court of Appeal to establish whether a defendant's actions when driving should be assessed in the manner described by the trial judge. The Court of Appeal took an entirely different approach. Stating very clearly that the driver's actions should be viewed as voluntary actions for which he should be held responsible:

> The *actus reus* of the offence with which we are concerned is the act of driving in a manner which is ... dangerous ... Furthermore, even adopting the approach of the judge, we regard this driver as conscious of the act his body was performing. He was aware that his body was performing the act of pressing the pedal.[44] [45]

43 *Attorney General's Ref No 4 2000* [2001] EWCA Crim 780.

44 *Attorney General's Ref No 4 2000* [2001] EWCA Crim 780 [13] per Woolf LCJ.

45 English case law had already established in driving cases, prior to this case, that for a sane automatism plea to succeed in relation to that part of the test in Bratty which refers to conscious control of action: "the defence of automatism requires that there was a total destruction of voluntary control on the defendant's part. Impaired, reduced or partial control is not enough." See *Attorney General's Reference* (No 2 of 1992) [1993] 3 WLR 982, 994. Though the application of the law in some of the cases where diabetic episodes have caused traffic accidents is to say the least a little harsh. See *Broome v Perkins* (1987) 85 Cr App R 321 and *Watmore v Jenkins* [1962] 3 WLR 463, both cases of diabetics who suffered diabetic comas without any warning.

There is scientific evidence about conscious states which supports this argument. Susan Greenfield in her examination of conscious states makes it clear that we are not conscious of every movement that we make. Greenfield writes that: "Many of the movements we make ... are in a sense, semi-automatic" (Greenfield 1997, 35). According to Greenfield, movements that fall into this category are those which do not require conscious thought (1997, 39). The question legally speaking relating to sane automatism becomes: "Did the mind have any control over the muscles?"[46]

Greenfield's review of neuroscientific research suggests that movement to press brake pedals "seems to be an automatic movement" and is controlled by the brain region known as the cerebellum (1997, 41). Earlier she writes: "Perhaps then the cerebellum is important for automated movements triggered by outside events rather than by internalized proactive thought processes" (1997, 38). The question this raises is whether the more accurate legal question with regard to the driver of the bus is whether the driver of the bus could have acted otherwise. The issue is not whether his body was pressing a pedal but whether the driver had the capacity to press the correct pedal. It seems from the evidence given on appeal that in fact what had happened was not that the driver of the bus was unconscious or that he did not have any control over his muscles, which he demonstrably did in that he could press the pedal. The issue in reality was that the accident was due to a mistake as to which pedal to press. In a sense the scientific evidence makes this issue clearer, by pointing to the fact that in acting we cannot consciously recall how we perform basic actions. This does not however mean, as the trial judge stated, that the driver's actions were not a deliberate act of the defendant. The pressing of the wrong pedal was a deliberate but mistaken act. This is a case which suggests that in terms of physical incapacity the criminal law and science may be in accord. But where the real problem arises is in relation to case law where the defendant's claim is that they were not conscious of their actions.

This type of automatism claim arises where the claim is that the actor falls into the second category of defendants utilizing the plea of automatism. This was explained by Lord Denning in *Bratty* as being "an act done by one who is not conscious of what he is doing".[47] Here the problem of requiring a narrator in the brain becomes very evident; one of the best illustrations of the problem is the Australian case of *Falconer*.[48] The defendant was a woman who had killed her husband. It was claimed on her behalf that these events happened whilst she was in a dissociative state. Evidence was presented at trial that her husband had abused her and their children, and that he had sexually assaulted her on the day on which she killed him.

The then relevant law was contained in the Western Australian Criminal Code. Section 23 stated "a person is not criminally responsible for an act or omission which occurs independently of the exercise of his will". Section 26 provided

46 See footnote 34 and accompanying text for a discussion of the definition of automatism.

47 *Attorney General for Northern Ireland v Bratty* [1963] AC 386, 409.

48 *Queen v Falconer* (1990) 171 CLR 30.

"every person is presumed to be of sound mind, and to have been of sound mind at the time which comes in question, until the contrary is proved". And section 27 stated that:

> A person is not criminally responsible for an act or omission if at the time of doing the act or making the omission he is in such a state of mental disease or natural mental infirmity as to deprive him of capacity to understand what he is doing, or of capacity to control his actions, or of capacity to know that he ought not to do the act or make the omission.

The question before the Australian High Court was whether evidence relating to the voluntariness of her actions should have been considered by the court of first instance as supporting the assertion that the shooting had "occurred independently of her will" and thus satisfied section 23 of the Criminal Code. The High Court was asked to determine how the common law related to the Western Australian Criminal Code.[49] The Crown argued that in Falconer's case section 23 related to section 27 via the medium of section 26. Thus in effect the presumption of sanity expressed in section 26 could only be displaced by evidence of unsoundness of mind. On the basis of the earlier Canadian case of *Rabey*[50] the Crown argued that where the blow was external, as in concussion, a defence of automatism was available, but where the cause of the blow was internal to the accused the only defence was disease of the mind.[51]

The decision of the court was unanimous as to the quashing of her conviction and the ordering of a retrial of Falconer. They were also in agreement as to the existence of a defence of sane automatism[52] under section 23 of the Western Australian Criminal Code. But three of the judges, a minority, favoured the introduction of an objective test based on soundness of mind in cases of psychological blow automatism. These judges[53] stated: "There seems to be no reason in principle why psychological trauma which produces a transient non-recurrent malfunction of an otherwise sound mind should be distinguished from a physical trauma which

49 "Before this Court, those questions were formulated by the Crown in the following way: '(a) whether involuntary acts performed in a state of dissociation resulting from emotional tension are excused by virtue of the operation of s. 23 of the *Criminal Code* (W.A.); (b) the relationship between ss. 23, 26 and 27 of the *Criminal Code* where the normal functioning of the mind is disturbed by emotional tension; and (c) the application to the *Criminal Code* of common law decisions dealing with automatism and insanity as they affect criminal responsibility'." *Queen v Falconer* (1990) 171 CLR 31, 65 (Toohey J.) For a case commentary see Ellard, (1995).

50 (1990) 171 CLR 31.

51 (1990) 171 CLR 31, 33.

52 In *Falconer* automatism is referred to both as sane or insane automatism (1990) 171 CLR 31, 55 and as non-insane and insane automatism (1990) 171 CLR 31, 77 depending upon which of the judges was giving judgment.

53 Mason C.J., Brennan and McHugh JJ.

produces a like effect."[54] However, this acceptance of a psychological blow as a trigger to automatism was strictly limited, in their view, to cases where the mental malfunction was "transient", the defendant's mind "otherwise sound", the cause "trauma" and the malfunction is "not prone to recur".[55] The problem of distinguishing between an unsound and sound mind was discussed:

> The problem of classification in a case of a transient malfunction of the mind precipitated by psychological trauma lies in the difficulty in choosing between the reciprocal factors – the trauma and the natural susceptibility of the mind to affection by psychological trauma – as the cause of the malfunction. Is one factor or the other the cause or are both to be treated as causes? To answer this problem, the law must postulate a standard of mental strength which, in the face of a given level of psychological trauma, is capable of protecting the mind from malfunction to the extent prescribed in the respective definitions of insanity. That standard must be the standard of the ordinary person: if the mind's strength is below that standard, the mind is infirm; if it is of or above that standard, the mind is sound or sane.[56]

The issue in *Falconer* involved an ethical evaluation of Falconer's criminal culpability for her response to a deeply shocking and traumatizing event. Scientific or medical arguments could be produced in court to support her assertion that she had no memory of her acts and that she was not conscious of what she was doing. In fact given her experiences, her loss of memory of the event was not uncommon. Writing of the connection between amnesia and crime, Parkin notes: "Surveys have shown that between 23% and 65% of murderers have, or claim to have, amnesia for their crime" (Parkin 1995, 162). Parkin then considers the effect of psychological blow automatism and comments that such cases "present courts with a particular difficulty kind of decision". Briefly, the difficulty is that of distinguishing between ordinary amnesia "which serves to repress the unpleasant memories of the violent act" where the "amnesia arises *after* the event" – from those where there is a "lack of conscious involvement during the amnesic period itself" (1995, 167, emphasis in original). Scientific explanations of why such memory loss occurs may assist in helping a jury to understand when deliberating as to guilt or innocence whether the psychological blow could have caused Falconer to behave as she did. Scientific evidence may assist in determining whether her lack of conscious recall in relation to her action is relevant to her criminal liability. The problematic issue for the criminal law is how her lack of conscious recall of the events impacts on her criminal liability. Could the psychological trauma have meant that she had no conscious involvement in the killing? This would arguably relieve her of criminal responsibility for her actions.

54 (1990) 171 CLR 31, 54.
55 (1990) 171 CLR 31, 55.
56 Ibid.

But here there is a real gap – the gap between what the law terms causal and what various strands of science and philosophy view as being of causal relevance. Scientifically, causation in the legal sense is not the appropriate focus of attention in determining the cause of events. To a scientist carrying out empirical observations, the word causation has a different value because in seeking causes the idea is not to attribute moral responsibility but to answer questions raised about how an act came about as the result of certain mental events. Causation in this scientific sense relates to how did this action happen, not to who is responsible for the fact that the prohibited result came about.[57]

Central to bridging the gap between legal and scientific explanations of behaviour is an acknowledgment that differences exist between legal and other approaches to causation as a means of attributing responsibility for actions. Legal causation seeks to establish whether the defendant's action is a substantial and operative cause of the prohibited result,[58] whilst for medicine the question is different again. Could the behaviour be linked to an underlying condition that is treatable? Are there markers in the brain that might explain how mental activity results in certain behaviours? The first is a question to which the answer will establish legal responsibility; the second and third questions are not concerned with responsibility for actions at all. Furthermore, the legal question with regard to the nature of the act – that is, whether it was a substantial and operating cause – is really a moral question.[59] Though, the precise status of moral judgment in relation to the criminal law is something which has been hotly debated.[60]

In a remarkable book entitled *Rationality in Action* (Searle 2001), John Searle investigates from a philosophical viewpoint how modern neuroscientific constructions of action might aid philosophical constructions of rationality in action. Searle examines in particular the apparent gaps in causal explanations of action. His aim in the book is to establish a more convincing philosophical explanation of practical reasoning. In order to achieve this Searle undertakes a critique of what he describes as the "classical model" of rationality in philosophical explanations of action. Searle's aim is to provide a more contemporary and workable model of rationality. His desire is to overcome the inherent difficulties which lie within the classical explanations of the meaning to be attributed to conscious states. What he has to say is of enormous assistance in bridging the gap between legal, philosophical and scientific explanations of action.

---

57 For a discussion of a scientific view of legal responsibility, see footnote 21 and accompanying text.

58 *R v Cheshire* [1991] 1 WLR 844, see Ashworth (2006, 122–35) for a discussion of how this requirement is utilized in the framework of criminal culpability.

59 Though legally speaking this is a moot point, the recent case law in relation to manslaughter in cases where death has resulted from the ingestion of illegal drugs by the victim suggests that a mixture of public policy and a view of the morality of a particular defendant's action may be relevant to the interpretation of whether a defendant's acts cause a result. See also footnote 15.

60 For a flavour of the debate, see Devlin (1965) and Hart (1963).

The reason why Searle's construction of rationality in action is so conceptually helpful is that he puts flesh on the bones of what it means to choose to act. He begins, *inter alia*, by examining what may be said to be causally effective in terms of action. He dismisses the classical explanations of philosophers such as Hume and concludes that desire independent states may be "causally sufficient" in determining the causes of action.

Earlier in the chapter consideration was given to Halpin's comment that the debate concerning whether all actions are determined is fruitless. However, arguably this debate is central to constructions of criminal liability which rest on the principle of individual autonomy. Clearly in the typical case people have reasons for choosing to act as they do and arguably those reasons are highly relevant to their criminal culpability. The suggestion is made that the traditional philosophical framework underpinning the criminal law should be revised. The question which follows from this is: "How should this be done?" One method of achieving this end is to utilize the work of John Searle, who strongly rejects that determinism has any basis. Searle writes:

> There is no way to think away your own freedom in the process of voluntary action because the process of deliberation itself can only proceed on the presupposition of freedom, on the presupposition that there is a gap between the causes in the forms of your beliefs, desires, and other reasons, and the actual decisions that you make (2001, 14).

Once it is admitted that capacity for making choices or for physical action is the foundation of liability, then it is possible to identify how reasoning in relation to an agent's acts takes place. Searle argues that rational decision-making takes place in stages. He identifies three gaps between thought and action. First, when there is deliberation as to a course of action or, in his words, "you try to make up your mind what you are going to do." Second, there is the gap between making up your mind in this sense and choosing to act on your decision or, as he describes it, "the decision is not of itself causally sufficient to produce the action" (2001, 14). Something else may interfere to make you change your initial decision to adopt a certain course of action. Searle's third gap exists where the decision to act relates to an action which takes place over an extended time frame. In which case there may be a further gap between the "initiation of the action and its continuation to completion". In this case Searle argues that "you have to make a continuous voluntary effort to keep going with the action or activity to its completion" (2001, 15). What is important to the legal conception of responsibility is that according to Searle an irreducible self operates in this gap; "'self' is simply the name for that entity which experiences its own activities as more than an inert bundle" (2001, 93).[61]

61 Searle makes this argument because he argues that "the Humean account of me as a sequence of impressions and ideas, even updated to include the physical body with

Philosophically what Searle achieves is the wresting of the concept of rationality in relation to action away from the determinist claims about choice and certain scientific approaches to the causal effectiveness of desire independent states of mind. In order to do this he utilizes the concept of intention-in-action. On the Humean explanation of action a gap cannot exist between the belief/desire states, which are causally effective, and the action itself. For Searle there has to be a gap in order for agency to have meaning. Searle sees two types of intention as operating in the gap: one is prior intention and the other intentionality-in-action. [62] The two concepts may be interrelated, as Searle explains in relation to the act of raising an arm in order to vote. In order to vote:

> I formed a prior intention (whose conditions of satisfaction are that it should cause the whole action) and then I perform the whole action, where the whole action consists of two components, the intention-in-action and the bodily movement (and the condition of satisfaction of the intention-in-action is that it should cause the bodily movement) (2001, 45).

Searle points out that on occasions when acting spontaneously all that is required for bodily movement is an intention-in-action whose condition of satisfaction is the achievement of that bodily movement. It is only in instances of action where deliberation is required that prior intention will be relevant. Importantly he says: "Intentions-in-action may or may not be conscious" (2001, 47).

The Humean view of causation, as Searle points out, makes the distinction between rational and irrational action hard to establish. Searle argues that this is because: if beliefs are an "efficient cause"[63] of behaviour rather than behaviour being caused by the choices of an irreducible self; then such behaviour based solely on beliefs and desires would be more akin to obsessional or addictive behaviour.

---

all its dispositions, does not capture the essential requirement for rational agency, namely selfhood." He adds flesh to the bones of his construction of a self as follows:

> It is characteristic of my conscious experience that I engage in deliberation and action, I have perceptions, I use my memories in deliberation, I make decisions, I carry out decisions (or fail to carry them out), and I feel satisfied or unsatisfied, guilty or innocent, depending on the net results of all these activities. The line I am following here is in a sense a fine line between Hume's skepticism and the naïve pretheoretical view that each of us is aware of himself or herself as a self. The point I am making is that though the self is not the name of an experience nor is it the name of an object of an experience, nonetheless there is a sequence of formal features of our experiences that are constitutive of ourselves as selves. (2001, 93–4, all quotations.)

62 Searle writes when discussing the concept of intention-in-action: "In ordinary English the closest word for an intention-in-action is 'trying'. If you had an intention-in-action but failed to achieve its conditions of satisfaction, you did at least try" (2001, 45).

63 Searle describes his use of this expression as "cases of actions for which the antecedent beliefs and desires really are causally sufficient". The sense of causation employed here is "as in: the explosion caused the building to collapse…" (2001, 12).

This is precisely because it lacks the deliberations of an irreducible self, selecting from a range of beliefs and desires and choosing how to act. Without this notion of an irreducible self the concept of a rational actor who may be held responsible for their actions becomes a chimera.

The law attributes responsibility for actions to an actor who may be held responsible for causing a prohibited result. The criminal law through the *mens rea* requirements of most offences and the underlying presumption of voluntariness assumes that there is a narrator in the brain who takes responsibility for choices made which bring about results prohibited by law. The law through the insanity and automatism defences permits an actor to claim that they were not criminally responsible for their actions because their actions were not those of a responsible agent. It does this in the case of insanity through denying that the agent had capacity for *mens rea* and in the case of automatism denying that the agent had the capacity to control their acts, or in some cases that the agent was not conscious of acting.

It is this sense of agency, or rather the lack of it, which is central to proving insanity or automatism pleas. However one views Humean causation, it is sceptical of the value of subjective explanations of causation. This scepticism poses a problem for the criminal law. Searle is not alone in finding the absence of the subjective view problematic when it comes to evaluations of agency. Hornsby argues that reductionist explanations which challenge subjective viewpoints make assessments of agency difficult.

In "Agency and Causal Explanation" Hornsby describes the relationship between the personal and impersonal viewpoints of action as follows:

> From the *personal* point of view, an action is a person's doing something for a reason, and her doing it is found intelligible when we know the reason that led her to it. From the *impersonal* point of view, an action would be a link in a causal chain that could be viewed without paying any attention to people, the links being understood by reference to the world's causal workings. We might take it for granted that there are truths available to be discovered from each of these points of view. The problems about agency surface when we start to wonder whether the impersonal point of view does not threaten the personal one" (1993, 161, emphasis in the original).

Hornsby concludes that "actions are not in fact accessible from the impersonal point of view" (1993, 162). She argues that this is because the personal and the impersonal are two different viewpoints and though they overlap they are not synonymous (1993, 182–5). Where Searle's explanation of rationality in action is invaluable to the criminal law is it gives value to each type of explanation and explains how it is that someone may be held responsible for their actions. It provides the structure that the criminal law requires to establish the framework of responsibility. Such a philosophical structure is necessary to assist in attributing responsibility for mental causes of events. Searle achieves this without falling foul of another issue much debated in philosophical circles in relation to mental causation, the idea of infinite regress.[64]

The philosophical framework has to be robust enough to encapsulate the requirements of criminal responsibility. The criminal law requires that differing levels of responsibility are imposed upon those convicted. It has already been established that some of this attribution of responsibility is dependent on an evaluation of the defendant's reasons for acting. To return to the case of *Falconer* and the issue before the court: were her actions voluntary when she took the gun and shot and killed her husband? In English law voluntary action has a fairly minimalist meaning. Arguably it relates to our capacity to control our actions. But the concept of criminal responsibility is broader than this. Interestingly and largely for policy reasons,[65] the criminal law ignores many of a defendant's reasons for acting when assessing culpability – hence some of the difficulty for the courts in deciding the level of culpability Falconer's actions should attract. The real issues in *Falconer* are twofold. They were outlined earlier; the difficulty lies in analysing whether the "amnesia arises after the event" – or whether there is a "lack of conscious involvement during the event itself".

To fit the events within Searle's framework, if evidence at trial could demonstrate a lack of conscious involvement during the event, then arguably Falconer would not be acting as a rational agent. The court would then have to consider the appropriate response to such persons who lacked causal agency. But if the issue was that the amnesia arises after the event, the question becomes: how much she should be excused for an arguably rational, but probably emotional and spontaneous, response to traumatic events[66] – events which it is possible to argue should lessen considerably, if not entirely diminish, her criminal responsibility. The issue is different to the first case scenario in which Falconer would have lacked capacity for conscious control of action, and would in Searle's explanation of action not have been a rational actor. Where the amnesia occurs after the event, the issue is not necessarily whether her action was irrational or insane or unwilled. The issue may be the nature of the emotional responses which caused

64 Infinite regress is defined in the *Oxford Companion to Philosophy* as follows:

> Suppose we define a voluntary act as one caused by an act of will: if acts of will are themselves voluntary then the definition requires that they themselves be caused by prior acts of will. But there is no limit to the number of times this train of reasoning can be reiterated: so either the definition is wrong or acts of will are not voluntary. The argument – deployed by Ryle in *The Concept of Mind* – shows that the proposed analysis of what it is for acts to be voluntary involves an infinite regress (Cohen 1995, 408).

65 For a discussion of the impact of policy on the development of the criminal law see Ashworth (2006) and Norrie (2001 and 2005).

66 This emotional reaction may well have psychological/psychiatric descriptions, e.g., dissociative disorders related to shock. Such states have been recognized by psychiatrists since the nineteenth century; see the work of Janet (1889; 1907). In England and Wales sleepwalking has been associated with dissociation and has led to the classification of sleepwalking as insanity or insane automatism; *R v Burgess* [1991] 2 All ER 769.

her behaviour. The English law has been very reluctant to enter into the discussion of these types of issues.[67]

This is precisely the concept that the law and traditional philosophical explanations eschew; the idea of reasons as having a causal relation to action, independent of desire/belief states.[68] Searle's answer to the question of action is to simply say that the explanation for actions lies within the actor's reasons for acting. That within each individual is an "irreducible self" that is causally responsible for the choices that individual makes when choosing to act. It is not possible in this chapter to deal with all the philosophical opposition that such an attack on the traditional philosophical position may attract but simply to say that Searle's defence of his arguments are robust and convincing and to examine how his model of "rationality in action" might assist attributions of responsibility in the criminal law, and how they link to the neuroscience of consciousness. Searle proposes that: "*Agency requires an entity that can consciously try to do something*" (2001, 83, emphasis in original).

Described briefly, Searle's argument is that mind and brain are not separable. The sense of choosing is a sense which arises from the activities of the brain – "it is just *the state that the brain is in*" (2004, 146, emphasis in original). This permits Searle to see consciousness as pivotal to practical reasoning and to the concept of rationality in action. Furthermore he links his account of rational action for which agents may be held responsible to neurobiological explanations of brain activity.

What Neurobiological Research into Conscious States Tells Us about the Gap

One of the bases of Searle's thesis is that "the gap" "is that feature of the consciousness of voluntary actions, whereby the actions are experienced as not having sufficient psychological causal conditions to determine them" (2001, 269). Searle goes on to investigate how viewing consciousness as an experience where "qualitativeness, subjectivity, and unity" provide a "'unified field approach'" (2001, 274) to the issue of the subjective experience of conscious states. Such an approach enables him to argue that this unified experience is the essence of conscious experience. This experience of a unified field of consciousness provides the necessary basis to enable the self to carry out voluntary actions. However, Searle admits that to explain how the unified experience of consciousness might be explained neuroscientifically using neurobiological evidence is somewhat problematic. Nonetheless Searle examines the explanations of action in relation

67 An example of this reluctance may be seen more generally in the treatment of battered women who kill their abusers. See for example the discussion of this issue by the Privy Council in *Attorney General for Jersey v Holley* [2005] UKPC 23.

68 For a discussion of the difficulties with traditional philosophical models of action in terms of voluntariness and the difficulty of describing actions as voluntary, see Duff's account of the relevance of different theories (1996, 75–106).

to conscious awareness through the work of Libet.[69] Here Searle's suppositions are controversial. Libet argues that the initiation of movement begins in the unconscious but that there is a time lag, a gap, between the neural correlates of the commencement of action and conscious awareness of the impending action. Libet takes this to establish that, in fact, "if all conscious awarenesses are preceded by unconscious processes, we are forced to conclude that we do not actually live in the present and that unconscious processes play a predominant role in the production of our conscious life" (2004, 222). But, as Searle points out, the explanation of the conscious initiation of action in the brain needs a more nuanced and subtle explanation. He argues that Libet's experiments may actually provide evidence of the subjective experience of choosing to act. Even on the limited evidence provided by Libet's experiments, it is clear that once action readiness potential appears as neural correlates it is always possible that subsequent action may be aborted by the actor.

Libet's interpretation of his own empirical research data is to conclude that there may be a "separable soul" – "'the ghost in the machine'", and asks: "How does Ryle *know* there is no ghost in our cerebral makeup?" (2004, 221, emphasis in original). Searle's proposed interpretation is very different. His answer is simply that the gap shows the neurobiological basis of the commencement of action. He locates and explains the gap as part of the unified experience of consciousness but points out that "the gap is not between the state of my neurons now and my conscious state now; the gap is between what is happening now in the conscious volitional component of the whole brain system and what is going to happen next" (2001, 293). This enables Searle to argue that consciousness is a biological phenomenon, but that free will and choice cannot be explained away in any convincing manner by the determinist thesis which, at its most extreme, would simply describe the experience of choosing to act as epiphenomenal. Searle does not find a clear answer in the scientific explanations of consciousness but he does find an examination of the data provided by scientists extremely useful. It is similarly useful to lawyers. Where its utility lies is in making clearer what issues need further clarification and where the law is actually incorrect in its construction of the voluntary actor or more correctly where involuntariness may excuse.

Conclusion

To conclude, the actual scientific research into conscious states may not at present provide a sustainable answer to constructions of criminal responsibility. However, it has a very important role to play. It is essential that lawyers understand the implications of new scientific and philosophical interpretations of consciousness and voluntary action, in order to develop the jurisprudential basis for constructions of responsibility in the criminal law. Scientific research has great use in providing

69 For an in-depth explanation of this thesis, see Libet (2004).

a focal point for the discussions about criminal responsibility. It is high time the law abandoned the evaluation of culpability in mental order defences through outmoded and illogical normative frameworks. If we are to construct a sustainable description to form the basis of criminal responsibility in the twenty-first century, it will be both worthwhile and necessary to widen the ambit of the debate; and to cross disciplinary boundaries in the search for a viable concept of agency which allows the correct attribution of responsibility for voluntary action. This is not to suggest that the criminal law can avoid the development of specialist principles but rather it needs to take cognizance of the broader contexts within which evaluations of agency take place. Or, as Searle would argue:

> We do not live in several different, or even two different, worlds, a mental world and a physical world, a scientific world and a world of common sense. Rather, there is just one world: it is the world we all live in, and we need to account for how we exist as a part of it (2004, 209).

References

Ashworth, A. (2006), *Principles of the Criminal Law*, 5th edition. (Oxford: Oxford University Press).

Cane, P. (2002), *Responsibility in Law and Morality*. (Oxford: Hart Publishing).

Chalmers, D.J. (1996), *The Conscious Mind*. (Oxford: Oxford University Press).

Churchland, P.M. (1995), *The Engine of Reason, the Seat of the Soul*. (Cambridge: MIT Press).

Cohen, M. (1995), "Infinite Regress" in Honderich, T. (ed.), *Oxford Companion to Philosophy*. (Oxford: Oxford University Press).

Dennett, D. (1991), *Consciousness Explained*. (London: Penguin).

Devlin, P. (1965), *The Enforcement of Morals*. (Oxford: Oxford University Press).

Duff, A. (1996), "Acting, Trying and Criminal Liability", in Shute, S., Gardner, J. and Horder, J. (eds), *Action and Value in the Criminal Law*. (Oxford: Oxford University Press).

Ebrahim, I., Fenwick, P., Wilson, W., Marks, R. and Peacock, K. (2005), "Violence, Sleepwalking and the Criminal Law: (1) The Medical Aspects", *Crim LR*, [2005] 601–12.

Ellard, J. (1995), "Some Notes on Non-insane Automatism and the Will", 69 *ALJ* 833–41.

Goodenough, O. and Prehn, K. (2006), "A Neuroscientific Approach to Normative Judgment in Law and Justice", in Goodenough and Zeki (eds), *Law & the Brain*. (Oxford: Oxford University Press).

Greenfield, S. (1995), *Journey to the Centres of the Mind*. (New York: W.H. Freeman).

—— (1997), *The Human Brain*. (London: Weidenfeld and Nicolson).
Halpin, A. (2004), *Definition in the Criminal Law*. (Oxford: Hart Publishing).
Hart, H.L.A. (1963), *Law, Liberty and Morality*. (Oxford: Oxford University Press).
—— (1992), *Punishment and Responsibility*. (Oxford: Oxford University Press).
Horder, J. (1996), "Criminal Law between Determinism, Liberalism and Criminal Justice", *Current Legal Problems* 159, 160–72.
—— (2004), *Excusing Crime*. (Oxford: Oxford University Press).
Hornsby, J. (1993), "Agency and Causal Explanation", in Heil, J. and Mele, A. (eds), *Mental Causation*. (Oxford: Oxford University Press).
—— (1997), *Simple Mindedness*. (Cambridge: MIT Press).
Hume, D. (1888), *Treatise of Human Nature*. (Oxford: Oxford University Press).
—— (1963), *Essays*. (Oxford: Oxford University Press).
Janet, P. (1889), *Psychological Automatisms*. (Paris: Alcan).
—— (1907), *The Major Symptons of Hysteria*. (New York: Macmillan).
Law Commission (2005), "A New Homicide Act for England and Wales?" *Law Commission Consultation Paper No 177*. (London: The Stationery Office).
Libet, B. (2004), *Mind Time*. (Cambridge: Harvard University Press).
Mackay, R.D. and Kearns, G. (1999), "More Fact(s) about the Insanity Defence", *Crim LR* [1999] 714–725.
Mackie, P.J. (1995), "Causality', in Honderich, T. (ed.), *Oxford Companion to Philosophy*. (Oxford: Oxford University Press).
McCall Smith, A. and Shapiro, C.M. (1997), "Sleep Disorders and Crime" in McCall Smith and Shapiro (eds), *Forensic Aspects of Sleep*. (Chichester: John Wiley & Sons).
Norrie, A. (2001), *Crime Reason and History*. (London: Butterworths).
—— (2005), *Law and the Beautiful Soul*. (London: Glasshouse Press).
Ormerod, D. (2005), *Smith and Hogan, Criminal Law*, 11th edition. (Oxford: Oxford University Press).
Ormerod, D. and Fortson, R. (2005), "Drug Suppliers as Manslaughterers (Again)", *Crim L R,* [2005] 819–833.
Parkin, A.J. (1995), *Memory and Amnesia*. (Oxford: Blackwell).
Penrose, R. (1995), *Shadows of the Mind*. (Oxford: Oxford University Press).
Raz, J. (1986), *The Morality of Freedom*. (Oxford: Oxford University Press).
Ryle, G. (1963), *The Concept of Mind*. (London: Peregrine).
Searle, J. (2001), *Rationality in Action*. (Cambridge: MIT Press).
—— (2004), *Mind*. (Oxford: Oxford University Press).
Simester, A.P. and Sullivan, G.R. (2003), *Criminal Law Theory and Doctrine*, 2nd edition. (Oxford: Hart Publishing).
White, A. (ed.) (1968), *The Philosophy of Action*. (Oxford: Oxford University Press).
Wilson, W., Ebrahim, I., Fenwick, P. and Marks, R. (2005), "Violence Sleepwalking and the Criminal Law: (2) The Legal Aspects", *Crim LR,* [2005] 614–23.

Chapter 5
Self-Exclusion Agreements: Should We Be Free not to Be Free to Ruin Ourselves? Gambling, Self-Exclusion Agreements and the Brain

Florian Wagner-von Papp[1]

Introduction

Traditional law and economics approaches have assumed that people act rationally at all times. This includes the assumption that people are not subject to motivational limitations, i.e., that they have perfect self-control and that their will power is unbounded. The approach of behavioural law and economics has criticized this attitude as being unrealistic: will power *is* bounded.

In order to cope with bounded will power, humans put up "self-paternalistic" safeguards to shield themselves from diminished self-control when faced with temptations.[2] Will power is especially bounded where "addictions" are concerned. In these cases, the need for effective safeguards against anticipated but "unwanted" behaviour is particularly pressing.

This chapter focuses on the legal treatment of one specific class of safeguards against limited self-control: self-exclusion agreements between casinos and problem gamblers, in which the gambler vows not to return to the casino.[3] As the gambling sector is liberalized in more and more jurisdictions, the need for protection of so-called

---

1 Lecturer in Law, University College London, Faculty of Laws. Ph.D. 2004 (University of Tuebingen, Germany), LL.M. 2002 (Columbia University), Bar Exam equivalent 2000 (Germany), LL.B./J.D. equivalent 1998 (University of Tuebingen). I gratefully acknowledge the helpful comments by many of the participants of the conference "Law, Mind & Brain" at UCL in 2006, and of the participants of the Gruter Institute's Annual Conference 2006 on "Law, Behaviour and the Brain'. I would especially like to thank Stefan Bechtold, Oliver Goodenough, James Grant, Morris Hoffman, Hannah Kütterer-Lang, Stephen Morse, Ernest Schonfield and Gerhard Wagner. The chapter was essentially completed in April 2006; as far as possible, it has been updated in February 2007.

2 For a plethora of examples of such safeguards, *see* Schelling (1985) and (2006) *at* 63–113; Elster (2000).

3 *See also* Eggert (2003) *at* 748; Rhea (2005); Weis (1999); Peters (2002); Schimmel (2006); Wagner-von Papp (2005, 2006).

problem gamblers[4] is increasingly recognized.[5] Self-exclusion is one form of such protection.

The common denominator of all "self-paternalistic" safeguards is that the actor tries to limit their future strategy space in order to maximize their perceived overall self-interest. The limitation of the future autonomy is itself autonomously chosen. This leads to the philosophical and legal question: to what degree (if at all) it is possible to limit one's future autonomy.

As have others before me, I posit that there is a trade-off between the autonomy at the time the decision to self-exclude is made (t_1) and the autonomy at the later time, when the actor "wants to" succumb to the temptation (t_2).[6] There are several possible ways to resolve this trade-off. One option would be to maximize autonomy in t_1: the actor would be entirely free in t_1 to limit their future autonomy in t_2 in any way they like. The opposite extreme would be to maximize autonomy in t_2: regardless what limitations were set up in t_1, the actor would be entirely free to do as they please in t_2. Yet another solution would be to maximize "overall autonomy"[7] or "vertical autonomy"[8] by adopting one of a whole range of intermediate solutions – the actor might be free to act in t_2, but only under certain conditions, or only after a certain period of time has lapsed between t_1 and t_2.

The chapter is divided into four parts. The first part will outline the dimensions of problem gambling and describe the mechanism of self-exclusion schemes ("Problem Gambling and Self-exclusion" below).

The second part will deal with the questions whether the law *should* allow the effective limitation of one's future autonomy, whether it *does* allow it, and – if the

4 The literature uses a number of different terms to describe what is – for the purposes of this chapter – essentially the same phenomenon, such as pathological, compulsive or addicted gamblers (for even more terms, *see* BMA Board of Science (2007) *at* 4). For the criteria for the terms "problem gambler" and "pathological gambler" *see infra* n. 9. This latter distinction is crucial when referring to prevalence studies, as some of them treat pathological gambling as the "hard core" and problem gambling as meaning (only) the borderline cases (Fisher (1996)), whereas others (such as Sproston, Erens & Orford (2000); Grinols (2004) *at* 201) use the term "problem gamblers" to include *both* categories. Whether gambling can lead to an addiction in a technical sense is subject to controversy, *see* the discussion in DCMS Gambling Review Body (2001) *at* 231 (Annex G); *see also* NGISC (1999) *at* 4-1; *infra* n. 86. The law adds to this terminological confusion by introducing the category of "other vulnerable persons", Gambling Act 2005, s.1(c), taken by the Gambling Commission (2006a *at* 55, para. 5.5.8.) to mean "people who gamble more than they want to, people who gamble beyond their means and/or people who may not be able to make informed or balanced decisions about gambling due to a mental impairment, alcohol, or drugs".

5 *See, inter alia,* Gambling Commission (2006b); DCMS Gambling Review Body (2001) *at* 7–10 (chapter 3), 85–96 (chapter 17), 173–177 (chapter 32) and 231–236 (Annex G and H); NGISC (1999) *at* 4-1 to 4-20 and *Exec.*-16 to 18.

6 *See, e.g.,* Eggert (2003); Smith (1996).

7 Eggert (2003) *at* 696.

8 Smith (1996) *at* 178.

answer to the latter question is in the affirmative – *to what extent* actors can limit their future strategy spaces ("Should We be Free not to be Free? – Introductory Examples" and "Should We be Free not to be Free? – Reasons for Preferring t_1 or t_2"). I reach the conclusion that although the law is usually reluctant to allow persons to limit their future autonomy, there are circumstances under which it is possible do so. One of the requirements for legitimate self-limitation is that there be some sort of defect at the later time (t_2) which is not present at the time the self-limiting agreement is entered into (t_1); another prerequisite is that the extent of the self-limitation be narrowly tailored to counterbalance this defect.

The third part of the chapter addresses the question if in the case of gambling and self-exclusion agreements there is such a relevant defect in t_2 ("The Relevant Defect in t_2: Problem Gambling and the Brain"). I will point to several studies which show that there are physiological dysfunctions suggesting that the gambler's decision in t_2 to gamble is indeed arrived at by different neural processes than the decision in t_1 to self-exclude. I submit that this constitutes a defect in t_2 which can legitimately be counterbalanced by the self-exclusion.

The fourth and final part ("Self-Exclusion: Extent of the Limitation of Autonomy" and "The Law and Self-Exclusion from Casinos: Regulatory Options") addresses the question of the permissible extent of the self-limitation. Several regulatory options are discussed and the self-exclusion arrangements proposed by the Gambling Commission in the United Kingdom are scrutinized against the background of the experience gained in Germany and the United States. I conclude that the enforcement of self-exclusion agreements by private litigation is preferable to the exclusively public enforcement currently envisaged.

Problem Gambling and Self-exclusion

Problem Gambling

Problem gambling is often defined as "gambling to a degree that compromises, disrupts or damages family, personal or recreational pursuits".[9] Its prevalence is difficult to assess: the definition of problem gambling is not clear-cut, and screening instruments rely on questionnaires, and thus self-assessment.[10] Studies

---

9 *See, e.g.,* Fisher (1996) *at* 2, 10; Sproston, Erens & Orford (2000) *at* iii, 41; DCMS Gambling Review Body (2001) *at* 87 (para. 17.25). The Gambling Commission (2006b *at* para. 6) defines problem gambling as "gambling that is not responsible gambling and so causes harm to the person concerned and others", where "[r]esponsible gambling ... means that on most gambling occasions the person will gamble within his or her means as regards both money and time."

10 Traditionally, the most commonly used screens are the South Oaks Gambling Screen (SOGS; Lesieur & Blume (1987)), which is based on the DSM-III-criteria, and screens based on the criteria of DSM-IV or DSM-IV-TR, *see* American Psychiatric Association

in various countries have generally shown a prevalence of lifetime pathological gambling between 1% and 2% in the general population; the past-year prevalence is slightly lower.[11] A large-scale prevalence study conducted in Great Britain in 1999 has put the past-year prevalence at 0.6% to 0.8% of the population,[12] a number which appears relatively low in an international comparison.[13] But even this low

(2000) *at* 312.31. In a new prevalence study in the United Kingdom, the Problem Gambling Severity Index (PGSI) is going to be used (BMA Board of Science (2007) *at* 3–4). A list and discussion of different screens can be found in Shaffer & Freed (2005) *at* 370–376; Orford et al. (2003) *at* 62–80; May-Chahal et al. (2004), *at* 14–15; *see also* Pallanti et al. (2005). The questions and criteria used in the SOGS and DSM-IV are reproduced in DCMS Gambling Review Body (2001), *at* 235–236; *see also* Sproston, Erens & Orford (2000) *at* 41–42 and Appendix 3, Questions C9–C28 and C29–37. "Problem gambling" is commonly assumed when a score of five in the SOGS is reached or three of the DSM-IV criteria are fulfilled (*e.g.*, Gambling Review Body *at* 234). "Pathological gambling" is assumed by the American Psychiatric Association when five or more of the DSM-IV criteria are fulfilled. The problem with self-assessment is that it is a common trait of problem gamblers to conceal their problems, *cf.* NGISC (1999) *at* 4–9.

11 An overview of prevalence studies can be found in Petry (2004) *at* 14–30. *See also* Shaffer & Freed (2005) *at* 346–355, 374–375; http://www.naspl.org/biblio10.html. The 1–2%-range comprises the "hard core" of pathological gamblers, around which a "soft core" of an additional 3–5% of the population of problem gamblers is positioned. The prevalence is substantially higher in certain subgroups (*e.g.*, adolescents (4.8% past-year pathological), homeless (5.4% pathological), prison inmates). The large variations in reported prevalence are partly due to differing standards, such as the question whether "lifetime" or "past year" prevalence is the appropriate measure (*see* May-Chahal et al. (2004) *at* 14; NGISC (1999) *at* 4-4), which of the "more than 27" (Shaffer & Freed (2005) *at* 370) different screens and which cut-off score is used; for additional reasons *see infra* n. 12. "Lifetime" measures are sometimes said to overestimate, "past year" measures to underestimate the problem; but, as Shaffer & Freed (2005) *at* 343–345 argue, absent a "gold standard", an independent and objective benchmark, it is difficult to know whether there is over- or underestimation, anyway. They also point out (*at* 346–347) that tests which produce an acceptable number of false positives in subgroups with a high base rate may lead to an overestimate when used in the general population in which the base rate is low. According to Shaffer & Freed, neurobiological research (*see infra* "The Relevant Defect in t_2: Problem Gambling and the Brain") will "likely" provide a gold standard (*op. cit. at* 340); if this is the case, one could then follow up on the screened positives.

12 Sproston, Erens & Orford (2000) *at* 45, 49. The follow-up "British Gambling Prevalence Study 2006" is currently being conducted under the aegis of the UK Gambling Commission; its final results are expected to be published in September 2007.

13 DCMS Gambling Review Body (2001), *at* 92 (para. 17.64) and *at* 94 (para. 17.69); BMA Board of Science (2007) *at* 5. Much has been made of this low prevalence rate in Britain. Additionally to the caveats mentioned by Sproston, Erens & Orford (2000) *at* 43, at least three further aspects should be taken into account. First, the low rate may be due to the traditional "unstimulated demand" policy that has hitherto governed the regulatory framework in the UK; if this were the explanation, the prevalence might be expected to rise after liberalization and the concurrently increased exposure of the population to gambling

estimate translates into approximately 275,000–370,000 problem gamblers in Britain alone.[14] And the figures about the prevalence in the general population may be understating the problem: when addressing the questions of whether and how to regulate gambling facilities, it is the prevalence among the patrons of such facilities that is of concern. There are indications that – for obvious reasons – the prevalence among the patrons of gambling establishments is much higher than in the general population.[15] The true scale of the problem emerges when one also

---

(BMA Board of Science (2007) *at* 18; DCMS Gambling Review Body (2001) *at* 94 (para. 17.69); Volberg (2000); for evidence for the fact that prevalence rates grow with the gambling opportunities *see* Petry (2004) *at* 30–33; *see also* NGISC (1999) *at* 4-1 and 4-4; Eggert (2004) *at* 225–226 and his citations in n. 45–49; Sproston, Erens & Orford (2000) *at* 53; for a harsh criticism of the British Government's failure to act on this insight, *see* Orford et al. (2003) *at* 257; more cautious: Shaffer & Freed (2005) *at* 351–352). Second, when comparing the British Gambling Prevalence Survey with other prevalence studies, it has to be taken into account that this study measured "past year" rather than "lifetime" problem gambling (Sproston, Erens & Orford (2000) *at* 41). Third, there may be cultural differences, which make international prevalence comparisons problematic, even if the same screen is used: as the questionnaires do not exclusively ask for objectively verifiable information, but also for purely subjective self-assessment, the more self-conscious the respondent is, the more likely he is to score higher; and self-consciousness concerning gambling may be influenced by cultural differences. For example, I would assume that in a society which condemns gambling for moral or religious reasons, the questions "Have you felt guilty about the way you gamble [..]?", "Have people criticised your gambling?" and "Do you feel you have a problem with betting money or gambling?" are, *ceteris paribus*, more likely to be answered in the affirmative than in societies in which betting is considered "part of the culture" (which Bellringer (1999) *at* 17–18 claims to be the case in Britain). – Another report, commissioned by the Office of the Deputy Prime Minister, mentioned a prevalence of 1% in Britain (Roger Tym and Partners (2006) *at* 19 (para. 3.3)). The ensuing criticism that this figure was "almost twice the number" given earlier to justify the Gambling Bill (*see* Coates (2006d), quoting Hugo Swire MP) is inapposite: the British Gambling Prevalence Survey gave a confidence interval of 0.6% to 1.0% from the start (Sproston, Erens & Orford (2000) *at* 45). Furthermore, the 2006 report does not even claim to present new data; it appears to simply have taken the upper bounds of the figures of the earlier survey. The prevalence estimates for Germany are even lower: the number of pathological gamblers is estimated to lie between 70,000 and 150,000 (*see* von Hippel (2001) *at* 559), which would constitute only between approx. 0.1% and 0.2% of the population. These numbers are based on an extremely thin factual basis and most probably understate the extent of the problem (*see* Kaiser (2004)).

14 Sproston, Erens & Orford (2000) *at* 49.

15 NGSIC (1999) *at* 4–5 reports the percentage of problem gamblers at US gambling facilities to be more than 13%. Fisher (1996) *at* 43 puts the number of past year "severe problem gamblers" (her category equivalent to pathological gamblers) among UK casino patrons at 2%, and of past-year "problem gamblers" at an additional 5%. Among *regular* (at least once a week) casino patrons (who make up 7% of all casino patrons, but account for 63% of the visits, Fisher (1996) *at* 65), there were 7% severe, and a further 7% problem gamblers (Fisher (1996) *at* 72). Fisher has downward-adjusted these numbers to account for the higher probability of regulars to be interviewed; Orford et al. believe that Fisher's data could more accurately be

takes into account that this relatively small fraction of problem gamblers generates a major part of the overall turnover of casinos;[16] it has even been suggested that without problem gamblers casinos might not operate profitably.[17]

Self-Exclusion Schemes

Today, most casinos offer the opportunity for problem gamblers to self-exclude. In some jurisdictions such self-exclusion schemes are made mandatory by regulation; in other jurisdictions the casinos have introduced the schemes voluntarily – presumably in order to show their goodwill, with the ulterior motive of forestalling more intrusive public regulation.[18]

The details of such self-exclusion schemes differ from jurisdiction to jurisdiction and from case to case. In their most basic form, the problem gambler picks up a form sheet provided by the casino, fills in their personal details, ticks the box "I want to be excluded from this casino for [x] years", and hands the form back to the casino. The casino then puts the self-excluded gambler on a blacklist. If the self-exclusion scheme works according to plan, the gambler will be denied access to the casino during the specified time period.

However, there have been numerous instances in which the scheme has failed.[19] Self-excluded gamblers were admitted to the casino despite the ban. They gambled, lost and sued. Should they be able to reclaim the lost stakes?

This question would be difficult to answer even if the agreements between the gambler and the casinos explicitly spelled out the intended consequences of a

---

stated as meaning that "of those people present in British casinos at any one time around 16 per cent might be expected to have gambling problems (8 per cent severe) […]" ((2003) at 77).

16 NGISC (1999), *at* 4-15/16, cites several studies which estimate that approximately 30% of the casinos' revenue is generated by problem gamblers, although one study put the figure at "only" 15%. Kindt (2004), *at* 545 and 586, even claims that 27% to 55% of the revenue comes from pathological gamblers. Igelmann & Kelly (2005) estimate that "problem gamblers are responsible for roughly 36 per cent of the revenue". A study cited by the Gambling Review Body (2001) *at* 93 (para. 17.68, n. 53) found that 65% of the turnover was generated by 7% of all gamblers; but although it may be indicative, this latter number in itself does not tell us much about problem gamblers; it may just as well result from a few very rich recreational gamblers. The same applies to the numbers mentioned by Grinols (2004) *at* 46 (citing a study which found that 10% "heavy bettors" account for 61% of the revenue). For further estimates of the turnover generated by problem gamblers *see* Eggert (2004) *at* 226 n. 51.

17 DCMS Gambling Review Body (2001) *at* 93 (para. 17.68); *see also* Fisher (1996) *at* 65.

18 The motives for which the industry should have a rational self-interest in contributing to a trust funding responsible gambling research cited in Arnold et al. (2003) *at* 35–36 can partly be transferred to the question why casinos may be interested in voluntarily offering self-exclusion schemes.

19 BMA Board of Science (2007) *at* 16 "Implementation of secondary prevention efforts by the gaming industry, such as […] exclusion programmes, have not always been of the highest quality and compliance has often been uneven."

relapse. Answering the question is complicated by the fact that the self-exclusion agreements regularly do *not* contain any such explicit promises; all consequences of a breach of the agreement need to be inferred from the communications "I want to be excluded" – "Agreed." Whether this can be understood as being an offer and an acceptance of a legally binding contract, and whether there is any mutual consideration to support this contract, depends upon the interpretation of the parties' communications.

But before we turn to the question of whether the requirements of a contract are fulfilled,[20] a more fundamental question needs to be answered. Even assuming, for the sake of argument, that the self-exclusion agreement can be understood to be a binding contract between the casino and the gambler by which the casino is obliged to repay any stakes lost by the excluded gambler on subsequent visits, the question remains as to whether this contract can bind the parties, if they *mutually agree to rescind* the self-exclusion contract when the relapsing gambler returns to the casino. And even if they do not *explicitly* rescind the self-exclusion contract, the conclusion of a gambling contract in itself may well be interpreted as an *implicit* rescission of the self-exclusion contract.

Should We be Free not to be Free? Introductory Examples

The question whether we should be able to limit our future autonomy is not a particularly new one. In the following, I shall mention a number of examples which are all structured around the question if the individual is "free" in a given time t_1 "not to be free" in a later period t_2.

Self-enslavement

John Stuart Mill coined the phrase that has inspired the title of this article, when he answered the question whether a person should be able to sell himself into slavery: "The principle of freedom cannot require that he should be free not to be free."[21] I would assume that, with regard to the specific question of slavery, most people would agree with Mill; courts would refuse to enforce such a contract on grounds of public policy.[22] The freedom in t_2 is deemed to prevail over the freedom to commit oneself to slavery in t_1.

Contract Modification/Rescission

Likewise, let us assume that two parties enter into a fixed-term – let us say 10-year – contract, but decide to rescind this contract on the very next day. Again, we

20 *See infra* "Self-exclusion agreements as contracts?").
21 Mill (1859/1997) *at* 125.
22 See Smith (1996) *at* 168–169.

honour the later agreement rather than the earlier one.[23] By doing this, we implicitly deem the autonomous decision in t_2 to prevail once more over the decision in t_1.

No-Oral-Modification Clauses (No Variation Except in Writing)

But the later agreement is not always entirely free from the shackles of a previous contract.

Consider the case of no-oral-modification clauses (also called NOM, or "no variation except in writing" clauses): two parties agree in a contract that any modifications to the contract should only be valid if agreed to in writing. Let us assume that a few days after this contract was concluded the parties *orally* agree to a modification.

The common law position The traditional common law position, at least in most states of the USA, is that an oral modification is valid despite the existence of a preceding no-oral-modification clause.[24] In the words of Benjamin Cardozo: "Those who make a contract may unmake it. The clause which forbids a change may be changed like any other. [...] What is excluded by one act is restored by another. You may put it out by the door; it is back through the window. Whenever two men contract, no limitation self-imposed can destroy their power to contract again."[25] In England, the same conclusion has only recently been – reluctantly – reached by the Court of Appeal: "[T]he parties have made their own law by contracting, and can in principle unmake or remake it."[26] In other words, the no-oral-modifications

23 Provided there was consideration for the modification or rescission of the contract.

24 *See, e.g.*, *Autotrol Corp. v. Continental Water Systems Corp.*, 918 F.2d 689, 692 (7th Cir. 1990) ("[A]n oral modification is enforceable under Texas law even if the contract forbids oral modifications [...]. The Texas approach [is] by no means idiosyncratic [...]."); *Beatty v. Guggenheim Exploration Co.*, 122 N.E. 378 (N.Y. 1919). *See also* Restatement (Second) of Contracts § 283, comment b; Farnsworth (2004) *at* 436–437 (§ 7.6). *But see* the discussion of contradictory precedent in the District of Columbia in *Ghahremani v. Uptown Partners, L.L.C.*, 2005 WL 3211463, slip copy *at* *13 (D.D.C. 2005). However, the cases cited in *Gharemani* in favour of the enforcement of the NOM-clause, such as Hildreth Consulting Engineers, *P.C. v. Larry E. Knight, Inc.*, 801 A.2d 967 (D.C. 2002), were already influenced by statutory law (*see infra* n. 28).

25 *Beatty v. Guggenheim Exploration Co.*, 122 N.E. 378, 381 (N.Y. 1919).

26 *World Online Telecom Limited (formerly known as Localtel Limited)* v *I-Way Limited* [2002] EWCA Civ 413 para. 10. Both Lord Justice Sedley (joined by Justice Charles) and Lord Justice Schiemann recognized the conflict between the freedom of contract at the time of the drafting of the no-oral-modification clause (in what I call t_1) and the freedom of contract at the time of the variation of the contract (in t_2): "[F]ar from fettering their freedom of contract, [the party invoking the NOM-clause] can legitimately say that a preclusive clause like [the NOM-clause] gives effect to this freedom. [...] But [...] no firm authority in this country closes the door upon fact-based arguments to the contrary. One reason may be that

clause contained in the earlier contract is of no relevance whatsoever, because the parties, by agreeing on an oral modification, can and do depart "autonomously" from the clause. Thus, under the common law, the autonomy in t_2 prevails, once again, over the autonomy in t_1.

Statutory provisions However, under a number of statutory provisions and model codes, the opposite solution is reached. No-oral-modification clauses are given effect, i.e., a subsequent oral modification is considered as not binding[27] under the Uniform Commercial Code,[28] some state statutes in the US,[29] the Convention on the International Sales of Goods,[30] and the UNIDROIT principles.[31] All these provisions state that the autonomous agreement in t_1 prevails over the agreement in t_2.

Preliminary Summary

The examples mentioned above show that the law usually favours the autonomous decision in t_2, even if this renders the contract concluded in t_1 nugatory. The self-

---

the principle itself is neither simple nor unitary. A consensual oral variation, after all, is also an exercise of freedom of contract." (Lord Justice Sedley *at* para. 10). *See also* Lord Justice Schiemann's opinion (*at* para. 17): "[The submission of the party invoking the NOM-clause is that] precisely that is allowed against which the parties may be regarded as having sought to safeguard themselves. I see a good deal of force in that submission; but for the reasons given by my Lord this appeal must be dismissed [...]." This judgment was delivered on an interlocutory appeal; for further developments see *I-Way Ltd.* v *World Online Telecom Ltd.* [2004] EWHC 244 (Comm). The issue was not addressed in *South Caribbean Trading Ltd.* v *Trafigura Beheer BV* [2005] 1 Lloyd's Rep. 128, where the variation by e-mail was found to satisfy the NOM-clause (*at* p. 150, para. 110). Prior to *World Online* the High Court seems to have subscribed to the opposite view, *see United Bank Ltd.* v *Masood Asif* 1999 WL 33285417 (Q.B.) (Justice Wright): "The real problem is that Mr Burgess is faced with a proposed oral variation of a situation created by the parties, which expressly provides that there shall be no variation of either deed unless made by one or more instruments in writing signed by the parties. With the greatest possible respect to Mr Burgess, I found his submissions, with respect, incomprehensible. He suggests that it is open to an officer of the bank to effectively disregard that express provision and to vary the provisions [...] without any document in writing, signed by either party at all. I simply cannot accept that submission."

27 Although an oral modification may still have a limited effect, *see, e.g.*, CISG Art. 29(2)2; UCC Art. 2-209(4) and (5); UNIDROIT Principles for International Commercial Contracts 2004, Art. 2.1.18(2). As convincingly argued by Jolls (1997) *at* 206, 230, the same reasons that weigh against an absolute preference for the agreement in t_2 also counsel for caution in the application of these reliance provisions.

28 UCC Art. 2-209(2).

29 *E.g.*, N.Y. Gen. Oblig. § 15–301 (McKinney); Cal. Civ. Code § 1698(c) (West) (*but see* § 1698(d)); D.C. Code § 28:2–209(2).

30 CISG Art. 29 (2).

31 UNIDROIT Principles for International Commercial Contracts 2004 Art. 2.1.18.

enslaved party is free in t_2 to do whatever she pleases (*supra* "Self-enslavement"); the parties can agree to modify or rescind their fixed-term contract before it has expired (*supra* "Contract Modification/Rescission"); and under common law, the parties can orally modify a contract containing a no-oral-modification clause (*supra* "The common law position"). This bodes ill for the self-excluded gambler: even if we assume that the self-exclusion agreement in t_1 is a binding contract, the law's preference for the freedom of contract in t_2 appears to lead to the conclusion that the gambler and the casino can rescind the self-exclusion contract once the relapsing gambler returns to the casino. There may be a question of whether the parties have to rescind the earlier contract *explicitly*, but, presumably, even the gambling contract concluded in t_2 would amount in itself to an *implicit* rescission of the earlier agreement not to gamble.

And yet, the example of the (quasi-) statutory treatment of no-oral-modification clauses (*supra* "Statutory provisions") has shown that the preference for the agreement in t_2 is not set in stone.[32] It is at least conceivable that an agreement in t_1 may prescribe rules for a later agreement in t_2, which implies that the parties can limit their freedom of contract in t_2 by an autonomous agreement in t_1.

Should We be Free not to be Free? Reasons for Preferring t_1 or t_2

What are the reasons for the law to usually prefer the later agreement, but to prefer the earlier one in other cases?

Starting Point: Full Autonomy/Rationality in Both Time Periods

The starting point of the analysis is the assumption in contract law that the parties are autonomous at all times.[33] This is mirrored in the traditional economic assumption that economic actors act rationally in a consistent manner.

32 For a comparison between no-oral-modification clauses and other self-binding agreements *see* Jolls (1997); Wagner-von Papp (2005). From a different point of view, *see* Davis (2006), arguing that there is no general need for "immutable contracts". Davis's main argument is that there is an indirect mechanism (the "Representative Trustee Technique") available to achieve the desired result, but that its rare use demonstrates a lack of demand for immutability (*see infra* "Possibility of an autonomous reversal of the self-limitation"). I agree with many of Davis's arguments concerning *absolutely* unmodifiable ("immutable") contracts; as I will argue, there needs to be *some* possibility of modification or rescission (ibid.). Davis is not averse to such less than absolute limitations on the freedom to modify a contract, *see* Davis (2006) *at* 528 ("Cardozo's prohibition [in Beatty] is probably not founded upon any clear principle of public policy against restrictions upon modification", pointing to UCC 2–209).

33 *See, inter alia*, *Printing & Numerical Registering Co.* v *Sampson*, (1875) L.R. 19 Eq. 462, 465: "[M]en of full age and competent understanding shall have the utmost liberty of contracting, and [...] their contracts when entered into freely and voluntarily shall be

From this premise, it would appear to follow that one should attach, at least in principle, the same weight to the agreements in t_1 and in t_2. But attributing the *same* weight to both agreements would result in the need for *balancing* the conflicting interests. Any increase in weight accorded to the agreement in t_1 would diminish the effects of the equally autonomous decision in t_2, and *vice versa*. Unlimited freedom in both t_1 *and* t_2 is impossible – you can't have your cake and eat it.

If a balancing of the conflicting interests is necessary, the result found above that the law usually favours the later agreement requires an explanation: why should the autonomy in t_2 (usually) *outweigh* the autonomy in t_1?[34]

Reason for Usually Preferring t_2: Improved Information Sets

In most cases, there is indeed a very good reason for preferring the later agreement: the passage of time often reveals previously unknown information. Thus, the parties in t_2 are usually acting on an improved informational basis. New and unforeseen events may have occurred between t_1 and t_2; previously existing, but undisclosed, information may have come to light in the meantime; or the parties expected in t_1 to have a preference for something in t_2, and then discover that in t_2 their preferences have changed.[35] In these cases, there is no reason why we should bind *consenting* parties, who mutually agree to alter a previously existing contract, to their earlier (and now refuted) estimate of their future payoffs, when they could receive a higher payoff by relying on the more current ("better") information acquired in t_2 – *volenti non fit iniuria.*

This aspect will account for a large number of cases in which the parties mutually agree to modify or rescind a previously existing contract (compare the example *supra* III.2.). In balancing between the agreements in t_1 and t_2, the aspect that the parties have improved information sets in t_2 justifies the outcome that

---

held sacred [...] [Y]ou are not lightly to interfere with this freedom of contract." See also Mental Capacity Act 2005, s.1(2): "A person must be assumed to have capacity unless it is established that he lacks capacity." and s.1(4): "A person is not to be treated as unable to make a decision merely because he makes an unwise decision."

34 If anything, the opposite result would be easier to explain: The later preferences need to be discounted, as the fulfilment of earlier preferences earns "interest" for the time between t_1 and t_2.

35 The latter presupposes that preferences change over time. Although traditional economics operates under the simplifying assumption that preferences are stable, it is acknowledged that in actual life preferences do change. So common is this latter criticism, that George Stigler included it in his list of standard comments heard at nearly every economic conference: "*The conclusion rests on the assumption of fixed tastes, but of course tastes have surely changed.*" (Stigler (1977) *at* 443). In the context of addictions, it has been argued that it is not actually tastes that change, but the influence of "*visceral factors*" (Loewenstein (2004)). I will use the more common terminology of preferences without prejudice to the possibility that Loewenstein's distinction has its merits.

the autonomy in t_2 outweighs the pre-existing arrangement which was based on information that is now out of date.

Exception: Anticipation of the Change in t_1

The argument that the parties' informational sets are improved in t_2, and that therefore the later agreement should prevail, loses considerably in strength if the parties have *anticipated* a *clearly defined change in circumstances* in the agreement concluded in t_1, and have *specifically addressed this issue*. If the parties to an agreement have foreseen a specific change in circumstances and dealt with this contingency in the earlier agreement, the mere fact that the change actually occurs does not convey any substantial new information.

This is the case of the no-oral-modification clause (*supra* "Contract Modification/ Rescission"): the parties have foreseen that they might later be tempted to agree to a modification orally, and have specifically addressed the question what to do in such a case, namely: consider the modification as not binding.

This does not necessarily lead to the conclusion that the self-limiting agreement established in t_1 actually *does* (or even should) prevail. However, it deprives the later agreement of its *inherent* informational advantage that makes us in the usual cases *automatically* attach greater weight to the agreement in t_2. The anticipation of a specific change in circumstances "levels the playing field" between the agreements in t_1 and t_2.

Why not Wholly Disregard the Autonomy in t_1?

However, even if the agreement in t_1 anticipates a change – and the additional value of the information that the change has actually occurred in t_2 is therefore minimal – there needs to be a substantive reason why we should attach *any weight at all* to the previous agreement in t_1. After all, presumably the parties remember in t_2 the preferences and information they had in t_1. Thus, one could deem the decision in t_2 to incorporate the interests in t_1.

Credible commitment in bilateral settings Why, in other words, should we ever allow an individual in t_1 to bind themselves in t_2? The answer is that the possibility to bind oneself for the future can actually *increase* the range of available options. This is the reason for the very existence of contract law: if one were not able to commit oneself to doing something in the future by giving a legally binding (and thus potentially state-enforced) promise, the only exchanges that would take place would be exchanges performed on the spot.[36] Legally non-enforceable promises to

36 This statement is vastly simplifying and needs to be qualified in at least two regards: (1) Private ordering may take the place of enforcement by the state in many cases (*see*, *e.g.*, Williamson (1985) *at* 164 et seq.). (2) Even absent an external (public or private) enforcement mechanism, cooperative solutions may be Nash equilibria if there is infinitely

do something in the future would usually lack credibility. By submitting oneself (in t_1) to the enforcement mechanism of a legally binding contract (in t_2), one deprives oneself of the option to renege on the promise[37] – and by doing this, makes one's promise to deliver in the future credible, opening up the option of contracts with delayed performance.[38] Pre-commitment to limit one's future options can actually increase one's freedom.[39]

Credible commitment in self-limiting agreements Transplanting this conclusion from bilateral contracts to self-limiting agreements requires some elaboration. In the case of bilateral contracts, the actor deprives themselves of their future option to defect from the agreement in order to make their promise credible *to the other party*. In the case of self-limiting agreements, it is not immediately obvious who the addressee of the "credible promise" could be. Let us again take the example of the no-oral-modification clause. Here, both parties restrict their future freedom (to modify the contract orally in t_2), *not* in order to make their present commitment credible to the other party – the other party does not need any such assurance, as their interests are already adequately protected by the requirement of their consent to modification. Rather, both parties want to assure *themselves* (not *each other*) by the no-oral-modification clause that they will not modify the contract orally later on.

There is a difference between the case of the bilateral contract (in which the assurance is reciprocal) and the no-oral-modification clause (in which the assurance is reflexive). In the case of the bilateral contract, the assurance for party A is necessary, because a change of mind of party B is outside A's control. In contrast, in the case of the no-oral-modification clause, it is far from obvious that the future behaviour of party A is outside A's control (or, *mutatis mutandis*, that B's future behaviour is outside B's control).

Why should A (or B) doubt that they will safeguard their interests in t_2 without the restriction imposed in t_1? There needs to be a reason why the pre-commitment in t_1 is a better decision than a decision made "on the spot" in t_2. The decision-making in t_2 needs to be *deficient* in one form or another.

Defective outcome? The question which immediately arises is what constitutes a "defect" in t_2. Intuitively, one is tempted to refer to the quality of the outcome of the decision: gambling, smoking, drinking, etc., are "bad for you",

repeated exchange between the parties (or, more realistically, an unknown number of future repetitions); in these latter cases, the agreement may be self-enforcing. I have omitted these alternatives (which replace state enforcement by private enforcement or self-enforcing arrangements) in the text for the sake of simplicity.

37 Or, to be more precise: one increases the costs of reneging to a point that the (discounted) costs of reneging would be higher than the (discounted) costs of complying.

38 *See, e.g.*, Schelling (2006) *at* 14; Elster (2000) *at* 42.

39 *E.g.* Elster (2000) *at* 1 and *passim*. It can also increase the parties' combined welfare, *see* Jolls (1997); *but see* Davis (2006).

hence the decision not to gamble, etc., is "more valuable" than the decision in t_2 to relapse. However, this approach would run counter to both the economic premise that utility functions are defined subjectively, not objectively, and the contract law premise that we honour the parties' autonomous decisions, even if they appear to be irrational to an outsider (*stat pro ratione voluntas*). The "defect" has to be identified without looking at the quality of the outcome.[40]

Self-evaluation in the self-limiting agreement While an objective outcome-oriented control would be paternalistic, the self-evaluation documented in the self-limiting agreement introduces a subjective element. The evaluation that the temptation of gambling or oral modifications should be subject to constraints is not imposed by a third party who "knows better". Rather, it is the actor themselves that decides on their preferred course of action, foreseeing a conflict between their preferences in a certain situation. In the self-limiting agreement, the actor reveals their preference about their own conflicting future preferences.

The possibility of such a hierarchy of preferences has been recognized and extensively dealt with in the literature.[41] In *Amartya Sen's* terminology, there is a meta-ranking of preference rankings.[42] In *Harry Frankfurt's* terminology, the self-excluding gambler may in t_2 have a *first-order desire* to gamble, but they may still at the same time be aware that gambling is bad for them and thus have a *conflicting first-order desire* not to gamble. Although they may compulsively act on the former rather than the latter first-order desire, they may still have the *second-order volition* not to gamble:[43] they may "want to gamble" and "want not to gamble" on the level of first-order desires, but on a higher level they may "want to want not to gamble".

In the self-limiting agreement, the actor reveals their second-order volition, their meta-ranking of preferences.[44] If the second-order volition or meta-ranking were the "highest internal authority", one could stop the analysis at this point: the second-order volition, revealed in the self-limiting agreement, would authoritatively define the true will of the actor. Unfortunately, there is nothing in the analysis that precludes the possibility of either the existence of a "third-order

40 I have to confess, though, to re-introducing an indirect outcome-oriented criterion in the balancing process later on (*infra* "Scope of the self-limitation").

41 Eggert (2003).

42 Sen (1977) *at* 339.

43 Frankfurt (1971) (*see especially* p. 12, discussing the case of an unwilling drug addict). I am not concerned here with Frankfurt's assertion that this second-order volition is "essential to being a person" (*ibid.*, p. 10).

44 This seems at first glance to contradict Sen's claim that people's actual choices reveal only their preference rankings and not their meta-rankings, and that there is therefore the need for introspection and communication (1977 *at* 339). However, as we will see in a moment (see the text following this footnote), the revelation of the meta-ranking (*e.g.*, not to gamble) does not preclude the possibility that there is a "meta-meta-ranking" on an even higher level of abstraction which is not revealed by actions.

volition"[45] (a meta-meta-ranking), or a changing of the second-order volition. Just as preferences may change, meta-preferences may change over time.[46]

This complicates matters further: just as the action in t_2 does not necessarily reveal the actor's second-order volition, the action of concluding the self-limiting agreement does not necessarily reveal the highest-order volition in t_1, and even if it did, it would not necessarily mean that this would remain the highest-order volition in t_2. This is the basis for the criticism against enforcing self-limiting agreements: "Indeed a presumption of a general worsening of preferences is necessary before we can safely side with the present self and promote the success of all its rulemaking over the future self."[47]

There are a number of ways around this objection. An apparent solution would be to point to the fact that the second-order desire is the highest-order decision that was actually *acted* upon (in concluding the self-limiting agreement), and that – relying on an extended version of the theory of revealed preferences, which we could call the "theory of revealed meta-preferences" – this evidence should be considered conclusive. However, this line of reasoning is unsatisfactory: It disregards that the self-excluded gambler has actually gambled in t_2. While gambling in t_2 *may* only be the revelation of the first-order desire which remains unwanted on the meta-level, there is no way to disprove the claim that the gambling also reveals a change of the second-order desire – the actor may now want to want to gamble.

---

45 *Cf.* Frankfurt (1971) *at* 16; Elster (2000) *at* 22 (text accompanying and in n. 63), and *at* 5 n. 9. We could construe an example for such a third-order desire as follows: X is a compulsive gambler who wants to quit gambling. At the same time, X is a staunch liberal who refuses to believe in anything but free will, and thus condemns all forms of restriction of options. Yet, foreseeing a financial predicament, he self-excludes. – X may "want to gamble" and "want not to gamble" as first-order desires; he may "want to want not to gamble" and "want to want to have free choice" as second-order desires; but he ultimately may "want to want to want to have free choice" (third-order volition). His decision to self-exclude would then reveal his second-order desire (*i.e.*, his wanting to want not to gamble), but may still not reflect his "true will', which would be to retain free choice. I am trying to make essentially the same point as Elster, who also treats the "the capacity for self-binding" (only) *to a first approximation* as a criterion for deciding "[w]hich self [...] is right".

46 Let us assume Romeo is a disappointed lover; Rosalind has rejected him. Romeo is on the verge of overcoming his disappointment over Rosalind and feels the first signs of falling in love with Juliet. The disappointment still lingering, he vows never to enter into a relationship with a woman again. Three months later, he decides to marry Juliet, and is entirely happy with his decision. – Although Romeo had initially wanted to refrain from succumbing to his love with Juliet (first-order desire), and at the same time wanted to succumb (conflicting first-order desire), and initially wanted to want not to succumb (second-order volition), this second-order volition has changed over time. He now wants to want to succumb and marry Juliet. A shorter way of putting the same thought would be: never say never.

47 Winston (1985) *at* 377.

A second option is to accept the revealed second-order volition tentatively as a kind of "rebuttable presumption": the self-limitation could be considered binding, unless it was demonstrated that it violated an even higher-order desire, or that the second-order volition had changed in the meantime.

A third option is to identify the "defect" of the decision in t_2 neither by looking at the self-evaluation (which may be indicative, but is in the end inconclusive as to the "true will"), nor by looking at the quality of the outcome (which would be paternalistic), but by discerning *procedural* defects in reaching the decision in t_2 (*infra* (3)).

A fourth option is to combine some (or all) of the above options.[48]

Procedural defects As suggested above, a further way to define a "defect" in t_2 would be to look at the quality of the decision-making process. Despite its basic premise that adults act autonomously and may thus make legally binding decisions, contract law provides for exceptions to this rule by taking into account vitiating factors, *e.g.*, if the person was incapacitated, unduly influenced or under duress; in the case of door-to-door selling, the defect lies in the mere fact that the buyer is taken by surprise.[49] These defences can be understood not to be outcome-oriented, but based on procedural defects in the decision-making process.[50]

In some, but few, of the cases considered here, the defences provided by contract law may be directly applicable; for example, the actor may be incapacitated or under duress at t_2, or holding the gambler to the gambling contract may be unconscionable.[51]

---

48 My own view is that (1) the self-evaluation in the form of the self-binding commitment is a very strong indication that the second-order desire is indeed the actor's true will (2) *as long as* the procedural defects in t_2 are greater than any procedural defects in t_1, but (3) even so, the self-binding effect should never be so complete that a higher-order volition or change in second-order volition cannot be taken into account at a later point.

49 In the European Union, *see* Council Directive 85/577/EEC of 20 December 1985 to protect the consumer in respect to contracts negotiated away from business premises, OJ 1985 L 372/31, implemented in the UK in the Consumer Protection (Cancellation of Contracts Concluded away from Premises) Regulations 1987, SI 2117/1987; in the US, *see* FTC Cooling-Off Rule, 16 C.F.R. § 429.

50 Sometimes the "bad" outcomes trigger a defence (*e.g.*, the defence of unconscionability). But even in these cases, it can be said that it is not the outcome itself which makes the promise unenforceable, but the assumption that this outcome would not have obtained if the procedure had not been tainted. For an account and criticism of this "classical approach" see, *e.g.*, Smith (2005) *at* 296–301; Chen-Wishart (2005) *at* 347.

51 *Lomonaco v. Sands Hotel Casino and Country Club*, 614 A2d 634, 637–638 (N.J. Super. Ct. Law Div. 1992): "There is no section of the Casino Control Act which states that the defense of duress, the elements of which plaintiff alleges would be present here if plaintiff suffered from the illness of compulsive gambling, may not be asserted to void a contract […]. Thus, this court must find that […] the common law contract defenses of incapacity, duress, and unconscionability still exist." The court in *Lomonaco* held that there were sufficient genuine issues of material fact concerning duress or unconscionability to deny defendants' motion for summary judgment. The court stressed, however, that there was "no support in legislation or case law that the disorder of compulsive gambling should, in

These cases are unproblematic from a dogmatic contract law point of view. The question of self-limitation is irrelevant, because even if there had been no self-limitation, the gambling contract concluded in t_2 would still be voidable or void.

In most cases of self-limitation, however, either the relatively high thresholds of the remedies provided by contract law are not reached, or even if they have been reached, this fact cannot be proven.[52] The compulsion in t_2 may have been strong, but not strong enough to incapacitate the actor; the oral modification may have been made hastily and under pressure, but under circumstances that do not yet amount to duress or undue influence. Nevertheless, one could argue that the legal exceptions show that the question of whether a decision is arrived at autonomously is not a dichotomous one ("either autonomous or not"), but one of degree.[53] The obvious objection is that even if the degree of autonomy can be mapped on a continuous scale, contract law has drawn a bright line to distinguish decisions that are "sufficiently autonomous" from those that do not pass muster. While a hurried decision may be "less autonomous" than one taken after thorough consideration, both are usually deemed "sufficiently autonomous" to bind the promisor. The argument here is that a procedural defect that may not be sufficient *in itself* to make a promise void or voidable, may still provide a sufficient justification *to enforce the self-limitation*. One could also say that the self-limiting agreement lowers the threshold of the "protection from oneself" that is afforded by contract law in general. Where neither the procedural defects nor the self-limitation in itself would suffice, the combination of both may achieve the desired result.

Preliminary summary The question at the outset of this section was why we should attribute any weight at all to the decision in t_1. The answer is that a credible promise to oneself in t_1 can be necessary if the decision in t_2 is feared to be defective. Whether a decision is defective could be judged on the quality of the outcome; I reject this approach as paternalistic. One might also argue that a defect in t_2 is conclusively established by the self-limiting agreement. However, while the self-

---

and of itself, be recognized as a defense to capacity to contract which will render a contract void." *Lomonaco* at 639. According to Kindt (2004) *at* 574 the case was later settled. *Kindt* speculates that "[Lomonaco's] defense would have more weight in the twenty-first century". *See also Seigel v. Merrill Lynch, Pierce, Fenner & Smith*, 745 A.2d 301, 305 (D.C. 2000); *Adamar of New Jersey v. Scandrett*, 2006 WL 3590057 (N.J. Super. A.D. 2006); *Hakimoglu v. Trump Taj Mahal Assoc.*, 876 F. Supp. 625, 634 (D.N.J. 1994) *aff'd* 70 F.3d 291 (3d Cir. 1995) (all in concord with *Lomonaco*). In Germany, some courts have accepted a defence based on incapacity due to pathological gambling, *e.g.*, Oberlandesgericht Zweibrücken, decision of March 12, 1998, 4 U 182/96, OLGR Zweibrücken 1998, 264; Oberlandesgericht Hamm, decision of October 7, 2002, 13 U 119/02, NJW-RR 2003, 971.

52 Or, the defences are excluded by statutory law: notably, Nevada has excluded "mental or behavioral disorder[s] involving gambling" from the list of permissible defences, *see* Nev. Rev. Stat. § 463.368(6)(a); *Stars' Desert Inn Hotel and Country Club v. Morgenstern*, 1996 WL 366602 (9th Cir. 1996).

53 *See* Eggert (2003) *at* 734.

limiting agreement may indeed reflect the "true will" of the party better than the decision in t_2, this does not follow conclusively; the actor may have higher-order desires or may change their "true will" by t_2. A final way to identify a defective decision would be to look at the decision-making process.

The solution favoured here is that a second-order decision, revealed in a self-limiting commitment, provides a presumption that this reflects the true will of the actor ("theory of revealed meta-preferences"). However, this presumption should be rebuttable by showing that any procedural defects in t_1 clearly outweigh the procedural defects in t_2; in this case, the higher-order desire may be better reflected in t_2. In any case, the pre-commitment should never be enforced to such an extent that it is impossible to accommodate a change in higher-order desires, because otherwise there would be no autonomy left in t_2 at all.

Balancing Autonomy in t_1 and t_2

The extent to which a pre-commitment should be enforced depends on a number of factors.[54]

Extent of the self-limitation of autonomy in t_2 First, the *extent of limitation of autonomy in t_2*, which the self-limiting agreement in t_1 tries to achieve, should be considered. This concerns the *scope* of the limitation as well as the questions if and how the self-limitation can be *reversed*.[55]

Possibility of an autonomous reversal of the self-limitation I propose that where the self-limitation derives its force from an autonomous agreement in t_1, there has to remain the possibility of an autonomous reversal of the self-limitation in t_2. Otherwise, there would be no *balancing*, but instead a complete domination of the autonomy in t_1 over the autonomy in t_2, for which there is no more substantive reason than for the opposite solution, the complete domination of autonomy in t_2 over the autonomy in t_1.

---

54 Eggert (2003), *at* 744–746, has suggested a more elaborate taxonomy of nine "interrelated questions" with which I largely agree (*see also ibid., at* 755–758 (application of his taxonomy to self-exclusion)). I depart from his analysis only in a small number of (albeit important) details: (1) Eggert is willing to introduce autonomous pre-commitment (in t_1) to heteronomy (in t_2). While I agree that this option could be helpful to obtain renegotiation-proofness, I believe that this is out of reach for *autonomous* self-binding, as it would leave no room at all for *autonomy in t_2* (*see infra* text accompanying n. 59–68). (2) I suspect Eggert is slightly more willing than I to introduce an (what I call) outcome-oriented yardstick. (3) As to the question of duration of the self-limitation, see the following footnote.

55 In my opinion, in order for there to be autonomy in t_2, there always has to remain *some* possibility of reversal of the self-limitation (see the text immediately following this footnote). Therefore, the *duration* of the self-limitation itself is not a question (*but see* Eggert (2003) *at* 744); the only question is how onerous and time-consuming the process for reversal is (*see also infra* n. 97 and accompanying text).

The lack of a possibility of autonomous reversal is one of the reasons[56] for which self-enslavement (*supra* "Self-enslavement") is impermissible. If the self-enslavement contract were enforced, the slave's future autonomy would be reduced to zero, as he would not be able to withdraw from the contract.[57]

Another classic case for the requirement that the limitation must be reversible is the one argued by Sir Karl Popper under the heading "the paradox of freedom": does democracy entitle the majority of voters to elect a tyrant?[58] Or, to exclude the element of heteronomy for the minority inherent in Popper's example: does democracy entail the freedom to elect a tyrant *unanimously*? As Popper correctly points out, there needs to be a sufficient possibility of reversing the decision which would not be present in a "freely elected tyranny".[59]

However, the possibility of reversal of the decision made in t_1 need not be immediate and costless. If it were, the self-binding effect would be illusory. Effective and credible self-binding can only be achieved by erecting "hurdles" (cost or delay) for the reversal of the self-limitation in t_2.

---

56 Another reason is, of course, the *scope* of the limitation. It is mainly the *combination* of these factors, rather than either one taken by itself, that makes slavery so repulsive. To exemplify: (1) An agreement in which one of the parties allowed the other to "do with me as you like" (*enormous scope*), but which contained a clause that the promisor could terminate his promise at will at any time without giving notice (*unlimited possibility of reversal*), cannot be considered an undue limitation of autonomy in t_2 (provided that actions which factually preclude the exercise of the option to reverse the limitation, such as shooting the promisor, are deemed impermissible). In fact, this promise contains no limitation of future autonomy at all and would thus be considered an *illusory promise*, unless the power to terminate the agreement "at will" was somehow, at least by implication, limited, *cf.* Farnsworth (2004) *at* 79–81 (§ 2.14); Treitel (2003) *at* 84. (2) An agreement that is more limited in scope (*e.g.*, obliging the promisor to do certain onerous tasks), but does not contain a termination clause, may be more detrimental to future autonomy; however, these agreements are usually upheld.

57 The slave could, of course, in t_2 renegotiate with the slave-owner to be freed. This would not be entirely autonomous, as the slave cannot *unilaterally* terminate the contract; he would depend on the slave-owner's consent. However, this element of heteronomy is usually accepted in bilateral contracts (*see infra* n. 59). However, the deprivation of the slave's liberty is so intense that even this element of heteronomy cannot be accepted (*see supra* n. 55 for the interaction between intensity of the limitation and the ease of its reversal).

58 Popper (1945/1966) *at* 123–125 (referring to an example from Plato's Republic). Popper defines the paradox of freedom as "the argument that freedom in the sense of absence of any restraining control must lead to very great restraint, since it makes the bully free to enslave the meek" (*ibid., at* 265 in n. 4). As Popper specifies in the endnote, the example given in the text is actually "the paradox of democracy", which is, however, logically isomorphic to the paradox of freedom.

59 Popper (1945/1966) *at* 124: "For we may distinguish between two main types of government. The first type consists of governments of which we can get rid without bloodshed – for example, by way of general elections; that is to say, the social institutions provide means by which the rulers may be dismissed by the ruled [...]. The second type consists of governments which the ruled cannot get rid of except by way of a successful revolution [...]."

But although one may require the self in t_2 to overcome certain hurdles before the self-limitation is lifted, these hurdles must themselves be subject to limitations. One aspect of these "limitations to the limitations to the reversal of self-limitation" is that the relationship between the scope of the self-limitation and the permissible hurdles to overcome is inversely proportional: The more intrusive the self-limitation is, the easier it must be to reverse the limitation.

Another aspect putting limits on the hurdles is that the autonomously erected hurdles may not make the reversal of the self-limitation *conditional on the will of a third party*,[60] because otherwise there would not be *autonomy* but *heteronomy* in t_2. To exemplify: it has been proposed by a number of commentators that the rescission or termination of gamblers' self-exclusion agreements could be made conditional on a certification by a mental health professional;[61] another suggestion might be to have the gambler's spouse or a relative agree to the rescission/termination. I believe that such requirements could not be imposed by an autonomous agreement alone.

It may be objected, and it is true, that adding a third party can be a powerful tool for making an agreement between two parties renegotiation-proof[62] (or, at any rate, less vulnerable to renegotiation[63]); in the example given, the requirement of a certification would prevent the gambler and the casino from rescinding the self-exclusion agreement prematurely. An option to introduce a third party would therefore enhance the autonomy in t_1: the self-limitation would gain credibility. However, it would leave *no room at all* for autonomy in t_2, as the actor would

60 The "third party" is to be distinguished from the "second party" with whom the self-limiting actor concludes the self-limiting contract. The second party has an interest of its own to have the self-limiting actor adhere to the contract (otherwise, the agreement would lack consideration). This need for consent by the second party introduces an element of heteronomy as well, as the self-limiting actor cannot "autonomously" depart from the self-limitation; however, this is a possibility offered by contract law to bind oneself in order to make one's promise credible *to the other party*. As to third party beneficiaries: see text *infra*.

61 Weis (1999) *at* 151–152; Peters (2002) *at* 181; *see also* Eggert (2003) *at* 757 (but *see ibid.* n. 255, 202, which may indicate that Eggert wants the "subordinator" to retain some review over the "authority's" decision [which comes close to my own view]; Eggert's main text seems to indicate the contrary). For another example of – in my view impermissible – heteronomy in t_2 *see* Elster (2000) *at* 57.

62 *See, e.g.*, the "Representative Trustee Technique" in Davis (2006) *at* 518–537.

63 The problem that the third party can be bribed is of little importance in the cases discussed here, as we may assume that a mental health professional would be bound by their professional ethics (which may, by those who prefer economic parlance, be taken as a short form for a profitable reputation). And where the gambler's spouse is the third party, the gambler will not be able to offer any pecuniary bribe, as their increased value placed on gambling in t_2 is derived from non-pecuniary utility, and any pecuniary bribe offered would not be the derived from the gambling, but out of the household budget. Of course, the casino could bribe the spouse by paying the gambler's expected losses in advance. But this would eliminate the casino's (expected) profits and hence its incentive to bribe in the first place; and considering that presumably the spouse is risk-averse, the bribe would need to be even higher than the gambler's expected losses.

always depend on the will of a third party, even if their highest-order volition changed. This is not to say that heteronomous elements in self-binding schemes are generally out of the question. However, they are limitations of a *truly paternalistic* nature which cannot be achieved by virtue of an autonomous agreement at an earlier time. If the freedom in t_2 is to be restrained paternalistically by subjecting the self to third-party decisions, this has to be done by public regulation (with the corresponding restraint by democratic accountability) rather than by contract.

Nevertheless, as Davis has recently argued, it is not inconceivable that a third party – such as, in our context, the gambler's spouse – could be made a beneficiary of a payment if the parties to the contract try to rescind the contract under the Contract (Right of Third Parties Act) 1999 (the "1999 Act").[64] The involvement of the third party could potentially strengthen the renegotiation-proofness of the contract, because the position of the third party under the 1999 Act is paradoxically in some respects stronger than that of the contract parties, most notably concerning the rescission of the contract (s. 2(1) of the 1999 Act).[65] However, it seems doubtful whether the courts would enforce such an agreement if the sole purpose of the involvement of the third party were the strengthening of the renegotiation-proofness by invoking s. 2(1) of the 1999 Act.[66] Firstly, there remains a doubt whether a contract clause could be made consistent with the purely derivative nature of the claim by the third party (s. 1(5) of the 1999 Act); but this obstacle could arguably be overcome by creative drafting. Secondly, and more importantly, the restraint on the contract party's autonomy in t_2 would probably raise concerns: essentially, the promisee would be at the whim of the third party beneficiary, and would be deprived of the possibility of legal pastime activities.[67]

A hurdle which I would certainly find permissible even in a purely autonomous, self-limiting agreement is third-party interference that is merely persuasive. For example, A and B agree that A is to be excluded from B's casino. This self-exclusion can be terminated only after giving a month's notice. Once given, the notice could be retracted.[68] Once B receives notice, he has to inform some third person close to A (*e.g.*, A's wife C), who can then try to persuade A to retract the notice. As C's

---

64 Davis (2006) *at* 528–529.

65 *See, e.g.,* Chen-Wishart (2005) *at* 647–648.

66 *But see* Davis (2006) *at* 526–530.

67 Consider the case that a wife takes her husband to the local public house and persuades him to sign an agreement with the publican that the wife is to be paid a certain sum (as liquidated damages) if the pub serves her husband. I am less than certain that an English court would enforce this clause (*see also* Schelling's quotation *infra* n. 89). For those not persuaded by the pub example: consider the case where a husband persuades his wife not to frequent the local library by such a contract. In essence, the third party beneficiary induces the promisor to boycott the promisee, an objective which courts are usually hesitant to help pursuing.

68 Note that up to this point, this is analogous to the scheme proposed by Schelling (2006) *at* 66, and does not contain third-party interference.

interference is merely *persuasive* rather than *authoritative*, A's decision to retract (or not) would remain autonomous.[69]

Scope of the self-limitation The scope of the self-limitation in t_2 is another important factor. The more restrictive the self-limitation in t_2 is, the more questionable is its enforcement. A very restrictive self-limitation may be acceptable if it can be reversed very easily, but not otherwise.

The question is how to define whether the self-limitation is "restrictive". At this point, I confess that I see no way out but to commit a heresy. Contract law and utility curves are subjective concepts. Yet, at this stage there seems to be no solution but to refer to an outcome-oriented ("objective")[70] yardstick: what "does one" consider to be important freedoms? The trouble with a subjective interpretation would be that *by definition* the self-limiting pre-commitment tells us that the actor wants to preclude themselves from exercising certain options – and thus reveals that they do not place a high value on them. But this self-evaluation in t_1 cannot be the relevant yardstick when the question has to be decided in t_2 whether the self-limitation is too restrictive; otherwise, the autonomy in t_1 would dominate absolutely.[71] Nor can we take the revealed preferences in t_2 as the yardstick, as this would render the self-limitation nugatory; this would be to treat the autonomy in t_2 as an absolute. So there is necessarily an outcome-oriented (objective) element in the analysis:[72] is the liberty foreclosed in the self-limiting agreement *generally* considered as being important? I believe this to be acceptable (though not entirely satisfactory), because the outcome-oriented element is only part of a balancing process. And if it is very easy to reverse the limitation, there may not even be a need to evaluate the importance of the actions foreclosed (*see supra* (1)), so that the question becomes critical only when the hurdles that must be overcome to reverse the self-limitation are substantial.

The procedural defect in t_2 Another factor in balancing the respective autonomies in t_1 and t_2 is the nature and extent of the procedural defect in t_2. If there were

69 In the terminology introduced by Schelling (1985) *at* 372–373, in my view "referees" allow for sufficient autonomy, while "judges" introduce an impermissibly element of heteronomy.

70 I prefer the term "outcome-oriented" to "objective", because the yardstick necessarily calls for a value judgment. And value judgments are always "subjective" – it is just not the subjective perspective of the person to whom the yardstick is applied that is relevant, but the subjective perspective of "reasonable person" (or, more accurately, of the person in charge of ultimately making the value judgment).

71 To exemplify: in the self-enslavement case, the slave in t_1 does not seem to value their freedom of action in t_2. Should we then say that in t_2, the limitation to their freedom of action is "not important'? The obvious answer is no.

72 Schelling (2006), *at* 73–78, raises the same point when he is troubled by the fact that in order to decide which self should dominate, the equivalent of an interpersonal utility comparison (more precisely, one could call it an intertemporal, intrapersonal utility comparison) becomes necessary.

no defect in t_2, self-limitation would be unnecessary in the first place. The more defective the decision-making process in t_2 is, the more urgent the need for effective self-limitation becomes.

Provided that there is at least a probability of a defect in t_2, the possibility of self-limitation increases autonomy in t_1 and, arguably, overall autonomy. As pointed out above, effective self-limitation requires that the reversal of the self-limitation is not possible without cost or delay ("hurdles"). These hurdles should be closely tailored to fit the need – *i.e.*, address the mischief, the defect in decision-making in t_2, in the least restrictive way – lest the autonomy in t_2 be unduly limited. If the defect in t_2 is "hot decision-making", the appropriate hurdle would be to require a cooling-off period before the self-limitation can be reversed. If the fear is that in t_2 an oral promise could be given rashly, the hurdle should be that the promise is only valid if put into writing. From this vantage point, it is unsurprising that it has been suggested that if the procedural defect in t_2 is an addiction, the appropriate hurdle should be proof that the addiction has been cured – proof that could, if at all, only be furnished by a medical expert. But this would constitute a hurdle of heteronomy, which – as discussed above – is impermissible if established by autonomous agreement (as opposed to state intervention). The aforementioned scheme[73] combining delay and persuasive interference of a third party may be a substitute, albeit admittedly an imperfect one.

Recapitulation

This section developed the general framework for deciding to what extent self-limiting agreements should be enforced. Such self-limitations can enhance the autonomy in t_1; but it has to be recognized that their enforcement necessarily limits autonomy in t_2. Neither the autonomy in t_1 nor the autonomy in t_2 should be treated as absolutes. It is necessary to strike a balance between the autonomies in t_1 and t_2.

In the usual cases of contract modification or rescission, the law is well-advised to let the autonomy in t_2 prevail over the autonomous agreement in t_1, because the parties have updated information in t_2. This automatic prevailing of the agreement in t_2 shapes our attitude towards the balancing process. I suggest that we have to get rid of this bias in favour of t_2 in those exceptional cases in which the substantive reason for preferring the decision in t_2 is missing, *i.e.*, in cases in which the actors have anticipated a narrowly defined contingency and have put up safeguards addressing this contingency. In these cases, the autonomous decisions in t_1 and t_2 have, at least conceptually, equal weight. Safeguards are only necessary, however, where the parties foresee a danger. This danger was identified as "defective" decision-making in t_2. The view that the *outcome* of the decision in t_2 could be the yardstick for deciding whether the decision was defective was rejected as being paternalistic. The self-evaluation contained in the self-limiting agreement was acknowledged as being indicative, but not conclusive for determining the "true

73 *See supra* text accompanying n. 67.

will" of the actor in t_2. The relevant defect in t_2 has to impair the decision-making *process*, resembling qualitatively (but not necessarily quantitatively) the defects that contract law acknowledges as making contracts void or voidable. It is the combination of the self-evaluation in the self-limiting agreement that the decision in t_2 will be defective on the one hand, and a procedural defect in t_2 on the other hand that legitimates enforcement of the self-limiting agreement. Yet, even if these conditions are met, self-limiting agreements should always leave room for a change of mind in t_2 (or for a higher-order volition). Therefore, self-limitations should always be reversible; if the express terms do not provide for such reversibility, a termination clause has to be supplied by implication. However, if self-limitation is to be effective at all, the reversal cannot be immediate and costless. Appropriate hurdles to the reversal may be put up. Which hurdles are "appropriate" is itself to be determined by balancing autonomy in t_1 and t_2. The hurdles should effectively address the procedural defect in t_2 in the least restrictive way; they may not include authoritative decisions (as opposed to persuasive suggestions) by third parties. The more important the behaviour foreclosed is, the easier it must be to reverse the self-limitation.

The Relevant Defect in t_2: Problem Gambling and the Brain

In assessing whether to enforce gamblers' self-exclusion agreements, the first step has to be to identify the defect in t_2 that makes such pre-commitment necessary in the first place. I assume that much of the reluctance to enforce self-exclusion agreements stems from the belief that the gambler could refrain from gambling in t_2 if he only really wanted to. This belief is formed largely by introspection, which might run along the lines: "I know that there is a temptation to gamble more than one should, but *I* would stop gambling before it got out of hand. So, if some gamblers do not stop when they should, they simply lack discipline; the financial loss may be the right punishment to make them mend their ways." The problem of such reasoning is that comparison by introspection presupposes *a priori* the essential equivalence of the subjects compared; it does not make allowance for varying individual predispositions.[74] A further problem is that this belief is largely resistant to countervailing *behavioural* evidence: behavioural studies can show (and have overwhelmingly shown) that a fraction of people *do not* sufficiently control themselves; however, these studies cannot show that these people *could not* control themselves *with the same quantum of effort* as the introspector.[75]

74 This is also true of an extended comparison: "The vast majority of people who gamble do so without experiencing loss of control as well (so-called "social" or "recreational gambling"). Therefore, problem gamblers could do the same."

75 *See* Orford et al. (2003) *at* 70: "Not only has confusion and controversy reigned over the meaning of addiction, but it has also not been difficult for the legal profession to pick holes in the DSM definitions. […] [T]he insanity defence of Torniero was damaged

This is where neurobiological evidence may become relevant. During the past decade, problem gambling has received more attention than before. The evidence is growing that compulsive gambling shares many attributes with substance-related addictions; there are even indications that not only the phenomenology, but also the causal mechanism of gambling dependence may resemble that of substance-related addictions.[76]

For present purposes, especially two neurophysiologic findings appear to be relevant. One is that the activity in the ventral striatum of problem gamblers is decreased in a gambling task as compared with controls, a phenomenon which has been known to be present in substance-addicted persons.[77] The dysfunction is thought to affect the processing of rewards and punishments:[78] while in non-addicted persons the stimulation provided by natural reinforcers usually suffices in order to maintain a homeostatic baseline of the neurotransmitter dopamine in the ventral striatum, in drug addicts and problem gamblers the decreased activity of this brain region calls for stronger reinforcers in order to achieve the same baseline.[79] There are competing, though not necessarily mutually exclusive, hypotheses about the neurobiology of problem gambling.[80]

---

by cross-questioning of expert witnesses [...] on the question of whether pathological gamblers were *unable* to resist or simply showed a *failure* to resist impulses to gamble. [...] Although the distinction may be too fine a one for clinicians to argue about, it is of course crucial in law."; *see also* Shaffer & Freed (2005) *at* 339, 340: "[P]eople will need to view [pathological gambling] as the consequence of (1) overwhelming and uncontrollable impulses, (2) compromised biobehavioral regulatory mechanisms, or (3) a combination of both. Anything short of this will leave people thinking that intemperate gambling is simply the result of people not controlling their 'habits'."

76 *Cf.* the studies cited below, and the overview in Petry (2004) *at* 117 et seq.; *see also* Leitzel (2005) *at* 24. *But see* Professor Jeffrey Gray, in DCMS Gambling Review Body (2001) *at* 233, and Elster (1999), who cautions against prematurely assuming causation from "superficial similarities". *See also* Orford et al. (2003) *at* 62–72. I am in no position to take sides in the controversy about whether pathological gambling is rather a "dependence" related to substance-dependence, or a disorder of impulse control; the truth may lie in the middle (*see infra* n. 79).

77 Reuter et al. (2005).

78 Delgado et al. (2000); Reuter et al. (2005).

79 Reuter et al. (2005); Robbins & Everitt (1999). *But see* Professor Jeffrey Gray, in: DCMS Gambling Review Body (2001) *at* 233, denying that pathological gamblers' "withdrawal symptoms" could be caused by homeostatic mechanisms similar to those at work in the case of heroin users; indeed, it is unclear whether there are any significant withdrawal symptoms which are not psychological (*see* Elster (1999) *at* 216–217; Orford (*c.* 2005) *at* 16).

80 For a discussion of a number of studies linking pathological gambling to defects in different neurotransmitter systems (dopaminergic, noradrenergic, and serotonergic systems) and the possible genetic causes, *see* Ibáñez et al. (2003); Petry (2004) *at* 117–133; *see also* Orford (*c.* 2005) *at* 14–16; Robbins & Everitt (1999). The non-exclusionary nature of the hypotheses, each supported by promising but not yet conclusive evidence, may best be

The second potentially relevant finding is that in certain tasks the ventromedial and ventrolateral prefrontal cortex shows less activity in substance addicts[81] and problem gamblers[82] as compared with controls. These brain regions are associated with an excessive focus on immediate rewards and impaired impulse control.[83]

The application of pharmacological treatment, informed by the studies on neurotransmittors affected by problem gambling and by the treatment of substance-related addictions, may provide yet more evidence that substance-related addictions and pathological gambling share more than the phenomenology, and may be caused in a similar way.[84] One recently published study, based on a double-blind, placebo-controlled experiment, has shown that a drug affecting the opioid receptors antagonistically (Nalmefene hydrochloride), which had already been known to be effective in the treatment of alcohol addicts, proved to reduce symptoms of pathological gambling.[85]

A significant number of questions remain. Although *correlation* of certain dysfunctions and pathological gambling has been established, the question of *causation* is not settled conclusively; co-morbidity leads to further complications.[86]

Nevertheless, the preliminary findings indicate that:

1. problem (or at least pathological) gambling may be due to dysfunctions in the neural processes, and shares sufficient elements with substance-related addictions to transfer knowledge about these addictions to problem gambling

---

captured by constructing pathological gambling as a syndrome, *see* Shaffer & Freed (2005) *at* 342–343.

81 Robbins & Everitt (1999) *at* 570 (noting differences between opiate and amphetamine users).

82 Reuter et al. (2005) (using a gambling task); Potenza et al. (2003) (using the Stroop paradigm).

83 Bechara (2003); Reuter et al. (2005); Potenza et al. (2003).

84 For an extensive overview *see* Petry (2004) *at* 137–152; *see also* Potenza et al. (2001) *at* 143–144 (describing promising, albeit not ultimately conclusive, experiments with the serotonin reuptake inhibitors fluvoxamine (*see* Hollander et al. (1998)) and paroxetine on the one hand, and naltrexone on the other hand).

85 Grant et al. (2006). An earlier experiment with a related drug (naltrexone) had found similar results (*ibid., at* 303).

86 *See* Shaffer & Freed (2005) *at* 355–361; BMA Board of Science (2007) *at* 10–11. Care has to be taken in conducting and interpreting the pharmacological studies. Effectiveness of medication does not necessarily indicate that problem gambling and drug-related addictions are of the same mould, because the medication might not address the cause of the gambling problem directly. The effect could be indirect, by alleviating either an underlying cause (such as depression) common to both gambling and a concurring substance-related addiction, or by affecting the concurring drug-related addiction (*e.g.* alcoholism) which is in turn cause of, or contributing factor to, the gambling problem. These are just some of the possible variations; *see* Shaffer & Freed (2005) *at* 356.

(and maybe even to use the term gambling *addiction*, although one should not become obsessed with or distracted by merely terminological questions[87]);

2. the problem gambler's decision-making process is impaired,[88] in that there is an excessive focus on immediate rewards; the decision in t_2 is impulsive, largely bypassing conscious weighting of benefits and costs.

This evidence may not be sufficient to establish that a pathological gambler *cannot* control their behaviour in t_2 at all; indeed, if this were the case, the logical consequence for the law would be to acknowledge a lack of capacity in t_2, regardless of any prior self-exclusion.[89] But the evidence does show that the reasoning from introspection ("*I* can control myself, hence *he* can control himself") or from interpersonal analogies may not be appropriate, because the essential equivalence of the neural processes of the compared subjects, which would be a prerequisite for such a comparison, is absent.

There is a relevant defect in t_2 in the sense of the above analysis (*supra* "Credible commitment in self-limiting agreements"). Once the gambler is confronted with

87 The dispute whether pathological gambling is an "addiction" has several facets, because the term addiction is ill-defined (*see* Shaffer & Freed (2005) *at* 334–335, 338–341). (a) For some, using the term "addiction" seems to imply taking sides in the dispute between the impulse-control-disorder- and the dependence-classification of pathological gambling (*see supra* n. 75, 79). (b) For others, it merely indicates that there is "(1) some element of craving or compulsion; (2) loss of control; and (3) continuing the behavior in question in spite of associated adverse consequences" (*see* Shaffer & Freed (2005) *at* 339, who do not, however, endorse this view). (c) In suggesting that the term addiction may be justified, I mean to imply that pathological gambling is not merely "the result of people not controlling their 'habits'", but is due to "overwhelming and uncontrollable impulses" or "compromised biobehavioural regulatory mechanisms" or both (Shaffer & Freed (2005) *at* 340). This view is less restrictive than (a), in that it is open to both the impulse-control-disorder- and the dependence-theory (or some middle ground), but it is more restrictive than (b) in that it focuses on neurobiological reasons for the loss of control.

88 Admittedly, there is a leap in deducing an *impairment* in the decision-making from finding a *difference* in the neural process of decision-making. While impairment refers to a normative category, the finding itself is merely descriptive. However, I believe that the value judgment establishing the necessary link between the descriptive and the normative – *i.e.*, that the short-term focus triggered by the dysfunction causes "worse" decision-making than that after conscious deliberation – should be sufficiently uncontroversial as to warrant the lack of elaboration in the main text. But considering the ongoing discussions about the body–mind problem, it may be premature to call anything in this area uncontroversial.

89 The "Cautionary Statement" in the DSM-IV-TR states the commonplace that the criteria for pathological gambling "may not be wholly relevant to legal judgments, for example, that take into account such issues as individual responsibility [...] and competency." (American Psychiatric Association (2000)). As Shaffer & Freed (2005) *at* 367–368 (and in n. 6) point out, this statement does more harm than good – its literal meaning is a matter of course, and it may well be (mis-) taken to imply that pathological gambling is not a "real" psychiatric disorder.

the relevant cues (or visceral factors) in t_2, the decision-making process is impaired. Of course, even without the neurological evidence, both common sense and the behavioural evidence about problem gamblers could have told us that the decision-making process of problem gamblers is impaired when it comes to gambling.

Self-Exclusion: Extent of the Limitation of Autonomy

Having determined that there is a relevant defect in t_2, we now turn to the extent of the limitation brought about by self-exclusion agreements, influenced by both the scope of freedom restricted in t_2 and the possibility of reversal.

As indicated above, there is necessarily an outcome-oriented element in evaluating whether the freedom foreclosed by the self-limitation is "important". Thus, it is hardly astonishing that value judgments differ. People sceptical of the merits of gambling might stress that gambling is one form of recreational activity which most people can do very well without. Others might argue that a ban from gambling facilities would deprive the self-excluded person of options available to everybody else, and that several such bans (at least cumulatively) could severely limit the self-excluded person's inalienable freedom of action.[90] However, there is no need to address this question in isolation; it has to be seen in conjunction with the possibility of reversal. The relevant question is not whether self-exclusion from gambling facilities infringes the inalienable freedom of action. The relevant question is what possibilities of reversal must be left open in order for the self-exclusion not to infringe this freedom. The issue is sometimes taken up under the heading "duration of the ban" – should the ban last a maximum of half a year, three or five years, or a lifetime? Although those asking the question recognize the necessity of balancing the autonomy in t_2 with the autonomy in t_1, the question misses the point. I would not take exception to a lifelong ban. I would, however, take exception to a lifelong *irrevocable* ban (more precisely, to basing such an irrevocable ban on an autonomous self-paternalistic decision rather than on democratically accountable state intervention).

What are the proper modalities for revocation of a self-paternalistic ban? As stated above, these modalities should be closely tailored to fit the defect in t_2 and should not contain authoritative third-party intervention. It has already been pointed out that the latter constraint rules out authoritative mental health professionals' certification before the self-exclusion can be revoked, while a requirement of receiving *advice* by a mental health professional or informing a spouse or relative could be put into place. An important device to tailor the need seems to me the introduction of delay. If the defect in t_2 is based on decreased impulse control, it has

90 *Cf.* Eggert (2003) *at* 754–755; Schelling (2006) *at* 112: "[I]t is constitutional for my state to forbid the sale […] of alcoholic drinks, but not to keep me home on weekends or out of bars that are open to the public, even if I have volunteered the authority to them, because some of my rights are not alienable, even by myself."

to be ensured that the self-exclusion cannot be revoked on the spur of the moment. This calls for a period of notice before the ban can be lifted. Ideally, this should be coupled with Schelling's suggestion that this notice should be retractable.

How long this period of notice should be, and what other restrictions (such as persuasive third-party participation) should be implemented, depends upon the defect in t_2. When addressing the loss of control in t_2, one has to have regard not only to what Elster calls the "within-episode phenomenon" (that a gambler gambles more in a gambling session than previously intended), but also to the "between-episode phenomenon" of relapse.[91] I suspect that the relapse might be triggered by a number of different factors, including the mental representation of a gamble which sets into train similar mechanisms that cause the loss of control in the within-episode phenomenon; or behavioural habits adopted while being addicted, connecting gambling to an environmental cue;[92] or maybe even the discomfort associated with the suspense about whether one will succeed in staying away from gambling.[93] The "hurdles" put up before the self-limitation can be terminated should have regard to all these possibilities. The one-day cooling-off period mentioned by the UK Gambling Commission[94] might be a first step in this direction. I suspect that it may be too short, however, because even if the urge to relapse vanishes within the 24-hour period, the gambler may not take immediate action to retract the notice within this period.[95] Consumers in door-to-door-sales, who can hardly be said to suffer from defects in decision-making equal to those of problem gamblers, are given at least seven (in the EU)[96] or three days (in the US)[97] during which they can revise their decision. As an absolute minimum, problem gamblers should be afforded the same period to change their minds. How long the period should be, should be determined by those with experience in treating problem gamblers. It may well be that the initial self-exclusion period envisaged by the Gambling Commission of between six months and several years is the appropriate period of notice, but it should start to run only from the moment in which the gambler has terminated their self-exclusion, and not from the moment in which the self-exclusion agreement was concluded.[98]

---

91 Elster (1999) *at* 208.

92 Robbins & Everitt (1999) *at* 569.

93 Schelling (2006) *at* 104.

94 Gambling Commission (2006a) *at* 26.

95 Note, however, that the Gambling Commission's proposal is actually far more "restrictive": it provides for an initial period (between six months and at least five years) during which the self-exclusion is *irrevocable*, and only *after* this period can the gambler reapply (with a 24-hour cooling-off period). *See infra* n. 97 and accompanying text.

96 *See* Council Directive 85/577/EEC (*supra* n. 48) Art. 5(1); in the UK: Consumer Protection (Cancellation of Contracts Concluded away from Premises) Regulations 1987, SI 2117/1987 s. 4(1),(5).

97 FTC Cooling-Off Rule, 16 C.F.R. § 429.1.

98 I simply fail to understand why this initial period should shrink to 24 hours once the initial period of self-exclusion has lapsed. This would suggest that in t_1 the restriction

The Law and Self-Exclusion from Casinos: Regulatory Options

Up to this point, the discussion of self-limiting agreements has commingled two problems that analytically should be treated separately. The discussion has treated the question of self-limitation simply as a question of how to make the promise of the self in t_1 not to gamble in t_2 credible to the self in t_2. Judging from the literature, it seems almost impossible to discuss this problem without mentioning the allegory of Homer's Ulysses being lashed to the mast.[99]

I would like to strain this already overstrained allegory even further: we must now put wax in the sailors' ears. By this, I mean the following: if the self-exclusion agreement works as it should, the casino will turn the self-excluded gambler away at the entrance. Thus, the mere existence of the self-exclusion agreement will make the promise by the t_1-self not to gamble *somewhat* more credible for the t_2- and t_3-selves. This is analogous to Ulysses being lashed to the mast. But being lashed to the mast is no good if the sailors unbind you as soon as they hear the Sirens' song and you pleading. Which brings us to the more interesting legal question: how can we make *the casino's* promise to stick to the agreement credible? If the wax is not in the sailors' ears, lashing Ulysses to the mast does hardly any good – if the casino's promise is not credible, neither is the promise by the t_1-self to the t_2-self.

Making the Casino's Promise Credible

Of course, one would not need to worry about the credibility of the casino's promise if enforcing the self-exclusion agreement were in the casino's self-interest; self-exclusion would be self-enforcing. Unfortunately, this is not the case, for at least two reasons. The first reason is that the casino's average house edge is nearly 20% of all monies staked.[100] Thus, losing any customer is a loss in revenue. Losing a problem or pathological gambler is even more of a loss, considering that such gamblers contribute disproportionately to the revenue.[101] Thus, the exclusion of

---

of being bound to a, *e.g.*, one-year ban would be an acceptable restriction, but after a year a 24-hour ban is all that is necessary. I find it far more convincing to establish an acceptable period of time (say, half a year, or a month), but start the countdown from the moment the gambler has given notice of terminating their self-exclusion (subject to retraction of the notice). In other words, the more sensible approach, in my opinion, is an indefinite duration of the self-exclusion coupled with a requirement for a fixed period of notice, rather than fixed-term self-exclusions.

99 See the titles of Elster (1984; 2000) and Eggert (2003); *see also* Kuklin (1992) *at* 656; Jolls (1997) *at* 210, 219, 223; Schulze (2004) *at* 1587; van Aaken (2006) *at* 11.

100 The Gambling Commission (2006d) *at* 46 reported a 17% house win for casinos in 2005/06. Likewise, the Gaming Board for Great Britain (2005) reported a 17% house win for casinos (GBP 715m of GBP 4.15bn staked), *at* 29, para. 2.41, and a 20% edge for gaming machines (GBP 2.17bn of GBP 10.71bn staked) in Great Britain in the year 2004–2005, *at* 49, para. 5.3.

101 *See supra* n. 15, 16.

a problem gambler results in significant opportunity costs consisting of foregone profits. The second reason is that the enforcement of the self-exclusion scheme is also costly in the accounting sense – monitoring the casino for the presence of self-excluded gamblers requires the expenditure of out-of-pocket costs. From the casino's point of view, the benefits of enforcing the agreement are externalities, they accrue to the gambler (or, more precisely: the gambler's t_1- and t_3-selves), while the costs of enforcement have to be borne by the casino. Conversely, permitting a self-excluded gambler to gamble internalizes the casino's benefits (house edge), requires no monitoring costs, and externalizes the costs which are in the end borne by the gambler's t_3-self. This is why in quite a lot of well-documented cases of self-exclusion, the self-excluded gambler ends up gambling in the casino without encountering any obstacles.[102]

If one wants the self-exclusion to be effective despite its lack of self-enforcement, one needs to employ external mechanisms of enforcement to make the casino's promise credible. It is, in other words, necessary to tinker with the incentives. Broadly speaking, one can achieve this aim by using two different enforcement mechanisms and by altering two different sets of incentives.

As to the enforcement mechanisms, one can rely on:

1. public action, *i.e.*, use state power to enforce the self-exclusion scheme; and/or
2. private enforcement, by distributing property rights among the parties, who are then in a position to enforce these property rights by appealing to the courts.

As to the sets of incentives to be altered, one can:

1. raise the stakes or lower the expected gain for the self-excluded gambler:[103] by making it less attractive for the gambler to return to the casino after self-exclusion, they (more precisely: their t_2-self) might be scared off; and/or
2. increase the casino's costs or decrease the casino's benefits of permitting the self-excluded gambler to enter the casino; this would induce the casino to prevent the gambler from entering in its own self-interest.

---

102 BMA Board of Science (2007) *at* 16 (see the quote *supra* n. 18). The self-exclusion scheme is ineffective because of the lack of credibility of the enlisted trusted party to stick to its promise; other situations of this sort are described in Elster (2000) *at* 66–68. That casinos do not have an incentive to support self-control can also be inferred from measures adopted to prevent self-control once the gambler is in the casino. *See* Elster (1999) *at* 217 (referring to other authors mentioning, *inter alia*, serving free alcohol, blocking out sunlight and refusing to tell the time in order to make self-imposed time-limits difficult to enforce, grouping slot-machines together in order to provide "vicarious reinforcement from the success of others").

103 This corresponds to pre-commitment device (ii) in Elster (2000) *at* 31.

This allows for (in a first step) four combinations, which are not mutually exclusive, and which have all been used in the context of self-exclusion agreements:

1. *Public action raising the stake of the gambler or lowering his expected gain*: Some self-exclusion schemes in the US explicitly provide that a self-excluded gambler who relapses commits a criminal offence.[104] And it would appear that, even in jurisdictions where this is not explicitly spelled out, the general criminal provisions pertaining to trespass apply. Furthermore, some self-exclusion schemes provide for the forfeiture/confiscation of the gambler's winnings, thus making a trip to the casino less attractive for the gambler.
2. *Public action increasing the casino's costs of permitting the gambler to return*: This seems to be the option currently favoured by the Gambling Commission in the United Kingdom. "Effective procedures for self-exclusion" are made a licence condition for most gambling facilities.[105]
3. *Private enforcement by making returning less attractive to the gambler*: Instead of the forfeiture by public regulation mentioned above (*supra* (1)), one could achieve a similar effect by denying the gambler his winnings by treating the gambling contract in t_2 as void or voidable. Alternatively, one could consider gambling in t_2 as a breach of the self-exclusion agreement by the gambler, the damages being the amount of any winnings paid.[106] The main difference to the forfeiture alternative is the recipient of the amounts won: while the state would receive such winnings under option (1), under option (3) the casino would be the recipient.
4. *Private enforcement by decreasing the casino's benefit of permitting the self-excluded gambler to gamble*: By treating the gambling contract in t_2 as void or voidable, or, alternatively, by considering the act of permitting the self-excluded gambler to gamble as a breach by the casino, one could award the self-excluded gambler a claim against the casino for repayment of their stakes lost on subsequent visits (either as a breach of contract claim or as a negligence claim, with the duty owed to the gambler derived from the contract).[107]

---

104 *E.g.* Mich. Comp. L. Ann. § 432.225(13)(West); Regulations of the Mississippi Gaming Commission sub III.J. s.7(b) (http://mgc.state.ms.us).

105 *See* Gambling Commission (2006a) *at* 57–60 (Section 5.6).

106 Theoretically, one could raise the stakes even higher for the gambler by introducing *punitive* damages against them.

107 As will be described below in more detail, the German Federal Court of Justice has recently adopted this approach (Bundesgerichtshof, decisions of December 15, 2005, III ZR 65/05 and 66/05, JuristenZeitung 2006, 468, favouring the award of damages for breach of contract over restitution), departing from its earlier decision denying such a claim, *see* BGH, decision of October 31, 1995, XI ZR 6/95, Entscheidungen des Bundesgerichtshofs in Zivilsachen [BGHZ] 131, 136). For a criticism of the earlier decision *see* Wagner-von

It should be noted that options (3) and (4) are essentially the ones chosen by the UK Gambling Act 2005 for the protection of *children*, see s. 83(1): they may not collect any winnings, but can reclaim their stakes when they lose.[108]

Comparing the Options

While space constraints prevent a full discussion of the respective merits and demerits of the options, a few cursory remarks are called for. Public action has the advantage of affording harsher sanctions, thus making the scheme potentially more effective.[109] However, two reservations should be made.

Criminal sanctions? First, it would seem inappropriate to raise the stakes for the gambler by introducing *criminal* sanctions. The rationale for making a relapse a criminal offence is clear: it is the attempt at raising the costs of a breach to such a prohibitive level that the problem gambler would rather refrain than suffer the consequences. This is a rationale deeply entrenched in rational choice theory. This approach has its greatest appeal in designing "optimal sanctions" for "rationally calculated" crimes (such as some forms of white collar criminality). If it is to be applied to "crimes of passion", it loses much of its appeal – at least the approach has to be so severely modified to take account of extremely hyperbolic discounting and non-pecuniary benefits, that the model, after it has been altered to fit the facts, may accurately *describe* the phenomenon, but loses its predictive power.[110] In the case of compulsive behaviour, it is – to say the least – of very limited value. To defend my view, it is not even necessary to claim that a compulsive gambler is completely reward-insensitive.[111] While this may be true in the case of such intense cravings as "uncontrollable" thirst,[112] it is at least doubtful whether the intensity of the cravings of a compulsive gambler is equivalent. But in any case, it can be assumed that the cravings are sufficiently severe that the reward-sensitivity of a gambler is significantly reduced. Indeed, there are numerous examples of compulsive gamblers committing embezzlement or other crimes in order to cover

---

Papp (2005); Peters (2002); Weis (1999); Grunsky (1996); *but see* Schulze (2004). For comments on the recent decisions *see* Wagner-von Papp (2006); Schimmel (2006).

108 This is achieved by subjecting the operating licence to a condition, which overrides any contractual provision (s. 83(3)(a)). However, under this section, the winnings cannot be reclaimed when already paid (s. 83(3)(b)); I would not suggest to extend this exception to self-excluded gamblers, as this would strengthen the incentive to try and opportunistically circumvent exclusion measures.

109 Private enforcement sanctions are necessarily more limited if one does not want to resort to punitive damages; *see supra* n. 105.

110 *But see* Posner (2003) *at* 220.

111 For the distinction between completely reward-insensitive selves and selves who are only incompletely motivated by rewards in t_2, *see* Elster (2000) *at* 8–11.

112 Schelling (2006) *at* 91.

their gambling debts.[113] This reveals that – even if, for the sake of the argument, we apply the rational choice approach – the (discounted) costs of the sanctions for *these* crimes do not outweigh the utility derived from the immediate pleasures (whatever they may be[114]) of gambling. This all-too-frequently revealed preference is a fact, and it hardly matters whether this preference ranking is due to (or modelled as) extremely hyperbolic discounting or a preference reversal.[115] If one wanted to draft "optimal sanctions" sufficient to deter compulsive gamblers from returning to the casino, these sanctions would need to be so harsh as to be clearly disproportionate from a human rights perspective. Thus, criminal sanctions for a violation of self-exclusion would be either ineffective or disproportionate.

Another argument against criminal sanctions for the violation of self-exclusion is that it may have a deterrent effect on gamblers deciding to enter a self-exclusion scheme in the first place (entry barrier, participation constraint).[116] It is probably unwise to build up additional hurdles for problem gamblers, who already need to take the crucial step of overcoming the self-denial commonly associated with dependent behaviour. A third reason why one should be hesitant to resort to criminal sanctions for relapsing gamblers is that criminalization can make rehabilitation even harder by adding to the criminal record, making it in turn more difficult for the gambler to find a job to pay off gambling debts.[117] A fourth reason is the disincentive for informing the regulator of a breach once it has occurred.[118]

Private cause of action foreclosed by public enforcement? A second reservation against public enforcement is not so much against using it at all, but against using it *exclusively*. The Court of Appeals of Indiana held that self-exclusion schemes which use public enforcement are presumed not to give rise to a private cause of action, in the absence of a clear indication to the contrary.[119] From a policy point of view, this presupposes that public enforcement does not need to be complemented

113 *See, e.g.*, Grinols (2004) *at* 168–174, 146–167.

114 For a discussion of the unfathomable reason for which people gamble at all, *see* Elster (1999) *at* 213–215.

115 For some observations on crafting optimal sanctions when faced with time-inconsistency, *see* Utset (2006).

116 Of course, this argument would hardly make sense if we conceived gamblers as having a *constant* hyperbolic discount rate, because then the gambler would presumably choose the immediate gratification of self-excluding in t_1, as the future criminal sanction (in t_3) would be significantly discounted. But I believe that the discount rate in t_1 is not nearly as hyperbolic as it is in t_2 (if the hyperbolic discount rate is indeed the explanation – or at least, an accurate model – for the compulsive behaviour); it is the presence of "visceral factors" (Loewenstein (2004)) which affects the discount rate in t_2.

117 Napolitano (2003) *at* 307–308.

118 *See infra* text accompanying n. 120.

119 *Stulajter v. Harrah's Indiana Corp.*, 808 N.E.2d 746, 748–749 (Ind. App. 2004). *See also Merrill v. Trump Indiana, Inc.*, 320 F.3d 729, 732 (7th Cir. 2003); *Brown v. Argosy Gaming*, 384 F.3d 413, 416 (7th Cir. 2004).

by private enforcement. Yet private enforcement may have comparative advantages over public enforcement. First, public enforcement may raise public choice issues – regulatory capture may be a real danger, especially where local or regional regulators (such as gambling commissions or licensing authorities) regulate an industry which contributes, in some cases significantly, to the public revenue by way of taxes and license fees.[120] Second, even if one does not want to call the regulators' proper motivation into question, there is still the problem of informational asymmetry. The casino and the gambler have the information about the violation of the self-exclusion scheme; yet they may not want to voluntarily share it with the regulator unless they stand to gain from such disclosure. The casino has a financial interest in letting the gambler gamble; the gambler's t_2-self certainly will not inform the regulator; and whether the gambler's t_3-self will inform the regulator seems doubtful – not only because of possible emotions such as shame and guilt, but also because of transaction costs and possible sanctions attached to a relapse of the gambler.[121] Therefore, it makes sense to provide financial incentives for the parties to share their information with the regulator, or to provide an incentive structure in which the parties themselves wish to comply with the self-exclusion agreement.

The private enforcement options mentioned above could provide such incentives. The self-excluded gambler who returned and lost may reveal the violation in t_3 if they stand to recover their lost stakes (and is not deterred by offsetting public sanctions).[122] Conversely, if the self-excluded gambler won, the casino could avoid paying out the winnings.[123] In both cases, one of the parties has an incentive to invoke the self-exclusion agreement, thus disclosing it to the regulator.

There is one countervailing argument that has been raised against this possibility of enforcing self-exclusion agreements, namely, that financially rewarding

120 *Cf.* the anecdotal evidence of lobbying by the gambling industry and resulting regulatory (and legislatory) capture reported by Grinols (2004) *at* 28–53; *see also* Orford et al. (2003) *at* 253–255, 257–265 (industry influence on the process leading up to the Gambling Act 2005) and 70; Kindt (2004); Coates (2006a), (2006b); for accounts of lobbying on behalf of the gambling industry *see* Coates (2006c); Baldwin & Stroman (2006); Reid (2006). The following passage from a decision of the 9th Circuit Court of Appeals (*Stars' Desert Inn Hotel and Country Club, Inc. v. Morgenstern*, 1996 WL 366602 (9th Cir.)) may also be considered somewhat revealing: "Moreover, the statute's legislative history supports this reading *[scil.: limiting the defences against gambling debts]*. A representative of the gaming industry, in remarks made to the legislature during consideration of the measure that became § 436.368, made it clear that the bill was aimed at individuals who seek to avoid liability by contending that they cannot control their gambling." This reliance on "remarks" of industry representatives for statutory construction may raise eyebrows not only in the UK, where even the question whether *Hansard* may be referred to as an aid to interpretation is subject to controversy (*see Pepper* v *Hart* [1993] 1 All ER 42).

121 This is yet another reason counting against too harsh sanctions (criminal or punitive) for relapsing gamblers.

122 For examples of such litigation *see infra* n. 125–136.

123 *See infra* n. 127.

gamblers who breach their commitment would impair the clinical benefits of these schemes. The argument runs as follows: if self-excluded gamblers could rely on the casino's enforcement of the scheme, this would convey the idea that it is the casino's responsibility to keep the gamblers away, whereas one of the crucial aspects of therapy for problem gamblers is to impress upon the gamblers that they have to accept their responsibility.[124] Without such acceptance of responsibility, much of the benefit of self-exclusion schemes would be lost. This argument may indeed have its merits. However, making the scheme enforceable in the described way (*i.e.*, making the gambler's losses recoverable and winnings unenforceable) would ensure that the casino has a sufficient self-interest in establishing strict access controls to the game. Even though the self-excluded gamblers' resolve not to return to the casino would probably be somewhat weakened, this would not result in direct harm, because the *technical* barriers most probably erected by the casinos would prevent self-excluded gamblers from re-entering the casino.[125] Moreover, when the benefits from joining the self-exclusion scheme are increased, more gamblers may want to join the scheme in the first place – thus, in turn, further increasing the casinos' incentives to actually introduce access controls.

Enforcing Self-exclusion in Germany, the USA and the UK: A Short Overview

Germany In Germany, there are currently no public regulations specifically addressing self-exclusion. For more than a decade, self-excluded gamblers have tried to turn to the civil courts for relief, both in order to reclaim their lost stakes, and in order to claim winnings. In 1995, the Federal Court of Justice decided that self-excluded gamblers had no claim to their lost stakes.[126] The Court denied that the casino had an intention to create legal relations when concluding the self-exclusion agreement.

During the following years, the lower courts based their rulings on this decision by the Federal Court of Justice. This resulted in several rulings which held that self-

---

124 O'Hare (2004); Napolitano (2003) *at* 312–313; Gambling Commission (2006a) *at* 58, para. 5.6.7: "[W]e have no objection to operators including a disclaimer of liability within any agreement of self-exclusion. We believe individuals must take responsibility for any self-exclusion agreements they have entered into [...].". As to the importance of accepting responsibility *see also* Bellringer (1999) *at* 89–90.

125 I do not believe that O'Hare (2004) is correct in postulating that "[self-exclusion programs] cannot be designed well enough, implemented well enough, monitored, nor enforced well enough to ever compensate for the lack of [...] the gambler's internal motivation to change." As the experience in Germany shows, casinos are able to implement effective controls very rapidly once they stand to lose profits if they fail to do so. *See also* Eggert (2003) *at* 753–754, noting that privacy concerns against access controls are somewhat misplaced, considering that casinos "are already using face recognition technology, though in an effort to protect their own purses, not to help pathological gamblers fight their addiction."

126 Bundesgerichtshof, decision of October 31, 1995, XI ZR 6/95, (1995) Entscheidungen des Bundesgerichtshofs in Zivilsachen 131, 136.

excluded gamblers could not reclaim their losses,[127] but could not claim their winnings either, because the casinos had extended their offer to gamble only to patrons who were not excluded.[128] It was a lose–lose situation for the self-excluded gamblers.

The literature criticized the 1995 decision and its progeny in near unison.[129] Of course, one could argue that the lose–lose situation provided maximum deterrence once a gambler had excluded themselves. However, neither did it make self-exclusion a particularly attractive option for gamblers to begin with, nor did it provide an incentive for the casinos to monitor the entrance and enforce the self-exclusion schemes. And, more importantly from a contract law perspective, it was hardly what the parties of the self-exclusion agreement had bargained for.

Lower courts started to depart from the 1995 decision.[130] They ruled that the self-exclusion agreement was a binding contract after all, and that this contract prevented gamblers from collecting their winnings on the one hand, but on the other hand allowed them to recover their lost stakes.

In December 2005, the Federal Court of Justice revisited the issue.[131] It now rejected its earlier decision's line of argument and conceded that the parties' intentions are better reflected when the self-exclusion is treated as a legally binding contract protecting the gambler from themselves. This contract obliges the casino to exert reasonable efforts to prevent self-excluded gamblers from gambling. A breach of this promise results in a damage award (equalling the lost stakes) to the self-excluded gambler. The Court left undecided whether a casino has a general

---

127 *E.g.*, Oberlandesgericht Hamm, decision of August 30, 2001, 22 U 39/01, NJW-RR 2002, 447; Landgericht Leipzig, decision of August 5, 1999, 10 O 4992/99, NJW-RR 2000, 1343.

128 *E.g.*, Oberlandesgericht Hamm, decision of July 17, 2002, 8 U 19/02, NJW-RR 2002, 1634; *see also* Kammergericht, decision of June 30, 2003, 8 U 237/02, NJW-RR 2003, 1359 (though this decision was mainly grounded on the existence of a self-exclusion contract).

129 Grunsky (1996), Weis (1999), Peters (2002), Wagner-von Papp (2005); *but see* Schulze (2004).

130 Oberlandesgericht Hamm, decision of October 7, 2002, 13 U 119/02, NJW-RR 2003, 971; Kammergericht, decision of June 30, 2003, 8 U 237/02, NJW-RR 2003, 1359; *see also* the decisions of the lower courts leading up to the 2005 decision of the Federal Court of Justice (*see* next footnote): Amtsgericht Münster, decision of May 12, 2004, 48 C 1117/03, and decision of February 11, 2004, 55 C 3513/03; Landgericht Münster, decisions of February 24, 2005, 8 S 224/04 and 8 S 81/04. This may seem a startling occurrence to a common law lawyer, but in Germany there is *de jure* no doctrine of *stare decisis* – lower courts may depart from precedents. *De facto*, this is a rare occurrence in Germany as well, as the lower courts risk reversal of their decisions on appeal, something which German judges tend to avoid by all means. In the self-exclusion cases, the lower court judges based their decisions also on alternative grounds, such as a lack of capacity due to compulsive gambling.

131 Bundesgerichtshof, decisions of December 15, 2005, III ZR 65/05 and III ZR 66/05, JuristenZeitung 2006, 468. For comments *see* Schimmel (2006) and Wagner-von Papp (2006).

duty to check the gamblers' identities at the entrance of the casino.[132] However, it ruled that at least when the casino acquires knowledge of a gambler's identity, reasonable efforts require a cross-reference to the list of self-excluded persons. In the cases before the Court, the casino could have noticed the gamblers' identities, because they had withdrawn cash from cash machines at the casino. The Court therefore permitted the gamblers – or, more precisely, their wives, to whom these claims had been assigned – to recover the lost stakes.

USA While self-excluded problem gamblers have instigated a number of lawsuits, by and large they do not seem to be successful. In some states, statutory provisions specifically insulate casinos from private litigation.[133] Even in the absence of such an express insulation, at least two courts have refused to accept a contract law claim arguing that where there was a detailed statutory scheme of public regulation, there would need to be clear evidence as to the legislature's intent to create a competing private cause of action.[134] One court indicated that it would have been willing to accept a negligence claim based on a contractual duty contained in a self-exclusion agreement,[135] but could not find such any such agreement on the facts of the case.[136] Apparently, some cases have settled.[137]

United Kingdom In the United Kingdom, the Gambling Act 2005, s. 1(c), has entrusted the Gambling Commission for the first time with the protection of "vulnerable persons". The Gambling Commission plans to oblige casinos to offer self-exclusion options to the gambler.[138] However, presently the Gambling Commission also plans to allow casinos to escape civil liability by including disclaimers of liability in the self-exclusion agreements.[139] The sole incentives for

---

132 The Oberlandesgericht Hamm, decision of December 4, 2006, 22 U 250/05, has now ruled that such a duty exists.

133 Mich. Comp. L. Ann. § 432.225(14) (West); N.J. Stat. Ann. § 5:12–71.2(c) (West); *see also* Moles (2001).

134 *Merrill v. Trump Indiana, Inc.*, 320 F.3d 729, 732 (7th Cir. 2003); *Stulajter v. Harrah's Indiana Corp.*, 808 N.E.2d 746, 748–749 (Ind. App. 2004). *But see* Bauer (2006).

135 *Merrill v. Trump Indiana, Inc.*, 2002 WL 1307304 (N.D. Ind. 2002) *at* 5.

136 This finding of fact was not contested on appeal, and all claims based on a contract were dropped, *see Merrill v. Trump Indiana, Inc.*, 320 F.3d 729, 731 (7th Cir. 2003).

137 *See* Kindt (2004) *at* 545–546, 574; Bauer (2006) *at* 91–94. For an overview of Canadian cases, *see* Igelmann & Kelly (2005).

138 Gambling Commission (2006b) *at* para. 2, 11; Gambling Commission (2006a) *at* 57–60, para. 5.6.

139 Gambling Commission (2006a) *at* 58, para. 5.6.7; *see also* the waiver and release prescribed by Regulations by the Mississippi Gaming Commission *sub* III.J. s.2(c)(3). This is based on the acceptance-of-responsibility argument described *supra* "Private cause of action foreclosed by public enforcement?". While this argument has its merits, for the reasons described above (*ibid.*) I believe that the increase in self-control, even if bolstered by the acceptance of responsibility, cannot compensate the reduced incentive for the casinos

the casinos to enforce the self-exclusion agreements appear to be the regulatory effects of a violation.[140] As compliance with such regulatory requirements is difficult (and costly) to monitor, and for the other reasons mentioned above, it would be preferable if this approach were reconsidered.

Self-exclusion agreements as contracts? In jurisdictions which have not (expressly or implicitly) excluded the application of contract law or granted immunity to the casinos, the question remains whether self-exclusion agreements can be considered binding contracts. The existence of offer and acceptance appears unproblematic; there are mutual declarations by the parties.[141] The real question is if there is consideration supporting these promises. While some answer the question in the affirmative,[142] others claim that there is no consideration.[143] The answer depends upon the interpretation of the mutual promises. If, as Napolitano suggests, the promises were to be interpreted as "I promise not to go on the casino premises" and "If we find you on the casino premises, we promise to have you removed [...]", respectively, then it would indeed be difficult to establish consideration. Nor do I find the view convincing that the consideration accruing to the casino should generally be seen in the advantage that it could use the self-exclusion scheme as a marketing instrument.[144]

---

to monitor access when they are allowed to escape civil liability. Sasso & Kalajdzic (2006) argue for a narrow reading of disclaimers in self-exclusion forms.

140 The Gambling Commission (2006c *at* 27 sub 3.5.14) has indicated that "a failure to ensure that employees were aware of their responsibilities in relation to problem gambling" will be considered as a *serious* breach.

141 There is, however, a question of the content of these declarations; this will be discussed in the following in establishing the nature of the consideration. There is yet another question: which communication is the offer, which is the acceptance? Rhea (2005) *at* 468 assumes the casinos' declarations (providing the self-exclusion forms) to constitute the offer, and the gamblers' declarations of the wish to be added to the self-exclusion list to constitute the acceptance. I would suppose that the distribution of self-exclusion forms is more likely to be considered an invitation to treat, rather than an offer. But if the casino is obliged by statute to accept a self-exclusion request, Rhea's interpretation may be right. In this case, there is (supplementary to the following observations) another way to establish consideration: if the casino's offer is interpreted as being "In consideration of your identifying yourself as a compulsive gambler, we promise to deny you access to the casino and to return any stakes lost on return visits", then the stepping forward might be considered the consideration sought by the promisor. However, this does arguably not work in jurisdictions where the consideration is required to be of a tangible benefit to the promisor. And it does not work if the self-exclusion forms are invitations to treat; in this case, the self-identification as a problem gambler would be past consideration at the time the contract is concluded.

142 Rhea (2005) *at* 468–469.

143 Napolitano (2003) *at* 304–305.

144 But see Rhea (2005) at 468–469 ("[I]n providing access to the [self-exclusion] programs, casinos are establishing goodwill and therefore conducting business with moral

Instead, the promise by the casino should be interpreted as meaning: "If you lose on a return visit to the casino, we promise to repay your lost stakes, and we will deny you access to our casinos". The promise by the gambler can be interpreted as conveying: "If I win on a return visit to the casino, I promise not to claim or else to repay the winnings". This interpretation does not overstrain the parties' declarations. These promises constitute a bargained-for exchange, with each promise constituting a detriment to the promisor and a benefit to the promisee. Although it may not be a particularly attractive deal for the casino, as it foregoes its house edge, there is a benefit to the casino in the gambler's promise, as the casino obtains a claim to monies won by the gambler on return visits which it would not have absent the agreement. It is irrelevant that the main reason for the casino may be to forestall public regulation that is more intrusive; if there is consideration, the presence of additional motives does not affect the validity of the contract.

Conclusion

I have argued in this chapter that from a policy point of view self-limitation in t_1 can be autonomy-enhancing when decision-making in t_2 is tainted by a procedural defect, and that such a defect is present when problem gamblers return to their casino against their "true will" as documented in a self-exclusion agreement. There is, therefore, a need for self-exclusion schemes, a need that has increasingly been recognized in the regulation of the gambling sector.

However, when self-limitation is to be realized by autonomous agreement, the autonomous decision in t_1 cannot entirely preclude the exercise of autonomy in t_2. There are limitations to self-limitation; the self-limitation must be reversible. Nevertheless, this reversal need not (and, if the self-limitation is to be effective, must not) be immediate and costless. I have tried to identify some of the "hurdles" that may be imposed on the reversal of a self-exclusion agreement.

The question for the law is how to enforce self-exclusion agreements. As the agreements are not self-enforcing, their effectiveness depends on sanctions. These

---

consideration to society. It also could be argued the casinos would be able to use these self-exclusion lists as advertisement"). While Rhea does not refer to *Merrill* for this proposition, I assume that is the origin of his argument. The situation in *Merrill*, where this argument was used before the District Court to establish consideration, was somewhat special: in this case it was alleged that a clinic with a programme for compulsive gamblers had contacted a casino and formed "an oral contract whereby Trump agreed to accept and honor Merrill's self-eviction request in exchange for the clinic and its patients publicizing Trump's support for recovering compulsive gamblers". While the argument seems appropriate under these special circumstances, I find it less convincing that the run-of-the-mill self-exclusion request by a single gambler can be read as the promise to provide (or lend themselves to be the object of) marketing services for the benefit of the casino. Also, the concept of "moral consideration" is a highly controversial one, rejected in many jurisdictions.

sanctions can be either public, or private, or both. I have tried to show that self-exclusion agreements can be considered binding contracts in which the parties promise each other that the other party may reclaim the stakes lost or the winnings, respectively. Private enforcement was shown to provide an advantageous incentive structure: regardless who wins, one of the parties will have an incentive to bring the breach to the attention of the regulator. At the same time, the participation constraint for problem gamblers in entering self-exclusion schemes is reduced, because they stand to profit from the agreement. Furthermore, there is an incentive for the casino to introduce effective supervision in order to prevent opportunism by returning gamblers; this effective supervision should eliminate any effects from an increased incentive for self-excluded gamblers to return in order to opportunistically profit from the self-exclusion. The participation constraint for the casino may be a problem. As it loses the house edge, it may not want to offer a self-exclusion scheme. This may be a cause for public intervention, requiring the casino to offer such a scheme, and prohibiting the use of disclaimers of liability. There may be further aspects that public regulations need to address. The supervision of effective control arrangements could be one of them, although the incentive structure, once private enforcement is implemented, should alleviate some of this regulatory burden. The approach of criminalizing relapsing self-excluded gamblers is, for several reasons, inadvisable.

It should be noted that this article is not to be taken to suggest that self-exclusion agreements are a panacea for problem gambling. Only a fraction of problem gamblers actually participates in self-exclusion schemes, although the latter may become more attractive once private enforcement is accepted by the courts. For the other problem gamblers, the question remains whether the casino owes a duty of care under tort law to identify and exclude them. Such an intervention would, however, not be *self*-paternalistic, but be a case of paternalism; the question is thus beyond the scope of this chapter.

Neither is there a danger that classifying self-exclusion agreements as binding contracts will lead to a flood of litigation. In fact, once the incentive structure is balanced correctly, there need not be any litigation. It is the hallmark of any credible and effective threat that it has never to be carried out. The casinos would monitor effectively and thus prevent self-excluded problem gamblers from gambling. Allowing private enforcement could thus lead to effective self-exclusion of problem gamblers. Should we be free not to be free to ruin ourselves? The short answer is: yes.

References

(Online resources last visited on February 28, 2007)

American Psychiatric Association (2000) *Diagnostic and Statistical Manual of Mental Disorders*, 4th ed., Text Revision (DSM-IV-TR). Washington, D.C.: American Psychiatric Association.

Arnold, Glen; Collins, Peter; Eadington, William R.; Remmers, Pieter; Ricketts, Tom (2003) *Towards a Strategy For Addressing Problem Gambling in the UK: A Report to the Gambling Industry Charitable Trust*. London: GICT.

Baldwin, Tom & Stroman, Anna (2006) "British Firms Top Foreign Spending on US Lobbyists", *The Times* January 20, p. 38, London.

Bauer, Justin E. (2006) "Self-Exclusion and the Compulsive Gambler: The House Shouldn't Always Win", *Northern Illinois University Law Review* 27: 63–94.

Bechara, Antoine (2003) "Risky Business: Emotion, Decision-Making, and Addiction", *Journal of Gambling Studies* 19: 23–51.

Bellringer, Paul (1999) *Understanding Problem Gambling*. London and New York: Free Association Books.

BMA Board of Science (2007) *Gambling Addiction and Its Treatment Within the NHS*, http://www.bma.org.uk/ap.nsf/Content/gamblingaddiction.

Chen-Wishart, Mindy (2005) *Contract Law*. Oxford: Oxford University Press.

Coates, Sam (2006a) "Casino Law Will Fuel Gambling Problems", *The Times* January 3, p. 1, London.

Coates, Sam (2006b) "Supercasinos Are No Big Deal, Says Gaming Watchdog", *The Times*, January 3, p. 2, London.

Coates, Sam (2006c) "Backroom Boys Who Influence Our MPs", *The Times*, January 5, p. 33, London.

Coates, Sam (2006d) "Tories Demand an Explanation on Super-Casinos", *The Times*, March 14, p. 13, London.

Davis, Kevin E. (2006) "The Demand for Immutable Contracts: Another Look at the Law and Economics of Contract Modifications", *New York University Law Review* 81: 487–549.

DCMS Gambling Review Body (2001) *Gambling Review Report*, http://www.culture.gov.uk/Reference_library/Publications/archive_2001/gamb_rev_report.htm.

Delgado, M.R.; Nystrom, L.E.; Fissell, C.; Noll, D.C. & Fiez, J.A. (2000) "Tracking the Hemodynamic Responses to Reward and Punishment in the Striatum", *Journal of Neurophysiology* 84: 3072–3077.

Eggert, Kurt (2004) "Truth in Gaming: Toward Consumer Protection in the Gambling Industry", *Maryland Law Review* 63: 216–286.

Eggert, Kurt (2003) "Lashed to the Mast and Crying for Help: How Self-Limitation of Autonomy Can Protect Elders from Predatory Lending", *Loyola of Los Angeles Law Review* 36: 693–775.

Elster, Jon (1984) *Ulysses and the Sirens*, rev. ed. Cambridge: Cambridge University Press.

Elster, Jon (1999) "Gambling and Addiction", pp. 208–234. In: *Getting Hooked: Rationality and Addiction*. Cambridge & New York: Cambridge University Press.

Elster, Jon (2000) *Ulysses Unbound*. Cambridge: Cambridge University Press.

Farnsworth, E. Allan (2004) *Contracts*, 4th ed. New York: Aspen Publishers.

Fisher, Susan E. (1996) *Gambling and Problem Gambling Among Casino Patrons*. University of Plymouth, Faculty of Human Sciences.

Frankfurt, Harry G. (1971) "Freedom of the Will and the Concept of a Person", *The Journal of Philosophy* 68: 5–20.

Gambling Commission (2006a), "Licence Conditions and Codes of Practice", November 2006, http://www.gamblingcommission.gov.uk/UploadDocs/Contents/Documents/LCCPFinal.pdf.

Gambling Commission (2006b), "Problem Gambling", *Issues Paper* IP01/06, March 2006, http://www.gamblingcommission.gov.uk/UploadDocs/Contents/Documents/Gambling Commission problem gambling issues paper.pdf.

Gambling Commission (2006c), "Licensing, Compliance and Enforcement – Consultation Document", May 2006, http://www.gamblingcommission.gov.uk/UploadDocs/Contents/Documents/Licensing,%20Compliance%20and%20Enforcement.pdf.

Gambling Commission (2006d) *Annual Report 2005–2006*, H.C. 1226 SE/2006/94. London: The Stationery Office, *available at*: http://www.gamblingcommission.gov.uk/UploadDocs/News/documents/annual_report_05_06.pdf.

Gaming Board for Great Britain (2005) *Report of the Gaming Board for Great Britain 2004–05*. H.C. 227 SE/2005/113. London: The Stationery Office, *available at*: http://www.gamblingcommission.gov.uk/UploadDocs/publications/Document/AnnualText.pdf.

Grant, Jon E.; Potenza, Marc N.; Hollander, Eric; Cunningham-Williams, Renee; Nurminen, Tommi; Smits, Gerard; Kallio, Antero (2006) "Multicenter Investigation of the Opioid Antagonist Nalmefene in the Treatment of Pathological Gambling", *American Journal of Psychiatry* 163: 303–312.

Grinols, Earl L. (2004) *Gambling in America*. Cambridge: Cambridge University Press.

Hollander, Eric; DeCaria, Concetta M.; Mari, Eduardo; Wong, Cheryl M.; Mosovich, Serge; Grossman, Robert; Begaz, Tomer (1998) "Short-Term Single-Blind Fluvoxamine Treatment of Pathological Gambling", *American Journal of Psychiatry* 155: 1781–1783.

Ibáñez, Angela; Blanco, Carlos; Perez de Castro, Ignacio; Fernandez-Piqueras, Jose; Sáiz-Ruiz, Jeronimo (2003) "Genetics of Pathological Gambling", *Journal of Gambling Studies* 19: 11–22.

Igelman, Alex & Kelly, Joseph (2005) "Status of Canadian Compulsive Gambling Litigation", *Gaming Law Review* 9: 116–133.

Jolls, Christine (1997) "Contracts as Bilateral Commitments: A New Perspective On Contract Modifications", *Journal of Legal Studies* 26: 203–237.

Kaiser, Alfons (2004) "Die Glücksspielmentalität wächst", *Frankfurter Allgemeine Zeitung*, December 15, p. 11, Frankfurt a.M./Germany.

Kindt, John Warren (2004) "'The Insiders' for Gambling Lawsuits: Are the Games 'Fair' and Will Casinos and Gambling Facilities Be Easy Targets for Blueprints for RICO and Other Causes of Action?", *Mercer Law Review* 55: 529–593.

Kuklin, Bailey (1992) "Self-Paternalism in the Marketplace", *University of Cincinnati Law Review* 60: 649–712.

Leitzel, James A. (2005) "From Harm to Robustness: A Principled Approach to Vice Regulation", available at SSRN, http://www.ssrn.com/abstracts=773030.

Lesieur, H.R. & Blume, S.B. (1987) "The South Oaks Gambling Screen (SOGS): A New Instrument for the Identification of Pathological Gamblers", *American Journal of Psychiatry* 144: 1184–1188.

Loewenstein, George (2004) "Out of Control: Visceral Influences on Behavior", pp. 689–723. In: *Advances in Behavioral Economics* edited by Colin F. Camerer, George Loewenstein & Matthew Rabin. Princeton: Princeton University Press.

May-Chahal, Corinne, et al. (2004) "Young People and Gambling in Britain", *DCMS Technical Report Series, Technical Paper No. 8*, November 2004, http://www.culture.gov.uk/NR/rdonlyres/F4941636-7790-44B2-A994-F963853B6F77/0/YoungPeopleandGamblinginBritain.pdf.

Mill, John Stuart (1859/1997) *On Liberty*. Edited by Currin V. Shields. Upper Saddle River, N.J.: Prentice Hall.

Moles, Nicholas F. (2001) "Fine-Tune the Plan Allowing Gamblers to Exclude Themselves From Casinos", *New Jersey Law Journal* 165: 135.

Napolitano, Francisco (2003) "The Self-Exclusion Program: Legal and Clinical Considerations", *Journal of Gambling Studies* 19: 303–315.

NGISC (1999) *National Gambling Impact Study Commission – Final Report*, http://govinfo.library.unt.edu/ngisc/reports/finrpt.html.

O'Hare, Carol (2004) "Self-Exclusion – Concept vs. Reality", *Gaming Law Review* 8: 189–191.

Orford, Jim (*c.* 2005) "Problem Gambling and Other Behavioural Addictions", *Foresight Brain Science, Addiction and Drugs project* V.1.0, http://217.33.105.254/Previous_Projects/Brain_Science_Addiction_and_Drugs/Reports_and_Publications/ScienceReviews/Problem%20Gambling%20and%20other%20Behavioural%20Addictions.pdf.

Orford, Jim; Sproston, Kerry; Erens, Bob; White, Clarissa & Mitchell, Laura (2003) *Gambling and Problem Gambling in Britain.* Hove and New York: Brunner Routledge.

Pallanti, Stefano; DeCaria, Concetta M.; Grant, Jon E.; Urpe, Mauro; Hollander, Eric (2005) "Reliability and Validity of the Pathological Gambling Adaptation of the Yale-Brown Obsessive-Compulsive Scale (PG-YBOCS)", *Journal of Gambling Studies* 21: 431–443.

Peters, Frank (2002) "Die Selbstsperre des Glücksspielers", *Juristische Rundschau* 2002: 177–182.

Petry, Nancy M. (2004) *Pathological Gambling – Etiology, Comorbidity, and Treatment*. Washington, D.C.: American Psychological Association.

Popper, Karl R. (1945/1966) *The Open Society and its Enemies – Vol. I: The Spell of Plato*, 5th rev. ed. London: Routledge.

Posner, Richard A. (2003) *Economic Analysis of Law*, 6th ed. New York: Aspen Publishers.

Potenza, Marc N.; Kosten, Thomas R.; Rounsaville, Bruce J. (2001) "Pathological Gambling", *Journal of the American Medical Association* 286: 141–144.

Potenza, Marc N.; Leung, Hoi-Chung; Blumberg, Hilary P.; Peterson, Bradley S.; Fulbright, Robert K.; Lacadie, Cheryl M.; Skudlarski, Pawel; Gore, John C. (2003) "An fMRI Stroop Task Study of Ventromedial Prefrontal Cortical Function in Pathological Gamblers", *American Journal of Psychiatry* 160: 1990–1994.

Reid, Tim (2006) "Lobbyist's Guilt Sets Stage for Fresh White House Scandal", *The Times*, January 4, p. 35, London.

Reuter, Jan; Raedler, Thomas; Rose, Michael; Hand, Iver; Gläscher, Jan & Büchel, Christian (2005) "Pathological Gambling Is Linked to Reduced Activation of the Mesolimbic Reward System", *Nature Neuroscience* 8: 147–148.

Rhea, Andy (2005) "Voluntary self-exclusion lists: How they work and potential problems", *Gaming Law Review* 9: 462–469.

Robbins, Trevor W. & Everitt, Barry J. (1999) "Drug addiction: Bad Habits Add Up", *Nature* 398: 567–570.

Roger Tym and Partners (2006) *The Use Classes Order, Casinos and the Gambling Bill*, http://www.communities.gov.uk/pub/67/TheUseClassesOrderCasinosandtheGamblingBillPDF361Kb_id1163067.pdf.

Sasso, William V. & Kalajdzic, Jasminka (2006), "Do Ontario and Its Gaming Venues Owe a Duty of Care to Problem Gamblers?", *Gaming Law Review* 10: 552–570.

Schelling, Thomas C. (1985) "Enforcing Rules on Oneself", *Journal of Law, Economics & Organization* 1: 357–374.

Schelling, Thomas C. (2006) *Strategies of Commitment and Other Essays*. Cambridge, Mass.: Harvard University Press.

Schimmel, Roland (2006) "Der Schutz des Spielers vor sich selbst", *Neue Juristische Wochenschrift* 59: 958–960.

Schulze, Götz (2004) "Verträge zum Schutz gegen sich selbst", pp. 1577–1587. In: *Festschrift für Erik Jayme, Vol. II*, edited by Heinz-Peter Mansel et al. Munich: Sellier European Law Publishers.

Sen, Amartya K. (1977) "Rational Fools: A Critique of the Behavioral Foundations of Economic Theory", *Philosophy and Public Affairs* 6: 317–344.

Shaffer, Howard J. & Freed, Christopher R. (2005) "Assessment of Gambling-Related Disorders", pp. 334–391. In: *Assessment of Addictive Behaviors*, edited by Dennis M. Donovan & G. Alan Marlatt, 2nd edn. New York and London: The Guilford Press.

Smith, Stephen A. (1996) "Future Freedom and Freedom of Contract", *The Modern Law Review* 59(2): 167–187.

Sproston, Kerry; Erens, Bob; Orford, Jim (2000) *Gambling Behaviour in Britain: Results from the British Gambling Prevalence Survey*. London: National Centre for Social Research.

Stigler, George J. (1977) "The Conference Handbook", *Journal of Political Economy* 85: 441–443.

Treitel, Guenter (2003) *The Law of Contract*, 11th ed. London: Sweet & Maxwell.

Utset, Manuel A. (2006) "When Good People Do Bad Things: Time-inconsistent Misconduct & Criminal Law", *University of Utah Legal Studies Paper No. 05-39*, http://ssrn.com/abstract=895734.

van Aaken, Anne (2006) "Begrenzte Rationalität und Paternalismusgefahr: Das Prinzip des schonendsten Paternalismus", *Preprints of the Max Planck Institute for Research on Collective Goods* 3/2006, http://www.coll.mpg.de/pdf_dat/2006_3online.pdf.

Volberg, Rachel A. (2000) "The Future of Gambling in the United Kingdom – Increasing Access Creates More Problem Gamblers", *BMJ (British Medical Journal)* 320: 1556.

von Hippel, Eike (2001) "Zur Bekämpfung der Spielsucht", *Zeitschrift für Rechtspolitik* 34: 558–561.

Wagner-von Papp, Florian (2005) "Die privatautonome Beschränkung der Privatautonomie – Gewillkürte Schriftformklauseln und Sperrverträge in Spielbanken als Ausprägungen des Freiheitsparadoxons", *Archiv für die civilistische Praxis* 205: 342–385.

Wagner-von Papp, Florian (2006) "Anmerkung zu BGH v. 15.12.2005, III ZR 65/05", *JuristenZeitung* 61: 470–473.

Weis, Christiane (1999) *Die Sperre des Glücksspielers*. Frankfurt a.M., Germany: Peter Lang Verlagsgruppe.

Williamson, Oliver E. (1985) *The Economic Institutions of Capitalism*. New York: The Free Press.

Winston, Gordon C. (1985) "The Reasons for Being of Two Minds: A Comment on Schelling's 'Enforcing Rules on Oneself'", *Journal of Law, Economics & Organization* 1: 375–37.

Chapter 6
The Problems with Blaming

Theodore Y. Blumoff[1]

> To ... blame is not to judge merely that what happened was a ... bad thing, but to judge the person for having done it, in view of the circumstances under which it was done. The difficulty is to explain how this is possible.[2]

Is this possible? That's the question.

The social practice of blaming today reflects a view of moral psychology that routinely overemphasizes the wrongdoer's wicked *character*. This view, which tends to disconnect the individual's settled disposition from the artefacts produced by their actual situation (as if nature and nurture were, in fact, dichotomous rather than sublimely coextensive), follows from a deeper anthropological presumption, which accepts without much debate that the wrongdoing actor virtually always possesses and retains sufficient cognitive and volitional capacity to choose other than the crime they have committed. The timelessness of the legal presumption that each individual actually possesses both intellectual and volitional capacity speaks volumes to our practical wisdom about individual capacity. But volumes don't encompass every case and the presumption, as defined and applied,[3] presents both moral and jurisprudential problems, and (ironically) the presumption is especially troublesome

---

1 Professor of Law, Adjunct Professor of Medical Education, Mercer University, Macon, Georgia. Portions of this chapter were delivered at a colloquium at Georgia State University College of Law, a Faculty Workshop at Washington University's School of Law, at the John Marshall Law School, and at a Mercer University Law School Faculty Development Colloquium. I also presented the main thesis of this work at a conference on "Law, Mind and Brain," University College London, co-hosted by the Gruter Institute on Law and Behavioural Research, on 13 February 2006. Many thanks to those colleagues and friends who offered friendly and helpful comments and suggestions on this and related projects, including Robert Audi, Karen Kovach, Harold Lewis, Stephen Morse and Jack Sammons. As always, I appreciate the financial and collegial support of Mercer Law School and Dean Daisy Floyd. Finally, special thanks to Rebecca McKelvey (Class of 2006) for timely and thorough research assistance.

2 Thomas Nagel, The View From Nowhere 120 (Oxford 1986).

3 *See e.g.*, Michael Moore, *The Moral and Metaphysical Sources of Criminal Law* in J. Roland Pennock and John W. Chapman (eds), Nomos XXVII: Criminal Justice 20 (New York: N.Y.U. Press, 1985). The existing standard, in practice, tends to measure only the capacity to move from *desire* to *belief* to *action*, which satisfies the requirements of a practical syllogism. *See* Terry A. Maroney, *Emotional Competence, "Rational Understanding," and*

in the categories that require us to adjudicate violent felonies, where dangerousness often signals the existence of substantial neuropsychological deficits.[4] To blame and punish damaged people who could not have done otherwise is immoral.

I cannot make the entire case I have outlined above in this chapter.[5] I limit my remarks here to a discussion of the importance of and problems associated with blaming in our culture, which exacerbate unhelpful tendencies inherent in the larger scheme. I begin by examining some of the moral rhetoric of blaming in light of a salient view that stresses the bad character of the wrongdoer. Next, I look at the semantics of the term *character* that support blaming generally; when we dig into the term, we discover that it describes an understandably abbreviated and, *just to that extent*, a woefully incomplete shorthand expression that conceals deep problems. Finally, I discuss some of those deep problems, which often show up as reflections of the social and cultural biases that we bring to the process of attributing blame. I present a synthesis on the practice of blaming from the rich data in the social sciences signalling that our blaming practices tend to overemphasize the actor's wicked disposition to wrongdoing in a process that, on balance, often fails to serve well our long-term goal of providing a safer society for ourselves and our children: by creating conditions that permit us to overfocus substantially on the *bad* person rather than the situation, by providing impetus to an unhelpful penchant for scape-goating, and, worst, by undermining our own moral and ultimately political responsibility for the world. We are strange

---

the Criminal Defendant, (March 15, 2006), ExpressO Preprint Series. Working Paper 1142, http://law.bepress.com/expresso/eps/1142.

In this respect, we are barely distinguishable (if at all) from lower primates: "Primary consciousness – the ability to generate a mental scene in which a large amount of diverse information is integrated for the purpose of directing present or immediate behavior – occurs in animals with brain structures similar to ours." Gerald M. Edelman and Giulio Tononi, A UNIVERSE OF CONSCIOUSNESS: HOW MATTER BECOMES IMAGINATION 103 (Basic Books 2000). *See also* Joseph LeDoux, THE EMOTIONAL BRAIN: THE MYSTERIOUS UNDERPINNINGS OF EMOTIONAL LIFE 126 (Simon & Schuster 1996). When we begin to refine our understanding of human intentionality, we necessarily move toward an appreciation of the benefits of compassion. On the need for a definition of rationality that includes empathic capacity, *see* Stephen J. Morse, *Rationality and Responsibility*, 74 S. CAL. L. REV. 251, 264–66 (2000) (arguing for a "generic partial excusing condition" for those who lack a well-developed conscience and capacity for empathy).

4 This is, of course, an empirical statement that at some point in time demands demonstration. For now, I will assume this to be true; a good deal of evidence supports it. *See, e.g.*, Laurence Tancredi, HARDWIRED BEHAVIOR: WHAT NEUROSCIENCE REVEALS ABOUT MORALITY esp. Ch. 11 (Cambridge 2005) (reviewing some of the neuroscientific data that measure incidents of aberrant criminal behaviour); Joshua Greene, *Cognitive Neuroscience and the Structure of the Moral Mind*, in Stephen Laurence, Peter Caruthers, and Stephen Stich, 1 INNATE MIND: STRUCTURE AND CONTENTS 338 (Oxford 2005) available at http://www.wjh.harvard.edu/~jgreene/Greene.

5 I have addressed these issues in BLAMING ANGRY MEN: THE PARADOX OF EVIL AND THE LIMITS OF CONTEMPORARY JURISPRUDENCE (copyright © 2006 by Theodore Y. Blumoff).

animals who sometimes tend to evade responsibility for our own situations. And, last, I address the role of blaming within the paradox of evil, which, in its most unintelligible forms, suggests that poor environmental conditions do in fact effect changes within an individual's cognitive and volitional control. I briefly present suggestions for modifying the extant practices.

The Place of Blaming

We devote substantial time and energy to blaming wrongdoers, as we must; we are social animals who are obliged to civilize our children.[6] In the process of blaming and punishing those who violate our public norms, however, we often brush aside our basic commitments to compassion; retributive emotions appear to take over. We cannot escape the practice of blaming; there is something in our nature and in the nature of morality that requires the attribution of fault;[7] but we must be able to harness it and use it to protect our children, ourselves and others. I thus do not understand those who oppose reformatory punishment because it supposedly interferes with the goal of retribution.[8] Protecting our children, ourselves and one another is, in my view, more important than retribution *qua* retribution, which may make us feel good but cannot bring about safer neighbourhoods.[9] I hope to show that we have reasons for adopting a stance that is fundamentally more pragmatic when it comes to protecting ourselves and future generations. This position appreciates in full the need to restrain certain wrongdoers; it's the edges that count. At the edges, it endorses the development of and genuine commitment to moral educational tools for those adjudicated wrongdoers and are capable of being helped – a point I develop briefly later.

---

6 Among secular theorists, both Aristotle and Kant understood appropriate child-rearing as obligations, either implicitly or explicitly. "It makes no small difference, then, whether we form habits [of anger or good temper] of one kind or another from our very youth. It makes a very great difference, or rather *all* the difference." Aristotle, Nicomachean Ethics Bk II, 1103b 23-25 (trans. by David Ross; Oxford, 1987) (emphasis in the original); Immanuel Kant, *General Introduction to the Metaphysics of Morals*, in The Philosophy of Law (trans. by W. Hastie; Edinburgh, Augustus M. Kelley, 1974 ed.) at 195 114–16 (discussing the parents' obligation to care for and maintain the well-being of children until they are able to do so for themselves as free individuals).

7 On the naturalist features of blaming, *see* Adam Smith, The Theory of Moral Sentiments Pt. II (Prometheus Books 2000) (Hereafter, Smith, TMS); Peter Strawson, *Freedom and Resentment*, Proc. Brit. Academy (1962), reprinted in Free Will 59 (ed. by Gary Watson; Oxford 1982).

8 Hastings Rashdall, *Punishment and the Individual*, in Gertrude Ezorsky, ed., Philosophical Perspectives on Punishment 6, 7 (State University of N.Y. Press 1972).

9 On the affective bases of retributive *see*, Joshua Greene, *The Secret Joke of Kant's Soul*, in Walter Sinnott-Armstrong, ed., 3 Moral Psychology: The Neuroscience of Morality (M.I.T., in progress) available at http://www.wjh.harvard.edu/~jgreene/GreeneWJH/Greene-KantSoul.pdf.

For now I can be clearer still: no one should advocate the elimination of blaming as a social practice; I am far too committed to understanding our neurobiological development to adopt such an either-or, unnatural stance. Blaming persists as a significant feature of our penal decision-making and moral culture because, more fundamentally, it permits us to tell all wrongdoers, as directly as the context allows, that they have committed wrongs that we disapprove of, that they should not have acted as they did on those occasions when we judge their conduct wrongful, and that they should not commit similar acts in the future (or, potentially, face substantial pain). In this sense, the need to cast blame is both a natural defensive stance and an essential one. To the question, then, "Is blaming *per se* inappropriate," where blaming instantiates an ascription of fault or demerit to an individual for producing an unwelcome outcome intentionally (at least usually[10]), the answer couldn't be much clearer: "Of course not. It can't be."

It can't be inappropriate as a general matter because blaming – telling an individual that he or she has done wrong and should not do so in the future – is a basic and essential rhetorical tool in our effort to advance our children's ethical and moral conditioning. As a child-rearing practice exercised with love and compassion, and employed with a long-term view of moral development,[11] blaming often helps us achieve the important goal of educating our children in shared moral, social, cultural and legal norms, thereby furthering the project of civilizing them in light of our status as primates.[12] Anyway you look at it, we are members of a species that needs civilizing care.[13]

---

10 I don't mean to suggest that inadvertently caused harms are entirely non-blameworthy, *see* Judith Andre, *Nagel, Williams, and Moral Luck*, 43 ANALYSIS 202 (1983), only that they typically occasion less blame than do intentionally caused harms.

11 It is now non-controversially understood that human brains don't reach full maturity until the individual reaches their mid-20s. *See, e.g.,* NIH Publication No. 01-4929, *Teenage Brain: A Work in Progress* (2001) at http://www.nimh.nih.gov/publicat/teenbrain.cfm. *See Roper v. Simmons*, 543 U.S. 551 (2005) (holding that the Eighth Amendment's prohibition on cruel and unusual punishment prohibits the execution of minors, in part, based on the fact that juvenile brain development is immature with respect to decision-making and impulse control).

12 In the child-rearing context, blame serves as a tool for teaching moral responsibility, including genuine feelings of shame and guilt and resentment and the like, on the one hand, and love and respect and compassion, on the other. Following Hume, therefore, I incline toward a utilitarian (even pragmatic) view of blame and punishment. *See* David Hume, *Of the Immortality of the Soul*, in SELECTED CLASSICS 324, 327–28 (Stephen Copley and Andrew Edgar (eds), Oxford 1996). *See generally* Paul Russell, *Hume on Responsibility and Punishment*, 20 CAN. J. PHIL. 539, 550–52 (1990).

13 *See, e.g.,* Robert Boyd and Peter J. Richerson, *Solving the Puzzle of Human Cooperation*, in, Stephen C. Levinson and Pierre Jaisson (eds), EVOLUTION AND CULTURE 105(MIT Press 2005); Robert Boyd and Peter J. Richerson, *Punishment Allows the Evolution of Cooperation (or Anything Else) in Sizeable Groups*, 13 ETHOLOGY & SOCIOBIOLOGY 171 (1992). Both are at www.sscnet.ucla.edu/anthro/faculty/boyd/Publications.htm.

As loving, conscientious parents, we routinely devise or borrow the basic outlines of our children's moral education. These outlines typically begin with a certain kind of discipline that requires, as a necessary condition, the neurobiological *capacity* to internalize the basic moral demands of our society, and (thereafter) some $\underline{x\pm}$ number of (genuine and non-abusive) *opportunities* to learn the basics, where $\underline{x\pm}$ represents the number of examples over a long period of time when we direct our best efforts at successful child-rearing. Often, in our own families, the number of opportunities required to achieve this education falls well outside our initial hopes and expectations, at least for some of our children some of the time. To meet our own intuitions about the developmental needs of our children, we employ educational strategies that require persistent efforts aimed at teaching the everyday material of values. Reaching that goal, in turn, dictates that we make available to every child variably graded exercises pointed at learning the nature of individual agency and its obligations: instilling within them the notion that each of us can (*prima facie*) recognize ourselves as sources of consequence on the world, and so inculcating practices that appropriately praise good and censure bad.[14] An adequate moral education permits the student with sufficient capacity and opportunity to internalize a substantial measure of what it means to *hold* oneself, and *be held*, responsible for chosen conduct.[15] We usually know (or at least believe we know)

14 This course follows multiple tracks, and not least one that describes form and another the substance of responsibility. There are, as Bernard Williams notes, many modalities for blaming. Some take the proleptic form, "If I were you I would have (or not have) …." This form of advising involves "treating the person who is blamed like someone who had a reason to do the right thing but did not do it". Bernard Williams, *Internal Reasons and the Obscurity of Blaming*, in Making Sense of Humanity and other Philosophical Papers 35, 42–3 (Cambridge 1995). On the substance side, we can and should expect a sufficient understanding of basic decency, one that takes into account Hillel's account of Torah: "What is hateful unto you, do not unto your neighbour. The rest is commentary – now go and study." *See, e.g.*, Karen Armstrong, A History of God: The 4000-year Quest of Judaism, Christianity and Islam 72 (Alfred A. Knopf 1993); Joseph Telushkin, Jewish Literacy: The Most Important Things to Know About The Jewish Religion, Its People, And Its History, 62–63 (William Morrow & Co. 1991). I have discussed this at length in *An Essay on Liberalism and Public Theology*, 14 J. Law & Relig. 229 (Winter 1999/2000).

15 John Martin Fischer & Mark Ravizza, Responsibility and Control: A Theory of Moral Responsibility 208–10 (Cambridge 1998). *See* Sharon Lamb, The Trouble With Blaming: Victims, Perpetrators, and Responsibility 133–39 (Harvard 1996). Bernard Williams describes this process as one that culminates in the implicit understanding that an agent knows what it means to act "*on* reasons", a stance that requires a sense of reciprocity which adjudicated wrongdoers, in light of their misconduct, may be unable to manage. Bernard Williams, Ethics and the Limits of Philosophy 65 (Boston: Harvard U. Press 1985). When it comes to blaming children, the point of blaming is the hope of creating self-correcting proleptic mechanisms so that ethical behaviour becomes a part of their everyday motivational set. Lamb, *supra* at 133 (describing the process as one of "internalization"). The practice appears to be an emotionally reactive expression at conduct (including speech acts) that produce or could produce unwelcome outcomes. *See* Strawson, *supra* note 7.

with respect to our own children that when they make morally relevant choices, they possess the fundamental capacity-in-fact to make important decisions with at least a reasonable measure of prudence if not yet genuine moral sensitivity.[16] This is a central concern for us as parents and bearers of our culture.[17]

But blame attribution processes also operate when we find fault with individuals who are not our own beloved children. We assign blame to these *others* when we are persuaded that they have engaged in misconduct that we, as a society, condemn and sometimes criminalize. Attributing blameworthiness and criminal wrongdoing to someone whose lives we visit only briefly and who often live in tragic circumstances – and whose childhoods and opportunities for moral development we view incompletely, with snapshots rather than lifelong motion pictures – are qualitatively different than those in which we instruct our own children, although they too are still fully human and entitled to learn appropriate lessons. With respect to these *others*, we tend to blame far too readily and too harshly, as if they were members of a natural rival tribe. For example, when we evaluate the conduct of our own children (to whom we offer unconditional love), our mistaken judgments, because they are rendered with love, are usually forgivable; these are *our* children and, for that reason if no others, we are almost always forgiven by them. The judgments we make about others, however, should be exercised with as much attention as we direct to the evaluation of our own children because decisions about the conduct of others often culminate in harsh, lasting punishment – in lost property and liberty and the pain attendant thereto.[18]

---

16 Throughout this work, I refer to "capacity-in-fact". What I mean by the phrase is defined, in part, by its goal: to establish a richer view of human potential than the extant legal view, one that understands, for example, that deficiencies in modelling and comforting, that environmental toxins, that disturbed parenting generally suffered in early childhood can affect profoundly the person who the child becomes. *See, e.g.,* Pratibhan Reebye, *Aggression During Early Years: Infancy and Preschool*, 14 Can. J. Child and Adolescent Psychiatry Rev. 16 (2005). The view advanced here conduces to treatment and compassion, and measures cognitive and volitional capacities that acknowledge the need for a more exacting assessment of the separation of humankind from lower primates. The new definitions far exceed the current test of minimal instrumental capacity, which measures only the ability to effect a simple syllogism. *See* note 4 *supra*.

17 On the relationship between moral development and the emotions, *see* Joshua Greene, *Cognitive Neuroscience and the Structure of the Moral Mind*, in Stephen Laurence, Peter Caruthers, and Stephen Stich, 1 Innate Mind: Structure and Contents 338 (Oxford 2005) available at http://www.wjh.harvard.edu/~jgreene/Greene. *Cf.* Dascher Keltner and Jonathan Haidt, *Social Functions of Emotions*, in Tracy J. Mayne and George A. Bonnano, Emotions: Current Issues and Future Directions 192 (Guilford Press 2001) (describing the problem-solving social functions served by the emotions and synthesizing evolutionary and social constructivist theories of emotion) at http://wsrv.clas.virginia.edu/~jdh6n/publications.html.

18 For a real, often wrenching description of how the blaming process affects children adjudicated guilty of violent crimes, *see* Mark Salzman, True Notebooks (Knopf 2003) (documenting the author's two years as a creative writing teacher in a youth detention centre in Los Angeles).

This need for great care and precision also arises because our collisions with the lives of these *others* are almost always sudden, almost always unbidden, and so always epistemically incomplete; from the blamer's perspective, moreover, they are evanescent. These attributions of blame lack the loving judgments we offer our children as we teach them our norms. These *others* are usually total strangers, a substantial number of whom, owing to bad moral luck,[19] reside in a province that lies outside the reach of the learned, ethically anticipatory mechanisms we routinely teach our kids, lessons we should envelop more in love than anger. Given these prominent deficits, if the practice of blaming the many others operated as it should – *with a genuine compassion that recognizes that these others have often lived tragic lives and with the hoped-for aim of moral and ethical development* – we would blame wrongdoers if, but only if:

a. we had more nearly complete information – a time lapse portrait instead of a quickly taken Polaroid – covering the antecedent conditions and events that preceded the wrongful act, Φ, than we now seek;
b. we were certain that the wrongdoers had the capacity-in-fact and opportunities to learn the need to avoid inflicting harm on others; and
c. we were confident that we had genuinely tried to set aside our own prejudices in the process of ascribing blame.[20]

We would, in short, demand for all children that which we insist upon unwaveringly for our own. That we are not close to meeting these requirements as a matter of routine criminal justice administration (and seem sometimes to lack the will even to question the settled ways[21]) requires us to rethink the role of blaming as a practice in our criminal law.

---

19 *See, e.g.*, Thomas Nagel, *Moral Luck*, in MORTAL QUESTIONS 24, 34 (Cambridge 1979) (discussing four species of moral luck, including *consequential luck*, *constitutive luck*, *antecedent circumstances*, and luck in the *testing circumstances* one has or has not confronted); Bernard Williams, *Moral Luck*, in MORAL LUCK: PHILOSOPHICAL PAPERS, 1973–1980, 29 (Cambridge 1981) (rejecting the Kantian hypothesis that good or bad will is "unconditioned" [or] … free from external contingency"); Bernard Williams, *Moral Luck: A Postscript*, in MAKING SENSE OF HUMANITY AND OTHER PHILOSOPHICAL PAPERS, 1982–1993, at 241, 241 (Cambridge 1995). *Constitutive luck*, which speaks directly to one's personality and character, is discussed *infra* text accompanying notes.

20 For an effort to apply a Rawlsian analysis to assure a more just justice, *see* James P. Sterba, *Retributive Justice*, 5 POL. THEORY 349, 353 (1977) (arguing that the "ignorance condition [might] guarantee fair decisions among persons with conflicting interests. … [because] fairness requires that we discount our own special interests in arbitrating conflict-of-interest situations, and imagining oneself to be ignorant of those special interests has the same effect"). I have embraced this approach in other works, including *An Essay on Liberalism and Public Theology*, 14 J. LAW & RELIG. 229 (Winter 1999/2000).

21 *See, e.g.*, Michael S. Moore, *Causation and the Excuses*, 73 CAL. L. REV. 1091, 1092 (1985) (arguing that "moral responsibility for an action should be ascribed to an actor even when that action was caused by factors over which he has no control").

A Theory of Blame

One way to pursue issues of moral psychology is to examine a "psychological phenomenon, and explore its links to normative concepts and assumptions".[22] As Jay Wallace notes, "If we wish to understand morality as a normative phenomenon, we must understand the psychological states and capacities that make it possible for it to regulate people's lives in the way it aspires to do."[23] The question here is on which factors, among the many that compose blaming, does its practice connect with complex psychological states and potential capacities. This section begins with an examination of the views of Judith Jarvis Thomson, a prominent moral philosopher, and then turns to the work of several contemporary jurisprudence scholars who advance character-based theories of punishment and excuse. On the view of moral psychology explored here, an actor is "bad" if they act in ways that (a) makes their conduct more blameworthy than that of a lucky someone else whose intentions are indistinguishable but produce no harm, and (b) cause us to believe that they act in such a way as to reveal an essential deficit in their character. It then moves on to consider the merits of this general approach in light of well-replicated social science data on blaming as a social practice.

Thomson presents her approach to our understanding of blame in an essay on the effects (or not) of moral luck on issues of personal accountability. She hopes to demonstrate that bad luck concerning one's antecedent and constitutive circumstances (roughly genetic and early socio-economic conditions, respectively) does not undermine the possibility of fully warranted individual responsibility.[24] Her analysis is helpful but incomplete, and her rhetoric brings into view some of the unexamined presuppositions that guide her (and us) to the semantics and attributive patterns of blameworthiness.

Thomson offers two intention-based definitions of blame in an effort to tame the determinist beast. The first blame formulation, **BF1**, states that *a person is to blame for an action that produces an unwelcome event or state of affairs where that person caused the event or state of affairs by some wrongful act or omission for which they had no adequate excuse*. The second, alternative formulation, **BF2**, holds that *a person is to blame for doing something to a greater or lesser extent*

22 R. Jay Wallace, *Moral Psychology*, in Frank Jackson and Michael Smith (eds), The Oxford Handbook of Contemporary Philosophy (Oxford University Press) (page cites unavailable), at www.ist-socrates.berkeley.edu/~jwallace/papers/rtf/Moralpsych.rtf.

23 *Id.*

24 Judith Jarvis Thomson, *Morality and Bad Luck*, in Moral Luck 195 (ed. by Daniel Statman; SUNY 1993). In his work on moral luck, Nagel notes that we commonly assert that "[a] person can be morally responsible only for what he does." At the same time, however, we know with certainty that "what he does results from a great deal that he does not do". In the end, then, we face a paradox: The actor "is not responsible for what he is and is not responsible for". On this view, the actor seems to be morally responsible for nothing, because for much that he does he bears no responsibility – a view which seems to be normatively intolerable despite its descriptive accuracy. Nagel, *supra* note 19, at 34.

where their doing that something gives us a stronger or weaker reason to think they are a "bad" person.[25] **BF2**, unlike **BF1**, stresses the effect on the viewer and raises questions about the compatibilist construct within which Thomson operates.[26]

Thomson's goal is to account for blame in a way that acknowledges causal determinism[27] without succumbing to it. In that spirit and in an effort to situate the practice of blaming, she offers two potential accounts of a world that's causal all the way down. The first, the strong determinist thesis, ***SDT***, holds that blaming is always improper because personal responsibility is, by definition, lacking: whatever happens must happen, and thus no misconduct can bring discredit to us.[28] She also offers a weak determinist thesis, ***WDT***, according to which events over which we have no control (luck) matter, but that nothing we do in consequence thereof sheds any more discredit on us than is shed on us by our mental acts.[29] ***WDT*** rests on

---

25 *Id.* at 200–02. The undefined term *bad* is Professor Thomson's choice. She offers a variation of this first formula that focuses instead on *being the kind of person who* causes an unwelcome event instead of focusing on causation; that is, a person is to blame for *being* in a certain way that produces unwelcome outcomes rather than *causing* the same. Although this formulation puts character more clearly into focus, I do not think the differences matter for present purposes; in the absence of describing "the kind of person who" in terms that explain *why* he is "the kind of person who", in her telling "causing the kind of event which" describes the same personality and character ensemble and set of antecedent events and conditions (or states and capacities). She makes no such distinctions, however.

26 For a discussion of the distinction between "hard" determinism, according to which freedom is an illusion because *all* of our conduct is *always* determined, and "soft" determinism, according to which one can acknowledge that events have antecedent causes, but maintain nonetheless that in an important sense agents control their own mental states, even though those states are themselves causally determined, *see* P. S. Greenspan, *Behavior Control and Freedom of Action*, in MORAL RESPONSIBILITY 191, 191 n. 1 (ed. by John Martin Fischer; Cornell 1986).

27 "Causal determinism is the thesis that, for any given time, a complete statement of facts about that time, together with a complete statement of the laws of nature, entails every truth as to what happens after that time." Fischer and Ravizza, *supra* note # –, at 14 (arguing, generally, that causal determinism, whether true or not, does not subvert our common sense understanding of moral responsibility). Although one could distinguish between determinism and mechanism, Hilary Bok, FREEDOM AND RESPONSIBILITY 4 (1998), whereby determinism describes one form of mechanism, I use the two terms synonymously here.

28 The basic analytic conclusion is that if determinism is correct, then blame is always undeserved. *See generally* A. J. Ayer, *Freedom and Necessity*, in Watson, *supra* note 11, at 15.

29 With Adam Smith, who famously discussed the "irregularity of sentiments" in THE THEORY OF MORAL SENTIMENTS, *supra* note 7, at 135, Thomson subscribes to the prevailing view that we judge blameworthiness based only on intentions and not consequences. *See, e.g.*, Joel Feinberg, *Equal Punishment for Failed Attempts: Some Bad But Instructive Arguments Against It*, 37 ARIZ. L. REV. (1995); Richard Parker, *Blame, Punishment, and the Role of Result*, 21 AM. PHIL. Q. 269, 271 (1984) ("The individual is blameworthy and

the reasonably hypothesized conclusion that anytime we can imagine a person, P, intentionally Φing, which causes a bad outcome, O, we can also imagine another person, P^2, identically Φing but, for a variety of reasons, P^2 *fortunately* fails to produce a negative result, Ø.[30] Accordingly, she concludes that we should blame P for Φing (where, initially, Φing consists of backing out of the driveway without looking and thereby running over a child) but no more than we blame P^2 (who also Φed but had the good fortune that no unseen child was crossing his vehicle's path). Both acted "wrongfully" although P^2 happily avoided the bad outcome.[31]

Thomson rejects ***SDT***, which she acknowledges rightly as holding that "whatever … [P or P^2] does, the event that consists in his or her doing it ha[d] to occur" – a hard determinist position that undermines moral responsibility entirely.[32] Under this view of the world, Thomson argues, the person who deliberately kills babies for amusement suffers no discredit and no blame. She disavows this view because, in her words, "of course" the baby killer, BK, is a "bad person".[33] Thomson does not deny that luck plays a formative role in who the actor is at *t*, the theoretical

---

punishable, on my view, only for conduct itself, where conduct is construed as a combination of overt action, state of mind (including intention, knowledge, etc.) and circumstances."). *See* Sanford H. Kadish, *Forward: The Criminal Law and the Luck of the Draw*, 84 J. Crim. L & Criminology 679 (1994) (arguing that the harm doctrine, whereby punishment varies based upon the chance that harm does or does not occur, is rationally indefensible). I have taken up Professor Kadish's challenge in *A Jurisprudence for Punishing Attempts Asymmetrically*, 6 Buff. Crim. L. Rev. 951 (2003).

30 In this context, "intentional" refers broadly to our mental interactions with and about the world, not to the narrow description of statutory criminal *mens rea*. *See, e.g.*, Model Penal Code §2.02 (2) (American Law Institute 1985) (defining levels of criminal intent including negligence, recklessness, knowledge and purpose) (hereafter, cited as "MPC").

31 Although she purports to be offering Thomas Nagel's explanation of moral luck, she takes it on as her own in an effort to challenge the notion that ordinary events undermine moral responsibility. Hence she frames the challenge this way: "Take any person who is engaging in *X* caused outcome *O*. We can always imagine a second person engaged in *X*, but whose engaging in *X* did not cause an outcome of kind *O*." *Id.* at 199. The "wrongful" conclusion is, of course, not incontestable from the perspective of tort law, as the debate between Holmes and Andrews makes clear. *Compare Palsgraf v. Long Island R.R.*, 162 N.E. 99 (Ct. App. N. Y. 1928) (Holmes, J.) *with id.* at 104 (Andrews, J., dissenting).

The theory of action she describes, which accounts for our intentions and potential fault, is fairly unexceptional, although thin, as she concedes: whatever a person does is either a purely mental act, or is a causing of some outcome by some mental acts or acts – and that something can be either an act or an answerable omission. On this account of action, if one forms the intention of washing clothes in the washing machine and does so, putting the clothes in the machine was causing the clothes to get washed, which was a product of one's mental acts, among which was the intention to wash clothes. *Cf. id.* at 199.

32 Thomson, *supra* note 24, at 208.

33 Thomson, *supra* note 24, at 208 (emphasis added). She notes that ***SDT*** cannot be true "if it's taken to deny the second notion of 'blame,'" according to which we have good "*reason to think* [BK] *is a bad person*." *Id.*

moment when bad act and culpable intent converge.[34] This acknowledgment leads her to adopt ***WDT***, a weak view of determinism that permits us to measure blame by those purely mental acts that produce the misconduct or a chargeable omission. **BF2**, because it is only comparative – do we have a stronger or weaker reason to believe P is a bad person compared to P^2? – is nonetheless inadequate. Instead of addressing **BF2**'s inadequacy directly, however, she lashes the two formulations of blame to a thin concept of an adequate excuse.

Thomson accomplishes this tie-in by constructing a theoretical compatibilist link between **BF1** and **BF2**, which she labels a "connecting thesis" (***CT***). ***CT*** states that *a person is to blame for some conduct* Φ *under* **BF1** (causing an unwelcome event) *if and only if he is in some way to blame for* Φing *under* **BF2** (causing us to think he is a "bad person") *for which there is no adequate excuse.*[35] Thus the wanton baby killer, BK, is blameworthy under ***CT*** because he caused an unwelcome event that causes us to think he is a bad person, and he has no excuse for the conduct "since his [killing babies] *does* give us reason … to think him a bad person".[36]

No one doubts that BK is a "bad" person, as a matter of ordinary usage the world over. Because ordinary language reflects only our pre-evaluative, intuitive beginning, it is defeasible; and ***CT*** is not the last word.[37] Thomson's use of the descriptor, *bad*, raises at least three questions: (a) What is an acceptable definition of *adequate excuse* so that what is *bad* conduct nonetheless escapes blame? (b) Do her hypothetically inadvertent and morally indistinguishable identical wrongdoers, whose conduct provides the model for her theory of blame, really apply to brutal BK, despite their different levels of criminal intent? Most importantly for present purposes, (c) What is entailed in concluding that a person is *bad*?[38]

---

34 *See, e.g.*, *Morissette v. United States*, 342 U.S. 246, 251 (1952) ("Crime, as a compound concept, generally constituted only from concurrence of an evil-meaning mind with an evil-doing hand."). The Model Penal Code reflects the prevailing wisdom by requiring convergence of a voluntary act with the statutorily prescribed level of culpability. *See* M.P.C. §§ 2.01(1), 2.02(1). Mark Kelman, *Interpretive Construction in the Substantive Criminal Law*, 33 Stan. L. Rev. 591 (1981), has demonstrated, however, that even this bedrock requirement is subject to manipulation: the courts often expand or contract the relevant time frame for this convergence to occur as a matter of public policy. *See, e.g., People v. Watson*, 637 P.2d 279 (Cal. 1981) (affirming a conviction for second degree murder where the defendant knew several hours earlier that he would be driving his car when he left the bar); *People v. Decina*, 138 N.E. 2d 799 (N.Y. 1956) (overruling a demurrer to the charge of culpable negligent homicide where the defendant, "knowing" that he was subject to seizure disorders, chose to drive his car, lost consciousness, and caused several deaths).

35 Thomson, *supra* note 24, at 211. The "adequate excuse" condition appears to be borrowed from **BF1.**

36 *Id.* at 211–12.

37 On the place of ordinary language, *see* J.L. Austin, *A Plea for Excuses*, 57 Proc. Aristotelian Socy. 1, 11 (1956).

38 There is also a meta-ethical problem that pervades her analogy and it involves her narrow definition of moral luck, namely, that it entails *only* consequential or resultant

One response to (a) is that she leaves substantially undefined the components of an adequate excuse. She defines excuse broadly (and admittedly tentatively) as a condition or event that annuls **BF2**, conduct that causes us to label the actor "bad". Even this hasty definition is just a tautology; it tells us nothing about the wrongdoer's capacity-in-fact to control their mental state.[39] Generally, an excuse annuls the wrongdoing because the actor is, for some reason, not blameworthy: their conduct reflects some incapacity such that Φing is viewed as involuntary or unknowing or unintentional. Excuses typically speak to involuntariness, not in the sense of the absence of a bodily act, but in the sense of absence of genuine choice, which "does not accurately reveal the actor's character", and thus makes punishment unjust.[40] In the case of blaming BK, often the first issue in question should be one of capacity-in-fact, a question philosophers tend not to pursue.

Thomson's slender definition of an "adequate excuse" is not the only problem. One additional difficulty concerns her effort to construct hypothetical examples that reflect different levels of intentionality that, in turn, produce equal culpable states among her paired, hypothetical wrongdoers. The hypothetical situations she constructs as a platform for her illustrations of comparative blameworthiness are too imprecise to support her all-purpose notion of *badness*. Her hypothetical examples of wrongdoing are intended to illustrate levels of individual blameworthiness that are, from the standpoint of moral accounting, comparatively indistinguishable across the broad expanse of culpable intent. Her examples are intended to meet the demands of ***CT***. The models, however, fall short of supporting her goal; their basic impulse is far too formal.

She begins convincingly by demonstrating that the hapless motorist, P, whose Φing consists of failing to look into his rearview mirror before backing out of the drive, is neither more nor less guilty of wrongdoing than fortunate P^2, whose identical Φing luckily inflicts no harm.[41] Her approach at the inadvertence end of

---

luck; that is, events that occur after the actor engages the mental processes that produce the action. But much of the luck that concerns both Nagel and Williams, her two targets, goes well beyond consequential luck; they include antecedent luck, constitutive luck, and luck in the testing circumstances an actor might face. *See* note 5 *infra*.

39 In fairness, I do not know what Professor Thomson's thoughts are about the presumptions of sufficient capacity for control. She does not qualify her observations with this question in mind. For a helpful approach in a book length treatment, *see* Bok, *supra* note 27, at 7, 8–9 & n. 10, who offers a comprehensive theory for acknowledging free will but states at the outset that she is leaving some questions unaddressed, including the moral responsibility of the addict who continues to abuse her drug of choice, of those who act under compulsions or "powerful unconscious motives", and issues of punishment.

40 George Fletcher, *The Individualization of Excusing Conditions*, 47 S. Cal. L. Rev. 1269, 1271 (1974). For a theory of excuses tied to the issue of choice, *see generally* Sanford H. Kadish, *Excusing Crime*, 75 Cal. L. Rev. 257 (1987).

41 Thomson's hypotheticals begin as attempts to anticipate how Nagel and Williams, who believe that moral luck exists, would respond to the luck and non-luck conditions. I have simplified the examples for purposes of this discussion.

the intent continuum is well taken; we all suffer from self-condemnation and with corresponding feelings of self-blame for our negligence but usually less, in varying degrees, than it might have been had the harm unfortunately come to pass.[42] Causing pain to others does and should bring pain to us even when the act producing the harm is unintentional and non-malevolent, that is, at least inattentive or insensitive. Her argument becomes more difficult, however, when she transports a description of blameworthiness created in the context of empty-headedness to the context of baby killing; the relative blameworthiness of these two instantiations of intention is unstable. No longer are we assessing the blameworthiness of an empty or other-directed but relatively normal mind of P or P^2; with BK we are viewing the impact of a mind filled with crazed deliberations of the most motivationally repugnant and unintelligible form: pain inflicted for its own sake or, equally deplorable, without any concern at all about the harm imposed relative to some perverse immediate benefits gained.[43] Stated otherwise, when we describe a person as *bad* in the context of inadvertence, we are mostly describing the unwelcome effect of their oversight. The example she uses initially to establish ***WT*** arises in a situation where P and P^2 have the same moral and legal duties to avoid Φing: that is, to keep a careful lookout. Thus the description of their misconduct as *bad* speaks mostly to the effect of their breach of duty and not (necessarily) to their general bad characters or dispositions;[44] for there but for the grace of God go any one of us. In stark contrast, when we talk about ***BK***, we are addressing a qualitatively different species of wrongfulness.

(Thomson also offers a mid-level, apparently transitional example of bad intent – between a motorist's inadvertence and perverse baby killing – when she includes within her moral model the mental acts of two hypothetical judges, J and J^2, both equally willing to accept a bribe and undermine justice. This reflects a level of criminal intent akin to "knowledge" at least.[45] Of the two, only J is

42 This is a point Smith fully elucidated in Smith, TMS, at 134 (concluding that the "intention or affection of the heart" is all that matters to assess blameworthiness, but that in "particular cases the actual consequences which happen to proceed from any action, have a great effect upon our sentiments concerning … merit or demerit, and almost always enhance or diminish our sense of both"). I have discussed this at length in terms of the aesthetics of retribution in *Aesthetics of Retribution*, *supra* note 12 at 243–47 (surveying some of the implications of the positions of Smith and Hume on the normativity of a naturalist approach to moral philosophy).

43 *Cf.* R.A. Duff, *Choice, Character, and Criminal Liability*, 12 L. AND PHIL. 345, 348 (1993) (stating that liability for criminal negligence does not require choice unless negligence is defined in the pluperfect – she would have chosen to avoid doing Φ if she had made a choice). And that conclusion would beget a "recklessness" charge from many quarters.

44 In fact, Thomson goes to some lengths to describe P, P^2, and P^3 (also inadvertent) as generally careful drivers who were momentarily distracted. Thomson, *supra* note 24, at 196–98. Thus she established the inappropriateness of discussing a character trait of inadvertence or haste or insensitivity.

45 *See* M.P.C. §2.02 (2) (a & b) (distinguishing between conduct that is undertaken with either the *purpose* – "conscious object" – or the *knowledge* – "practical certainty" – that prohibited conduct or results will occur).

actually approached with and offered a bribe, which he accepts. Thomson argues that J^2's mental acts make him equally as culpable as J because J^2 also was willing to accept the bribe; he simply lacked the opportunity. This example of advertent, intentional wrongdoing moves her thesis closer to a general approach that supports ***CT*** than does the example of the distracted drivers, but the case of the corruptible judges also presents a different characterological matter than does the case of the gleeful baby killers. The case of J and J^2 illustrates uncommon but motivationally intelligible greed, a form culpability and a tendency many people have had to tame at one time or another.[46] The comparison with the enraptured Jeffrey Dahmer-like,[47] motivationally unintelligible butchery fails, however, because it raises all sorts of psychopathological and neurobiological issues that the conduct of J and J^2 does not implicate. Put simply, we more clearly understand J than we do BK.)

Baby killing as sport is undeniably "bad", and providing a reason for it is beyond the imaginations of most of us.[48] The baby killer causes great (if brief) pain to the deceased child, and massive theretofore inconceivable, life-changing pain to the baby's parents, families and friends. This unvarnished description of pain produces an emotional aesthetic that is often uncabinable and immeasurable.[49] But is BK "blameworthy" in the same way as are P and J? Can we even imagine what neuropsychological deficits produced this character? Here the hypothetical contexts for Thomson's formulations of blame blur important distinctions. First, unlike P and P^2 (the negligent drivers) or even the corruptible judges, J and J^2, it is difficult even to imagine a BK^2 for every BK; that is, we can only barely imagine a BK, much less BK^2, whose misconduct consists in only *attempting* to kill babies for fun; and unlike the distracted driver or the greedy judge, we cannot imagine at

46 There is also anecdotal evidence that greed-motivated crimes are more susceptible to reformation. *See, e.g., United States v. Bergman*, 416 F. Supp. 496, 500 (S.D.N.Y. 1976) (noting that brief period of incarceration for wealthy, well-educated older man who pled guilty to multiple state and federal counts of criminal non-impulsive fraud "are among the most likely to be generally deterrable") (citations omitted).

47 *See, e.g., Insanity Defense By Dahmer Fails*, N. Y. Times, Feb. 16 1992, sec. 1, part 1; col.6; *Report Documents Dahmer's Cannibalism*, U.P.I., Aug., 4, 1991; online at www.geocities.com/donnysmith.geo/dahmer.html; www.arminm.com/jeffrey_dahmer.htm.

48 In the Nicomachean Ethics, 1110a5, Aristotle noted that some conduct is simply too base to be performed no matter what the consequences. The conduct of *BK* seems to me clearly to fall into this category and so the conduct Thomson attributes to *BK* is not, it seems to me, very useful for constructing a general theory of blame that stamps out the determinist brute. Christopher Rowe, Trans., Aristotle Nicomachean Ethics 123 (Oxford 2002).

49 And so the retributive emotion that's triggered by the idea of frivolous baby killing is undeniable in its existence (even if the conduct Thomson describes is, thankfully, rare.) I take this topic up directly in *Some Thoughts on the Aesthetics of Retribution*, 17 Can. J. L. & Juris. 233 (2004). It is true that negligent killings also may evoke retributive emotions but not (ordinarily) vengeful ones; we tend to address negligent deaths through money damages rather than incarceration or worse.

all what motivates these hypothetical baby killers.[50] Second, excuses speak only indirectly to the *bad* label we place on the actor's conduct – that is, to whether we have a stronger or weaker reason to think they're a bad person. Rather, they speak to the actor's mental state, traditionally whether they were ignorant or coerced or mistaken or the like. We excuse them, in part, *because* they were not acting like themselves – they were not *in* character – or they were acting involuntarily or they lacked significant cognitive ability or suffered a significant deficit in volitional control. Short of something like an unforeseen heart attack or other genuinely involuntary act, there simply is little excuse for the inadvertent drivers, P or P^2.[51]

The same, paradoxically, cannot be said of BK. No one doubts the *badness* of BK's character or of Dahmer's or of the barbarity of their crimes, at least as a matter of common expression; and no one believes that BK or Dahmer, because of their deficits, be permitted freely to roam the streets. No feeling, caring, even marginally empathic human can harbour such a desire, much less the demand that it be gratified with such gruesomeness.[52] If that conclusion is accurate, then we should pursue a deeper question, which Thomson omits: what aberrant synergies of poor environment and faulty neurocircuitry make it possible for any actor to achieve a state of mind that produces the insatiable desire to kill precious innocent babies? So framed, to call the actor *bad* or *evil* is to say, metaphorically, that they are theologically irredeemable, a statement we cannot make about P or P^2. Thus we should ask the common-sense question: how did this person BK get *so* sick? And if we agree that BK (or Dahmer and others) are sick, what ingredient in the nature of blaming is served by blaming them? Blaming those who lack the capacity-in-fact for moral understanding is pointless, not in all instrumental senses because, as noted above, we do blame our children when we ascribe accountable fault to them for producing an unwelcome event or state of affairs. Rather, to blame BK is an empty gesture inasmuch as the point of blaming is to communicate resentment, and no communication is possible with certain people,[53] at least without an effort

---

50 Moreover, unlike the careless but fortunate driver, with whom we can all sympathize *and* advance some reproach, there is no deliberate baby killer who has the good fortune of not killing – or at least of causing grave harm to – an infant he hopes to kill, unless BK^2 is caught prior to inflicting harm.

51 It is possible that some emergency triggered a duty that trumped ordinary caution but that occurs rarely. In a legal context, under appropriate circumstances a defendant may seek a "sudden emergency" instruction, according to which the jury may find that defendant had insufficient time to exercise ordinary care. *See, e.g., Whicher v. Phinney*, 124 F.2d 929, 932–33 (1st Cir. 1942).

52 The account of reactive attitudes I describe below begins with Strawson, *supra*, note 7. For chilling portraits of psychopathic personalities, *see* R.D. Hare, Without Conscience: The Disturbing World of The Psychopaths Among Us Ch. 1 (New York: Simon and Schuster, 1993).

53 Gary Watson, *Responsibility and the Limits of Evil*, in Responsibility, Character, and the Emotions, 265 (ed. by Ferdinand Schoeman; Cambridge 1987) (hereafter, "Watson, *Responsibility*")).

at offering substantial long-term assistance. Why then do we so quickly determine *badness* without considering the conditions and events – the whole biographies, insofar as that information is available – of actors who behave badly? What conditions and events produced these wretched being?[54]

The deficiencies they experience combine unfortunate events with unfortunate conditions.[55] Reflect momentarily on the background of Andrea Yates, who suffered from a psychotic state that was induced by repeated, tragically underexamined bouts of postpartum depression;[56] or on Robert Alton Harris's, whose childhood was as devoid of love as it was occupied with hate and abuse;[57] or on Jeffrey Dahmer's, whose undiagnosed genetic defects caused him to commit totally unfathomable acts: carving, storing and cannibalizing his victims.[58] These tragic figures could

---

54 Thomson does recognize this point; she addresses it only in passing by noting that her analysis implicates deep issues of causality. Thomson, *supra* note 24, at 212–13.

55 *See* Matt Ridley, Nature via Nurture: Genes, Experience, & What Makes us Human (HarperCollins 2003) (describing that we are genetically coded to responded to environmental stimuli) [hereafter, "Nature via Nurture"]. For a survey of the neuroimaging studies of psychopathy, *see* Greene, *Cognitive Neuroscience*, *supra* note 17 6–10 (online page cites).

56 *See* Sheri L. Beinstock, *Mothers Who Kill Their Children Postpartum Psychosis*, 32 Sw. U. L. Rev. 451 (2003).

57 On Harris's life, *see* Miles Corwin, *Icy Killer's Life Steeped in Violence*, Los Angeles Times, May 16, 1982 (reprinted in Watson, *Responsibility*, *supra* note 53, at 268–71, 272–74). Corwin presents the following portrait: Harris was the product of cruelly abusive chronic alcoholic parents. His mother not only refused to permit him to make any physical contact with her ever, she blamed him, the youngest of nine children, for all her suffering. His father, never willing to accept that his youngest child Robbie was his progeny, kicked his mother in the stomach while the child was *in utero*. Later that same night the child was born and nearly died. His sister recalled that as a beautiful young child all Robbie had ever wanted was love from someone – anyone. He never received it. Twenty-five years after his rude birth, Harris brutally and senselessly murdered two young teens and then calmly ate their lunches. His fellow death row inmates were so disconcerted by Harris's demeanor that they cheered his impending death.

On the issue of environmental effects, *see* Ridley, Nature via Nurture, *supra* note 55. *See also* Antonio R. Damasio, Descartes' Error: Emotion, Reason, and the Human Brain (HarperCollins 1994) (discussing the somatic marker thesis); Joseph LeDoux's, Synaptic Self: How Our Brains Become Who We Are (2002).

58 According to one analysis, Dahmer's homicidal behaviour was "intrinsically associated with autistic spectrum psychopathology, specifically Asperger's disorder." J.A. Silva, M.M. Ferrari, and G.B. Leong, *The Case of Jeffrey Dahmer: Sexual Serial Homicide from a Neuropsychiatric Developmental Perspective*, 47 J. Forensic Sci.1347 (2002). *See also* Carey Goldberg, *Inside the Psychopath: Moving Ahead on Diagnosis and Possible Treatment*, Boston Globe, July 15, 2003 at C1 (citing a Swedish study of serial killers which concluded that psychopaths like Dahmer suffer from imbalances in the neurotransmitters, serotonin and dopamine). Both articles are available online.

not have caused their own deranged characters, at least not in an easily identifiable fashion. In fact, if we accept the determinist premise that Thomson hopes to corral, that every event has a cause and that every cause has a prior cause all the way down, the very notion of self-causation is either absurd or meaningless. Galen Strawson explains why:

> [T]o be truly deserving of ... praise or blame for our actions, ... we must be truly responsible for how we are mentally [for our intentions.] We must be genuine 'originators' of ourselves. ... But the attempt to describe how we could [possibly] be true originators of ourselves ... leads to infinite regress ... for even if one could somehow choose how to be, ... one would ... already have to have existed prior to that choice, with a certain set of preferences about how to be. But then the question would arise: where did these preferences come from? Or were they just there, unchosen preferences for which one was not responsible? And so on.[59]

Self-causation, Aristotle's hook on character and its impact, ultimately makes no sense. And still, the irregularity of our sentiments being what they are, *we* blame Yates and Harris and Dahmer and BK for acts produced by their grossly deficient dispositions. Why? Clearly, neither determinism nor indeterminism as heuristic categories provides a clear-cut answer. In fact, when we contemplate the breakdown that occurred in the lives of these individuals, we should be concerned with determining the sources of their crazy preferences. There may be no complete answers to this inquiry, but I think there are at least some good questions, including why we blame those who often lack the necessary capacity-in-fact for volitional control.

Character and the Semantics of Blame

What, then, do we mean when we say that an actor is "bad"? That they have a bad character? That they deserve our condemnation? That they should be blamed and punished for their wrongdoing? One response to these questions is that they have done an unwelcome harmful or potentially harmful act that causes us to believe they are a *bad* person – Thomson's conclusion, but it is incomplete. Many commentators go well beyond Thomson's modest proposal, which stresses a regime of normatively comparative culpability judgments, and insists that we

59 Strawson, *Consciousness, Free Will, supra* note 7, at (1989). *Accord e.g.*, Thomas Nagel, WHAT DOES IT ALL MEAN? 55–7 (Oxford 1987); Hilary Bok, FREEDOM AND RESPONSIBILITY 201 (1998) ("The supposition that we were caused to choose as we did by something other than ourselves implies that we are not free. The supposition that we caused them to occur simply pushes the problem back."); Stephen J. Morse, *The Moral Metaphysics of Causation and Results*, 88 Calif. L. Rev. 879, 881 (2000) ("No one is a prime mover unmoved.").

should punish actors only (and always) when their misconduct and subsequent bad choices reflect a defect of character.[60] The persistence of this view implies the existence of a non-controversial rule or standard of measurement. The need to temper this view is acute because for many people the conclusion that a wrongdoer is "bad" or "just bad" provides a sufficient justification not only to blame but to imprison as well: lock up defendants who have been adjudicated guilty and throw away the keys! There are at least two replies to the questions that begin this paragraph: one combines a contemporary rule-utilitarian outlook on excuses with a thin and formal Kantian view of capacity-in-fact; the other proceeds cautiously, responding to widespread semantic and social psychological phenomena entailed in our practice of blaming. I address the two responses and then take up an issue hinted at and implied throughout my critique: the paradoxical nature of evil and its relation to the regime of excusing misconduct.

A Brief Look at Jurisprudential Accounts of Character

In his NICOMACHEAN ETHICS, Aristotle maintained that individuals are responsible for their own characters because their actions establish their character.[61] Hume advanced this idea in the TREATISE to account not only for the source of our actions, but also for our reactions to the conduct of others: "Actions are by their very nature temporary and perishing; and where they proceed not from some cause in the characters and disposition of the person, who performs them, they … can neither redound to his honor, if good, nor infamy, if evil."[62] He elaborated the dispositional viewpoint with an example of homicide.

> Take any action allow'd to be vicious: Wilful murder, for instance. Examine it in all lights, and see if you can find that matter of fact, … which you call *vice*. In which-ever way you take it, you find only certain passions, motives, volitions and thoughts. There is no other matter of fact in the case. The vice entirely escapes you … till you turn your reflexion into your own breast, and find a

60 For useful surveys and critiques of character theories generally, *see* R.A. Duff, *Do We Want an Aristotelian Criminal Law?*, 6 BUFF. CRIM. L. REV. 147 (2002); Duff, *Choice, Character, and Criminal Liability*, *supra* note 43.

61 Aristotle, NICOMACHEAN ETHICS iii.5.1114a3-11 (Trans. by David Ross Oxford, 1987), maintained that by virtue of their slackardly dispositions, men are "responsible for becoming men of that kind." For a neurologically informed critique of this view, *see* Carl Elliott, THE RULES OF INSANITY: MORAL RESPONSIBILITY AND THE MENTALLY ILL OFFENDER 29–31 (Suny 1996) (noting that "in many ways we are clearly *not* responsible for our characters, at least as Aristotle implies"). *Id.* at 30.

62 David Hume, A TREATISE OF HUMAN NATURE 411 (L.A. Selby-Bigge and P.H. Nidditch (eds); Oxford 2nd ed. 1978). On Hume's particular brand of utilitarian thinking, *see* Paul Russell, *Hume on Responsibility and Punishment*, 20 CAN. J. PHILOS. 539 (1990).

sentiment of disapprobation, which arises in you, toward this action. It lies in yourself, not in the object.[63]

Hume's view is that we disapprove of BK's conduct not because it is vicious; rather, we identify the conduct as vicious because, in turning to our own dispositions (our "breasts"), we disapprove of it.[64] Morality, according to the Humean view, resides in us, in our characters and dispositions – a view with which I largely concur. [65] Emotions, on this view, seem to propel normativity as much as cognition does. Such a determination seems generally correct and would be rationally and morally unimpeachable if all who are judged "bad" possessed control-in-fact over their characters.[66]

In his frequently cited work, *A Utilitarian Theory of Excuses*, Richard Brandt follows this Humean line, arguing for a rule-utilitarian theory of excuses according to which moral demerit is judged by the following dictum:[67] "An agent is morally blameworthy … for an act if, and to the degree that, the moral code the currency of which in that society would maximize utility would condemn … him for it."[68] Condemnation is appropriate, on this view, whenever the actor

---

63 *Id.* at 468–69.

64 Christine M. Korsgaard, The Sources of Normativity 50 (Cambridge 1996).

65 This claim is, of course, just the opposite of Kant's, who argued that free will is a necessary condition for moral responsibility. *See* Kant's Groundwork, *supra* note 6.

66 *See* Keltner and Haidt, *Social Functions of Emotions*, in Emotions: Current Issues and Future Directions *supra* note # – (presenting an insightful synthesis of primordial and socially constructed views of how and why our emotions function as they do).

67 On rule-utilitarian thought, *see* John Rawls, *Rule Utilitarianism*, in Philosophical Perspectives on Punishment 82 (ed. by Gertrude Ezorsky State University of N. Y. Press 1972) (originally published as *Two Concepts of Rules*, 44 Philos. Rev. 3 (1955) (distinguishing between justifications for the practice of punishment generally, and particular applications, and defending utilitarianism as an explanation for moral judgments thereunder); John Rawls, *Legal Obligation and the Duty of Fair Play*, in Law and Philosophy: A Symposium 3, 9–10 (N.Y.U. Press 1964) (defining the duty of fair play as a scheme in which everyone benefits by mutual social cooperation and in which everyone or nearly everyone accepts certain restrictions on liberty to enjoy the benefit which is, in a sense, free, that is, the situation is unstable to the extent that one person knows that he can fail to cooperate but still enjoy the benefit).

68 Richard B. Brandt, *A Utilitarian Theory of Excuses*, 78 Philos. Rev. 337, 354 (1969) (emphasis in the original). Although I believe that the debate between character and choice theorists is substantially overinflated, *see, e.g.*, Duff, *Choice, Character, and Criminal Liability*, *supra* note 43, I am assuming that character is a relevant factor in the search for blame, especially when the issue of excusing misconduct arises. *See, e.g.*, M.P.C., cmt. to §2.04, at 275 (noting that the excuse of mistake of law applies when the "act charged is consistent with the entire law-abidingness of the actor"); *id.* §210.3, at 55 (stating that provocation acknowledges that "one who kills in response to certain provoking events should be regarded as demonstrating a significantly different character deficiency than one who kills in their absence").

lacks an internalized motivational system that should produce appropriate feelings of guilt or shame or dishonour in response to conduct that violates the existing preference maximizing moral code, absent a traditional assessment of excuse. Motivation is key: an agent's conduct is excusable if, but only if, "an objectively wrong action (or an action in some way out of order) ... *does not manifest some defect of character*."[69] Brandt's description of character, which he distinguishes from a "trait of personality",[70] is terse; it is some internal quality that goes beyond a mere trait to include more or less permanent dispositions, so that for Brandt the crucial moral question is whether or not people *would* be "trained to be motivated, and to feel, in certain ways about certain things, namely, to have an aversion to breaking a promise, to feel guilty about doing so," that is, to act according to utility-maximizing rules of conduct. Implicit in this approach is the Aristotelian–Humean belief that the explanation for conduct reflecting character is internal to the actor and their desires, even if not fully within their control. On Brandt's view, "a defect of character is, or includes, a defect of motivation."[71] Presumably this means that the actor *could* have learned appropriate conduct but failed to do so because they lacked the appropriate motivational reinforcement. (In fact, whether any particular individual *could* be so trained, in the sense that they have adequate capacities-in-fact for cognition and volitional control and have had the opportunity to learn same, is not an issue on which Brandt opines.[72]

---

69 Brandt, *supra* note 68, at 354 (emphasis added).

70 *Id.*

71 Brandt, *supra* note 68, at 355 (emphasis added). Brandt's survey of excusing conditions is fairly typical except insofar as he presses the motivational button: "All the considerations traditionally recognized as exculpating excuses are ones evidencing adequate motivation – or at least showing absence of evidence of inadequate motivation." *Id.* at 357. Notably absent is serious consideration of volitional deficits or how they are acquired. In fact, his understanding of a motivational defect begs the question how it came about: "For part of what it is to *blame* a person is to impute a *defect* to him – and a defect is a dispositional feature of him, an incapacity or deleterious tendency." *Id.* at 385 (emphasis in the original).

72 Part of my critique of Brandt's view is a reaction to its neurobiological naivete. No serious neuroscience scholar doubts that genetic endowment, for example, plays a substantial role in the construction of personality. *See, e.g.* David Wasserman and Robert Wachbroit, *Introduction: Methods, Meaning, and Morals*, in Genetics and Criminal Behavior 1, 12–13 (ed. by David Wasserman and Robert Wachbroit: Cambridge 2001); Kenneth Taylor, *On the Explanatory Limits of Behavioral Genetics*, in Genetics and Criminal Behavior, *supra* at 117, 125–26 (summarizing data that suggest that some criminality reflects defects in an individual's "basic cognitive or affective architecture", citing B. Maughan, *Childhood Precursors of Aggressive Offending in Personality-Disordered Adults* in S. Hodgins, Mental Disorder and Crime (1993) (noting that while only 7% of the general population suffers from antisocial personality disorder, 45% of a population of convicted violent felons so suffer)); M. Virkkunnen and M. Linnoila, *Serotonin in Personality Disorders with Habitual Violence and Impulsivity* in Hodgins, *supra* (linking habitual aggressive behaviour with reduced serotonin levels); and J. Volavka, D. Martell, and A. Convit, *Psychobiology of the*

I suspect, though, that the dual requirements of capacity-in-fact do not present him with a forbidding hurdle.[73])

Working in a similar vein, Norvin Richards dismisses the importance of constitutive luck on our assessments of human conduct.[74] (Constitutive luck describes the conventional understanding that our "inclinations, capacities, and temperament" – those relatively permanent qualities that go some distance towards composing us – are to some immeasurable extent outside our control.[75]) Along with Brandt, Richards argues that such factors would count as exculpating only "if one's character is *to no extent* one's own artefact. But if the individual makes *any contribution whatever* to the sort of person he is, that contribution can be the basis of his deserving ... blame for what he does."[76] Although he concedes that bad luck may play some role in determining one's character, he defends the idea that we can also make wrong *choices*, and it is the "*wrong* part" of human conduct that he wants to take "seriously".[77]

Richards's explicit proposition – that excuses are proper only if our character is "*to no extent*" of our own making and are inappropriate, therefore, if one's character makes *any contribution whatsoever* to one's own authorship – raises at least three separate but related questions that intrude directly upon our judgments about blameworthiness and criminality. The questions implicate (a) the ontological proposition that we are to some extent the authors of our own lives; and (b) the

Violent Offender, 7 J. Forensic Sci. 237 (1992) (suggesting that reduced serotonin follows from a genetic mutation)). Yet it is precisely these developments that our jurisprudence is just now beginning to take any cognizance of.

73 Brandt, *supra* note 68, at 351–52, states that excuses entail societal costs insofar as the wrongdoer or potential wrongdoer believes that the clever lawyer will help them use the excuse to avoid incarceration. At the same time, he expressly acknowledges the role of learning as a condition for motivational propriety.

74 Norvin Richards, *Luck and Desert*, 95 Mind 198 (1986).

75 Thomas Nagel, *Moral Luck*, *supra* note 24, at 38.

76 Richards, *supra* note 74, at 202 (emphasis in the original).

77 *Id.* (emphasis added). George Fletcher's approach to excuses indicates similar views, although his final account is unclear. Stated in summary form, Fletcher contends that because punishment is justified only if measured in terms of desert, where desert is a measure of character, we are required to make a judgment about the actor's character whenever we adjudicate the propriety of excusing certain conduct. George Fletcher, Rethinking Criminal Law §10.3.2, at 800 (1978). The points of view taken here are akin to, if not instantiations of, what Professor Susan Wolf describes as the "deep-seated view" of the free self, according to which we are responsible for our actions not only because they are intentional, but also because they are necessary reflections of a will that expresses our deep-seated character traits. Susan Wolf, *Sanity and the Metaphysics of Responsibility*, in Responsibility, Character, and the Emotions, *supra* note 70, at 46, 47–50 (discussing the work of Harry Frankfurt, Gary Watson and Charles Taylor). As Wolf points out, these positions, like those discussed above, leave open the question: "Who, or what, is responsible for this deeper self?" *Id.* at 51 (concluding that the ability to step back and contemplate our own actions, the standard reply, is insufficient).

epistemologically informed metaethical/ethical questions of (i) whether we possess the tools to *recognize* correctly those features over which we do and do not have authorial control, and (ii), if so, whether we can accurately *attribute* particular instances of misconduct to those circumstances over which we have such control and, thereafter, impose justifiable penalties on account of that over which we do exert control.[78] Richards does not, of course, advocate that we separate out these strands; he assumes authorship implicitly, thereby pretermitting very difficult questions of capacity. But simply to clarify, much less disentangle the polycentric issues embedded within the phrases "*to no extent*" or "*makes any contribution whatever*" illustrates the difficulties with this position.[79] Thus the notion of "any control", Richards's bottom line, cuts too wide a swath. For while I readily accept the "authorial" premise (a) as given, I do so but only when an agent has sufficient cognitive capacity and sufficient opportunities to develop a mature conscience. I cannot embrace propositions (b)(i) or (b)(ii) because recognizing those features for which we bear genuine individual responsibility is far more difficult than the Brandt–Richards position allows, a point that I pursue shortly. The question thus remains: how much control does one have over one's own character?

All of the basic questions raised by this view of character rest on the problematic assumption that all those wrongdoers whom the law deems sane and competent – BK, Yates, Harris, Dahmer and the like – have both control over their character and that character in general is relatively stable over time.[80] Although the latter

78 Perhaps Professor Richards meant no such thing. Perhaps he has or would recommend issues related to cub-pathological capacity deficits be dealt with at sentencing. *See, e.g.,* §5K.2.13, SENTENCING GUIDELINES MANUAL (permitting a departure for "significantly reduced mental capacity," provided, *inter alia*, that the offence charged is non-violent). If that is the case, then, we must (at the very least) reappraise the propriety of the assumptions in our fairly non-discretionary Sentencing Guidelines. *See, e.g.,* Thomas W. Hutchison, David Yellen, Deborah Young, and Matthew R. Kipp, FEDERAL SENTENCING LAW AND PRACTISE, ch. 5, pt. H (St. Paul: West, 1999) (excluding from consideration the conditions in which wrongdoers, through accidents of birth alone, are raised and receive – or do not receive – a moral education). At worst, we must ask if he hasn't buried issues related to the presumption that we can genuinely ascribe moral responsibility more deeply and less rationally than it is presently.

79 The idea of law as reflecting polycentric phenomena was introduced to law by Lon L. Fuller, THE MORALITY OF LAW (New Haven: Yale University Press 1969).

80 *Cf.* Elkhonon Goldberg, THE EXECUTIVE BRAIN: FRONTAL LOBES AND THE CIVILIZED MIND 150 (Oxford, 2001) (suggesting that data from neuroscience require a "new legal construct of 'inability to guide one's behavior despite the availability of requisite knowledge' may be needed to capture the peculiar relationship between frontal lobe dysfunction and the potential for criminal behavior"). *See id.* at 108–09 (describing a phenomenon characterized by the "non-pathological diminution of the ability to form a [common sense] theory of the mind," i.e., the inability to sense how others are reacting internally to us as reflecting "normal variability" in frontal lobe functioning). For a thoughtful legal perspective on this issue as it informs criminal law, *see* Terry A. Maroney, *Law and Emotion: A Proposed*

point is vigorously contested,[81] assume for now that individual moral development goes through something like Kohlbergian stages and becomes more or less fixed at some point in time with respect to at least some areas of conduct.[82] Even if this is correct, the point overlooks (or dismisses as unimportant) an incontrovertible fact: who we are at *t*, the moment of wrongdoing on which we focus for rendering moral and legal accounts, is a function of all the antecedent influences whose impact on the decision made at *t* are certain, albeit not fully discernible.[83] Nor will it do to claim, as many do, that because determinism is universal and affects all of us, it can be dismissed from the moral and jurisprudential compass.[84] For now, suffice it to say that "universal", as in causal theories of behaviour, is not the same as "uniform". And how to address the lack of uniformity is *the* legal issue. (That "We are all created equal" is, of course, a social construct albeit a necessary one.) We are each affected uniquely – some for better (and some much better), some for worse

Taxonomy of an Emerging Field, 28 L. & Human Behav. (2006), available at http:// papers.ssrn.com/sol3/papers.cfm?abstract_id=726864.

81 *See* John M. Darley and Thomas P. Shultz, *Moral Rules: Their Content and Acquisition*, 41 Annu. Rev. Psychol. 525, 541–45 (1990) (discussing research on how children learn moral rules); Yoram Shachar, *The Fortuitous Gap in Law and Morality*, 6 Crim. Just. Ethics 12, 24 (1987) (surveying Piaget's work among others and speculating that "human morality, once autonomously developed and formed, remains so in *some* areas of conduct, while other authorities replace parental authority in other areas and create in the human mind the same subservient nonautonomous opinion which is a mere reflection of external manifestations of attitude by such authorities"). As Daniel Goleman, Emotional Intelligence xiii (1995) notes, "the neurological data suggest [the existence of] a window of opportunity for shaping our children's emotional habits."

82 *See, e.g.*, Lawrence Kohlberg, *Stages of Moral Development* (1971) at http://www.xenodochy.org/ex/lists/moraldev.html.

83 Bernard Williams makes this point about the instability of character judgments made at, or in reference to, a fixed point in time, in terms of the criteria needed to make such a determination:

> [W]hat one does and the sort of life one leads condition one's later desires and judgments. The standpoint of that retrospective judge who will be my later self will be the product of my earlier choices. So there is no set of preferences both fixed and relevant, relative to which the various fillings of my life-space can be compared. If the fillings are to be evaluated by reference to what I variously … want, the relevant preferences are not fixed, while if they are to be evaluated by what I now … want, this will give a fixed set of preferences, but one that is not necessarily relevant.

Bernard Williams, *Moral Luck*, in Moral Luck: Philosophical Papers, 1973–1980, 29 (Cambridge 1981) (rejecting, generally, the Kantian hypothesis that good or bad will is "unconditioned" [or] … free from external contingency").

84 *See, e. g.*, Moore, *Causation and the Excuses*, *supra* note 21, at 1092 (arguing that "moral responsibility for an action should be ascribed to an actor even when that action was caused by factors over which he has no control"); Morse, *Moral Metaphysics*, *supra* note 59, at 886.

(and some much worse).[85] This brute existential fact challenges our conception of freedom because the conventional wisdom posits that free actions "should not be determined by antecedent conditions and should be fully explained only intentionally, in terms of justifying reasons and purposes".[86] Yet antecedent events and conditions obviously *do* matter greatly, and everyone knows it; our observations and well-nurtured intuitions shout out this basic understanding routinely.[87] Even our discourse about character and personality betrays the incompleteness of our current understanding of blameworthiness, an incompleteness in its expressions and judgments and, ultimately, in its practical wisdom.

The Abbreviated Semantics of Character

Perhaps it is not surprising that character theorists tend not to define character with great rigour.[88] It is a wobbly term, the contours of which are just now giving way to serious study. So, like the late United States Supreme Court Justice Potter Stewart, they assume that they recognize the impact of character when they see it,[89] and they know it for certain that they have seen it when it produces an unwelcome outcome; that is to say, character theorists tend to reason in a *post hoc ergo propter hoc* manner.[90] The task of attributing blame based on misconduct that reflects the bad content of one's character is, it turns out, a tricky business, as likely to reveal those cognitive biases of the observer as it is the bad character of the actor. In

85 This is a basic fact of our genes and neurobiology. *See, e.g.*, Ridley, *supra* note 55; Damasio, *supra* note 57.

86 Nagel, The View From Nowhere *supra* note 2, at 115. *See also* Thomas Nagel, What Does It All Mean?, *supra* note 37, at 51.

87 Even our ordinary, everyday usage underscores this fact. We routinely talk to our friends and neighbours across fences – and without ever second-guessing ourselves (a human quality of mixed virtue) – about our genetic make-ups, including our likenesses to Mom or Dad ("like father, like son," "the acorn never falls far from the tree," and so on), to our sisters or brothers, and the variations nature has carved out among our siblings. On the importance of family selection studies, *see, e.g.,* Robert Plonim, Nature and Nurture: An Introduction to Human Behavioral Genetics 38–41 (Pacific Grove, Cal: Brooks/Cole Publ. Co. 1990).

88 *See, e.g.,* Richards, *supra* note 74, at 200 (defining character as a person's "set of preferences, in so far as these are relatively stable over time").

89 *Jacobellis v. Ohio*, 378 U. S. 184, 197 (1964) (declining to define the term "obscenity," but noting that "I know it when I see it.") (Stewart, J., concurring).

90 Brandt, for example, fully discusses character as a factor in making moral assessments, but gives short shrift to its definition by declaring that it reflects "relatively enduring response tendenc[ies]" revealed in contexts rife with moral implications. Richard Brandt, Ethical Theory 466 (Prentice Hall 1959). Note that this "definition" moves backwards from effect to cause; it follows from a purported unwelcome effect to the assumption of bad character as its cause. For a generally sympathetic (but not fully convinced) view of Brandt's theory, *see* Andrew E. Lelling, *A Psychological Critique of Character-Based Theories of Criminal Excuse*, 49 Syracuse L. Rev. 35, 47–59 (1998).

this section, I look first at the complex nature of describing fully one's character. Thereafter I report on the empirical data from the social psychology of bias that accompanies attributions of blame.

The search for an individual's bad character commonly appears in our folk psychological usages as familiar shorthand expressions that serve as proxies for rich descriptions of complex human behaviour. This idiomatic simplicity meets *our* immediate needs to release anger, define blame, evoke shame and (too often) move on. We use naive terms to describe one's "character" – such as "sweet" or "shy" or "considerate" or "clumsy" or "surly" or "vicious" or "bad" – when we want to say something about the observed actor's apparent intentions sufficiently general so that we then can use our own experiences and imaginations to fill in the epistemic gaps in our attributions of character. That is, we use familiar metaphors in lieu of fully informed psychological explanations. These semantic shortcuts serve us well enough in everyday conversation, but they fall well short as accurate descriptions and thus fail to meet our goal as a compassionate, justice-seeking community.

The semantic case is made in part by Adam Morton, who notes that the function of conceptions of character in psychological explanation is "to block, qualify, or emphasize the connection between beliefs and desires that an explanation appeals to and the actions it explains".[91] We use general descriptions of character traits that reveal *some* relatively common patterns of observation relevant to the peculiarities of different incidents. In this partially informed way, our common metaphors permit the attributor to avoid describing character in adequate behavioural terms. The simple explanation for this process is that fully described behavioural states always seem too complex and difficult for an immediate account. So terms like "brutal" or "vicious"or "angry" or "short-tempered" or "bad" generally truncate discussions about the compound states that actually generate behaviour. Instead, we find quick, familiar (apparently visible) connections between complex internal states and the actions we observe. We use distancing "character" terms in lieu of dealing with the "person" of the accused.

In a general though still incomplete way, we follow this condensed approach because the "ultimate perfect character term," *T,* for describing one's character would go something like this:

> A set of states *S* and the term [*T*] would jointly hold only when one of a defining range of actions was performed, and given an action there would be a set of combinations of *S* and [*T*] which account for it.[92]

---

91 Most of the discussion in this section is based on Adam Morton, *Character and the Emotions*, in EXPLAINING EMOTIONS 153, 155 (ed. by Amélie O. Rorty; Cal 1980). Doubtless Morton would disagree with some of my conclusions.

92 *Id.* at 156.

Something close to *T*, a more accurate (if not perfect) character description, requires that we describe these *states* with care, as the products of unique world experiences that emerge from details far greater than can be revealed by a snapshot taken at *t*. A more fully descriptive term or phrase would encompass a substantial record of the various states that produced this unique person: the *events*, *conditions* (including not least genetic endowment, significant early trauma[93] and so on) and, as importantly, the *opportunities* to trigger appropriate responsive "states". Acting together, these are the circumstances that generate one's "character", and it is critical to note that the environment – each individual's *own* peculiar environment – incites genetic change and neuronal growth and death in a process of constant self-origination.[94] We are, in crucial part, a reflection of our genetic adaptation to our unique environments.

A more fully reported *S*, therefore, would include analyses of both intentional behaviours and their related neurobiological adaptive processes.[95] An *S* that

---

93 On the potentially severe effects on development due to early childhood rejection and abuse, *see, e.g.,* Dorothy Lewis, *From Abuse to Violence: Psychophysiological Consequences of Maltreatment*, 32 J. Am. Acad. Child Adolescent Psychiatry 221 (1993) (noting nearly 15 years ago that "[a]lthough violence does not invariably beget violence, there is abundant evidence that a history of maltreatment is often associated with aggressive behaviors") (citation omitted); Adrian Raine et. al., *High Rates of Violence, Crime, Academic Problems, and Behavioral Problems in Males with both Early Neuromotor Deficits and Unstable Family Environments*, 53 Arch. Gen. Psychiatry 544 (1996). *See generally* Avshalom Caspi et al., *Role of Genotype in the Cycle of Violence in Maltreated Children*, 297 Science 851(2002) (finding a neurotransmitter that suggests an explanation for why some abused children escape the moral deficits that often follows childhood abuse).

94 The point here is that whereas some genes guarantee that the overwhelming majority of individuals are born with all and only the right parts in the right places, other genes have different functions. "The function of many genes is … to switch other genes on or off. And the susceptibility of a gene to be switched on or off depends on the sensitivity of its promoters," that is, on a species of genetic material that facilitates the production of proteins when other genetic materials ("transcription factors") attach themselves. Ridley, Nature via Nurture, *supra* note 55, 31. What causes such genes to switch other genes on or off? Put simply, the environment, defined broadly in terms of the unique, non-genetic experiences each individual encounters. An individual's *S* (or motivational set) includes at least one's "desires, evaluations, attitudes, projects, and so on". Williams, *Internal Reasons, supra* note 40 at 35. Thus, describing the composition of a *state* is itself a complex task. *Cf.* David C. Rowe and Kristen C. Jacobsen, *In the Mainstream: Research in Behavioral Genetics* 23–4, in Ronald A. Carson and Mark A. Rothman, Behavioral Genetics: The Clash of Culture and Biology (Johns Hopkins 1999) (describing *state dependence* as part of a developmental model according to which "past behavior affects future behavior", such that the commission of a crime increases the likelihood of future criminality). I discuss this in considerably more detail in *On the Potential of Neuroscience: A Comment on Greene and Cohen's For the Law, Neuroscience Changes Nothing and Everything*," http://law.bepress.com/expresso/eps/844 (posted 10/28/05).

95 *See* Allan Gibbard, *Genetic Plans, Genetic Differences, and Violence: Some Chief Possibilities*, in Wasserman and Wachbroit, Genetics and Criminal Behavior, *supra* note

genuinely incorporates the antecedent circumstances affecting character development over time – the individual's person – would reveal a complicated, interconnected network of traits, but it is a process over which we should seek maximum understanding in the context of criminal culpability because doing so will yield policies and decisions that embrace genuine compassion and move towards greater safety over time.[96] The *T* that more fully describes one's characters and so reflects an appreciation for an individual's intentions is undoubtedly complex, but it is no more complex than are the basic ideas of fairness and justice. Again, what is remarkable (mind-boggling, really) about this debate is that *no one* seriously doubts the influences of such antecedent events and conditions on the development of character as a matter of observation and common intuition; it is only as a matter of our penal law and its expectations that we disregard these insights. Taking cognizance of these facts in our criminal justice system demands far more honesty than it now exhibits and much more goodwill than our politics currently allow.

Instead of using more precise compound descriptions, which requires an expanded narrative of life – a sensitive inquiry into the adaptations that the actor's environment required for survival – we substitute "fixed patterns of explanation in terms of beliefs, desires, and other well-behaved states", which move us in this direction but stop well short of accuracy, thereby encouraging us freely to fill in the epistemological chasms in light of patterns of character attributions we

---

72, at 177–78 (noting the theoretical deficiencies of folk psychological explanations of causal relations).

96 *See* Joshua Greene and Jonathan Cohen, *For the Law, Neuroscience Changes Nothing and Everything*, 359 Phil. Trans. Soc. Lond. 1775–85 (2004).

It is true that if the jurisprudence of excuses were taken to its logical conclusion, it reasonably could produce an environment in which all intelligible rationales for misconduct would produce an excuse, and that this environment is normatively unacceptable, at least without changing that jurisprudence. *See* Michael S. Moore, *Causation and the Excuses*, 73 Cal. L. Rev. 1091, 1094 (1985) ("If one accepts the determinist thesis that all events, including all human behavior, are caused, and if one believes that causation excuses, then one must believe that moral responsibility is an illusion on which liability to criminal punishment cannot be built."). So our jurisprudence concerning punishment and incarceration needs to be debated once again. "Punishment" and "incarceration" can be achieved more humanely with noun substitutes, like "treatment", where both normatively and descriptively appropriate, in lieu of the current punishment default, and "incapacitation" when the risk of future dangerousness so requires.

This would be a daunting task if the prosecution were required to bear the burden of proof on "treatability", and if, failing to carry that burden, required a not "guilty" verdict. "Treatability", for example, asks whether the defendant is more likely to achieve a more law-abiding status as a person undergoing extensive counselling and education than he is to emerge (if ever) as a hardened career criminal. We should strive to measure such tendencies with the best available medical and psychological standards and rules. I address the neurobiological basis of the measurement problem at length in *Blaming Angry Men, supra*, mss in the author's possession.

have already assimilated.[97] What we require, if we hope to find and reinforce the wrongdoers' redemptive features, is the ability "to capture in one's ascriptions of character the *reasons* why this particular person, at this time, is moved by these motives".[98] Sadly, we do not, in general, follow this course in our substantive law. The complexities always seem too great. Instead, Morton points out, "we invent a labyrinth of character terms interacting in their effects and stratified in complicated ways, to capture more and more of the particularity of people."[99]

Within the highly cropped terms we use to describe character are patterns of conduct that we attribute to the bad character of wrongdoers in light of *our* collective aspirations, which may or may not be accurate in light of *their* relative capacities-in-fact. In everyday matters, it seems "implausible and inaccurate to explain an inappropriate attitude by attributing a belief or desire that would rationalize it, because the apparently anomalous emotion is embedded in a system of … inappropriate attitudes or false beliefs".[100] To assess these inappropriate (and often criminal) systemic attitudes with greater precision enjoins us to trace an individual's causal history, and an apparent problem with this prescription is determining the biographical starting point. For a full explanation one has to go all the way back "to explain the prepropositional but intentional habits of salience, organization, and interpretation. It is these which, through later intervening beliefs and attitudes – many of them false and inappropriate – explain the conservation of emotions,"[101] that is, the persistence of evidently inappropriate and disadvantageous emotional (and thus behavioural) states.[102] We might call these phenomena maladaptations.[103]

---

97 Morton, *supra* note 91, at 156. On the systemic biases we bring to the attribution of blame, *see infra* text accompanying notes 91.

98 Morton, *supra* note 91, at 156. One apparent exception to this point is the nascent defence of diminished capacity. *See, e.g., United States v. Brawner*, 471 F.2d 969 (D.C. Cir. 1972) (approving the admissibility of evidence of reduced mental capacity for the purpose of showing that the defendant was incapable of forming the requisite intent). One wonders, however, why a separate doctrine is required to address what is primarily an evidentiary issue. *See* M. P. C. § 4.02, at 219.

99 Morton, *supra* note 91, at 156.

100 Amélie O. Rorty, *Explaining Emotions*, in Explaining Emotions, *supra* note 100, at 103, 104.

101 *Id.* at 103 (seeking to explain the "unexpected conservation of emotions", that is, why people fail to change their emotional commitments when circumstances seem to warrant it).

102 For a description of how such an evaluation might be made, *see* Gibbard, *supra* note 95, at 188–92.

103 Some of the most creative work in this area has been done by Owen D. Jones. *See, e.g., Time-Shifted Rationality and the Law of Law's Leverage: Behavioral Economics Meets Behavioral Biology*, 95 Nw. L. Rev. 1141 (2001); *On the Nature of Norms: Biology, Morality and the Disruption of Order,* 98 Mich. L. Rev. 2072 (2000); *Evolutionary Analysis in Law: An Introduction and Application to Child Abuse*, 75 N. C. L. Rev. 1117, 1200–04 (1997).

The Troubling Nature of Blame Attribution

Unfortunately, the problem that *is* the everyday use of incomplete semantic descriptions of character in criminal law only begins to state the profound problems with blaming. In order to factor in the many variables that would produce a more complete understanding of one's character, we must first cross another hurdle on the road to an accurate assessment of blameworthiness: namely, overcoming our own biases in the construction of blame attribution, a difficulty which, if overcome, could produce a reconfiguration of the order of proof on issues such as basic competency.[104] Cognitive social psychologists use the phrase "fundamental attribution error" (FAE) to describe a well-studied phenomenon that reflects the existence of common biases in our attributions of wrongdoing: there is a significant likelihood that in any instantiation of our ordinary assessments of wrongdoing we significantly overattribute negative outcomes to character and disposition of the actors rather than the situations in which they find themselves. In this section, I briefly explain attribution theory (AT) and describe the biases that inhere in the process, i.e., FAE. In the following section, I describe how these biases operate pervasively to produce socially undesirable (even counterproductive) results in the domain of punishment.

AT describes how ordinary individuals explain causation, the *whys* of human conduct that we routinely question: why did this human act occur? When an actor performs an act that produces an unwelcome event, Φ, the observer often wants to know whether Φing occurred because of something within the actor – that is, was it "dispositional"? – or whether it occurred because of something within the actor's environment – that is, was it "situational"?[105] AT evaluates the assessment procedure of ordinary individuals – jurors and judges, for example. Fritz Heider, the Gestalt psychologist who developed the theory, described his approach to AT as "naive psychology" because it addresses how the person-in-the-street explains observed behaviour.[106] Heider maintained that individuals account for the conduct of others based on the observer's own beliefs, whether those beliefs validly describe

104 Because we use second order "avoidance" techniques to ascribe blame when doing so appears to be consistent with our world views, *see, e.g.,* Lawrence M. Solan, *Cognitive Foundations of the Impulse to Blame*, 68 BROOKLYN L. REV. 1003, 1004–05 (2003), we might need to rethink our default tests of competency and modifications to the burden of proof to counteract these tendencies.

105 These phenomena are sometimes referred to as "internal attribution", which examines the causative forces internal to the actor that contribute to *X* doing Φ; and "external attribution", which examines the causative forces external to the actor that contribute to *X* doing Φ. Taken to their extremes, the former assigns only internal motivators to *X* doing Φ, and the latter assigns only external motivators to *X* doing Φ. Attribution Theory (I): Fundamentals, at www.psyc.abdn.ac.uuk/homedir/amilne/Social.

106 Attribution Theory, http://hsc.uusf.edu/~kmbrown/Attribution_Theory-overview.htm.

the actor's conduct or not.[107] The "alert perceiver" makes inferences about another person's intentions and dispositions based on their observations; the inferences drawn are deemed to be "correspondent" when the observed behaviour and the inferred disposition can be assigned similar labels.[108] For example, the observer might conclude that because Mr. *X* did an act, Φ, that they, the observer, views as mean-spirited (or kind), Mr. *X* is viewed as a mean-spirited (or kind) person, one who Φs. Observers seek correspondence between their predilections and the conduct they observe.

But is the observer's naive psychological assessment of character correct? The answer is resounding and unsettling: usually not. To begin with, attributing misconduct to an individual's disposition or character raises the familiar problem of free will: the observer assumes that the actor being blamed enjoyed freedom of choice: he could have done otherwise.[109] The more difficult the action observed, moreover, the more likely the observer is to attribute it to free choice. For example, although it is probably not easy to split someone's skull in half with a ball pean hammer, an observer provided with little or no information before deciding whether a severe head injury resulted from accidental or intentional conduct is more likely to attribute the injury to an actor's bad character (or disposition) and the choices emanating therefrom than to the situation.[110] This tendency to overascribe harm to disposition is a constant phenomenon, and so there is a consistent "fundamental attribution error" running through the process: we tend to underestimate situational influences and overestimate dispositional influences on behaviour.[111]

---

107 For a still useful summary of Heider's early work in Gestalt theory, *see* Morton Deutsch and Robert M. Krauss, THEORIES IN SOCIAL PSYCHOLOGY 29–36 (Basic Book 1965). According to Heider, "the attribution of personal responsibility involves a decision as to which of several conditions of action – the intentions of the person, personal power, or environmental factors – is to be given primary weight for the actual outcome. In general, the more the environmental factors are thought to influence the action, the less the person is held responsible for an action with which he is connected." *Id.* at 32.

108 Attribution Theory, *supra* note 105 (attributing the phrase "alert perceiver" to disciples of Heider, E.E. Jones and K.E. Davis).

109 There are at least two aspects to "free will", although neither is sufficient to explain free will. The first is *freedom of action*, the second is *freedom of choice*. Freedom of action speaks to capacity: an actor could lack free will simply because they lack a certain capacity to act freely. For example, a person with profound cerebral palsy lacks the capacity to undertake certain freely chosen activities, like playing basketball or serving as a stenographer. Freedom of choice, in contrast, speaks to opportunity. A person may have the evident capacity to choose, but lack the opportunity at the relevant time. *See* John Martin Fischer, *Introduction: Responsibility and Freedom*, in John Martin Fischer, ed., MORAL RESPONSIBILITY 9, 10–15 (Cornell 1986).

110 *Cf.* Em Griffin, A FIRST LOOK AT COMMUNICATION THEORY (McGraw-hill, 2d ed. 1994).

111 *Id.* (quoting Lee Ross, *The Intuitive Psychologist and His Short-Comings: Distortions in the Attribution Process*, 10 ADVANCES IN EXPERIMENTAL PSYCHOL. 184 (1977)

When we attribute blame and responsibility to an individual for Φing, which invariably results from a number of substantial causative factors, we tend to "cite the cause for which an actor is most blameworthy, that is, we search for the cause containing the most indelible stain" on the actor's character.[112] It is certainly not clear why this tendency to point and attribute fault to character has evolved and with what rewards and anguish, but it is an omnipresent feature of the blaming practice.[113] Nor is it entirely clear what to do about this tendency beyond the good that might come from honestly recognizing it. That something must be done, however, follows from the obvious fact that this systemic tendency does not reflect our more compassionate natures, and it does not produce a safer society.

Professor Mark Alicke has demonstrated this dispositional preference in an artfully designed study that asked subjects to review one of several experimental narratives that ended with the exact same bad outcome. Alicke asked subjects ("observers") to evaluate the identical conduct of four individuals. The motives of the individuals involved in the narratives varied from favourable to benign to culpable; their motives, however, were relevant only to when the harm occurred, and not to its material causation. Despite the absence of this causal relevancy, the subject-observers significantly attributed fault to the actors whose motives for action were perceived as more blameworthy (less worthwhile) than to those actors whose motives were neutral or favourable. To reiterate, the observers made the negative character attributions notwithstanding the fact that motivation was causally unrelated to the unwelcome outcomes.[114]

(page cite omitted). It is also worth noting that FAE is more prominent when we judge others than it is when we judge ourselves. *See, e.g., Focus on Attribution Theory*, at www.ua1vm.ua.edu/~droskos/Attribution%20theory/sld002.htm.

112 Mark D. Alicke, *Culpable Causation*, 63 J. PERSONALITY & SOC. PSYCHOL. 368, 369 (1992) (describing the "stain theory" of Joel Feinberg, *Sua Culpa*, in Feinberg (ed.) DOING AND DESERVING: ESSAYS IN THE THEORY OF RESPONSIBILITY 187 (Princeton 1970)).

113 It might be that we use blame to channel retributive urges that many people cannot control. Nonetheless we understand intuitively that at the soul of retribution is anger and the potentially vicious conduct it can generate. *See Some Thoughts on the Aesthetics of Retribution*, note 42 *supra*.

114 For example, in one experimental setting, a driver (D1) was exceeding the speed limit (driving 40 mph in a 30 mph zone) when hit an oil slick on the road (or failed to see a stop sign that was covered by a tree branch, or was faultlessly unable to brake his car. As a result, he hit a car travelling in the opposite direction; the "other" driver (D2) suffered multiple cuts, a broken collar bone and a fractured arm. Observers were then told that the accident occurred in one of four contexts: as D1 (a) was rushing home to celebrate his anniversary; (b) was rushing home to hide a vial of cocaine he had left in the open at his parent's home; or (c) was trying to avoid D2 who had run through a stop sign. The study showed that causation was attributed to D1 as a function of his motive, and that D1 was more likely to be held responsible (and pay enhanced damages) depending on the negative circumstances in which the accident occurred. As Alicke noted, "in the socially undesirable motive condition [the desire to hide cocaine], the focal actor [D1] was … cited more frequently as a cause than any

There are several ways to explain and cabin these and similar findings, and none is necessarily exclusive of any (or all) others for they can be synthesized based on existing research data. Fincham and Schultz, for example, advance an "entailment model" to explain FAE. According to their basic rationale, the tendency to blame (in general) occurs whenever observers discover some causal link between the actor and the harm inflicted. Importantly, *that* causal linkage is sufficient to impose retributive punishment on these actors, because the observer's attribution of causal control establishes not only the necessary evidential link between the actor and the harm inflicted; it also serves in the process of justifying punishment.[115]

Weiner moves the explanation further along with his identification of a "stage theory", according to which our assessments of responsibility generally move in stages from "an evaluation of personal and impersonal causation (based on an analysis of intent) and considers the extent to which the actor controlled the harmful outcomes and [then to] whether mitigating circumstances exist[]."[116] Weiner provides empirical support for a basic assumption that is formally embedded (if not always actually honoured[117]) in our law: a direct relationship between levels of criminal intent and desert. According to a third theory, described as a "sequential stage model", observers typically move "into sequential stages of causal attribution, responsibility attribution, and finally blame", where blame is broken down further into moral responsibility (knowing, voluntary action) modified (when appropriate) by an excuse or justification.[118]

---

other factor, even when [D2] was clearly negligent in running through the stop sign." Alicke, *Culpable Causation, supra*, note 114, at 369–70. For similar findings *see* F.D. Fincham and T.R. Shultz, *Attribution of Responsibility: From Man the Scientist to Man as Lawyer*, in 13 Advances in Experimental Social psychology 81 (L. Berkowitz, ed., 1981).

115 Mark D. Alicke, *Culpable Control and the Psychology of Blame*, 126 Psychol. Bull. 556, 557 (2000) (describing Fincham and Shultz, *Attribution of Responsibility: From Man the Scientist to Man as Lawyer, supra* note # –) (hereafter, "*Culpable Control*"). Put otherwise, "a judgment of blameworthiness presupposes a judgment of causation." Kathleen M. McGraw, *Conditions for Assigning Blame: The Impact of Necessity and Sufficiency*, 26 Brit. J. Soc. Psychol. 109, 114 (1987); *accord* John M. Darley and Thomas R. Schultz, *Moral Rules: Their Content and Acquisition*, 41 Annual. Rev. Psychol. 525, 531 (1990). This does not mean, however, that judgments of causation, blame and punishment are identical – only that they are closely interrelated.

116 Alicke, *Culpable Control, supra* note 115, at 557 (summarizing B. Weiner, Judgments of Responsibility: A Foundation for a Theory of Social Conduct (NY: Guilford Press 1995)).

117 For a useful work that ties FAE to the doctrinal anomalies of felony murder, to the attempt/completed crime asymmetry in punishment, and to its effect on different theories of punishment that defy the formal principle of grading, *see* Donald A. Dripps, *Fundamental Retribution Error: Criminal Justice and the Social Psychology of Blame*, 56 Vand. L. Rev. 1383 (2003).

118 Alicke, *Culpable Control, supra* note 115, at 557 (discussing the work of K.G. Shaver, The Attribution of blame; Causality, Responsibility, and Blameworthiness (NY: Springer-Verlag 1985)).

Alicke's contribution to this line of research is an extension of sequential stage theory called the "culpable control model". This work adds two dimensions to the earlier research. First, it provides empirical support for the presence of a strong spontaneous affective component in the process of attributing blame. Second, it adds a "blame-validation" component, where evidential and motivational biases are deployed to validate the prior spontaneous ascriptions of blame. "Because cognitive shortcomings and motivational biases are endemic to blame," Alicke writes, "a psychological treatment of this model requires a model in which personal expectations and emotional reactions are central components."[119] This affective/emotional component nourishes the three interrelated elements of personal control assessment: "mental states, behaviors, and consequences", where the mental element encompasses intentions, the behavioural element includes acts and culpable omissions, and the consequences include both immediate and extended attributions.[120]

Alicke's model assumes that observers "deliberately and consciously" assess the links between (1) choice and conduct, (2) the actor's apparent impact and the harmful outcome, and (3) their desire for and anticipation of the unwelcome consequences: all staples of criminal law. The novelty he contributes from the perspective of criminal law – and what puts him in the camp with those who study FAE – is his demonstration that individual observer judgments are influenced by "relatively unconscious, spontaneous evaluations" in the assessment of each of the three elements. "Spontaneous evaluations are affective [emotionally induced] reactions to the harmful event and the people involved."[121] They are driven by two sources: the information the observer possesses about the actor's "intentions, behaviors, or the consequences they produce", and "extra-evidential factors" such as the actor's reputation and social status.[122]

What is of central concern here is the finding that our attribution biases are nearly universal and difficult to eradicate: the construction of blame follows from the perception of inappropriate motivation, even when motivation is irrelevant to the cause of harm. This tendency continues to plague us even when observers attempt to validate their initial spontaneous attributions of blame, which occurs when the stress of observation is lowered and the blame attributors (presumably) make their assessments more soberly; that is to say, when the rational analysis model would predict better judgment, observers still review the evidence of

---

119 Alicke, *Culpable Control*, *supra* note 115, at 557.

120 *Id.* Griffin, *supra* note 110, describes a similar three-part process of attribution, including perception of action, judgment of intention and attribution of intention. This approach to determinations of blameworthiness goes back at least to Smith, TMS, at 133.

121 Alicke, *Culpable Control*, *supra* note 115, at 558; *accord* Bargh and Chartrand, *supra* note # –, at 465 ("The idea that social perception is a largely automated psychological phenomenon is now widely accepted."). *See generally* Russell H. Fazio, David M. Sanbonmatsu, Martha C. Powell and Frank R. Kardes, *On the Automatic ActivatiPon of Attitudes*, 50 J. PERSONALITY AND SOC. PSYCHOL. 229 (1986).

122 Alicke, *Culpable Control*, *supra* note 115, at 558.

linkage from intention to behaviour to consequences in the same biased manner.[123] Alicke's work indicates that observers continually exaggerate the actor's volitional control over unwelcome outcomes either "by lowering their evidential standards for blame or by seeking information to support their blame attribution bias".[124]

This phenomenon is reflected in our tendency to overimpute causal control to human agency, namely, in FAE.[125] As a result of blame-validation processing, "observers are inclined to blame the actor or actors who arouse the most negative affect or whose behavior confirms unfavorable expectations".[126] The upshot is that "expectations and affective reactions [are] conflated with assessments of personal control".[127] Because of these deep-seated, non-idiosyncratic reactions, we tend to alter our judgments of blameworthiness, generally assessing more blame on the putative wrongdoer than the context requires. This tendency to construct blame as reactions to perceived agential motivation and control is significant and significantly harmful.

Why FAE Matters

The price we pay for a practice of blame assessment that overattributes wrongdoing to character is the subject of an important recent article by Garth Williams. Williams notes that our current culture of blaming generates three counterproductive features that undermine the potential benefits our punishment regime might produce for our culture generally and wrongdoers specifically. Each of the three costs arises by virtue of the unwillingness of the blamer (or observer, which includes all of us individually and collectively, and not least jurors and judges) to confront the complexities that underlie our attributions of blame and responsibility.[128]

---

123 *Id.* On rational analysis, *see* Robert Nozick, THE NATURE OF RATIONALITY 74 (Princeton 1993) (stating that the "rational person will try to be aware of whether the reasons she has are a biased indicator of truth and will accordingly shape her estimate of the truth from the reasons she has. If she judges her reasons to be unrepresentative in some particular direction, she will correct for this.").

124 Alicke, *Culpable Control*, *supra* note 115, at 558. The phenomenon I'm elucidating here is an instantiation of cognitive dissonance. I have examined this well-researched human reaction in a legal context in *The Third Best Choice: An Essay on Law and History*, 41 HASTINGS L.J. 537 (1990).

125 The factors involved in assessing causal and volitional control vary as a function of the observer's perception of whether (and to what extent) the actor's conduct is seen as willful and purposive as opposed to accidental: the greater the perception of purpose, the greater the assessment of volitional control. Issues of personal control also vary as a function of assessments of individual capacity and situational constraints, roughly corresponding to cognitive capacity (diminished capacity, for example) and justifications and excuses. Alicke, *Culpable Control*, *supra* note 115, at 559–61.

126 *Id.*

127 *Id.*

128 Garth Williams, *Blame and Responsibility*, 6 ETHICAL THEORY AND PRACTICE 427 (2003). And, of course, the crabbed, binary understanding of capacity-in-fact often

The first negative effect attributable to overemphasizing the individual's character is a tendency to demonize the actor. By failing to consider adequately the situational factors in which wrongdoing occurs, we come to hold unwarranted beliefs concerning the truth value of our assumptions about what an actor *could have done other than* Φing, engaging in wrongdoing.[129] The result of this inclination threatens to focus all of our attention on the actor's dispositions and intentions and, in so doing, yields a *practice* that simply does not serve our long-term goal of making our neighbourhoods safer places. By focusing on the actor's character, observers (Williams call them "finger-pointers") leave us with few opportunities to offer constructive help. (This might explain politicians' disdain for reformative practices; politicians generally want to present themselves as not just tough on crime but the opposite of "them".[130]) The wrongdoer is too often reduced to a label: "just the kind of person who Φs", a designation that transforms the actor in the observer's consciousness into someone who regularly acts inappropriately if not invariably criminally. After describing the culprit in such hopeless terms, the alternatives left to the many finger-pointers among us concerning the actor's future are narrow and gravitate towards "manipulation", which could be broadly or narrowly conceived and is always prone to moving towards "outright coercion", thus running the gamut from a slap on the wrist to death by gas or electrocution or lethal injection.[131]

Designating the wrongdoer as "*just the kind of person who*" shows the troubling metaphysical problem discussed previously: it threatens to render absurd our legal culture's nearly irrebuttable presumption of free will, at least in many instances. It is not strictly a violation of the law of non-contradiction to use this offputting characterological description *and* simultaneously to avow that the wrongdoer commands free will, but it is at least puzzling and troubling.[132] Williams elaborates:

---

disables fact-finders even from considering (at least formally) the effects of substandard non-pathological cognitive and volitional deficiencies.

129 *Id.* at 432; McGraw, *supra* note 115, at 115. Alicke also considers the effect of counterfactual reasoning and attributions of control, noting that if the harmful outcome would have occurred independent of the actor's causal contribution, the perception of "effective causal control" is reduced but [as he shows] ... not eliminated. Alicke, *Culpable Control*, *supra* note 115, at 561. This assessment appears to occur in two stages: first, the observer contemplates how the harmful outcome could have been avoided. Next, he accords causal priority to causal events that could have been avoided and uses that priority as a basis for attributing blame. *See* Neal J. Roese, *Counterfactual Thinking*, 121 Psychol. Rev. 133 (1997).

130 Even so-called "moderate" to "liberal" politicians embrace "get tough" policies when it comes to discussions of punishment in election politics. *See, e.g., The Cost of the Incarceration Boom: Correction Expenditures Rise, While Programs and Oversight Are Cut*, at http://home.comcast.net/~lwva/Harshba.htm (quoting former Massachusetts Governor William Weld stating that "prison should be like a tour through the circles of hell").

131 *See id.* at 434–35.

132 The law of non-contradiction holds that propositions *p* and *not-p* cannot both be true. *See* David Wiggins, *Towards a Reasonable Libertarianism*, in Essays on Freedom of Action 48 (ed. by Ted Honderich (1973) (quoted in Bok, *supra* note 27, at 69).

> [I]t is somewhat odd to say that the culprit "*just does that sort of thing*" (dispositional attribution) and also freely, that is, *deliberately*, chose to act in that undesirable way. These are only consistent, and this is not at all coincidental, if we picture a more or less demonic agent, one who chooses wrong for wrong's sake.[133]

Stated otherwise, the overemphasis of dispositional blaming tends to transform wrongdoers into creatures like Melville's Claggert, the personification of pure evil. The likes of Claggert, Melville wrote, are capable of:

> apprehending the good [they possess theoretical reasoning], but [are] powerless to *be* it [they lack full-throated practical reasoning]; a nature like [Claggert's] surcharged with energy as such natures almost invariably are, what recourse is left to it but to recoil upon itself and like the scorpion for which the Creator alone is responsible, act out to the end the part allotted to it.[134]

This view runs counter to a significant feature of our moral and theological values – compassion.

This distancing, which is constitutive of a fundamental attribution error, produces the second cost of FAE, "tunnel vision": a narrowing of the perspective we bring to bear on our judgments about the actor. Overattributing unwelcome outcomes to the actor's character or disposition devolves into a refusal to take cognizance of the other's perspective, which (in turn) undermines the wrongdoer's ability to receive honest constructive criticism.[135] What is important is that blaming usually reflects an emotionally laden reactive attitude that accents our negative view of the actor to the detriment of situational considerations, and its narrowing tendency makes clear a point this chapter began with: blaming is a complex social process in which all of us, actors and observers alike, are engaged and about which we must continuously ask questions. As such, it requires that we give to it its own commanding attention; we do not focus only on what appears to lie behind Φ because the process generates contradictions that appear not to serve us well. Nor can we simply "lock 'em up and throw away the keys", as our overlapping retributive inclinations would often have us do.[136]

The affective/emotional aspect of FAE clarifies that rather than merely assessing and responding to the many Φs of wrongdoing, we as observers and finger-pointers discharge our own emotions towards the actor; blaming reflects the internal mental states that we project onto an external reality. Another negative outcome of this

---

133 Williams, *supra* note 128, at 435 (first emphasis added).

134 Herman Melville, BILLY BUDD 39 (Signet ed. 1998).

135 *Id.* at 436–37.

136 *See, e.g.*, Markus Dirk Dubber, *Recidivist Statutes as Arational Punishment*, 43 BUFF. L. REV. 689 (1995) (concluding that "three strike" statutes were passed and remain on the books despite the absence of a logical nexus between the punishment and its legitimate purposes).

practice is one that Joel Feinberg has described: we indelibly stain the wrongdoer by ratcheting up our disapproval, which rarely produces a beneficial encounter between blamer and actor.[137] At the same time and possibly more damning still, we suffer the tendency of reducing assessments of the wrongdoer's conduct to naive, oversimplified truth claims about their character, which are reflected in our abbreviated semantics. The production of tunnel vision permits the blamer to dismiss the wrongdoer's perspective and (worse, I think) to search for an audience with which we can share our self-certain truth about the wrongdoer.[138] The actor whose conduct we deplore – and whom we should hope to reform for the better – is now emotionally and actually forsaken.[139]

The third cost of FAE reveals the final act in the blaming process: the abandonment of an individual based on their bad character. This appears in part as the familiar practice of scapegoating, which succeeds emotionally (if not rationally[140]) when we target a wrongdoer's character based on the simplified, biased and other-directed stories of wrongdoing we routinely tell ourselves.[141] The most troubling aspect of this destructive and unintended interpersonal process is that it provides us with licence to deny our own responsibility in the wider web of relationships of which we and our targets are a part. The other becomes an *"it," – just the sort of person who*; we are excused as a part of our social epistemology (what we take as a "usual, normal and invisible" part of membership in our community[142]); and we license ourselves to deny the "co-responsibility and contingency" in our lives and engage in a very troubling sort of moral accounting. When we blame without accounting as fully as we reasonably can for the "complex history of involvement in the events before, during, and after the 'blameworthy' deed", we lose sight of the

137 *See* note 112 *supra*.

138 Williams, *supra* note 128, at 437. As Williams notes, the certainty of truth makes the actor's misdeeds all the more unthinkable to the observer who purports not merely to have an accurate picture of the reproved; they have a sufficient picture to condemn them with little if any appreciation for their perspective. "The speaker addresses the world, but refuses to engage with its realities: by what right, then, does he speak at all?" *Id.* at 438.

139 For a dated but still helpful survey of early research on the variables that affect the biases in the social observer assessments *see* Gary Marks and Norman Miller, *Ten Years of Research on the False-Consensus Effect: An Empirical and Theoretical Review*, 102 Psychol. Bull. 72 (1987).

140 Understanding that "rationality" is itself a construct, here I'm opting for a definition that includes some measurable and enduring capacity for empathy, which includes some sense of what Rawls describes as "reasonable principles ... – those that regulate how a plurality of agents ... are to conduct themselves in their relations with one another. Principles of fairness or justice that define the fair terms of cooperation are standard examples. So are principles associated with the moral virtues recognized by common sense: truthfulness, fidelity, and so on." Rawls, Lectures, *supra* note # – at 47.

141 Williams, *supra* note 128, at 439.

142 For a rich description of how this process operates, *see* Allen Buchanan, *Political Liberalism and Social Epistemology,* 32 Phil. & Pub. Aff. 96 (2004).

good and loving use of blaming. This denial of biographical narrative (of the need to determine *who* this person is from a broader perspective) and the corresponding dismissal of co-responsibility becomes suspicious, I think, in direct proportion to the self-righteous certainty one brings to the process.[143]

Blaming as a social practice is deeply and too often tragically flawed; it fails to acknowledge an inalienable truth: that unaccountable contingencies mediate all inputs and outcomes in significant ways. As a result, compassion fails; we tend to assess the wrong committed based on the need to determine guilt in a simplified, biased culpability assessment according to which every unwelcome outcome is equated with or projected onto an appropriately "guilty" individual. (This may account in part for the reluctance of many theorists to acknowledge the existence of moral luck.[144] It demands a willingness to invest substantial personal energy to fight against deeply ingrained retributive urges.[145]) When we engage in the process of hypothesizing the wrongdoer's intentions in a moral audit to which we bring our own biases, we empower ourselves to disregard the fact that we bear some responsibility for the conditions that undermine for many the possibility of developing normatively appropriate practical reasoning skills.[146] When we disregard our own responsibility for the creation or continuation of the kinds of antecedent conditions and events that produce inappropriate conduct, we heap blame on the individual alone. But determinations of guilt are not simple matters of matching intentions with misconduct on a scale of comparative adversity,[147] something like Thomson's connecting thesis, ***CT***. It may be that this simplistic accounting of moral matching works at one level of attribution and of retribution – finding *a* causal agent and discharging the feeling of release among others[148] – but that it fails to chronicle faithfully the myriad contingencies that "inhere between will and deed, between character and situation, between choice and result".[149] We often opt for some reductive form of condemnation: We foist all such unwelcome contingencies on the individual, label them *bad*, and hope to be done with them.

143 *See* Williams, *supra* note 128, at 439.

144 Among the many theorists who reject either the concept or importance of moral luck are Jeremy Horder, *Criminal Law: Between Determinism, Liberalism, and Criminal Justice*, 49 CURRENT L. PROBS. 159 (1996); Kadish, *Forward: The Criminal Law and the Luck of the Draw*, *supra* note # –; Moore, *Causation and the Excuses*, *supra* note 21, at 1092 (acknowledging the pressure of determinist forces but arguing that "moral responsibility for an action should be ascribed to an actor even when that action was caused by factors over which he has no control"); Morse, *The Moral Metaphysics of Causation*, *supra* note 21, at 883–86.

145 *See* Greene *supra* note 96.

146 *See* John L. Hill, (Note) *Freedom, Determinism and the Externalization of Responsibility in the Law: A Philosophical Analysis*, 76 GEO. L. J. 2045, 2059 (1988).

147 Williams, *supra* note 128, at 439.

148 *See* my *Some Thoughts on the Aesthetics of Retribution*, *supra* note 42 *passim*.

149 Williams, *supra* note 128, 441. For a description of the multiple levels of moral attribution in criminal law, *see* George Fletcher, BASIC CONCEPTS OF CRIMINAL LAW 82–4 (Oxford 1998).

In light of the costs associated with FAE, it is at least appropriate to ask *who* the audience is for such unforgiving attributions of blame, *why* we choose this or that audience, and *what* we hope to accomplish on their behalf and ours when we engage in a process that so distances *us* (the good guys) and *them* (the bad ones) in a Whig culture committed to the idea of human progress and improvement. Among the systemic issues this flawed approach embodies is the failure to acknowledge that if God had thrown the dice just one more time, the culprit being blamed *might* have been you or me.[150] On such matters as our genetic makeup and the socio-economic conditions into which we are born, for example, we have only good or bad fortune, and more or less of it. We certainly know that the world today is not always a just place, and we know that current notions of objectivity often are nothing more than yesterday's enlightened standards and tomorrow's *ancien regime*. We cannot claim widespread intersubjective normative agreement sufficient to inflict pain on all those wrongdoers who fail to meet our prescriptive standards if we neglect to reconsider the actual facts that inform normativity and, in the process, honour our obligation to appreciate all the players in a contingent world as best we can. Blaming – and especially the process that transports our biases into legal practice – discounts the need for accurate appraisal prior to blaming, and assumes a justness that simply does not exist in fact.[151]

Confronting the Paradox of Evil

Accounting for the destructive features of blaming will advance our pursuit of a more accurate determination of desert; the process requires great care in combining situational and dispositional factors without bias – a daunting task. As Amélie Rorty suggests, the task often requires that we go "all the way back".[152] This retrieval process is not simply a matter of deciding *whether* an unsavoury actor caused (even in a substantial way) an unwelcome event with sufficient cognitive capacity to attribute to them "knowledge" of its wrongfulness; or of finding the putatively applicable statutory *mens rea* mirrored in our reconstructed vision of the wrongdoer's brain at or attributably near *t*;[153] or, conversely, of determining whether some hyperpathology demands an excuse.[154] Rather, we also must commit to determining as best we can *how* they got to be that way; for without an answer to the *how* question, we have no hope of preventing the rush of what seems to be

150 *Cf.* Watson, *Responsibility*, *supra* note 53, at 276-77 (ultimately rejecting the "throw of the dice" metaphor but acknowledging the sensation).

151 *See* Williams, *supra* note 128, at 442–43.

152 *See* text accompanying note 100 *supra*.

153 Fletcher, Basic Concepts, *supra* note 149, at 82.

154 Under the Model Penal Code, for example, an actor's cognitive process must have completely decomposed; he is (without differentiation) deemed insane, if he "believes he is squeezing lemons as he chokes his wife." M.P.C. to § 4.01, at 166.

an unending supply of wrongdoers. This approach implicates a far richer view of both the potential and reality of human nature than settled jurisprudential doctrine recognizes, and it imposes attendant costs. The practical difficulty with this suggestion is that it also produces an unsettling paradox:

> The more egregious one's misconduct, the more likely he is to be damaged; the more likely he is to be damaged, the more likely he is to cause an unwelcome outcome, the more likely he is to cause an unwelcome outcome based on that damage, the more likely he is to take advantage of an excuse; and the more likely he is to take advantage of an excuse, the more likely he is to avoid suffering the full penalties the law prescribes, which are themselves based on our collected folk wisdom.

To the extent, therefore, that excuses are viewed as beneficial, because they permit the wrongdoer to escape some quantum of punishment, any proposal that might increase the availability of excuses might produce perverse incentives to engage in the misconduct.[155]

This result would present a very serious problem if accounting for wrongdoing accurately was not consistent with our moral and theological commitments to compassion, and if the only alternative to the default recipe of imprisonment was permitting dangerous actors to roam the streets. But retributive imprisonment cannot be the only alternative; civil commitment, or some more humane middle-way, must exist as an alternative to imprisonment. Civil commitment is one potential alternative but it, too, depends on the goodwill of the entire system, from top to bottom.[156] But there's a deeper problem as well, and it concerns our razor-thin understanding of the propriety of blame. This understanding ought to evoke some emotional tension.

Using the biographical highlights of the psychopath, Robert Alton Harris, as his test case, Gary Watson describes the source of a basic, intuition-based, moral conflict:

---

155 I thank the participants at a Washington University Law School faculty research programme, where I first presented some of these ideas, for pointing out this potential problem.

156 Foucault has described the layers of authority that must be brought on board to achieve any such revamping:

> Small-scale legal systems and parallel judges have multiplied around the principal judgment: psychiatric or psychological experts, magistrates concerned with the implementation of sentences, educationalists, members of the prison service, all fragment the legal power to punish. … [A]s soon as the penalties and the security measures defined by the court are not absolutely determined, from the moment they may be modified along the way, … one is handing over to [these individuals] mechanisms of legal punishment to be used at their discretion.

Michel Foucault, Discipline & Punish: The Birth of the Prison 21 (Trans. by Alan Sheridan; New York: Vintage Books, 1978). That this is an undoubtedly daunting task cannot provide an excuse to forgo it.

"To be homicidally hateful and callous in Harris's way [to eat the lunch of the innocent teen he has just brutally and senselessly killed] is to lack moral concern to an extent that comes as close to *entirely* as one can, and to so lack moral concern is to be incapacitated for moral community."[157] This explanation, which is clearly consistent with one fork in the stream that our moral intuitions follow, potentially exempts every hateful and callous criminal from moral disapprobation; and these exemptions might seem to arise more or less independently of any particular wrongdoer's unique background. But in the case of Harris we know he had a hideous, loveless and brutalizing background.[158] In the case of Andrea Yates, we know she had suffered severe depressive conditions that erupted more than once into full-blown psychotic episodes following childbirth. The conduct of Jeffrey Dahmer can be explained only as the manifestation of a catastrophic genetic defect: the taste for human flesh is well beyond the comprehension of individual intentions that any of us can imagine. Logically, he could not have caused his own desire to cannibalize his unsuspecting victims; only grave neurobiological imperfections and environmental catalysts can explain this desire.[159] Some form of incapacitation, therefore, is obviously necessary and appropriate in some cases beyond any reasonable doubt.

The facts bearing on lack of capacity-in-fact and environmental opportunities represent a fundamental conundrum for the metaphysics that undergird our jurisprudence of punishment.[160] For example, compatibilists justify punishment within a determinist world.[161] For utilitarian compatibilists, what matters is that

---

157 Watson, *supra* note 53, at 274. What to do with psychopaths has evoked a variety of reactions from health care specialists, philosophers and jurisprudence scholars. The premier researchers in this area of psychology are Hervey Cleckley, THE MASK OF SANITY (5th ed. 1988), and more recently Robert D. Hare. *See, e.g.,* Robert D. Hare and Michael J. Quinn, *Psychopathy and Autonomic Conditioning*, 77 J. ABNORMAL PSYCHOL. 223, 224 (1971), who suggests that psychopaths commit approximately 50% of all major crimes. R.D. Hare, WITHOUT CONSCIENCE: THE DISTURBING WORLD OF THE PSYCHOPATHS AMONG US 87 (Simon and Schuster, 1993). On Hare's contribution to our understanding of psychopathy, *see, e.g.,* Ian Pitchford, *The Origins of Violence: Is Psychopathy an Adaptation?,* available online at http://human-nature.com/nibbs/01/psychopathy.html. *See also* Elliott, *supra* note # –, at Ch. 5 (concluding that some of their misconduct is blameworthy despite acknowledging their lack of volitional control); Walter Glannon, *Psychopathy and Responsibility*, 14 J. APPLIED PHILOS. 263, 268 (1997) (noting that psychopaths lack the capacity to reason prudentially, which is a necessary condition for assessing one's long-term interests; Stephen J. Morse, *Rationality and Responsibility*, 74 S. CAL. L. REV. 251, 254 (2000) (stating that if "the emotional capacity for empathy" is deemed to be part of rationality, then psychopaths would not be considered rational; and concluding that psychopaths *are* "morally irrational" and thus should be excused).

158 *See* note 157 supra.

159 The extent to which our genes are triggered and destroyed by the actual events in our lives is the subject of Ridley, *supra* note 55.

160 *See* note 80 *supra.*

161 H.L.A. Hart, *Legal Responsibility and Excuses*, in PUNISHMENT AND RESPONSIBILITY 28, 44 (Oxford 1968).

holding people responsible for their actions has efficacy in regulating behaviour.[162] For others within this school, what matters is that blaming expresses and confirms community resentment.[163] In both cases the sought-after penal goal is achieved whether or not the conditions of epistemologically informed, full moral assessment are met. To the question – "Here we are today; what should we do now?" – different answers appear. For the regulator or expressivist, the answer is, "How he got to the point of blameworthy misconduct makes no difference."[164] For incompatibilists and hard determinists,[165] in contrast, Harris's biography seems to prove their case: his background, if only in retrospect, seemed to doom him; for if we view him as the mechanistic product of an egregious childhood, we cannot hold him responsible. (This does not necessarily mean that Harris *had* to turn out as he did; his siblings did not become vile, hateful killers, although they did have different genetic make-ups.[166]) Given the level of abuse he suffered and what we know about the potential effects of abuse, and given Yates' history of postpartum psychotic depressive episodes, our intelligible reactions to such cases ought to be and often is, "No wonder they turned out that way."[167]

Our ability to appreciate their emotionally and physically challenged backgrounds should cause us to react with appropriate moral uncertainty. We see their capacities for brutality and respond to them as the killers they are: they have inflicted unimaginable pain and suffering on wholly undeserving victims. But we also should see them as tragic figures caught within the web of uncontrollable antecedent events and conditions that trapped them within brutal lives, and so we sense that they too are victims. How many children suffer such a total absence of love and cruelty as did Harris and thrive as "normal"? Of Harris's crimes Watson writes, "Our sympathy toward the boy he was is at odds with the outrage toward the man he is."[168] We obviously have good cause to fear him and to fear his kind of violence, at least absent substantial successful treatment; and we have reason to require, as necessary, a long period of confinement (and even

162 *See* Richard W. Burgh, *Do the Guilty Deserve Punishment*, 79 J. Philos.193, 194 (1982) (noting that there is a belief among utilitarians that "the greater good of punishment serves to mandate compliance with rules").

163 *See, e.g.,* Joel Feinberg, The Moral Limits of the Criminal Law: Harmless Wrongdoing 149 (Oxford 1990) (stating that the relevance of moral blameworthiness "derives from its correspondence to an essential function of legal punishment which, as a symbolic device for expressing public reprobation, automatically stigmatizes the condemned offender").

164 *See* Watson, *supra* note 53, at 274.

165 A useful discussion of the distinctions among compatibilists and determinists is found in P.S. Greenspan, *Behavior Control and Freedom of Action*, in Moral Responsibility 191, 191 n. 1 (ed. John Martin Fischer; Cornell 1986).

166 On the suspicion that a certain genotype may explain why some children who suffer abusive childhoods become criminals and others do not, *see* Caspi et al., note 93 *supra*.

167 *See* Watson, *supra* note 53, at 275.

168 *Id.*

indefinite incapacitation, provided adequate process).[169] But we should also be conflicted. Harris's formative years were inflicted on him without any choice; at the same time, he "unambivalently endorse[d] suffering, death, and destruction, and that is what (one form of) evil is."[170] Following the birth of her firstborn, Yates suffered from a debilitating depressive episode through no fault of her own, and yet she viciously killed all her children. That we can understand these actions as predictable responses to horrifying conditions suggests both the fragility of our moral judgments and the need for compassion.

On Coping With Our Irregular Sentiments

This chapter began by noting that the urge to blame is an original emotional sentiment. In his classic treatise, THE THEORY OF MORAL SENTIMENTS, Adam Smith observed that our judgments about blameworthiness (and praiseworthiness) hinge on three elements: (a) the *intent* with which an action is done, (b) the *action* that the intention produces, and (c) the good or bad *consequences* that follow from the action.[171] He argued that elements (b) and (c) – acts and consequences – were logically unrelated to our assessments of blame.[172] Smith was presaging later "subjectivist" theorists who contend that harm should not be relevant to assessing blame:[173] the consequences, Smith opined, are "indifferent either to praise or blame". He concludes that (a) – the "intention or affection of the heart" – is all that matters; and asserts strongly that this "maxim … [reflects] self evident justice."[174]

Smith was a utilitarian.[175] He might have disparaged the retributive urge centuries ago as unnecessary idealism. Instead, he explained the salience of harmful consequences and our tendency to respond thereto with blame:

169 By this I mean that no one should be confined absent, at a minimum, clear and convincing evidence that the subject presents a genuine danger of substantial physical harm to himself or, more importantly, to others. *Addington v. Texas*, 441 U.S. 418 (1979). The nature of the allegations, which must vary as a function of dangerousness and controllability (on balance), may impose a higher burden on the state.

170 Watson, *supra* note 53, at 275.

171 Smith, TMS, at 133.

172 *Id.* The irony that we require both (at least formally) as epistemological requisites to a procedurally sound conviction is beyond the scope of this article. *See Aesthetics of Retribution, supra* note 42 (concluding that genuine harm to a first order interest will be a feature of our criminal jurisprudence for the foreseeable future).

173 The "subjectivist" approach measures culpability based solely on the actor's subjective intent. *See, e.g.,* Joshua Dressler, UNDERSTANDING CRIMINAL LAW 378–80 (3d ed. 2001) (distinguishing between "subjectivist" and "objectivist" approaches to attempts).

174 TMS, at 134.

175 In fact, Smith's consequentialism in this instance operates indirectly; that is, he embraces a positive form of retribution, understanding that it would have a regulatory effect on deterrable conduct. *See* Russell, *supra* note 27, at 550–52.

> What chiefly outrages us against the man who injures or insults us is the little account which he seems to make of us, the unreasonable preference which he gives to himself above us, and the absurd self-love, by which he seems to imagine that other people may be sacrificed at any time to his convenience or his humor.[176]

Many of us experience something like this as an instance of "road rage", the (sometimes nearly uncontrollable) anger that often ensues after someone cuts off or otherwise endangers another driver in traffic.[177] My normal (unprintable) reaction is likely to be: "How dare you *fr#%*g* jackass imagine that I might be sacrificed at any time for your *fr#%*g* convenience?" Smith's analysis is right, of course.[178]

But this tendency to transform harm-committed into an over ascription of blame that reflects the wrongdoer's evil character is not only unfair.[179] We should know that it is also counterproductive to the goal of an increasingly more rational and sensible system of criminal justice because the extant view makes little room for meaningful efforts at rehabilitation, which raises the never well-answered question that began this chapter: how can we charge the reformatory view of punishment with disrespecting human personality, simply because it acknowledges humankind's primate genesis with our imperfect neuropsychological natures and hopes to use such information as a means to the good of our higher selves, remains incomprehensible? I say this understanding that no sane, fully flourishing person would advocate for a system that permits dangerous actors to roam the streets and threaten our families, our children and ourselves. The means and end I propose are pragmatic *and* compassionate; those two natural human qualities cannot easily be opposed. A humane practice of commitment, which avoids the regime of punishment, could provide an alternative,[180] because we need a regime that suspends blame, at least as a reflexive default social practice.

---

176 TMS, at 139.

177 For a popular discussion of this phenomenon, *see* Patti Davis, *If You Can''t Say Something Nice ...*, NEWSWEEK, Aug. 3, 2001, at www.keepmedia.com/ShowItemDetails.do?itemID=315977&extID=10043&data=road_rage.

178 I don't mean to suggest that the errant driver necessarily intended to endanger me or anyone else on the road. Often, I suspect, carelessness (or perhaps even recklessness) provoked the dangerous driving. Nonetheless, we often tend to react as if the driver had elevated their priorities over ours in an unacceptable manner. I have addressed some of these questions in *An Essay on Vengeance and Forgiveness*, mss in author's possession.

179 It is also ironic that those theorists who attempt to explain our jurisprudence in terms of character overlook the bias that inheres in blaming even as they would eliminate differences in penalties for attempts as opposed to completed harms.

180 *See, e.g.*, Lawrence O. Gostin, *Public Health Theory and Practice in the Constitutional Design*, 11 HEALTH MATRIX 265, 308–10 (2001) (arguing for strict tests for civil commitment with meaningful treatment). *Cf. O'Connor v. Davidson*, 422 U.S. 563,

The system I envision turns the normal process for dealing with violent felonies on its head. Today, the process generally saves for the sentencing phase (if then) questions about the convicted defendant's (non-pathological) capacity-in-fact and opportunity. I suggest that these questions be answered on the front end of the process rather than the back end, rather than collecting information in the discovery process that is always gathered with an eye clearly focused on conviction. The proposal I advance retains a role for blame and educated blaming, but it does so only as part of a pre-trial procedure that, in cases of violent felonies, make inquiries on two axes. The *X* axis measures capacity-in-fact, in which the court seeks to determine, with the best diagnostic tools and information-gathering processes available, whether the individual has the cognitive and volitional capacities necessary for learning basic moral lessons. The *Y* axis asks an essentially historical/biographical question about the defendant's past opportunities for moral education and the uses made of that education in light of the quality and quantity of those opportunities. Essentially, the question is: what educational opportunities were available as this person matured, and what opportunities to advance were actually used?

Under this proposal, meeting the current demands of minimal instrumental rationality, the ability to reason from desire to belief to action,[181] simply indicates that the actor should remain in the criminal justice system. For those unable even to effect a simple practical syllogism, cognitive competency is no longer an issue; that is to say, the actor with such profound deficits clearly needs some useful treatment and may need incapacitation. And if the actor has little or no volitional control (the psychopath being the model for such incapacity) they are relegated to a system that implements minimally coercive procedures to effectuate necessary constraint.

After these assessments are made, and assuming some minimal capacities, a modified blaming and punishment practice takes over. Those who have ample cognitive capacity, affective control and good fortune but fail to make use of them are, *prima facie*, the most culpable both morally and intuitively for they (when compared with those who are cognitively, emotionally or experientially deprived) more likely *could and thus should have done otherwise.* (I also suspect their crimes are typically the more intelligible and deterrable as well.) In contrast, those who lack these minimal capacities and suffer bad antecedent luck are the least blameworthy for it is more likely that despite appearances, they *could not have done otherwise.* In the middle are those who possess sufficient cognitive skill and capacity-in-fact but lack the opportunity to adapt to minimal social norms appropriately or those who lack the capacities but have been blessed with good opportunities; all may well require restraint, but little or no blame, and certainly not vengeful, retributive treatment. For all such groups, appropriate moral education

575–76 (1975) (holding that a state cannot confine a non-dangerous, mentally ill person without providing meaningful treatment).

181 *See* my *Justifying Punishment,* 14 CAN. J. L. & JURIS. 161, 175–77 (2001).

during their period of incapacity is the only meaningful moral alternative we can choose if protecting future generations is our basic penal goal and demonstrating compassion is an elemental human duty.

Conclusion

I have tried to link our concepts of blame to the psychological phenomena that support it. I have examined one theory of the moral philosophy of blaming, which rests on the underexamined idea that the actor who causes harm is *bad*. In large part, that conclusion both inspires and rests on an abbreviated semantic description of character, which in turn both animates and supports the social and cultural biases we bring to the practice of attributing blame. We thus tend to overlook or devalue the striking nature of the conditions within which many wrongdoers reach maturity.[182] This endemic tendency to overattribute wrongdoing to the actor's bad character is at best unfortunate for it casts the wrongdoer as the target of our scorn, undermines efforts to make society safer by educating the actor and removes us from responsibility for the social conditions that conduced to wrongdoing initially. At worst, it creates a subculture of *others* whom we tend to view as an irreclaimable Claggert.

In lieu of blaming as a routine practice applicable to all instances of wrongdoing, I propose that we consider a new regime that suspends blaming pending an analysis of capacity-in-fact and opportunity. For those who lack capacity-in-fact and opportunity, the emphasis should be on education, although incapacitating those who present obvious dangers still may be warranted. For those who have ample capacity and opportunity, blame is appropriate for we have good reason to believe that they could have made choices other than those they made and thus should have. In the end, the system I have outlined rests on compassion and the unwillingness to do to others what we would not want done to us, had God rolled the dice differently.

182 For an original understanding of the influence of background, *see* Richard Delgado, "*Rotten Social Background*": *Should the Criminal Law Recognize a Defense of Severe Environmental Deprivation?*, 3 J. L. & Inequality 9 (1985).

Chapter 7
Why Distinguish "Mental" and "Physical" Illness in the Law of Involuntary Treatment?

John Dawson and George Szmukler

Why do most Western legal systems operate two distinct streams of law to cover the treatment without consent of "physical" and "mental" disorders respectively? We favour the fusion of these two streams of law into one comprehensive involuntary treatment scheme. Under this unified scheme, the decision to intervene in a person's life would be squarely based on their incapacity (or incompetence)[1] to consent to medical treatment, regardless of the cause of their incapacity. Consistent ethical principles would then be applied to all forms of health care.

In Australasia and Britain, the jurisdictions considered here, treatment for mental disorder is largely governed by mental health legislation. Under that legislation, the usual criteria for intervention – by way of both detention and involuntary treatment – are that the person concerned is "mentally disordered" (or "mentally ill') in the necessary sense and that they present a serious threat of harm to themselves or others or have a seriously diminished capacity for self-care. If a person meets those complex criteria, the legislation will usually authorize their certification by medical practitioners, their emergency detention and transportation to a hospital or clinic, their compulsory assessment, their involuntary psychiatric treatment, and perhaps their compulsory community care, provided the person's involuntary status as a whole is kept under regular, continuing review by a court or tribunal. In these jurisdictions' mental health regimes, no sharp distinction is made between the criteria applicable to the detention and involuntary treatment decisions. So, generally speaking, when a person is lawfully detained under the mental health legislation, they may also be treated for their mental disorder without their consent. The origins of these mental health statutes can be traced to the establishment of the asylums and particularly to the lunacy legislation of nineteenth-century Britain.[2]

When it comes to the treatment without consent of non-psychiatric medical conditions, on the other hand, different criteria and different procedures are followed that are grounded in different sources of law. Here we rely on common law powers

1 The terms incapacity and incompetence will be used here interchangeably. The former term is commonly used in Europe, the latter in North America.

2 Unsworth, C. (1987). *The Politics of Mental Health Legislation*. Clarendon Press: Oxford.

(or justifications) for intervention whose origins lie in the defence of necessity in the law of crime and tort,[3] or we act under adult guardianship (or incapacity) legislation.[4] This legislation is a modern expression of the ancient *parens patriae* powers of the Crown that have long since been delegated to the courts.

Under these latter regimes, which are applied to the treatment without consent of non-psychiatric conditions, the fundamental criterion for intervention is not the presence of any specific disorder or the imminent threat of harm. Instead, the test for intervention is the incapacity of the person to make necessary treatment decisions, regardless of its cause. If the person lacks that capacity, treatment that is in their "best interests" may generally be provided without their consent. And, although the mental health legislation discussed earlier expressly covers involuntary psychiatric treatment, many people with mental disorders who lack the necessary capacity, such as elderly people with advanced dementia, are now managed under these alternative common law or adult guardianship schemes.

The question we want to pose, which we believe might become *the* major question in the design of the law governing involuntary treatment in the coming decades throughout the Western world as the distinction between physical and mental illness becomes increasingly untenable, is whether we should continue to operate two distinct legal streams of this kind, one for involuntary psychiatric treatment *only*, the other for the involuntary treatment of *any* medical condition provided the person lacks the capacity to consent. Is the maintenance of two regimes desirable, and is it principled? In particular, is the two-track approach consistent with general principles of health care ethics and with basic notions of human rights, particularly the right of people with mental disorders to be free of unnecessary discrimination in the law?

The alternative approach, which we advocate, is to abandon the two-track approach, and, instead, to fuse the two together into a single comprehensive involuntary treatment scheme. This scheme would not rely on any specific reference to "mental disorder". Instead, it would rely squarely on the criterion of incapacity to make necessary treatment decisions, *but* it would still authorize both a person's detention and their involuntary treatment. We call this the "fusion" proposal.[5] Under it, the incapacity of a person to consent would be *the* fundamental criterion governing *all* involuntary health interventions, and that criterion would be applied to *both* detention *and* involuntary treatment, of *both* "physical" *and* "mental" conditions.

Note that we are not advocating the intermediate (or hybrid) legal position now followed in many parts of North America and continental Europe that involves the

3 Re F [1990] 2 AC 1; *R* v *Bournewood Community and Mental Health NHS Trust, ex parte L* [1998] 3 WLR 107.

4 E.g., Mental Capacity Act 2005 (England and Wales); Protection of Personal and Property Rights Act 1988 (NZ).

5 Dawson, J. and Szmukler, G. (2006). The fusion of mental health and incapacity legislation. *British Journal of Psychiatry*, 188, 504–509.

application of different legal criteria to the detention and involuntary treatment decisions. Under that approach, mental disorder and threat of harm criteria may be applied to a person's detention, while incapacity criteria may be applied to their treatment.[6] That approach has the significant disadvantage that it can lead to a position wherein a person may be lawfully detained in a psychiatric facility on the basis of their mental disorder, but they cannot be treated if they retain or regain their capacity to consent to psychiatric treatment.[7] For that reason, it is not an approach that has been widely supported in Australasia or Britain.

Instead, we would argue that the test of incapacity to consent should be applied to both a person's detention and their involuntary treatment. The aims of this proposal are to:

- avoid the problematic distinction between mental and physical illness
- acknowledge that mental disorder is *not* always associated with incapacity to consent, while also acknowledging that patients with many other medical conditions *may* lack the capacity to consent
- acknowledge that the capacity of mentally disordered people is already assessed for many other legal purposes
- reduce discrimination against mentally disordered people (and perhaps against mental health professionals) by not making psychiatric treatment, unnecessarily, the subject of special legislation, and
- apply consistent ethical principles across medical law.

Illustrations of the Two-Track Approach

A couple of examples may be useful to illustrate the problematic nature of the current, two-track approach. One of the current authors, Dr Szmukler, a community psychiatrist, was consulted in London about the following case. A 61-year-old man was lying at home, in his own bed, delirious and vomiting blood: a potentially fatal consequence of chronic alcoholism. He had no previous psychiatric history and he was adamantly resisting the suggestion that he be taken to hospital. An ambulance had been called, but the ambulance officers would not take the man to hospital over his objections, despite the frantic requests of his wife, because the officers doubted they had the authority to seize and restrain him, even in his grave condition, when he had not been certified under the Mental Health Act. Dr Szmukler was urged to provide the necessary medical certificate under civil commitment legislation, to

6 See, e.g., Dawson, J. and Kampf, A. (2006) Incapacity principles in mental health laws in Europe. *Psychology, Public Policy and Law*, 12, 310–331.

7 See, e.g., Appelbaum, P. (1994). *Almost a revolution: mental health law and the limits of change*. OUP: New York; Kelly, M., Dunbar, S., Gray, J., and O'Reilly, R. (2002). Treatment delays for involuntary psychiatric patients associated with reviews of treatment capacity. *Canadian Journal of Psychiatry*, 47, 181–185.

permit the man to be taken forcibly with police assistance to a psychiatric ward to which he would be admitted briefly and then immediately transferred to another ward for general medical care.

The ambulance officers may not have fully understood their own legal position. The common law of necessity may well have authorized immediate intervention in such a case, because a delirious person may be considered to lack the capacity to decide on their own emergency medical care, which may therefore proceed without their consent in their best interests.[8] But it is not to be expected that ambulance officers will always understand the details of the common law.

What does this example show, then? It shows that different sources of law, different criteria and a different process would apply to this man's involuntary treatment depending on whether we view his condition as a "mental" or a "physical" disorder. If we view his condition as a purely physical disorder, his emergency treatment would be governed by incapacity criteria under the common law, and there may be no statute that provides clear powers to detain, restrain and transport him to hospital, nor any formal certification process created by law. Nor would his detention be reviewed, automatically and swiftly, by a tribunal or court. If we were to view his condition as a mental disorder, on the other hand, which would be a perfectly valid description of a delirious state of mind, intervention would be authorized under the different criteria established by the Mental Health Act. There would be a clear certification process. Powers of emergency detention, restraint, transportation and involuntary treatment would be clearly provided by the statute. And in most jurisdictions his detention would be automatically reviewed by a court or tribunal within a reasonable period of time.

So why have two separate legal regimes of this kind, with different criteria and different procedures? Why tolerate a situation in which this kind of case would usually be handled under common law incapacity principles, when a severely depressed person, who has slashed themselves, and is also slowly bleeding to death, would usually be handled under the Mental Health Act? Why not fuse these schemes into one comprehensive involuntary treatment regime based on a single set of standards and procedures?

Another useful example is the well-known case of *In re C*.[9] This case concerned an elderly Jamaican man who had been detained as a psychiatric patient in Broadmoor for the previous 30 years. He had a psychiatric diagnosis of paranoid schizophrenia, characterized by delusions, but he also had an ulcerated, gangrenous leg whose amputation was proposed. Involuntary treatment of his schizophrenia was authorized by the Mental Health Act, but the amputation of his leg fell to be determined by the application of incapacity principles under the common law. The same person, therefore, could be treated simultaneously, for the two different conditions, under

---

8 *R v Bournewood Community and Mental Health NHS Trust, ex parte L* [1998] 3 WLR 107; Dawson, J. (1999). The law of emergency psychiatric detention. *New Zealand Law Review*, 275–303.

9 *In re C* [1994] 1 WLR 290.

two distinct legal regimes. But why apply different criteria to the treatment without consent of the two conditions? Why not apply incapacity principles in both cases?

In our view, no clear case has been made that the impairment of a person's capacity – where it exists – differs in any essential respect in mental and physical disorders. Impairment of decision-making capacity may be more commonly encountered in people with mental disorders, but in both cases *some impairment or disturbance of mental function is the cause* of the patient's incapacity, and legal criteria sufficiently flexible to cover all relevant situations can be devised.[10] Whatever the cause of the person's incapacity, whether it be unconsciousness, delirium, intense pain, trauma, gross intoxication, brain poisoning, or psychosis, *some* impairment or disturbance of mental function is the cause of their incapacity, regardless of whether those conditions are described as mental or physical disorders: hence our fusion proposal.

The Potential Contents of a "Fused" Statutory Scheme

So, what kinds of provisions would a comprehensive involuntary treatment statute contain? Our suggestion is that it should draw on the strengths of both adult guardianship and mental health legislation, and that it should authorize both detention and involuntary treatment, under certain conditions. We therefore need to identify the central features of both the adult guardianship and the mental health schemes.

Under the current adult guardianship schemes of Australasia and Britain, incapacity to make decisions of the relevant kind is the central test for intervention. That test is not linked to the presence of any specific disabling condition. It is a purely functional incapacity test, which preserves the autonomy over treatment of patients whose capacity is *intact.*

Various models of substitute decision-making are then available:

- a "private" model, under which family members or friends of an incapacitated person may be appointed to make decisions on their behalf
- a "public" model, under which a public official, such as a public guardian or public advocate (or a member of their staff) is appointed to act
- a clinical model, under which a treating clinician is empowered to make the necessary decisions, and
- a judicial model, under which a court or tribunal will itself make the necessary decisions on the person's behalf.

In addition, various models of independent review are followed, based on the choice between a court and a specialist tribunal as the forum for review.

10 Grisso, T. and Appelbaum, P. (1998). *Assessing Competence to Consent to Treatment.* New York: Oxford University Press.

On the other hand, this kind of legislation may not expressly authorize the *detention* of an incapacitated person, or their emergency treatment before their incapacity has been formally determined, nor may it authorize the use of "reasonable force" for treatment purposes. These matters are usually left to be handled under common law principles, or the necessary powers are delegated to the substitute decision-maker, but the use of those powers may not then be subject to rigorous independent review.

Under mental health legislation, on the other hand, at least in Australasia and Britain, intervention is based on "mental disorder" and "dangerousness", not on incapacity criteria, and formal assessment of an involuntary patient's capacity to consent to psychiatric treatment is rarely required by law. This kind of legislation is therefore weak on patient autonomy principles in comparison with the usual adult guardianship scheme. So patients who retain, or regain, their capacity to consent may still be provided with most forms of psychiatric treatment without their consent under the mental health legislation as long as they remain involuntary patients under the scheme. Nevertheless, the use of force, and the detention and involuntary treatment of objecting patients, is clearly authorized and *regulated* by the mental health regime. Comprehensive independent review procedures will also be provided, including perhaps mandatory peer review, by independent clinicians, of the treatment regime.

Furthermore, the mental health legislation will usually interact in a number of complex ways with the criminal justice system. The prison-to-hospital transfer process, the making of hospital orders following a person's conviction, the position of forensic patients reclassified to civil status, and the treatment of forensic patients generally, may all be governed by the mental health legislation. No equivalent interaction with the criminal justice process, or with the prison system, is usually built into the structure of an adult guardianship scheme.

How, then, could we fuse the central elements of these two distinct schemes into one comprehensive piece of legislation? We suggest the following general framework could be employed. The basic criteria for intervention under "fused" legislation could be incapacity to make necessary treatment decisions. The usual meaning of "incapacity" or "incompetence" would apply: that is, inability to understand, recall, process, use or weigh relevant information; inability to communicate a decision; or inability to reach a decision that is sufficiently stable for it to be followed. This incapacity test must be defined in a manner that is sufficiently flexible to cover the complex and subtle forms of incapacity found in some mental disorders, as may arise from subtle delusions or denial of illness. The test need not be linked to any specific disabling condition, even if it might be linked in a general manner to some "impairment or disturbance in the function of the mind or brain", as provided by section 2(1) Mental Capacity Act 2005 for England and Wales. In addition, for intervention under this test to occur, no less restrictive resolution of the apparent problems should be available.

In emergency circumstances, a "reasonable belief" that the patient lacked capacity in this sense should be sufficient to authorize intervention, before the patient's capacity could be fully assessed. Suitably qualified professionals could then intervene, using similar powers to those provided by a civil commitment scheme: that is, powers of entry, detention of the person, transportation to assessment, use of reasonable force, and so on. The patient would then enter a staggered compulsory assessment process, during which immediately necessary treatment would be authorized, as is now permitted under the common law. A more structured assessment of the patient's capacity would then take place.

If the patient's involuntary treatment was to continue, further downstream decisions about the details of their treatment would be required: decisions, for instance, concerning the need for their detention for treatment purposes or to protect the safety of others; the appropriate place of treatment; the contents of the treatment plan; and the value of any continuing outpatient care.

Comprehensive review and accountability mechanisms would also apply. All involuntary patients should have ready access to rights advice and to independent review of their status before a court or tribunal. A substitute decision-maker for treatment could be appointed (and parameters for the patient's treatment set), and the full range of substitute decision-making models could be available, including the option of appointing the responsible clinician to make treatment decisions, as is typical under British and Australasian Mental Health Acts. Some particularly controversial forms of treatment could still be regulated in a more stringent manner, through mandatory peer review of treatment, for instance. But that kind of requirement should not apply only to psychiatric treatment; it should apply to all treatments of a similarly controversial or intrusive kind. Finally, any "oversight" commission, akin to the Mental Health Act Commission for England and Wales, should have jurisdiction over all involuntary patients under the scheme.

Two Potential Lines of Objection

Those are the central elements of our fusion proposal. The question is not whether such legislation would be perfect, of course, but whether it would be preferable to the current, two-track approach. Before we can assess that matter, however, a number of potential objections to our proposal must be entertained. At least two main lines of objection are likely. The first involves the argument that assessing the capacity of people with mental disorders presents special difficulties, the second the argument that the application of incapacity principles may be specially problematic in the context of forensic care.

With regard to the first of these objections, the argument might be made that assessing the capacity of people with mental disorders is especially difficult for a number of reasons. It may be said that it requires special training, for instance; that it is hard to assess in the emergency circumstances typical of civil commitment; or that particularly subtle forms of incapacity may be present in some forms of mental disorder; and so on. If this is so, the argument may continue, this could lead to the unreliable application of incapacity principles to people with mental disorders, or it could produce considerable disagreement between clinicians on capacity matters, and that in turn could lead to "arbitrary detention" contrary to human rights norms. Moreover, there is the special problem, so central to mental health law, of the fluctuating capacity of people with fluctuating mental conditions.

How, then, would we respond? First, we would acknowledge that capacity assessment is a difficult task requiring special training and knowledge. But we are not convinced that there is something particularly difficult about assessing the capacity of "mentally disordered" people to consent to psychiatric treatment that would not already arise in other contexts where capacity assessment is now required. Very similar difficulties may arise, for instance, when assessing the capacity of an elderly person, who has a serious and fluctuating physical illness, to consent to surgery, or when assessing the capacity of a confused patient with ischaemic heart disease to refuse continuing medication.

The objections listed above are all really objections to the capacity assessment process *in general*, or they point to problems in assessing the capacity of people with mental disorders *in general*, rather than pointing to particular problems in assessing the capacity of "mentally disordered" people to consent to psychiatric treatment in particular. We therefore do not find these objections very convincing, both because we consider that assessing the capacity of general medical patients can be equally difficult, and because it is already necessary to assess the capacity of psychiatric patients for many legal purposes other than the provision of psychiatric care. We assess their capacity to drive, stand trial, make a will, be a parent, sell property, and so on. These are all complicated matters whose resolution is already required under current law, and they may require separate resolution – via specific capacity assessments – even in relation to people who are simultaneously being treated under the Mental Health Act. The empirical evidence to date supports the view that capacity can be assessed reliably in both patients with "physical" and "mental disorders".[11]

Furthermore, the need for special training and expertise is not limited to the capacity assessment process. It is also required to apply the criteria of mental disorder and serious risk of harm established by the mental health legislation, and there is no current research evidence that those criteria are applied any more reliably, between clinicians, hospitals or regions, than incapacity tests. So there is no compelling case to be made at present that assessing the capacity to consent to psychiatric treatment of people with mental disorders is particularly problematic. There are simply problems in all capacity assessment fields, as there are in applying the criteria for intervention established by the Mental Health Act.

Application to Forensic Care

As to the second line of objection: what would be the consequences of applying capacity principles to forensic care? Here the matter is complicated by the

11 Cairns, R., Maddock, C., Buchanan, A., et al. (2005) Reliability of mental capacity assessments in psychiatric in-patients. *British Journal of Psychiatry,* 187, 372–378.

existence of many different categories of forensic patient, some of whom have been convicted of criminal offences, while some have not because they have been found not guilty by reason of insanity, or unfit to stand trial, instead. The matter is also complicated by the fact that some forensic patients can be returned to prison if they regain their capacity and refuse treatment, while others cannot be returned to prison, because they are not currently subject to a prison sentence. If the detention of a person in that latter group was no longer authorized, they would have to be immediately released, which is not an outcome that is likely to be politically or socially acceptable if the person concerned still presents a serious threat of harm.

This points to the fact that protecting the autonomy over treatment of patients with capacity is not the only important ethical principle in this field. Another important principle concerns the need to protect other people from serious harm. So some modification of pure capacity principles may be required in the forensic field.

Nevertheless, we suggest that most of the difficulties in the forensic area could be finessed if the following legal principles were applied. First, any mentally disordered offender *with* capacity who *consents* to their treatment could be treated in an appropriate facility (and any sentence they were under could continue to run). Secondly, any mentally disordered offender *who lacks* capacity could be treated *involuntarily* like any other patient. Thirdly, any criminal defendant found unfit to stand trial or not found guilty due to insanity might still be treated without their consent, *even if they retain or regain their capacity*, under the following conditions. There is reliable evidence that:

- the person has committed acts constituting a serious offence, and
- a serious mental disorder has contributed significantly to that conduct, and
- an effective treatment can be offered that could be expected to reduce the risk of that disorder's reoccurrence.

This would compromise pure incapacity principles, in narrowly defined circumstances, in order to prevent harm to others.

Furthermore, any mentally disordered offender who had been *convicted* of a serious criminal offence could be sentenced to the usual period of imprisonment, and if they were then found to lack capacity and need treatment, they could be transferred to hospital for necessary care. Alternatively, a convicted person could be placed under a hospital order on disposition from the criminal court, and be directed immediately to psychiatric treatment, but such an order should always be for a limited term, proportionate to the seriousness of their offence. During that limited term involuntary treatment could proceed on the same conditions, specified above, as would apply to those found not guilty by reason of insanity or unfit to stand trial. But at the end of that term, only a patient who lacked capacity could be treated without consent, as would be the case with other, non-forensic patients under the comprehensive involuntary treatment scheme.

In that manner, capacity principles could be followed in most forms of forensic care, subject to some limited modifications that would be required to respect the competing ethical principle of preventing serious harm to others.

Conclusion

It is our conclusion, therefore, that adult guardianship (or incapacity) schemes show proper respect for personal autonomy, but they do not address the detention or treatment of objecting patients, nor do they address necessary interactions with the criminal justice system. Mental health legislation, on the other hand, places less emphasis on patient autonomy, but it clearly regulates emergency intervention, detention and involuntary treatment, and it establishes necessary connections with forensic care.

The fusion of these two regimes into one comprehensive involuntary treatment statute that retained the strengths of both is readily conceivable, even if some minor departures from pure incapacity principles may still be required. It is our hope that implementation of this fusion proposal would reduce unnecessary discrimination in the law against people with mental disorders, and that it would apply consistent ethical principles across medical law.

Chapter 8
A Stable Paradigm: Revisiting Capacity, Vulnerability and the Rights Claims of Adolescents after *Roper* v. *Simmons*

Catherine J. Ross[1]

Scientific advances are confirming what parents have long known: the teenage brain is "a very complicated and dynamic area" (National Institute of Mental Health, 2001). When the United States Supreme Court considered the death penalty as applied to crimes committed by a person under the age of 18 in *Roper* v. *Simmons* (2005) it received summaries of recent neurological evidence showing that teenage brains are not fully developed. Newly available magnetic resonance imaging (MRI) research, several briefs argued, established that teenagers as a group lack the capacity of the typical adult to make decisions, avoid risks and understand the consequences of their actions and that they are therefore less culpable for violent acts than adults. In *Roper* the Supreme Court held that persons may not be subjected to capital punishment for crimes they committed between the ages of 16 and 18. Dissenting, Justice Scalia zeroed in on a key analytical problem. He challenged the majority to explain how it is possible to reconcile the view of teenagers as too young to be "treated as adults" when they commit capital offences because they "lack the ability to take moral responsibility for their actions" with the jurisprudence and scholarly literature justifying rights for minors, including the position that adolescent girls are "mature enough to decide whether to obtain an abortion without parental involvement" (*Roper* v. *Simmons*, 2005 (Scalia, J., dissenting, p617)).

Framed more broadly, to the extent that the *Roper* v. *Simmons* majority reflected awareness of a scientific consensus that teenagers lack the requisite capacity to be held fully accountable for criminal acts, does that finding justify or even mandate a retreat from recognizing classical rights for minors? To answer this fundamental

1 Catherine J. Ross, Yale B.A., Ph.D., J.D., is Professor of Law at George Washington University Law School and, during 2008–9, a Member of the Institute for Advanced Study in Princeton, NJ. The author thanks participants at the interdisciplinary symposium on juvenile justice and brain science held at the Ohio State University Moritz College of Law on 10–11 March 2005 and at the Gruter Institute conference on the brain held February 2006 for comments on earlier drafts, and Dean Frederick Lawrence for his comments and for the generous support of the George Washington Law School.

question we must ask what the proper relationship ought to be between capacity and rights, vulnerability and voice. On closer examination, I argue, things are not as simple as Justice Scalia proposes they should be.

The second part of this chapter provides a brief summary of the scientific information that has recently emerged as a result of technological advances in the study of the human brain and that was presented to the Court in *Roper*. The third section reviews the dominant schools of thought about the relationship between capacity and children's legal rights and considers whether emerging scientific knowledge requires a reconsideration of these theories. The fourth section argues that scientific validation of cultural perceptions regarding the vulnerability of adolescents is consistent with theories supporting constitutional rights for minors and indeed supports increased voice and empowerment for teenagers, along with procedural protections that account for their developmental limitations.

Advances in Scientific Understanding of the Teenage Brain

MRIs allow scientists to study both the structure of the brain and how it functions by non-invasive imaging and provide quantitative data about brain development that was previously unobtainable (Anderson et al., 2006, p2). In 2003 the researchers who developed MRI technology won the Nobel Prize (Anderson et al., 2006). Neuroscientific research on the teenage brain using this new technology provided information to the Supreme Court in 2004 that had not been available when the Court had last considered the application of the death penalty to juveniles in the late 1980s. Although a plurality of the Court had ruled in 1988 that capital punishment for crimes committed when defendants were under the age of 16 constituted cruel and unusual punishment barred by the Eighth Amendment (*Thompson* v. *Oklahoma*, 487 U.S. 815, 1988), the next year the Court refused to bar the death penalty for crimes committed when the defendant was between the ages of 16 and 18 (*Stanford* v. *Kentucky*, 492 U.S. 302, 1989).

The very same day it declined to hold the death penalty unconstitutional for acts committed by persons aged 16 to 18, however, the Court held that the evolving standards of decency implicated by the Eighth Amendment barred the execution of the mentally retarded: their impairments diminish personal culpability, making it "less defensible to impose the death penalty as retribution for past crimes and less likely that the death penalty will have a real deterrent effect" (*Roper*, 2005, p563, summarizing *Penry* v. *Lynaugh*, 492 U.S. 302, 318–20 (1989)). The resemblance between the lack of full capacity demonstrated by teenagers, albeit temporary, and by the mentally retarded, albeit life-long, lent support to the continuing movement to abolish the death penalty for crimes committed by teenagers, no matter how heinous, and strengthened the trend towards abolition cited by *Roper* as evidence of a growing national consensus that the death penalty is disproportionate when applied to juveniles (*Roper*, pp564–68). Indeed, in 2003 the Governor of the State of Kentucky commuted the death sentence of Kevin Stanford (the defendant whose conviction the Supreme Court had upheld in 1989) on the ground that "[w]e ought not be executing people who, legally, were children" (*Roper* v. *Simmons,* 2005, p565).

Although no evidence concerning the capacity of adolescents as a group had been presented at the trial or state court appeal (*Roper,* Transcript of Oral Argument 2004, pp31–34) of Christopher Simmons, a confessed, callous teenage murderer, the Supreme Court received, among other filings, two briefs *amicae curiae* that presented scientific evidence about the adolescent brain. (*Amicae curiae* are "friends of the court" who are not parties to an action, but are able to provide information that will be useful to the court's deliberations.) The first brief, submitted by the American Medical Association (AMA) and seven other professional groups, presented evidence from numerous refereed articles in neuroscience and psychology that the behavioural differences between adults and adolescents have an anatomical basis (AMA et al., 2004). A second amicus brief filed on behalf of the American Psychological Association (APA) and the Missouri Psychological Association also summarized recent neuropsychological research as well as an array of behavioural studies from the psychological literature (APA, 2004).

Justice Kennedy's opinion for the Court began his discussion of the nature of adolescence with the comment that "as any parent knows and as the scientific and sociological studies respondent and his *amici* cite tend to confirm … ." He then summarized the "three general differences between juveniles under 18 and adults" that undermine the "reliability" of determinations that a juvenile is "among the worst offenders" for whom the death penalty is reserved: (i) lack of maturity, impetuousness and recklessness; (ii) special vulnerability to "outside pressure, including peer pressure"; and (iii) the transitory nature of a juvenile's personality traits, which are still in formation (*Roper*, p569). As Justice Kennedy's prefatory comment suggests, the scientific data before the Court may be more significant for the way in which it bolsters or confirms embedded cultural understandings of development than for paradigm-shifting significance.

One could argue that there is not much new in the notion that teenagers are different from adults. Even the ancient philosophers and Shakespeare identified youth as a stage of life characterized by impulsiveness (consider Romeo and Juliet) and, in Aristotle's terms, unable to understand "moral lectures" (Brooks, 2006, p643). Similarly, the Supreme Court has long weighed youth as a special factor when considering criminal acts committed by teenagers, beginning with the Court's 1932 decision to overturn the conviction of the "Scottsboro boys", black youths who were sentenced to death for raping a white woman, after a trial at which they did not have legal representation (Ross, 1996; *Powell* v. *Alabama*, 1932). In 1947 the Court referred to a 15-year-old defendant as "a mere child – an easy victim of the law" who could not be expected to withstand police interrogation, and "cannot be judged by the more exacting standards of maturity … This is the period of great instability which the crisis of adolescence produces" (*Haley* v. *Ohio*, 332 U.S. 596, 1947 p599).

Although it fits within the rubric the Court had long acknowledged, the new scholarship on adolescent brain development seems to have influenced the Court (*see e.g.* Haider, 2006; Denno, 2006) and is often credited as the persuasive evidence leading to the decision in *Roper* (Gruber & Yurgelin-Todd, 2006, p331). Concededly, Justice Kennedy's opinion did not cite the neuroscience evidence, perhaps because of issues raised at oral argument about the fact that it had not been tested at trial through cross-examination of the experts (*Roper* v. *Simmons*, Transcript, 2004), but his opinion cited liberally to the social science data from the briefs, including articles that, in turn, cited the neuroscience.

Critical findings from MRI research set forth in the *amicus* briefs included evidence that the dorsal-lateral frontal lobe of the brain, which handles "judgments and values, long-term goals, the weighing of risks and consequences – what parents call wisdom or common sense and what science calls 'executive function'," (Williamson, 2005) is among the last areas of the brain to mature, and does not reach full maturity until well after the age of 18 (AMA, 2004, p16, 16 n. 55, citing authorities). Another line of research documented that teens process emotions differently than adults, in distinct areas of the brain (Williamson, 2005). Teenagers process a great deal of information in the amygdala, which, according to the AMA's brief, "is associated with aggressive and impulsive behavior" and "dictates instinctive gut reactions" in comparison with the frontal lobes, which handle "'more complex' information-processing functions" including "thinking" and "reasoning" (pp25, 26).

As teens grow older, brain activity tasks tend to shift gradually to the frontal lobe and communication between the frontal lobe and the amygdala improves (AMA, 2004, p15), reflecting increased reliance on reasoning rather than emotion, more reasoned perceptions, and improved performance of tasks and life skills. The evidence makes clear that "[o]ne of the last areas of the brain to reach full maturity ... is the part associated with regulating behavior, stifling impulses, assessing risks, and moral reasoning" (AMA, 2004, p20). And, this process may last into the early to mid-twenties (Arshagouni, 2004, p351), long past the age at which the laws of various states allow young people to marry, vote, drink or drive (*Roper*, 2005, Appendices).

As exciting as it is to view the brain at work through MRIs, the new data are entirely consistent with longstanding legal presumptions about youth. Throughout the twentieth century Supreme Court decisions about the young expressly proceeded from an understanding that young people are different from adults (Ross, 1996) as did the rulings that captured the rehabilitative vision of the juvenile justice system (Ross, 1995). Contemporary scholarship on juvenile justice emphasizes knowledge of child development as being essential to best practices (Scott & Steinberg, 2003; Scott & Grisso, 1997) in stark contrast to the mounting trend in state courts and federal legislation to treat juvenile offenders as adults (Johnson et al., 2004).

The new data from brain imaging are, however, critically important to the broader debate about the accountability of juveniles within the justice system in at least one respect: they establish that an individual teenager is not responsible for an inability to exercise certain kinds of self-control or to reflect upon the consequences of actions. Scientific research points to neurological bases for the impulsivity and shortsightedness that predominates among adolescents. It suggests that a teenager's failure to consider consequences does not lie in personal deficiencies but is attributable, at least in part, to neurobiology, beyond the control of any typical individual. This analysis, which led to a categorical ban on capital punishment for crimes committed by teenagers, may also be extended to support a distinction between moral culpability and legal accountability that results in harsh, inflexible legal punishment for lesser offences. This sort of extension would be comparable to the Court's adjustment of its initial line-drawing for accountability for death penalty purposes from 16 (*Stanford* v. *Kentucky*, 1989) to 18 as the Court in *Roper*.

One of the issues on which the *Roper* majority and the dissenters differed was the question of whether individualized consideration of the defendant's maturity by the jury was a sufficient safeguard against the unjust execution of any particular person who committed a heinous act. The Justices disagreed about the implications of the evidence presented in the briefs showing that most persons under the age of 18 do not have the capacity to be held fully accountable under law for their crimes (compare *Roper*, pp572–73 to p588, p618, 620). Justice Scalia framed the issue by stark contrast of the death penalty cases to the Court's rulings in the context of abortion, in which the APA had submitted an *amicus* brief arguing that "[b]y middle adolescence" minors "are mature enough to decide whether to obtain an abortion without parental involvement" (*Roper*, 2005, p617 (Scalia, J. *dissenting*), *quoting* APA, 1989, p18 in *Hodgson* v. *Minnesota*, 1990). How, Justice Scalia asked, can a minor be mature enough to obtain an abortion without parental consent but not mature enough to be held accountable for a heinous murder: "Whether to obtain an abortion," he posits, "is surely a much more complex decision for a young person than whether to kill an innocent person in cold blood" (*Roper*, 2005, p620).

The simple answer to Justice Scalia's challenge is that the Court's jurisprudence on abortion rights for minors presumes, first, that most minors will consult their parents, and that only a small group of girls who feel they cannot do so will need to avail themselves of the procedural rights the Constitution guarantees. The Court has held that no state may require that a minor receive parental consent to obtain an abortion unless the state provides a judicial framework in which a judge may substitute her consent for that of the parent (known as a "judicial bypass" procedure) (*Bellotti* v. *Baird*, 1979; *Hodgson* v. *Minnesota*, 1990). Properly understood, a minor's right to abortion involves substitution of one adult's supervisory power (the judge's) for another's (the parent's). A bypass hearing requires a judge to ask two questions. First, is the particular minor seeking an abortion "mature" enough to understand the decision? If so, the judge should consent to the abortion. If not, the judge reaches the second question: is it in the minor's best interests to have the abortion? Given that the judge has already determined that the girl is too immature to make the decision to abort herself, she is presumably too immature to have and raise a baby. In neither event is the girl treated as fully mature and independently accountable.

One immediate distinction between abortion and imposition of the death penalty involves the impact of the two decisions on the young person's future. It is generally agreed that the primary justification for paternalism toward the young is that adults will try to make wise decisions that serve the child's best interests by preserving the child's options in life. For example, the state may intervene where a child's parents or guardians withhold life-preserving medical treatment, engage in abusive behaviour that threatens the child's physical or emotional health, or withhold education.

In the context of abortion, as Justice Powell cogently observed, "the potentially severe detriment facing a pregnant woman [citation omitted] is not mitigated by her minority. Indeed, considering her probable education, employment skills, financial resources, and emotional maturity, unwanted motherhood may be exceptionally burdensome for a minor" (*Bellotti* v. *Baird*, 1979, p642, *quoted* in *Hodgson* v. *Minnesota*, 1990, p434). Indeed, having a baby effectively terminates the teenage girl's adolescence and propels her, prepared or not, into adulthood (*Bellotti* v. *Baird*, 1979, p642). Because the consequences of childbirth are potentially so far-reaching, the option of abortion must be available to teenagers who seek it in order to preserve their options in life. The contrast to the imposition of the death penalty could not be starker: it goes without saying that the death penalty terminates life itself, while alternative harsh penalties such as life imprisonment effectively diminish the quality of life (and render many or most options unavailing) but does not completely extinguish it.

The Supreme Court's conclusion in the abortion context "that a minor may be very much an adult in some respects does not mean that his or her need and opportunity for growth under parental guidance and discipline have ended" (*Bellotti* v. *Baird*, 1979, p644) is confirmed by recent social science as well as neuroscience. Furstenberg et al. (2004) have documented that the transition from adolescence to adulthood, measured by life events such as completing education, becoming self-supporting and developing a clear sense of self takes much longer today than it did in 1900 or even in 1960. They estimate that the period of transitional, or incomplete, adulthood lasts into the thirties for more than two-thirds of men, and into the late twenties for three-quarters of women.

Arguably Justice Scalia's challenge was more in the nature of a debater's dismissive quick jab than a weighty question, for it implies a reductionist portrait of the arguments on behalf of rights for minors. It is, however, worth exploring whether *Roper* poses a serious challenge for advocates of children's legal rights. The remainder of this chapter considers the implications of the emerging knowledge about the teenage brain for competing theories of children's rights.

Theories of Children's Rights

The inherent tension between children's vulnerability and voice has been a central theme in academic discussions of children's rights, particularly in the United States.

The philosophical tension is less pronounced among the other nations, all of which, with the exception of Somalia, have undertaken to comply with the United Nations Convention on the Rights of the Child (1989). The UN Convention incorporates provisions that recognize children's vulnerabilities (*e.g.*, the *right* to education, housing, health services and other needs-based services and to be protected from abuse and exploitation, generally referred to as "welfare rights") side by side with articles that guarantee civil and political rights for minors (*e.g.*, the *right* to be heard in matters affecting them, freedom of thought, speech and religion) (UN Convention, 1989; *see also* Buck, 2005). Of course, many signatories do not in fact provide either set of rights, but that set of problems is beyond the scope of this chapter.

The Convention's organizing principles embrace the notion that the view of children as having needs is entirely compatible with the position that they have rights as defined by the liberal political tradition. Under this view, Justice Scalia's challenge to children's advocates might be a non-starter. But in the United States, and perhaps elsewhere, it appears essential to explain how we may reconcile the acknowledged vulnerabilities of minors with rights claims.

In light of the interdisciplinary nature of this volume, this section briefly introduces the major schools of thought regarding the relationship between children's level of competency and their claims to both kinds of rights recognized by the UN Convention. The literature can be roughly divided into four schools of thought, with the caveat that three of the four schools may not be mutually exclusive: (i) the nurturance model; (ii) the "liberationist" model; (iii) the classic "rights model" applied to minors; and (iv) the "empowerment" model. Each of these models, discussed in more detail below, requires distinctions among sub-groups of minors delineated by factors including age and capacity. With the exception of the liberationists, all have attempted to account for the ways in which children and teenagers differ from adults, have accordingly proposed sliding scales of rights, and have considered the distinctions that arise based on the varying contexts in which rights and interests may be asserted.

The Right to Nurture

Who can seriously argue that children do not need to be nurtured? As Woodhouse's (1993) classic article underscores, the starting point for discussions of children in legal systems is children's dependency and vulnerability. The issue is how we respond to that dependency – which for infants is literally a matter of life and death. Woodhouse proposed what she called a "generist perspective" in which both private stewardship (parenthood) and communal responsibility for children would be evaluated based on how well they fulfil their obligations to the next generation in contrast with the current emphasis in the United States on the rights of biological parents. The concept that children require essential care is embodied both in laws allowing states to intervene to prevent child abuse and in the welfarist provisions of the UN Convention. Children are distinguished by their "double dependency on parents and on the state" (Minow, 1986, p24). Since children are not just mini-adults, such laws and covenants are designed to protect their "development rights" – the rights that allow them to achieve their potential (Minow, 1995). Whether a society can mandate loving parents – which the psychological sciences argue are necessary to healthy development (Goldstein et al., 1996) – is more controversial (Ross, 2006a).

David Archard (2004) suggests that children have what he terms "moral rights", including rights available only to children and resting on their special status as children. Such rights, however, having their origin in communal ideals, become more than moral exhortation and are transformed into legal rights when the state establishes a floor beneath which the standard of care accorded children by their legal guardians may not fall without endangering the terms and existence of the guardianship. Where each society draws that line, how the line is enforced, by whom and how successfully are critical questions that lie beyond the scope of this chapter.

In a similar vein, Minow (1990) and others have emphasized the interdependency of family members rather than giving primacy to the individual rights claims of family members. This view suggests that the neediest in the family (the children, or those with disabilities rendering them vulnerable) receive the attention and support they need even at cost to the caregivers. The obligation flows from the adult to the child as a matter of responsibility, without any legally implied reciprocity or reward. The Scotts (1995) go one step further, positing that parents may be regarded as having a legally enforceable fiduciary duty to care for their offspring.

With the possible (and wholly theoretical) exception of radical liberationists, all advocates for children and their rights presumably adopt the precepts of the nurturance school. The question is how much we want to add to it, the content of those additional arguments, and when certain rights or claims should be triggered.

The Liberationist Model

This approach, entirely attributable to social scientists and largely related to the broader social trends of the 1960s, took the view that families and other authoritarian structures oppressed children. Children, its proponents argued, should be accorded all of the legal rights held by adults, including the right to self-determination (Archard, 2004). Since none of the leading children's liberation theorists (Holt, 1974; Farson, 1974; Neill & Fromm, 1960) were legal scholars, it may not even be necessary to acknowledge liberationists as a serious school of legal thought about children and rights. To the extent that we take liberationists at face value, if they mean that children of all ages should be left to their own devices, recognition that children need caretaking diminishes, and the emerging scientific evidence about the brain would seem to demolish, the school's legitimacy.

The Liberal Rights Model

A third school of thought, while recognizing that children need nurturance, argues that children should nonetheless share in the classical liberal rights available to adults in their society. In the United States, this view has prevailed at least in part in Supreme Court decisions such as *In re Gault* (1967), which established a minor's right to counsel, adequate notice, confrontation and cross-examination of witnesses and freedom from self-incrimination in proceedings that might result in confinement, and *Tinker* v. *Des Moines Independent Community School District* (1969), frequently cited for the proposition that "[i]t can hardly be argued that students or teachers shed their constitutional rights to freedom of speech or religion at the schoolhouse gate" (p506), implying that students, who are presumably minors, share in such rights.

None of these cases suggest, however, that the rights of minors are co-extensive with those of adults, and indeed the Court has expressly stated they are not:

> Viewed together, our cases show that although children generally are protected by the same governmental guarantees against governmental deprivations as are adults, the State is entitled to adjust its legal system to account for their vulnerability ... These rulings have been grounded in the recognition that, during the formative years of childhood and adolescence, minors often lack the experience, perspective and judgment to recognize and avoid choices that could be detrimental to them (*Bellotti* v. *Baird*, 1979, p635).

From this perspective, the new science about the adolescent brain may be viewed as merely confirming what the Court already understood and integrated into its vision of children's rights: a scaled version of adult constitutional rights, adjusted for minors – and generally restricted to teenagers.

The autonomy rights of minors may be constrained by the state's deference to the views of their parents and guardians in matters such as freedom of speech, receipt of information and religious exercise (Ross, 1999). Whether or not these restrictions are justified may depend on such factors as the child's age (two or seventeen), the context in which the minor wishes to assert independence and the nature of the perceived risks. Indeed, the ability of minors to assert their rights generally depends on the support of the adults who have responsibility for them.

This brings us to the question of capacity that lies at the heart of Justice Scalia's challenge to children's rights advocates. If adolescents are characterized by diminished capacity to make reasoned choices, can they still claim classical rights on their own behalf? Archard (2004) identifies three components of rational autonomy that are generally regarded as a precondition to the exercise of rights: "rationality, maturity and independence". The evidence from neuroscience would seem to undermine the pure autonomy claims of minors in that the parts of the brain related to rational decision-making and other behaviours our society associates with maturity appear not to be fully functional in teenagers. If rationality requires cognitive competence, the science underscores that teenagers, as a group, lack it.

As Archard (2004) and others argue, however, many adults also fall short of J.S. Mill's idealized prudent and rational citizen and are nonetheless allowed to exercise rights of self-determination. Moreover, in most instances the state does not categorically bar people over the age of 70 or 80 from driving, voting, working or living independently. Since independence (if defined as independent living and financial self-sufficiency) comes later and later for the young, independence premised on competency might be regarded as a shrinking stage of life. But we might also ask who in the modern world is truly independent and self-sufficient?

Limitations on the affirmative civil rights of minors (such as the right to express political views at school in a non-disruptive manner recognized in *Tinker*), based on arguments that young people are not yet fully cogent, must presumably be based on arguments that parallel the justifications for paternalistic protections of the sort discussed above. That is, for any argument in support of limiting rights to succeed under this model it would need to rest on the notion that exercise of certain rights now would ultimately diminish the range of choices available to the child in the future.

Taken to its outer edge, the rights model would seem to require granting suffrage to minors, since the vote is the critical recognition of citizenship. I am unaware of any legal commentator who has proposed that all children be able to vote, though many observe that some minors may be far better qualified to vote (by virtue of interest in and information about politics) than some adults who have the privilege, including the illiterate, the uninterested and those who fail to exercise their franchise. Archard (2004) observes that people may vote at age 16 in several countries, and argues that teenagers are capable of exercising the franchise.

So too I am unaware of any scholar who has argued that small children lacking in capacity should be able to exercise independent liberty claims *vis a vis* the state. Instead, the portrait of a school of thought premised on the assumption that capacity is irrelevant seems to flower in the assertions of those who criticize granting legal standing and authority to the young. Buss (1999), for example, challenges lawyers for children to show greater awareness of socio-cognitive development. Certainly incorporating longstanding knowledge of child development into legal theories has been critical from the earliest days (*e.g.*, Wald, 1979), and it will now be complemented by new knowledge about the brain, much of which confirms what we long knew or suspected from observation. Buss's comments were largely directed at proponents of empowerment, within the context of litigation, particularly proceedings arising out of abuse and neglect. The next section considers the empowerment approach to children's rights in a broader context.

Empowerment

The empowerment perspective shares with the caretaking approach an acceptance of children's developmental dependency, especially in the early years, and their needs for nurturance. It shares with the classical liberal model a recognition that rights have "intrinsic worth" (Federle, 1995, p1595) because once rights are recognized those who would intrude on those rights must, at a minimum, justify the intrusion, and/or take the rights-holder's perspective into account. Federle (1995) has correctly identified capacity as a central dilemma for this approach. To the extent that classical liberal theories of rights demand that rights-holders satisfy the requirement of capacity (as discussed above), presumptively established by achieving a certain birthday (18 or 21), how do children successfully claim rights? Federle, for example, rejects delegation of children's rights to adults standing as their proxies, because, in her words, "a caretaker ideology ... promotes the powerlessness of children" (p1590). The implications are practical as well as symbolic. The very adults who would normally stand as proxies for minors (their parents and guardians) may be the adults who stand between children and their rights as in the context of abortion, unwarranted psychiatric hospitalization or independent religious expression (Ross, 1996, 1999). Or, even if parents are well intentioned and share their children's goals, they may not be the most capable representatives of their children's interests (Ross, 1996).

Empowerment means the right to be heard about important decisions in the public sphere that affect a child's future, whether directly or through a representative who presents the child's viewpoint (Ross, 2006). Proponents of this approach may differ on the extent to which the child's ability to formulate and articulate their views matters, and the extent to which such ability tracks normative definitions of capacity. But they tend to emphasize that participation in process protects rights and assuages the sting of powerlessness even if the ultimate decision does not conform to the child's expressed preferences.

Because the leading theorists of children rights – whether from the caretaking, classical liberty or empowerment approaches – recognize that children are not the same as adults in critical respects related to capacity and competency, the new science does not seem to call for the paradigm shifts Justice Scalia envisions. Brain imaging may, however, bolster arguments for children's rights based on – rather than in spite of – the vulnerabilities and analytical deficiencies of the young, as discussed in the next section.

A Strengthened Paradigm

With the pronounced exception of the liberationists, doctrinal debates about the rights of minors have already taken into account a presumed lack of capacity and the very gradual nature of maturation. Brain imaging underpins this understanding with science, but for purposes of legal analysis at most it calls merely for recalibration, not paradigm shifts.

By giving a physiological basis to some of the indicia of immaturity in teenagers, however, the new findings accentuate three features of what we may broadly term lack of fully developed capacity. First, for teenagers as a group the capacity to make reasoned decisions may not be readily amenable to increased logic and information to the extent that the brain is not equipped to process that information. This is perhaps a starker statement than reflected in some of the legal literature to date. Second, the research suggests peaks and valleys in development rather than a linear progression. Third, while we have always acknowledged that 18 is merely a heuristic bright line the research suggests that as a physiological matter adolescence extends far beyond the age of 18.

Finally, brain MRIs mesh with the notion of youth as a "stage" which we all pass through. Scientist Jay Giedd reminds us that teenage brains are not broken, they are just under construction (Williamson, 2005). This generality is not disqualifying under any of the rights models because adults are not uniformly graced with capacity. Proponents of empowerment have always reminded their critics that adults who do not appear to think rationally or make choices others think wise nonetheless receive the full panoply of legal rights. The notion of the teenage brain as being in formation also supports the advocates of rights as caretaking and the importance of relational rights highlighted by feminist scholars.

Acknowledgement of teenagers' limited capacity does not necessarily support diminishment of their rights, because vulnerability and voice are not always diametrically opposed. Instead of treating vulnerability and rights as mutually exclusive, the vulnerability of young people can be turned to their advantage and used to bolster their rights claims (Ross, 1996). In several contexts, children's vulnerabilities may justify expanding rights and procedural protections rather than constricting them. To the extent that maturing minors lack the full executive functioning usually associated with complete autonomy, MRI discoveries about the adolescent brain may support expansion of rights designed to protect the vulnerable, particularly in court proceedings. Consider, for example, the adolescent's need in some circumstances, for appointed counsel in civil litigation, and, more frequently, for adult guidance and other special protections in navigating the justice system.

Children's vulnerabilities may in some instances argue for expanding their rights, for example by building on the parallels between the incapacities normatively associated with childhood and the situations in which courts appoint counsel for *pro se* litigants such as prisoners in civil litigation (Ross, 1996). Federal courts in the United States have the discretion to appoint counsel in civil cases, though it is rarely exercised outside the context of petitions from prisoners, whose lack of autonomy while incarcerated may resemble the position of minors in some authoritarian families, or at least the teenager's perception of the limits on their autonomy. Judges considering applications for counsel generally look to such factors as lack of financial resources, the merits of the claim, and the applicant's "ability to investigate the crucial facts … ability to present the case [and] the complexity of the legal issues" bearing in mind issues such as the level of education attained, maturity and judgment, all of which would favour making counsel available to teenagers based on their common analytical deficits. (Ross, 1996 p1598). MRI findings also bolster the argument that where teenagers or courts perceive that parents are not appropriate spokespersons for their children (for example, where children are committed to psychiatric hospitals over their objections) or their interests conflict with their parents' choices in other ways (Ross, 1999) or children in foster care whose parents are not presumed to speak for them (Ross, 2006), courts should appoint counsel to help young people tell their stories.

Similarly, I have argued that although "children's vulnerability is commonly used to justify state paternalism rather than to promote rights for minors" (Ross, 2003, p86) recognition of the cognitive and experiential limitations of minors should support zealous protection of their procedural rights. In particular, I have argued that a parent–child evidentiary privilege (which is not currently recognized under federal law or in more than a handful of states) is necessary so that parents may serve as conduits for their children's assertion of rights in court proceedings. How can teenagers solicit their parents' guidance about such issues as whether to waive their right to appointed counsel, or ask their parents to invest in private counsel without telling their parents what really happened in the activities leading up to the court appearance?

In contrast to most or all of Europe (Ross, 2003), under current law in the United States when a parent asks "what happened", the parent is at risk of being called as a witness against their own child. So too, parents might not urge children to "tell the truth" to police officers, as they frequently do, if they knew what the child was about to say. Psychological research, now supported by brain MRIs, indicates that the young are particularly vulnerable during interrogations (Grisso, 2006) and need help with the critical decisions made in the course of a trial, including whether to accept a plea bargain. To the extent that parents and children share the same goals in a child's court proceeding, a parent's advice and mediation of the judicial system may be the most effective means of preserving a child's procedural rights, and will undoubtedly be more effective if the child is assured that their confidences to a parent are protected by law. It is perverse to recognize the vulnerability of children on the one hand, and to acknowledge that children have constitutional rights with the other, without recognizing how the vulnerabilities of youth may diminish the exercise of rights and then to take responsive measures.

In *Roper*, *amici* APA argued that the MRI studies and other new data demonstrate that "adolescent immaturity undermines a defendant's ability to make meaningful and fully informed decisions to manage his or her own defense" (APA, 2004, p23). Teenagers need special protections because they cannot effectively navigate the justice system on their own, and must confide in their parents to get meaningful advice. Similarly, emerging knowledge about the teenage brain and its role in impulsivity and difficulty resisting collective wrongdoing reinforces authoritative arguments against the trend in the United States to try and sentence teenagers as young as age 13 in adult courts and even to incarcerate them with adults (*see* Campaign for Youth Justice, 2007; Corriero, 2006; Zimring 1998).

The hard science supports what we have long observed, and cautions us to remember that immaturity disadvantages youth at every stage from committing an offence through trial, sentencing and punishment. It also may help us, as a community, to anticipate and meet children's needs in the first instance, and, when some young people get off track, to acknowledge and facilitate the rehabilitative possibilities that exist for many individuals. In such a world, when their brains finally mature, the young may still be in a position to realize life's possibilities.

References

American Medical Association et al. 2004. Brief of the American Medical Association [et al.]... as *Amici Curiae* in Support of Respondent, *Roper* v. *Simmons*, No. 03-633.

American Psychological Association & the Missouri Psychological Association. 2004. Brief for the American Psychological Association and the Missouri Psychological Association as *Amici Curiae* Supporting Respondent, *Roper* v. *Simmons*, No. 03-633.

American Psychological Association. 1989. Brief for the American Psychological Association as *Amicus Curiae* Supporting Petitioner/Cross-Repondent, *Hodgson* v. *Minnesota*, No. 88-805.

Anderson, D.R. et al. 2006. Brain Imaging – An Introduction to a New Approach to Studying Media Processes and Effects. Media Psychology 1–6.

Archard, D. 2004. Children, Rights and Childhood. 2d ed. Routledge: London.

Arshagouni, P. 2004. "But I'm an Adult Now … Sort of": Adolescent Consent in Health Care Decision-Making and the Adolescent Brain, 9 J. of Health Care Law and Policy 315.

Brooks, R.O. 2006. "The Refurbishing": Reflections Upon Law and Justice Among the Stages of Life, 54 Buffalo L. Rev. 619–692.

Buck, T. 2005. International Child Law. London: Cavendish Publishing Ltd.

Buss, E. 1999. Confronting Developmental Barriers to the Empowerment of Child Clients, 84 Cornell L. Rev. 895.

Campaign for Youth Justice. 2007. The Consequences Aren't Minor: The Impact of Trying Youth as Adults and Strategies for Reform.

Corriero, M.A. 2006. Judging Children as Children: A Proposal for a Juvenile Justice System. Philadelphia: Temple University Press.

Denno, D.W. 2006. The Scientific Shortcomings of *Roper* v. *Simmons*, 3 Ohio State Journal of Criminal Law, 379–396.

Farson, R. 1974. Birthrights. London: Collier, MacMillan.

Furstenberg, F.F., Jr. et al. 2004. Growing Up Is Harder to Do, 3 Contexts: Understanding People in Their Social Worlds 1. http://www.contextsmagazine.org/content-sample-v3-3.php.

Goldstein, J., Solnit, A.J., Goldstein, S. & Freud, A. 1996. The Best Interests of the Child: The Least Detrimental Alternative. New York: The Free Press.

Gruber, S.A. & Yurgelin-Todd, D.A. 2006. Neurobiology and the Law: A Role in Juvenile Justice?, 3 Ohio State J. of Criminal Law, 321–340.

Haider, Aliya. 2006. *Roper* v. *Simmons*: The Role of the Science Brief. 3 Ohio State Journal of Criminal Law 369, 369–377.
Haley v. *Ohio*, 332 U.S. 596 (1947).
Hodgson v. *Minnesota*. 1990. 497 U.S. 417.
Holt, J. 1974. Escape From Childhood: The Needs and Rights of Children. Harmondsworth: Penguin.
In re Gault. 1967. 387 U.S. 1.
Johnson, D.L. et al. 2004. The Violent Youth Offender and Juvenile Transfer to the Adult Criminal Court, 2004 Journal of the Institute of Justice and International Studies 84.
Minow, M. 1995. What Ever Happened to Chldren's Rights? 80 Minnesota Law Review 267.
Minow, M. 1990. Making All the Difference: Inclusion, Exclusion and American Law. Ithaca: Cornell University Press.
Minow, M. 1986. Rights for the Next Generation: A Feminist Approach to Children's Rights. 9 Harvard Women's Law Journal 1.
National Institute of Mental Health. 2001. Teenage Brain: A Work in Progress. Available at http://www. Nimh.nih.gov/pubcat/teenbrain.cfm. (last visited 21 June 2007).
Neill, A.S. & Fromm, E. 1960. Summerhill: A Radical Approach to Child Rearing. Harmondsworth: Penguin.
Penry v. *Lynaugh*. 1989. 492 U.S. 302.
Powell v. *Alabama*, 287 U.S. 45 (1932).
Roper v. *Simmons*. 2005. 543 U.S. 551.
Roper v. *Simmons*, 2004. . Transcript of Oral Argument, October 13, 2004. 2004 U.S. Trans LEXIS 55.
Ross, C.J. 2006. A Place at the Table: Creating Presence and Voice for Teenagers in Dependency Hearings. 6 Nev. L. J. 1362.
Ross, C.J. 2006a. Review of James Dwyer's The Relationship Rights of Children, 16 Law and Politics Book Review 975.
Ross, C.J. 2003. Implementing Constitutional Rights for Juveniles: The Parent–Child Privilege in Context. 14 Stanford Law & Policy Review 85.
Ross, C.J. 1999. An Emerging Right for Mature Minors to Receive Information. 2 U. Pa. J. Const. L. 223.
Ross, C.J. 1996. From Vulnerability to Voice: Appointing Counsel for Children in Civil Litigation, 64 Fordham Law Review, 1571–1620.
Ross, C.J. 1995. Disposition in a Discretionary Regime: Punishment and Rehabilitation in the Juvenile Justice System. 36 Boston College Law Review 1037.
Scott, E. & Grisso, T. 1997. The Evolution of Adolescence: A Developmental Perspective on Juvenile Reform. 88 The Journal of Criminal Law and Criminology 137.
Scott, E. & Steinberg, L. 2003. Essay: Blaming Youth. 81 Texas Law Review 799.

Scott, E.S. & Scott, R.E.1995. Parents as Fiduciaries, 81 Va. L. Rev. 2401.
Stanford v. *Kentucky*. 1989. 492 U.S. 302.
Thompson v. *Oklahoma*, 487 U.S. 815, 1988.
Tinker v. *Des Moines Indep. Community Sch. Dist.* 1969. 393 U.S. 503.
United Nations. 1989. Convention on the Rights of the Child.
Wald, M. 1979. Children's Rights: A Framework for Analysis? 12 U.C. Davis L. Rev. 255.
Williamson, E. 2005. Brain Immaturity Could Explain Teen Crash Rate; Risky Behavior Diminishes At Age 25. The Washington Post. Feb. 1, A-1
Woodhouse, B.B. 1993. Hatching the Egg: A Child-Centered Perspective on Children's Rights, 14 Cardozo L.Rev. 1747.
Zimring, F. 1998. American Youth Violence. New York: Oxford University Press.

Chapter 9

Thinking Like a Child: Legal Implications of Recent Developments in Brain Research for Juvenile Offenders

Katherine Hunt Federle and Paul Skendelas

Over the last decade, advances in brain-imaging technology have revealed important details about the developmental stages of the human brain and how functioning is impacted during this process. The parts of the brain that are critical to judgment, foresight and decision-making are the last to mature. The prefrontal cortex, which is the focal point of these processes, does not develop until late adolescence or early adulthood. As a result, adolescents are physiologically less able to reason than adults; they process information and make decisions with a different part of the brain. Because they are at a more primitive developmental stage, adolescents lack judgment, are more prone to peer influence and impulsivity, and cannot understand the consequences of their actions.

Paralleling these recent developments was the criminalization of the American juvenile court system. On 1 March 2005, the United States Supreme Court decided *Roper v. Simmons*,[1] which struck down the use of the death penalty for crimes committed before age 18. Noting that evolving standards of decency, as embodied in legislative enactments, determine which punishments are so disproportionate as to be cruel and unusual, the Court found that because the majority of states had rejected the juvenile death penalty, "our society views juveniles … as 'categorically less culpable than the average criminal'".[2] While the decision in *Roper* does not rest on any of the recent developments in brain research, the Court's conclusions are consistent with the growing body of scientific evidence that recognizes that there are fundamental differences in the ways juveniles process information and make decisions.

The research in brain development has wide-ranging implications for juvenile offenders, some of whom are as young as seven to twelve years of age. It raises questions about current concepts of culpability, accountability and punishment, especially with regard to imposing adult terms as part of a blended sentence, transferring or relinquishing jurisdiction to adult courts, and labelling minors as sexual offenders or predators. The research raises moral and legal issues about the

1 543 U.S. 551 (2005).

2 *Id.* at 567 (quoting *Atkins v. Virginia*, 536 U.S. 304, 316 (2002)).

juvenile justice system in light of the majority holding in *Roper,* which found that imposing society's harshest penalties on those who are less culpable because of age, maturity and level of emotional and psychological development violated the prohibition against cruel and unusual punishment set forth in the United States Constitution.

The trend to treat juvenile delinquents as adult offenders runs counter to recent findings about the development of the human brain. What is indisputable is the essential fact that the mind of a child is different. Because the brain reaches 95% of its adult size by the time a child is six, it was thought to be fully developed.[3] Technological advances in brain scanning and mapping, however, show that brain development is marked by waves of proliferation and pruning of brain cells moving from the back to the front of the brain.[4] Thus, the brain regions that mature earliest are those responsible for controlling sensory functions like vision, hearing and spatial processing, while the last part of the brain to fully develop – the prefrontal cortex – is the region responsible for planning, organizing, suppressing impulses and weighing the consequences of one's actions.[5] These findings suggest that the human brain does not reach its full adult capacity until the individual is in their early twenties.[6]

This new brain development research, especially when considered in conjunction with the increasing criminalization of the juvenile justice system and the concomitant imposition of adult sanctions on increasingly younger offenders, raises questions about the culpability and accountability of juveniles. When a child is between the ages of six and twelve, the brain's grey matter, the "thinking" part of the brain, thickens as brain cells make connections to neurons and create new pathways for nerve signals.[7] The thickening of all this grey matter – the neurons and their branch-like dendrites – peaks when girls are about 11 and boys 12½, at which point the brain then alters the number of connections, or synapses, between them.[8] As the grey matter is pruned, the brain's white matter, which makes nerve-signal transmissions faster and more efficient, thickens. This thickening process continues well into adulthood, possibly up to the age of 40.[9]

---

3 "FRONTLINE: Inside the Teenage Brain, Adolescent Brains are Works in Progress" available at www.pbs.org/wgbh/pages/frontline/shows/teenbrain/work/adolescent.html (2002).

4 Elizabeth Sowell et al., *Mapping Continued Brain Growth and Gray Matter Density Reduction in Dorsal Frontal Cortex: Inverse relationship During Postadolescent Brain Maturation,* The Journal of Neuroscience 21(22): 8819–8829 (Nov. 2001).

5 Elizabeth Sowell et al., *Mapping Cortical Change Across the Human Life Span*, 6 Nature Neuroscience 309–315 (March 2003).

6 The International Justice Project, "Brain Development, Culpability and the Death Penalty."

7 "FRONTLINE: Interview Jay Giedd" available at www.pbs.org.wgbh/pages/frontline/shows/teenbrain/interview/giedd.html (2002).

8 *Id.*

9 Bruce Bower, *Teen brains on trial: the science of neural development tangles with the juvenile death penalty*, Science News (2004).

The thickening of this grey matter peaks roughly around the time of puberty and its subsequent pruning occurs during adolescence. This pruning process results in a significant and "massive" loss of brain tissue. So, while the brain of a teenager between the ages of 13 and 18 is maturing, it nevertheless loses 1–2% percent of its grey matter per year.[10] This pruning process, however, is critical to the brain's development. Brain scanning and mapping studies thus reveal that there is relatively subtle growth in the brain's frontal lobes after adolescence.[11]

Because the brain is developing from back to front, the part of the brain that is most affected by this wave of proliferation and pruning is the prefrontal cortex, the part involved in organization, planning, judgment and strategizing. Recent developments in brain research have established a link between the frontal lobe and the maturation of judgment and impulse control. By comparing adult brain scans with scans of adolescent brains, scientists have been able to contrast the relative differences in decision-making abilities, thereby highlighting distinct dissimilarities between adults and adolescents. Thus certain abilities associated with the frontal lobes, like response inhibition, emotional regulation, planning and organization, continue to develop between adolescence and young adulthood while cognitive functioning like learning, which also is linked to the frontal system, improve throughout adolescence.[12] This means that even as they become fully capable in other areas, adolescents cannot reason as well as adults; "maturation, particularly in the frontal lobes, has been shown to correlate with measures of cognitive functioning".[13]

These studies indicate that during the teenage years, the frontal lobe of the brain that is supposed to help organize and strategize is not done being built.[14] The brain consolidates learning by pruning away synapses and wrapping white matter, myelin, around other connections and strengthening them. The accumulation of this fatty tissue, which fosters transmission of electrical signals, develops especially slowly in the frontal lobe. Those parts of the brain that "govern impulsivity, judgment, planning for the future, foresight of consequences, and other characteristics that make people morally culpable" are not developed until the early twenties.[15] Thus, with respect to controlling aggression and other impulses, "[i]f the neural substrates of these behaviours have not reached maturity before adulthood, it is unreasonable to expect the behaviors themselves to reflect mature thought processes".[16] It would be "unfair to expect [teens] to have adult levels of organizational skills or decision making before their brain is finished being built".[17]

---

10 *Adolescence, Brain Development and Legal Culpability*, Jan. 2004 A.B.A. Criminal Justice Section.

11 *Id.*

12 *Id.*

13 *Id.*

14 *Id.*

15 *Id.*

16 *Id.*

17 *Id.*

This evidence provides a neural basis for assuming that teens are less blameworthy than adults for the commission of criminal acts.[18] To compensate for the relative immaturity of the frontal lobe, the teenage brain places heavy reliance on an almond-shaped inner-brain structure called the amygdala, a more primitive part of the brain that is responsible for gut reactions.[19] Studies conducted at Harvard Medical School used functional MRI scans to show that adolescents rely on the amygdala in interpreting emotional information, while adults rely on the prefrontal cortex, the brain's rational decision-making region.[20] In order for adolescents to appreciate the consequences of a behaviour, they have to understand the potential outcome. Since adolescents cannot always rely on the frontal lobe, they may not be able to appreciate these outcomes and consequences the way an adult may. As a result, the information received by the brain, how it is organized, and the ultimate response may all be different in adolescents.

Adolescents also lag behind in the development of other critical areas of the brain. For example, the corpus callosum, the cable of nerves that connects and relays information between the two hemispheres of the brain, develops in waves.[21] This is significant because the corpus callosum, which is involved in problem-solving and creativity, continues to grow and change through adolescence.[22] Moreover, the lack of a properly formed corpus callosum as well as a prefrontal cortex suggests that an adolescent brain relies heavily on the amygdala.[23] Similarly, the cerebellum, involved in the coordination of our thinking processes, also continues to change well into adolescence. The cerebellum is "not essential for any activity … but it makes any activity better. Anything we can think of as higher thought, mathematics, music, philosophy, decision-making, social skill, draws upon the cerebellum … To navigate the complicated social life of the teen and to get through these things … seems to be a function of the cerebellum."[24]

Recognizing the process in which teenage brains develop might also give us a better understanding of teen behaviour. Studies indicate that it may be harder for juveniles than adults to foresee the consequences of their actions.[25] In these experiments, adults and teens were shown scenarios on a computer screen, like swimming with sharks, and were asked whether each scenario was a good idea or a bad idea. It took juveniles 0.15 seconds longer than adults to reach a decision. Brain scans conducted during the study showed more activity in the prefrontal cortex of

---

18 Bower, supra note 9.

19 "FRONTLINE: Interview with Deborah Yurgelun-Todd," available at http://www.pbs.org/wgbh/pages/frontline/shows/teenbrain/interviews/todd.html.

20 *Id.*

21 "FRONTLINE: Inside the Teenage Brain," supra note 3.

22 The International Justice Project, supra note 6.

23 *Id.*

24 "FRONTLINE: Interview Jay Giedd," supra note 7.

25 Helen Philips, *Teenagers fail to see the consequence,* New Scientist, Dec. 04, 2004 available at www.newscientist.com/article.ns?id=dn6738

juveniles' brains, indicating that they may be making a greater effort to judge the results of each scenario.[26] Adults, however, had more basal ganglia activity, which indicates a more automatic response.[27] Adults also had more activity in the parts of the brain that create mental imagery and often signal internal distress.[28] The results suggest that juveniles try to use the frontal lobe to reason but it is not automatic and may actually be a difficult process.[29]

Physiological differences in the teenage brain raise serious questions about juvenile culpability and punishment. Juveniles are less likely to be deterred from committing crimes because of the threat of harsh punishment. The inability of adolescents to understand the longer-term consequences of their actions means they look only to the immediate future, perhaps a period of one to three days, when assessing choices.[30] Although such limitations do not negate knowledge and a basic understanding of right and wrong, they nevertheless suggest that teenagers are not yet adults and should not be treated in the same way.[31] The developmental evidence also overwhelmingly demonstrates just how different the brains of pre-pubescent children are and how baseless it is to treat offenders under the age of 12 or 13 in the same way as older teens, since in most instances the brains of these children are still growing.

What does the brain research tell us, then, about our approach in juvenile court? First, we must be clear what the research does not do. It does not tell us whether children ought to and do have rights. Some might argue that because the research indicates children lack sufficient brain maturity, they therefore lack the capacity to have and exercise rights. From this perspective, we are correct to delay the extension of rights until children's brains are sufficiently mature. I have always maintained, however, that having capacity is not a prerequisite to having and exercising rights. Rather, I have argued that rights themselves are a form of power, a means of empowering the powerless.[32]

From this perspective – what I have called elsewhere the empowerment perspective[33] – rights are concerned exclusively with the dynamics of power in personal and institutional interactions and with equalizing power within those relationships. Consequently, empowerment rights flow, somewhat paradoxically, to the least powerful; thus, while having a right accords the rights-holder power, obtaining the right suggest the disempowerment of the claimant. In other words,

26 *Id.*

27 *Id.*

28 Abigail Baird, *Why do teens do "stupid" things?*, www.theteenbrain.com/latest

29 A NewsHour with Jim Lehrer, Transcript, "The Teen Brain." (Oct. 13, 2004) available at www.pbs.org/newshour/bb/science/july-dec04/brain_10-13.html.

30 The International Justice Project, *supra* note 6.

31 *Id.*

32 See, e.g., Katherine Hunt Federle, *Looking Ahead: An Empowerment Perspective on the Rights of Children*, 68 Temple L. Rev. 1585 (1995).

33 See *id.*

rights are valuable because they provide the powerless with access to political and legal hierarchies and with a means of challenging their oppression and subordination. By rejecting the capacity of the rights-holder as a prerequisite to having and exercising rights, empowerment rights allow us to reconsider the status of children as rights-holders and to see how other accounts of rights fail to accommodate the powerlessness of children. An empowerment perspective thus seeks to remedy the exclusion and marginalization of the powerless through the redistribution of power. By recognizing that rights are a form of power, this perspective ensures that the powerless may capture the attention of powerful elites by demanding that they, too, be respected as powerful rights-bearing individuals. Thus, the brain research does not constrain our accounts of children's rights because the fact of the right is not dependent on a construct of capacity.

What does this mean in context? Consider the issue of competency. The adversarial process is premised on a conception of fairness embodied in the Due Process Clause of the United States Constitution. This notion of fairness necessarily entails the accused's cognizance of the proceedings against them. Otherwise, the mere presence of the accused without this understanding not only would be meaningless but would also undermine the integrity of the trial process if the accused is unaware of what is happening to them. Thus, the accused must understand the nature of the proceedings, be able to communicate with counsel and be capable of making rational choices. If the accused is incapable of participating in any meaningful way because of mental incompetence, mental illness or some other mental disability, then the proceedings are unjust. To convict an incompetent person, then, is not only inequitable but unfair as a constitutional matter.

In *Dusky v. United States*,[34] the United States Supreme Court articulated the standard by which a court should determine the accused's competence to stand trial. According to the Court, the test is "whether the defendant has sufficient present ability to consult with his lawyer with a reasonable degree of rational understanding – and whether he has a rational as well as a factual understanding of the proceedings against him."[35] The Court has held this to mean that the defendant must be able to assist in preparing his defence. Thus, the issue of the defendant's competency to stand trial may be raised at any time prior to or during the proceeding. Moreover, many jurisdictions permit any party or even the judge to raise the issue of the accused's competence. All of the states have adopted the test articulated by the Court in *Dusky* or some variation of it.

Unlike insanity, incompetency involves the defendant's mental state at the time of the relevant proceeding and focuses only on two narrowly defined areas: the defendant's ability to understand the proceedings and their ability to communicate with their lawyer. According to the courts, the accused must have a basic understanding of the charges against them, of the consequences of conviction on those charges and of the nature of adversary process. If the case goes to trial, the

34 362 U.S. 402 (1960).

35 *Id.* at 402.

defendant must have the capacity to understand various rights that may be waived during the trial process, like the right to counsel or the right to remain silent. As to whether they have a rational as well as a factual understanding of the proceedings against them, the defendant should be able to recount pertinent facts surrounding the time of the offence. The government may require the defendant to prove their incompetency.

Because the test is stringent, most criminal defendants are found to be competent to stand trial. A finding of incompetency, however, does not mean the defendant will be released; in most jurisdictions, the state will hospitalize the defendant in order to restore them to competency. This may result in periods of confinement in excess of any possible sentence that could be imposed for the underlying offence. Although some jurisdictions do limit the length of hospitalization, a majority of jurisdictions do not impose any limits on the length of confinement for incompetency. Nevertheless there are some constitutional limits on the length of time the defendant may be hospitalized.

The question remains whether due process mandates a different standard of competence when the accused is in juvenile court. We do know that adolescent brains are far less developed than we previously thought. The prefrontal cortex provides us with an advanced level of consciousness – an ability to prioritize thoughts, think in the abstract and anticipate consequences. But because the prefrontal cortex is not fully developed until the early twenties, adolescents cannot rely on that part of their brains when making decisions. Rather, they rely on the amygdala – that more primitive part of the brain responsible for gut reactions, the part that processes emotions.

The point is that the human brain is still developing – and developing in important ways. Thus children under 14 may be more likely to misread emotional signals because they rely on their gut reactions – not their judgment. Moreover, adolescents may be more prone to taking risks in the presence of their friends and more responsive to immediate pay-offs. If, as the research suggests, the immature brain relies on the amygdala rather then the prefrontal cortex, then we might wonder how children have the present ability to understand the proceedings and to communicate with their attorneys.

How likely is it that children may be incompetent to proceed? In one large-scale study, researchers in the United States interviewed 927 youths in four communities.[36] Two subgroups, matched for age, gender and ethnicity, were identified: those in the juvenile justice system and those without justice system involvement.[37] The study participants were further divided into three age categories: children ages 11–13 (constituting 20% of the study population); children ages 14–15 (constituting 37% of the study group); and 16- and 17-year-olds (representing

---

36 Elizabeth S. Scott & Thomas Grisso, *Developmental Incompetence, Due Process, and Juvenile Justice Policy*, 83 North Carolina L. Rev. 793, 820 (2005).

37 *Id.*

43% of the study population).[38] All participants were given a standard intelligence test and a measure of symptoms of mental or emotional disturbance.[39] Researchers also administered two tests to assess the abilities relevant to competence to stand trial. The first was a specially designed instrument for the study called the MacArthur Competence Assessment Tool-Criminal Adjudication to assess an understanding of the charges, penalties, pleas and roles of trial participants.[40] The second instrument, the MacArthur Judgment Valuation, was designed to assess psychosocial influences on decision-making related to trial participation.[41]

The researchers found that children between the ages of 11 and 13 had a poorer understanding of trial matters, poorer reasoning and recognition of the relevance of information for a legal defence than did the 14- and15-year-olds who, in turn, performed significantly more poorly than the 16- and 17-year-olds.[42] The researchers, however, found no significant differences between the 16- and 17-year-olds and young adults.[43] Intelligence scores also were significantly related to the competence assessment, an important fact because a greater proportion of the detained youths were in lower IQ ranges compared with youths not in system.[44] While there were no significant differences based on race and gender, there was a relationship between age and performance that was important independent of intelligence.[45]

The study also indicated that adolescents were much more likely to make choices in compliance with the perceived desires of authority figures – thus they were more likely to recommend waiving constitutional rights in interrogation than adults or to accept a plea offer.[46] Thus, even if youths in the study were found to be significantly impaired, it does not necessarily mean they were incompetent to stand trial since the study does not probe communication and other abilities that might be important to assisting counsel. Nor did the study take into account how these individuals would fare if given proper assistance. Moreover, standard treatments to restore competency simply do not work for a minor who has never attained competency in the first place.[47] Nevertheless, the study does indicate that developmental competence is real and should be accounted for when dealing with juvenile offenders.

Ultimately, the recent developments in brain research may say both too much and too little. It may say too much because it suggests that most children may lack

38 *Id.* at 820–821.
39 *Id.* at 821.
40 *Id.*
41 *Id.* at 821–822.
42 *Id.* at 822.
43 *Id.*
44 *Id.* at 822–823.
45 *Id.* at 823.
46 *Id.* at 824.
47 *Id.* at 830.

the ability to think abstractly and to anticipate consequences – the very kind of thinking we ask of our clients when assisting us in the preparation of their cases. It may also suggest that the paradigm client simply may not exist – at least if they are under the age of 25. The problem of course may be that our competency standard is an unrealistic one – and in fact we may know this already. It could explain why, for example, so few criminal defendants are found incompetent to stand trial.

As a practical matter, even juveniles routinely are found competent. Assessments of juvenile competence further adult control and state regulation of children. The brain research thus may be seen along this spectrum. The willingness to find that children are competent increases the likelihood that these children will remain in the justice system and thus be subject to state control and governmental involvement in their lives. Analogously, one could extrapolate from the research the suggestion that most children lack the ability to think abstractly and to anticipate consequences, the very kind of thinking we ask of our clients when assisting us in the preparation of their cases. Claiming that children lack the ability to articulate their legal interests also promotes further state intervention.

There nevertheless are limits on what we might draw from the research. For example, the findings do not truly explain why some youths commit crimes and others do not. Similarly, the studies cannot tell us whether our clients are legally competent. It would be disturbing to think that all our juvenile clients are incompetent because then we would be placed in the anomalous situation of asking for a finding of incompetency in almost every case involving a juvenile offender. That in turn may expose our juvenile clients to longer periods of institutionalization.

Perhaps it is easiest to see how the research would apply to dispositions. Because medical evidence suggests that juveniles are less culpable for their actions, this evidence is relevant to considerations of treatment and punishment. But it also poses some risks because the suggestion of immaturity carries with it the suggestion of future dangerousness. The science has not advanced far enough to quantify its effect, necessarily limiting its use. This problem is less important on the dispositional side, as a mitigating factor, where courts consider all relevant factors in deciding an appropriate sentence. Certainly, the research comes at a crucial time, in light of the United States Supreme Court decision in *Roper v. Simmons*, holding that it is cruel and unusual punishment to execute a person for crimes committed under the age of 18.

Nevertheless, it is very clear that in the United States, we have taken an increasingly punitive approach to the treatment of juvenile offenders. For example, state legislatures amended their juvenile codes to emphasize juvenile accountability and punishment in addition to or even in lieu of rehabilitation and protection. Six states have enacted statutes that explicitly articulate traditional criminal goals, like deterrence, punishment, accountability and public safety.[48]

48 Patrick Griffin, Linda Szymanski, & Melanie King, "National Overviews," *State Juvenile Justice Profiles* (2006) available at http://www.ncjj.org/stateprofiles/. The six states are Connecticut, Hawaii, North Carolina, Texas, Utah and Wyoming.

Another 17 jurisdictions embrace "balanced and restorative justice" principles.[49] While less aggressively punitive, these statutes nevertheless focus on restoration of the victim through offender accountability while balancing the need to return the offender to law-abiding status.[50] Although many jurisdictions, including some of those already mentioned, still retain language suggesting rehabilitation as a goal, only three states emphasize the best interests of the child as the primary purpose of the juvenile court.[51]

Simultaneously, state legislatures redefined the juvenile court's jurisdictional authority, permitting criminal courts to assume jurisdiction over more offences and ever younger offenders. Known as waiver or transfer, these provisions allow certain juveniles to be tried in the criminal court system and held accountable as if they were adults. Although mechanisms to exclude certain youthful offenders from the juvenile court's jurisdiction have always existed, perceptions of a juvenile crime wave in the 1990s spurred sweeping changes in state transfer laws.[52] Between 1992 and 1997, 44 states and the District of Columbia passed new laws that would send more juveniles to criminal court.[53] Most states simply excluded certain offenders by virtue of age or the charged offence from the juvenile court's original jurisdiction.[54] Thus, 28 states expanded the list of offences to be excluded from juvenile court jurisdiction while seven states lowered the age at which a youthful offender could be transferred to criminal court.[55] Some jurisdictions even shifted the burden of proof to the child to rebut the presumption of transfer.[56]

Despite clear statistical evidence of a significant downturn in juvenile offending, state legislatures continued to amend their transfer laws. Between 1998 and 2002, 31 states enacted amendments to their transfer laws.[57] Of these, 18 states extended their transfer laws, primarily by expanding the number of transfer-eligible offences.[58] The most dramatic changes occurred in California with the passage of Proposition 21, which created new mechanisms for transfer initiated

49 *Id.* They include Alabama, Alaska, California, the District of Columbia, Florida, Idaho, Illinois, Indiana, Kansas, Maryland, Minnesota, Montana, New Jersey, Oregon, Pennsylvania, Washington and Wisconsin.

50 *Id.*

51 *Id.* For example, one statute states that juveniles should be "treated not as criminals, but as children in need of aid, encouragement, and guidance."

52 Howard N. Snyder & Melissa Sickmund, *Juvenile Offenders and Victims: 2006* National Report 96 (2006).

53 OJJDP Statistical Briefing Book, available at http://ojjdp.ncjrs.gov/ojstatbb/structure_process/qa04107.asp?qadate=19990701.

54 Patricia Torbet & Linda Szymanski, *State Legislative Responses to Violent Juvenile Crime: 1996–97* Update 2 (1998).

55 OJJDP Statistical Briefing Book, *supra* note 53.

56 Torbet & Szymanski, *supra* note 54, at 3.

57 Patrick Griffin, "National Overview," State Juvenile Justice Profiles (2006) available at http://www.ncjj.org/stateprofiles/overviews/transfer9.asp.

58 *Id.* available at http://www.ncjj.org/stateprofiles/overviews/transfer9t.asp.

by prosecutors and new categories of minors excluded from juvenile court jurisdiction.[59] Only six states narrowed their transfer provisions, yet these changes were relatively minor.[60]

Currently, every state and the District of Columbia rely on a combination of mechanisms to transfer juveniles to criminal court; these include judicial waiver provisions, direct file laws and statutory exclusions. Forty-six states have enacted judicial waiver laws in which juvenile court judges enter an order authorizing the transfer of the juvenile to criminal court.[61] Fifteen states have direct file laws which allow the prosecutor to decide whether to file in criminal or juvenile court.[62] An additional 29 states rely on statutory exclusion provisions to exclude certain classes of juveniles from juvenile court jurisdiction *ab initio* while vesting original jurisdiction over these cases in the criminal courts.[63]

As a general matter, most transfer mechanisms do not involve a determination of the individual juvenile's competence or developmental abilities. For example, statutory exclusion provisions do not permit either the juvenile court judge or the prosecutor to consider the individual attributes of the juvenile.[64] These exclusions generally redefine who is a delinquent child for the purposes of juvenile court jurisdiction and thus automatically exclude certain offenders based on age, the current offence and prior record.[65] Similarly, direct file laws authorize the state to choose the prosecuting forum.[66] Although typically the statutes require that the juvenile be of a certain age and charged with a certain offence, direct file laws often authorize filing in criminal court for a broader range of offences.[67] Moreover, in 34 states, once a juvenile has been transferred to criminal court, the minor will be treated as an adult for all subsequent criminal prosecutions.[68] Most states do not make any distinctions based on the age of the offender, although many states do at least require that the transferred minor be convicted of the transferred offence.[69]

Although 45 states do authorize discretionary judicial waiver based on broad statutory criteria that permit the court to take individual characteristics of the juvenile into account,[70] many states nevertheless preclude the juvenile court from making an individualized determination about the appropriateness of waiver. For example, 15 states mandate the transfer of a juvenile to criminal court if the juvenile

---

59 *Id.* available at http://www.ncjj.org/stateprofiles/overviews/transfer9.asp.

60 *Id.* available at http://www.ncjj.org/stateprofiles/overviews/transfer9t.asp.

61 Patrick Griffin, *Trying and Sentencing Juveniles as Adults: An Analysis of State Transfer and Blended Sentencing Laws 2* (2003).

62 *Id.*

63 *Id.*

64 *Id.*

65 *Id.* at 8.

66 *Id.* at 10.

67 *Id.*

68 *Id.* at 11.

69 *Id.*

70 *Id.* at 4.

is of a certain age and is charged with committing a specified offence.[71] In these jurisdictions, the juvenile court merely verifies that the articulated statutory criteria have been met and then authorizes waiver.[72] Four of these states, in addition to 13 other jurisdictions, also have presumptive waiver laws.[73] Under these provisions, waiver is to be presumed appropriate if the statutory criteria have been satisfied; the burden then is shifted to the juvenile to show that transfer is not warranted.[74]

While discretionary judicial waiver is the most common provision for transfer, there nevertheless is every indication that far more – and ever younger – children are being waived to criminal court through other transfer mechanisms. In 2000, juvenile court judges across the country transferred fewer than 6,000 minors to criminal court.[75] The number of juveniles waived has been declining, a trend that may largely be attributable to increasing reliance on other methods of waiver.[76] Although no federal data exist on the actual numbers of children waived through direct file or statutory exclusion mechanisms, some estimates indicate that as many as 200,000 juveniles are tried each year as adults.[77] Moreover, all kinds of transfer provisions permit younger children to be tried as adults. Two states, for example, permit children as young as 10 to be waived to criminal court,[78] while another 25 states permit transfer of children under the age of 16.[79] Additionally, at least one transfer mechanism specifies no minimum age at which a minor may be sent to criminal court in 23 states.[80]

Once in the criminal system, juvenile offenders typically are treated no differently than adult defendants for the purposes of punishment. Although juveniles may no longer be sentenced to death in the United States, they nevertheless could face life imprisonment without the possibility of parole. Sixteen states impose mandatory life imprisonment without the possibility of parole on juveniles who have been tried and convicted as adults in criminal court.[81] While the majority of these jurisdictions authorize the imposition of a life sentence only on juveniles who are 14 years of age or older,[82] one jurisdiction would permit the imposition of life without parole on a 10-year-old offender while three other states have no age limitations at all.[83] Another six states mandate the imposition of life without

---

71 *Id.* at 7.

72 *Id.*

73 *Id.* at 6–7.

74 *Id.* at 6.

75 Snyder & Sickmund, *supra* note 52, at 113.

76 *Id.* at 114.

77 *Id.* at 114. The two states are Kansas and Vermont.

78 *Id.*

79 *Id.*

80 *Id.*

81 Victor Streib & Bernadette Schrempp, *Life Without Parole for Children,* Crim. J. 4, 10 (Winter 2007).

82 *Id.*

83 *Id.* South Dakota permits the imposition of life without parole on a 10-year-old offender. In Delaware and Florida, there is no statutorily defined age limit and in Pennsylvania, there is no age limit if the juvenile offender is convicted of murder.

parole on finding certain statutorily enumerated factors.[84] An additional 19 states permit, but do not require, the imposition of a life sentence without the possibility of parole on juvenile offenders.[85]

But even those juveniles who remain in the juvenile justice system may be subject to criminal penalties. These laws, known as blended sentences, permit juvenile courts to impose adult sanctions on certain qualifying juvenile offenders. To date, 15 states have enacted provisions authorizing blended sentences.[86] Typically, these laws authorize a juvenile judge to impose a criminal sentence, usually in addition to the juvenile disposition, that the court then suspends on condition that the juvenile successfully completes their juvenile term. In three of these states, however, the court may directly impose an adult sentence in lieu of a juvenile disposition.[87] In three other states, the court has the authority to impose a term of incarceration that may extend years beyond the age limits of the court's jurisdiction without reference to the minor's adjustment or rehabilitation.[88]

In 10 states, the blended sentencing provisions are more expansive than the waiver laws, so more juveniles are at risk of adult sanctions because of these broader eligibility requirements.[89] For example, in some states the age at which a child may be eligible for a blended sentence is lower than for transfer.[90] Thus, Colorado, Michigan, Rhode Island and Texas limit the class of juveniles eligible for transfer by requiring that they be of a certain age but nevertheless permit the imposition of a blended sentence on a child of *any age*.[91] Even juveniles in those states that have expansive waiver provisions may be at higher risk for actual imposition of adult sanctions through the blended sentencing laws. Because in most jurisdictions, once a minor has been waived to criminal court they will be treated as an adult for all subsequent criminal prosecutions, waiver is generally an irrevocable and final decision; thus, the decision to pursue a blended sentence may be a way to reach juveniles who would not otherwise warrant transfer.[92]

Adult sanctioning may occur even in the absence of transfer or blended sentencing provisions. Minors convicted of certain sexual offences, for example, may be subject to sex offender registration requirements for terms lasting well beyond the maximum age of the juvenile court's jurisdiction. These measures, commonly called "Megan's Laws" were passed after the rape and murder of seven-year-old Megan Kanka by a convicted sex offender who was living across the street from her. They are based, in large part, on a philosophy that sex offenders

84 *Id.* at 11.
85 *Id.* at 9.
86 Snyder & Sickmund, *supra* note 52, at 115.
87 Griffin, *supra* note 61, at 13–14.
88 *Id.* at 14.
89 *Id.* at 15.
90 *Id.*
91 *Id.* at 13.
92 *Id.* at 15.

cannot be cured and that they will pose a risk to society throughout their lives. For political, more than scientific reasons, states have increasingly extended these adult restrictions to juvenile sex offenders.

Generally, these provisions require the offender to provide identifying information, and sometimes even a photograph, to the designated authority within a specified time period.[93] The offender also is required to periodically update that registration on threat of further prosecution. Local authorities may be required to notify the members of the community in which he lives of his status as a sexual offender or predator.[94] In some states, a period of incarceration may be followed by indefinite civil commitment for those individuals who are found to be sexually violent predators.

Thirty-two states require juveniles who have been adjudicated delinquent for or criminally convicted of specified sexual offences to register with a local law enforcement agency.[95] Most of these jurisdictions do not distinguish between juvenile and adult registrants, and thus require that juveniles register for the same term of years. The duration of the registration period varies, but can be as long as life.[96] Moreover, the registration requirements in some states may require all juveniles to register regardless of age or type of offence, even when the sexual activity is arguably consensual.[97] Nor are juvenile registrants necessarily exempt from community notification requirements that result in the publication of the names of juvenile sex offenders, raising real issues about the confidentiality of juvenile court records.[98]

There currently are no concrete definitions within the behavioural sciences for what constitutes sexual misconduct in juveniles.[99] Scientific studies suggest that even though the behaviour of juvenile sex offenders may appear similar to the conduct of adult sex offenders, the underlying mechanisms triggering the behaviour may be different. This may account for studies showing distinct differences in recidivism rates. Recidivism rates for juvenile sex offenders, as measured across studies, range from 8% to 12%, while rates for adults generally range from 20% to 40%.[100] Rates of recidivism may differ because "deviant patterns of sexual behavior may be less established in juvenile sex offenders", who have "greater developmental fluidity, having not yet developed a stable pattern of sexual arousal and interest".[101]

93 Adam Shajnfeld & Richard B. Krueger, *Reforming (Purportedly) Non-Punitive Responses to Sexual Offending*, 25 Developments in Mental Health Law 81, 85 (2006).

94 Lisa Trivits & N. Dickon Reppucci, *Application of Megan's Law to Juveniles,* 57 American Psychologist 690, 691 (September, 2002).

95 *Id.* at 694.

96 *Id.* at 691.

97 Timothy E. Wind, *The Quandary of Megan's Law: When the Child Sex Offender is a Child*, 37 J. Marshall L. Rev. 73, 112 (2003).

98 *Id.* at 117–118.

99 Trivits & Reppucci, *supra* note 94, at 695.

100 *Id.* at 700.

101 *Id.* at 697.

Treating juvenile sex offenders in the same manner as adults raises not only legal and scientific questions about culpability and punishment, but the registration and notification requirements are also inconsistent with concepts of treatment and rehabilitation. The community notification requirements subject the juvenile to social ostracism, limit access to educational and work opportunities, make it more difficult for juveniles to be placed with family or friends, and limit residential treatment options. In addition to lease restrictions imposed by private landlords, some states have also restricted where juveniles are permitted to reside – preventing them from living within a specified distance of the school that they might attend. The notification requirements are often contrary to the traditional goal of non-punitive intervention and rehabilitation. Moreover, it is especially problematic that sex offender laws tend to treat juvenile sex offenders in the same manner as adult sex offenders with respect to reporting, notification and length of classification, even though juveniles have fewer legal rights and protections than adults.

The purposes and goals of the juvenile system are often schizophrenic, focused more on safety and punishment than rehabilitation and treatment. Moreover, the system withholds rights from juveniles because of their perceived level of immaturity yet views them as having the same degree of culpability as adults when they commit delinquent acts. In recent years, we have seen an increasing use of judicial waivers, prosecutorial discretion and legislation mandating transfer of youth to criminal courts, along with the use of blended sentencing provisions, which allow courts to impose adult terms on juvenile offenders as young as 10 years of age. This trend, which comes at a time of decreasing juvenile crime rates, is legally and morally contrary to what we are learning about patterns of brain development in minors.

The brain research provides strong evidence that we should not hold minors as accountable as adults because their brains are different and they do not have the same decision-making capacity as adults. They lack judgment, are impulsive, have limited ability to understand and plan for the future, are more susceptible to peer influence and cannot foresee the consequences of their actions. Recent comparisons between the conduct and decision-making ability of juveniles and adults demonstrate that these differences can be substantial. Juveniles process information and react to situations differently because the pre-frontal cortex, which controls decision-making and judgment is not sufficiently developed, thereby requiring juveniles to rely on the more primitive processing of the amygdala.

As the United States Supreme Court recognized in *Roper*, the traditional goals of sentencing are less appropriate for juvenile offenders. Harsher sentences cannot deter juveniles because they do not fully understand the consequences of their actions and are less affected by the threat of sanctions. Moreover, taking retribution against an individual who is less culpable because of developmental immaturity would, for any civilized society, be immoral. The old formula of dealing with crime through stiffer sentences and restrictions, while politically popular, is an oversimplistic approach that lacks social and scientific validation as a way of dealing with juveniles. The scientific research on brain development is sufficiently compelling as to require us to reconsider our views on juvenile punishment as it is morally wrong and scientifically unsound to hold juveniles to the same degree of responsibility as adults who commit similar offences.

Chapter 10
Legal Implications of Memory-Dampening

Adam Kolber

Introduction[1]

Suppose we could erase memories we no longer wish to keep. In such a world, the victim of a terrifying assault could wipe away memories of the incident and be free of the nightmares that such memories often cause. Some memories, however, even quite unpleasant ones, are extremely valuable to society and ought not be eliminated without due consideration. An assault victim who hastily erases memory of a crime may thereby impede the investigation and prosecution of the perpetrator. In a world with memory erasure, our individual interest in controlling our memories may conflict with society's interest in maintaining access to those memories.

While true memory erasure is still the domain of science fiction,[2] less dramatic means of dampening the strength of a memory may have already been developed. Some experiments suggest that propranolol, a drug already approved by the United States Food and Drug Administration (FDA), can dull the emotional pain associated with the memory of an event when taken within six hours *after* the event occurs. Furthermore, by reducing the emotional intensity of a memory, propranolol may be capable of dampening its factual richness as well.[3] Together, the research holds out the possibility that, under some circumstances, propranolol may dampen both emotional and factual components of memory.

Researchers are now conducting larger studies with propranolol to test these preliminary results[4] and to examine whether propranolol might alleviate traumatic

1 This chapter is condensed and adapted from Adam J. Kolber, Therapeutic Forgetting: The Legal and Ethical Implications of Memory-dampening, 59 Vand. L. Rev. 1561 (2006).

2 See, e.g., Eternal Sunshine of the Spotless Mind (Focus Features 2004); Paycheck (Paramount 2003); Men in Black (Sony Pictures 1997); Total Recall (Artisan Entertainment 1990); see also Steven Johnson, The Science of Eternal Sunshine, Slate, Mar. 22, 2004, http://slate.msn.com/id/2097502.

3 See Kolber, supra note 1, at 1574 (describing an experiment that suggests that propranolol may dampen factual recall of emotionally arousing events when taken soon before those events); see also Physicians' Desk Reference 3423 (60th ed. 2006) (listing short-term memory loss as a side effect of Inderal LA, the manufacturer's name for a long-acting version of propranolol).

4 See Robin Marantz Henig, The Quest to Forget, N.Y. Times Mag., Apr. 4, 2004, at 32, 34–36 (describing plans for a larger study supported by the National Institute of Mental Health).

memories from the more distant past.[5] Meanwhile, even though propranolol was originally granted FDA approval to treat hypertension, clinicians may already use it to treat traumatic memories because doctors are permitted to prescribe it for off-label purposes.[6] Whether or not further research supports the use of propranolol to treat traumatic memories or focuses on some more potent successor, the quest for drugs to "therapeutically forget" is under way, and the search is starting to show promise.

Those susceptible to post-traumatic stress disorder (PTSD), an affliction characterized by invasive, painful memories, stand to gain the most from memory-dampening drugs. Attention to PTSD has increased in recent years as a result of terrorist attacks, military conflicts in Iraq and Afghanistan, and natural disasters like Hurricane Katrina and the Asian tsunami of 2004. These events have left thousands of survivors gripped by traumatic memories. The Department of Veterans Affairs has raised particular concerns about the cost of treating PTSD in soldiers. Veterans received PTSD benefit payments totalling $4.3 billion in 2004, up from $1.7 billion in 1999.[7] Any drug that can consistently and cost-effectively prevent or ease the suffering of PTSD will be of great interest not only to doctors and patients, but also to federal and state governments, private insurers and pharmaceutical companies.

Despite the potentially huge market for memory-dampening drugs, the subject has received surprisingly little scholarly attention,[8] appearing primarily in brief news articles.[9] It is already clear, however, that people have remarkably divergent

5 For example, researchers have sought to alleviate older traumatic memories by having subjects recall those memories after ingesting propranolol. Marilynn Marchione, A Pill to Fade Traumatic Memories? Doctors Are Working on It, Jan. 14, 2006, http://www.signonsandiego.com/news/science/20060114-0917-traumapill.html. The theory behind this research, according to neuroscientist Joseph LeDoux, is that "[e]ach time you retrieve a memory it must be restored," and "[w]hen you activate a memory in the presence of a drug that prevents the restorage of the memory, the next day the memory is not as accessible." *Id.* (quoting LeDoux).

6 Citizen Petition Regarding the Food and Drug Administration's Policy on Promotion of Unapproved Uses of Approved Drugs and Devices; Request for Comments, 59 Fed. Reg. 59820, 59821 (Nov. 18, 1994) (quoting 12 FDA Drug Bull. 4–5 (1982)) (alteration in original).

7 Dep't of Veterans Affairs, Office of Inspector Gen., Review of State Variances in VA Disability Compensation Claims vii, Rep. No. 05-00765-137 (2005), available at http://www.va.gov/oig/52/reports/2005/VAOIG-05-00765-137.pdf. The numbers in the text are based on the Department's fiscal year which begins 1 October of the preceding calendar year.

8 See David Wasserman, Making Memory Lose Its Sting, 24 Phil. & Pub. Pol'y Q. 12 (Fall 2004); Gilbert Meilaender, Why Remember?, 135 First Things 20 (2003), available at http://www.firstthings.com/ftissues/ft0308/articles/meilaender.html. The subject is also discussed at length by the President's Council on Bioethics.

9 *See, e.g.*, Greg Miller, Learning to Forget, 304 Science 34, 34 (2004); Erik Baard, The Guilt-Free Soldier, Village Voice, Jan. 22, 2003, at 32; Sharon Begley, A Spotless Mind May Ease Suffering, But Erase Identity, Wall St. J., Aug. 19, 2005, at B1; Scott LaFee,

intuitions about the desirability of memory-dampening. For example, in response to an article on the subject in the *New York Times Magazine*, one mother wrote the following letter to the editor:

> Six years ago, I watched both of my teenage boys die, several hours apart, after our car was struck by a speeding patrol car ... I don't mean to judge the way in which others should treat (or be treated for) their own personal tragedies. But for me, I needed to retain every detail of my memory, not only for the manslaughter trial that followed a year and a half later but also for my own well-being ... Although it's painful to relive that night and its aftermath, doing so helps me feel that I am doing something positive with this tragedy. As for erasing the memories of that night, I would never want to take a chance that even an iota of all the positive memories of my wonderful sons would disappear along with the painful ones.[10]

By contrast, in an online discussion of memory-dampening, one participant commented:

> I really feel that this could help a lot of people heal ... the pain that stays in their mind. I for one would go through with it because I can hardly go on through life with all this pain. I have been dealing with multiple traumas in my life and its [sic] going on almost 14 years now.[11]

Another participant added, "[I] have severe [PTSD] and would sell my soul to the devil himself to be rid of my 24/7 hellish flashbacks and night terrors."[12]

These heartfelt but dramatically different points of view highlight the numerous legal and ethical issues raised by memory-dampening. The President's Council on Bioethics (the Council)[13] explored many of these issues in a series of hearings in

---

Blanks for the Memories, San Diego Union Trib., Feb. 11, 2004, at F1; Rob Stein, Is Every Memory Worth Keeping?, Wash. Post., Oct. 19, 2004, at A1.

10 Michelle Norton Spicer, Letter re: Quest to Forget, *N.Y. Times Mag*., Apr. 18, 2004, at 66.

11 Posting of Michelle to CogNews, http://cognews.com/1072217907/index_html#11092 85564 (Feb. 15, 2005, 9:48 A.M.).

12 Posting of Lisa to CogNews, http://cognews.com/1072217907/index_html#1109285564 (Mar. 7, 2005, 5:13 A.M.).

13 In 2001, President George W. Bush created the Council by executive order. Exec. Order No. 13237, 66 Fed. Reg. 59851 (Nov. 28, 2001), available at http://www.whitehouse.gov/ news/releases/2001/11/20011128-13.html. According to the order, "the Council shall be guided by the need to articulate fully the complex and often competing moral positions on any given issue, rather than by an overriding concern to find consensus." *Id.* The Council has been renewed by subsequent executive orders.

2002 and 2003.[14] By and large, the Council was sceptical of the merits of memory-dampening, raising concerns that memory-dampening may: (1) prevent us from truly coming to terms with trauma, (2) tamper with our identities, leading us to a false sense of happiness, (3) demean the genuineness of human life and experience, (4) encourage us to forget memories that we are obligated to keep, and (5) inure us to the pain of others.[15]

I have elsewhere addressed the Council's ethical concerns, arguing that research into memory-dampening should be encouraged, free of the fear that it is generally wrong to dampen memories.[16] In this essay, I merely discuss some of the legal issues that could be raised by future memory-dampening technology. Given how frequently traumatic events like assaults and motor vehicle accidents lead to legal proceedings, drugs that affect memories of such events can have widespread legal implications. I pay particular attention to issues of informed consent, obstruction of justice and the mitigation of emotional distress damages.

Legal Issues

While propranolol-style memory-dampening is itself sufficiently novel to raise a host of legal and ethical questions, the President's Council on Bioethics focused less on our current capabilities and more on the direction in which further research will take us. The Council is principally concerned with the "psyche-altering agents of the future, devised unlike those of the past on the basis of exact knowledge of the brain [that] will permit more refined and effective interventions."[17] Thus, the Council addresses memory-dampening quite broadly, sometimes speaking more dramatically of memory-blunting[18] or even memory-erasing,[19] without always

14 See Remembering and Forgetting: Physiological and Pharmacological Aspects: Hearings Before the President's Council on Bioethics (Oct. 17, 2002 and Mar. 6, 2003), http://bioethics.gov.

15 Since the publication of the Council's report, the Council's composition and leadership have changed somewhat. Most notably, Edmund Pellegrino has taken over the position of Council chair from Leon Kass, who remains a member of the Council. See Dan Vergano, Bioethics Hits a Crossroads, USA Today, Sept. 29, 2005, at D1.

16 *See* Kolber, *supra* note 1.

17 President's Council on Bioethics, Beyond Therapy: Biotechnology and the Pursuit of Happiness 209 (2003) [hereinafter "Beyond Therapy"].

18 *Id.* at 276 ("blunting painful memories"); *id.* at 226 ("Use of memory-blunters at the time of traumatic events could interfere with the normal psychic work and adaptive value of emotionally charged memory.").

19 *See, e.g.*, id. at 286 ("Many people are probably repelled by the idea of drugs that erase memories ..."); *id.* at 230 ("If there are some things that it is better never to have experienced at all – things we would avoid if we possibly could – why not erase them from the memory of those unfortunate enough to have suffered them?").

distinguishing whether the memory degradation applies to the factual content of memory, the emotions we attach to those memories or some combination of both.

I will follow the Council's lead in broadening the discussion of memory-dampening beyond the limits of propranolol-style memory-dampening. By not tying the analysis to any particular therapy (including the side effects of any real world therapy), we can address more generally the underlying legal issues that therapeutic forgetting may present. While we do not know the exact nature of these more advanced technologies to come, the Council warns that "if we wish to act responsibly regarding the biotechnical future that we might be, willy-nilly, in the midst of creating for ourselves and our descendants",[20] we must to some extent anticipate the advances of new biotechnical interventions, so that we have time to consider the pertinent questions raised.[21]

Overview of Legal Issues

Memories serve two distinct roles in the legal system. First, they play an indispensable role in fact-finding. We gather memories in depositions, trial testimony, police investigations, line-ups and more to help establish the underlying facts that set the entitlements of disputing parties. We value these memories principally for the information they can provide. Second, memories and their associated affective states can themselves form part of a claim for damages. If you injure me and cause me to have upsetting memories, I can sometimes seek redress for the intentional or negligent infliction of the emotional distress associated with those memories.[22] While the existence of emotional distress must be proved just like other facts in a cause of action, the memories causing that distress are significant not only for their fact-finding role in assessing liability but also because of the negative feelings attached to them.

The informational value of memory Let us turn first to the role of memory as a source of information. There is little evidence so far as to how much, if at all, propranolol affects the informational content of traumatic memories formed before the drug is consumed. Assume, however, that propranolol or a future memory-dampening drug dampens both informational and emotional aspects

20 *Id.* at 209.

21 *Id.*

22 *See, e.g.*, *Henricksen v. State*, 84 P.3d 38, 55 (Mont. 2004) (stating that "where there is a physical manifestation of bodily harm resulting from emotional distress, such as PTSD, this bodily harm is sufficient evidence that the emotional distress suffered by the plaintiff is genuine and severe" enough to count as legally cognizable damage); *Hegel v. McMahon*, 960 P.2d 424, 426, 431 & n.5 (Wash. 1998) (allowing bystander claims for emotional damages if plaintiffs demonstrate "objective symptoms of their emotional injur[ies]," for example, "intrusive memories," where the collection of symptoms constitutes "a diagnosable emotional disorder" such as "post traumatic stress disorder").

of memories. If a witness to a recent gruesome crime uses such a drug, it will have two effects: first, it will ease the witness's suffering and help them resume a normal life. Second, it will reduce the socially valuable information contained in the witness's memories – information that may be vitally important to prosecuting the perpetrator and protecting others from harm. These two effects reveal a trade-off that memory-dampening may pose between our individual autonomy interests in controlling what happens to our bodies[23] and society's interest in preserving evidence that benefits others.[24]

In related contexts, the law tries to strike a balance between these interests. For example, we limit the government's power to recover physical evidence of a crime, a bullet for example, when it is lodged inside a defendant and can only be recovered by invading the defendant's body.[25] More generally, the law balances our obligations to report information that we have with our freedom to control that information. For example, while the government can use the subpoena power to force us to testify about our memories,[26] we are generally not required to report crimes we witness in the absence of a subpoena.[27]

The traditional balance of information control is upset to some degree if memory-dampening drugs give individuals incentives that conflict with society's best interests. Without memory-dampening, a crime or car accident victim

23 Such autonomy interests are frequently noted in important constitutional law cases. *See, e.g.*, *Cruzan v. Director, Mo. Dep't of Health*, 497 U.S. 261, 278 (1990) ("The principle that a competent person has a constitutionally protected liberty interest in refusing unwanted medical treatment may be inferred from our prior decisions."); *Washington v. Harper*, 494 U.S. 210, 229 (1990) ("The forcible injection of medication into a nonconsenting person's body represents a substantial interference with that person's liberty.").

24 *See generally* Christopher Slobogin, *Subpoenas and Privacy*, 54 DePaul L. Rev. 805, 805–26 (2005) (describing the subpoena power).

25 *See Winston v. Lee*, 470 U.S. 753, 760 (1985) ("The reasonableness of surgical intrusions beneath the skin depends on a case-by-case approach, in which the individual's interests in privacy and security are weighed against society's interests in conducting the procedure."); *cf. United States v. Crowder*, 543 F.2d 312, 316 (D.C. Cir. 1976) (finding no Fourth Amendment violation when a bullet was surgically removed from the defendant, against his will, where the bullet was superficial and the surgery was comparatively minor).

26 *See, e.g.*, *Branzburg v. Hayes*, 408 U.S. 665, 682 (1972) ("Citizens generally are not constitutionally immune from grand jury subpoenas; and neither the First Amendment nor any other constitutional provision protects the average citizen from disclosing to a grand jury information that he has received in confidence.").

27 Gerard E. Lynch, *The Lawyer as Informer*, 1986 Duke L.J. 491, 492 (1986). Many states do, however, have statutes that require bystanders to report certain kinds of crimes. *See, e.g.*, Mass. Gen. Laws Ann. ch. 268, § 40 (West 1990); Eugene Volokh, *Duties to Rescue and the Anticooperative Effects of Law*, 88 Geo. L.J. 105, 106 n.6 ("[A] duty to tell the police about crimes is not far removed from the traditionally accepted duty to testify in court when subpoenaed. The fact that we consider the duty to testify to be a permissible – even a generally uncontroversial – infringement of personal liberty suggests that duties to report might likewise be permissible infringements.").

typically remembers their traumatic experience, and society as a whole can use that information to better protect itself from a dangerous person. Thus, the gains from memory preservation are widely shared. By contrast, the victim, suffering great emotional distress, disproportionately bears the cost of retaining the memory. In a world with memory-dampening, however, victims need not bear this disproportionate cost, and so memory-dampening might lead to suboptimal levels of memory retention from a societal perspective.[28]

In order to better align individual incentives with societal interests, the government could use new or existing laws to penalize those who dampen socially valuable memories. For example, numerous civil and criminal provisions already make it illegal to alter evidence. In some cases, tampering with one's memory could be deemed to "spoliate evidence". When evidence is spoliated, the fact-finder is typically entitled to presume that the lost or otherwise unavailable evidence was unfavourable to the spoliator.[29] In more severe cases, discussed below, those who dampen a memory may be deemed to have obstructed justice, when they know (or perhaps even when they should have known) that their unadulterated memories would be needed at an upcoming judicial proceeding. However, when a person alters their memory to further a legitimate therapeutic purpose, they may be able to claim a defence of medical necessity.[30]

Assuming that a potential witness has dampened memories, courts will have to decide when to nevertheless permit that witness to testify in court. The Federal Rules of Evidence and similar state laws require testifying witnesses to have "personal knowledge" of the facts about which they testify.[31] Under current law, those with foggy memories usually satisfy the personal knowledge

---

28 In some cases, a witness will also have a unique interest in seeing that a perpetrator is punished or that a tortfeasor is held liable, and so their interests may substantially align with those of society more generally.

29 *See Brown & Williamson Tobacco v. Jacobson*, 827 F.2d 1119, 1134 (7th Cir. 1987) ("A court and a jury are entitled to presume that documents destroyed in bad faith while litigation is pending would be unfavorable to the party that has destroyed the documents."); Dale A. Oesterle, *A Private Litigant's Remedies for an Opponent's Inappropriate Destruction of Relevant Documents,* 61 TEX. L. REV. 1185, 1232–39 (1983) ("[A] party's bad faith destruction of relevant documents is an admission by conduct that he believes his case is weak and cannot be won fairly."). *See generally* 2 JOHN HENRY WIGMORE, EVIDENCE § 291 (James H. Chadbourn rev. ed., 1979) (discussing evidence spoliation). Occasionally, spoliation of evidence has been recognized as an independent tort. *See Smith v. Howard Johnson*, 615 N.E.2d 1037, 1038 (Ohio 1993) (recognizing "a cause of action ... in tort for interference with or destruction of evidence"); James T. Killelea, Note, *Spoliation of Evidence Proposals for New York State*, 70 BROOK. L. REV. 1045, 1048 (2005) (advocating an independent tort to discourage third-party spoliation).

30 *See, e.g.*, MODEL PENAL CODE § 3.02 (1985) (choice of evils defense); N.Y. PENAL LAW § 35.05 (McKinney 1998) (general justification defense).

31 *See* FED. R. EVID. 602 ("A witness may not testify to a matter unless evidence is introduced sufficient to support a finding that the witness has personal knowledge of the matter.").

requirement,[32] so except in cases of thorough memory erasure, this requirement is unlikely to prevent admission of memory-dampened testimony. Expert testimony might be permitted, however, to impeach the quality of the witness's testimony or to suggest that the extent of the witness's purported failure to recall is inconsistent with the use of memory-dampening drugs.[33] In some cases, litigants may seek to record a witness's testimony before their memory is dampened.[34] In such cases, courts will still have to decide under what circumstances to admit the recorded hearsay in a subsequent trial.[35]

There are a variety of ways one might exploit memory-dampening to eliminate damaging evidence. For example, the perpetrator of physical or sexual abuse could try to dampen their victim's memory, making it harder for the victim to assist police and provide incriminating testimony.[36] There is already much scepticism about the accuracy of such eyewitness memories;[37] pharmaceutical memory-alteration will

---

32 "[M]emory gaps and doubts caused by the lapse of time go to the weight to be given the testimony. So long as the witness has some recollection, a jury could reasonably give the testimony some weight and this aspect of the personal knowledge requirement is satisfied." 27 Charles Alan Wright & Victor James Gold, Federal Practice and Procedure, Evidence § 6023 (1990) (footnote omitted); *see Tucker v. State*, 721 P.2d 639, 642 (Alaska Ct. App. 1986) (finding it proper to admit testimony in a murder case despite the purportedly defective memory of the witness, stating that "[d]efects in a witness' recollection are proper subjects for cross-examination and impeachment, but the defects do not generally render the witness' testimony inadmissible").

33 *See* Fed. R. Evid. 702 (allowing expert witness testimony that assists the fact-finder where "(1) the testimony is based upon sufficient facts or data, (2) the testimony is the product of reliable principles and methods, and (3) the witness has applied the principles and methods reliably to the facts of the case").

34 If the time window to commence memory-dampening is a short six hours or so, it is unlikely that courts can intervene before dampening must begin. With a longer window, however, litigants might seek to depose witnesses before they begin treatment. In criminal cases, "[a] party may move that a prospective witness be deposed in order to preserve testimony for trial. The court may grant the motion because of exceptional circumstances and in the interest of justice." Fed. R. Crim. P. 15.

35 Such hearsay evidence might be permitted as a recorded recollection, *see* Fed. R. Evid. 803(5). If the declarant is deemed unavailable to testify at trial because of their lack of memory, *see* Fed. R. Evid. 804(a)(3), or because they are deemed to have a mental infirmity, *see* Fed. R. Evid. 804(a)(4), then there may be additional options for admitting the evidence, particularly for oral statements that would not fall under the recorded record exception. *See* Fed. R. Evid. 804(b) (describing hearsay exceptions that apply when the declarant is deemed unavailable).

36 Similar issues may arise in cases of drugged rape. *See, e.g.*, National District Attorneys Association, *The Date Rape Drug: The Difficulty in Obtaining Convictions*, Prosecutor, Apr. 31, 1997, at 28 (noting that prosecutions can be difficult in date rape drug cases where victims were not conscious during the crime).

37 *See generally* Elizabeth Loftus & James M. Doyle, Eyewitness Testimony: Civil and Criminal (1997).

only create more doubt. In the particularly dreadful scenario where the victim is a child, memory-dampening drugs could further muddle the much-debated issues surrounding the accuracy, prevalence and, some would add, existence of repressed childhood memories.[38]

Furthermore, memory-dampening drugs might be taken, not just by victims and witnesses, but by perpetrators as well. A perpetrator might do so in order to cope with feelings of shame and guilt associated with their crime.[39] Alternatively, a perpetrator might cold-heartedly dampen their memories in order to more convincingly deceive police and a jury. It might be more advantageous to do so than to claim a Fifth Amendment privilege to remain silent and face the negative inference that jurors often draw from that silence.[40] Even without memory-dampening drugs, those accused of a crime frequently claim to have no recollection of committing it.[41] While many of these claims are undoubtedly spurious, the availability of a powerful memory-dampening drug could increase the rate of both genuine and malingered claims of forgetting by criminals.[42] Thus, in order to ease painful memories or to deliberately eliminate damaging evidence, those who dampen memories may degrade our shared pool of socially valuable information and may require us to strengthen laws governing evidence preservation.

The affective disvalue of memory Memory-dampening drugs also raise new legal issues associated with memory's connection to negative emotional states. For example, under some circumstances, doctors could be liable for malpractice for failing to dampen a patient's distressing memory and, perhaps too, for dampening a memory that should have been left alone. If so, we would face difficult questions about how to calculate damages for memories that are tortiously dampened or retained. Furthermore, as I discuss in more detail in the next section, questions may arise as to the sorts of disclosures that health professionals must make in order to obtain informed consent to dampen the memories of a recently traumatized person.

---

38 *See generally* Daniel Brown et al., Memory, Trauma Treatment, and the Law 578–612 (1998) (discussing repressed memory litigation in the courts).

39 Wasserman, *supra* note 8, at 14.

40 As a practical matter, criminal defendants may be hesitant to exercise their right to silence for fear that jurors expect an innocent defendant to testify in their own defence. *See* Anne Bowen Poulin, *Evidentiary Use of Silence and the Constitutional Privilege Against Self-Incrimination*, 52 Geo. Wash. L. Rev. 191, 197 (1984).

41 Of those convicted of homicide, one source estimates that 25% to 45% claim amnesia for the killing. *See* M.D. Kopelman, *The Assessment of Psychogenic Amnesia*, *in* Handbook of Memory Disorders 427, 428–29 (Alan D. Baddeley et al. eds, 1995).

42 Courts are, not surprisingly, suspicious of defendants' assertions of memory loss. See *Fajeriak v. State*, 520 P.2d 795, 802 (Alaska 1974) ("The potential for fraudulent allegations of memory loss is so great that we would for this reason alone be reluctant to follow amnesia as a ground for a finding of incompetency even if we were otherwise inclined to do so.").

In the torts context more generally, courts may have to decide the effect of memory-dampening in the already controversial area of damage calculations for emotional distress. In addition to the valuation issues just noted, one thorny problem, discussed in more detail below, concerns whether a person with tortiously-caused physical and emotional trauma fails to mitigate damages if they decide not to dampen. While courts have generally not required plaintiffs to mitigate emotional damages, if indeed memory-dampening proved popular and successful, the tendency might change.

Regular clinical use of memory-dampening drugs would also raise a familiar set of concerns over access to and distribution of expensive medical resources. For example: would the drugs be covered by various forms of health insurance and, if so, to what extent? How would reimbursements for memory-dampening compare with those available for other methods of treating traumatic memories, like psychotherapy? While these issues are familiar, they are also unique in this context. If insurance programmes were to provide better reimbursement for memory-dampening pharmaceuticals than for more labour-intensive, expensive psychotherapy, patients could feel pressured to dampen memories they would have preferred to keep and wrestle with the old-fashioned way in therapy. Thus, policy questions over insurance coverage will implicate deeper questions about how people should deal with psychic distress and how much freedom they should have to select the form of their mental health treatments.

If we liberate ourselves entirely from existing technology and look to the distant future, we can imagine a number of interesting, if fanciful, scenarios for courts to decide. For example, the invasion of privacy tort has been used to recover damages for "unreasonable intrusion upon the seclusion of another".[43] It has been used in suits against those who install hidden video cameras in bathrooms[44] or listening devices in the bedroom of a married couple.[45] In such cases, damages can be awarded for emotional distress, but one can never take away the voyeuristic memories the defendant retains. Never, that is, unless one has very sophisticated memory-erasing technology along with very few protections of our rights to be free from forced memory-dampening.[46]

Many of the issues raised by memory-dampening, science fiction or otherwise, implicate some provision of the Constitution,[47] and the risk of constitutional violations

43 Restatement (Second) Torts § 652A (1977); *see also id.* § 652B & cmt. A.

44 *See, e.g.*, *Harkey v. Abate*, 346 N.W.2d 74, 76 (Mich. Ct. App. 1983) (holding that the installation of hidden viewing devices "can itself constitute a sufficient wrongful intrusion" into a plaintiff's seclusion to permit recovery).

45 *Hamberger v. Eastman*, 206 A.2d 239, 241–42 (N.H. 1965).

46 Similar science fiction scenarios could be crafted to remedy trade secret violations or to untaint juries that have been inadvertently exposed to lurid and prejudicial inadmissible evidence.

47 This is a vast topic in itself. To offer just an example, the First Amendment could be construed to protect us against certain kinds of government interference with memory.

would be particularly high if the government forced a person to dampen memories. Weaker forms of coercion might also violate the Constitution, if, for example, a municipality tried to save money by requiring its police, firefighters and paramedics to use memory-dampeners to prevent the formation of traumatic memories on the job. As government employees, they could claim that certain pressures to dampen are unconstitutional conditions of employment.[48] Much more can be said about the broad liberty interests implicated by intentional memory manipulation, and I briefly return to the subject at the end of the "Freedom of Memory" section.

Some Specific Legal Issues

In this section, I address three legal issues in greater detail. First, I address the claim, raised by Council member Gilbert Meilaender and echoed by the Council in its report on memory-dampening, that it may be difficult or impossible to obtain informed consent from patients to undergo propranolol-style memory-dampening. Second, I describe how existing obstruction of justice provisions may criminalize memory-dampening in certain cases. Lastly, I discuss the mitigation of emotional damages in tort to show how the doctrine requires us to establish norms of behaviour in the memory-dampening context.

Informed consent The doctrine of informed consent, in both its legal and ethical formulations, is typically understood to require healthcare personnel to make certain disclosures to patients prior to beginning medical procedures and to obtain the patient's permission to proceed.[49] Such disclosures should include "the nature of the pertinent ailment or condition, the risks of the proposed treatment

---

See, e.g., *Stanley v. Georgia*, 394 U.S. 557, 565 (1969) ("Our whole constitutional heritage rebels at the thought of giving government the power to control men's minds."); Charles Fried, *Perfect Freedom, Perfect Justice*, 78 B.U. L. Rev. 717, 735–36 (1998) ("The First Amendment as freedom of thought … protects against government interfering with the process of judgment itself, the judgment by which we may conclude that all the other commitments we make are wise or not." (footnote omitted)); Bruce J. Winick, *The Right to Refuse Mental Health Treatment: A First Amendment Perspective*, 44 U. Miami L. Rev. 1, 17–19 (1989) (arguing that the First Amendment limits intrusive forms of government interference with our mental processes). Government authority over memory-dampening may also implicate privacy protections of the Fourth, Fifth, Ninth and Fourteenth Amendments, as well as the Eighth Amendment protection against cruel and unusual punishment.

48 *But cf. Greenawalt v. Indiana Dep't of Corr.*, 397 F.3d 587, 589–90 (7th Cir. 2005) (holding that requiring a state employee to take an invasive psychological test as a condition of employment does not unconstitutionally burden her Fourth Amendment right to be free from unreasonable searches and seizures).

49 *See, e.g.*, *Canterbury v. Spence*, 464 F.2d 772, 786–87 (D.C. Cir. 1972) ("[T]he test for determining whether a particular peril must be divulged is its materiality to the patient's decision: all risks potentially affecting the decision must be unmasked."); *Schloendorff v. Soc'y of N.Y. Hosp.*, 105 N.E. 92, 93 (N.Y. 1914) ("Every human being of adult years and

or procedure, and the risks of any alternative methods of treatment, including the risks of failing to undergo any treatment at all".[50]

The doctrine has formed the basis of a criticism particular to propranolol-style memory-dampening. As noted earlier, memory-dampening using propranolol is currently thought most likely to be effective in the first six hours after a traumatic event while the memory is still in the process of consolidating. During this period, however, we cannot accurately predict whether a given patient will eventually develop PTSD or otherwise develop severe traumatic memories. This means that doctors would have to prescribe propranolol and seek informed consent to the treatment before they can predict with confidence whether a particular patient would go on to develop PTSD in the absence of the drug.

In an essay on memory-dampening,[51] Council member Gilbert Meilaender suggests that the time limitation on propranolol-style memory-dampening makes it difficult, if not impossible, for patients to give their informed consent to the treatment because they would not yet know the role that their painful memories would ultimately play in their lives.[52] The Council elaborates on the same point:

> [I]n the immediate aftermath of a painful experience, we simply cannot know either the full meaning of the experience in question or the ultimate character and future prospects of the individual who experiences it ... Will he be cursed forever by unbearable memories that, in retrospect, clearly should have been blunted medically? Or will he succeed, over time, in "redeeming" those painful memories by actively integrating them into the narrative of his life?[53]

The quality of informed consent to propranolol-style memory-dampening can thus be challenged on two grounds. First, almost by definition, traumatized patients will have some level of psychological disturbance that may cloud their decision to consent. Second, as Meilaender suggests, even if they are capable of making sound medical decisions, they will only have limited information as to the relative costs and benefits of undergoing the therapy. Given that propranolol is not risk-free (because it may cause side effects and because some patients may regret having used it to dampen their memories), it would be preferable to allow patients

---

sound mind has a right to determine what shall be done with his own body and a surgeon who performs an operation without his patient's consent ... is liable in damages.").

50 W. Page Keeton et al., Prosser and Keeton on the Law of Torts 190 (5th ed. 1984).

51 Meilaender, *supra* note 8. The essay was written in Meilaender's individual capacity and does not speak for the Council. *Id.* at 21.

52 *Id.* (asking whether recently traumatized patients contemplating memory-dampening could "know or decide in that moment whether doing so was wise? Is that the moment in which to decide whether one wants to carry such painful memories along throughout life or to erase them?").

53 Beyond Therapy, *supra* note 17, at 227.

and psychiatrists time to determine the scope and severity of a patient's traumatic memories before deciding to dampen them.[54]

Despite these concerns, the doctrine of informed consent does not pose a general obstacle to the use of propranolol-style memory-dampening. We frequently use preventative medicines on people who are unlikely to develop the illnesses we seek to prevent. We make such decisions by weighing expected costs and benefits, even when these decisions dramatically alter people's lives. For example, some women with a known genetic predisposition to develop breast cancer opt for preventative mastectomies even though many of them would never have actually developed the disease.[55] Part of the role of physicians is to inform patients of the costs and benefits of medical interventions, particularly when the outcome of a proposed intervention is uncertain. Thus, physicians prescribing propranolol have obligations to obtain their patient's consent after describing the probabilistic costs and benefits of treatment. Assuming they do so, the fact that the treatment involves probabilistic decision-making is otherwise irrelevant.

Furthermore, while it is true that many of those asked to consent to memory-dampening, having just recently suffered emotional trauma, will not have the full benefit of their faculties of contemplative reflection, we ordinarily require no such thing before commencing serious medical treatments. For example, suppose a person is severely injured in a motor vehicle accident and is rushed to the emergency room, conscious and aware but emotionally shaken. Suppose further that the patient must decide whether to have part of a limb amputated to reduce the probability of amputating the entire limb later on. Despite the patient's emotional turmoil, both from the accident itself and the prospect of amputation, if the patient satisfies rather minimal standards of competence, health professionals will seek the patient's consent to the operation.[56]

Assume now that this same patient must decide not only whether to amputate but also whether to dampen their memory of the accident. If they can consent to the amputation by making a probabilistic determination after recently suffering trauma, then they can make the same sort of determination about memory-dampening. While memory-dampening is a more novel and unfamiliar therapy than is amputation, every significant medical innovation is novel and unfamiliar for some period of

---

54 As noted, researchers are testing propranolol's efficacy when taken more than six hours after a traumatic experience. Future forms of memory-dampening may not have the limitations that propranolol-style memory-dampening appears to have.

55 Timothy R. Rebbeck et al., *Bilateral Prophylactic Mastectomy Reduces Breast Cancer Risk in* BRCA1 *and* BRCA2 *Mutation Carriers: The PROSE Study Group*, 22 J. Clinical Oncology 1055, 1055 (2004); *see also* Carl T. Hall, *Surgery Cuts Risk of Breast Cancer: Study Supports Use of Preventive Mastectomies*, S.F. Chron., Feb. 24, 2004, at A2 ("The first major study of preventive breast-removal surgery in women with a high genetic risk for breast cancer showed the radical step may reduce cancer risk by 90 percent.").

56 Similarly, parents who are emotionally traumatized from witnessing their children's traumatic injuries can ordinarily still give informed consent to their children's medical treatment.

time, and that is not ordinarily enough to vitiate the quality of patient consent.[57] In any event, a patient's state of trauma cannot be a complete hindrance to obtaining their informed consent, for if we truly thought a patient incompetent to consent, we typically still seek consent from close relatives or the courts.[58]

Obstruction of justice As noted earlier, there are already a variety of laws that, in effect, limit our rights to dampen memories. Under certain circumstances, for example, use of a memory-dampening drug that affects factual recall could constitute obstruction of justice.[59] Obstruction of justice refers to a "medley of crimes"[60] with a variety of names in federal and state statutes, such as "tampering with a witness" or "tampering with physical evidence". Among the federal government's obstruction statutes, an omnibus clause in 18 U.S.C. § 1503 provides for the imprisonment of anyone who "corruptly or by threats or force, or by any threatening letter or communication, influences, obstructs, or impedes, or endeavors to influence, obstruct, or impede, the due administration of justice".[61] The catch-all nature of the clause is intended to prohibit "novel and creative

57 In addition, as Meilaender himself acknowledges, those who have the greatest likelihood of experiencing traumatic events – rescue workers, for example – can be informed in advance about the pros and cons of memory-dampening and need not address the issue for the first time while experiencing the immediate aftermath of a traumatic event. *See* Meilaender, *supra* note 11, at 21 (noting that rescue workers could consent before they are traumatized, but asking rhetorically whether one can "actually think this through knowledgeably in advance of the experience").

58 *See, e.g., Strunk v. Strunk*, 445 S.W.2d 145, 145, 149 (Ky. Ct. App. 1969) (authorizing a kidney transplant, with parental approval, from "an incompetent ward of the state" to his brother). *See generally* Stewart G. Pollack, *Life and Death Decisions: Who Makes Them and By What Standards*, 41 Rutgers L. Rev. 505 (1989); John Robertson, *Organ Donations by Incompetents and the Substituted Judgment Doctrine*, 76 Colum. L. Rev. 48 (1976). In general, emotionally traumatized patients are competent to consent to treatment. In cases where a traumatized patient is incompetent, however, it would indeed be difficult to reach family members and virtually impossible to commence meaningful judicial proceedings within the preferred six-hour window to begin propranolol-style memory-dampening.

59 *See generally United States v. Buckley*, 192 F.3d 708, 710 (7th Cir. 1999) ("The term 'obstruction of justice' refers to efforts to impede the processes of legal justice."); *United States v. Cihak*, 137 F.3d 252, 262 (5th Cir. 1998) ("Obstruction of justice involves any attempt to impede the due administration of justice."); Sarah Roadcap, *Obstruction of Justice*, 41 Am. Crim. L. Rev. 911 (2004) (surveying the law of obstruction of justice, particularly federal law).

60 *Buckley*, 192 F.3d at 710.

61 18 U.S.C. § 1503 (2006); *see also United States v. Brenson*, 104 F.3d 1267, 1275 (11th Cir. 1997) ("[T]he omnibus clause is broad enough to cover any act committed corruptly, in an endeavor to impede or obstruct justice." (quoting *United States v. Brand*, 775 F.2d 1460, 1465 (11th Cir. 1985))).

schemes"[62] to obstruct justice that are not listed by name in § 1503's more specific prohibitions.[63]

In some cases, memory-dampening could be one of those novel and creative schemes. Long before our recent interest in memory-dampening, it was held to be obstruction of justice to intentionally get a witness drunk in order to prevent the witness from testifying in court.[64] By analogy, one may obstruct justice by pharmaceutically tampering with another's memory in order to prevent that person from testifying in court. If a rapist forces their victim to consume a memory-dampening drug so that the victim cannot later testify as a witness when the rapist is on trial, then, among their crimes, the rapist might be convicted of obstruction under the broad language of § 1503.

A potentially more common scenario could occur as follows: the victim of an armed robbery takes a powerful memory-dampening drug to ease their painful memories of the incident. They regret that doing so will greatly diminish the value of their testimony at an upcoming judicial proceeding against the perpetrator, but they do not want to bear the full strength of their painful memories in the interim. Under these circumstances, let us assume, the victim is well aware that the drug will impede the administration of justice, though this is not their goal. In the language of the Model Penal Code, the victim has "knowledge" that their conduct will impede the administration of justice, though this is not their "purpose".[65]

While courts have not established a uniform mental state requirement to convict a defendant for obstruction under § 1503, it is clear that a defendant can be convicted even when it is not their purpose to obstruct. For example, in *United States v. Neiswender*,[66] Neiswender told the attorney of a criminal defendant in a high-profile case that, for the sum of $20,000, he could ensure the defendant's acquittal because he had one of the jurors in that case under his control.[67] It appears that Neiswender was merely seeking to extract money from the attorney, as there was no evidence that Neiswender actually had communicated or intended to communicate in any way with any member of the jury.[68] Nevertheless, the government charged

62 *United States v. Tackett*, 113 F.3d 603, 607 (6th Cir. 1997).

63 *See United States v. Griffin*, 589 F.2d 200, 206–07 (5th Cir. 1979) ("The obstruction of justice statute was drafted with an eye to the variety of corrupt methods by which the proper administration of justice may be impeded or thwarted, a variety limited only by the imagination of the criminally inclined." (citation and internal quotation marks omitted)); *United States v. Cueto*, 151 F.3d 620, 630 (7th Cir. 1998) (citing *Griffin* and *Tackett*).

64 *State v. Holt*, 24 A. 951, 952 (Me. 1892) (holding that it is obstruction of justice to "[i]ntentionally and designedly ... get a witness drunk, for the express purpose of preventing his attendance before the grand jury, or in open court"); *see also Commonwealth v. Berry*, 133 S.W. 212, 213 (Ky. Ct. App. 1911) (quoting *Holt*); *State v. Jones*, 48 P.2d 403, 405 (N.M. 1935) (same).

65 *See* Model Penal Code § 2.02 (1985).

66 590 F.2d 1269 (4th Cir. 1979).

67 *Id.* at 1270.

68 *Id.* at 1271.

Neiswender with obstruction of justice, arguing that "[h]ad Neiswender convinced [the attorney] that he had a juror under his control and induced [the attorney] to participate in the scheme, the natural consequence would have been to reduce [the attorney's] efforts in defending his client."[69] In reply, Neiswender argued that he had absolutely no intent to obstruct justice. In fact, he claimed that his "motivation was directly at odds with any design to obstruct justice since a guilty verdict would have revealed [his] fraud."[70] The Fourth Circuit upheld Neiswender's conviction, stating that Neiswender "need only have had knowledge or notice that success in his fraud would have likely resulted in an obstruction of justice".[71] Similarly, in *United States v. Silverman*,[72] the court stated that "[t]he government is not required to prove … that the defendant harbored the specific purpose of obstructing the due administration of justice; all the government has to establish is that the defendant should have reasonably foreseen that the natural and probable consequence of the success of his scheme would achieve precisely that result."[73]

Such cases aside, it seems unlikely that a prosecutor would consider it obstruction to use memory-dampening in good faith to alleviate traumatic memories. Nevertheless, if courts merely require that defendants have knowledge or reasonably foresee that their acts will impede justice, the memory-dampened robbery victim described above could be convicted under § 1503 (assuming they have no necessity defence) because they knew that they drastically devalued their future testimony when they chose to dampen their memory.

Mitigation of emotional distress damages Many share the intuition that the government should not limit our freedom to control something as deeply personal

69 *Id.* at 1272.

70 *Id.* at 1272–73.

71 *Id.* at 1273; *see also United States v. Buffalano*, 727 F.2d 50, 54 (2d Cir. 1984) ("[W]hile the statutory term 'corruptly endeavors' requires intent, such intent may be inferred from proof that defendant had knowledge or notice that his corrupt actions would obstruct justice then actually being administered.").

72 745 F.2d 1386, 1389–95 (11th Cir. 1984) (holding that a criminal defence attorney obstructed justice when he told his client that, for the sum of $25,000, he could pay "some very powerful people" at the Department of Justice to "fix" the client's case and secure favourable sentencing after a guilty plea).

73 *Id.* at 1393; *see also United States v. Cueto*, 151 F.3d 620, 630–31 (7th Cir. 1998) ("The government only has to establish that the defendant should have reasonably seen that the natural and probable consequences of his acts was the obstruction of justice."). *But cf. United States v. Aguilar*, 515 U.S. 593, 599 (1995) ("[I]f the defendant lacks knowledge that his actions are likely to affect the judicial proceeding, he lacks the requisite intent to obstruct.").

To add to the hodgepodge treatment of obstruction *mens rea*, some courts hold that defendants can only be convicted if they impeded justice with a corrupt motive. *See, e.g.*, *United States v. Thomas*, 916 F.2d 647, 651 (11th Cir. 1990) ("Although the government is not required to prove that the defendant had the specific purpose of obstructing justice, it must establish that the conduct was prompted, at least in part, by a 'corrupt motive.' " (citation omitted)).

as our own minds and, hence, that the government should not be in the business of regulating our control over our memories.[74] While this intuition may provide answers to many public policy questions, even if it is correct, it does not resolve all of the wide-ranging legal issues that could arise in a world with memory-dampening. Even if the government allows people to make dampening decisions for themselves, the law would still need to establish background expectations about the reasonableness of decisions to dampen or to refuse to do so.

The tort doctrine of damage mitigation illustrates how expectations as to the reasonableness of dampening could seep into the law. Consider an easy case first. Suppose that a defendant negligently drives their car into the plaintiff such that the plaintiff is hospitalized with both physical and emotional damages. Suppose further that when the plaintiff enters the hospital, for whatever reason, they refuse to allow the medical staff to set their leg in a cast for a week. As a result, the plaintiff needs more medical attention prior to the setting of their leg and more physical therapy afterwards. These additional costs, however, need not be compensated by the defendant. Under longstanding principles of damage mitigation, the defendant need not compensate the plaintiff for damages that could have been prevented had the plaintiff taken reasonable steps after the commission of the tort to avoid them.[75]

A more difficult case would arise if the plaintiff failed to mitigate the emotional, rather than the physical, aspect of their injuries.[76] Thus, suppose that the plaintiff promptly attended to their physical injuries but declined a psychiatrist's reasonable advice to dampen their memories. In such a case, the defendant could assert that, according to general principles of mitigation, the plaintiff's recovery for emotional damages should be reduced by whatever portion of those damages is attributable to the plaintiff's failure to dampen their memories.

The plaintiff might argue in response that they have a deeply held interest in not altering their memory. In an arguably related context, however, such arguments have largely failed to persuade courts. In cases where plaintiffs have refused medical treatment on religious grounds, where, for example, a Jehovah's

74 *See, e.g.*, Richard Glen Boire, *Forget About It?*, http://www.corante.com/brainwaves /20030801.shtml (last visited 1 September 2006). According to Boire, a director of the Center for Cognitive Liberty and Ethics, "[t]he right to cognitive liberty posits that the power to enhance, erase, or otherwise modify one's own memory ought to be an individual decision; something that is neither compelled nor prohibited by laws." *Id.* He further states that "[g]overnment may rightfully police our actions, but it does not, and should not, have the power to police our minds." *Id.*

75 *See generally* Restatement (Second) of Torts, § 918(1) (1979) (stating the general rule that "one injured by the tort of another is not entitled to recover damages for any harm that he could have avoided by the use of reasonable effort or expenditure after the commission of the tort").

76 *See* Kevin C. Klein & G. Nicole Hininger, *Mitigation of Psychological Damages: An Economic Analysis of the Avoidable Consequences Doctrine and Its Applicability to Emotional Distress Injuries*, 29 Okla. City U. L. Rev. 405, 439 (2004); Eugene Kontorovich, Note, *The Mitigation of Emotional Distress Damages*, 68 U. Chi. L. Rev. 491, 492, 513–20 (2001).

Witness refuses to undergo surgery to correct an injury caused by the defendant, the prevailing approach refuses to compensate the religious plaintiff for damages that would have been avoided by a reasonable person who lacked those religious beliefs.[77] Even though the religious plaintiff has a deeply held interest in following their religious tradition – the free exercise of which is constitutionally protected[78] – the damage mitigation doctrine does not consider their idiosyncratic interests, deeply held as they may be. Thus, the plaintiff in our example is not likely to get much help for their argument by appealing to the mitigation doctrine in the context of plaintiffs who refuse medical care on religious grounds.

Fortunately for our hypothetical plaintiff, courts are disinclined to require plaintiffs to treat their emotional injuries. While courts have not categorically held that emotional damages need not be mitigated, most courts do not reduce plaintiffs' emotional distress damages when plaintiffs fail to adequately treat them.[79] Only on rare occasions have courts mitigated emotional damages where plaintiffs fail to undergo psychotherapy[80] or refuse to take recommended antidepressants.[81] As

---

77 *See Williams v. Bright*, 658 N.Y.S.2d 910, 912–16 (N.Y. App. Div. 1997) (requiring a jury to consider whether a "reasonably prudent person" would have undergone hip and knee surgery to mitigate damages rather than considering whether a reasonably prudent Jehovah's Witness would have done so); *see also Munn v. Algee*, 924 F.2d 568, 574–75 (5th Cir. 1991) (finding no First Amendment violation where the mitigation of damages doctrine was applied without an exemption for a religiously motivated failure to mitigate). *But cf.* Comment, *Medical Care, Freedom of Religion, and Mitigation of Damages*, 87 YALE L.J. 1466, 1468 (1978) (arguing that prevailing approaches violate the First Amendment).

78 U.S. CONST. amend. I ("Congress shall make no law … prohibiting the free exercise of religion.").

79 For example, most courts do not require plaintiffs to treat their emotional injuries with psychiatric medication. In *Baker v. Dorfman*, the plaintiff was erroneously informed that he was HIV-positive. No. 97 Civ. 7512, 1999 WL 191531, at *1 (S.D.N.Y. Apr. 5, 1999), *aff'd*, 239 F.3d 415 (2d Cir. 2000). While misinformed, he was in a state of emotional distress and received psychiatric attention but refused psychiatric medication. *Id.* at *6. The court refused to mitigate damages because "[t]he jury could have reasonably concluded that [the plaintiff] did what he could to alleviate his distress." *Id.* This issue was not pursued on appeal. 239 F.3d 415, 418 n.1 (2d Cir. 2000). *See also Demary v. United States*, 982 F. Supp. 1101, 1111–12 (D.S.C. 1997) (holding that the decision not to take antidepressants by plaintiff flight-attendant who was physically and emotionally scarred in a place crash was not a "wholly unreasonable choice" and was not a failure to mitigate damages given that "[h]e has, instead, made major efforts in other ways"); *Salas v. United States*, 974 F. Supp. 202, 211–12 (W.D.N.Y. 1997) (finding no failure to mitigate where plaintiff received psychiatric treatment but refused to take certain psychiatric medications that caused negative side effects).

80 *See Skaria v. State*, 442 N.Y.S.2d 838 (N.Y. Ct. Cl. 1981) (mitigating rape-victim-plaintiff's recovery because she failed to follow her psychologist's advice to continue treatment after moving to a new city).

81 *See Neal v. Director*, No. CIV.A.93-2420, 1995 WL 517249, at *15 (D.D.C. Aug. 9, 1995) (reducing plaintiff's award for front pay where mental health specialists "agreed that medication would probably improve [plaintiff's] mental state to a significant degree" and

mental health treatments become more effective, however, a plaintiff's failure to use them may appear more unreasonable, and courts may become more willing to penalize plaintiffs who fail to mitigate emotional damages.

Assuming that memory-dampeners were part of mainstream medical practice, courts would be asked to decide whether and under what circumstances a plaintiff could be put to the choice of either dampening painful memories or else foregoing compensation for the pain attached to those memories that could have been dampened. Whatever the best solution may be, the issue cannot be resolved simply by saying that individuals should be free to decide whether or not to dampen memories. For even if they were free to choose, we would still have to make societal determinations (or, at least, court and jury determinations) as to the reasonableness of such decisions.

Of course, the issue of damage mitigation in the memory-dampening context is largely mooted if plaintiffs must maintain their memories in order to effectively prepare and pursue their claims. Some jurisdictions help amnesic plaintiffs by creating a presumption that they were exercising due care at the time of an accident;[82] it is doubtful, however, that courts would apply such a presumption to a plaintiff who *intentionally* dampened memories. Therefore, as a practical matter, the mitigation issue might only arise if plaintiffs can dampen emotional aspects of their memories without affecting their evidentiary content. Alternatively, plaintiffs may dampen memories when those memories are not needed to prove a cause of action or when plaintiffs are able to adequately record their memories prior to dampening for purposes of future litigation. Such wrinkles demonstrate, however, that the principal roles that memory plays in the law – an evidentiary role and an affective role – may be hard to separate if some plaintiffs are effectively forced to preserve a memory's emotional pain in order to preserve its evidentiary value.

Freedom of Memory

I have only scratched the surface of the many legal issues that might confront us in a world with effective ways of deliberately forgetting. Yet, these issues are not so terribly complicated or invidious that they require broad legal restrictions on memory-dampening. If that's true, then we should have at least a limited right to dampen our memories.

---

that, were plaintiff "to take therapeutic doses of one of the currently available medications, such as Prozac, it is likely she could return to work in four to six months").

82 *See, e.g.*, *Brown v. Connolly*, 398 P.2d 596, 597 (Cal. 1965) ("Under ordinary circumstances if a party cannot testify because of amnesia induced by injuries suffered in the accident involved in the litigation, he is entitled to a presumption that he acted with due care."); *Anderson v. Schulz*, 527 P.2d 151, 152 (Wyo. 1974) (finding error in a grant of summary judgment on the basis of contributory negligence where the plaintiff, a passenger in the car defendant was driving, did not recall the facts surrounding the accident).

Such a right may be a small part of a much broader, as-yet-poorly-defined bundle of rights to control what happens to our memories. For example, we may have some right to be free from forced memory-dampening were the government to try to make us forget a trade secret or a voyeuristic memory. Neuroscientists are also hard at work developing drugs to enhance memory retention to treat Alzheimer's disease, as well as less severe age-related memory problems.[83] In the context of memory enhancement, we might have rights to enhance the emotions we attach to our memories (perhaps to increase affect attached to positive memories) as well as rights to enhance the factual content of the memories we store (to avert memory disorders or, more controversially, to perform better in school). We may also have rights to prevent forced enhancement of the factual richness of our memories by those who would make us better spies, soldiers, students or employees or to prevent forced enhancement of our memory-related affect by those who think doing so would make us more responsive to conscience and less likely to violate social norms.[84]

In addition to enhancing and dampening memories, we may have rights to keep memories private. Such a right is already circumscribed by the government's subpoena power – the power to demand that we answer (or at least try to answer) certain questions, under oath, about the content of our memories.[85] Advances in neuroscience, however, have led to the creation of neuroimaging technologies, like functional magnetic resonance imaging (fMRI), which will make questions about the privacy of memory even more important.[86] For example, neuroscientists are trying to develop brain-imaging techniques to determine if an experimental subject recognizes a person in a photograph (that is, has a memory of that person) using brain imaging alone, without relying on the subject's own (possibly deceptive) report.[87] The emergence of such technologies recently led one group of researchers to make the controversial claim that "[f]or the first time, using modern

---

83 *See* James McGaugh, Memory and Emotion 68–79 (2003) (describing a variety of drugs that may enhance memory).

84 *See* Wasserman, *supra* note 11, at 14 ("Some might suggest that for particularly heinous crimes, enhancement of guilt-ridden memory could serve as a form of punishment, a kind of forced internalization.").

85 *See generally* Slobogin, *supra* note 24, at 805–26 (describing the subpoena power).

86 One company, "No Lie MRI" has already begun selling fMRI-based lie detection services and another, "Cephos Corp.," plans to do so soon. *See* No Lie MRI, Inc., http://www.noliemri.com (last visited Sept. 21, 2006); Cephos Corp., http://www.cephoscorp.com (last visited Sept. 21, 2006); *see also* Associated Press, *Your Lying Brain: Scanners Dig for Truth from Deep Inside the Mind*, Chi. Trib., Jan. 30, 2006, at 26.

87 *See* Sean Kevin Thompson, Note, *The Legality of the Use of Psychiatric Neuroimaging in Intelligence Interrogation*, 90 Cornell L. Rev. 1601, 1602 (2005) (suggesting that neuroimaging could someday be used to detect whether a person being interrogated recognizes the subject of a photograph). *See generally* Charles N.W. Keckler, *Cross-Examining the Brain: A Legal Analysis of Neural Imaging for Credibility*

neuroscience techniques, a third party can, in principle, bypass the peripheral nervous system – the usual way in which we communicate – and gain direct access to the seat of a person's thoughts, feelings, intention, or knowledge."[88]

Related to the right to keep memories private is the right to make memories public. One such "publicity right", if it may be called such, concerns the means by which we can voluntarily demonstrate the content of our memories in court. In *Harrington v. State*,[89] convicted murderer Terry Harrington sought to offer unconventional evidence of his memories in the form of so-called "brain fingerprinting",[90] a kind of electroencephalography.[91] The brain fingerprinting results purportedly showed that Harrington did not have memories of the crime scene that the actual perpetrator would have had and that Harrington did have memories that supported his alibi.[92] At a post-conviction proceeding in Iowa District Court, the court took seriously some of the electroencephalographic evidence Harrington presented, though the court determined that Harrington "failed

---

Impeachment, 57 HASTINGS L.J. 509 (2006); Nicholas Wade, *Improved Scanning Technique Uses Brain as Portal to Thought*, N.Y. TIMES, Apr. 25, 2005, at A19.

88 Paul Root Wolpe et al., *Emerging Neurotechnologies for Lie-Detection: Promises and Perils*, 5 AM. J. OF BIOETHICS 39, 39 (2005); *see also* Yukiyasu Kamitani & Frank Tong, *Decoding the Visual and Subjective Contents of the Human Brain*, 8 NATURE NEUROSCIENCE 679, 679 (2005) (using fMRI as a method of "mind-reading" to enable investigators to determine the orientation of images shown to subjects). The reason the claim in the text is controversial is that it is not clear that one can ever, even in principle, have direct access to these features of another's mind.

89 659 N.W.2d 509, 515 (Iowa 2003) (seeking post-conviction relief). Harrington was convicted of first degree murder in the late 1970s, *State v. Harrington*, 284 N.W.2d 244 (Iowa 1979), and was then sentenced to life imprisonment without possibility of parole, Harrington, 659 N.W.2d at 512, 515–16.

90 The "brain fingerprinting" technique used in the case was developed by Lawrence Farwell. It may be more hype than substance, as the technology is proprietary and has not been subjected to rigorous peer review. *See* Wolpe et al., *supra* note 88, at 44 (raising concerns about the reliability of the studies examining Farwell's technique because they had small sample sizes and potential conflicts of interest). *See generally* Deborah Denno, *Crime and Consciousness: Science and Involuntary Acts*, 87 MINN. L. REV. 269, 331–35 (2002); U.S. GEN. ACCOUNTING OFFICE, FEDERAL AGENCY VIEWS ON THE POTENTIAL APPLICATION OF "BRAIN FINGERPRINTING," REP. NO. GAO-02-22 (2001), *available at* http://www.cognitiveliberty.org/pdf/goa_bfp.pdf; Nell Boyce, *Truth and Consequences: Scientists Are Scanning The Brain for Traces of Guilty Knowledge*, U.S. NEWS & WORLD REP., Jan. 15, 2001, at 40; Chris Clayton, *"Brain Fingerprints" As Defense?*, NAT'L L.J., Nov. 20, 2000, at A4.

91 Electroencephalograms measure brain signals known as "event related potentials" that can be detected "on the scalp 300–500ms after the subject is exposed to a stimulus." Wolpe et al., *supra* note 88, at 41. Farwell's brain fingerprinting technique is supposed to use electroencephalography to determine whether a subject is exposed to a familiar or unfamiliar stimulus by measuring event-related potentials that are "associated with novelty and salience of incoming stimuli." *Id.*

92 *Harrington*, 659 N.W.2d at 516 n.6.

to meet his burden to prove that the … evidence probably would have changed the result of his trial".[93] Harrington's conviction was ultimately overturned on grounds unrelated to this evidence.[94]

Prior to recent advances in neuroimaging and in neuropharmaceuticals, it made little sense to speak of a "freedom of memory".[95] There was simply too little we could do as human beings to affect our own memories to warrant clarifying our rights. In light of these developing technologies, however, we can begin to envision a bundle of rights associated with memory, including perhaps: rights to dampen memories; rights to enhance memories or memory-retention skills; rights to keep memories private (or to allow us to publicize them in court); and rights to be free of certain invasions of our memories by forced enhancement, forced dampening or even the secret implantation of false memories.[96]

Conclusion

Recent research suggests that primitive methods of therapeutic forgetting may be close at hand. Early methods have focused on efforts to dampen the affective qualities of memory but even such methods may have collateral effects on the recall of factual matters. Given how important memory is to the law, if even primitive forms of memory-dampening enter widespread use, it will not take long for such drugs to raise interesting legal questions.

If it turns out that effective forms of memory-dampening are on the more distant horizon, then many of the legal issues such therapies raise are less pressing. Nevertheless, the mere possibility of memory-dampening raises fundamental questions about who owns our memories and how we should balance the rights of memory-holders against society as a whole. Answers to such questions will ultimately shape the contours of our freedom of memory, a bundle of rights that

93 *Harrington v. State*, No. PCCV 073247, at 11 (Iowa Dist. Ct. Mar. 5, 2001); *see also Slaughter v. State*, 108 P.3d 1052, 1054 (Okla. Crim. App. 2005) (finding that the issue of brain fingerprinting "could have been previously raised in the direct appeal" and that there was "insufficient evidence to support a conclusion that brain fingerprinting, based solely upon the MERMER effect, would survive a *Daubert* analysis"). Farwell claims that brain fingerprinting has confirmed the guilt of one individual as well. *See* Beth Dalbey, *Brain Fingerprinting Testing*, Fairfield Ledger, http://www.brainwavescience.com/FairfieldLedger.php. (last visited Sept. 1, 2006).

94 *Harrington*, 659 N.W.2d at 512, 516.

95 There are no court opinions on Westlaw containing the phrase "freedom of memory", although the somewhat broader concept of "freedom of mind" appears in a number of opinions, principally in the area of First Amendment law.

96 Elizabeth Loftus and her research team have implanted so-called false memories into experimental subjects under a variety of conditions. *See* Elizabeth Loftus, *Our Changable Memories: Legal and Practical Implications*, 4 Nature Reviews Neuroscience 231 (2003); Elizabeth Loftus, *Make-Believe Memories*, 58 Am. Psychologist 867 (2003).

will take on greater importance and develop greater coherence as we confront new neuroscience technologies that improve our ability to manipulate memory. While each of these technologies will implicate somewhat different concerns, the central issues discussed here will constantly reappear, for all of these technologies will raise questions about the social value of memory and our willingness as a society to restrict individual control over intimate features of the mind.

Chapter 11

Reframing the Good Death: Enhancing Choice in Dying, Neuroscience, End-of-Life Research and the Potential of Psychedelics in Palliative Care

Robin Mackenzie

Introduction

What is a good death? I will suggest that there are ways in which we could dispel some of the uncertainties which prevent our answering this question with more specificity. While what happens after death remains, and seems likely to remain, contentious, research into the neuroscience of the dying brain offers us the potential to enhance choice in death by enhancing dying. So far, this constitutes unknown territory. Our knowledge of the neurochemistry of various brain states is growing (Johnson 2004), but does not yet include an evidence base which would enable us to orchestrate our dying from this perspective. Whereas palliative care research has isolated factors associated with our feeling more comfortable about the dying process, like a belief that our life has had meaning and relief from physical suffering (Woodruff 1999), technologies which would enable us to chart the subjective experiences of dying have, until now, been unavailable. Brain-imaging tools which measure neurological activity associated with moods, emotions and bodily processes now afford neuroscientists with the means to measure, record and compare sufficient varying subjective experiences of dying to establish an evidence base. Research on how specific substances and processes impact upon and determine subjective experiences of dying could thus provide a foundation from which choices over how our dying might be enhanced could be offered. This chapter will explore some of the legal and ethical issues associated with such a quest.

An important initial caveat is that this modest proposal does not imply a fixed position in relation to ongoing social negotiations over how far we should permit medically assisted dying, the legalization of unlawful psychoactive substances or human genetic enhancement. As I shall argue, ethical and legal justification may be found within aspects of current palliative care, the clinician's obligation of beneficence and many spiritual practices. Hence research into the neuroscience of dying should be undertaken in order to enable us to choreograph our deaths in this way.

End-of-life Research: The Need for an Evidence Base to Enhance Choice in Dying

How far those who are about to die might become the subjects of research into end-of-life treatments, palliative care options or various characterizations of the good death remains contentious. Ethical approval of research involving the dying or the terminally ill hinges upon interpretations of legal criteria which seek to offer protection to groups of categorized as vulnerable. Those who are seen as inherently lacking in capacity, such as children and the mentally infirm, may lawfully become research subjects only where stringent ethical and legal protections are in place. These commonly centre about normative judgments over consent and capacity, assessments of risk, harm and benefit, and issues associated with decisions being made by third parties on the behalf of those seen as unable to do so for themselves.

End-of-life research on human subjects has characteristics which compound these complexities. As we embark upon the final portion of our earthly lives, many of us are in a state of poor physical health, mirrored in declining or fluctuating mental powers. The terminally ill are likely to be receiving medical treatment to ameliorate symptoms, control pain and preserve life until only palliative care is seen as clinically appropriate. Both side effects of treatment and the inherent characteristics of the dying process render end-of-life research problematic. Symptoms we may experience include breathlessness, nausea and vomiting, loss of appetite, depression, constipation, anxiety, nervous tremors, pain, confusion, weakness and various degrees of dementia. Treatments for one of these, such as the use of opiate-based analgesics for pain, typically impact upon others, as in engendering constipation or affecting alertness. Hence our ability to participate in research, or to agree to do so, is likely to be inherently compromised. It may be hampered by an inability to communicate, through the adverse effects of pain, disease and multiple medications or by the dying process itself. We are unlikely to have discussed research participation should we become incompetent with our families (Bravo et al.. 2003) and those who may make decisions on our behalf are unlikely to be able to assess our views on research participation should we lose capacity with complete accuracy (Kim and Kiebutz 2006; Stocking et al.. 2006). Finally, should we, towards the end of our lives, become research subjects, there is a significant likelihood that we will die before the project is complete.

In addition, while iatrogenic multifactorial confounding factors such as the side effects and mutual interactions of medications render assessing the effects of alternative treatments difficult, placebo trials present specific ethical difficulties (Hardy 2001; Kirkham and Abel 2001). Understandably, then, what end-of-life research there is has tended to focus upon symptomatic relief, disease-specific treatments or palliative care. One of the consequences of this is that we know comparatively little about subjective experiences of the dying process in itself, or neurochemical activities which take place in the brain at end of life. Without the evidence base customary amongst most areas of clinical treatment, the ability of clinicians to evaluate alternative means of providing appropriate care for the dying is compromised.

Thus, in an important sense, when we die we do so without an appreciation of choices we might exercise here. My suggestion in this chapter is that the current debate over how far it might be seen as ethically and legally permissible to request hastened death as part of medical treatment has artificially restricted perceived possibilities. The resulting binary opposition between palliative care and medical assistance to die thus constrains unduly our choices over our dying. On this basis, I will put forward the argument that current developments in neuroscience demonstrate the potential to enhance choice in dying through the option of enhancing the dying process. For reasons of space, I will focus only on the potential of psychedelics to enhance our dying through enhancing our ability to find meaning in our lives. In order to support this position, I will consider the legal and ethical factors associated with end-of-life research upon human subjects, arguing that this may be justified within appropriate safeguards. The potential of neuroscience to ameliorate some of the previous difficulties associated with such endeavours will be explored as a preliminary to demonstrating how enhanced choice in the experience of dying might be afforded.

Neuroscience and End-of-life Research

Advances in medicine have given rise to situations where clinicians, families and the legal profession must make decisions not over whether very ill human entities can be kept alive, but whether they should be. Current controversies over such decisions at the beginning of life concern the stage of a pregnancy wherein termination should be lawful, the cut-off point at which a baby who has been born prematurely with a poor prognosis should not necessarily be resuscitated and when it can be seen as in the best interests of a severely damaged baby to be allowed to die. The impact of new medical technologies – particularly imaging techniques which provide information on internal states of being in unprecedented depth – on public involvement in policy-making has been significant. Images of foetuses in the womb sucking thumbs, reportedly able to feel pain and to recognize the voices of family members, have influenced public perceptions of the beginning of life as well as official policies. Medical imaging has become domesticated as a result, as expectant parents routinely make copies of ultrasound images of their future offspring, and know whether to anticipate a boy or a girl. Thus, while imaging technologies provide evidence to underpin guidelines and policies on controversial beginning-of-life issues, they also raise specific ethical dilemmas over the broad personal and social meanings attributed to neuroimages (Racine et al. 2006). Yet the clinical evidence neuroscience provides may be drawn upon to construct nuanced ethical foundations for policy deliberations. This potential has been demonstrated in the Nuffield Council on Bioethics' highly impressive recent report on critical care decisions in foetal and neonatal medicine, where the emphasis on evidence bases rests in part on a measured appreciation of the potential of medical technology to support ethical decision-making (Nuffield Council of Bioethics 2006). In my view, neuroscientific techniques afford a similar potential for providing information to underpin ethical decision-making at the end of life, and to expand the range of choices available here. The remainder of this section will sketch out this claim.

Neuroimaging techniques permit brain activities and mechanisms to be matched with subjective experiences and behaviour patterns. While first-person accounts of subjective experiences cannot be authenticated using objective, third-person measurements, multimodal functional brain-imaging techniques (EEG, ERP, MEG, fMRI and PET), now may map brain mechanisms and alterations in such a way as to correlate these with cognition and consciousness (Harneroff 2005). Degrees of activity in specific areas of the brain are associated with experiences of particular feelings like happiness, spiritual enlightenment, or fear (Haidt 2006). Engaging in specific behaviours may trigger such activity deliberately: Tibetan monks meditating on universal compassion demonstrated an ability to manifest gamma wave synchrony associated with a higher form of consciousness, as measured by EEG (Harneroff 2005; Lutz et al. 2004). In addition, stimulation of specific areas of the brain provokes characteristic responses. For instance, the feeling of a sensed presence, or sentient being, associated in many cultures and times with subjective experiences of spirituality and mysticism, may be provoked by stimulation of the right hemisphere with weak complex magnetic fields, and measured in terms of alpha waves and temporal lobe activity (Booth et al. 2005). Neuroimaging technologies also have the capacity to map subjective experiences as they manifest in neurotransmitter activity. Human behaviour and moods are largely mediated by dopminergic and serotonergic systems, where rewards, motivations and arousal are associated with regulatory neurotransmitter mechanisms (Saah 2005). These vary with circumstance and medical condition. Those addicted to alcohol, or suffering from certain mental disorders, are likely to evidence characteristic disruptions in serotonin and dopamine processing in the brain (Kapur and Lecrubier 2003). Thus the therapeutic potential of neuroscientific means of assessing neurotransmitter mechanisms in order to restore health and homeostasis holds much promise as a basis for future clinical treatments based on detailed knowledge of such brain structures and mechanisms.

These techniques of measurement and stimulation also afford the possibility of investigating the neuroscience associated with end of life, including the experience of the dying process. My suggestion here is that in the same way as beginning-of-life policies are informed by the impact of imaging techniques, equivalent evidence over end-of-life mechanisms should be accumulated as underpinning for salient ethical, legal and medical decision-making. Given that developmental factors influence not only the beginning, but also the ending of our lives, it makes sense to investigate both. By and large, our knowledge of the neuroscience of what happens as we embark on the dying process is partial at best. Rather than focus on the dying process itself, neuroscientists have tended to investigate specific clinical conditions associated with ethically problematic states of being. Nonetheless, researchers have recently begun to draw upon neuroscientific technology in an attempt to provide detailed, integrated explorations of the neural, behavioural and computational correlates of altered states of consciousness such as brain death, coma, vegetative states, minimally conscious state, locked-in syndrome, dementia, epilepsy, schizophrenia, hysteria, general anesthesia, sleep, hypnosis and hallucinations as a basis for ethical decision-making in these areas (Laureys et al. 2006). I would argue that such investigations should be extended to how we die and the neuroscience of the dying process, not only to ensure better medical care, but also to provide us with enhanced choices which include enhancing the dying process in order to achieve what we would regard as a good death.

Neuroscience, Psychedelics and Reframing the Good Death

What, then, is a good death? I would suggest that there are ways in which we could dispel some of the uncertainties which prevent our answering this question with more specificity. While what happens after death remains, and seems likely to remain, contentious, research into the neuroscience of the dying brain offers us the potential to enhance choice in death by enhancing dying. So far, this constitutes unknown territory. How, then, might our dying process be enhanced? Neuroscience has much to offer here in that it also possesses the potential to extend our knowledge of how end-of-life states of being relate to psychoactive substances. In that these may be both produced internally, or endogenous, as opposed to taken in from external sources, or exogenous, their role in health is of central importance. Indeed, medical treatments at end of life commonly rely upon exogenous psychoactive substances in the form of opiates and their derivatives to control pain, as well as psychiatric medications to ameliorate dementia, depression, anxiety and agitation. Research involving exogenous psychoactive substances which are also used as unlawful recreational drugs has been seen as permissible only recently (Check 2004; Mackenzie 2006; Nichols 2006). Recent clinical trials seek to assess the potential of otherwise unlawful psychoactive substances to ameliorate depression and anxiety in the terminally ill (Morris 2006), cluster headaches (Sewell 2006), post-traumatic stress disorder and other forms of psychotherapy including treating addictions (Sessa 2006). Psychoactive substances such as LSD, psilocybin, mescaline, ibogaine, ayahuasca, MDMA or ecstasy and salvia divinorum have all been found to have clinical potential as a result. For the purposes of this chapter, and for reasons of space, only the possibility of enhancing subjective experience of end-of-life processes with psychedelics will be considered further.

Psychedelic, or mind-manifesting, psychoactive substances are also known as hallucinogens (producing hallucinations), psychotomimetics (mimicking psychosis) and entheogens (revealing the God within) (Kleber 2006). Neuroscientists have recently conducted rigorously constructed double-blind active and inactive placebo controlled studies characterizing subjective, physiological and perceptual effects of various psychedelics, with follow-ups to evaluate long-term effects (Griffiths et al. 2006; Nichols 2006). These have revealed not only the role of neurotransmitter mechanisms in their effects (psychedelics are serotonergically mediated, but may resemble norepinephrine and dopamine as well as serotonin) but also demonstrate the promise of neuroimaging for explaining the sites and mechanisms of action of hallucinogens and the workings of consciousness (Snyder 2006). The effects of psychedelics on the neurobiology of body perception and awareness (interoception) and emotional processing has also been demonstrated using SPECT and PET imaging techniques (Riba et al. 2006). Such studies have consistently demonstrated that psychedelics promote spiritual or mystical experiences which tend to have long-lasting positive effects on the subjective experience of life. These resemble spontaneously occurring mystical states associated with the dissolution of ego boundaries and feelings of transcendence, or merging with the universe, and it is postulated that both are mediated by changes in serotonin mechanisms (Haidt 2005; Snyder 2006). Their therapeutic potential is seen as highly promising for treatment of intolerable pain, refractory depression and the sufferings of the terminally ill, as well as for humanistic psychology, substance abuse and dependence (Friedman 2006; Kleber 2006; Kolp 2006).

Naturally there are caveats. Considerations of dosage, efficacy of different psychedelics, individual differences in response as mediated by genetics or context, and other issues associated with clinical judgments over risks and benefits would need to be addressed. Research into possible negative subjective experiences resulting from ingesting psychedelics would be essential before providing them as treatment or enhancement might be seen as lawful. Nonetheless, the promising nature of the results so far has led to calls for continuing research on the basis of probable therapeutic benefit, as well as increased insights into the nature of consciousness and cognition (Griffiths et al. 2006; Kleber 2006; Nichols 2006; Saah 2005; Schuster 2006; Sessa 2006; Snyder 2006). The positive effects of spiritual experiences promoted by psychedelics in enhancing subjective feelings that life has meaning possess obvious potential for palliative care, including the possibility of reducing or replacing medication for pain, anxiety and depression, as well as the associated unwelcome side effects.

Spiritual convictions that one's life is meaningful have the highest correlation with subjective assessments of quality of life amongst cancer patients and their spouses (Axelsson and Sjoden 1998). The current orientation within palliative care is to improve quality of life and to relieve suffering (Kim et al. 2005). Positive psycho-spiritual well-being is seen as central to patients' ability to find meaning in the experience of terminal illness by clinicians involved in palliative care throughout the world (Lin and Bauer-Wu 2003). Palliative care ethicists distinguish between the intrinsic aim of palliative care, to bring about a medical good; and the extrinsic aim, to promote the patient's psychological, emotional, relational and spiritual good. Randall and Downie (1999) argue that phronesis, or the practical wisdom to deal with a range of issues relating to the extrinsic aims, is the controlling moral component in all palliative care. Phronesis is essential if clinicians are to appreciate the meaning of the disease, suffering and treatment for each particular patient, and to respect how that meaning fits into the patient's conception of their total good (Randall and Downie 1999, 1–28). From this perspective, the possibility of including the administration of clinically approved psychedelics on request in palliative care provision as coming within the ethical aegis of beneficence or phronesis seems initially plausible. Yet allowing us to request psychedelics to enhance a spiritual sense of meaning at end of life may not be simply accepted as clinical treatment. Should providing this choice be framed as enhancement, many are likely to find such an option objectionable. The following section will consider the reasons why this might be so.

Reframing the Good Death to Enable Enhanced Choice and Enhanced Dying

I wish to argue in this section that the discourses surrounding choice in dying and notions of the good death are currently impoverished. My suggestion is that the good death be reframed to include enhanced choice in death by providing us with options over how our dying might be enhanced. Such a prospect may seem odd. I shall argue that this is so because of an historical relationship between the discursive strategies adopted within the separate debates surrounding assisted dying, enhancement, the regulation of psychoactive substance use and how these should relate to medical treatment. In my view, concerns over risks associated with hereditary enhanced genetic characteristics and the controversies surrounding medically assisted death, taken together with troubled cultural relationships with pleasure, have resulted in a degree of rhetorical capture. As a consequence, any association between medical treatment, enhancement, pleasure and death has been rendered, to a degree, unthinkable. Enhancement has been discursively constructed as applicable largely to inherited characteristics, pleasure through psychoactive substances read as addiction and medically assisted dying equated with hastening death in response to patients exercising a tightly constrained autonomy. I have no desire to retraverse the arguments in each of these debates. Instead, I wish to draw from them in order to propose a reframing of the good death as one wherein we could choose to receive medical assistance to enhance our dying.

How far, and in what way, if at all, we should place ethical and legal limits on enhancement technologies is not self-evident. Ethicists, politicians, the bioscience industry and the public seem unlikely to arrive at a negotiated consensus here (Fukuyama 2002; President's Council on Bioethics 2003; Smith 2005). Opponents of enhancement tend to proscribe it as interfering with nature, or to argue that medical treatment is ethically permissible, but enhancement is unethical (Sandel 2004). Psychoactive substances constitute a special category where the enhancement of human capacities and moods is concerned (Foresight 2005). While pharmaceuticals like Prozac, Modafinil and their progeny demonstrate the commercial potential of such products, ethical and legal limits have been placed on their availability. Nonetheless, many such drugs, ostensibly used to ameliorate difficulties associated with medical conditions, have crossed over into the off-label mainstream where they are used to enhance performance or mood. Pharmaceutical manufacturers holding a multitude of patents nearing the ends of their useful lives need to find new markets and new products in order to sustain profitability. Yet the relationship between psychoactive substances which lead us to feel better as well, and better than well, is a troubled one. Many, like the opiates, are controlled substances whose use is prohibited unless prescribed. Nonetheless, much non-prescription use of these takes place outside the law, either through diversion of prescribed medications or illegal manufacture. The lack of congruence between the legality of psychoactive substances and their favourable or harmful effects on our health is problematic for the public health and criminal justice authorities which seek to persuade us to maintain our health and to respect the law (Mackenzie 2006; WHO 2004). For pharmaceutical companies, though, the salient problem is that patent protection extends only as far as new effects of old substances, or to new substances. Where the latter function to enhance the moods or capacities of the healthy, they are liable to be designated as unlawful designer drugs. This leaves the industry in a situation of moral hazard, where yielding to the temptation to create new disease entities cured by new "lifestyle" drugs has been condemned as "disease-mongering" and strategic deployment of the rhetoric of choice and need (Biggs and Mackenzie 2000; PLOS Medicine 2006).

All this has deleterious effects where research into enhancing dying through pharmaceutical means is concerned. Since most psychoactive substances which might do so are not new or, frequently, lawful, their ability to attract patent protection would be uncertain, so that the financial incentive for pharmaceutical companies to place research and development funds into this area is minimal. As palliative care organizations are usually charities, their resources from which to fund research are limited, as well as their orientation being to soothe rather than enhance the dying process. In addition, as outlined above, research into dying is acknowledged to raise special issues (Field et al. 2001; Jubb 2002). Yet these practical difficulties are outweighed by ethical and legal factors. It is upon these I wish to focus for the remainder of this chapter.

My starting point is the assertion that current debate over end-of-life decision-making has been curtailed by a degree of rhetorical capture. Self-evident concerns over the integrity of the medical profession, the appropriate limits on autonomy and the protection of the vulnerable have ensured that considerations of patient choice in relation to our dying have been restricted to whether and in what circumstances medically assisted dying might receive ethical and legal approval. As a consequence, the means by which clinicians might provide treatment which would enhance our subjective experience of the dying process has received scant consideration. In particular, the opportunity for a role for patient choice in medically enhanced dying has not, as far as I am aware, been mooted previously. In my view, a salient additional factor is that ethical discourse over enhancement has been overdetermined by that already put in place by controversies over the new reproductive technologies. Together with this, research into the neurochemistry of the promise for enhancement afforded by psychoactive substances has been compromised by injudicious past practices (Mackenzie 2006; Nicols 2006). My suggestion is that severing criteria for permitting enhancement from an association with inheritable characteristics should permit a focus on how the dying process might be enhanced in ways which might prove beneficial to many. This would be anchored by an evidence base obtained via research into the neuroscience of the dying process, as providing the potential for an investigation of the subjective effects of psychoactive substances in this context, as outlined above.

Should this be framed as optional clinical treatment rather than consumer demand, there is the potential for enhancement of the dying process, based upon highly structured ethical studies, to be viewed as falling within healthcare professionals' obligation to treat their patients with beneficence, as an extension of current palliative care measures. Future possibilities, and how these might relate to legal issues and patient choice, will be explored in this light.

Decision-Making, Death and Dying and the Law

Most of us would like some choice over how, where and when we die. While such decisions are inherently restricted by the vagaries of incarnation and the mishaps of fate, we are able to exercise a degree of choice over dying where healthcare is concerned. We may refuse medical treatment altogether or eschew specific measures, although we cannot request and receive those which are seen as clinically unjustified (*R (On the Application of Burke)* v *General Medical Council (Official Solicitor and Others Intervening*) [2005] 3 WLR 1132 and the European Court of Human Rights decision to refuse Mr Burke the chance to appeal against this judgment http://cmiskp.echr.coe.int/tkp197/view.asp?item=2&portal=hbkm&action=html&highlight=burke&sessionid=8546023&skin=hudoc-en). Nor can we, in the United Kingdom, ask for, and receive, assistance to die. Should some future version of the Lord Joffe's Assisted Dying for the Terminally Ill Bill become law, those of us who are terminally ill, suffering unbearably and competent may be lawfully provided with the means by which we might end our own lives by healthcare professionals provided certain safeguards are in place (Parliament 2006). Although assisted suicide, voluntary and involuntary euthanasia are available within the law in certain countries in Europe, common law jurisdictions almost universally prohibit assisted suicide and all forms of active euthanasia (Marker 2006). This stance is associated with a reading of death as appropriately falling within the aegis of medicine; logically enough in that most of us die subject to clinical judgments, either that treatment has failed to save us or that further treatment would be futile. From this perspective, a good death involves the caring healthcare professional's relieving suffering, providing palliative care and hastening death, without the intention to do so, only where there has been a refusal of treatment or where pain relief does so as a side effect. Thus, medical assistance in our dying is subsumed under beneficence, the duty to relieve patients' suffering. The correlative duty to respect patients' autonomy applies insofar as patients may refuse treatment, but clinical judgment prevails over autonomous requests for either hastened death or specific treatments which are regarded as clinically unjustifiable.

Many believe that a good death should be interpreted otherwise. Requesting assistance to die has been framed in terms of autonomy, dignity and relief of intolerable suffering (Biggs 2001). All of these terms have contested meanings (Pullman 2002; Singer 1996). Widespread agreement on what they signify, or how they should relate to clinical judgment and patient or human rights is highly unlikely (Williams 2005). I have no wish to traverse these well-rehearsed positions yet again. Instead, I wish to propose a widening of the debate to reframe the good death as incorporating the possibility of enhancing the dying process.

In my view, our choices over dying need not be restricted to whether or not it should be seen as ethically acceptable and lawful for patients to request medical assistance in dying only in the sense of actively hastening death. This is essentially a negative choice to avoid specific consequences like ennui, dependency or feeling like a burden. Reading ennui, dependency or feeling like a burden as suffering might lead to a view of medically assisted death as ethically acceptable, through a combination of respecting patient autonomy, in terms of allowing a choice to die, and providing beneficence, in terms of relieving suffering. Yet concerns over the integrity of the medical profession, preserving trust as an element of the clinician/patient relationship and affording protection for the vulnerable have so far prevented active medical assistance in dying from becoming lawful in most jurisdictions. Even in those where it has become lawful, the good death has not been reframed to enhance choice through providing means to enhance dying. I shall now explore reasons why this has not taken place, in order to argue that a degree of rhetorical capture has prevented this.

Reproductive Technologies, Enhancement and Death: Rhetorical Capture

It is now a truism to say that death has replaced sex as spectacle as the transgressive impact of the latter declines (Carnell 2000). The resurgence of public autopsies, exhibitions of corpses and an unrelenting media focus on mortality induced by others denotes a [re]current cultural fascination, following on from the demystification of sex and reproduction which preceded it (Kuppers 2004; Tait 2006; van Dijck 2001). I wish to suggest here that the deconstruction of death and dying parallels that of sex and reproduction, specifically in that the ethical and legal controversies over choice and autonomy exhibit the same rhetorical concerns. Debates tend to centre about an opposition constructed between a quest for secular ethics and a positioning of technology as the enemy of the sacred. Of note here is that technology as enabling the deconstruction of "life itself" fosters specific rhetorical tropes wherein life, nature and the sacred are regarded as threatened by autonomy and choice (Mackenzie 2007). This has been explicated in relation to debate over the regulation of the new reproductive technologies, the Warnock report and the Human Fertilisation and Embryology Act 1990. Feminists have demonstrated how resolution was achieved via strategies involving the creation of a new entity, the pre-embryo, the medicalization of infertility and the sacralization of motherhood, which together rendered acceptable the new reproductive technologies (Franklin 1993; Mulkay 1997; Spallone 1996).

One argument I am making here is the assertion that much of the current debate over death and dying has been subjected to rhetorical capture. The discursive rhetoric surrounding reproductive technologies has been transferred to ethical considerations of death and dying. This rhetorical capture of how we die has foreclosed and constrained the symbolic universe within which we currently conceive of the dying process. By and large, the new reproductive technologies have faded into the background of our ethical landscape. Cultural dissension where sex and reproduction is concerned tends to be sited in the rearguard actions mounted by those who oppose abortion as part of family planning and support marriage as a solely heterosexual institution. Much of the shock of the new has transferred to finding a common language for ethical discourse over "death itself" as opposed to "life itself". Thus the extension of the dying process made possible by technology, in-between states like persistently vegetative states and the varying medical and legal ways in which death itself may be defined have together produced a discursive environment very similar to that which surrounded the new reproductive technologies around 30 years ago.

Enhancement is one arena where controversy over reproduction remains. Condemned along with cloning and stem cell technologies as unnatural, against human dignity and a crime against humanity by influential bioethicists, enhancement as deliberate alteration of inheritable human genetic characteristics is also proscribed in significant international agreements (Annas et al. 2002; Fukuyama 2002; Kass 2002; President's Council on Bioethics 2003). Transhumanists and others who favour such enhancement, or who see it as inevitable given its technological temptations and commercial potential, regard such bioconservatism as philosophically suspect in that it is based upon overly narrow conceptions of humanity, dignity and autonomy (Bostrom 2005; Smith 2005; Stock 2002). In addition, all concerned disagree upon how best to assess and evaluate the risks of altering the human germline.

My point here is that the rhetoric of the cultural debate over "life itself" is misleading for ethical and legal decision-making over "death itself". For a start, medically enhanced dying would not involve unforeseeable hereditary change in the human germline. In addition, where "life itself" is concerned, the disparate groups whom Brownsword has designated as the "dignitarian alliance" rely upon the concept of dignity to constrain rather than extend choice (Brownsword 2004). "Designer babies", reproductive cloning and manipulation of the human germline are all seen as offending against human dignity and the proper relationship between humans, nature and life itself (Lauritzen 2005; Sandel 2004). While some philosophical inquiries into dignity have concluded that predetermination of human genetic characteristics and some manipulations of the genetic heritage of humans need not be seen as offending against human dignity, despite statements of principle in various international instruments, this is not a common viewpoint (Bostrum 2005; Smith 2005). Brownsword characterizes the stance of the dignitarian alliance as in opposition to a pragmatic reduction of the salient ethical issues to the secularized touchstone of a risk/benefit analysis based upon the precautionary principle. From the latter perspective, choice over enhancement in reproduction would be subject to restrictions based upon interpretations of the idea of dignity as well as those posed by unforeseeable inherited consequences. Yet it is not self-evident that this need be so where dying is concerned.

Enhancement, dignity and choice can all be seen to have context-specific meanings. Should the rhetoric of new reproductive technologies be simply transferred to decisions governing "death itself", it would therefore constrain them in an inappropriate fashion. I would argue that this transfer has taken place, with consequent limits being placed upon how we conceive of the ethics of possibilities associated with our dying. Notions of dignity are currently deployed to shape choices over how we reproduce in a way which excludes enhancement. This is commonly achieved through linking the idea of dignity to a naturalized sacralization of the current human genome which defines humans with enhanced genetic characteristics as lacking in human dignity (Smith 2005). The human genome becomes linked to nature as sacred human tissue properly immune to technical manipulation (Lauritzen 2005; Sandel 2004). Even where the ethics of enhancement aside from reprogenetics is in question, an ostensibly secular debate is embued with terms and symbology associated with religion and the sacralization of nature by those who oppose it (Strong 2005).

I would argue that this conflation of the natural, the sacred and the viewing of technical intervention as offending against dignity, as developed in the discourses of reproductive technologies and enhancement, impoverishes the current debate over how far and in which ways we should be able to exercise choice in dying. The terms, perspectives and ways of thinking associated with dissension over reproductive technologies and the limits which should be placed on enhancement with respect to reproduction have created a rhetorical symbolic universe which has been applied to debates over end-of-life issues in ways which create confusion. An example of this may be seen in the ongoing dissension over whether artificial nutrition and hydration constitute medical treatment, which may be withdrawn on request or according to clinical judgment, or basic care, which should continue. Guidelines over hospice and palliative care typically characterize dying as a natural process wherein artificial nutrition and hydration form part of basic care until the dying process begins, whereupon artificial nutrition and hydration become categorized as intrusive technological intervention (Frederick 2002). The dying process, from this perspective, thus becomes sanctified, naturalized and ideally subject to minimal medical intervention. Thus the concept of dignity, when applied to death and the dying process in the context of withdrawal of treatment, sanctifies the natural and opposes it to intervention. Both legal and medical professionals speak of providing dignity in death in terms of "letting nature take its course" as part of respecting the sanctity of life (Keown 2005). Dignity here is equated with not taking heroic measures to preserve life when to do so would be futile, but allowing the naturalized dying process to proceed. The extent to which this use of both dignity and nature represents rhetorical strategy may be seen when we consider that medical intervention inherently interferes with the natural processes associated with ill health, and that is indeed why we seek it when we are unwell. Certainly once we begin to die we lose our appetites and our fluid intake diminishes. Yet how far away the rhetoric of "letting nature take its course" might be from most understandings of dignity is revealed by the fact that the result of the decision to do so often results in conceptually distinct situation of patients, who were not otherwise dying, slowly doing so from starvation and dehydration once artificial nutrition and hydration has been withdrawn (Brogden 2001). Thus drawing upon cultural conceptions of dignity which sacralize and naturalize the process of dying with minimal medical intervention circumscribes debate over when and by what means we should die when we are not expected to recover.

Brownsword's model of a policy opposition between the dignitarian alliance and autonomy-driven risk/benefit libertarianism as traversed above fits the discursive dissension over reproductive technologies better than that over death and dying. Here both those who oppose and those who support medically assisted dying lay claim to the term dignity, the former as outlined above and the latter as exemplified in the recent decision by the Voluntary Euthanasia Society to change its name to Dignity in Dying. Strong conceptions of autonomy in this context sever notions of dignity from the natural where death is concerned. Thus, when those who conceive of a good death as potentially incorporating active medical assistance in dying wish to be able to request death, or claim a right to die, once they feel that to continue living would involve an intolerable lack of dignity, they do so on the grounds that dignity is compatible with autonomy but not dependence. Such a death, then, is denaturalized not only in terms of incorporating medical care, but also in relying upon it to curtail the dying process. The merits of medically assisted death and its relation to dignity have been debated elsewhere often, and I do not propose to revisit them. Nonetheless, this position suggests that while dignity might act as a fetter upon choice where reproduction is concerned, once the concept of dignity is separated from that of nature in relation to how we die, its use within debates over medically assisted dying is both strategic and incoherent. Thus, in my view, there is no reason why conceptions of dignity should restrict how we exercise choice here. Indeed, despite its presence in many international agreements, human rights jurisprudence and cases concerning death such as *Pretty v United Kingdom* (Application 2346/02) [2001] 2 FCR 97), the value of the concept of dignity as an ethical tool may be seen as limited without specific definition (Hayry 2004; Hayry and Takala 2005).

I have suggested above that choice over medically enhanced dying need not be circumscribed by conceptions of dignity, since in the context of death and dying these are so various as to lack persuasive force, and that ethical objections against enhancement which are mounted within reprogenetics debates do not apply here. Nonetheless, were these suggestions to be found acceptable, the way forward to enhancing the dying process is not clear, as cultural attitudes towards pleasure and suffering come into play. I shall consider these first in relation to sex and reproduction before assessing their impact on my arguments.

The nexus between sex, reproduction, pleasure and suffering possesses contested cultural significance. Sex, birth, death and dying are all processes which are part of life for most of us. The degree to which they should be medicalized, given that they are not, strictly speaking, illnesses, and the amount of choice we should be able to exercise over them remains contentious. These questions have been mapped onto other debates over the appropriate reach of medical services, consumerism and enhancement. As a consequence, arriving at consensus over how they should be associated with already culturally overladen experiences such as suffering and pleasure is not a straightforward process. An example here is the biblical association between childbirth and suffering as punishment for Eve's yielding to the snake's temptation: "in sorrow shalt thou bring forth children" (Genesis, 3:16). While it is now accepted that pain relief in childbirth is appropriate medical care, how far requests for elective caesarians might be seen as acceptable remains unsettled. That sex and reproduction are no longer necessarily causally connected has facilitated the commodification and celebration of sexual pleasure which characterizes our times. Yet their deconstruction has also been accompanied by an encroachment of medicalization, as in the creation of the disorder female sexual dysfunction, a condition allegedly suffered by almost half of the women in the United States (Laumann et al. 1999). Thus the enhancement of bodily processes which are not in themselves illnesses ends up being characterized in these terms, with the medical profession as gatekeepers or overseers, in circumstances requiring compromises between medical ethics and consumer choice.

This impacts on enhancing dying as follows. While the deconstruction of sex and reproduction has permitted an open personal and commercial focus upon sexual pleasure and its enhancement, cultural differences mean that this has proven a troubled pathway. Historic associations between sexual pleasure, perceptions of immorality and tawdry commerce tainted and delayed research until the mid-twentieth century. Similar associations hamper the accumulation of an evidence base on enhancing dying. The combination of pleasure and death calls forth memories of serial killers, snuff movies and similar forms of popular entertainment which it is easy to decry. Psychoactive substances and dying are linked not only to the relief of suffering in medical treatment but also with entertainers and addicts taking lethal overdoses and imprudent practices involving hallucinogens within academia in the 1960s and 1970s. Yet the deconstruction of dying and death affords opportunities for enhancement which parallel those associated with sexual pleasure today. If we are to be granted more autonomy over the dying process when recovery is no longer possible, should we also not have some say into the means by which we do so?

A logical response here is that while pleasure is the biologically driven response to sexual activity, the same cannot be said for our dying. It is here that I wish to turn to the neuroscience of daily life, in order to argue that our biological substrates and many reports of dying experiences suggest that the situation may be more complex. In everyday life, to be happy is to be healthy, other things being equal. Research into the neuroscience of health reveals that enhanced health is associated with an overall sense of coherence, or a global orientation to view the world and the individual environment as comprehensible, manageable and meaningful. Instruments for measuring how such beliefs and practices are associated with good health have proven cross-cultural validity and reliability (Eriksson and Lindstrom 2005). In addition, pleasure not only enhances our health but forms a basis of action and interaction in our daily lives. For example, recent research suggests that the release of endogenous opiates ensures that we enjoy one another's company, providing evidence for a postulated human trait of affiliation (Depue and Morrone-Strupinsky 2005).

Associations between certain states of being or beliefs and practices and good health are now accepted, while investigations into the neurocircuits in the brain associated with functional mechanisms that contribute to health via specific beliefs and practices are ongoing. For instance, maintaining good health despite stressful situations is associated with the belief that things will work out as well as can reasonably be expected, being mutually in love, believing in God and expecting things to change for the better (Smith 2002). Such beliefs need not be rational or realistic for them to function in this way, as evidenced by the placebo effect, which involves the brain's reward pathways and stimulates feelings of well-being (Esch and Stefano 2004). Neuroscientists recommend being in lust or in love as the associated pleasures reduce anxiety and stress, enhance health and promote sociality (Esch and Stefano 2005a). In fact, all varieties of love accompanied by pleasure appear to offer health benefits (Esch and Stefano 2005b). This first came to the attention of neuroscientists through research projects associated with the love of the divine (Lee and Newberg 2005). Investigations into spiritual practices, medicine and neurotheology previously associated such health-promoting effects specifically with religion and religious activities such as prayer (Sloan et al. 2000). More recently, however, subsequent research suggests that any shared strong belief system accompanied by regular rituals will produce identical health benefits (McGuire and Tiger 2006). Thus a congregation of atheists who meet regularly to affirm their beliefs in ritualistic fashion could be expected to experience similar feelings of well-being as would those of an equivalent group of those with religious faith. What these findings tell us is that good feelings promote good health. If we feel that life makes sense, that we can deal with its difficulties, and are able to love at least some of our lives, our gods and our fellow men and women, then we are more likely to be healthy than if we do not, and to recover better from ill health (Mackenzie 2006).

This neurochemical model of how we live suggests that feelings of bodily produced pleasure underpin happiness, sociality and health (Depue and Morrone-Strupinsky 2005; Katz, 2005; Smith 2002). In addition, experiences of subjective meaning, whether these are produced by love, belief or social rituals, enhance how we experience our lives as well as promoting health. Indeed, many mental and mood disorders, as well as many of the effects of the ageing process, may be explained in terms of neurotransmitter dysfunction within the brain which interfere with the ability to experience life as pleasurable (Charney and Nestler 2004; Keverne and Ray 2005; Reynolds 2005). Psychoactive substances may enhance or substitute for these mechanisms, as their effects on the brain frequently mimic the neurochemical mechanisms involved. For instance, opiates administered as part of medical treatment to ameliorate pain do so as correlative endogenous opioids also effect analgesia (Li et al. 2004). The endogenous cannibinoid system is involved in the reward circuitry which provides the experience of pleasure, as well as affecting appetite, pain and the immune system. Evidence that this malfunctions as a result of certain medical conditions like advanced cancer, diminishing the ability of patients to experience pleasure (Lissoni et al. 2003), adds force to the argument I am making here that providing us with the choice to enhance our dying might be ethically compatible with both beneficence and palliative care.

If the substrate of daily life, health and well-being is based upon the neurochemistry of pleasure and subjective experiences of meaningfulness, it becomes more difficult to argue that the clinical administration of substances which produced such effects at end of life should be seen as unnatural. While some may argue that producing spiritual experiences through psychoactive substances denigrates from their validity compared with those which arise of themselves, those who tell of the former, whether these take place in sacramental or experimental contexts, tend to express no such doubts (Griffiths et al. 2006; Riba et al. 2006). Nonetheless, where the intention is to provide an option of enhancing the subjective experience of dying, this could be proscribed as enhancement rather than treatment. Several ethical issues are salient here. Those who argue that an ethical distinction between treatment and enhancement is sustainable (Sandel 2004; Schwartz 2005) are opposed by those who find this position incoherent (Kamm 2005). Others argue that the context and meaning of enhancement should govern its ethical acceptability (Martin and Peerzada 2005; Robert 2005). In addition, the relationship between enhancement and professional integrity is a troubled one. Those who have concerns over what they see as inappropriate patient choice over enhancement, where the doctor/patient relationship becomes one of consumer and service provider, seek to prevent a future where medical ethics reduces to the ethics of marketplace transactions (Miller and Brody 2005).

Given the flexibility of disease taxonomies when commercial opportunity beckons, as sketched out above, it seems likely that research into the neuroscience of end of life would reveal processes and mechanisms which might be framed as in need of clinical treatment. In the same way as the manifestations of ageing, such as pigmentation anomalies, may be categorized as forms of ill health, aspects of end of life could lead it to be seen as a disorder of some kind. Options to enhance end-of-life care could then include the provision of clinically approved psychedelics to promote feelings of meaningfulness associated with quality of life, as well as ameliorating symptoms of anxiety, depression and ennui. Taxonomies at end of life could prove central to the legalities of research on human subjects at end of life. It is to these complexities that I will now turn.

Legal and Ethical Considerations in Research on End-of-life Human Subjects and Enhancing the Dying Process

Research on human subjects at the end of their lives as outlined above would involve neuroimaging to measure both the neuroscience of the dying process and the impact on the subjective experience at end of life of administering psychedelics and active or inactive placebos. The ethical and legal requirements for gaining research ethics committee approval for such research, involving firstly the neuroscience of the dying process and secondly the neuroscience of the impact of the administration of psychedelics at end of life will now be considered. The salient features of the research governance structures will be outlined, then applied to each case.

Research on human subjects in the United Kingdom is governed by a combination of legislation, regulation and guidelines. While all research trials on human subjects should be approved by an ethics committee, clinical trials of pharmaceuticals and research on those without mental capacity are subject to specific regulation. Good clinical practice over research into medicines for human use is governed by the Medicines for Human Use (Clinical Trials) Regulations 2004, which incorporate European Directive 2001/20/EC into domestic law. Regulation 28, which provides that clinical trials must be carried out "in accordance with the conditions and principles of good clinical practice", gives lawful force to criteria contained in international codes of research ethics, such as the Declaration of Helsinki. In addition, Schedule I, Part 2, specifies that trials should take place only where anticipated benefits for the trial subject and other present and future patients outweigh foreseeable risks (s.2); that the rights, safety and well-being of the trial subjects should prevail over the interests of science and society (s.3); and that freely given informed consent should be obtained from competent trial subjects (s.9). Schedule I, Part 3, elaborates on the requirement for informed consent for research subjects who are either able to consent, or who have given their consent prior to the onset of incapacity.

Mentally incapacitated adults who are incapable of giving consent are not necessarily precluded from becoming research subjects. Provided that it is impossible to carry out the research on those capable of giving consent; that the research is likely to benefit either the individual concerned or members of the group to which they belong; that efforts to gain assent have been made; that evidence of a desire not to participate in the research should be decisive; and that the risks involved in non-therapeutic research are no more than minimal unless there are exceptional circumstances; such research may be conducted lawfully provided consent has been obtained from the incompetent person's legal representative. This consent should be based upon both information about the trial, the presumed will of the proposed research subject and a continuing evaluation of how far participation in the research remains appropriate.

Under Schedule I, Part 4, additional conditions and principles which apply to incapacitated adults specify that the proposed research subject must have received information about the risks and benefits of the trial tailored to their ability to understand it; that where any capacity to understand this information is present, any explicit wish to refuse to participate or be withdrawn from a trial must be considered by the investigator; that no incentives or financial rewards be provided to them or their legal representative; that there are grounds for expecting that the medical product to be administered would produce a benefit to the subject outweighing the risk or produce no risk; and that the trial relates directly to a life-threatening or debilitating clinical condition suffered by the proposed research subject.

These concerns are mirrored in professional guidelines. For instance, s.48 of the guidelines on research produced in 2002 by the General Medical Council specify that research on incapacitated adults should not be carried out where it could equally well be carried out on other adults (General Medical Council 2002). It should be limited to their incapacity or physical illnesses linked to this. Such research may be carried out only where it has been demonstrated that: it could be of direct benefit to the health of the research subject or to that of people of the same age group with the same state of health; that it would significantly improve the scientific understanding of their incapacity leading to a direct benefit to them or to others with the same incapacity; and that the research is ethical and will not cause emotional, physical or psychological harm to participants; and there is no physical or verbal expression of objections. Any sign of distress, pain or indication of refusal is to be considered as an implied refusal. Guidance issued by COREC, the Central Office for Research Ethics Committees, elaborates on finer points outside the Clinical Trials Regulations. For instance, should a capable adult give informed consent to take part in a clinical trial, then subsequently lose capacity, the consent will remain legally valid (COREC 2006).

Additional statutory provisions for research carried out on incapacitated adults may be found in the Mental Capacity Act 2005, which comes into force in October 2007. Many of the safeguards and principle in the Clinical Trials Regulations are mirrored in the portions of the act dealing with research. A key principle of the Mental Capacity Act is that individuals are presumed to have capacity unless otherwise demonstrated. Once incapacity has been established, the consent of a third party, based upon the past and present wishes of the incapacitated individual, must be obtained before research may proceed. Under s.30 of this act, "intrusive" research carried out on, or in relation to, a person who lacks capacity to consent to it is unlawful unless certain conditions are fulfilled. Research defined as "intrusive" under s.30(2) of the Mental Capacity Act 2005 is research of a kind which would be unlawful if it were carried out without consent on a person with the capacity to consent. Unless "intrusive" research is subsumed under the Clinical Trials Regulations, it is unlawful under s.30 unless it meets criteria in ss.32 and 33. Section 31 provides that: the research could not be carried out on adults with capacity; that no more than minimal risk is involved; and that the proposed subject or others with the same condition will benefit. Section 32 lists criteria for consultation with carers or those with lasting power of attorney over the incompetent adult's participation in the proposed research and their powers and responsibilities, whereas s.33 provides additional safeguards allowing for withdrawal where there are demonstrations of a wish not to participate, or where the research involves things which would be contrary to previously expressed wishes. Where research does not have the potential to benefit the subject, any additional risk or discomfort should be negligible or nil and should not significantly interfere with their freedom or privacy.

Not all of the ethical and legal criteria intended to form part of the Act's guidance are yet in place. Part 4 of the draft Mental Capacity Act Code of Practice, which formed the basis for a consultation exercise and which will appear in final form in late 2007, identified the processes that need to be followed in order to ensure research on incapacitated adults was lawful (Department of Constitutional Affairs 2006). These provisions were intended to apply to "intrusive" research not covered by the Clinical Trials Regulations, which included participants who have an impairment of, or disturbance in, the functioning of the mind or brain that results in incapacity to consent to the research. The Department of Health also sought views on whether provisions in the Act which proposed arrangements for research involving people who gave their informed consent to participate then lost capacity found the appropriate balance between the need to allow long-term research to continue while respecting the past and present wishes of the participants. In its response to the consultation exercise, the Department clarified that there was no requirement for researchers to constantly check the capacity of their participants (Department of Health 2006).

How might this structure of research governance apply to the end-of-life research proposed in this chapter? Where neuroimaging alone was involved, this would fall outside the Clinical Trials Regulations. In that neuroimaging would constitute "intrusive" research under s.30(2) of the Mental Capacity Act, should capacity be lost consent from a third party might have to be obtained for continued participation. There is some uncertainty here, which may be resolved in the final Code of Practice. Given that there is a presumption of capacity under the act, and that the Department of Health confirmed that researchers were not required to constantly check on the capacity of research participants, it seems probable that the initial consent provided by a competent person at end of life might suffice for much of the time. However, should capacity be clearly lost, there are several possibilities. One is the use of advance research directives specifying a desire to participate in research after the onset of incapacity. While these do not feature in the regulatory scheme sketched out above, many scholars support their use, often as a supplement for third-party consent as evidencing intention (Backlar 1998; Berghmans 1997; Bravo et al. 2003; Dukoff and Sunderland 1997; Gevers 2006; Rosenstein and Miller 2003). Where the onset of incapacity is anticipated during a research study, the consent procedure might include a statement of the participant's wishes should this occur. While these methods of providing advance consent are uncommon, given that third party's assessments of the wishes of those whom they represent are often incorrect (Berghmans 1997; Bravo et al. 2003; Wendler 2000), building them into the research protocol seems sensible. Indeed, Alzheimer

Europe favours campaigns to educate people to make advance directives which cover research participation (Gevers 2006).

However, these would not be the only hurdles. As end of life is likely to involve eventual incapacity, since no more than minimal risk is involved in neuroimaging (Rosen and Gur 2002), and that the research results have the potential to benefit others at end of life, the criteria of s.30 might be fulfilled. One caveat here is that the others who may receive such benefits should suffer from the same condition. If end of life is accepted as a condition, as I have suggested above given the flexibility of medical taxonomies, this too might prove non-problematic. Provided the past and present wishes were clearly to participate in the research, it should also fall within ss.32 and 33. As neuroimaging involves negligible risk or discomfort, and protocols are in place to ensure that the incompetent are made comfortable during procedures involving scanning, the research should not significantly interfere with freedom or privacy. Overall, then, it is likely to receive ethical approval.

Where neuroimaging accompanied the administration of psychedelics at end of life, the research would fall under the Clinical Trials Directive. Hence consent given while competent would ensure that participation remained lawful even should capacity be lost, provided assent to the procedures continued. Other ethical dimensions would centre about demonstrations of the safety of the psychedelics, favourable risk/benefit ratios and freely given consent. A central factor would be establishing the credentials of psychedelics as medicines, but given the accumulating evidence of their potentially beneficial effects as outlined above, this should prove possible. The increasing role of spiritual meaning within palliative care could then ground an ethical justification for the administration of psychedelics as an optional part of end-of-life care.

Conclusion

This inquiry into how we might enhance choice in dying is a contribution to the current debate over how much choice we should have over how and when we die. My central argument is that enhancing choice over death should include medically enhanced dying, and that as neuroscience has the potential to allow us to reframe the "good death" according to criteria drawn from an expanded evidence base, research into the neuroscience of the dying brain should become a priority. I began by considering pragmatic contextual reasons why this research has not taken place before arguing that there has been a degree of rhetorical capture of "death itself" by the discourses surrounding "life itself". Resistance to reproductive enhancement and notions of dignity have been explored in this light. The neuroscience of pleasure, subjective experiences of personal meaning and psychoactive substances have been drawn upon as a background for proposals over how research on dying human subjects might take place within appropriate ethical and legal safeguards. My conclusion is to propose a reframing of the good death to include medically enhanced dying as an option.

References

Annas, G. et al. (2002), Protecting the Endangered Human: Towards an International Treaty Prohibiting Cloning and Inheritable Alternations. *American Journal of Law & Medicine* 28:2&3, 151–78.

Axelsson, B. and Sjoden, P. (1998), "Quality of Life of Cancer Patients and Their Spouses in Palliative Home Care", *Palliative Medicine* 12:1, 285–97.

Backlor, P. (1998), "Advance Directives for Subjects of Research Who Have Fluctuating Cognitive Impairments Due to Psychotic Orders (Such As Schizophrenia)", *Community Mental Health Journal* 34:3, 229–40.

Berghmans, R. (1997), "Advance Directives for Clinical Research in Dementia: Some Ethical and Policy Considerations", *International Journal of Neurology. Supplement* 5, 29–33.

Biggs, H. (2001), *Euthanasia: Death with Dignity and the Law* (Oxford: Hart).

Biggs, H. and Mackenzie, R. (2000), "Viagra is Coming! The Rhetoric of Choice and Need", in Freeman, M. and Lewis, A. (eds), *Law and Medicine: Current Legal Issues* (Oxford: Oxford University Press).

Black, H. and Rubinstein, R. (2004), "Themes of Suffering in Later Life", *The Journals of Gerontology Series B: Psychological Sciences and Social Sciences* 59: s17–s24.

Booth, J. et al. (2005), "Increased Feeling of the Sensed Presence and Increased Geomagnetic Activity at the Time of the Experience of the Exposure to Transcerebral Weak Complex Magnetic Fields", *International Journal of Neuroscience* 115:7, 1053–79.

Bostrom, N. (2005), "In Defence of Posthuman Dignity", *Bioethics* 19(3): 202–214.

Bravo, C. et al. (2003), "Advance Directives for Research: Prevalence and Correlates", *Alzheimer Disease & Associated Disorders* 17:4, 215–22.

Brogden, M. (2001), *Geronticide: Killing the Elderly* (London: Jessica Kingley).

Brownsword, R. (2004), "Reproductive Opportunities and Regulatory Challenges", *Modern Law Review* 67(2): 304–321.

Carnell, D. (2000), "Death and Dying", *British Medical Journal* 320:1, 194.

Caulfield, T. and Chapman, A. (2005), "Human Dignity as a Criterion for Science Policy", *PLOS Medicine* 2(8) http://medicine.plosjournals.org/perlserv?request=get-document&doi=10.1371/journal.pmed.0020244, accessed 2 February 2007.

Central Office for Research Ethics Committees (2006), *Medicines for Human Use (Clinical Trials Regulations) 2004. Informed Consent in Clinical Trials* (London: COREC).

Charney, D. and Nestler, E. (eds) (2004), *The Neurobiology of Mental Illness* (Oxford: Oxford University Press).

Check, E. (2004), "Psychedelic Drugs: the Ups and Downs of Ecstasy", *Nature* 429:20, 126–8.

Chen, D. et al. (2002), "Enrolling Decisionally Impaired Adults in Research", *Medical Care* 40:9, 20–9.
Chidester, D. (2002), *Patterns of Transcendence: Religion, Death and Dying* (Belmont: Wadsworth).
Coors, M. and Hunter, L. (2005), "Evaluation of Genetic Enhancement: Will Human Wisdom Properly Acknowledge the Value of Evolution?", *American Journal of Bioethics* 5:3, 21–2.
Department of Constitutional Affairs (2006), *Mental Capacity Act Code of Practice Consultation Paper* (London: DCA).
--- (2006), *Mental Capacity Act Draft Code of Practice* (London: DCA).
Department of Health (2006), *Government response to Consultation on Mental Capacity Act 2005: Draft Research Regulations* (London: DoH).
Depue, R. and Morrone-Strupinsky, J. (2005), "A Neurobehavioral Model of Affiliative Bonding: Implications for Conceptualizing a Human Trait of Affiliation", *Behavioral and Brain Sciences* 28:3, 313–385.
Dukoff, R. and Sunderland, T. (1997), "Durable Power of Attorney and Informed Consent with Alzheimer's Disease Patients: a Clinical Study", *American Journal of Psychiatry* 154:8, 1070–5.
Eriksson, M. and Lindstrom, B. (2006), "Antonovsky's Sense of Coherence Scale and the Relation with Health: a Systematic Review", *Journal of Epidemiology and Community Health* 60:5, 376–81.
Esch, T. and Stefano, G. (2005a), "The Neurobiology of Love", *Neuroendocrinology Letters* 26:3, 175–192.
Esch, T. and Stefano, G. (2005b), "Love Promotes Health", *Neuroendocrinology Letters* 26:3, 265–268.
Esch, T. and Stefano, G. (2004), "The Neurobiology of Pleasure, Reward Processes, Addiction and Their Health Implications", *Neuroendocrinology Letters* 25:3, 235–251.
Field, D. et al. (eds) (2001), *Researching Palliative Care* (Buckingham: Open University Press).
Foresight (2005), *Brain Science, Addiction and Drugs Project* (London: Dept Trade and Industry).
Franklin, S. (1993), "Making Representations: the Parliamentary Debate on the Human Fertilisation and Embryology Act" in Edwards, J. et al. (eds), *Technologies of Procreation: Kinship in the Age of Assisted Conception* (Manchester: Manchester University Press).
Frederick, M. (2002), "Artificial Nutrition and Hydration in the Terminally Ill", *American Academy of Hospice and Palliative Medicine Bulletin* 8–10.
Friedman, H. (2006), "The Renewal of Psychedelic Research: Implications for Humanistic and Transpersonal Psychology", *The Humanistic Psychologist* 34:1, 39–58.
Fukuyama, F. (2002), *Our Posthuman Future: Consequences of the Biotechnological Revolution* (London: Profile).
Garwood-Gowers, A. (2006), *Journal of Mental Health Law* 7:1, 7–25.

General Medical Council (2002), *The Role and Responsibilities of Doctors* (London: GMC).

Gevers, S. (2006), "Dementia and the Law", *European Journal of Health Law* 13:2, 209–17.

Griffiths et al. (2006), "Psilocybin Can Occasion Mystical-type Experiences Having Substantial and Sustained Personal Meaning and Spiritual Significance", *Psychopharmacology* 187:3, 268–83.

Grof, S. and Halifax, J. (1977), *The Human Encounter with Death* (London: Souvenir).

Guinn, D. (2002), "Mental Competence, Caregivers, and the Process of Consent: Research Involving Alzheimer's Patients or Others with Decreasing Mental Capacity", *Cambridge Quarterly of Healthcare Ethics* 11:2, 230–45.

Hardy, J. (2001), "Placebo-controlled Trials in Palliative Care: the Argument For", in Field, D. et al. (eds) (2001), *Researching Palliative Care* (Buckingham: Open University Press).

Hayry, M. (2004), "Another Look at Dignity", *Cambridge Quarterly of Healthcare Ethics* 13:1, 7–14.

Hayry, H. and Takala, T. (2005), "Human dignity, bioethics and human rights", *Developing World Bioethics* 5:3, 225–233.

Horgan, J. (2003), *Rational Mysticism: Spirituality Meets Science in the Search for Enlightenment* (Boston: Houghton Mifflin).

Johnson, C. and McGee, M. (eds) (1998), *How Different Religions View Death and the Afterlife* (Philadelphia: Charles Press).

Johnson, S. (2004), *Mind Wide Open: Why You Are What You Think* (London: Penguin).

Jubb, A. (2002), "Palliative Care Research: Trading Ethics for an Evidence Base", *Journal of Medical Ethics* 28:3, 342–346.

Kamm, F. (2005), "Is There a Problem With Enhancement?", *American Journal of Bioethics* 5:3, 5–14.

Kapur, S. and Lecrubier, Y. (2003), *Dopamine in the Pathophysiology and Treatment of Schizophrenia: New Findings* (London: Taylor & Francis).

Kass, L. (2002), *Life, Liberty and the Defense of Dignity* (San Francisco: Encounter).

Katz, L. (2005), "Opiod Bliss as the Felt Hedonic Core of Mammalian Prosociality – and of Consummatory Pleasure More Generally?", *Behavioural and Brain Sciences* 28:3, 356–356.

Kaufman, S. et al. (2006), "Old Age, Life Extension and the Character of Medical Choice", *The Journals of Gerontology Series B: Psychological Sciences and Social Sciences* 61:1, s175–s184.

Kaufman, S. et al. (2004), "Revisiting the Biomedicalisation of Aging: Clinical Trends and Ethical Challenges", *The Gerontologist* 44:4, 731–738.

Keown, J. (2006), "Restoring the Sanctity of Life and Replacing the Caricature: a Reply to David Price", *Legal Studies* 26:1, 109–119.

Keown, J. (2005), "A Futile Defence of *Bland*: a Reply to Andrew McGee", *Medical Law Review* 13:3, 393–402.

Keverne, J. and Ray, M. (2005), "The Neurochemistry of Alzheimer's Disease", *Psychiatry* 4:1, 40–42.

Kim, A. et al. (2005), "Palliative Care: Optimising Quality of Life", *Journal of the American Osteopaths' Association* 105:5, 9–14.

Kim, S. and Kiebutz, K. (2006), "Appointing a Proxy for Research Consent After One Develops Dementia: the Need for Further Study", *Neurology* 66:9, 1298–9.

Kirkham, S. and Abel, J. (2001), "Placebo-controlled Trials in Palliative Care: the Argument Against", in Field, D. et al. (eds) (2001), *Researching Palliative Care* (Buckingham: Open University Press).

Kleber, H. (2006), "Commentary on 'Psilocybin Can Occasion Mystical-type Experiences Having Substantial and Sustained Personal Meaning and Spiritual Significance' by Griffiths et al.", *Psychopharmacology* 187:3, 268–83.

Kolp, E. (2006), "Ketamine Enhanced Psychotherapy: Preliminary Clinical Observations on Its Effectiveness in Treating Alcoholism", *The Humanistic Psychologist* 34:4, 399–422.

Kuppers. P. (2004), "Visions of Anatomy: Exhibitions and Dense Bodies", *Differences: a Journal of Feminist Cultural Studies* 15:3; 123–156.

Laumann, E. et al. (1999), "Sexual Dysfunction in the United States: Prevalence and Predictors", *Journal of the American Medical Association* 281:3, 537–544.

Laureys, S. et al. (eds) (2006), *The Boundaries of Consciousness: Neurobiology and Neuropathology* (New York: Elsevier).

Laurie, G. and Mason, J. (2000), "Negative Treatment of Vulnerable Patients: Euthanasia by Any Other Name?", *Juridical Review* 3, 159–178.

Lauritzen, P. (2005), "Stem Cells, Biotechnology, and Human Rights: Implications for a Posthuman Future", *Hastings Center Report* 35(2): 25.

Lee, B. and Newberg, A. (2005), "Religion and Health: a Review and Critical Analysis", *Zygon* 40:2, 443–468.

Lewis, P. (2002), "Procedures that are Against the Medical Interests of Incompetent Adults", *Oxford Journal of Legal Studies* 22:4, 575–615.

Li, et al. (2004), "Opioid-mediated Pain Sensitivity in Mice Bred for High Voluntary Wheel Running", *Physiology & Behaviour* 83:4, 515–524.

Lin, H. and Bauer-Wu, S. (2003), "Psycho-spiritual Well Being in Patients with Advanced Cancer: an Integrative Review of the Literature", *Journal of Advanced Nursing* 44:1, 69–80.

Lissoni, P. et al. (2003), "Psychooncology and Cancer Related Alterations of Pleasure Associated Neurochemical System: Abnormal Neuroendocrine Response to Apomorphine in Advanced Cancer Patients", *Neuroendocrinology Letters* 24:1/2, 50–4.

Lutz, A. et al. (2004), "Long-term Meditators Self-induce High-amplitude Gamma Synchrony During Mental Practice", *Proceedings of the National Academy of Sciences* 101:46, 16369–16373.

Mackenzie, R. (2007), "Regulating Reprogenetics: Strategic Sacralisation and Semantic Massage" *Health Care Analysis.* Forthcoming.

Mackenzie, R. (2006), "Addiction in Public Health and Criminal Justice System Governance: Neuroscience, Enhancement and Happiness Research", *Genomics, Society and Policy* 2:1, 92–109.

Marker, R. (2006), "Euthanasia and Assisted Suicide Today", *Society* 43:4, 59–67.

Martin, A. and Peerzada, J. (2005), "The Expressive Meaning of Enhancement", *American Journal of Bioethics* 5:3, 25–6.

Mason, S. et al. (2006), "Brief report on the Experience of Using Proxy Consent for Incapacitated Adults", *Journal of Medical Ethics* 32:1, 61–2.

McGuire, M. and Tiger, L. (2006), "The Neurobiology and Behaviour of Belief", Paper presented at Law, Mind and Brain: Interdisciplinary Colloquium, London, February.

Miller, F. and Brody, H. (2005), "Enhancement Technologies and Professional Integrity", 5:3, 15–6.

Mount, B. (2003), "Existential Suffering and the Determinants of Healing", *European Journal of Palliative Care: Supplement* 10:2, 40–42.

Mulkay, M. (1997), *The Embryo Research Debate: Science and the Politics of Reproduction* (Cambridge: Cambridge University Press).

Nicols, D. (2006), "Commentary on "Commentary on ""Psilocybin Can Occasion Mystical-type Experiences Having Substantial and Sustained Personal Meaning and Spiritual Significance" by Griffiths et al.", *Psychopharmacology* 187:3, 268–83.

Parliament (2006), Assisted Dying for the Terminally Ill Bill (London: HMSO) http://www.publications.parliament.uk/pa/ld200506/ldbills/036/2006036.htm accessed 2 February 2007.

Pattinson, M. (1977), *The Experience of Dying* (Englewood Cliffs: Prentice-Hall).

PLOS Medicine (2006) *Special Supplement On Disease Mongering, April 2006* http://medicine.plosjournals.org/perlserv?request=get-toc&issn=1549-1676&volume=3&issue=4 accessed 2 February 2007.

President's Council on Bioethics (2003), *Beyond Therapy: Biotechnology and the Pursuit of Happiness* (Washington: PCB).

Price, D. (2001), "Fairly Bland: an Alternative View of a Supposed New 'Death Ethic'", *Legal Studies* 21:4, 618–643.

Pullman, D. (2002), "Human Dignity and the Ethics and Aesthetics of Suffering", *Theoretical Medicine* 23:1, 73–94.

Racine, E. et al. (2006), "Brain Imaging: a Decade of Coverage in the Print Media", *Science Communication* 28:1, 122–43.

Randall, F. and Downie, R. (1999), *Palliative Care Ethics: A Companion For All Specialities* (Oxford: Oxford University Press).

Reynolds, D. (2005), "The Neurochemistry of Schizophrenia", *Psychiatry* 4:1, 21–25.

Riba, J. et al. (2006), "Increased Frontal and Paralimbic Activation Following Ayahuasca, the Pan-Amazonian Inebriant", *Psychopharmacology* 186: 3, 93–8.

Robert, J. (2005), "Human Dispossession and Human Enhancement", *American Journal of Bioethics* 5:3, 27–8.

Rosen, A. and Gur, R. (2002), "Ethical Considerations for Neuropsychologists as Functional Magnetic Imagers", *Brain and Cognition* 50:3, 469–81.

Rosenstein, D. and Miller, F. (2003), "Ethical Considerations in Psychopharmacological Research Involving Decisionally Impaired Subjects", *Psychopharmacology* 171:1, 92–7.

Saah, T. (2005), "The Evolutionary Origins and Significance of Drug Addiction", *Harm Reduction Journal* 2:1, 1–8.

Sandel, M. (2004), "The Case Against Perfection", *The Atlantic Monthly* 293:3, 51–62.

Schroepfer, T. (2006), "Mind Frames Towards Dying and Factors Motivating Their Adoption by Terminally Ill Elders", *The Journals of Gerontology Series B: Psychological Sciences and Social Sciences* 59:1, s129–139.

Schwartz, P. (2005), "Defending the Distinction Between Treatment and Enhancement", *American Journal of Bioethics* 5:3, 17–8.

Scott, Y. et al. (2004), "Proxy and Surrogate Consent in Geriatric Neuropsychiatric Research: Update and Recommendations", *American Journal of Psychiatry* 161:5, 797–806.

--- (2002), "Impaired Decision Making Ability in Subjects with Alzheimer's Disease and Willingness to Participate in Research", *American Journal of Psychiatry* 159:5, 797–802.

Sessa, B. (2006), "Is There a case for MDMA-assisted Psychotherapy in the UK?", *Journal of Psychopharmacology* 18 October Epub ahead of print http://jop.sagepub.com/cgi/rapidpdf/0269881106069029v1.pdf accessed 2 February 2007.

Sewell, R.A. (2006), "Response of Cluster Headaches to Psilocybin and LSD", *Neurology* 66:3, 1920–2.

Singer, P. (1996), *Rethinking Life and Death: the Collapse of Our Traditional Ethics* (London: St Martins Press).

Sloan, R. et al. (2000), "Should Physicians Prescribe Religious Activities?" *New England Journal of Medicine* 342:12, 1913–1921.

Smith, D. (2002), "The Functional Salutogenic Mechanisms of the Brain", *Perspectives in Biology and Medicine* 45:3, 319–324.

Smith, K. Mark (2005), "Saving Humanity: Counter-Arguing Posthuman Enhancement", *Journal of Evolution and Technology* 14(1): http://jetpress.org/volume14/smith.html accessed 2 February 2007.

Smith, R. (2000), "A Good Death: an Important Aim for Health Services and for Us All", *British Medical Journal* 320:1, 129–130.

Snyder, S. (2006), "Commentary on 'Commentary on "Psilocybin Can Occasion Mystical-type Experiences Having Substantial and Sustained Personal Meaning and Spiritual Significance" by Griffiths et al.'", *Psychopharmacology* 187:3, 268–83.

Spallone, P. (1996), "The Salutary Tale of the Pre-embryo", in Lykke, N. and Braidotti, R. (eds) (1996), *Between Monsters, Goddesses and Cyborgs: Feminist Confrontations with Science, Medicine and Cyberspace* (London: Zed Books).

Stock, G. (2002), *Redesigning Humans: Choosing Our Children's Genes.* (London: Profile).

Stocking, C. et al. (2006), "Speaking of Research Advance Directives: Planning for Future Research Participation", *Neurology* 66:9, 1361–6.

Strong, C. (2005), "Lost in Translation: Religious Arguments Made Secular", 5:3, 29–30.

Tait, S. (2006), "Autopic Vision and the Necrophiliac Imaginary in CSI", *International Journal of Cultural Studies* 9:1; 45–62.

Van Dijck, J. (2001), "Bodyworlds: the Art of Plastinated Cadavers", *Configurations* 9:1, 99–126.

Wattach, G. (2000), "The Near Death Experience as a Product of Isolated Subcortical Brain Function", *Journal of Near Death Studies* 19:2, 71–90.

Wendler, D. (2000), "Informed Consent, Exploitation and Whether It is Possible to Conduct Human Subjects Research Without Either One", *Bioethics* 14:4, 310–39.

Wendler, D. and Prasad, K. (2001), "Core Safeguards for Clinical Resarch with Adults Who are Unable to Consent", *Annals of Internal Medicine* 135:10, 514–23.

Williams, M. (2005), "Death Rites: Assisted Suicide and Existential Rites", *International Journal of Law in Context* 1:2; 183–198.

World Health Organisation (2004), *Neuroscience of Psychoactive Substance Use and Dependence* (Geneva: World Health Organisation).

Woodruff, R. (1999), *Palliative Medicine: Symptomatic and Supportive Care for Patients with Advanced Cancer and AIDS* (Oxford: Oxford University Press).

Yarborough, M. (2002), "Adults Are Not Big Children: Examining Surrogate Consent to Research Using Adults With Dementia", *Cambridge Quarterly of Healthcare Ethics* 11:2, 160–8.

Chapter 12
Equality in Exchange Revisited: From an Evolutionary (Genetic and Cultural) Point of View[1]

Bart Du Laing

Introduction

The goal of this chapter could be described as an attempt to construct a small part of what has been called a bio-legal history of contractual promises and their laws.[2] However, this enterprise necessarily entails a prior reflection on how to go about best when attempting to construct these bio-legal histories. Indeed, I mainly hope to show why evolutionary analysis in law could benefit considerably from incorporating culture – and its accompanying evolutionary theory – more explicitly into its models than at present seems to be the case.

To this end, I will draw on the legal example of equality in exchange in contract law on the one hand and on recent research on human cooperative behaviour on the other hand. I will start by making some remarks on the issue of substantive fairness in legal contract theory and in legal anthropology (section 2). I will then briefly sketch some results of some of the experiments commonly used in behavioural economics to shed light on human prosocial behaviour (section 3). These two introductory sections actually cover topics that are quite broad in their own right. Hence, it should be noted that they are not meant to provide a complete overview of either of these two approaches to the phenomenon of (substantive) fairness. They should, however,

1 Some of the ideas expressed in chapter paper were presented at the Current Legal Issues: Law, Mind & Brain Interdisciplinary Colloquium (University College London in association with the Gruter Institute for Law and Behavioral Research, London, 13–14 February 2006), the 8th Annual Society for Evolutionary Analysis in Law Scholarship Conference (Vanderbilt University Law School, Nashville, 1–2 April 2006) and the 18th Annual Human Behavior and Evolution Society Conference (University of Pennsylvania, Philadelphia, 7–11 June 2006). I would like to thank the participants, especially Owen Jones, Oliver Goodenough and Kimmo Eriksson, for their helpful suggestions and questions. I would also like to thank Andreas De Block, for introducing me to evolutionary theory in the first place.

2 For the concept of "bio-legal histories", see Owen D. Jones [2001], "Proprioception, Non-Law, and Biolegal History", 53 *Florida Law Review* 831, 857–859 (target paper with commentaries), Owen D. Jones and Timothy H. Goldsmith [2005], "Law and Behavioral Biology", 105 *Columbia Law Review* 405, 471–475.

set the stage for an exposition of a particular encompassing evolutionary theoretical framework underlying a particular interpretation of the experimental data.

Indeed, a great deal of the literature associated with evolutionary analysis in law appears to be quite heavily premised upon – only – one of the contemporary evolutionary approaches to human behaviour, namely evolutionary psychology – in its narrower sense that is.[3] Notwithstanding the fact that this somewhat unilateral approach will be criticized here, I want to stress from the onset that this chapter is meant to be squarely placed within the field of evolutionary analysis in law, as a positive contribution to this steadily developing field.[4], [5] I will try to make this contribution by drawing attention to some other candidates likely to provide us with useful pieces of the evolutionary puzzle of human behaviour (section 4).

By way of conclusion, I will argue that a gene-culture coevolutionary framework is of particular relevance for law and legal theory, at least if one purports to address *both* the behaviour that is supposed to be regulated – in my case exchange behaviour – *and* the phenomena that could be called the behaviour by which the former is regulated – in my case rules or standards with regard to exchange or contract law. Finally, I will provide some preliminary speculations on how this framework could eventually help to illuminate the issues surrounding universality and diversity in comparative legal theory (section 5).

Substantive Fairness in Modern Western Contract Law Theory and in Exchange in Pre-commercial Societies

In legal (contract law) theory, the issue of equality in exchange seems to have attracted by far the most attention by (moral) philosophically inclined

3 This means "narrow" in the cautiously optimistic sense given to it by, e.g., David Sloan Wilson [2003], "Evolution, Morality and Human Potential", in Steven J. Scher and Frederick Rauscher (ed.), *Evolutionary Psychology: Alternative Approaches*, Boston, Kluwer Academic Publishers, 2003, 55, 57–60, David Sloan Wilson [1999], "Tasty slice – But where is the rest of the pie? (Book Review of David Buss, Evolutionary Psychology: The New Science of the Mind)", 20 *Evolution and Human Behavior* 279.

4 Recent more (or less) negative views on the relevance of evolutionary theory for law and legal theory – resulting from an interpretation by their authors of some of the same source material I will use in this chapter – can be found elsewhere. See, e.g., Brian Leiter and Michael Weisberg [forthcoming], "Why Evolutionary Biology is (So Far) Irrelevant to Law" (February 2, 2007), University of Texas School of Law, Law & Economics Research Paper No. 81, Public Law & Legal Theory Research Paper No. 89, Available at SSRN: http://ssrn.com/abstract=892881, Amy L. Wax [2004], "Evolution and the Bounds of Human", 23 *Law and Philosophy* 527.

5 Throughout, I will assume some familiarity with the existing recent legal literature inspired by evolutionary theory. See for an introductory bibliography Owen D. Jones and Timothy H. Goldsmith [2005], "Law and Behavioral Biology", 105 *Columbia Law Review* 405, 409–410, footnote 4.

scholars.[6] James Gordley most notably is an ardent defender of "the ancient idea that in an exchange the value of what each party gives should be equal to the value of what he receives".[7] He also notes however that this idea that contracting parties should exchange performances of equal value, or that contracts should be substantively fair, is far from being generally acknowledged in legal scholarship.[8] He then goes on to trace this principle back to the Aristotelian conception of commutative (or corrective) justice.

One of the questions addressed in this chapter then is whether it is possible to trace this principle back somewhat further on an evolutionary timescale and, if so, how to proceed best in doing this. However, the question I would like to answer is not so much if or why people should exchange performances of equal value, but rather whether people generally are likely to perform this type of behaviour themselves – so to speak "naturally" – and expect others to do the same, and, if so, how this rather peculiar behavioural pattern could be adequately explained from an evolutionary – ultimate – perspective. In other words, in this chapter I will not concern myself too much with the distinctively moral dimension of the issue of equality in exchange.[9]

For my purposes, it is more interesting to note that Gordley also addressed the issue of substantive fairness in exchange in so-called pre-commercial societies. The ethnographic literature surveyed by Gordley sketches a different picture of what substantive fairness tends to look like in these societies. Speaking very generally, he is able to assert that "(t)he rules or standards that govern personalized transactions are shaped by the fact that every party is a repeat player in a series of

6 See, e.g., James Gordley [1981], "Equality in Exchange", 69 *California Law Review* 1587, James Gordley [2001], "Contract Law in the Aristotelian Tradition", in Peter Benson (ed.), *The Theory of Contract Law: New Essays*, Cambridge, Cambridge University Press, 2001, 265, 297–326, James Gordley [2006], *Foundations of Private Law: Property, Tort, Contract, Unjust Enrichment*, Oxford, Oxford University Press, 2006, 361–368, James Bernard Murphy [2002], "Equality in Exchange", 47 *American Journal of Jurisprudence* 85, Stephen A. Smith [1996], "In Defence of Substantive Fairness", 112 *Law Quarterly Review* 138, Patrick S. Atiyah [1985], "Contract and Fair Exchange", 35 *University of Toronto Law Journal* 1. Compare also Francis H. Buckley [1990], "Three Theories of Substantive Fairness", 19 *Hofstra Law Review* 33, Thomas A. Smith [2001], "Equality, Evolution and Partnership Law", 3 *Journal of Bioeconomics* 99.

7 James Gordley [1981], "Equality in Exchange", 69 *California Law Review* 1587, 1587.

8 Compare, e.g., Stephen A. Smith [1996], "In Defence of Substantive Fairness", 112 *Law Quarterly Review* 138, 138 ("Substantive fairness, it is widely believed, is either meaningless, indistinguishable from procedural fairness (fairness in the formation of a contract), impossible to assess, not valuable, beyond the competence of the courts to protect, or some combination thereof.").

9 Which also, more generally, means that I will not go into the possibilities and limitations of evolutionary ethics and its relation to natural law theories.

transactions. One consequence is that these standards need not ensure that every single transaction is fair; they may ensure that the series of transactions is fair."[10]

A few cursory examples taken from a classic legal ethnography may further clarify this phenomenon. Max Gluckman, who studied the law of the African Barotse, notes that:

> (t)rials over ownership of land may become inquiries into how the kinsfolk concerned have dealt with one another through long periods; whether the junior gave the senior fish from his catches and money from his earnings in European enterprises, or let him take poles, mats, and so forth, and whether the senior had contributed, for example, to his juniors payments of cattle for brides.[11]

Moreover, this phenomenon appears not restricted to relationships between kinsfolk. Indeed:

> (a) noteworthy fact of Barotse life is the tendency to expand isolated transactions between strangers into multiplex associations that resemble kin relationships. (…) (O)nce (two people have) made several bartering exchanges (…), they consider they have entered into a pact of friendship (…). Thereafter they do not barter item for item, but they are under a general obligation to help each other and to outdo each other in generosity (…).[12]

In a more recent contribution on comparative legal theory, Gordley himself offers some thoughts on how these differences with regard to substantive fairness in exchange could be accounted for using – in his own words – "an approach to law which is at least two centuries out of fashion",[13] namely a (quite nuanced) natural law approach. According to Gordley:

---

10 James Gordley [1997], *Contract in Pre-Commercial Societies and in Western History*, in *International Encyclopedia of Comparative Law*, VII, *Contracts in general*, 2, Tübingen, Mohr Siebeck, 1997, 4.

11 Max Gluckman [1972], *The Ideas in Barotse Jurisprudence*, Manchester, Manchester University Press, 1972, 172–173.

12 Max Gluckman [1972], *The Ideas in Barotse Jurisprudence*, Manchester, Manchester University Press, 1972, 173–174. Compare for similar observations, e.g., Paul Bohannan [1955], "Some Principles of Exchange and Investment among the Tiv", 57 *American Anthropologist* 60, Paul P. Howell [1954], *A Manual of Nuer Law: Being an account of Customary Law, its Evolution and Development in the Courts established by the Sudan Government*, Oxford, Oxford University Press, 1954/1970, 198. See also Laura Nader and June Starr [1973], "Is Equity Universal?", in Ralph A. Newman (ed.), *Equity in the World's Legal Systems: A Comparative Study*, Brussels, Bruylant, 1973, 125, 127–128.

13 James Gordley [2003], "The universalist heritage", in Pierre Legrand and Roderick Munday (ed.), *Comparative Legal Studies: Traditions and Transitions*, Cambridge, Cambridge University Press, 2003, 31, 31.

> it is important to see that sometimes the choice of which law to enact is not a matter of indifference even though the underlying principles are the same. Indeed, even when they are, the choice of which law to enact may be one which we rightly regard as shaping our values and culture. There are two reasons this may be so. The first is that circumstances differ and the laws appropriate in one set of circumstances may not be appropriate in the other. The second is that even when the circumstances are the same, laws can differ even when they are based on the same principles.[14]

As to the first type of reason he mentions, Gordley interestingly enough makes a connection between this phenomenon and the problem of insurance,[15] a connection that is equally present in some of the evolutionary literature on cooperation and exchange.[16]

Finally, it has to be noted that the personalized transactions to be found in what Gordley calls pre-commercial societies bear at least some resemblance to the by now relatively well-documented phenomena of relational contracting and non-contractual relations in business in our "modern" industrialized societies.[17]

---

14 James Gordley [2003], "The universalist heritage", in Pierre Legrand and Roderick Munday (ed.), *Comparative Legal Studies: Traditions and Transitions*, Cambridge, Cambridge University Press, 2003, 31, 41.

15 James Gordley [2003], "The universalist heritage", in Pierre Legrand and Roderick Munday (ed.), *Comparative Legal Studies: Traditions and Transitions*, Cambridge, Cambridge University Press, 2003, 31, 41–42. See also James Gordley [1997], *Contract in Pre-Commercial Societies and in Western History*, in *International Encyclopedia of Comparative Law*, VII, *Contracts in general*, 2, Tübingen, Mohr Siebeck, 1997, 6–7.

16 See, e.g., Leda Cosmides and John Tooby [1992], "Cognitive Adaptations for Social Exchange", in Jerome H. Barkow, Leda Cosmides and John Tooby (ed.), *The Adapted Mind: Evolutionary Psychology and the Generation of Culture*, Oxford, Oxford University Press, 1992, 163, 209–218.

17 A point also made by Simon Deakin [2003], "Evolution For Our Time: A Theory of Legal Memetics", in Michael D.A. Freeman (ed.), *Current Legal Problems 2002*, Oxford, Oxford University Press, 2003, 1, 24. Reference should be made here to Ian R. Macneil [1974], "The Many Futures of Contracts", 47 *Southern California Law Review* 691, Ian R. Macneil [1980], *The New Social Contract: An Inquiry into Modern Contractual Relations*, New Haven, Yale University Press, 1980, Stewart Macaulay [1963], "Non-Contractual Relations in Business: A Preliminary Study", 28 *American Sociological Review* 55, Stewart Macaulay [1985], "An Empirical View of Contract", 1985 *Wisconsin Law Review* 465; Lisa Bernstein [1992], "Opting out of the Legal System: Extralegal Contractual Relations in the Diamond Industry", 21 *Journal of Legal Studies* 115; Janet T. Landa [1981], "A Theory of the Ethnically Homogeneous Middleman Group: An Institutional Alternative to Contract Law", 10 *Journal of Legal Studies* 349. Compare also Iris Bohnet, Bruno S. Frey and Steffen Huck [2001], "More Order with Less Law: On Contract Enforcement, Trust, and Crowding", 95 *American Political Science Review* 131; Bernd Irlenbusch [2006], "Are Non-Binding Contracts Really Not Worth the Paper?", 27 *Managerial and Decision Economics* 21.

Similarly, the above does not mean that contractual promises (much) like (we think) we know them were or are necessarily totally absent in pre-commercial societies.[18] It would presumably be much more correct to speak of a difference in emphasis than of a difference in kind.[19] Much the same for that matter could be said regarding the absence or presence of anonymous interactions, or the relative importance of personal and impersonal exchange.[20]

How do these findings relate to fairness as it can be found – at least according to some – in the results of certain economic experiments that have been going on for quite some time now?

Fairness in (Cross-cultural) Economic Experiments

For some decades, behavioural economists have used a variety of experimental games to examine human (cooperative) behaviour, mostly in student populations from industrialized countries. Recently, however, some researchers have ventured somewhat further in order to start assessing the results gained from previous experiments in a cross-cultural fashion. Hence, the following can also be interpreted as an attempt to reconnect with some of the more recent developments in economic anthropology,[21] much like Gordley and others before him did in their writings on the subject.

For reasons of brevity, I will not go too deep into the details of these experiments.[22] Suffice it to say that one of these games, the Ultimatum Game, is

18 See, e.g., Nicholas Mahoney [1977], "Contract and Neighbourly Exchange among the Birwa of Botswana", 21 *Journal of African Law* 40.

19 See for further discussion Norbert Rouland [1994], *Legal Anthropology*, London, Athlone Press, 1994, 228–234. Compare also Alan Page Fiske [1991], *Structures of Social Life: The Four Elementary Forms of Human Relations*, New York, The Free Press, 1991, 51–60.

20 Compare, e.g., Wolfgang Fikentscher [2000], "Reziprozität als Begriff der Rechtsanthropologie – einige Bemerkungen", in Raimund Jakob and Wolfgang Fikentscher (ed.), *Korruption, Reziprozität und Recht: Grundlagenwissenschaftliche und rechtsdogmatische Forschungsbeiträge, Schriften zur Rechtspsychologie 4*, Bern, Stämpfli Verlag, 2000, 129, 137–139 and Ernst Fehr and Joseph Henrich [2003], "Is Strong Reciprocity a Maladaptation?: On the Evolutionary Foundations of Human Altruism", in Peter Hammerstein (ed.), *Genetic and Cultural Evolution of Cooperation*, Cambridge, MIT Press, 2003, 55, 69–76.

21 See Jean Ensminger [2002], "Experimental Economics: A Powerful New Method for Theory Testing in Anthropology", in Jean Ensminger (ed.), *Theory in Economic Anthropology*, Walnut Creek, Altamira Press, 2002, 59, Joseph Henrich [2002], "Decision Making, Cultural Transmission, and Adaptation in Economic Anthropology", in Jean Ensminger (ed.), *Theory in Economic Anthropology*, Walnut Creek, Altamira Press, 2002, 251.

22 See for overviews Colin F. Camerer and Ernst Fehr [2004], "Measuring Social Norms and Preferences Using Experimental Games: A Guide for Social Scientists", in Joseph Henrich et al. (ed.), *Foundations of Human Sociality: Economic Experiments and Ethnographic Evidence from Fifteen Small-Scale Societies*, Oxford, Oxford University

believed by a great deal of researchers to tap into the subjects' notion of fairness. Colin Camerer and George Loewenstein for instance call it "a useful workhorse for identifying departures from self-interest".[23]

In an Ultimatum Game, one person, the proposer, gets to decide on the division of a sum of money between himself and another person, the responder. The latter can then decide to accept the offer, in which case it is executed, or to reject it, in which case neither party gets anything. Rational self-regarding proposers are expected to offer the smallest amount possible, and responders are expected to accept this amount, since it still exceeds nothing. This is not what has been observed, though. Generally, the most common offer is around 40–50% of the total amount. These offers are rarely rejected, but offers below 20–30% often are.

Since the results of these types of experiments in "modern" student populations are quite robust, one could infer that a lot of people here do care about substantive fairness, making it more likely that this consideration does have its place in our laws or in our legal principles governing "industrialized" contractual exchanges.

Besides this, it has been shown experimentally that a sizeable number of people who play cooperate in one-shot Prisoner Dilemma Games, and engage in costly punishment of those who defect in Public Goods Games.

Herbert Gintis coined the term "strong reciprocity" for these phenomena,[24] although others, such as Joseph Henrich, seem to prefer to speak, perhaps more generally, of "social norms, punishment and prosociality".[25], [26] Gintis's "strong reciprocity" in any case could be defined as "a predisposition to cooperate with others and to punish those

Press, 2004, 55; Simon Gächter and Benedikt Herrmann [2006], "Human cooperation from an economic perspective", in Peter M. Kappeler and Carel P. van Schaik (ed.), *Cooperation in Primates and Humans: Mechanisms and Evolution*, Berlin, Springer, 2006, 279.

23 Colin F. Camerer and George Loewenstein [2004], "Behavioral Economics: Past, Present, Future", in Colin F. Camerer, George Loewenstein and Matthew Rabin (ed.), *Advances in Behavioral Economics*, Princeton, Princeton University Press, 2004, 3, 27.

24 Herbert Gintis [2000], "Strong reciprocity and human sociality", 206 *Journal of Theoretical Biology* 169.

25 Joseph Henrich and Natalie Henrich [2006], "Culture, evolution and the puzzle of human cooperation", 7 *Cognitive Systems Research* 220, 239.

26 The notion of "strong reciprocity" itself has indeed provoked a wide variety of reactions. Randolph Nesse for instance notes the similarities (and differences) between "strong reciprocity" and what he refers to as "commitment". See Randolph M. Nesse [2001], "Natural Selection and the Capacity for Subjective Commitment", in Randolph M. Nesse (ed.), *Evolution and the Capacity for Commitment*, New York, Russell Sage Foundation, 2001, 1, 25–26. Still others regard "strong reciprocity" simply as something of a misnomer. See, e.g., Richard Alexander [2006], "The Challenge of Human Social Behavior (Book Review of Peter Hammerstein (ed.), Genetic and Cultural Evolution of Cooperation)", 4 *Evolutionary Psychology* 1, 10, who continues to favour his well-known distinction between direct reciprocity and indirect reciprocity. Compare also Robert Trivers [2006], "Reciprocal altruism: 30 years later", in Peter M. Kappeler and Carel P. van Schaik (ed.), *Cooperation in Primates and Humans: Mechanisms and Evolution*, Berlin, Springer, 2006, 67, 78–81.

who violate the norms of cooperation, at personal cost, even when it is implausible to expect that these costs will be repaid by others or at a later date".[27]

Cross-cultural data obtained from conducting these types of experiments in various small-scale societies show a great deal of behavioural variability across groups in this respect. This variation is to a large extent correlated with group-level differences in economic organization and the degree of market integration, rather than to individual-level differences in economic and demographic variables.[28] More recent cross-cultural experiments seem to indicate that a similar type of reasoning applies to the punishment of non-cooperative norm violators.[29]

How could all of this be explained from an evolutionary point of view? As is more often than not the case, there are various competing evolutionary explanations – and of course a host of non-evolutionary ones as well – on offer for these phenomena.[30] Although I am well aware of this, and of the fact that the phenomenon of "strong reciprocity" is as such quite controversial, I would like to focus in the larger part of the next section on one of these explanations and particularly on the larger evolutionary theoretical framework within which it can be situated, namely dual inheritance or gene-culture coevolutionary theory. As I already mentioned, one of the reasons for this is that this encompassing framework seems to be unduly neglected in most current evolutionary analysis in law.

Evolutionary Approaches to Social (Fairness) Norms, Punishment and Prosociality in Humans

General Observations

Human populations cooperate on an unusually large scale, in dyadic interactions as well as in multi-person interactions, and with distantly related and even

27 Herbert Gintis, Samuel Bowles, Robert Boyd and Ernst Fehr [2003], "Explaining altruistic behavior in humans", 24 *Evolution and Human Behavior* 153, 154.

28 See Joseph Henrich et al. [2005], "'Economic man' in cross-cultural perspective: Behavioral experiments in 15 small-scale societies", 28 *Behavioral and Brain Sciences* 795 (target paper with commentaries and reply). See for a shorter version Joseph Henrich et al. [2001], "In Search of Homo Economicus: Behavioral Experiments in 15 Small-Scale Societies", 91 *AEA Papers and Proceedings* 73 and for a book-length treatment Joseph Henrich et al. (ed.) [2004], *Foundations of Human Sociality: Economic Experiments and Ethnographic Evidence from Fifteen Small-Scale Societies*, Oxford, Oxford University Press, 2004.

29 See Joseph Henrich et al. [2006], "Costly Punishment Across Human Societies", 312 *Science* 1767. Compare also Helen Bernhard, Urs Fischbacher and Ernst Fehr [2006], "Parochial altruism in humans", 442 *Nature* 912.

30 See for an introduction to the discussion, e.g., the various commentaries to Joseph Henrich et al. [2005]'s target paper "'Economic man' in cross-cultural perspective: Behavioral experiments in 15 small-scale societies", 28 *Behavioral and Brain Sciences* 795, 815–838.

unrelated individuals – a phenomenon often referred to as human ultra-sociality.[31] Now as has been pointed out by others, there are many evolutionary pathways to cooperation, which are by no means mutually exclusive.[32] In order to explain cooperative patterns in animal, including human, behaviour, reference is however most often made to kin selection and reciprocal altruism. Quite a lot of evolutionary social scientists are convinced that human social behaviour is to a very large extent based upon these processes having operated in the relatively small groups of our evolutionary past.[33]

However, while there is little doubt that kin selection and reciprocal altruism do play an extremely important role in human behaviour and although it is true that "(r)eciprocal altruism in the form of tit-for-tat or similar cooperation-sustaining strategies in the repeated prisoners' dilemma is a powerful ultimate explanation for human altruism in small and stable groups",[34] there appears to be a problem in extending these results to large-scale multi-person interactions. Indeed, mathematical models involving multi-person interactions strongly suggest that these solutions are unlikely to be able to sustain cooperation in other than quite small groups.[35] Samuel Bowles and Herbert Gintis recently provided us with

---

31 See, e.g., Donald T. Campbell [1983], "The Two Distinct Routes beyond Kin Selection to Ultrasociality: Implications for the Humanities and Social Sciences", in Diane L. Bridgeman (ed.), *The Nature of Prosocial Development: Theories and Strategies*, New York, Academic Press, 1983, 11, Peter J. Richerson and Robert Boyd [1998], "The Evolution of Human Ultra-Sociality", in Irenäus Eibl-Eibesfeldt and Frank K. Salter (ed.), *Indoctrinability, Ideology, and Warfare*, New York, Berghahn, 1998, 71.

32 See perhaps most notably Jack Hirshleifer [1999], "There are Many Evolutionary Pathways to Cooperation", 1 *Journal of Bioeconomics* 73, Lee Alan Dugatkin [2002], "Cooperation in animals: An evolutionary overview", 17 *Biology and Philosophy* 459. See more recently, e.g., Laurent Lehmann and Laurent Keller [2006], "The evolution of cooperation and altruism – a general framework and a classification of models", 19 *Journal of Evolutionary Biology* 1365 (target article with commentaries and reply), Martin A. Nowak [2006], "Five Rules for the Evolution of Cooperation", 314 *Science* 1560. Compare in a more legally oriented context, e.g., Oliver R. Goodenough [2001], "Law and the Biology of Commitment", in Randolph M. Nesse (ed.), *Evolution and the Capacity for Commitment*, New York, Russell Sage Foundation, 2001, 262, 262063.

33 This refers to the so-called "Environment of Evolutionary Adaptedness" or "EEA". See, e.g., John Tooby and Leda Cosmides [1990], "The Past Explains the Present: Emotional Adaptations and the Structure of Ancestral Environments", 11 *Ethology and Sociobiology* 375, Edward H. Hagen [2005], "Controversial Issues in Evolutionary Psychology", in David M. Buss (ed.), *The Handbook of Evolutionary Psychology*, Hoboken, Wiley, 2005, 145, 152–157.

34 Ernst Fehr and Urs Fischbacher [2003], "The nature of human altruism", 425 *Nature* 785, 788.

35 See, e.g., Robert Boyd and Peter J. Richerson [2005], *The Origin and Evolution of Cultures*, Oxford, Oxford University Press, 2005, 136–138. Compare also Robert Kurzban [2003], "Biological Foundations of Reciprocity", in Elinor Ostrom and James Walker (ed.), *Trust and Reciprocity: Interdisciplinary Lessons from Experimental Research*, New York,

the following summary of some of the problems to be overcome when shifting from dyadic to multi-person interactions:

> Critical differences between dyadic and *n*-person interactions in this respect are that (a) the number of accidental defections or perceived defections increases with *n*, and such "trembles" dramatically increase the cost of punishing defectors; (b) probability that a sufficiently large fraction of a large group of heterogeneous agents will be sufficiently forward-looking to make cooperation profitable decreases exponentially as *n* rises; and (c) coordination and incentive mechanisms required to ensure punishment of defectors by self-regarding group members become increasingly complex and unwieldy as *n* increases. Although many important human interactions are dyadic (e.g., mutualistic exchange of goods), many important examples of cooperation (e.g., risk reduction through co-insurance, information sharing, maintenance of group-beneficial social norms, and group defense) are large group interactions.[36]

Reputation-based approaches like indirect reciprocity and costly signalling do seem to support cooperation based upon reciprocal altruism in larger groups, but do not appear sufficient on their own to fully explain large-scale cooperation.[37] Confronting this difficulty, Robert Boyd and Peter Richerson started looking for a different kind of answer to the puzzle of large-scale cooperation in humans, an answer involving *culture*.

Before addressing in the next subsection some of the crucial features of their by now rather well-elaborated theoretical framework, I would like to stress the following. Whether the behaviour observed in experiments and in real life is or was adaptive or maladaptive, or whether it is "genuinely altruistic" or not, one of the – for my purposes at least – most interesting features of this alternative explanation is the plausible and genuine link it offers between human nature and culture. This important aspect of the theory tends to be overlooked in the recent "either-or" polemics that seem to focus, once more, on the relative merits of individual selection and group selection,[38] as well as on the explanatory scope of the so-called mismatch or adaptive-lag hypothesis.

Russell Sage Foundation, 2003, 105, 119–120. Compare in a more legally oriented context, e.g., Roger D. Masters [1992], "Naturalistic Approaches to Justice in Political Philosophy and the Life Sciences", in Roger D. Masters and Margaret Gruter (ed.), *The Sense of Justice: Biological Foundations of Law*, Newbury Park, Sage Publications, 1992, 67, 83.

36 Samuel Bowles and Herbert Gintis [2003], "Origins of Human Cooperation", in Peter Hammerstein (ed.), *Genetic and Cultural Evolution of Cooperation*, Cambridge, MIT Press, 2003, 429, 432.

37 See, e.g., Ernst Fehr and Urs Fischbacher [2003], "The nature of human altruism", 425 *Nature* 785, 789. Compare also Joseph Henrich and Natalie Henrich [2006], "Culture, evolution and the puzzle of human cooperation", 7 *Cognitive Systems Research* 220, 236–238.

38 The literature on group selection versus individual selection (in humans) is suitably large. See for – in my view – as useful an introduction as any to the (ongoing) debate,

Actually, there appear to be two distinct but related controversies going on with respect to the experimental data addressed in section 2 of this chapter. One controversy could be called "evolutionary"[39] and the other could be referred to as "economic",[40] even though there seems to be no – nor should there be any – clear dividing line between the two of them – which should come as no surprise, given the recurrent cross-fertilizations between economic theory and evolutionary theory.[41, 42]

The – "evolutionary" – mismatch or adaptive-lag hypothesis would seem to imply that the behaviour observed in the economic experiments I just mentioned results from a "misfiring" of our ancient evolved psychological mechanisms.[43], [44] Others have argued against this hypothesis, in favour of an adaptive explanation for the experimental results on offer.[45]

---

e.g., David Sloan Wilson and Elliott Sober [1994], "Reintroducing group selection to the human behavioral sciences", 17 *Behavioral and Brain Sciences* 585 (target article with commentaries and reply).

39 Exemplified by, e.g., a recent theme issue of *Analyse & Kritik* [2005/1], including papers by Ernst Fehr and Urs Fischbacher, Herbert Gintis, Robert Frank, Terence Burnham and Dominic Johnson, and Jon Elster.

40 Exemplified by, e.g., a recent theme issue of *Politics, Philosophy & Economics* [2006/2], including papers by Herbert Gintis, Paul Seabright, Don Ross, and Ken Binmore.

41 See Peter Hammerstein and Edward H. Hagen [2005], "The second wave of evolutionary economics in biology", 20 *TRENDS in Ecology and Evolution* 604.

42 As is perhaps already apparent from the law and economics-related literature cited – admittedly sparsely – in this chapter, much the same would seem to apply for evolutionary analysis in law and law and economics (behavioural or otherwise). I will not, however, further pursue this connection here.

43 See, e.g., Terence C. Burnham and Dominic D.P. Johnson [2005], "The Biological and Evolutionary Logic of Human Cooperation", 27 *Analyse & Kritik* 113, Edward H. Hagen and Peter Hammerstein [2006], "Game theory and human evolution: A critique of some recent interpretations of experimental games", 69 *Theoretical Population Biology* 339, 341–343.

44 Note that, under the heading of "time-shifted rationality", this hypothesis also figures prominently in current evolutionary analysis in law. See, e.g., Owen D. Jones [2001], "Time-Shifted Rationality and the Law of Law's Leverage: Behavioral Economics Meets Behavioral Biology", 95 *Northwestern University Law Review* 1141, Owen D. Jones and Timothy H. Goldsmith [2005], "Law and Behavioral Biology", 105 *Columbia Law Review* 405, 446–449.

45 See, e.g., Ernst Fehr and Joseph Henrich [2003], "Is Strong Reciprocity a Maladaptation?: On the Evolutionary Foundations of Human Altruism", in Peter Hammerstein (ed.), *Genetic and Cultural Evolution of Cooperation*, Cambridge, MIT Press, 2003, 55, Henrich et al. [2005], "Models of decision-making and the coevolution of social preferences", 28 *Behavioral and Brain Sciences* 838, 844–846 (reply to commentaries on target paper), Herbert Gintis, Samuel Bowles, Robert Boyd and Ernst Fehr [2005], "Moral Sentiments and Material Interests: Origins, Evidence, and Consequences", in Herbert Gintis, Samuel Bowles, Robert Boyd and Ernst Fehr (ed.), *Moral Sentiments and Material*

The second – "economic" – controversy appears to be centred on the question whether or not these experimental results (are sufficiently anomalous to) necessitate a major revision of the prevailing economic methodological framework and its underlying model of man. Ken Binmore, for instance, frames the debate as one between present day Hobbists and contemporary Butlerians.[46] In questioning the relevance of one-shot experiments as well as the actual scope of experimental anonymity, he appears to side with most evolutionary psychologists dealing with the subject, against people like Gintis.[47] According to Don Ross, however, this is not the case. A lot of their differences in opinion would have rather to do with a mutual misunderstanding about, or a different view on, the various timescales of interest.[48]

Moreover, at least some of the differing interpretations of these experimental results appear to agree on the relevance of culture and cultural capacities in trying to provide them with an appropriate explanation. For instance, both Binmore and Boyd and Richerson seem to acknowledge that their approaches are, at least in certain respects, not too dissimilar.[49] Indeed, a major point of agreement is the emphasis they place on what is called the equilibrium selection problem. By this is meant that the games commonly used to study cooperative behaviour can often lead to a multiplicity of stable outcomes, begging the question of how eventually one out of them gets settled on. I will return to this problem, and to the role culture has to play in its solution, in the next subsection.

In any case, the existing controversy over the interpretation of certain experimental results would not seem to necessarily invalidate the entire pre-existing theoretical evolutionary framework that has become associated with a particular interpretation of these experimental results.[50] At least as important seems to be

---

Interests: The Foundations of Cooperation in Economic Life, Cambridge, MIT Press, 2005, 3, 25–26.

46 See Ken Binmore [2006], "Why do people cooperate?", 5 *Politics, Philosophy & Economics* 81.

47 See Herbert Gintis [2006], "Behavioral ethics meets natural justice", 5 *Politics, Philosophy & Economics* 5.

48 See Don Ross [2006], "Evolutionary game theory and the normative theory of institutional design: Binmore and behavioural economics", 5 *Politics, Philosophy & Economics* 51, 60–65.

49 See and compare Robert Boyd and Peter J. Richerson [2005], *The Origin and Evolution of Cultures*, Oxford, Oxford University Press, 2005, 135–144, Robert Boyd and Peter J. Richerson [2002], "Group Beneficial Norms Can Spread Rapidly in a Structured Population", 215 *Journal of Theoretical Biology* 287, 288, Robert Boyd and Peter J. Richerson [2006], "Solving the Puzzle of Human Cooperation", in Stephen C. Levinson and Pierre Jaisson (ed.), *Evolution and Culture*, Cambridge, MIT Press, 2006, 105, 114–117 with Ken Binmore [2005], *Natural Justice*, Oxford, Oxford University Press, 2005, 11–14.

50 Compare also Edward H. Hagen and Peter Hammerstein [2006], "Game theory and human evolution: A critique of some recent interpretations of experimental games", 69 *Theoretical Population Biology* 339, 346.

that, although evolutionary theorists generally seem to acknowledge the relevance of something which could be called "culture" for the human species, there still remain quite different ways to connect it to the still perhaps somewhat more generally and more forcefully acknowledged species-typical human nature.[51] One way to try to establish this important connection is provided by dual inheritance theory or gene-culture coevolutionary theory.

Dual Inheritance Theory or Gene-culture Coevolutionary Theory

In a recent book by Kevin Laland and Gillian Brown, meant among other things as a "guide for the bewildered" to the variety of *different* contemporary evolutionary approaches to human behaviour,[52] dual inheritance theory or gene-culture coevolutionary theory is briefly, but all things considered rather even-handedly,[53] characterized as follows:

> Gene-culture coevolution is like a hybrid cross between memetics and evolutionary psychology, with a little mathematical rigour thrown into the pot. Like memeticists,[54] gene-culture coevolution enthusiasts treat culture as

---

51 See for a very readable overview Maria G. Janicki and Dennis L. Krebs [1998], "Evolutionary Approaches to Culture", in Charles Crawford and Dennis L. Krebs (ed.), *Handbook of Evolutionary Psychology: Ideas, Issues, and Applications*, Mahwah, Lawrence Erlbaum Associates, 1998, 163.

52 Kevin N. Laland and Gillian R. Brown [2002], *Sense and Nonsense: Evolutionary Perspectives on Human Behaviour*, Oxford, Oxford University Press, 2002, 8–10. See for a shorter survey Eric Alden Smith [2000], "Three Styles in the Evolutionary Analysis of Human Behavior", in Lee Cronk, Napoleon Chagnon and William Irons (ed.), *Adaptation and Human Behavior: An Anthropological Perspective*, Hawthorne, Aldine de Gruyter, 2000, 27.

53 "All things considered" refers mainly to the fact that at least Laland seems partial to dual inheritance theory in some of his own (earlier) writings. See, e.g., Marc W. Feldman and Kevin N. Laland [1996], "Gene-culture coevolutionary theory", 11 *TRENDS in Ecology and Evolution* 453, Kevin N. Laland [1993], "The mathematical modelling of human culture and its implications for psychology and the human sciences", 84 *British Journal of Psychology* 145. Compare also Kevin N. Laland, John Odling-Smee and Marcus W. Feldman [2000], "Niche construction, biological evolution, and cultural change", 23 *Behavioral and Brain Sciences* 131 (target paper with commentaries and reply).

54 For a general exploration of the significance of memetics for legal thought, see, e.g., Simon Deakin [2003], "Evolution For Our Time: A Theory of Legal Memetics", in Michael D.A. Freeman (ed.), *Current Legal Problems 2002*, Oxford, Oxford University Press, 2003, 1. The approach outlined in this chapter appears certainly not (necessarily) incompatible with Deakin's (very) broad conception of memetics, with the exception perhaps of Deakon's reliance on Luhmann's specific brand of sociological systems theory – which by the way is also often referred to as being "evolutionary".

Laland and Brown, however, carefully distinguish between memetics and gene-culture coevolutionary theory in their overview of evolutionary approaches to human behaviour,

> an evolving pool of ideas, beliefs, values, and knowledge that is learned and socially transmitted between individuals. Like evolutionary psychologists, these researchers believe that the cultural knowledge an individual adopts may sometimes, although certainly not always, depend on his or her genetic constitution. (…) For gene-culture coevolutionary theorists, the "leash" that ties culture to genes tugs both ways. The advent of culture was a precipitating evolutionary milestone, generating selection that favoured a reorganization of the human brain that left it specialized to acquire, store, and utilize cultural information. It was culture, loosely guided by genes, that allowed humans the adaptive flexibility to colonize the world.[55]

In the remainder of this section, I will focus on one of these dual inheritance or gene-culture coevolutionary theories, namely the one developed by Boyd and Richerson over the past three decades.[56]

In order to avoid oversimplifying the external field upon which I would like to draw to help explain certain legal or legally relevant phenomena, it has to be noted that there are other gene-culture coevolutionary theories available.[57] Similarly, it needs to be stressed that theirs is only one of the theories David Sloan Wilson assembles under the umbrella of what he calls "evolutionary social constructivism".[58] Focusing for now on the work of Boyd and Richerson and their

---

something, I guess, Boyd and Richerson themselves would surely approve of. See Robert Boyd and Peter J. Richerson [2003], "Memes: Universal acid or a better mousetrap?", in Robert Aunger (ed.), *Darwinizing Culture: The Status of Memetics as a Science*, Oxford, Oxford University Press, 2003, 143.

55 Kevin N. Laland and Gillian R. Brown [2002], *Sense and Nonsense: Evolutionary Perspectives on Human Behaviour*, Oxford, Oxford University Press, 2002, 242–243.

56 See for a recent strictly verbal treatment of their argument Peter J. Richerson and Robert Boyd [2005], *Not by Genes Alone: How Culture Transformed Human Evolution*, Chicago, University of Chicago Press, 2005. Older and more recent (more) formalized versions can be found in Robert Boyd and Peter J. Richerson [1985], *Culture and the Evolutionary Process*, Chicago, University of Chicago Press, 1985 and Robert Boyd and Peter J. Richerson [2005], *The Origin and Evolution of Cultures*, Oxford, Oxford University Press, 2005.

57 Other classical works include Charles J. Lumsden and Edward O. Wilson [1981], *Genes, Mind, and Culture: The Coevolutionary Process*, Cambridge, Harvard University Press, 1981, Luigi L. Cavalli-Sforza and Marcus W. Feldman [1981], *Cultural Transmission and Evolution: A Quantitative Approach*, Princeton, Princeton University Press, 1981, William H. Durham [1991], *Coevolution: Genes, Culture, and Human Diversity*, Stanford, Stanford University Press, 1991. The enumeration to be found in Wolfgang Wickler and Wolfgang Fikentscher [1999], "System und Aussenanbindung epigenetischer Verhaltenssteuerung", 30 *Rechtstheorie* 69, 76, footnote 5, however, appears to cast the coevolutionary net too widely (for now). But see also Jan-Hendrik Röver [2000], "Epigenetics and the Social Sciences: The Issue of Triple Inheritance", in Martin Usteri (ed.), *Gene, Kultur und Recht, Schriften zur Rechtspsychologie 5*, Bern, Stämpfli, 2000, 125.

58 See David Sloan Wilson [2005], "Evolutionary Social Constructivism", in Jonathan Gotschall and David Sloan Wilson (ed.), *The Literary Animal: Evolution and the Nature of*

various collaborators,[59] however, is in my view justifiable, since it seems to hold a lot of quite obvious "legal potential". This should readily become clear in the remainder of this section or, at least, in the next and final one.

Capacity for culture and biased social learning Boyd and Richerson's theoretical framework "emphasizes the additional possibility that adaptation to rapidly shifting evolutionary environments may have favored evolved psychological mechanisms that were specialized for various forms of learning, particularly complex forms of imitation".[60] These social learning mechanisms then gave rise to a second – cultural – system of inheritance that interacts with the genetic system of inheritance. Hence their theory also goes by the name of dual inheritance theory.

Within their theoretical framework, "(c)ulture is information capable of affecting individuals' behavior that they acquire from other members of their species through teaching, imitation, and other forms of social transmission",[61] so a

---

Narrative, Evanston, Northwestern University Press, 2005, 20, David Sloan Wilson [2004], "Evolutionary social constructivism: Narrowing (but not yet bridging) the gap", *Metanexus Anthropos* 2004.11.17, downloadable at http://www.metanexus.net/metanexus_online/show_article2.asp?ID=9167. Others include Henry Plotkin [2002], *The Imagined World Made Real: Towards a Natural Science of Culture*, London, Penguin, 2002, F. John Odling-Smee, Kevin N. Laland and Marcus W. Feldman [2003], *Niche Construction: The Neglected Process in Evolution*, Princeton, Princeton University Press, 2003, Christopher Boehm [1999], *Hierarchy in the Forest: Egalitarianism and the Evolution of Human Altruism*, Cambridge, Harvard University Press, 1999, and David Sloan Wilson [2002]'s own *Darwin's Cathedral: Evolution, Religion, and the Nature of Society*, Chicago, University of Chicago Press, 2002. Compare also Jerome H. Barkow [2006], "Introduction: Sometimes the Bus Does Wait", in Jerome H. Barkow (ed.), *Missing the Revolution: Darwinism for Social Scientists*, Oxford, Oxford University Press, 2006, 3.

59 The (unfortunately short and incomplete) account below is largely pieced together from the following quite accessible sources: Peter J. Richerson and Robert Boyd [2005], *Not by Genes Alone: How Culture Transformed Human Evolution*, Chicago, University of Chicago Press, 2005, Joseph Henrich and Natalie Henrich [2006], "Culture, evolution and the puzzle of human cooperation", 7 *Cognitive Systems Research* 220 (for the book-length version, see: Joseph Henrich and Natalie Henrich [2007], *Why Humans Cooperate: A Cultural and Evolutionary Explanation*, Oxford, Oxford University Press, 2007), Joseph Henrich and Richard McElreath [2003], "The Evolution of Cultural Evolution", 12 *Evolutionary Anthropology* 123.

60 Henrich et al. [2005], "Models of decision-making and the coevolution of social preferences", 28 *Behavioral and Brain Sciences* 838, 842 (reply to commentaries on target paper).

61 Peter J. Richerson and Robert Boyd [2005], *Not by Genes Alone: How Culture Transformed Human Evolution*, Chicago, University of Chicago Press, 2005, 5. Compare also Henry Plotkin [2002], *The Imagined World Made Real: Towards a Natural Science of Culture*, London, Penguin, 2002, 100–112.

This concept of "culture" appears to map onto what evolutionary psychologists John Tooby and Leda Cosmides have called "transmitted culture" or "epidemiological culture". See John

concept that "encompasses all the things that we learn from each other as opposed to learn for ourselves or inherit genetically".[62]

The resulting cultural transmission itself is likely to be biased by the decision rules that individuals apply, such as a (pay-off dependent) prestige bias – "do what successful individuals in the population are doing" – and a (frequency dependent) conformity bias – "do what the majority of the population is doing". Although other forces of cultural transmission undoubtedly have to be taken into consideration too,[63] much of their efforts have been concentrated on modelling these two transmission biases, which both can help to maintain stable variation between different cultural groups.

Biased social learning and moralistic punishment can lead to social norms Boyd and Richerson also investigated the evolutionary properties of moralistic punishment. These properties appear to differ fundamentally from those of reciprocal altruism. Although both can be regarded as public goods problems, moralistic punishment appears to have the edge on reciprocal altruism when it comes to sustaining cooperation in large-scale multi-person interactions. One of

---

Tooby and Leda Cosmides [1992], "The Psychological Foundations of Culture", in Jerome H. Barkow, Leda Cosmides and John Tooby (ed.), *The Adapted Mind: Evolutionary Psychology and the Generation of Culture*, Oxford, Oxford University Press, 1992, 19, 88–93 and 114–122. Tooby and Cosmides distinguish between "metaculture", "evoked culture" and "epidemiological culture". "*Metaculture*" comprises "the system of universally recurring relationships established and constituted by (1) our universal evolved species-typical psychological and physiological architectures, (2) the interaction of these architectures with each other in populations, (3) their interaction with the developmentally relevant recurrent structure of human natural and cultural environments, and (4) their patterned standard impact on human phenomena" (91). "*Evoked culture*" refers to "functionally organized, domain-specific mechanisms (…) triggered by local circumstances", which "leads to within-group similarities and between-group differences" (121). "*Epidemiological culture*" is used to refer to the "(o)bserver's inferential mechanisms construct(ing) representations similar to those present in others", whereby "domain-specific mechanisms influence which representations spread through a population easily and which do not" (121). I think it is fair to say that, in practice, evolutionary psychology as a discipline (in its narrower sense) focuses on what is called "metaculture".

However, it would be interesting to compare the notion of "evoked culture" with Gordley"s first type of reason for why there can be different laws based upon the same underlying principles. The second reason Gordley mentions would seem more related to the notion of "transmitted culture" (see above, section 2).

62 Peter J. Richerson and Robert Boyd [2000], "Evolution: The Darwinian Theory of Social Change – An Homage to Donald T. Campbell", in Waltraud Schelkle, Wolf-Hagen Krauth, Martin Kohli and Georg Elwert (ed.), *Paradigms of Social Change: Modernization, Development, Transformation, Evolution*, Frankfurt, Campus Verlag, 2000, 257, 257 (target paper with commentaries).

63 See for a short overview Peter J. Richerson and Robert Boyd [2005], *Not by Genes Alone: How Culture Transformed Human Evolution*, Chicago, University of Chicago Press, 2005, 68–71.

the reasons for this lies in the fact that "punishers don't have to pay the costs of punishing very often if being punished is more costly than the costs associated with sticking to the norm".[64]

However, their models equally suggest that moralistic punishment can stabilize not only individually costly *group-beneficial* behaviour in large-scale multi-person interactions, but also *any other* arbitrary behaviour, be it neutral or even harmful. A combination of biased cultural transmission and moralistic punishment can then lead to the adoption of a very wide variety of locally stable social norms in different cultural groups.

I believe this emphasis on a plausible evolutionary theory of social norms in any case is of particular relevance for any evolutionary analysis in law aiming at incorporating regulating behaviour or rule-making and rule-following behaviour in its analyses.[65]

Cultural group selection can lead to prosocial or cooperative social norms What is then needed, however, is a mechanism that is able to select among the wide variety of possible individually costly social norms – the equilibrium selection problem again. Boyd and Richerson argue that cultural group selection can plausibly provide such a mechanism and that it is likely to favour prosocial or cooperative social norms (in the longer run).

The necessary "competition" between groups involved with this evolutionary process can take various forms. Henrich mentions – of course – warfare, but also "demographic production (some social groups reproduce faster than others), or more subtle forms in which individuals learn decisions and strategies by preferentially observing more successful individuals, many of whom are more successful because they live in groups at stable cooperative equilibria".[66]

---

64 Joseph Henrich and Natalie Henrich [2006], "Culture, evolution and the puzzle of human cooperation", 7 *Cognitive Systems Research* 220, 240. See also Robert Boyd, Herbert Gintis, Samuel Bowles and Peter J. Richerson [2003], "The evolution of altruistic punishment", 100 *Proceedings of the National Academy of Sciences* 3531. Compare also Chandra Sekhar Sripada [2005], "Punishment and the strategic structure of moral systems", 20 *Biology and Philosophy* 767. See, however, for a different evolutionary view on punishment and multi-person exchange John Tooby, Leda Cosmides and Michael E. Price [2006], "Cognitive Adaptations for *n*-person Exchange: The Evolutionary Roots of Organizational Behavior", 27 *Managerial and Decision Economics* 103, 119–126.

65 See, e.g., Robert Boyd and Peter J. Richerson [2002], "Norms and Bounded Rationality", in Gerd Gigerenzer and Reinhard Selten (ed.), *Bounded Rationality: The Adaptive Toolbox*, Cambridge, MIT Press, 2002, 281, Robert Boyd and Peter J. Richerson [1994], "The Evolution of Norms: An Anthropological View", 150 *Journal of Institutional and Theoretical Economics* 72 (target paper with commentaries), Joseph Henrich and Natalie Henrich [2006], "Culture, evolution and the puzzle of human cooperation", 7 *Cognitive Systems Research* 220, 239.

66 Joseph Henrich [2006], "Cooperation, Punishment, and the Evolution of Human Institutions", 312 *Science* 60, 60–61, referring to Robert Boyd and Peter J. Richerson

Gene-culture coevolution could have led to "tribal social instincts" A human capacity to live in larger-scale forms of tribal social organization could then have evolved through a process involving the interaction of genetic and cultural evolution.[67] The rather far-reaching implications of this possibility are clearly illustrated by the following citation:

> Because the tribal instincts are of relatively recent origin and because our genes still fall under selection pressures obeying Hamilton's rule, they are not the sole regulators of human social life. The tribal instincts are laid on top of more ancient social instincts rooted in kin selection and reciprocal altruism. These ancient social instincts conflict with the tribal. We are simultaneously committed to tribes, family, and self, even though the conflicting demands very often cause us the great anguish as Freud (...) described in *Civilization and Its Discontents* (...). So long as reproductive competition among the cooperators exists, people still have to look out for their personal fitness interests even as they try to do their civic duty.[68], [69]

[2002], "Group Beneficial Norms Can Spread Rapidly in a Structured Population", 215 *Journal of Theoretical Biology* 287. See also Joseph Henrich [2004], "Cultural group selection, coevolutionary processes and large-scale cooperation", 53 *Journal of Economic Behavior & Organization* 3, 28–29 (target paper with commentaries and reply). Compare for recent experimental results Özgür Gürerk, Bernd Irlenbusch and Bettina Rockenbach [2006], "The Competitive Advantage of Sanctioning Institutions", 312 *Science* 108.

67 See Peter J. Richerson and Robert Boyd [2001], "The Evolution of Subjective Commitment to Groups: A Tribal Instincts Hypothesis", in Randolph M. Nesse (ed.), *Evolution and the Capacity for Commitment*, New York, Russell Sage Foundation, 2001, 186. See also Herbert Gintis, Samuel Bowles, Robert Boyd and Ernst Fehr [2005], "Moral Sentiments and Material Interests: Origins, Evidence, and Consequences", in Herbert Gintis, Samuel Bowles, Robert Boyd and Ernst Fehr (ed.), *Moral Sentiments and Material Interests: The Foundations of Cooperation in Economic Life*, Cambridge, MIT Press, 2005, 3, 22–24.

68 Peter J. Richerson and Robert Boyd [2001], "Culture is Part of Human Biology: Why the Superorganic Concept Serves the Human Sciences Badly", in Sabine Maasen and Matthias Winterhager (ed.), *Science Studies: Probing the Dynamics of Scientific Knowledge*, Bielefeld, Transcript, 2001, 147, 169. Perhaps it is telling in light of what preceded that in another, more recent contribution, Boyd and Richerson refer to these instincts as "Aristotelian social instincts". See Robert Boyd and Peter J. Richerson [2006], "Solving the Puzzle of Human Cooperation", in Stephen C. Levinson and Pierre Jaisson (ed.), *Evolution and Culture*, Cambridge, MIT Press, 2006, 105, 130.

69 It is worth noting that this seems to resonate quite well with Ian Macneil's (legal) views on relational contracting. See Ian R. Macneil [1983], "Values in Contract: Internal and External", 78 *Northwestern University Law Review* 340, 348 ("As students of man in society, we are faced with an illogicality. Man is both an entirely selfish creature and an entirely social creature, in that man puts the interests of his fellows ahead of his own interests *at the same time* that he puts his own interests first. Such a creature is schizophrenic, and will, to the extent that it does anything except vibrate in utter frustration, constantly

Again, whether or not this specific "tribal social instincts" hypothesis of theirs will turn out to be (the most) correct is beside the point I wish to make here. Indeed, in any case, a firmly evolutionary grounded theory of culture seems to be needed to be able to even begin to address the issues raised in the previous subsection. Quoting Henrich (only) slightly out of context, all of the above "by no means suggests that we cannot generalize about human behavior. Rather, it suggests we need a theory of culture, or of cultural transmission, to do so."[70]

To summarize then, culture exists, so we are in need – if we are interested in evolutionary explanations that is – of a plausible evolutionary explanation for culture and cultural capacities. If these capacities can, amongst other things, help in sustaining cooperation on a scale elsewhere only seen in social insects, I think it is only logical to try to combine them with other evolutionary theories bearing on the subject – thus providing a more complete picture of human social behaviour. In other words, I do not believe the scientific requirement of parsimony as such to be a sufficient reason to – implicitly or explicitly – exclude cultural capacities from evolutionary approaches to human behaviour, including evolutionary analysis in law.[71] So from this point of view culture appears more as a part of the solution than as a part of the problem.

Moreover, it is worth reminding that the theory I presented is of course far from complete, and does not present itself as such either. Indeed, according to Richerson and Boyd, "(t)he only thing about the project that (they) care to assert with utter conviction is that the Darwinian approach is *worth pursuing*",[72] which is, I think, a rather healthy attitude towards this and any other kind of theorizing. More specifically, trying to achieve some measure of integration with the evolutionary psychologically inspired cognitive anthropology represented by, amongst others, Dan Sperber would seem to be a particularly promising line of enquiry.[73]

---

alternate between inconsistent behaviors – selfish one second and self-sacrificing the next."), (incidentally also referring to Freud for that matter).

70 Joseph Henrich [2000], "Does Culture Matter in Economic Behavior? Ultimatum Game Bargaining Among the Machiguenga of the Peruvian Amazon", 90 *American Economic Review* 973, 978, footnote 3.

71 Compare also Charles Efferson and Peter J. Richerson [2007], "A prolegomenon to nonlinear empiricism in the human behavioral sciences", 22 *Biology and Philosophy* 1.

72 Peter J. Richerson and Robert Boyd [2005], *Not by Genes Alone: How Culture Transformed Human Evolution*, Chicago, University of Chicago Press, 2005, 254 (emphasis in original).

73 See most recently for attempts in this direction Dan Sperber and Nicolas Claidière [2006], "Why Modeling Cultural Evolution Is Still Such a Challenge", 1 *Biological Theory* 20, Dan Sperber and Nicolas Claidière [forthcoming], "Defining and explaining culture (comments on Richerson and Boyd, *Not by genes alone*)", in press *Biology and Philosophy* ("In particular we share the goal of developing a "population thinking" approach to cultural evolution that sees it neither as a mere extension of biological evolution (as in pop sociobiology), nor as a mere analog of biological evolution (as in pop memetics)."). See also Dan Sperber and Lawrence A. Hirschfeld [2004], "The cognitive foundations of cultural stability and diversity", 8 *TRENDS*

All of this, however, leaves the question of the importance of this theoretical framework for law and legal theory largely unanswered – or perhaps better only implicitly answered. Hence, by way of conclusion, I will now render more explicit some of the elements pertaining to this question.

Conclusion: Dual Inheritance Theory or Gene-culture Coevolutionary Theory and Evolutionary Analysis in Law

How indeed does this gene-culture coevolutionary or dual inheritance theoretical framework relate to law and legal theory, and, more specifically, their already evolutionary-minded exponents?

Well, when applying evolutionary theory to law and legal theory, I think it can be very useful to distinguish the behaviour supposed to be regulated from the behaviour *by which* it is regulated. In other words, evolutionary analysis in law should also be able to tell us something about "law"[74] itself.

The main reason for this is that whereas for example contracting behaviour is – at least in its archetypical case – a dyadic form of cooperation, the behaviour regulating this dyadic form of cooperation bears more resemblance to a large-scale multi-person form of cooperative dilemma or public goods problem – in which cooperation appears unlikely to have evolved on the basis of kin selection and reciprocal altruism alone.

Some sort of dual inheritance theory or theory of gene-culture coevolution thus seems to me the most likely candidate to begin to explain *both* the evolutionary origins of the behaviour which is regulated *and* those of the regulating behaviour and of the social norms the latter often expresses.[75]

---

in Cognitive Sciences 40, Dan Sperber [2001], "Mental Modularity and Cultural Diversity", in Harvey Whitehouse (ed.), *The Debated Mind: Evolutionary Psychology versus Ethnography*, Oxford, Berg, 2001, 23, Dan Sperber and Lawrence Hirschfeld [1999], "Culture, Cognition, and Evolution", in Robert A. Wilson and Frank C. Keil (ed.), *The MIT Encyclopedia of the Cognitive Sciences*, Cambridge, MIT Press, 1999, cxi, Dan Sperber [1996], *Explaining Culture: A Naturalistic Approach*, Oxford, Blackwell, 1996.

74 In this chapter, I have intentionally refrained from even trying to give a (working) definition of "law". I have preferred using instead the perhaps rather weak concepts of "regulating behaviour" and "rule-making and rule-following behaviour" (Margaret Gruter [1992], "An Ethological Perspective on Law and Biology", in Roger D. Masters and Margaret Gruter (ed.), *The Sense of Justice: Biological Foundations of Law*, Newbury Park, Sage Publications, 1992, 95), but am aware of the fact that these concepts could use further elaboration. Indeed, it is at present not clear to me what evolutionary theory has to add, if anything, to the enterprise of answering the question of what *distinguishes* law from other tools or systems of social ordering.

75 Compare Ernst Fehr and Urs Fischbacher [2004], "Social norms and human cooperation", 8 *TRENDS in Cognitive Sciences* 185, 185 ("Legal enforcement mechanisms cannot function unless they are based on a broad consensus about the normative legitimacy

After all, law not only *affects* human behaviour, in a very important way it also *is* human behaviour.[76]

Returning to the issue of equality in exchange, a theory like the one proposed by Boyd and Richerson and their collaborators provides a plausible explanation for the different manifestations of substantive fairness in both industrialized and pre-commercial societies within one and the same evolutionary framework.

First, it could be argued that the pattern we see in pre-commercial societies amongst the members of relatively small groups can to a large extent be adequately explained on the basis of reciprocal altruism and the mechanisms that are known to sustain it in dyadic interactions. Much the same would seem to apply for so-called relational contracts and the fact that they are largely self-regulating.[77] Indeed, Oliver Goodenough's warning that "(t)he theoretical discussions of contract law and evolutionary science are highly congruent, indeed so closely related that the possible infection of evolutionary theory by legal ideas seems a caution worth remembering",[78] seems well worth repeating here.

Secondly, however, the fairness norms underlying impersonal isolated exchange transactions in current Western contract law – as well as other similar norms elsewhere for that matter – are in need of a different kind of evolutionary explanation.[79] To account for these prosocial social norms would indeed seem to require that human cultural capacities be added to the evolutionary mix. Put

---

of the rules – in other words, unless the rules are backed by social norms. Moreover, the very existence of legal enforcement institutions is itself a product of prior norms about what constitutes appropriate behaviour."), Joseph Henrich [2004], "Reply to Commentaries on 'Cultural group selection, coevolutionary processes and large-scale cooperation'", 53 *Journal of Economic Behavior & Organization* 127, 127 ("However, assuming 'institutions', 'organizations', or some undefined ability to build these, grants too much of the solution, if one (such as I) is interested in evolutionary origins. Such assumptions merely push the question back to 'what evolutionary processes explain the emergence of these institutions and who is paying the evolutionary costs for maintaining them?'"). See also Jeroen C.J.M. van den Bergh and Sigrid Stagl [2003], "Coevolution of economic behaviour and institutions: towards a theory of institutional change", 13 *Journal of Evolutionary Economics* 289.

76 Something Owen Jones for that matter acknowledges in some of his contributions. See, e.g., Owen D. Jones [2005], "Evolutionary Psychology and the Law", in David M. Buss (ed.), *The Handbook of Evolutionary Psychology*, Hoboken, Wiley, 2005, 953, 970.

77 Compare also, e.g., Robert E. Scott [1987], "Conflict and Cooperation in Long-Term Contracts", 75 *California Law Review* 2005; Robert E. Scott [2003], "A Theory of Self-Enforcing Indefinite Agreements", 103 *Columbia Law Review* 1641; Simon Deakin, Christel Lane and Frank Wilkinson [1994], "'Trust' or Law? Towards an Integrated Theory of Contractual Relations between Firms", 21 *Journal of Law and Society* 329.

78 Oliver R. Goodenough [2001], "Law and the Biology of Commitment", in Randolph M. Nesse (ed.), *Evolution and the Capacity for Commitment*, New York, Russell Sage Foundation, 2001, 262, 277.

79 Compare also Janet T. Landa [1999], "The Law and Bioeconomics of Ethnic Cooperation and Conflict in Plural Societies of Southeast Asia: a Theory of Chinese Merchant Success", 1 *Journal of Bioeconomics* 269, 276–280.

somewhat differently, when attempting to go from dyadic contracts to social contracts, culture and cultural capacities inevitably seem to enter into the evolutionary picture, whether we may like it or not.

In other words, I believe much is to be gained for evolutionary analysis in law by taking seriously some of evolutionary biologist David Sloan Wilson's remarks in his book on the evolutionary origins of religion, *Darwin's Cathedral*. According to Wilson, "we need to reconcile two seemingly contradictory facts: the fact that moral systems require innate psychological mechanisms, and the fact that they can rapidly evolve by cultural evolution."[80] As Wilson seems to acknowledge towards the end of the book,[81] much the same could be said for the study of law and legally relevant phenomena from an evolutionary perspective. Even if the reconciliation he speaks of is far from achieved, it would seem incomplete at best for evolutionary analysis in law to focus rather exclusively on one of Wilson's pair of seemingly contradictory facts, namely innate psychological mechanisms.

A gene-culture coevolutionary enquiry into the cross-cultural similarities and differences regarding human cooperative behaviour could then also "offer a new foundation for the comparative analysis of human cultures and social institutions",[82] and hence provide for a useful external point of entry into the field of comparative legal theory and its perennial problem of reconciling legal universality and legal diversity. Mechanisms like the ones Boyd and Richerson describe can for instance provide very useful additional insights into how similar problems are solved differently in various legal systems or systems of rules, with various degrees of cooperativeness as a result.

The cross-cultural experimental economic research I mentioned in section 3 of this chapter already appears to lead in that direction.[83] Indeed, according to Efferson and Richerson, "(e)xperimental economic games in essence offer the possibility of a theory-driven, quantitative ethnographic map of human cultural variation. Such a map would bring anthropology and economics, perhaps the two most distant of the

---

80 David Sloan Wilson [2002], *Darwin's Cathedral: Evolution, Religion, and the Nature of Society*, Chicago, University of Chicago Press, 2002, 25.

81 David Sloan Wilson [2002], *Darwin's Cathedral: Evolution, Religion, and the Nature of Society*, Chicago, University of Chicago Press, 2002, 225 ("In this book I have tried to show how a theory of innate psychology can inform the study of religion and how it can clarify, rather than deny, the essential role of culture. The same theory can be applied to any other modern human social organization.").

82 Geoffrey Miller [2000], *The Mating Mind: How Sexual Choice Shaped the Evolution of Human Nature*, London, William Heinemann, 2000, 318.

83 Compare also Raffaele Caterina [2006], "Comparative law and economics", in Jan M. Smits (ed.), *Elgar Encyclopedia of Comparative Law*, Cheltenham, Edward Elgar, 2006, 161, 166–170, Thomas S. Ulen [2001], "Evolution, Human Behavior, and Law: A Response to Owen Jones's Dunwody Lecture", 53 *Florida Law Review* 931, 946 ("by studying the similarities and differences in the legal systems and other methods of social ordering among (different) cultures, one might greatly advance the cause of showing the relationship among evolution, law, and human behavior").

social sciences, closer together and probably bring psychology, political science, and sociology into the fold along the way."[84] Given that "in human zoology the law represents a rich, if somewhat idiosyncratic, pool of data on the wild behavior of Homo Sapiens",[85] one is left wondering why legal researchers should remain excluded from this endeavour.

References

ALEXANDER, Richard [2006], "The Challenge of Human Social Behavior (Book Review of Peter Hammerstein (ed.), Genetic and Cultural Evolution of Cooperation)", 4 *Evolutionary Psychology* 1.

ATIYAH, Patrick S. [1985], "Contract and Fair Exchange", 35 *University of Toronto Law Journal* 1.

BARKOW, Jerome H. [2006], "Introduction: Sometimes the Bus Does Wait", in Jerome H. BARKOW (ed.), *Missing the Revolution: Darwinism for Social Scientists*, Oxford, Oxford University Press, 3.

BERGH, Jeroen C.J.M. van den and STAGL, Sigrid [2003], "Coevolution of economic behaviour and institutions: towards a theory of institutional change", 13 *Journal of Evolutionary Economics* 289.

BERNHARD, Helen, FISCHBACHER, Urs and FEHR, Ernst [2006], "Parochial altruism in humans", 442 *Nature* 912.

BERNSTEIN, Lisa [1992], "Opting out of the Legal System: Extralegal Contractual Relations in the Diamond Industry", 21 *Journal of Legal Studies* 115.

BINMORE, Ken [2005], *Natural Justice*, Oxford, Oxford University Press.

BINMORE, Ken [2006], "Why do people cooperate?", 5 *Politics, Philosophy & Economics* 81.

BOEHM, Christopher [1999], *Hierarchy in the Forest: Egalitarianism and the Evolution of Human Altruism*, Cambridge, Harvard University Press.

BOHANNAN, Paul [1955], "Some Principles of Exchange and Investment among the Tiv", 57 *American Anthropologist* 60.

BOHNET, Iris, FREY, Bruno S. and HUCK, Steffen [2001], "More Order with Less Law: On Contract Enforcement, Trust, and Crowding", 95 *American Political Science Review* 131.

BOWLES, Samuel and GINTIS, Herbert [2003], "Origins of Human Cooperation", in Peter Hammerstein (ed.), *Genetic and Cultural Evolution of Cooperation*, Cambridge, MIT Press, 429.

---

84 Charles Efferson and Peter J. Richerson [2007], "A prolegomenon to nonlinear empiricism in the human behavioral sciences", 22 *Biology and Philosophy* 1, 10.

85 Oliver R. Goodenough [2001], "Law and the Biology of Commitment", in Randolph M. Nesse (ed.), *Evolution and the Capacity for Commitment*, New York, Russell Sage Foundation, 2001, 262, 272.

BOYD, Robert and RICHERSON, Peter J. [1985], *Culture and the Evolutionary Process*, Chicago, University of Chicago Press.
BOYD, Robert and RICHERSON, Peter J. [1994], "The Evolution of Norms: An Anthropological View", 150 *Journal of Institutional and Theoretical Economics* 72.
BOYD, Robert and RICHERSON, Peter J. [2002], "Group Beneficial Norms Can Spread Rapidly in a Structured Population", 215 *Journal of Theoretical Biology* 287.
BOYD, Robert, and RICHERSON, Peter J. [2002], "Norms and Bounded Rationality", in Gerd GIGERENZER and Reinhard SELTEN (eds), *Bounded Rationality: The Adaptive Toolbox*, Cambridge, MIT Press, 281.
BOYD, Robert and RICHERSON, Peter J. [2003], "Memes: Universal acid or a better mousetrap?", in Robert AUNGER (ed.), *Darwinizing Culture: The Status of Memetics as a Science*, Oxford, Oxford University Press, 143.
BOYD, Robert and RICHERSON, Peter J. [2005], *The Origin and Evolution of Cultures*, Oxford, Oxford University Press.
BOYD, Robert, and RICHERSON, Peter J. [2006], "Solving the Puzzle of Human Cooperation", in Stephen C. LEVINSON and Pierre JAISSON (eds), *Evolution and Culture*, Cambridge, MIT Press, 105.
BOYD, Robert, GINTIS, Herbert, BOWLES, Samuel and RICHERSON, Peter J. [2003], "The evolution of altruistic punishment", 100 *Proceedings of the National Academy of Sciences* 3531.
BUCKLEY, Francis H. [1990], "Three Theories of Substantive Fairness", 19 *Hofstra Law Review* 33.
BURNHAM, Terence C. and JOHNSON, Dominic D.P. [2005], "The Biological and Evolutionary Logic of Human Cooperation", 27 *Analyse & Kritik* 113.
CAMERER, Colin F. and FEHR, Ernst [2004], "Measuring Social Norms and Preferences Using Experimental Games: A Guide for Social Scientists", in Joseph HENRICH et al. (eds), *Foundations of Human Sociality: Economic Experiments and Ethnographic Evidence from Fifteen Small-Scale Societies*, Oxford, Oxford University Press, 55.
CAMERER, Colin F. and LOEWENSTEIN, George [2004], "Behavioral Economics: Past, Present, Future", in Colin F. CAMERER, George LOEWENSTEIN and Matthew RABIN (eds), *Advances in Behavioral Economics*, Princeton, Princeton University Press, 3.
CAMPBELL, Donald T. [1983], "The Two Distinct Routes beyond Kin Selection to Ultrasociality: Implications for the Humanities and Social Sciences", in Diane L. BRIDGEMAN (ed.), *The Nature of Prosocial Development: Theories and Strategies*, New York, Academic Press, 11.
CATERINA, Raffaele [2006], "Comparative law and economics", in Jan M. SMITS (ed.), *Elgar Encyclopedia of Comparative Law*, Cheltenham, Edward Elgar, 161.

CAVALLI-SFORZA, Luigi L. and FELDMAN, Marcus W. [1981], *Cultural Transmission and Evolution: A Quantitative Approach*, Princeton, Princeton University Press.

COSMIDES, Leda and TOOBY, John [1992], "Cognitive Adaptations for Social Exchange", in Jerome H. BARKOW, Leda COSMIDES and John TOOBY (eds), *The Adapted Mind: Evolutionary Psychology and the Generation of Culture*, Oxford, Oxford University Press, 163.

DEAKIN, Simon [2003], "Evolution for Our Time: A Theory of Legal Memetics", in M.D.A. FREEMAN (ed.), *Current Legal Problems 2002*, Oxford, Oxford University Press, 1.

DEAKIN, Simon, LANE, Christel and WILKINSON, Frank [1994], "'Trust' or Law? Towards an Integrated Theory of Contractual Relations between Firms", 21 *Journal of Law and Society* 329.

DUGATKIN, Lee Alan [2002], "Cooperation in animals: An evolutionary overview", 17 *Biology and Philosophy* 459.

DURHAM, William H. [1991], *Coevolution: Genes, Culture, and Human Diversity*, Stanford, Stanford University Press.

EFFERSON, Charles and RICHERSON, Peter J. [2007], "A prolegomenon to nonlinear empiricism in the human behavioral sciences", 22 *Biology and Philosophy* 1.

ELSTER, John [2005], "Fehr on Altruism, Emotion, and Norms", 27 *Analyse & Kritik* 197.

ENSMINGER, Jean [2002], "Experimental Economics: A Powerful New Method for Theory Testing in Anthropology", in Jean ENSMINGER (ed.), *Theory in Economic Anthropology*, Walnut Creek, Altamira Press, 59.

FEHR, Ernst and FISCHBACHER, Urs [2003], "The nature of human altruism", 425 *Nature* 785.

FEHR, Ernst and FISCHBACHER, Urs [2004], "Social norms and human cooperation", 8 *TRENDS in Cognitive Sciences* 185.

FEHR, Ernst and FISCHBACHER, Urs [2005], "Human Altruism – Proximate Patterns and Evolutionary Origins", 27 *Analyse & Kritik* 6.

FEHR, Ernst and HENRICH, Joseph [2003], "Is Strong Reciprocity a Maladaptation?: On the Evolutionary Foundations of Human Altruism", in Peter HAMMERSTEIN (ed.), *Genetic and Cultural Evolution of Cooperation*, Cambridge, MIT Press, 55.

FELDMAN, Marc W. and LALAND, Kevin N. [1996], "Gene-culture coevolutionary theory", 11 *TRENDS in Ecology and Evolution* 453.

FIKENTSCHER, Wolfgang [2000], "Reziprozität als Begriff der Rechtsanthropologie – einige Bemerkungen", in Raimund JAKOB and Wolfgang FIKENTSCHER (eds), *Korruption, Reziprozität und Recht: Grundlagenwissenschaftliche und rechtsdogmatische Forschungsbeiträge, Schriften zur Rechtspsychologie 4*, Bern, Stämpfli Verlag, 129.

FISKE, Alan Page [1991], *Structures of Social Life: The Four Elementary Forms of Human Relations*, New York, The Free Press.

FRANK, Robert H. [2005], "Altruists with Green Beards: Still Kicking?", 27 *Analyse & Kritik* 85.

GÄCHTER, Simon and HERRMANN, Benedikt [2006], "Human cooperation from an economic perspective", in Peter M. KAPPELER and Carel P. VAN SCHAIK (eds), *Cooperation in Primates and Humans: Mechanisms and Evolution*, Berlin, Springer, 279.

GINTIS, Herbert [2000], "Strong reciprocity and human sociality", 206 *Journal of Theoretical Biology* 169.

GINTIS, Herbert [2005], "Behavioral Game Theory and Contemporary Economic Theory", 27 *Analyse & Kritik* 48.

GINTIS, Herbert [2006], "Behavioral ethics meets natural justice", 5 *Politics, Philosophy & Economics* 5.

GINTIS Herbert, BOWLES, Samuel, BOYD, Robert and FEHR, Ernst [2003], "Explaining altruistic behavior in humans", 24 *Evolution and Human Behavior* 153.

GINTIS Herbert, BOWLES, Samuel, BOYD, Robert and FEHR, Ernst [2005], "Moral Sentiments and Material Interests: Origins, Evidence, and Consequences", in GINTIS Herbert, BOWLES, Samuel, BOYD, Robert and FEHR, Ernst (eds), *Moral Sentiments and Material Interests: The Foundations of Cooperation in Economic Life*, Cambridge, MIT Press, 3.

GLUCKMAN, Max [1972], *The Ideas in Barotse Jurisprudence*, Manchester, Manchester University Press.

GOODENOUGH, O.R. [2001], "Law and the Biology of Commitment", in Randolph M. NESSE (ed.), *Evolution and the Capacity for Commitment*, New York, Russell Sage Foundation, 262.

GORDLEY, James [1981], "Equality in Exchange", 69 *California Law Review* 1587.

GORDLEY, James [1997], *Contract in Pre-Commercial Societies and in Western History*, in *International Encyclopedia of Comparative Law*, VII, *Contracts in general*, 2, Tübingen, Mohr Siebeck.

GORDLEY, James [2001], "Contract Law in the Aristotelian Tradition", in Peter BENSON (ed.), *The Theory of Contract Law: New Essays*, Cambridge, Cambridge University Press, 265.

GORDLEY, James [2003], "The universalist heritage", in Pierre LEGRAND and Roderick MUNDAY (eds), *Comparative Legal Studies: Traditions and Transitions*, Cambridge, Cambridge University Press, 31.

GORDLEY, James [2006], *Foundations of Private Law: Property, Tort, Contract, Unjust Enrichment*, Oxford, Oxford University Press.

GRUTER, Margaret [1992], "An Ethological Perspective on Law and Biology", in Roger D. MASTERS and Margaret GRUTER (eds), *The Sense of Justice: Biological Foundations of Law*, Newbury Park, Sage Publications, 95.

GÜRERK, Özgür, IRLENBUSCH, Bernd and ROCKENBACH, Bettina [2006], "The Competitive Advantage of Sanctioning Institutions", 312 *Science* 108.

HAGEN, Edward H. [2005], "Controversial Issues in Evolutionary Psychology", in David M. BUSS (ed.), *The Handbook of Evolutionary Psychology*, Hoboken, Wiley, 145.

HAGEN, Edward H. and HAMMERSTEIN, Peter [2006], "Game theory and human evolution: A critique of some recent interpretations of experimental games", 69 *Theoretical Population Biology* 339.

HAMMERSTEIN, Peter and HAGEN, Edward H. [2005], "The second wave of evolutionary economics in biology", 20 *TRENDS in Ecology and Evolution* 604.

HENRICH, Joseph [2000], "Does Culture Matter in Economic Behavior? Ultimatum Game Bargaining among the Machiguenga of the Peruvian Amazon", 90 *American Economic Review* 973.

HENRICH, Joseph [2002], "Decision Making, Cultural Transmission, and Adaptation in Economic Anthropology", in Jean ENSMINGER (ed.), *Theory in Economic Anthropology*, Walnut Creek, Altamira Press, 251.

HENRICH, Joseph [2004], "Cultural group selection, coevolutionary processes and large-scale cooperation", 53 *Journal of Economic Behavior & Organization* 3.

HENRICH, Joseph [2006], "Cooperation, Punishment, and the Evolution of Human Institutions", 312 *Science* 60.

HENRICH, Joseph and HENRICH, Natalie [2006], "Culture, evolution and the puzzle of human cooperation", 7 *Cognitive Systems Research* 220.

HENRICH, Joseph and HENRICH, Natalie [2007], *Why Humans Cooperate: A Cultural and Evolutionary Explanation*, Oxford, Oxford University Press.

HENRICH, Joseph and MCELREATH, Richard [2003], "The Evolution of Cultural Evolution", 12 *Evolutionary Anthropology* 123.

HENRICH, Joseph, BOYD, Robert, BOWLES, Samuel, CAMERER, Colin, FEHR, Ernst, GINTIS, Herbert and MCELREATH, Richard [2001], "In Search of Homo Economicus: Behavioral Experiments in 15 Small-Scale Societies", 91 *AEA Papers and Proceedings* 73.

HENRICH, Joseph, BOYD, Robert, BOWLES, Samuel, CAMERER, Colin, FEHR, Ernst and GINTIS, Herbert (eds) [2004], *Foundations of Human Sociality: Economic Experiments and Ethnographic Evidence from Fifteen Small-Scale Societies*, Oxford, Oxford University Press.

HENRICH, Joseph, BOYD, Robert, BOWLES, Samuel, CAMERER, Colin, FEHR, Ernst, GINTIS, Herbert, MCELREATH, Richard, ALVARD, Michael, BARR, Abigail, ENSMINGER, Jean, HENRICH, Natalie Smith, HILL, Kim, GIL-WHITE, Francisco, GURVEN, Michael, MARLOWE, Frank W., PATTON, John Q. and TRACER, David [2005], "'Economic man' in cross-cultural perspective: Behavioral experiments in 15 small-scale societies", 28 *Behavioral and Brain Sciences* 795.

HENRICH, Joseph, BOYD, Robert, BOWLES, Samuel, CAMERER, Colin, FEHR, Ernst, GINTIS, Herbert, MCELREATH, Richard, ALVARD, Michael, BARR, Abigail, ENSMINGER, Jean, HENRICH, Natalie Smith, HILL,

Kim, GIL-WHITE, Francisco, GURVEN, Michael, MARLOWE, Frank W., PATTON, John Q. and TRACER, David [2005], "Models of decision-making and the coevolution of social preferences", 28 *Behavioral and Brain Sciences* 838.

HENRICH, Joseph, MCELREATH, Richard, BARR, Abigail, ENSMINGER, Jean, BARRETT, Clark, BOLYANATZ, Alexander, CARDENAS, Juan Camilo, GURVEN, Michael, GWAKO, Edwins, HENRICH, Natalie, LESOROGOL, Carolyn, MARLOWE, Frank, TRACER, David and ZIKER, John [2006], "Costly Punishment Across Human Societies", 312 *Science* 1767.

HIRSHLEIFER, Jack [1999], "There are Many Evolutionary Pathways to Cooperation", 1 *Journal of Bioeconomics* 73.

HOWELL, Paul P. [1954/1970], *A Manual of Nuer Law: Being an account of Customary Law, its Evolution and Development in the Courts established by the Sudan Government*, Oxford, Oxford University Press.

IRLENBUSCH, Bernd [2006], "Are Non-Binding Contracts Really Not Worth the Paper?", 27 *Managerial and Decision Economics* 21.

JANICKI, Maria G. and KREBS, Dennis L., "Evolutionary Approaches to Culture", in Charles CRAWFORD and Dennis L. KREBS (eds), *Handbook of Evolutionary Psychology: Ideas, Issues, and Applications*, Mahwah, Lawrence Erlbaum Associates, 163.

JONES, Owen D. [2001], "Proprioception, Non-Law, and Biolegal History", 53 *Florida Law Review* 831.

JONES, Owen D. [2001], "Time-Shifted Rationality and the Law of Law"s Leverage: Behavioral Economics Meets Behavioral Biology", 95 *Northwestern University Law Review* 1141.

JONES, Owen D. [2005], "Evolutionary Psychology and the Law", in David M. BUSS (ed.), *The Handbook of Evolutionary Psychology*, Hoboken, Wiley, 953.

JONES, Owen D. and GOLDSMITH, Timothy H. [2005], "Law and Behavioral Biology", 105 *Columbia Law Review* 405.

KURZBAN, Robert [2003], "Biological Foundations of Reciprocity", in Elinor OSTROM and James WALKER (eds), *Trust and Reciprocity: Interdisciplinary Lessons from Experimental Research*, New York, Russell Sage Foundation, 105.

LALAND, Kevin N. [1993], "The mathematical modelling of human culture and its implications for psychology and the human sciences", 84 *British Journal of Psychology* 145.

LALAND, Kevin N. and BROWN, Gillian R. [2002], *Sense and Nonsense: Evolutionary Perspectives on Human Behaviour*, Oxford, Oxford University Press.

LALAND, Kevin N., ODLING-SMEE, John and FELDMAN, Marcus W. [2000], "Niche construction, biological evolution, and cultural change", 23 *Behavioral and Brain Sciences* 131.

LANDA, Janet T. [1981], "A Theory of the Ethnically Homogeneous Middleman Group: An Institutional Alternative to Contract Law", 10 *Journal of Legal Studies* 349.

LANDA, Janet T. [1999], "The Law and Bioeconomics of Ethnic Cooperation and Conflict in Plural Societies of Southeast Asia: a Theory of Chinese Merchant Success", 1 *Journal of Bioeconomics* 269.

LEHMANN, Laurent and KELLER, Laurent [2006], "The evolution of cooperation and altruism – a general framework and a classification of models", 19 *Journal of Evolutionary Biology* 1365.

LEITER, Brian and WEISBERG, Michael [forthcoming], "Why Evolutionary Biology is (So Far) Irrelevant to Law" (2 February 2007), University of Texas School of Law, Law & Economics Research Paper No. 81, Public Law & Legal Theory Research Paper No. 89, Available at SSRN: http://ssrn.com/abstract=892881.

LUMSDEN, Charles J. and WILSON, Edward O. [1981], *Genes, Mind, and Culture: The Coevolutionary Process*, Cambridge, Harvard University Press.

MACAULAY, Stewart [1963], "Non-Contractual Relations in Business: A Preliminary Study", 28 *American Sociological Review* 55.

MACAULAY, Stewart [1985], "An Empirical View of Contract", 1985 *Wisconsin Law Review* 465.

MACNEIL, Ian R. [1974], "The Many Futures of Contracts", 47 *Southern California Law Review* 691.

MACNEIL, Ian R. [1980], *The New Social Contract: An Inquiry into Modern Contractual Relations*, New Haven, Yale University Press.

MACNEIL, Ian R. [1983], "Values in Contract: Internal and External", 78 *Northwestern University Law Review* 340.

MAHONEY, Nicholas [1977], "Contract and Neighbourly Exchange among the Birwa of Botswana", 21 *Journal of African Law* 40.

MASTERS, Roger D. [1992], "Naturalistic Approaches to Justice in Political Philosophy and the Life Sciences", in Roger D. MASTERS and Margaret GRUTER (eds), *The Sense of Justice: Biological Foundations of Law*, Newbury Park, Sage Publications, 67.

MILLER, Geoffrey [2000], *The Mating Mind: How Sexual Choice Shaped the Evolution of Human Nature*, London, William Heinemann.

MURPHY, James Bernard [2002], "Equality in Exchange", 47 *American Journal of Jurisprudence* 85.

NADER, Laura and STARR, June [1973], "Is Equity Universal?", in Ralph A. NEWMAN (ed.), *Equity in the World"s Legal Systems: A Comparative Study*, Brussels, Bruylant, 125.

NESSE, Randolph M. [2001], "Natural Selection and the Capacity for Subjective Commitment", in Randolph M. NESSE (ed.), *Evolution and the Capacity for Commitment*, New York, Russell Sage Foundation, 1.

NOWAK, Martin A. [2006], "Five Rules for the Evolution of Cooperation", 314 *Science* 1560.

ODLING-SMEE, F. John, LALAND, Kevin N. and FELDMAN, Marcus W. [2003], *Niche Construction: The Neglected Process in Evolution*, Princeton, Princeton University Press.

PLOTKIN, Henry [2002], *The Imagined World Made Real: Towards a Natural Science of Culture*, London, Penguin.

RICHERSON, Peter J. and BOYD, Robert [1998], "The Evolution of Human Ultra-Sociality", in Irenäus EIBL-EIBESFELDT and Frank K. SALTER (eds), *Indoctrinability, Ideology, and Warfare*, New York, Berghahn, 71.

RICHERSON, Peter J. and BOYD, Robert [2000], "Evolution: The Darwinian Theory of Social Change – An Homage to Donald T. Campbell", in Waltraud SCHELKLE, Wolf-Hagen KRAUTH, Martin KOHLI and Georg ELWERT (eds), *Paradigms of Social Change: Modernization, Development, Transformation, Evolution*, Frankfurt, Campus Verlag, 257.

RICHERSON, Peter J. and BOYD, Robert [2001], "The Evolution of Subjective Commitment to Groups: A Tribal Instincts Hypothesis", in Randolph M. NESSE (ed.), *Evolution and the Capacity for Commitment*, New York, Russell Sage Foundation, 186.

RICHERSON, Peter J. and BOYD, Robert [2001], "Culture is Part of Human Biology: Why the Superorganic Concept Serves the Human Sciences Badly", in Sabine MAASEN and Matthias WINTERHAGER (eds), *Science Studies: Probing the Dynamics of Scientific Knowledge*, Bielefeld, Transcript, 147.

RICHERSON, Peter J. and BOYD, Robert [2005], *Not by Genes Alone: How Culture Transformed Human Evolution*, Chicago, University of Chicago Press.

ROSS, Don [2006], "Evolutionary game theory and the normative theory of institutional design: Binmore and behavioural economics", 5 *Politics, Philosophy & Economics* 51.

ROULAND, Norbert [1994], *Legal Anthropology*, London, Athlone Press.

RÖVER, Jan-Hendrik [2000], "Epigenetics and the Social Sciences: The Issue of Triple Inheritance", in Martin USTERI (ed.), *Gene, Kultur und Recht, Schriften zur Rechtspsychologie 5*, Bern, Stämpfli, 125.

SCOTT, Robert E. [1987], "Conflict and Cooperation in Long-Term Contracts", 75 *California Law Review* 2005.

SCOTT, Robert E. [2003], "A Theory of Self-Enforcing Indefinite Agreements", 103 *Columbia Law Review* 1641.

SEABRIGHT, Paul [2006], "The evolution of fairness norms: an essay on Ken Binmore's *Natural Justice*", 5 *Politics, Philosophy & Economics* 33–50.

SMITH, Eric Alden [2000], "Three Styles in the Evolutionary Analysis of Human Behavior", in Lee CRONK, Napoleon CHAGNON and William IRONS (eds), *Adaptation and Human Behavior: An Anthropological Perspective*, Hawthorne, Aldine de Gruyter, 27.

SMITH, Stephen A. [1996], "In Defence of Substantive Fairness", 112 *Law Quarterly Review* 138.

SMITH, Thomas A. [2001], "Equality, Evolution and Partnership Law", 3 *Journal of Bioeconomics* 99.

SPERBER, Dan [1996], *Explaining Culture: A Naturalistic Approach*, Oxford, Blackwell.

SPERBER, Dan [2001], "Mental Modularity and Cultural Diversity", in Harvey WHITEHOUSE (ed.), *The Debated Mind: Evolutionary Psychology versus Ethnography*, Oxford, Berg, 23.

SPERBER, Dan and CLAIDIÈRE, Nicolas [2006], "Why Modeling Cultural Evolution Is Still Such a Challenge", 1 *Biological Theory* 20.

SPERBER, Dan and CLAIDIÈRE, Nicolas [forthcoming], "Defining and explaining culture (comments on Richerson and Boyd, *Not by genes alone*)", in press *Biology and Philosophy.*

SPERBER, Dan and HIRSCHFELD, Lawrence [1999], "Culture, Cognition, and Evolution", in Robert A. WILSON and Frank C. KEIL (eds), *The MIT Encyclopedia of the Cognitive Sciences*, Cambridge, MIT Press, cxi.

SPERBER, Dan and HIRSCHFELD, Lawrence A. [2004], "The cognitive foundations of cultural stability and diversity", 8 *TRENDS in Cognitive Sciences* 40.

SRIPADA, Chandra Sekhar [2005], "Punishment and the strategic structure of moral systems", 20 *Biology and Philosophy* 767.

TOOBY, John and COSMIDES, Leda [1990], "The Past Explains the Present: Emotional Adaptations and the Structure of Ancestral Environments", 11 *Ethology and Sociobiology* 375.

TOOBY, John and COSMIDES, Leda [1992], "The Psychological Foundations of Culture", in Jerome H. BARKOW, Leda COSMIDES and John TOOBY (eds), *The Adapted Mind: Evolutionary Psychology and the Generation of Culture*, Oxford, Oxford University Press, 19.

TOOBY, John, COSMIDES, Leda and PRICE, Michael E. [2006], "Cognitive Adaptations for *n*-person Exchange: The Evolutionary Roots of Organizational Behavior", 27 *Managerial and Decision Economics* 103.

TRIVERS, Robert [2006], "Reciprocal altruism: 30 years later", in Peter M. KAPPELER and Carel P. VAN SCHAIK (eds), *Cooperation in Primates and Humans: Mechanisms and Evolution*, Berlin, Springer, 67.

ULEN, Thomas S. [2001], "Evolution, Human Behavior, and Law: A Response to Owen Jones's Dunwody Lecture", 53 *Florida Law Review* 931.

WAX, Amy L. [2004], "Evolution and the Bounds of Human", 23 *Law and Philosophy* 527.

WICKLER, Wolfgang and FIKENTSCHER, Wolfgang [1999], "System und Aussenanbindung epigenetischer Verhaltenssteuerung", 30 *Rechtstheorie* 69.

WILSON, David Sloan [1999], "Tasty slice – But where is the rest of the pie? (Book Review of David Buss, Evolutionary Psychology: The New Science of the Mind)", 20 *Evolution and Human Behavior* 279.

WILSON, David Sloan [2002], *Darwin's Cathedral: Evolution, Religion, and the Nature of Society*, Chicago, University of Chicago Press.

WILSON, David Sloan [2003], "Evolution, Morality and Human Potential", in Steven J. SCHER and Frederick RAUSCHER (eds), *Evolutionary Psychology: Alternative Approaches*, Boston, Kluwer Academic Publishers, 55.

WILSON, David Sloan [2004], "Evolutionary social constructivism: Narrowing (but not yet bridging) the gap", *Metanexus Anthropos* 2004.11.17, downloadable at http://www.metanexus.net/metanexus_online/show_article2.asp?ID=9167.

WILSON, David Sloan [2005], "Evolutionary Social Constructivism", in Jonathan GOTSCHALL and David Sloan WILSON (eds), *The Literary Animal: Evolution and the Nature of Narrative*, Evanston, Northwestern University Press, 20.

WILSON, David Sloan and SOBER, Elliott [1994], "Reintroducing group selection to the human behavioral sciences", 17 *Behavioral and Brain Sciences* 585.

Chapter 13
Just (and Efficient?) Compensation for Governmental Expropriations

Jeffrey Evans Stake[1]

Introduction

London has won the right to host the Olympics in 2012. To host the Olympics, London needs to obtain a large and unbroken parcel of land, perhaps £700,000,000 worth. Unlike private real estate projects, which can properly be kept secret while the property is acquired, most governmental projects should be discussed openly in a democratic political system. The Olympics are no exception; planning cannot be done in secret. London has identified a large area encompassing derelict industrial land as well as poor housing. Much of the land is fragmented and divided by waterways, overhead pylons, roads, the London Underground network and heavy rail lines. The area also comprises one of the most deprived communities in the United Kingdom, one having among the worst public health records. Unemployment is high, running at 35% in some areas; skills levels are low.

Given the necessity of the project now that London has won the contract, London is in no position to rely on voluntary sales by landowners as they might hold out for far more than their reservation prices. To solve the holdout problem, and "to ensure the regeneration of the Lower Lea Valley, alongside the Olympic, Legacy and Stratford City developments", the London Development Agency (LDA) has issued a Compulsory Purchase Order (CPO), which allows the government to buy the needed land without the owner's consent.

The CPO power will also be used in the Thames Gateway project, straddling the Thames Estuary from East London to South Essex and North Kent. This project is expected to deliver 120,000 new homes and 120,000–180,000 new jobs by 2016. Wide CPO powers will similarly be needed for completion of the Crossrail project, which will create an underground rail line going east–west across London from Maidenhead to the Isle of Dogs.

---

1 I thank the organizers of the Law, Mind, and Brain Interdisciplinary Colloquium at University College London 13 February 2006, especially Oliver Goodenough and Michael Freeman, for giving me the opportunity to present this paper and the participants in the colloquium for helpful comments. I thank William Baude for his helpful remarks, especially regarding the problem of political capture.

Moving from old London to new, New London, Connecticut, had seen better times. It was once a prosperous American industrialized city with a substantial military presence. By the 1990s the Navy had closed its base and unemployment was on the rise. The state government declared the city to be economically distressed. In 2000, New London decided that it could revitalize itself, drawing in new businesses and creating 1,000 jobs, if it were to redevelop the once thriving waterfront area. To that end, it created a private, not-for-profit, redevelopment corporation and invested it with the power to coordinate a large-scale improvement in the centre of the city. It also delegated to the redevelopment agency the city's power to condemn land for the project, if necessary. The redevelopment agency worked up a plan and began acquiring the land needed for the project. The agency offered to buy the privately held parcels, but some owners were not interested in selling. Suzette Kelo, who owned a tidy little pink house, and her neighbour Wilhelmina Dery, who had lived in her house for her entire 87 years of life, refused the offers. So the city asserted its power to take land without the consent of the owner, called the "power of eminent domain" in the United States. Kelo took her case to the United States Supreme Court, which held against her in the summer of 2005 (*Kelo* v. *City of New London*, 545 U.S. 469 (2005)).

Perhaps in part because of the efforts of property rights groups such as the Castle Coalition, which called the *Kelo* decision the "the most reviled Supreme Court decision of our time" (Castle Coalition 2007), much of the US press misreported the case as having greatly expanded the power of eminent domain. In the US, the power to expropriate has been extremely broad since *Berman v. Parker* was decided in 1954 (*Berman* v. *Parker* 1954) and has been essentially unfettered by the US constitution at least since the *Midkiff* opinion was issued in 1984 (*Hawaii Housing Authority* v. *Midkiff* 1984). Nevertheless, *Kelo* ignited a firestorm of criticism resulting in new legislation in 42 states, much of which was designed to cabin the power of eminent domain (Castle Coalition 2007). Indeed, the public backlash was sufficient to convince New London to compromise with Kelo, agreeing to move her house to a new location if she would sell her land.

Far to the east, in Kalinga Nagar, Orissa, India, land has been expropriated from tribal owners to be used for steel plants and extraction of natural resources. Families who have farmed the land for centuries have been displaced and the government has allegedly profited by selling land for ten times' what it had given the residents. According to Amnesty International, on the morning construction was to begin on a 6 million tonne capacity Tata project, hundreds of residents gathered at the construction site to protest the inadequate financial compensation and other related problems. Violence erupted at this protest, and the police killed 12 protestors, including women and children.

Consider one final example from the US. Before he became Governor of Texas and long before he became President, George W. Bush served as the managing general partner of the Texas Rangers baseball team. While he was with the team and his father was employed in the White House, George W. Bush helped to persuade the City of Arlington to obtain land for a new ball park for the team.

Arlington used the power of eminent domain to acquire land from unwilling owners. When asked about the propriety of taking government and private land for the purpose of granting to private owners, Bush responded, "This is a case where there is established law, established process and established procedures, so I see no problem with that ..."

What Compensation is paid for Expropriated Land?

Around the world, governments use the power of expropriation to acquire land from private citizens. This power is at least as old as the Bible, in which King Ahab exercised his sovereignty to take the vineyard of Naboth (I Kings 21, v2). The question in most cases of wholesale expropriation is not whether the government has such power, but how much compensation will be paid. Although there are many difficult issues that arise in connection with the power of expropriation, such as whether regulations trigger compensation and what to do with partial expropriations and expropriations of personal property, this chapter is limited to the relatively simple situations in which the government intentionally acquires all of an owner's land.

In Commonwealth countries, there is a common law presumption in favour of compensation (*Attorney-General* v. *De Keyser's Royal Hotel, Ltd.* 1920). In the United Kingdom, the law requires compensation for the interest acquired and for disturbance (Moore 1990). Compensation includes market value plus an extra 10 per cent for loss of home, up to a maximum that changes yearly (Department for Communities and Local Development 2006). The Home Loss Payments Regulations 2006 lift to £40,000 the maximum amount of compensation payable in England under the Land Compensation Act 1973 to a person whose home is acquired by compulsory purchase (Stat. 1658 Regulations 2006). This amount is designed to compensate for the distress of moving from home at a time not of the owner's choosing. The same is true in Wales (Stat. 1789 Regulations 2006), and some Canadian provinces offer residential owners *solatium* to compensate for the compulsory nature of the transfer (Dukeminier et al., 2006; Todd 1990).

In India, the Twenty-fifth Amendment of 1971 requires only that an "amount" be paid for compulsory acquisition (van der Walt 1999), vesting the question of compensation in the legislature. But the legislature has generously offered 30 per cent *solatium* in consideration of the compulsory nature of the acquisition in addition to the usual market value plus relocation expenses (Singh 1990). To compensate the owner for their lack of consent to the government's acquisition, South Africa also adds *solatium,* in the amount of a capped 10 per cent, to market value (Jacobs & Gildenhuys 1990). In Japan, ordinary expropriations require full market compensation, and legislation provides assistance to reconstruct lifestyles of those who suffered from expropriations (van der Walt 1999). Although it is possible for compensation to be set at something less than market value (van der Walt 1999), the German Government pays market value in the typical case

(Alexander 2006), relocation costs and temporary losses are also recoverable (Schmidt-Aßmann 1990). In France, the Declaration of the Rights of Man and the Citizen 1789 mandates just compensation before expropriation, and just compensation means full value of the property (van der Walt 1999). In addition to market value, owners are given compensation for relocating, which can be a lump sum of 15–25 per cent (Picard 1990).

The Fifth Amendment to the United States constitution requires, at a minimum, that "just compensation" be paid to owners for lands taken. "Just compensation" has been interpreted by the US Supreme Court to mean fair market value (*United States* v. *50 Acres of Land* 1984; Alexander 2006), what a willing buyer would pay a willing seller. As in most nations, the focus is on the pecuniary loss to the owner, not the gain to the government (*Brown* v. *Legal Foundation of Washington* 2003). That does not mean that owners in the US have always been paid fair market value for condemned land. It appears that some governmental units have viewed it as their job to pay less than what the Supreme Court has determined to be just compensation. In a study of condemnation practices in Nassau County, New York, Berger and Rohan (1967) found that the first county official to approach the owners was a professional negotiator authorized to settle only for less than 85 per cent of fair market value. Only one in six owners who settled received even the amount of the county's appraisal, and one in twelve received less than half. Losses incurred because of relocation also went uncompensated (Hartman 1971).

In 1970, the US Congress improved matters by enacting the Uniform Relocation Assistance and Real Property Acquisition Policies Act. That law requires that agencies receiving federal funds offer relocation assistance and often has the effect of procuring replacement value or more for displaced homeowners (Garnett 2006). In addition, various states offer more than the amount required by the federal constitution. For example, Minnesota offers some compensation to business owners for "going concern" value (*City of Minneapolis* v. *Shutt* 1977), and state laws offer compensation for relocation costs (Mass. Gen. Laws Ann. Ch 79, Section 6A). One recent study concludes that, in practice, undercompensation is not as common as commonly thought; residential owners and tenants are frequently entitled to substantially more than fair market value, although businesses often suffer uncompensated losses (Garnett 2006).

What Compensation ought to be Paid?

According to a number of scholars (e.g., Michelman 1967; Heller & Krier 1999), the two central concerns of the United States' Takings Clause are efficiency and justice. Arguments sounding in both of those policy goals can be made for the proposition that market value is not enough and owners should be paid subjective value for their lands.

Efficiency

If efficiency is defined by the Pareto criterion, a change is efficient only if all parties are at least as well off after the change as they were before. That criterion can be satisfied only if compensation is based on the owner's minimum asking price, for any lesser compensation will leave the deprived owner feeling worse. Unless it is assumed that the owner does not know their own best interests, only complete subjective compensation can turn a governmental action from one that benefits the public overall to one that satisfies the Pareto test (Epstein 1985).

Efficiency arguments can be made for subjective compensation even if the criterion for determining efficiency is relaxed from the Pareto definition to the Kaldor-Hicks definition, also known as "potential Pareto superiority", under which a change is efficient if the net benefits outweigh the net losses. Most of these arguments fall into one of three groups, those that focus on the efficiency of government actions, those that focus on the efficiency of landowner behaviour and those that relate to the behaviour of other economic actors.

Government Consider first the efficiency of government actions. One of the most common arguments, sometimes called "fiscal illusion", goes as follows. If the price paid by the government for compulsory purchases is below subjective value, the government will not recognize the true cost of its project, either failing to consider or failing to accurately assess costs it does not bear. Not seeing the true cost, it may use its power of expropriation to shift land to new uses that are *less* valuable than existing uses (Posner 1972; Knetsch & Borcherding 1979; Merrill 1986). To put it another way, if the costs of acquisition are external to the decision-makers, acquisitions will occur at an inefficiently high level. Conversely, if the price paid by the government is too high, a ransom value above true subjective value, the government may fail to condemn land when society would get more value out of the land in its redeveloped use. This missed opportunity for social gain is also inefficient.

The fiscal illusion argument against undercompensation assumes the government decision-maker takes into account the public benefits from its projects but not the public costs (Levinson 2000). Under a competing model of government decision-making, government actors consider all the costs and benefits of government projects and take only those actions that are justified by cost–benefit analysis. Assuming this model more accurately describes reality, efficiency does not require that the government pay subjective value, or indeed anything at all, for taking land without consent. It is even conceivable that a compensation mandate shifts decision-makers from an administrative process in which the costs and benefits would be considered equally to an adversarial process in which the fair market value requirement short-circuits the administrative inquiry into the costs of the acquisition, resulting in less efficient decisions than if no compensation were required.

However, there are reasons to doubt that decision-makers in a democracy will give equal weight to all costs and benefits. If the functionary sets a price too high, the taxpayers (including the functionary, to a tiny degree) will have to pay more than they should. If they set the price too low, the taxpayers gain and landholders lose. The group of landholders is necessarily smaller than the group of taxpayers and, thus, if the functionary is directly or indirectly sensitive to the concerns of the majority, they will underpay the owner. They might hear fewer complaints and be more secure in their job if they pay less. It should not come as a surprise that some officials seem to view it as their job to pay as little as possible for properties acquired.

Under some conditions, full compensation can reduce the chances of reaching the efficient outcome. The example immediately above assumed that anyone adversely affected by the government decision would make their opposition known. By picking the right threshold of concern necessary for an individual to exercise influence in the decision process, one can create an example to show the opposite possibility, that full compensation reduces the chances of reaching the efficient outcome. Assume, for instance, that a politically powerful group would enjoy special benefits from an inefficient governmental project. If the government pays less than full compensation, a group of geographically concentrated and highly interested owners has an incentive to oppose the project and bring it to the attention of the polity, under which it might die of exposure. Full compensation eliminates the concentrated opposition to the project, leaving only a diffuse group of adversely affected owners, none of whom lose enough to make it worth their while to fight the project (Farber 1992; Levinson 2000; Fischel 2004). Incomplete compensation gives owners reason to expend resources to oppose the inefficient project in proportion to the degree of shortfall. Note, however, that expenditures in opposition will occur with efficient projects as well. Moreover, the argument just made can be summed up by saying that it is beneficial for a few individual owners to lose in some cases in order that the public be saved from inefficient projects in other cases. Setting aside efficiency for a moment, that is exactly the kind of unjust redistribution from an individual to the collective that the compensation requirement was designed to avoid. But I am getting ahead of myself.

Private landholders Consider next an efficiency argument focusing on the decisions of private actors. If compensation is offered only for objective value, and subjective value remains unprotected from destruction by governmental acquisitions, private parties will invest too little in land resources. In some cases, prospective purchasers will fail to buy when their value is substantially subjective because they know that they will not be compensated for their subjective losses if the government expropriates the land. In other cases, owners will fail to make subjective improvements to lands they own. There is already a bias against subjective purchases and improvements because subjective value is often not insurable against other forms of loss. Insurance can be purchased to cover objective losses from fire and natural disasters, but subjective value cannot be recovered and thus is subject to loss in ways that objective value is not. Between two investments, one of which would yield an objective benefit and the other of which would yield a greater subjective benefit, it could be more sensible to choose the lesser objective gain because it can be secured by insurance. Expropriation strengthens this inefficient bias against subjective purchases and improvements.

There is a counterargument to this argument that failure to compensate for subjective value will lead to underinvestment by owners. For locations and situations in which the frequency of expropriation is low, the degree of underinvestment will be small. In the remaining situations, where expropriation is likely, paying subjective value for government acquisitions may result in owners inefficiently investing in subjective improvements in the face of a likely expropriation (Blume & Rubinfeld 1984; Posner 2003). In the extreme case, if no compensation is given at all for expropriations, owners have a healthy incentive to keep abreast of public works, and to avoid investing in improvements when there is a chance the land might be expropriated. The greater the compensation accorded, the less the incentive to predict the path of government-sponsored development and stay out of the way (Knetsch & Borcherding 1979). In this regard, the arguments of whether to pay for a taking that could have been anticipated (Levmore 1999) and how much to pay traverse common ground, and the similarity of considerations suggests that whether to pay depends in part on how much will be paid if compensation is due.

Governmental compensation for takings can be seen as an alternative to private insurance against takings, as both spread risks (Posner 1972; Blume & Rubinfeld 1984). Such a comparison, however, brings to light some of the disadvantages of publicly provided insurance. The benefits of this governmentally provided insurance against compulsory acquisitions accrue to some landowners that are not risk averse and would not wish to purchase this insurance if they had to pay for it (Levinson 2000). In addition, this publicly provided insurance against expropriation is paid for not just by landowners but by taxpayers generally or beneficiaries of alternative government programmes forsaken for lack of funds. Because the benefits accrue to landholders, with those holding more valuable lands receiving greater benefits, providing publicly funded insurance instead of leaving landowners to the private insurance market redistributes wealth somewhat haphazardly.

Shifting attention from efficiency concerns about paying too little compensation to concerns about too much, above-market compensation might cause some owners to try to influence the government to take their property, since doing so would bring more than a sale. Although this is possible, the problem is not unique to expropriations. Whenever the government has the power to procure goods and services, that power can be corrupted in favour of those with sufficient influence. Rather than paying less than subjective losses, the better solution is to establish procedural safeguards, monitoring and punishments that will make pilfering of the public purse less likely to be undertaken and succeed.

Ulen (1992) notes that payment of a supermarket value for expropriations could result in a bidding frenzy for lands likely to be taken by the government. If the market anticipates that the government will expropriate a parcel and pay more than market value, the market value will move up to meet that, resulting in an artificial spiral. To prevent that, full subjective compensation would have to be determined as of a date prior to the discussion of the government plan and then increased by some inflation factor for the period between that assessment and the date of payment for the expropriation.

Other economic actors There is one final efficiency point against full compensation, one that focuses on the behaviour of neither government nor private landholders, but on the broader economy. If the owners get more, the government pays more. In order to fund such payments, the government must raise taxes, reduce production of public goods or print more money. Printing money is inflationary, reducing public goods may be inefficient and raising taxes will often distort private economic decisions.

Justice

Compared with the empirically unconfirmed arguments from Kaldor-Hicks efficiency, arguments grounded in the goal of maintaining an appearance of justice offer a more compelling justification for compensating lost subjective value. The argument from justice starts with the proposition that the purpose of requiring the government to compensate for its involuntary acquisitions is to prevent "Government from forcing some people alone to bear public burdens which, in all fairness and justice, should be borne by the public as a whole" (*Armstrong* v. *United States* 1960). In the United States, this is sometimes called the "*Armstrong*" principle.

A government usually takes land for a project for one or more of three reasons: because it has been influenced to acquire the land for the benefit of some private party; because it sees an opportunity to grab wealth from a minority; or because it views the project to be in the interests of the public. In the first two cases, the government should not acquire the property at all. The requirement of full subjective compensation, which is typically greater than objective value, would reduce the likelihood that the government will use its power illegitimately to shift wealth from one group of politically weak citizens to a group that has its hands on the levers of power. Even if the increased compensation fails to dissuade the government, the aggrieved minority will suffer a smaller loss at the hands of the majority if paid subjective value.

In the third case, involving legitimate use of the power to acquire land by compulsion, the government makes a decision that benefits the public but burdens an individual. If government fails to compensate landowners for their losses when a governmental project creates a special burden, the deprived owners have, in effect, paid a greater share of the cost than the rest of the public for the advancement of the community interest. If the owners deprived of property are nearly always the wealthiest, the result might be defended on redistributive grounds. But in most developed nations today, wealth takes a variety of forms; there is little correlation between wealth and ownership of land that the government wants to acquire. It is unjust to treat holders of land wealth worse than holders of other wealth and the situation is manifestly more unfair when those suffering the expropriation are the poor. Compulsory purchases for the London Olympics might provide an example of the affirmative injustice done when poor owners shoulder a greater part of the cost of increasing social welfare than others. In short, in nations having enough total wealth to afford it, a concern for fairness requires that the public compensate owners of expropriated land so as to make them whole, and that means paying full subjective value.

Some have argued that compensation should also include an increment for the insult of having land taken against one's will (Rubenfeld 1993; Fennell 2004), and that such an increment ought to be larger when the land will be transferred to private purposes (Garnett 2006). The empirical basis for this claim is yet to be established. It is not clear whether there is any insult to autonomy if the government pays full subjective value, at least if that is measured by the price the owner would demand in a sale. An owner's asking price assumes someone might offer the asking price and, therefore, when a government acquires at that price, there is no insult to be compensated. Even if sellers would choose to discriminate among buyers, charging more to the government, it is not clear that such an anti-community sentiment deserves legal respect. In addition, there may be better ways to reduce the insult to dignity. For example, it may possible to mitigate the insult by training government officials to avoid being arrogant and unfair during the negotiations and educating citizens to the holdout problems that justify expropriations. Such training might cost less and do more to mitigate the perceived insult to dignity than paying for the insult.

Problems with Proposals for Determining an Owner's Subjective Value

The basic problem with paying subjective value is that it is hard to measure (*United States* v. *564.54 Acres of Land* 1979). Owners have an incentive to claim a value higher than their true subjective price, and no incentive to set a low value. In one recent English case, the owner asked for about £9,000,000, but the court awarded £121,000. It is possible that the owner was telling the truth and that his subjective value was 75 times the market price, but it seems more likely that he was exaggerating. This difficulty may be surmountable, but so far the solutions are incomplete.

Self-assessment, coupling compensation to taxation One way to balance the incentives and improve the accuracy of owners' assessments is to make property taxes turn on the same subjective valuation used for compensation. The government could require owners to state a single value to be used in both kinds of situation, taxes and expropriation. Stating a price that is too high would increase taxes, while stating a price that is too low would reduce the compensation for an expropriation. There are two versions of this idea, one in which the government can exercise the right to buy for the price stated by the owner, and the Athenian alternative, which allowed private parties to purchase land at whatever price the owner declared (Posner 2003; Ulen 1992).

Although these are elegant proposals, they raise serious questions of both fairness and efficiency. For one thing, they would result in taxing people on the subjective value of their homes, which is inconsistent with income tax principles, under which subjective income is not taxed. Taxing subjective income would discourage its production. In addition, a shift to taxing subjective value would be regressive to the extent that the ratio of subjective to objective value is higher for poor owners than for wealthy owners. Adoption of either version would also mean that those who are more risk averse and those who live in their houses longer, who tend to be older owners, would pay greater property taxes. Owners without other assets and income sufficient to pay the high property taxes might be forced to reduce their declared value below their true asking price. Moreover, any owner confident that their political power is sufficient to fend off or delay expropriation could value their property at zero and pay no property taxes at all.

Coupling taxes to compensation for governmental expropriation would result in higher taxes being paid by those who live in areas more likely to be subject to governmental expropriation. Because the wealthy tend to be more powerful politically, and sometimes because it makes economic sense, expropriation is often used in areas of poverty. Therefore, owners in such areas will have a larger incentive to state a proportionately higher value than owners in areas where expropriation is unlikely. Having poorer owners pay proportionately greater taxes is unfair and lowers social welfare if marginal utility declines as income rises.

Forcing owners to declare their subjective value also raises opportunities for mistake and consequential unfairness. For many people, subjective value is related to objective value. They know that they place a special subjective premium on their property and they would want compensation of a certain amount, say Y, above and beyond what it would take to buy comparable property. If such persons are told that their house is worth X, they will say they value it at X plus Y because it would take X to replace it objectively, and Y would represent the subjective increment. If such persons mistakenly think the market value is much lower than it is, they will set their value too low and be severely disappointed when the land is taken through public or private expropriation. These inefficient results would be realized much more often if the power to purchase were extended to the public.

Even if inefficient transfers occurred rarely, the costs of uncertainty would be high. Especially under the more radical proposal that anyone could buy any land for the declared value, few owners could feel secure in the ownership of their homes. Most landowners would spend many hours each year trying to determine how to adjust the declared value of their lands to account for both changes that have occurred since the previous valuation and changes that will likely occur before the next. Self-assessment does not appear to be a viable option.

Scientific measurement Another approach to determining subjective value would be to use some scientific measurement of actual subjective loss or gain. With experiments in brain imaging, for example, it is conceivable that we could discover that different regions of the brain activate when an owner is offered more than their subjective value and other regions activate when they are offered less than their subjective value. Subjects might be told, we are taking your house and you will be given compensation. There are two conditions, one group is told $10,000, and the other is told $1,000,000. Their brains might react differently, one with an "injustice" reaction and the other with a reaction involving rational calculation of what to do with the proceeds. If there is a reliable difference, owners' brains could then be scanned as they were offered various prices for their lands. The subjective value could be set at the price at which the owner's brain shifted from one pattern to the other. In other words, brain scans could be used as subjective value detectors.

Unfortunately, there is a serious problem that arises with all attempts to determine an owner's true subjective value. The problem is that subjective value might be changed by actions taken by its holder. If subjective value is determined in part by testimony at a hearing, the process of testifying to a large loss might have the effect of increasing the actual loss. If subjective value is determined by brain imaging, owners might prepare for testing by attempting to shift their internal response so that they would feel, and hence show, more outrage. Such efforts would exacerbate losses. Moreover, under a truly subjective approach, the raging get richer and the placid get poorer. Justice is not served by giving greater compensation to those who have increased their own loss.

Normal Neutral Compensation[2]

The solution for these problems of valuation is not to fall back from subjective value to market value, but rather to moderate to some measure of central tendency, such as the median or average. Setting compensation at the average subjective loss for a given parcel rather than the median would assure that the government would pay for all subjective losses. Although some owners would, of necessity, receive less than their subjective value, many of them would be overcompensated and the net expected gain or loss from a governmental acquisition would be zero. Putting the standard more precisely, those aggrieved by compulsory governmental acquisitions should be awarded such compensation as would make the normal person neutral as to the acquisition. Such a compromise, allowing the average person to anticipate the acquisition of their land without concern, may be the best that can be achieved.[3]

---

2 Perhaps "normally neutralizing compensation" would be a better name despite the additional syllables.

3 The same approach might be advisable for determining the extent of losses from torts and crimes. Rather than having individuals testify to the extent of their loss, brain imaging or other testing might help us to determine the median or average subjective loss. Standardization of losses is implemented in workers' compensation laws.

How Might Normal Neutral Compensation be Determined?

Brain Imaging

As suggested above, experimentation could be done to determine whether there are reliable differences in brain reaction between subjects offered large compensation and those offered small compensation for their land. If there is a difference in reactions, from satisfaction to outrage perhaps, the amounts might be narrowed to find the transition point. If such a point or range could be found, it could be compared with market value of the subjects' lands. A formula could be worked up to estimate the average subjective value of an owner of a parcel having certain attributes.

Perhaps, in the future, brain imaging or other scientific advances will make it possible to get inside the owners' heads and determine how to adjust market value in order to reach average subjective value. Until that day, normal neutral compensation will have to be approximated with other tools, including economics, psychology and biology.

Economics

Initially, it should be noted that in the vast majority of situations, the owner's price will be equal to or greater than the market price less the costs of selling. If the owner's price were less than that, the owner would sell (Posner 1972). Market price is limited to the value of the second most appreciative owner on the planet, less transaction costs. Often, owners do not sell their lands because they derive greater value than any buyer would.

Sometimes, the very action of the government changes the price of land similar to the land being acquired by expropriation. For example, if the government takes enough land suitable for farming in a given district and the demand for farming land is sufficiently inelastic, the price of comparable land after the taking will be higher than the price of similar land before the taking. Should the owner get the lower value before the project started, the higher value at the end, or some intermediate value? If the owner is to be made whole, the owner should receive enough to be able to buy a similar parcel after the expropriations for the project are completed. However, as compensation is often calculated by reference to sales of comparable parcels that were negotiated before the project affected the market, the owner will often be undercompensated.

Expropriations reduce the supply to the private sector without reducing demand, resulting in an increase in price. In the case of India, for example, many of the displaced farmers apparently could not buy new farms with their compensation. Hence, the common administrative necessity of referring to past prices is not neutral, overall, but rather biases the process towards undercompensation. The unfairness in this bias is most obvious in cases like *Kelo*, where parcels taken by the government will be transferred to private parties for profitable uses (Krier & Serkin 2004; Serkin 2005).

There is another bias in the compensation process that might work against poor owners and in favour of the wealthy. The variance in the resources spent contesting valuation will be greater on the owner side than on the government side. To argue for a low valuation of the parcel, the government will nearly always be prepared to allocate a basic staff and, even for valuable parcels, will probably not allocate a large staff. By contrast, because the owners are mostly one-shot players, they will allocate to the effort of establishing a high valuation only the staff that is economically justified for that single case. For a valuable parcel, that might mean a staff that is larger and better equipped than the government's opposing staff. For a modest parcel, the owner might not be justified in spending anything on lawyers and other advocates because the increase in compensation that they would obtain would not be enough to pay their fees. Thus the owners of valuable properties will be more willing to spend money to establish full market value, while the poor owners will be less willing to do so. In the cases that are actually heard, the owners of valuable property are likely to get a larger portion of the value than the owners of modest parcels. Moreover, the government knows this, and might decide from the beginning, in light of those facts, to grant a larger portion of market value to the owners of more valuable parcels.

In addition to market value, and simply to make owners whole, governments should pay owners of condemned land the costs of relocating to other lands. The high failure rate for businesses after relocation (Frieden & Sagalyn 1989; Elwood 1994) indicates that relocating increases costs or reduces revenues. English law recognizes that relocation costs ought to be included in the expropriation award. According to the London Development Agency (LDA):

> [t]he principle of the CPO code is to ensure that you should be no worse off as a result of the compulsory acquisition of your property. Typical items of compensation for disturbance and relocation include removal expenses, legal fees arising from the acquisition of a new property and fitting out costs for new premises. The LDA will pay reasonable fees associated with your relocation, your surveyor will negotiate this on your behalf.

Relocation costs have not been recognized as an essential part of just compensation by the United States Supreme Court in its interpretations of the US constitution. Nevertheless, relocation costs are often underwritten for residential owners, albeit less so for business owners (Garnett 2006).

One of the possible costs of relocation for individuals is the cost of changing employment. Some jobs do not pay enough to justify commuting from a more distant residence acquired after expropriation. In such cases, the award should cover the lost work time and other costs of transition to a similar job in a new location. In other cases, the owner will not be able to find similar employment. For the displaced Indian farmers, the loss of farms meant the loss of their livelihoods. India is considering providing housing and perhaps trying to find jobs for the displaced tribal farm owners. By contrast, the US constitution does not require that the displaced resident be compensated for loss of his job.

Experimental Psychology

Are there any other systematic differences between the owner's subjective value and market value? Experiments by a number of researchers support the claim that owners should be paid more than the amount buyers are willing to pay. In one set of experiments by Kahneman, Knetsch and Thaler, student subjects were divided into three groups, "sellers", "buyers" and "choosers". Sellers were given a coffee mug; buyers were given a chance to buy a mug; choosers were given an option to get a mug. The students were then offered the opportunity to make purchases or sales. The buyers were asked to state the most they would pay for a mug. The sellers were asked to state the least they would take to sell their mug and the choosers were asked to state the least they would take to sell their option. In one of the studies, the median valuations for the mug were sellers: $7.12; choosers: $3.12; buyers: $2.87. In another study, the valuations were sellers: $7.00; choosers: $3.50; buyers: $2.00. The amounts the sellers were willing to accept was systematically higher than the amounts the buyers were willing to pay. Owner-possessors of mugs valued them about 100% more than owners of financially equivalent options to get mugs.

The experiments were not made for the purpose of determining compensation for expropriations, but analogies can be made. In some ways, the buyers are like the land buyers whose offers form the basis of market value. Although they are familiar with the attributes of the item, they do not own it and must give up their cash to obtain it. The choosers are owners of the item, and their valuations are systematically higher than the buyers', by a ratio of something like two to one. This suggests that a landowner's subjective value might be much higher than the market value, in the average case.

The implications can be taken another, more important, step. Some landowners are in possession; others are not. Those who are not in possession are like the choosers in the experiments, having paper rights of ownership or title. Landowners in possession are like the sellers, who have both title and possession. In the experiments, the owners in possession valued their mugs at nearly twice the price of owners out of possession. If the experimental results can be extended to real cases of land being taken by the government, landowners in possession should be paid twice the compensation paid landowners out of possession.

These experiments on exchange asymmetry have been replicated many times and in many contexts (Kahneman, Knetsch & Thaler 1990, 1991; Knetsch & Sinden 1984). However, Knez and Smith (1987) found that these effects did not persist in repeated market situations. Their findings would appear to be inapplicable to expropriation cases, however, as the landowners are usually not repeat traders of land. Plott and Zeiler (2005) have recently contended that the differences between willingness to accept (WTA) and willingness to pay (WTP) found in earlier studies are not due to irrational human psychology but rather are artifacts of the experiments. For example, in the mug experiments the students give mugs special value because the teacher intentionally made the gift and because it saves transaction costs to keep what you have. More replications need to be done, with refinements appropriate to the compulsory purchase context.

Even assuming that further research confirms that there is a disparity between WTP and WTA and that the disparity is heightened by possession, there are situations in which it might not be appropriate to increase the compensation above market value. When the owner is a publicly held corporation, for example, the disparity between WTP and WTA might be small or might not exist at all, and possession should not lead to greater compensation (Stake 1995).

Biology

Elderly humans get sick more easily and do not recover as well after being moved from their homes. Displacement is harmful, and biological experiments show that the costs of displacement vary with circumstances.

Krebs (1982) studied territorial defence in the great tit. He removed birds from their territories, allowed newcomers to occupy the territories and then released original possessors. Upon meeting, the new and old possessors would often fight and Krebs noted how long they fought. His results show that the longer an invader has possession, the longer it will fight to retain possession.

It is possible, however, that while birds fight longer, they do not fight as hard, with the result that they actually spend less energy trying to retain possession as time passes. A study of European robins by Tobias (1997) indicates otherwise. Like Krebs, he removed possessors and released them after their territories had been occupied by others. Tobias found that the longer birds possess, the more likely they will successfully resist eviction. After 10 days have passed, newcomers always won. These findings, suggesting that birds fight harder with time in possession, reinforce the Krebs finding that birds fight longer to retain possession as their time of possession increases.

As time in possession increases, birds fight longer and with more success. This increased willingness to expend resources to retain possession is a measure of an increased subjective value of the land to them. Thus value to the birds increases with time in possession. Justice Oliver Wendell Holmes, Jr. knew this to be true for men as well. "[M]an, like a tree in the cleft of a rock, gradually shapes his roots to his surroundings, and when the roots have grown to a certain size, can't be displaced without cutting at his life" (Holmes 1907). But the core of that idea was not new to him, for Jeremy Bentham (1789) had said, "[O]ur property becomes a part of our being, and cannot be torn from us without rending us to the quick."

The principles confirmed by the bird experiments, though long recognized by writers deeply influential in the law, have not yet been imported into the law of just compensation. If for humans as for birds, value increases with length of possession, the compensation due residents evicted from their homes should increase with the duration of their possession (Knetsch & Borcherding 1979). In the New London condemnation, Wilhelmina Dery should get some extra compensation for her 87 years of residence in her New London home. Suzette Kelo, by contrast, would get a lower supplement, given that she had been in possession for only 13 months.

Fee (2006) proposed a statutory schedule of personal detachment awards. That schedule adds 2 per cent of the market value for each additional year of home ownership, up to 30 years. To prevent longstanding owners in the path of a highway from taking advantage of this law by inefficiently improving their lands and receiving a multiple of their investment back from the government upon expropriation, the increased market value from improvements after notice of the possible expropriation would have to be excluded. Even with such an exclusion, there is some risk that owners in areas with appreciable potential for expropriation would overdevelop their lands.

In addition to that potential for inefficiency, a simple multiplier for duration of possession might be unfair. It is possible that deprivation of home causes similar feelings of loss to all owners, regardless of the market value of the home. The home triggers fond memories in the minds of the poor the same as in the minds of the rich. Furthermore, the poor owner, deprived of home by expropriation, will have far fewer choices for a replacement home, and thus might be less able to find a satisfactory replacement. Developing new social connections might also be more difficult for the poor. Thursz (1966) found that five years after the destruction of a neighbourhood in Southwest District of Columbia for urban renewal, one quarter of the displaced residents had not made a single new friend. For these reasons, a fixed monetary increment for each year of possession might be more appropriate than a percentage increment.

Another implication from the bird studies is that the attachment to a home grows for each person in possession, not just the owner. When they are forced to move, children will have to learn how to negotiate a new school and, like their parents, will often need to make new friends.

Spouses, like owners, will need to develop a new web of neighbours, and perhaps find a new job. Because expropriation breaks up communities and severs ties for all residents, compensation ought to be awarded to every displaced member of the household with sufficient tenure to form ties to social networks and physical structures. Doing so would compensate family members for losses of friends and school and work.

Similarly, biological analysis suggests that tenants, like freeholders and their families, ought to be paid for their loss of possession upon expropriation, as was provided in the Land Compensation Act 1973 (Moore 1990), unless those rights are reassigned (Goldberg, Merrill & Unumb 1987). Payments for each displaced person, including family members along with tenants, could be justified on other grounds as well. In a study of eminent domain used for urban renewal in Chicago, Munch (1976) found that owners of low-value parcels systematically received less than market value. If low-value parcels have relatively high occupancy rates, paying compensation for each displaced person could partially correct the imbalance.

Tobias's experiments with European robins showed that time in possession affects willingness to fight and success in defending possession. Tobias's experiments also indicate that time out of possession has opposite effects. He varied the removed bird's time out of possession while controlling for the replacement's time in possession. As the removed bird is kept away from home longer, it loses interest. It becomes less willing to fight protracted battles and less likely to regain possession from the replacement bird. The implications for just compensation policy are obvious. The possessory increment should be rolled back during periods of extended absence.

Krebs summed up his findings with a graph showing the change in value of territory with possession and absence. As possession lengthened, value increased. As absence lengthened, value decreased. Absence did not make the great tit heart grow fonder. These findings support the conclusion that compensation paid to those who suffer compulsory purchase orders should increase with their time in possession, but that possessory increment should decrease with time out of possession.

Another issue related to just compensation is raised by experiments with our close animal cousins. Brosnan and de Waal (2003) found that capuchins and chimpanzees react differently to exchanges depending on what is offered to other subjects. They taught the subjects to exchange tokens for food, both cucumbers and grapes. The subjects preferred grapes to cucumbers, but were happy to exchange the token for either type of food in the baseline condition. Then the condition was altered so that the subjects were given a cucumber after seeing another animal receive a grape for their token. The behaviour of the subjects changed dramatically. Once they had seen another capuchin or chimp receive a grape for a token, they were no longer happy to exchange their token for a cucumber.

The implication for just compensation is not hard to deduce. When the government expropriates more than one parcel, the fairness of compensation given each owner in the area depends on what the others receive. That principle has temporal consequences as well: the compensation scheme for the whole development should be decided before anyone is paid.

Brosnan and de Waal's fairness experiments suggest another point. It is possible that owners who lose property through compulsory purchase compare their lot not only to that of their neighbours but also to that of the new owners of the land. If it is the government that uses the land, it might be difficult to make such a comparison and owners might not feel they have been treated unfairly. But if the government turns the property over to private persons, the former owners might feel much like the capuchins that received only cucumbers while seeing the new owners receive grapes.[4] To prevent the resentment that would accompany such feelings, the old owners should be granted an opportunity to be among the new

4 The government might be like the experimenter. It would be interesting to know whether the capuchins or chimps would react the same way if there were a person in the adjoining cage making exchanges instead of the con-specific in the adjoining cage.

residents if there are private homes included in the project. Alternatively, and less tangibly, the old landowners should have an opportunity to own a share of the new development, so that if private individuals are going to profit by the expropriation, those who lost land, especially homes or businesses, should be among them. Such a requirement, as a component of normal neutral compensation, could go far to reduce the incentives for rent-seeking, which can cause private developers to employ the government's power of expropriation rather than pursue private negotiations for the land they want.

Experimental studies done to date have established a number of principles that should be applied in determining the compensation to be paid owners: owners should be paid more than the average buyer would pay; possessors should be paid more than mere owners; each possessor should be paid, not just the owner; longer possession should trigger greater compensation; longer absence should reduce the possessory increment; owners should be paid similarly; and owners should be given a cut of the action if private profits are possible.

Evolutionary analysis suggests one further point. Humans may form particularly strong loyalties to groups the size of the bands in which our ancestors hunted and gathered. For that reason, owners may feel special losses when an expropriation destroys their community in addition to removing them from it. Surveying those displaced from Boston's West End, Gans (1962) found that 46 per cent of women and 38 per cent of men suffered "fairly severe grief" after their community was obliterated by expropriation (Garnett 2006). Similarly, residents of Poletown, Michigan, were distraught at the destruction of their local church. If attachments are stronger when group size is smaller, we should expect those displaced to discount the benefits to the larger nation more than the losses imposed on the smaller tribe. As a result of this differential discounting, the owners might feel that the losses outweigh the gains even in cases where, as a matter of accounting, the gains are actually greater. Perhaps large-scale projects should pay additional compensation to owners for the destruction of their local communities.

Future Research

Future research on exchange asymmetry should focus more closely on the amounts to be added to market value in order to reach just compensation. How much more should owner-occupiers receive than mere owners, and should that be a ratio or a fixed sum? Should loss of home or farm or small business receive a fixed amount of extra compensation for those losses, on top of the increment given to all owners in actual occupation? Should the government pay each dispossessed person a fixed sum on the theory that they all suffer similarly upon the loss of home? How quickly should the fixed increments increase as possession lengthens, and how quickly should they decrease as absence continues? Does our sense of justice require that evicted owners be given a part of the profits if the developer will be making a profit? Answers to these questions might be found in further experiments along the lines of those discussed above. In addition, survey research using hypothetical questions might shed light on the perceived justice of various levels of compensation in varying situations.

Conclusion

Law influences behaviour by setting prices on behaviours. Equally important, it influences behaviour by setting norms to be followed not out of a sense of fear but out of a sense of community. Expropriations breed a sense of community, but not necessarily a healthy one. From Detroit to Orissa, undercompensated owners have taken to the streets in protest. One aggrieved American owner said she would not send her boys to fight for the country because they would not be fighting for freedom. High dissatisfaction with expropriations may undermine public faith in the law and increase disrespect for the government. If the law is to serve its coordinating and civilizing functions, it needs the respect of the people, and to receive respect it needs to be worthy of respect.

Getting compensation closer to right could increase efficiency and will increase perceived justice, while also reducing the pressure on the divisive question of when governments should be permitted to exercise the power to expropriate. Making compensation just will foster the law's ability to coordinate human behaviour for the welfare of all. Biological experiments indicate that owners should be given more than market value when their lands are taken against their will. Further research, building our knowledge about the brain's attachment to property, will help determine how much compensation needs be added to market value in order to achieve justice.

Bibliography

Uniform Relocation Assistance and Real Property Acquisition Policies Act of 1970, 42 U.S.C. §§ 4601–4655 (1982); 42 U.S.C. §§ 4601–4655 (2000).

Armstrong v. *United States*, 364 U.S. 40, 49 (1960).

Attorney-General v. *De Keyser's Royal Hotel, Ltd.*, A.C. 508 (H.L.) 1920.

Berman v. *Parker*, 348 U.S. 26 (1954).

Brown v. *Legal Foundation of Washington*, 538 U.S. 216 (2003).

City of Minneapolis v. *Shutt*, 256 N.W.2d 260 (Minn. 1977).

Hawaii Housing Authority v. *Midkiff*, 467 U.S. 229 (1984).

United States v. *564.54 Acres of Land*, 441 U.S. 506, 511 (1979).

United States v. *50 Acres of Land*, 469 U.S. 24, 29 (1984).

Department for Communities and Local Development, Explanatory Memorandum to the Home Loss Payments (Prescribed Amounts) (England) Regulations 2006 No. 1658, available at: www.opsi.gov.uk/si/em2006/uksiem_20061658_en.pdf (last visited 27 April 2008).

Statutory Instrument 2006 No. 1658, Compensation, England, Home Loss Payments (Prescribed Amounts) (England) Regulations 2006, available at: http://www.opsi.gov.uk/si/si2006/20061658.htm (last visited 27 April 2008).

Welsh Statutory Instrument 2006 No. 1789 (W.185), Acquisition of Land, Wales, The Home Loss Payments (Prescribed Amounts) (Wales) Regulations 2006, available at: http://www.opsi.gov.uk/legislation/wales/wsi2006/20061789e.htm (last visited 27 April 2008).

Alexander, Gregory S. (2006), *The Global Debate over Constitutional Property*, University of Chicago Press, Chicago.

Bentham, Jeremy (1789), *The Theory of Legislation, Principles of the Civil Code*, pt. I, ch. 10, at 115 (C.K. Ogden ed., Richard Hildreth trans., Routledge & Kegan Paul Ltd. 1950).

Berger, Curtis J. & Rohan, Patrick J. (1967), The Nassau County Study: An Empirical Look into the Practice of Condemnation, 67 *Columbia L. Rev.* 430.

Bible, I Kings 21

Blume, Lawrence & Rubinfeld, Daniel L. (1984), Compensation for Takings: An Economic Analysis, 72 *Cal. L. Rev.* 569–624.

Brosnan, S.F. & de Waal, F.B.M. (2003), Monkeys Reject Unequal Pay, 425 *Nature* 297–299. (doi:10.1038/nature01963)

Castle Coalition (2007), *Fifty State Report Card*, available at: http://www.castlecoalition.org/pdf/publications/report_card/50_State_Report.pdf (last visited 20 April 2008).

Dukeminier, Jesse, Krier, James E., Alexander, Gregory S. & Schill, Michael H. (2006), *Property*, Aspen Publishers, New York.

Ellickson, Robert C. (1989), Bringing Culture and Human Frailty to Rational Actors: A Critique of Law and Economics, 65 *Chi-Kent L. Rev.* 23, 35–39.

Elwood, John P. (1994), Rethinking Government Participation in Urban Renewal: Neighborhood Revitalization in New Haven, 12 *Yale L. & Pol. Rev.* 138, 179.

Epstein, Richard A. (1985), *Takings: Private Property & the Power of Eminent Domain*, Harvard U. Press, Cambridge Massachusetts.

Farber, Daniel A. (1992), Public Choice and Just Compensation, 9 *Const. Commentary* 279.

Fee, John (2006), Eminent Domain and the Sanctity of Home, 81 *Notre Dame L. Rev.* 783–819.

Fennell, Lee Anne (2004), Taking Eminent Domain Apart, 2004 *Mich. St. L. Rev.* 957.

Fischel, William A. (2004), The Political Economy of Public Use in *Poletown*: How Federal Grants Encourage Excessive Use of Eminent Domain, 2004 *Mich. St. L. Rev.* 929.

Frieden, Bernard J. & Sagalyn, Lynne B. (1989), *Downtown, Inc.: How America Rebuilds Cities*. MIT Press.

Gans, Herbert J. (1962), *The Urban Villagers: Group and Class in the Life of Italian-Americans*, The Free Press, New York; Collier-Macmillan Limited, London.

Garnett, Nicole Stelle (2006), The Neglected Political Economy of Eminent Domain, 105 *Michigan L. Rev.* 101.

Goldberg, Victor P., Merrill, Thomas W. & Unumb, Daniel (1987), Bargaining in the Shadow of Eminent Domain: Valuing and Apportioning Condemnation Awards Between Landlord and Tenant, 34 *UCLA L. Rev.* 1083–1021.

Hartman, Chester W. (1971), Relocation: Illusory Promises and No Relief, 57 *Va. L. Rev.* 745.

Hoffman, Elizabeth & Spitzer, Matthew L. (1993), Entitlements, Rights, and Fairness: An Experimental Examination of Subjects' Concepts of Distributive Justice, 14 *J. Leg. Stud.* 259.

Holmes, Oliver Wendel (1907) Letter from Oliver Wendel Holmes, Jr. William James (Apr. 1, 1907), in *The Mind and Faith of Justice Holmes: His Speeches, Essays, Letters and Judicial Opinions*, 417, 417–418 (Max Lerner ed., 1943).

Jacobs, Marcus & Gildenhuys, Antonie (1990), Expropriation in South Africa, pp 373–399 in volume I of *Compensation for Expropriation: a comparative study* (Gavin M. Erasmus ed.) Published by Jason Reese in association with The United Kingdom National Committee of Comparative Law, Oxford, 1990.

Kahneman, Daniel & Tversky, Amos (1984), Choices, values and frames, 39 *Am. Psychol.* 341–350.

Kahneman, Daniel, Knetsch, Jack L. & Thaler, Richard H. (1990), Experimental Tests of the Endowment Effect and the Coase Theorem, 98 *J. Pol. Econ.* 1325–1348.

Kahneman, Daniel, Knetsch, Jack L. & Thaler, Richard H. (1991), The Endowment Effect, Loss Aversion, and Status Quo Bias: anomalies, 5 *J. Econ. Persp.* 193–206.

Knetsch, Jack L. (1983), *Property Rights and Compensation: Compulsory Acquisition and Other Losses*, Butterworths, Toronto.

Knetsch, Jack L. & Borcherding, Thomas E. (1979), Expropriation of Private Property and the Basis for Compensation, 29 *U. Toronto L. J.* 237–252.

Knetsch, Jack L. & Sinden, J.A. (1984), Willingness to Pay and Compensation Demanded: Experimental Evidence of an Unexpected Disparity in Measures of Value, 99 *Q.J. Econ.* 507.

Knez, Marc & Smith, Vernon L. (1987), Hypothetical Valuations and Preference Reversals in the Context of Asset Trading, in *Laboratory Experimentation in Economics*, 132 (Alvin E. Roth ed., 1987).

Krebs, John R. (1982), Territorial Defence in the Great Tit (Parus major): Do Residents Always Win? 11 *Behav. Ecol. Sociobiol.* 185–194.

Heller, Michael A. & Krier, James E. (1999), Deterrence and Distribution in the Law of Takings, 112 *Harv. L. Rev.* 997–1025.

Krier, James E. & Serkin, Christopher (2004), Public Ruses, 4 *Mich. St. L. Rev.* 859–875.

Levinson, Daryl (2000), Making Government Pay: Markets, Politics, and the Allocation of Constitutional Costs, 67 *U. Chi. L. Rev.* 345.

Levmore, Saul (1999), Changes, Anticipations, and Reparations, 99 *Columbia L. Rev.* 1657–1700.

Merrill, Thomas W. (1986), The Economics of Public Use, 72 *Cornell L. Rev.* 61, 83–85.

Merrill, Thomas W. (2002), Incomplete Compensation for Takings, 11 *N.Y.U. Envtl. L.J.* 110, 111.

Merrill, Thomas W. (2005), Brief for the American Planning Association, et. al. as *Amici Curiae*, Supporting Respondents, *Kelo* v. *City of New London*, 2005 WL 166929.

Michelman, Frank I. (1967), Property Utility, and Fairness: Comments on the Ethical Foundations of "Just Compensation" Law, 80 *Harv. L. Rev.* 1165.

Moore, Victor (1990), Compulsory Purchase in the United Kingdom, pp1–31 in volume I of *Compensation for Expropriation: a comparative study* (Gavin M. Erasmus ed.) Published by Jason Reese in association with The United Kingdom National Committee of Comparative Law, Oxford, 1990.

Munch, Patricia (1976), An Economic Analysis of Eminent Domain, 84 *J. of Political Economy* 473–497.

Picard, Etienne (1990), Expropriation in France, pp33–80 in volume I of *Compensation for Expropriation: a comparative study* (Gavin M. Erasmus ed.) Published by Jason Reese in association with The United Kingdom National Committee of Comparative Law, Oxford, 1990.

Plott, Charles R. & Zeiler, Kathryn (2005), The Willingness to Pay-Willingness to Accept Gap, the "Endowment Effect," Subject Misconceptions, and Experimental Procedures for Eliciting Valuations, 95 *Am. Econ. Rev.* 530.

Posner, Richard A. (1972), *Economic Analysis of Law*, Little, Brown and Company, Boston.

Posner, Richard A. (2003), *Economic Analysis of Law*, 6th ed., Aspen Publishers, New York.

Rachlinski, Jeffrey J. & Jordan, Forest (1998), Remedies and the Psychology of Ownership, 51 *Vand. L. Rev.* 1541.

Rubenfeld, Jed (1993), Usings, 102 *Yale L.J.* 1077, 1133–34.

Schmidt-Aßmann, Eberhard (1990), Expropriation in the Federal Republic of Germany, pp81–103 at 90–91 in volume I of *Compensation for Expropriation: a comparative study* (Gavin M. Erasmus ed.) Published by Jason Reese in association with The United Kingdom National Committee of Comparative Law, Oxford, 1990.

Serkin, Christopher (2005), The Meaning of Value: Assessing Just Compensation for Regulatory Takings, 99 *Nw. U. L. Rev.* 679.

Singh, Mahendra P. (1990), Expropriation in India, pp34–57 in volume II of *Compensation for Expropriation: a comparative study* (Gavin M. Erasmus ed.) Published by Jason Reese in association with The United Kingdom National Committee of Comparative Law, Oxford, 1990.

Stake, Jeffrey Evans (1995), Loss Aversion and Involuntary Transfers of Title, Chapter 10 in Robin Paul Malloy and Christopher K. Braun, *Law and*

Economics New and Critical Perspectives, volume 4 in *Critic of Institutions*, (Robert Kevelson general editor) Lang, New York.

Thaler, Richard H. (1980), Toward a Positive Theory of Consumer Choice. 1 *J. Econ. Behav. & Org.* 39–60.

Thursz, Daniel (1966), *Where Are They Now?* Health and Welfare Council of the National Capital Area, Washington, D.C.

Tobias, Joe (1997), Asymmetric Territorial Contests in the European Robin: The Role of Settlement Costs. 54 *Anim. Behav.* 9–21.

Todd, Eric C.E. (1990), Compensation for Expropriation in Canada, pp 321–357 in volume 1 of *Compensation for Expropriation: a comparative study* (Gavin M. Erasmus ed.) Published by Jason Reese in association with The United Kingdom National Committee of Comparative Law, Oxford, 1990.

Ulen, Thomas S. (1992), The Public Use of Private Property: A Dual-Constraint Theory of Efficient Governmental Takings, in *Taking Property & Just Compensation: Law & Economics Perspectives of the Takings Issue* 168–198 (Nicholas Mercurio ed.) Kluwer Academic Publishers, London, 1992.

van der Walt, A.J. (1999), *Constitutional Property Clauses: a comparative analysis*, Kluwer Law International, Juta & Co. Ltd., Cape Town, South Africa, 1999.

Chapter 14
Examining the Biological Bases of Family Law: Lessons to be Learned for the Evolutionary Analysis of Law

June Carbone[1] and Naomi Cahn[2]

This chapter examines the insights that the biology of attachment (including evolutionary analysis and neuroscience data) offers for understanding the relationship between family law and family stability and then analyses the limitations of this analysis. The chapter initially considers evolutionary analysis, comparative anatomy and neuroscience data to conclude that while the pair bond appears to be a universal feature of human sciences, long-term fidelity is not. The second part of the chapter considers the benefits and limitations of evolutionary analysis concluding, first, that evolutionary analysis, without connection to modern neuroscience or sociological data, remains highly speculative; second, that where the evolutionary analysis is borne out by modern neuroscience and/or sociological data, it is more persuasive, but often obvious; and third, that undertaking this type of examination nonetheless leads to new insights or new questions that should prompt productive research.

If evolutionary analysis has any salience for law, it is likely to have important insights for family law. Families, after all, are about the most biologically based of human activities: sex and reproduction. Indeed, some would say the very concept of family starts with a biological construction rooted in the ordering and regulation of biological relationships. Yet, precisely for this reason, evolutionary analysis, to be influential, must overcome resistance to the very idea of the undertaking. Some of these objections are present whenever the issue of evolutionary analysis of law is raised, but they are often asserted with more emotion in the context of the family for understandable reasons.

Take, for example, one of the most basic objections, that of the naturalistic fallacy. This doctrine posits that an "ought" should not be derived from an "is". Evolutionary analysis might suggest, for example, that 1) it takes a man and a woman (or at least an egg and a sperm) to produce a child, 2) adults are more likely to look out for children who are biologically theirs, 3) men and women tend to form pair-bonds that

---

1 Edward A. Smith/Missouri Professor of Law, the Constitution and Society, University of Missouri-Kansas City.

2 Professor of Law, George Washington University.

facilitate reproduction, 4) human children take longer to raise than the offspring of other closely related species, and 5) the pair-bond is therefore likely to have arisen to facilitate human child-rearing. Some authors might then conclude that children should be raised in two-parent biological families, and law should stigmatize and discourage the formation of single-parent, same-sex, step-parent or other less favoured families. While almost all scholars recognize that any simple-minded move from evolutionary observations to societal prescriptions is a misuse of evolutionary analysis,[3] the very fact that the family orders indisputably biological activities inflames fears of misuse. After all, any number of commentators who do not pretend to endorse evolutionary analysis argue that the family of biologically related mothers, fathers and children is naturally (if not divinely) ordained, and certainly better for the well-being of children. In the context of such a debate, greater emphasis on biology, critics fear, can only serve to increase intolerance for alternative families.

We believe that such fears are well founded, and we and many others who would undertake evolutionary analysis have addressed them.[4] In this chapter, however, we wish to take on a different issue, that is, whether at the end of the analysis, after all of the qualifications and disclaimers have been added, evolutionary analysis has anything to add and, if so, whether the insights it supplies make it a worthwhile subject of endeavour for law professors. Take, for example, the issue of family composition. Casual observation suggests, without any evolutionary analysis at all, that 1) it takes a man and a woman (or at least an egg and a sperm) to produce a child, 2) adults are more likely to look out for children who are biologically theirs, 3) men and women tend to form pair-bonds that facilitate reproduction and child-rearing, 4) human children take longer to raise than the offspring of other closely related species, and 5) children whose parents stay together and care for them tend to do better than children whose parents do not. Whether or not these observations are true, however, is more a matter for conventional sociology than a biology lab. Studies show, for example, that American children who are adopted or whose mothers are widowed do about as well as children in conventional two-parent families, but the same is not true of either hunter-gatherers (where the survival of both parents may have a dramatic impact on the children's life expectancy) or children raised by never-married Americans. Moreover, even determining that it is sometimes true that two-parent biological families produce better outcomes for children raises a host of additional causal issues. Never-married mothers, for example, are different from widowed mothers in ways that may be more important than the fact they head a single-parent family. Within the context of such a complex debate, what can evolutionary analysis add for law professors?

Owen Jones has provided the most considered answer. He argues that the most critical contribution evolutionary analysis makes is what he calls the "Law of Law's Leverage":

3 See, e.g., Pope (2005 p. 56).

4 See, e.g., Jones (2001, p. 207); Jones & Goldsmith (2005, p. 405); Carbone & Cahn (2004, p. 223) (the analysis in this chapter is adapted from the fuller study of the biological issues in this article).

> The magnitude of legal intervention necessary to reduce or to increase the incidence of any human behaviour will correlate positively or negatively, respectively, with the extent to which a predisposition contributing to that behaviour was adaptive for its bearers, on average, in past environments.[5]

We believe that Jones's statement is correct both in its description of human behaviour, and its conclusion that correctly identifying human behaviour likely to be resistant to change is a worthwhile endeavour. The problems arise, however, in determining 1) when we want to develop an appropriate "legal intervention"; and 2) whether a "predisposition" that contributed to the behaviour was "adaptive". And these issues may be more central to family law than the origins of the behaviour at issue. We thus are not certain how useful Jones's law concerning evolutionary analysis will turn out to be for law professors.

In this chapter, we plan to describe our own adventures in considering the role of evolutionary analysis in family law. In the process, we have learned a fair amount, educated others and become cautious proponents of the enterprise. Our experiences, however, have convinced us that the most important question is not whether evolutionary analysis is necessarily accurate, precise or provable, but whether it takes a worthwhile path of inquiry along which we would otherwise not have travelled.

Our ultimate answer is that for evolutionary analysis to be useful we must lower our expectations. We believe that evolutionary analysis is unlikely to provide a wholesale substitute for other social science techniques or for traditional legal analysis. Instead, at its best, it may lead us to ask different questions, to adopt different techniques and to continue to questioning the received wisdom of more conventional research. Once we have formulated the right questions, the process of answering them might not be different at all from conventional legal, sociological or ethical analysis involving positive descriptions of behaviour followed by norm development. The question must therefore be whether these questions are worth asking. We present our own ventures in family law as support for a tentative conclusion that they are.

In this chapter, we will describe our initial family law hypothesis, the time sink involved in exploring the full range of data that might support our speculation, the risks of overgeneralization and reductionism to be avoided, the refining of the question into a more productive form, and the final result of the inquiry: commitment to an exciting new project that involves only the slightest incorporation of biological inquiry.

Evolutionary Analysis: Law Professors Beware

We began our inquiry into an evolutionary analysis of family law with a simple hypothesis.[6] We speculated that the evolutionary literature would show that the

5 Jones and Goldsmith (2005, p. 461).

6 We have completed papers that incorporate evolutionary analysis of family law, one that examines the role of step-fathers and a second on the biological basis of commitment.

pair-bond[7] is a universal of the human species, but that long-term fidelity is not. We expected to conclude therefore that while people could be expected readily to form pair-bonds, it would require far greater societal intervention to produce long-term fidelity and that, indeed, the history of "civilization" would bear us out.[8]

We approached our hypothesis in a manner that evolutionary analysts might have recommended: we tried to determine the evolutionary conditions that produced the pair-bond in the first place. Doing so may have been a mistake on two grounds. First, we took the universality of the pair-bond as a given, and considered "universality" to mean that couples form pair-bonds in virtually all societies, and that virtually all (90% or more) individuals who have the opportunity to form a pair-bond will do so at some time in their life. The interdisciplinary sources we consulted supported the assertion and no legal audience has questioned it.[9] When we presented the work to an audience that included anthropologists, however, the first question was whether we maintained that such a thing as human nature existed? We think the question is a good one that it has taken us a long time to answer. Our starting assumption that the pair-bond is a universal of the species was intended as a positive assertion that the human pair-bond is species-typical behaviour. Evolutionary biologists start with an assumption that closely related species exhibit different behaviour because of genetic differences that arose in the context of the factors related to the divergence from a common ancestor.[10] Some anthropologists, however, maintain that all human behaviour is culturally determined, and reject any assertion that human behaviour differs from that

---

In this chapter, we will focus only on the second, which undertook a more in-depth evolutionary examination. The comments on the second project, however, also apply to the first. Carbone & Cahn (2003, 2004).

7 We spent several successive drafts trying to define the pair-bond, and settled on "intense emotional attachments to a single partner". Carbone & Cahn (2004, p. 224). We did not specify either sexual activity or sexuality exclusivity because we thought it appropriate to leave open chaste but emotionally intense attachments (though we expected the emotional intensity to involve sexual attraction) and sexually promiscuous but emotionally faithful pairings. We also did not specify length, though if we had we would have suggested "for a period longer than that necessary to insure the woman's pregnancy".

8 Our hypothesis is hardly original. See, e.g., Jones's comment that: "Evolutionary analysis predicts and explains why the slope of the demand curve for adulterous behavior is likely to be comparatively steep, as is the slope for most sexual behavior, and thus comparatively insensitive to the imposition of legal prohibitions, or other costs, such as effect on career. It also predicts and may help explain why marriage, separation, divorce, and remarriage behavior will be less sensitive to legal changes – at least in moderately democratic cultures – than will be many other forms of behavior." Jones & Goldsmith (2005, p. 463–64).

9 Carbone & Cahn (2004, p. 230).

10 In Darwin's original work, for example, he examined the development of separate species of finches that rose as the original species settled on different, isolated islands with slightly different habitats and food sources. Darwin (1839, ch. XVII).

of chimpanzees because of innate characteristics. To engage the research on evolutionary biology required acceptance of the notion that species-typical behaviour exists and has genetic roots. After some consideration, however, we have concluded that as law professors we have no basis on which to take a position in the controversy, and the assertion that such a thing as human nature exists may not be necessary to our family law conclusions. Nonetheless, we remain troubled by the question of how many interdisciplinary controversies are embedded in our assumptions, and how many we need to resolve to have a credible product. Law professors who start with the question of whether a given behaviour is "adaptive to its bearers" may wish to explore (as we did not) whether they are taking a position on the issue of whether a particular methodology makes it possible to determine what is adaptive and what is not in a rigorous way.[11]

Our second reason for hesitation is that, putting methodology aside, we are now quite convinced that law professors (at least *qua* law professors) are in no position to determine when and why the pair-bond arose – period. Reaching that point nonetheless took us through a fascinating and time-consuming inquiry. No one without tenure should attempt it. Researchers speculate that the human species diverged from a common primate ancestor approximately 6–7 million years ago. No record exists, of course, that makes it possible to determine early human behaviour, so anatomical remains provide the best clues. Biologists hypothesize that "the more mates a male can expect to have in comparison with other males, the larger he is likely to be in comparison with females of the species".[12] A high degree of sexual dimorphism is therefore inconsistent with the existence of a sexually exclusive pair-bond. Some of the earliest hominid remains are those of *Australopithecus afarensis*, a species that lived approximately 3½ million years ago. Initial investigation of the bones concluded that the species exhibited a high degree of sexual dimorphism. More recent publications suggest that males and females exhibited no greater differences than modern humans.[13]

The stakes in this research are enormous – at least for scientists and social scientists. Some researchers maintain that the pair-bond arose soon after the human line diverged from other primates, and is therefore an important element driving the evolution of the species. Others contend that the pair-bond did not arise until much later in human development. Bi-pedalism, and not the pair-bond or larger brains, then becomes the more critical evolutionary development.[14] Still others argue that the pair-

11 As we explore to a greater degree below, however, asking the question about what was likely to be adaptive may lead to other, more productive, inquiries, whether or not the scholar is willing to take a position on the issue.

12 Carbone & Cahn (2004, p. 236 & nn. 102–105).

13 Reno et al. (2003, pp. 9404–9409).

14 In these accounts, the narrower pelvises that come with upright posture produce less mature young, who require more care, which makes their caretakers more dependent, which in turn makes the pair-bond and with it the ability to better secure food and protection from a mate more of an evolutionary advantage. See, e.g., Lewin (1998, pp. 215–29).

bond arose together with greater human intelligence, but that both occurred a long time after the divergence from other primates. To the extent that the pair-bond and greater intelligence occurred at the same time, they may have influenced each other.

This debate is enthralling, in part, because it addresses the intersection of gender and the rise of human intelligence. The original speculation about the origins of human intelligence focused on "man the hunter". In this account, evolutionary biologists argued that "the transition from mere foraging to large-game hunting provided a major impetus for human evolution, with a cascading set of consequences including a rapid expansion of tool making and tool use, the development of a large human brain, and the evolution of complex language skills necessary for communication on cooperative hunts."[15] Feminists objected that this made women no more than passive beneficiaries of the increased importance of male activities, and they countered with scenarios that focused attention on the evolution of gathering and cooperative patterns of childcare. The most recent theories substitute emphasis on mate selection. Darwin had demonstrated in his initial work on evolution that some developments (e.g., the peacock's tail) could better be explained in accordance with their attractiveness to potential mates than in terms of their advantages for survival. With the rise of the pair-bond, humans may have become more inclined to look for witty, empathetic or entertaining mates, conferring a competitive reproductive advantage on the more intelligent or verbally adept. The pair-bond itself would then explain the rapid rise of human intelligence and dominion over other species.

Indeed, the successive waves of information that we – and the scientists upon whom we relied – discovered helped reinforce the significance of who is asking the questions, and how they are framing them before drawing any conclusions on how the law could be affected. The grandmother hypothesis provides another fascinating example of this: why do women, unlike men, live much longer than they can reproduce? Feminist anthropologists have found female gathering, not male hunting, often contributes the majority of the groups' sustenance in hunter-gatherer societies, with 60–80 per cent of some groups' calories coming through women's gathering of food from plants.[16] Given that hunting produced food at uneven intervals, and societies typically functioned at a subsistence level, women's gathering provided a more consistent source of food, and men may have needed women for their own survival.[17] Other researchers have suggested that scavenging, by both men and women, contributed more than big-game hunting. More recent research has added that among contemporary hunter-gatherers the most successful hunters share their spoils with other men as much or more than with their mates or children.[18] And, in

15 Buss (2004, p. 75).

16 Buss (2004, p. 338).

17 See de Waal (2001, p. 63) (suggesting that men may have benefitted from women's gathering and from their fine motor coordination in tool use).

18 See Hrdy (citing research of Marion Petrie) (articulating the "showoff hypothesis") (1999, pp. 228–29). See Ridley (2003, p. 19).

these tribes, mothers are more likely to turn to "alloparents", that is, grandparents, aunts and cousins, than to their lovers for assistance with their newborns.[19] Indeed, for females, pair-bonding may not be in their evolutionary interest;[20] women in contemporary hunter-gatherer societies report that men may be a net drain on their resources by consuming food and requiring care. Kristen Hawkes suggests that these alternative explanations based on cooperation may even suggest that "more exclusive pair bonds may [have been] added to a set of older interdependencies … the assumption that nuclear families are units of common interest may hamper our explanations of classic patterns in ethnography as well as of 'newly emerging' family forms in the postindustrial world."[21] Helping question the "naturalness" of any forms of human behaviour itself may be a productive route for inquiry.

Which view is correct? We certainly don't know. Considering the possible role of the clitoris in distinguishing between committed mates and opportunistic cads may be a better way to spend professional time than contemplating the role of dissomaster in child support awards, but law professors are not trained and should not be expected to weigh in on the former. Indeed, it is unlikely that any researcher today can determine the rise of the pair-bond with confidence. And if no answers exist, then it is not possible to identify the degree to which the pair-bond "was adaptive in past environments". While we suspect and most evolutionary biologists maintain that the pair-bond is likely to have conferred a reproductive advantage, we certainly cannot say that the advantage arises from the meat provided, the assistance with the child, the protection of the mother from possible dangers, or the advantages that come with in-laws.[22] For law professors, productive inquiry must lie elsewhere.

Modern Biology and Human Behaviour: A More Fruitful Inquiry?

Our hypothesis about human mating practices, of course, did not originate with observations of the Pleistocene. In similar fashion, we have found summarizing the evidence from contemporary biology texts more productive than attempting to evaluate the finds from archaeological digs. Once we let go of the efforts to understand the origins of the species, we found two types of less controversial evidence that strongly supported our argument.

---

19 The other possible male contribution – direct assistance with childrearing – is also under assault. Sarah Hrdy and others maintain that male contributions to infant care are likely to have been less important than the contributions of grandmothers, aunts and other "alloparents". Group-based rather than pair-bond care is likely to have been the norm. See Miller (2000, p. 190) (summarizing Hrdy's argument and concluding that "male help may have been a welcome luxury, but it was not a necessity").

20 Fisher (1992, p. 150).

21 Hawkes (2001, p. 704).

22 See, e.g.,Coontz (2005) (arguing that marriage is more about cementing extended family relationships than about the relationship between the couple.)

Comparative Anatomy

As we mentioned above, biologists use relative differences in body size and structure to better understand differences in closely related species. Three such differences between humans and other primates provide strong evidence that serial monogamy has long characterized human behaviour. First, biologists find that testicle size correlates inversely with female fidelity. Males mating with faithful females enjoy exclusive access. They are able to reproduce so long as the quality and quantity of sperm they produce is sufficient to impregnate their partner. In species with promiscuous females, male sperm competes with the sperm of other males within the female's body. In such species, the quantity and quality of male sperm confers a significant reproductive advantage. Among primates, male chimpanzees have some of the largest testicles in proportion to their body weight and trained observers have found that female chimps in heat mate with many males. The testicles of male gorillas in contrast are 16 times smaller in proportion to their body weight than those of male chimps, and observers of gorillas in the wild report that dominant males maintain harems in which they have exclusive access to many females. In humans, male testicles are almost five times as large as those of gorillas, but about one-third as big as those of chimpanzees.[23] The size of human male testicles accordingly suggests that human females are more monogamous than chimpanzee females, but less faithful than female gorillas.[24]

The second difference concerns the degree of sexual dimorphism. In species like gorillas where males compete to establish harems, bigger males may win big while smaller males fail to reproduce. As a result, size is a bigger factor in male than female reproductive success.[25] Among primates, gorillas, who gain and police exclusive access to groups of females, show the largest sexual dimorphism, orangutans are next, humans are in the middle, while chimps and bonobos, with their equally promiscuous males and females, show the smallest differences.[26] This suggests at least some human polygamy, with larger males having the opportunity to have more mates than others.[27]

Finally, female anatomy offers some, albeit more ambiguous, evidence. In other primates, females tend to experience periods of oestrus, which correspond to the most fertile period of the sexual cycle, and both enhance female capacity for arousal and advertise that availability to males. Sarah Hrdy observes, for example,

23 Ridley (2003, pp. 20–21).

24 Ridley (2003, p. 21). Chimps' larger testicle size and an ability to produce high-quality sperm allows them to compete within the female's reproductive system, rather than by mating with only one female and fending off other males. *Id.*

25 Buss (2004, pp. 285–86).

26 Buss (2004, pp. 285–86). (Chimp males weigh twice the average weight of females; human males weigh 12 per cent more than females.)

27 Lewin (1998, p. 165) (stating that "all species characterized by significant sexual dimorphism exhibit some degree of polygamy").

that while female primates "range from being sexually receptive for just a few hours right about midcycle to being able to copulate … across extended periods of the cycle, human females fall at the extreme end of this continuum, at the far edge of flexible, situation-dependent receptivity."[28] The question is why?

The primary advantage of concealed ovulation is that it made it virtually impossible to know when a woman is ovulating, and thus when it is best to mate with her. Early speculation focused on the advantages of retaining a mate. If women were sexually available longer, men were less likely to stray.[29] Later researchers suggested that if men were uncertain of the period of receptivity, securing paternity required policing access.[30] More recent scholars have maintained that concealed ovulation permitted women to convince more men that they were fertile, thereby persuading multiple partners to invest in the resulting child.[31] All of the arguments suggest that the disappearance of oestrus corresponded to the increased importance of the pair-bond, while the disagreements concern the resulting level of female fidelity.

The issue again arises should law professors engage in this type of speculation as to the evolutionary advantages of observed species-typical divergences? Here, at least, other evidence exists. Anthropologists document that in some contemporary hunter-gather societies, children with mothers who mated with more than two (though not necessarily more) men had the highest survival rates.[32] Multiple potential fathers in the face of uncertain paternity guaranteed that if one potential father died, another might step in. Overly promiscuous behaviour, however, deterred all of the men from investing in a child unlikely to be theirs. Simply reporting the results of this type of research has tantalizing implications for family law.

Neuroscience

The newest type of research into human proclivities involves neuroscience or the study of the brain. This type of inquiry examines the hormonal basis of human behaviour and the neural pathways that MRIs and CAT scans can reveal. While we can never assess the quality of the pair-bonds that existed before the dawn of recorded history, modern neuroscience allows us to discern something about the extent to which our evolutionary history has primed for us human attraction today.

---

28 Hrdy (1999, pp. 219–20). Primates, however, have been observed using force to compel females not in oestrus to mate. See Smuts & Smuts (1993, pp. 1, 6) (Captive chimpanzees and lowland gorillas have been observed "forcing females to copulate throughout the estrous cycle").

29 Diamond (1997, p. 84).

30 Fisher (1982, p. 187).

31 See Hrdy, (1999, pp. 247–49).

32 Hrdy (1999, pp. 237–249). "Among the Ache [one of the Amazonia tribes], Hill observed that children with just one father received less help, but when a mother lined up too many fathers, the extreme uncertainty of paternity dissuaded all candidates from helping. Children identified as having one primary and one secondary father had the best survival rates." Hrdy (1999, p. 248).

These studies confirm that while *homo sapiens* is clearly capable of experiencing "love", that love may not be designed for permanence.

Neuroscience studies suggest that three different biochemical systems underlie feeling of romantic attachment. The first involves "lust", or sexual attraction, and it is associated with testosterone. The second system involves "romantic love", or intense obsessive highs associated with the operation of the chemicals dopamine and nor-epinephrine, the same biochemicals associated with addiction. The third set of emotions, which involve long-term attachment, are identified with vasopressin in men and oxytocin in women. These systems may operate in tandem: partners can simultaneously feel lust towards one potential partner, romantic love towards a second and long-term attachment towards a third.[33] Evolutionary biologists speculate that this would provide all of the benefits of long-term pair-bonding, while giving men the opportunity to sire more children and women access to better genes and additional protection and support.

The existence of three distinct, yet overlapping, systems, suggests that human behaviour is designed to permit a fair amount of flexibility – and that it cannot be reduced to biochemistry kit. Nonetheless, a better understanding of the biochemical basis of behaviour may shed light on patterns of human behaviour. Some of the most intriguing studies involve nature's natural experiments. High levels of testosterone, for example, can reduce oxytocin and vasopressin, making attachment less likely,[34] and "men with high baseline levels of testosterone marry less frequently, have more adulterous affairs, commit more spousal abuse, and divorce more often[]" than men with lower baseline levels.[35] Researchers further speculate that some people may be addicted to the adrenaline rush that comes from infatuation – and the corresponding brain saturation with chemicals like dopamine.[36] Anti-depressants typically block the effect of dopamine and scientists have discovered that Prozac may allow patients who seem addicted to love, who move from relationship to relationship, to become better able to settle comfortably with a single mate, while other patients taking anti-depressants may find it harder to fall in love and therefore become less likely to enter into relationships at all.[37]

The effect of environment on the interaction of these chemicals is also well documented. A man's testosterone levels, for example, will tend to be higher when single than married, and if a given marriage becomes less stable, testosterone levels rise.[38] At the same time, ejaculation may be associated with higher levels

33 The statistics on fidelity support this dual strategy hypothesis.

34 Fisher (2004, p. 90).

35 Fisher (2004, p. 90).

36 Indeed, one of the mysteries of addiction is that it can be triggered by many different types of substances from stimulants like cocaine to sedatives like heroin. The answer is that both stimulate the release of dopamine, causing a series of effects within the brain. See generally Nestler & Malenka (2004).

37 Fisher (1992, pp. 53–54).

38 Fisher (2004, p. 90).

of vasopressin in monogamous male prairie voles[39] and higher levels of oxytocin in human females.[40] Researchers accordingly speculate that consummating a sexual relationship may promote attachment.[41] If the sexual relationship produces children, the fathers of newborns experience falling levels of testosterone, making them less likely to stray.[42] Indeed, simply holding a baby can cause testosterone levels to fall.[43] Similarly, the production of "dopamine and norepinephrine can stimulate the release of vasopressin and oxytocin",[44] suggesting that romantic love contributes to bonding.[45] And the effects of these chemicals may be different in men than in women: the mothers of newborns, influenced by the increased presence of oxytocin, often feel calm, relaxed, serene and focused on their babies while new fathers, more influenced by the presence of vasopressin, may become more vigilant, protective and anxious.[46] These are not three discrete systems, but overlapping ones that underscore the potential flexibility of human behaviour, and its sensitivity to environmental as well as genetic factors.

Science or Speculation?

What is a law professor to do with this research? Writing a marriage advice manual did enter our minds. And we still might do so. More relevantly, we concluded that an examination of comparative anatomy combined with the results of the modern understanding of neuroscience does provide significant support for our thesis that humans are primed for pair-bonding, but not necessarily long-term fidelity. The very existence of romantic love, as an addition-like state separate from lust and long-term attachment, suggests that the pair-bond is an important factor in human society. Moreover, a range of evidence from neuroscience data to sociological documentation to everyday human observation provides support for the idea that it is a common occurrence.[47] Separating the existence of the behaviour from the question of its origins makes greater certainty possible.

---

39 Fisher (2004, p. 88). Fisher notes that in male rats, "sexual activity can increase brain levels of dopamine and norepinephrine." Fisher (2004, p. 86).

40 Johnson (2004, p. 111).

41 Fisher (2004, p. 195) (suggesting that men release vasopressin and women oxytocin with sexual climax.). See also Johnson (2004, p. 237) (suggesting that oxytocin plays a different role in men than women).

42 In the time around the birth of a child, testosterone levels drop, and cortisol levels increase in men. Laurence (2004, pp. 141, 147) (quoting Dr Marianne Legato, Columbia University).

43 Fisher (2004, p. 90).

44 Fisher (2004, p. 91).

45 Johnson (2004, p. 132).

46 Johnson (2004, pp. 130–31, 236).

47 See, e.g., Coontz (2005, p. 24). ("We know of only one society in world history that did not make marriage a central way of organizing social and personal life.")

Nonetheless, the idea that humans form pair-bonds of uncertain duration is hardly an earth-shattering assertion. For evolutionary analysts, the more controversial issues are the details. Helen Fisher, for example, has asserted that pair-bond duration is tied to the period of greatest mother-child dependence, *viz.*, the three- to four-year period of lactation in hunter-gather societies.[48] Other researchers suggest that the period is shorter, perhaps eighteen months to two years. While the evidence that romantic highs wane is compelling, the average length of the corresponding relationship, and the role of biochemicals in the break-up, remain matters of speculation.

Moreover, even if the evolutionary assertions that the pair-bond arose to secure paternal investment in newborns could be established with certainty, it would not automatically follow that romantic love is critical to paternal investment, or that romantic love is the factor around which societies necessarily organize family life. Indeed, the opposite is more likely to be true. Stephanie Coontz argues that most societies before the modern era rejected the idea of romantic love as too flimsy or disruptive a basis for marriage, and we suspect that almost all societies would find that romantic love alone, for the reasons we have discussed, does not provide a lasting foundation for long-term relationships.[49] As natural law theorists have long recognized, marriage has served not so much to allow the expression of our biological inclinations as to constrain them. The purpose of understanding the biological bases of commitment for a law professor must be to better understand the extent to which human societies – and law – have any hope of directing (or redirecting) such behaviour. To what degree have human societies been successful in promoting long-term fidelity? What strategies work? Can we say anything about the role of law in promoting family stability? Can law professors successfully engage history, anthropology and sociology to find out?

Historical, Anthropological and Sociological Inquiry: Should Law Professors Apply?

The hominid line diverged from other primates more than 5 million years ago, erect hominids with modern features have been around for roughly 1 million years, and *homo sapiens* have been in Africa for more than 100,000 years.[50] "Civilization", in contrast, dates back no more than a few thousand years, and the history of civilization could arguably be cast in terms of the effort to secure family regularity. For law professors who wish to test the hypotheses that emerge from evolutionary analyses against the recorded history of human institutions, establishing the

48 Fisher (1992, pp. 153–54).

49 Fisher (1992, pp. 5–9).

50 Fisher (1982, p. 63); Frans B.M. de Waal, *Introduction to Tree of Origin*, *supra* note 65, at 2 (suggesting that humans separated from gorillas about 6 million years ago, and from bonobos about 5 million years ago).

origins of an evolutionary past may be less daunting than examining the extent to which it is possible to alter the resulting behaviour. For those who would test these hypotheses in the context of the family, two immediate obstacles arise: the literature is vast and the very effort to identify general patterns of behaviour may be in disrepute.

The history and anthropology of the family arguably start with Frederick Engels's argument in the late nineteenth century that monogamy followed the rise of agriculture and served to ensure the husband that all of his wife's children were "his".[51] Yet, while Engels's theories of patriarchy (and its association with monogamy) remain influential among feminists, he was wrong in most of his particulars. Moreover, these errors have discredited the effort to find universals about family development. He was certainly inaccurate in associating hunter-gatherers with wholesale promiscuity. He was wrong (and condescendingly moralistic) in his description of the family practices of non-European societies. And anthropologists have thoroughly rejected his claim of unilinear patterns of family evolution.[52]

What did replace Engels's study of the family was much more particularized discussion of the practices of different societies at different times. On the one hand, this makes any comprehensive study of different cultures over different times daunting, if not impossible. General statements about the role of biology, or

---

51 Engels (1891/1964). Engels's methodology reflected the influence of Darwin and Marx. He sought to tie domestic arrangements to material changes in society and argued that human development had "progressed" through three distinct stages of family development:

1. The first linked "savagery", or the hunter-gatherer stage of human existence, with group marriage. Promiscuity was the norm, and descent was traced exclusively through the female line.
2. The "barbarism" stage associated the early periods of herding and farming with the pair-bond. One man lived with one woman, occasionally tolerating polygamy and the man's, but not the woman's, infidelity. Divorce was readily available, with the mother retaining custody of the children.
3. The third stage produced "civilization", large-scale agriculture, industry, the accumulation of wealth – and monogamy. Monogamy, in Engels' scheme, differed from pair-bonding in its insistence on lifelong family ties and a shift from female to male lines of descent. He observed that "the sole exclusive aims of monogamous marriage were to make the man supreme in the family, and to propagate, as the future heirs to his wealth, children indisputably his own." Engels (1891/1964, p. 125).

52 Laslett & Hall (1972, p. 5). The authors conclude that:

> Much of value has, of course been taken into the social sciences from these earlier thinkers, but there can be no doubt of their systems being consciously cast aside. Indeed there are those who would say that when nineteenth-century evolutionism was rejected, the only comprehensive theory of family development disappeared without anything being put in its place.

inquiries about the transition from hunter-gathers to modern arrangements, become as much of a morass for law professors as explorations of sexual dimorphism during the Pliocene. (Indeed, it took us almost as long to rework and mostly discard a lengthy digression on the family changes that accompanied the rise of agriculture as it did to determine that we would never reach closure on the evidence for the pair-bond in early hominids.)

Yet, just as we found when we abandoned archaeology for neuroscience, the interdisciplinary studies that focus on more particularized accounts of behaviour in our own culture provide a potentially rich and more relevant basis for considering the role of biology than overly generalized historical claims. More recent historians, for example, have refined Engels' discussion of monogamy to transform it from a universal statement about the hallmarks of civilization to an examination of the distinctive culture of northwestern Europe.[53] These records show illegitimacy rates in England and other parts of northwestern Europe to be extraordinarily low, rising in the eighteenth century from less than 1 per cent to under 7 per cent only with greater urbanization.[54] Moreover, Edward Shorter's extensive review of evidence ranging from birth records to rural doctors' diaries similarly concludes that the level of sexual activity over several centuries of northwestern European history may have been remarkably low in comparison with either hunter-gatherer or modern sexual practices.[55] These records, of course, cannot determine whether marital children were in fact the biological offspring of their mothers' husbands, but the more general accounts of the policing of sexuality in these societies suggest that the rates of falsely identified paternity are likely to be much lower than the 10–20% of children who have been found not to be biologically related to their legal fathers in some more recent studies.[56] They suggest that the assumption that marriage, separation, divorce and adultery may not be as "insensitive to the imposition or legal prohibitions, or other costs" as our assumptions about evolutionary history might suggest.[57]

53 See discussion in Carbone (2000, pp. 58–62). Indeed, Stone emphasizes that "the sublimation of sex among male adults may well account for the extraordinary military aggressiveness, the thrift, the passion for hard work, and the entrepreneurial and intellectual enterprise of Western man." Carbone (2000, p. 61) (citing Stone (1977, p. 408)). Particularity can be of use to Western notions of superiority as easily as generality.

54 Stone (1977, p. 631)

55 Shorter (1975, p. 99).

56 Fisher (2004, p. 151) (10 per cent of children tested in a 1998 programme which screened for genetic diseases); Ridley, *The Red Queen* (1993, p. 226) (less than 80 per cent of sons tested in Liverpool and southern England were the children of their fathers). Given high rates of extra-marital affairs, the numbers may be higher. Approximately 25 per cent of men and 15 per cent of women surveyed by National Opinion Research Center in 1994 admitted to extra-marital copulation. Fisher (1992, p. 151).

57 See Jones & Goldsmith (2005, pp. 463–64) (Evolutionary analysis predicts and explains why the slope of the demand curve for adulterous behaviour is likely to be

Nonetheless, the comparisons with today's society are startlingly. We have gone from non-marital birth rates of under 7 per cent in the eighteenth century to one-third of all US births today. Divorce, which was virtually unknown in some time periods, has plateaued at one of every two marriages. The majority of American children may now spend some part of their childhood in a single-parent family. While high death rates in earlier centuries make comparisons of divorce rates less exact, historians can document the exertion of considerably more energy (with greater likelihood of success) in the policing of sexuality activity in earlier periods. Differences of this magnitude necessarily reflect the flexibility of human society rather than biologically mandated behaviour. Does a better understanding of biology have anything to add?

What Does Biology Contribute to Legal Research? The Lightbulb Goes On

In examining this kind of data, the fascinating parts are not the commonalities in human behaviour, but the variations. Some contemporary writers, convinced that the behaviour we observe in today's societies reflect universals of human behaviour, simply reject the claims that historical times were different.[58] If Stone and Shorter are accurate, however, the contribution of biology may be to help us focus on the factors that make societies regulate sexuality differently. To further this understanding the Law of Law's Leverage, which we discussed at the beginning of this chapter, is extremely useful. For example, if romantic love is biologically primed to be fleeting, then laws that help that romantic love endure, such as mandatory periods of separation, as observant Jews prescribed for certain times of the month for women, or that make it more difficult to leave a marriage after the first two years, may promote family stability. Speculation as to why there are different stages of "love" is useful and interesting, but we also must acknowledge that the science is still in its infancy. We began our inquiry into the evolutionary basis of family stability, after all, not to resolve scientific disputes about human biology, but to critique family law. Family law in the United States and elsewhere has historically served to reinforce the values on which family stability rests. Can biology help to make sense of the transformation of the modern family that is now taking place and of the possibilities for guiding it?

The secret, we believe, lies not with developing a new, biologically based model of sex, marriage, gender differences, divorce or reproduction, but of revisiting our existing models. The conventional account of family change, to which both of us have contributed, ties the reorganization of the family to the changes wrought by the post-industrial economy.[59] To oversimplify: the older

---

comparatively steep, as is the slope for most sexual behaviour, and thus comparatively insensitive to the imposition of legal prohibitions, or other costs, such as effect on career.)

58 See, e.g., Patterson (1998, p. 36).

59 For a much fuller account, see Carbone (2000, pp. 48–49; 63–66; 108–09).

Anglo-American system linked family wealth, first, to land ownership, then to the husband's workforce participation. Within this system, women's chastity was a closely guarded commodity,[60] and marriage occurred at or relatively soon after the beginning of women's sexual activity. Earlier societies then placed the wife under her husband's supervision, as both contributed to economic production within the home. The nineteenth century remade that bargain for the American middle class, as increased male specialization rewarded greater investment in children, commercial production increasingly occurred outside of the home or farm, and women's roles were redefined in terms of primary emphasis on children. Financial interdependence and social stigma made it difficult for women to leave improvident relationships, and men were imbued with responsibility for their families' financial well-being while the double standard sometimes permitted some leeway for male affairs that did not threaten family stability.[61]

If nineteenth-century changes turned on increasing specialization among men and greater distinctions between home and market, then the twentieth century's post-industrial economy brought with it increasing specialization among women and dissolution of the distinctions between home and market. Demand increased for women's market services, and rewarded greater investment in women. Women then reorganized themselves, as higher-earning women hired other women (and McDonald's and frozen foods) to provide the less specialized services they had once performed within the home. As women joined men in securing higher education, the average age of marriage increased. As women married later and their income rose, they also became less dependent on men and marriage, and as the consequences of divorce and improvident pregnancies became less devastating, men felt less responsible for the negative consequences that did occur. The economic coercion that complemented the moral suasion of the older family system gave way, and so did the effectiveness of the mechanisms that promoted family stability for centuries.[62]

What can biology add to this analysis? We have concluded that it may shed indispensable light on the evaluation of the possible alternatives. Adding biology to our older analysis has led us to a new thesis: managing attachment in the modern era requires a re-examination of the interaction between family formation and different stages in the adult life cycle. The result is a research agenda that we hope will bring new insight, not into evolutionary analysis, but into what Justice Scalia has termed "the culture wars". The thesis that has emerged from our biological inquiries is that our story of the contemporary reorganization of

60 Many historians emphasize, moreover, that protection of women's "virtue" was not a universal, but rather varied with class and race. This may be consistent, however, with an evolutionary approach that suggests greater investment in women's fidelity, the more that is at stake. Wealthier men may have more reason to care whether the children who inherit their wealth or receive the results of their largesse are in fact biologically their own.

61 Fisher (1992, pp. 75–81).

62 See generally, Carbone (2000).

family life is only half right. Instead, it appears that states have adopted different strategies to respond to the impact of the post-industrial world. "Blue states" have adopted a new family strategy that places a premium on postponing child-rearing until the peak periods of testosterone production have passed, and couples can be expected to form stable relationships with a minimum of external coercion. "Red states" in contrast continue to link family stability to the control of sexuality, and internalized values that associate sexuality exclusively with marriage and reproduction.[63] They do so in the context of more traditional, often more rural, and more working class cultures in which adults are ready to begin child-bearing at younger ages, and expect to marry shortly after women become sexually active. The Bible Belt and Utah – the reddest of red states – also have the highest rates of divorce in part because the degree of coercion necessary to keep couples together increases inversely with the age at which they begin marriage. The result is an irreconcilable clash between two very different moral and family systems.

Our new thesis takes us into a more discrete examination of biology. We wish, first, to examine more thoroughly the biological changes that occur in early adulthood and the impact of the different legal strategies on the manifestation of these changes. An extensive literature ties risk-taking, crime, adultery and divorce to age. Testosterone levels and brain chemistry are the expected causal agents, and we wish to take a closer look at the strength of the studies that support these assertions. Evolutionary analysis, however, is ready to supply an explanation: testosterone levels may peak during the prime periods for child-bearing and, if so, they may suggest a trade-off between ease of conception and relationship stability.

Second, we have completed a preliminary examination of the relationship between physical maturity, marriage and child-bearing. We have found that in 1840, the average age of menarche was 16[64] and the average age of marriage for women was 19. In the US today, based on better nutrition and health, the average age of menstruation has fallen to 12,[65] while the average age of marriage is now well over a decade later.[66] We believe that it will be relatively easy to maintain that at least part of the reason for the blue state shift is the impossibility of containing female sexuality for a decade or more while "unsupervised" women complete their education and enter the workforce.[67]

Third, what role does jealousy play in the new system? Does the availability of effective contraception simply lower fears about paternity, or does jealousy affect the patterns in ways we have not anticipated?

---

63 See Carbone (2000, p. 60) (discussing northwestern Europe).

64 Planned Parenthood (2001) (average age of menarche was 16.5); see also Wyshak & Frisch (1982, pp. 1033–1035); Tanner (1981, p. 604).

65 See Planned Parenthood (2001) (average age today of menarche is 12.8).

66 The average age of marriage for women is 25, and it is 27 for men. Carbone & Cahn (2004, n. 215). See also Fields & Casper (2001).

67 Carbone (2000, 261, n.6).

Fourth, we would like to consider the evidence for the permanent impact of upbringing on brain patterns. If we were able to conduct our own MRI experiments, we would propose comparing the responses of those raised in repressive sexual environments with those brought up in more liberal surroundings. Do modern researchers have a different view of what Freud discovered when he tried to analyse the repressive child-rearing practices of central Europe?

These inquiries, however, are tangential to what we expect to be the main subject of our research: documenting the divergence of family law systems that still attempt to pass judgment on sexual activity from those that do not. This examination involves the traditional methodology of the legal academy – looking at statutes and cases – and some relatively simply statistical analysis. We believe that such a study will show a correlation between lower ages of marriage, higher levels of divorce and stricter efforts to limit access to abortion, denying recognition to same-sex relationships, and considering non-marital cohabitation as a significant negative factor in custody awards. In the process, we expect to consider whether other demographic variables, such as religious observation, race, class and income, independently affect the outcomes. We believe, however, that if we find the correlations we expect to find, a significant difficulty with the research will be a chicken-and-egg problem: do states have younger average ages of marriage because of the efforts to control sexuality, or do the efforts to control sexuality lower the age of marriage from what it might otherwise be?

As law professors, however, we believe that the research will have been worthwhile if we can simply show that two, internally coherent and incompatible family law systems are emerging. Establishing a link to age of marriage will be a significant plus, but identification of the implications of two such systems is the traditional stuff of legal analysis. If we had arrived at the thesis from the more conventional analysis described above, our interdisciplinary inquiries might have focused in greater depth on economic change. With this agenda, we expect to focus to a greater degree on demographic differences, and the implications of divergent rather than converging normative systems. Biological observations may not be determinative, but they have the potential to fundamentally reframe the inquiry.

Conclusion: Is It Worth It?

We remain excited by this research despite the dead ends we have encountered. Nonetheless, we do have doubts about recommending it to others. Some of us believe that law and economics, at least in its early stages, became so popular because the barriers to entry were low, and the results easily supported the predetermined positions of some of the proponents. The result was to change the parameters of discussion in ways that enhanced the status of some, and skewed the resulting outcomes at least until the rest of the academy caught up.

Evolutionary analysis of law risks a similar fate, but there are nonetheless significant differences. If evolutionary analysis simply encourages speculation about evolutionary origins, speculation, for example, that men are more likely to commit adultery than women,[68] the barriers to entry will be low, but the proponents are likely to encounter the charged opposition that now faces proponents of the older generation of law and economics. Instead, we believe that the integration of this type of analysis into legal scholarship involves the steps we have tried to describe here.

First, tying the origins of human behaviour to hunter-gather reproductive advantages is more likely to inspire speculation and amusement than satisfying resolutions, particularly for the law.

Second, overly general statements like ours, i.e., that *homo sapiens* are primed for pair-bonding, but not long-term fidelity, are not likely to be terribly useful, even if true. Either they cannot be proven or they restate the obvious.

Third, more nuanced statements (e.g., couples who marry as testosterone levels begin to wane are more likely to stay together) need to be empirically tested even if they correspond to evolutionary theories about reproductive advantage.

Fourth, evolutionary analysis will become persuasive as it is integrated with biological studies that identify the causal mechanisms (e.g., testosterone) that more immediately influence human behaviour.[69]

Fifth, biological insights do not stand alone; they must be integrated with more traditional legal and/or sociological analysis.

In the end, however, what these insights do most effectively is to change the questions that are asked and the framework used to evaluate the answers. We are convinced that we could explore the differences between family law systems that mediate child-bearing at 19 and at 29 without reference to biology at all, and that most of our legal and normative discussion would be the same. But we are not sure that without the lengthy inquiry described in this chapter, we would have ever focused on the questions of age, and we are certain that we would not have framed our inquiry in the same way.

References

Buss, David M. (2004) *Evolutionary Psychology: The New Science of the Mind.* Boston: Allyn and Bacon.

Carbone, June & Cahn, Naomi (2004) 'The Biological Basis of Commitment: Does One Size Fit All?' *Women's Rights Law Reporter*. 25: 223.

Carbone, June & Naomi Cahn (2003) 'Which Ties Bind? Redefining the Parent-Child Relationship in an Age of Genetic Certainty,' *Wm. & Mary Bill Rts. J.* 11:1011.

68 Something we believe, by the way, is true, but which nonetheless varies considerably by culture.

69 Jones's insightful observation on this point is that the two complement each other.

Carbone, June (2000) *From Partners to Parents*. New York: Columbia Univ. Press.

Coontz, Stephanie (2005) *Marriage, a History: From Obedience to Intimacy, or How Love Conquered Marriage*. New York: Penguin.

Darwin, Charles (1839) *Voyage of the Beagle* available online at http://www.infidels.org/library/historical/charles_darwin/voyage_of_beagle/Chapter17.html

Diamond, Jared M. (1997) *Why is Sex Fun? The Evolution of Human Sexuality*. New York: Basic Books.

Engels, Frederick (1891/1964) *The Origin of the Family, Private Property and the State*. New York: International Publishers.

Fields, Jason & Casper, Lynne (U.S. Census Bureau) (2001) 'America's Families and Living Arrangements: Population Characteristics', Current Population Reports.

Fisher, Helen (2004) *Why We Love: The Nature and Chemistry of Romantic Love*. New York: Henry Holt.

Fisher, Helen (1992) *Anatomy of Love: The Natural History of Monogamy, Adultery, and Divorce*. New York: W.W. Norton & Co.

Fisher, Helen E. (1982) *The Sex Contract: The Evolution of Human Behavior*. New York: William Morrow.

Hawkes, Kristen. (2003) 'Grandmothers and the Evolution of Human Longevity', *Am. J. Human Biology* 15: 380, 382.

Hawkes, Kristen et al. (2001) 'Reply', *Current Anthropology* 42: 702, 704.

Hrdy, Sarah Blaffer (1999) *Mother Nature: Maternal Instincts and How They Shape the Human Species*. New York: The Ballantine Publishing Group 2000, 228–29.

Johnson, Steven (2004) *Mind Wide Open: Your Brain and the Neuroscience of Everyday Life*. New York: Scribner 111.

Jones, Owen (2001) 'Evolutionary Analysis in Law: Some Objections Considered', *Brooklyn L. Rev.* 67: 207.

Jones, Owen D. & Timothy H. Goldsmith (2005) 'Law And Behavioral Biology', *Colum. L. Rev.* 105: 405.

Laslett, Peter and Richard Hall (eds) (1972) *Household and Family in Past Time*. Cambridge: Cambridge University Press.

Laurence, Leslie (2004) 'His and Her Stress,' *Ladies Home Journal*, May, pp. 141, 147.

Lewin, Roger (1998) *Principles of Human Evolution*. Malden, MA: Blackwell Science Publishing.

Miller, Geoffrey (2000) *The Mating Mind: How Sexual Choice Shaped the Evolution of Human Nature*. New York: Doubleday.

Nestler, Eric J. & Malenka, Robert C. (2004) 'The Addicted Brain', *Scientific American* 78: Available from http://www.sciam.com/article.cfm?chanID=sa006&articleID=0001E632-978A-1019-978A83414B7F0101&pageNumber=2&catID=2.

Patterson, Orlando (1998) *Rituals of Blood: Consequences of Slavery in Two American Centuries*. New York: Civitas.

Planned Parenthood (2001) Adolescent Sexuality [Internet], available at http://www.plannedparenthood.org/library/sexuality/AdolescSexual.html.

Pope, Stephen J. (2005) 'Sex, Marriage and Family Life: The Teachings of Nature,' in *Family Transformed: Religion Values, and Society in American Life*, Steven M. Tipton and John Witte, Jr., (eds) Washington, D.C.: Georgetown University Press.

Reno, Phillip L. et al. (2003) 'Sexual Dimorphism in Australopithecus afarensis was Similar to that of Modern Humans'. Proceedings of the National Academy of Sciences [Internet], 5 Aug. 2003, 100(16), 9404–9409. Available from: <http://www.pnas.org/cgi/content/full/100/16/9404?maxtoshow =&HITS=10 &hits=10&RESULTFORMAT=&fulltext=Reno &searchid=1099865503006 3821&stored search=&FIRST INDEX=0> [accessed 24 March 2005].

Ridley, Matt (2003) *Nature via Nurture: Genes, Experience & What Makes Us Human*. New York: Harper Collins.

Ridley, Matt (1993) *The Red Queen: Sex and the Evolution of Human Nature*. New York: Macmillan.

Shorter, Edward (1975) *The Making of the Modern Family*. New York: Basic Books.

Stone, Lawrence (1977) *The Family, Sex and Marriage in England 1500–1800*. London: Harper and Row.

Smuts, Barbara B. & Smuts, Robert W. (1993) 'Male Aggression and Sexual Coercion of Females in Nonhuman Primate and Other Mammals: Evidence and Theoretical Implications', in Peter J.B. Slater et al. (eds) *Advances in the Study of Human Behavior*. New York: Academic Press.

Tanner, J.M. (1981) 'Menarcheal Age', *Science* 214: 604 [letter].

Trivers, Roberts L. (1972) 'Parental Investment and Sexual Selection' in Bernard Campbell (ed.) *Sexual Selection and the Descent of Man: 1871–1971*. Chicago: Aldine.

van Schaik, Carel & Dunbar, Robin (1990) 'The Evolution of Monogamy in Large Primates: A New Hypothesis and Some Crucial Tests', *Behavior* 115:30. Cited in de Waal, Frans B.M. (2001) 'Apes from Venus: Bonobos and Human Social Evolution' in Frans B.M. de Waal (ed.) *Tree of Origin: What Primate Behavior Can Tell Us About Human Social Evolution*. Cambridge: Harvard University Press.

de Waal, Frans B.M. (2001) 'Apes from Venus: Bonobos and Human Social Evolution' in Frans B.M. de Waal (ed.) *Tree of Origin: What Primate Behavior Can Tell Us About Human Social Evolution*. Cambridge: Harvard University Press.

Wrangham, Richard (2001) 'Out of the Pan, Into the Fire: How our Ancestors' Evolution Depended on What they Ate' in Frans B.M. de Waal (ed.) *Tree of Origin: What Primate Behavior Can Tell Us About Human Social Evolution*. Cambridge: Harvard University Press.

Wyshak, G. & Frisch, R.E. (1982) 'Evidence for a Secular Trend in the Age of Menarche', *N. Engl. J. Med.* 305: 1033–1035.

Chapter 15
Why Do Good People Steal Intellectual Property?

Oliver R. Goodenough[1] and Gregory Decker, J.D.

Why do good people steal intellectual property? You know who we mean. The person (perhaps even yourself) who feels deep remorse if she mistakenly walks off with your pencil, who takes a wallet she found on the street, full of money but with no identification, to the police, and who without a qualm or any thought of payment, downloads copyrighted music off the Internet or from a friend to put onto her iPod. What is going on here? Some suggest ignorance of the law, but that is generally not the case. She knows about copyright. Some suggest a lack of enforcement, but that doesn't stop her from turning in the wallet. No, something else is going on – some failure of a normally law-abiding, "good" person to feel any compulsion to obey this set of laws.

The emerging discipline of cognitive science can help us understand this challenge to our intellectual property system. This chapter will pursue this line of inquiry, both for its own sake, and as an example of how we can look into the brain for answers to some of the law's persistent conundrums. In the process, it will provide an introduction to an approach we might call cognitive jurisprudence,[2] exploring its potential and its methodology. In this context, the role of emotion in our thought and action will be of particular importance. The chapter will conclude with a return to our problem of intellectual property, offering a hypothesis that gives us answers to our core question and sketching possible paths towards both concrete research and law reform.

Looking for Answers in the Brain: The Cognitive Revolution

The past 20 years have marked a startling change in our understanding of human thought and behaviour: the cognitive revolution. Not so long ago, it was received wisdom that the human brain was an unknowable "black box" (Goodenough 2006). We might gain some insights through philosophical introspection and

1 Professor of Law, Vermont Law School, USA.

2 The name of the combined fields of law and cognitive neuroscience is still "up for grabs". Some are linking it to the term "neuroethics". See, e.g., http://www.neuroethicssociety.org/.

analysis, or through the study of our behavioural linkages and social patterns, but the underlying mechanisms of thought were impenetrably opaque, what Skinner called "private events" (Skinner 1953).

In keeping with the ethos and limits of the times, legal studies focused on doctrinal study, on procedural matters, and, in the hands of the legal realists and their successors, on the effects of law in society. There was an emphasis on achieving policy goals, often with the help of the social sciences, such as sociology and economics (Ellsworth 2005; Goodenough and Prehn 2004; Goodenough 2001a).

The merging of neurological advances with more traditional psychology has produced a new synthesis – cognitive science and its branches cognitive neuroscience and cognitive psychology (e.g., Goodenough and Prehn 2004; Gazzaniga et al. 2002). Some cite the seminal vision of David Marr at MIT in his 1982 book *Vision* as a key catalyst for this merger (Marr 1982; Gazzaniga et al. 2002); others cite a taxi ride conversation in the late 1970s where the term "cognitive neuroscience" was first coined (Gazzaniga et al. 2002); the Cognitive Neuroscience Society was formed as recently as 1994.[3] The advances of cognitive science have been driven by complementary sets of developments in theory and technology, providing both a greatly improved model of thought and action and exciting new tools to construct and test the model.

Advances in Theory

The emerging model of thought rests on a few key points. First of all, thought is a computational process, made possible by the physical structures and workings of the human brain (e.g., Marr 1982; Gazzaniga et al. 2002). There is, therefore, a fundamental link between the physiology of our nervous systems and how we think and translate thought into action (e.g., Kosslyn and Andersen 1995; Gazzaniga et al. 2002; Goodenough and Prehn 2004). Second, our cognitive processes involve a mix of localized centres, often with particular functions or capacities, and interactions across many parts of the brain. While there is still considerable debate around the details of specialization and generalized functionality, there is broad agreement that our thinking is the product of a synthesis of the two (e.g., Barrett and Kurzban 2006; Goodenough and Prehn 2004; Mundale 2002). A third key is the importance of formal approaches such as game theory for understanding the strategic basis of cognition in a social context involving human interaction (e.g., Goodenough and Prehn 2004; Fehr and Fischbacher 2004). A fourth element is recognizing the multiple inputs that shape our decision-making, ranging from the genetic basis of our brain organization and function, through the influence of our physical, social and cultural environment, both shaping the development of the brain and informing its memories and habits, and onto such capacities as conscious thought, logic and the ability to create and shape external institutions

3 See www.cogneurosociety.org.

such as the law (e.g., Goodenough and Prehn 2004; Goodenough 2006). Each of these principles will be examined in more detail below.

Advances in Technology

The technology has centred on increasingly powerful, non-invasive methods for identifying and studying the anatomical aspects of brain function and for linking anatomy to specific cognitive tasks. Brain scanning holds a particular, but by no means exclusive, importance in these advances. The techniques have a daunting set of names and acronyms, including positron emission tomography (PET), functional magnetic resonance imaging (fMRI) and near infrared spectroscopy. Their common feature is that they provide a measure of blood flow to specific regions of the brain. Localized increases in blood flow have been correlated with increased activation of that portion of the brain, and such activation, in turn, can generally be linked to some involvement in the mental task posed to the subject at the time of the increase. By using sophisticated analytical tools, it is possible to make increasingly targeted associations between particular kinds of thought processes and specific centres and networks in the anatomy of the brain. Increases in the resolution of imaging techniques are permitting ever more finely grained associations of function and structure. Studies of individuals with brain injuries had already given some means of linking anatomy and activity, and these unfortunate natural experiments continue to be important "cross checks" on data from imaging.

In addition to imaging based on metabolism and blood flow, measurements of electrical activity, both generalized and localized, give important information about the timing and structure of brain processes. These techniques include the electroencephalogram (EEG) and magneto encephalogram (MEG). Here, too, exciting technical advances hold out promise of using non-invasive methods to identify electrical excitation down to the level of individual neurons, something now only possible with intrusive methods confined largely to animal subjects (Glimcher 2003).

Another area of advance involves the monitoring of the neurochemistry of thought and action. At this writing, measurement is still only possible at a fairly generalized level, such as blood serum levels. Even this relatively crude approach is providing useful information on questions such as trust (e.g., Kosfeld et al. 2005; Zak et al. 2005), aggression (e.g., Simpson 2001) and love (e.g., Lucentini 2005).

For the purposes of this chapter, a deeper understanding of the *technologies* is unnecessary. Those with an interest in additional detail can consult a number of other sources, ranging from relatively concise summaries in popular journals such as *Scientific American Mind* to a graduate-level review (e.g., Frackowiack et al. 2004). What is important here is an understanding that existing tools, despite some limitations and the potential for improvement, are both supporting the advances in our model of thought and permitting the unravelling of the physical basis of specific kinds of mental work.

Relating the Cognitive Revolution to the Law

The advances of the cognitive revolution are reshaping many fields of study; it has a particular potential to foster a better understanding of questions of concern to law. Indeed, traditional legal scholarship can be viewed as a capable, if somewhat naive, science of thought and behaviour. This idea draws on an insight of the noted neurologist of vision Semir Zeki about the nature of art. In his book *Inner Vision,* Zeki (1999) argues that art is only effective if it interacts with our visual processing capacities in ways that we can perceive and ascribe meaning to. An artist, therefore, is a kind of untutored cognitive scientist, seeking effective avenues of interacting with human physiology to produce her effect.

In a similar way, the study of law is, at its heart, a cognitive inquiry (Goodenough 2001; Winter 2001). The law is keenly focused on analysing and categorizing our deeds and mental processes in particular contexts of social interaction, and in matching that categorization to consequences of punishment and enforcement. Over the years, jurisprudence has borrowed the best available tools for undertaking this job, whether from religion, philosophy, social science or psychiatry. The jurisprudence of the twenty-first century will incorporate the cognitive revolution in its turn. Just as in Moliere's "*Le Bourgeois Gentilhomme*" Monsieur Jourdain is astonished to discover that he's been speaking prose all his life, so too will legal scholars, as they become more and more familiar with the new findings about the brain, discover that they have been brain scientists all along. An understanding of neuroscience will just make them much better at it.

The normal processes of feedback in the law have been effective in shaping much of its doctrine to the contours of the human cognitive landscape. Whether through common-law evolution, or legislative or regulatory revision, the process of trial and error, application and adaptation, provide a persistent, if not infallible, tug towards an institution that fits with human psychology. Some in law and economics have claimed a similar trend towards efficiency in legal solutions (e.g., Posner 1998; Cooter and Ulen 1988; Kaplow and Shavell 2002), but that is at best a more removed goal; working with the human brain is a first-order requirement. Therefore, it is to be expected that some areas of law will provide a pretty good fit, even if the rationales and labels are sometimes poorly articulated (Goodenough 1997; Greene and Cohen 2004). Other areas of doctrine, even those with good logical cohesion, may not work as well with our fundamental mental architecture. We would expect this kind of problem to be more salient in relatively recent legal enactments. Intellectual property, we believe, is just such a field. Applying the understandings of the brain and the methodology provided by cognitive science can help us in designing more psychologically effective legal institutions.

Before turning in more detail to applications of cognitive approaches to the law, we will review the approaches of neuroscience in further detail.

The Strategic Role of Thought

Understanding the formal strategic situation is an important step in studying a social judgment such as whether taking the creative product of another is blameworthy. Most law-relevant thought will be about behaviour with a social dimension. If an action doesn't affect other people in some way, either by its impact or through some evaluative judgment, it is probably of little interest to the law. Therefore, the underlying rationale for a cognitive process drawing the attention of the law is probably rooted in the dynamics of social interplay. The strategic dimension of a decision will be reflected in its functional instantiation in the brain, and vice versa.

Although many kinds of social science provide insight into the dynamics of motivation, game theory strips away a lot of the clutter and noise and provides a particularly helpful means of analysis, both formal and descriptive, for evaluating strategic decision-making (Binmore 1998; Gintis 2000). Game theory suggests that our social judgments are often rooted in dilemmas around cooperative opportunities or the allocation of scarce resources among potentially competitive actors. These opportunities and challenges present themselves in many different forms. In some cases plus-sum cooperative solutions will fall naturally from the pursuit of each actor's self-interest. In such a case the positive solution is said to be "dominant". In others, such as the broadly recognized "prisoner's dilemma", self-interest will lead to less optimal results, and the positive solution is "dominated" by the negative (Dixit and Skeath 2004). While people are not perfect Nash calculators (thank goodness), the strategic options available to actors in multi-player social interactions shape much of our thought (Gintis 2000; Goodenough 2007).

Although it is not always recognized in the game theory literature, humans are not necessarily prisoners of the prisoner's dilemma itself. Maynard Smith and Szathmáry (1995) have charted how each of the major transitions in evolutionary biology have coincided with some restructuring of the physical nature of life that has given access to dominant cooperative solutions within and between living actors. They argued that human societies are extensions of this same principle.

By further extension, we can recognize the human capacity to avoid prisoner dilemma-style games, with their likelihood of poor outcomes. In a process sometimes called "mechanism design", people both choose and change the strategic properties of their social interaction (Goodenough 2007). Some of this is done at the level of our evolved psychology, with ready access to the reinforcement of emotion and compulsion; choices can also be created anew and embedded in our cultural inheritance. Law can be seen as a further step in this chain, creating institutionalized game structures with which attractive, plus-sum outcomes become dominant. In this way humans can be seen as "outwitting" Nash (Goodenough 2007).

Multiple Inputs

Until recently, reasonably intelligent scholars and authors were arguing over whether our behavioural motivations and responses are a product of nature or of nurture. A much better picture of our composite human nature arises from the understanding that the answer is both, and even more (e.g., Ridley 2003). Information-to-action pathways get established in many ways. Some of our perceptions, capacities and responses can be thought of as relatively hard-wired, or at least predisposed, traits, present in our genetic heritage and shaped over evolutionary time. Of course, few if any of these are independent of environmental influence; almost all are shaped to a greater or lesser degree during development by interaction with the non-genetic world. Others are the product of our non-genetic, social inheritance, received through cultural learning. Rules of behaviour ranging from customs and social mores through to tradition-based law can be transmitted this way. Conscious and unconscious conclusions drawn from our individual history and experience add to the mixture, as do the workings of our special human capacity for rationality and hypothetical thinking. Finally, we create physical and social institutions such as codes, protocols and even architecture that use externalized information and structures to help guide us (Goodenough 2007; Goodenough and Prehn 2004).

One motivation for the nature/nurture argument has been the assumption by some in the competing camps that there was an innate priority or superiority that went with a particular location in the motivational composite. Cognitive science by and large rejects any such conclusion. Culture and rationality constrain our genetic heritage and vice versa. The human project is a collective partnership and a continuous negotiation, and no one source holds the leash. From this standpoint, "biological determinism" and "social determinism" are inflammatory insults in a turf fight broken loose from reality (e.g., Skull 2007), rather than useful categories of thought.

That does not mean, however, that the actual mechanisms and their location in the composite are unimportant – far from it. Nor does it mean that the different components will always work in concert. Embodying these insights, Owen Jones (2001) has propounded what he calls the "law of law's leverage". This approach recognizes that law, as an institutionalized, cultural force, will seek to move behaviour that may be rooted in relatively unreflective, internalized motivational pathways. Understanding the strengths, strategic contours and mental attributes of both the law and its target will help us to create effective legal intervention.

Decision-Making: Multiple Steps and Paths from Sensory Input to Behaviour

Most of us have a folk image of decision-making in the mind that looks a bit like the captain of a ship, standing on the bridge, weighing the reports from the various members of the crew, choosing a course of action, and then barking out orders which the somewhat befuddled and emotional crew, in turn, sometimes follows

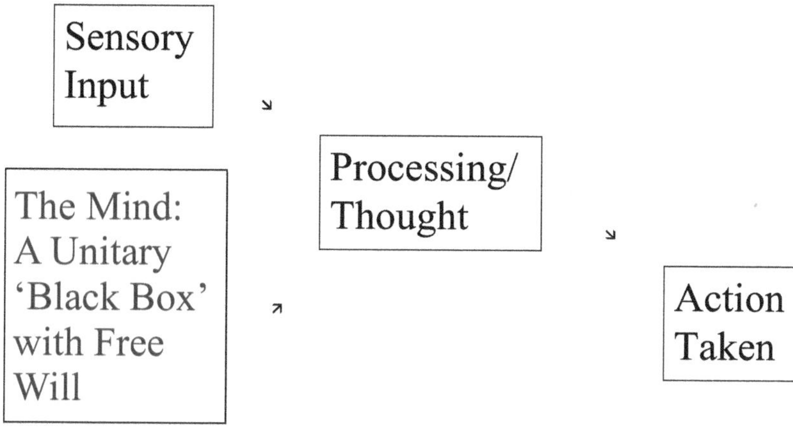

Figure 15.1 Traditional, Massively Over-simplified Model of the Movement from Sensory Input to Action in the Brain

and sometimes doesn't hear or disregards. Put graphically (Figure 15.1), there appears to be a simple line from sensory input to decision-processing to action. While this notion may have some subjective appeal, it is a poor model for what is in fact happening in our brains.

If the informational sources of human decision-making and action are not unitary, neither is the brain which does the processing. First of all, there are a number of steps along the road. Figure 15.2 lays out a better, if still simplified, schematic. Sensory input is first subject to primary processing, which sorts out basic elements like shape, colour, motion, etc., then secondary processing applies meaning, identifying the input in some way. With recognition can come a step like desire formation, where a generalized wish is created. Then may come an inhibition moment. The brain works as much by inhibition as by affirmative processes; if the desire is judged inappropriate it can be stopped in its tracks. If the decision process goes forward, then, in this model, a more specific strategy would be created, and an action plan to put it in place. Once again, however, there can be a chance for inhibition – the plan could work, but it would create trouble in some other way.

Consider, for instance, the decision on whether or not to eat some *hors d'oeuvres*. If they were in front of you on a plate, you would need to identify them as having a certain look and smell, and then ascribe meaning to that combination. Food, you would conclude. That conclusion could lead to a desire to eat, a desire that might be blocked, either unconsciously if you were intent on some absorbing task, or consciously if you were on a diet. If no inhibition came at that point, you might think about moving over and taking it off the plate to put in your mouth. Then, another consideration could intrude: someone is holding the plate in a proprietary fashion. It is tasty and desirable, but it belongs to someone else – inhibition intrudes once again.

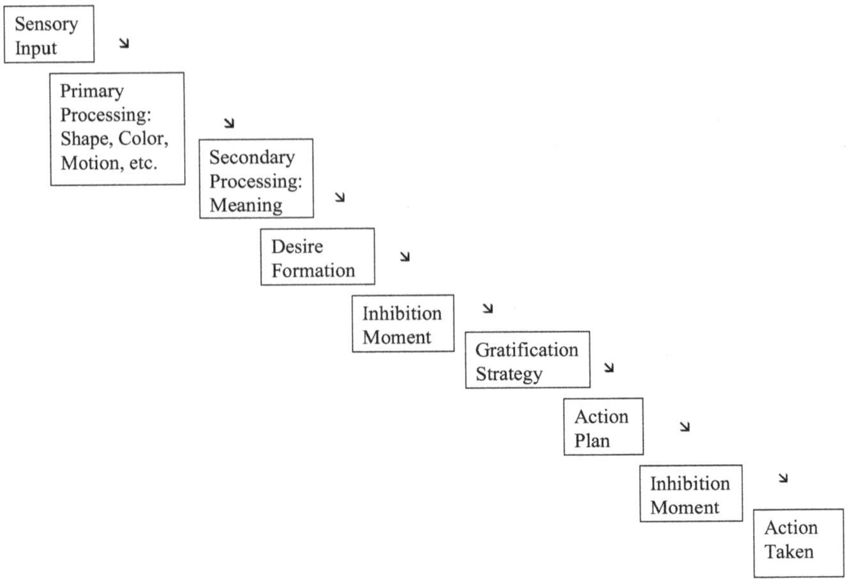

Figure 15.2 Plausible, Less Over-simplified Model of the Movement from Sensory Input to Action in the Brain

Even here the model is too simple, however. Often, several tracks are running simultaneously, influencing each other, and being influenced, in turn, buy the neurochemical state of the brain, attention-grabbing alternatives, stress and a host of other factors. The model set out in Figure 15.3 is still at best an approximation of the actual chain of processes, but it serves to suggest the complexity and multiplicity of the real thing.

Specialization in Function and Anatomy

This complexity is reflected in the emerging anatomical picture of the functioning brain, which looks to be a mix of specialized and multi-purpose structures, tied together in systems that follow typical patterns in many humans, but allow some variation as well. As with the nature/nurture argument, there is ongoing debate around the specialized/general issue as well (e.g., Barrett and Kurzban 2006). The vision of extreme functional generality and plasticity that accompanied "black box" behaviourism gave way early in the cognitive revolution, at least in some scholarship, to a kind of hyper-modularity and specialization that in turn has proven overstated. Current scholarship recognizes a balance, nicely summed up as early as 1992 by Stephen Kosslyn:

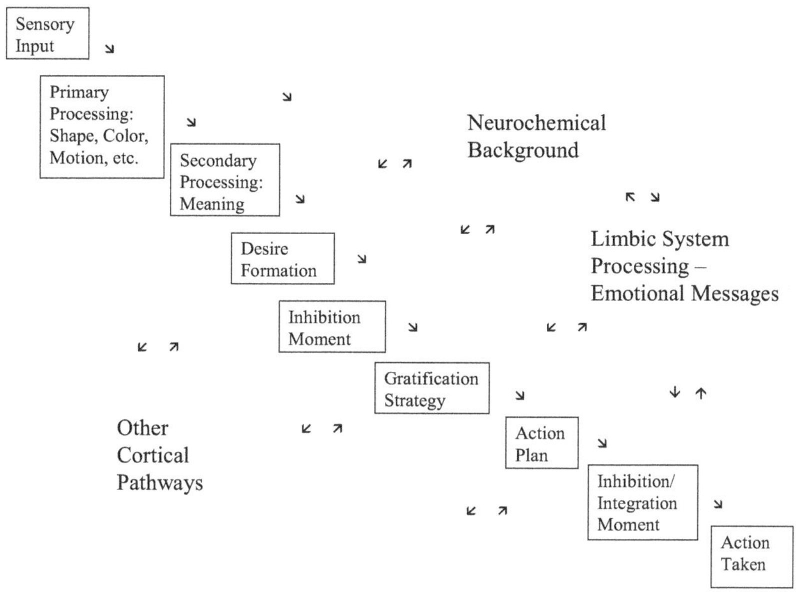

Figure 15.3 Combine the Model with Other Systems and Effects

> Any complex ability, then is not accomplished by a single part of the brain. So, in this sense, the globalists were right. The kinds of functions posited by the phrenologists are not localized in a single brain region. However, simple processes that are recruited to exercise such abilities are localized. So in this sense, the localizationists were right (quoted in Gazzaniga et al. 2002 at 14).

By way of example, the primary processing of visual information from the eye is done by some very specialized areas in the visual cortex, with selective sensitivity to properties such as line, colour and motion (Frackowiak et al. 2004; Zeki 1999). The assembly of this data into that meaningful amalgam we call sight pulls these different processing strands together, first through interactive "concurrent processing" (Gazzaniga et al. 2002), and then through the recruitment of an even wider anatomical network including the equipment involved with memory, emotion, etc.

Even at this more general level, however, there remains specialization. For instance, humans are heavily primed, even overprimed, to see faces. If you have ever stared at a knotty board and watched as face after face pops out from the random patterns, you will know what I mean. The efficacy of the ☺ symbol in generating the "it's a face" response is unquestionable (see generally, Svoboda 2007). This face recognition capacity has been traced, at least in part, to a brain formation called the fusiform gyrus. There has been some continuing debate over its degree of specialization. For instance, the fusiform gyrus is also involved in reading – an example of recruitment of an existing system for a new culturally constructed practice (McCandliss et al. 2003). There is also continuing research into how much experiential learning is necessary to prime this region's functions (Johnson 2004; Halit et al. 2003; Pascalis and Slater 2003). Nonetheless, the localization of critical aspects of facial processing in this area is well established (e.g., Gazzaniga et al. 2002). Some researchers call a functionally specialized structure such as the fusiform gyrus a "primitive" (Goodenough and Prehn 2004). Returning to the Kosslyn quote above, these primitives embody the pieces of the process that are indeed physically localized and functionally specialized.

Functional specialization can also occur in a distributed process employing a network of capacities. Language use, for instance, is a complex behaviour that is partly localized in "language centres", such as Broca's and Wernicke's areas in the left brain of most individuals. It is also distributed over other areas, including the motor control areas used in speech production. Moral judgment, of more direct interest to law, appears to have no unique locus in the brain, but a number of studies have identified a reasonably well-defined anatomical network that is implicated in this kind of thought: the ventromedial prefrontal cortex, orbitofrontal cortex, posterior cingulate cortex and posterior superior temporal sulcus (Goodenough and Prehn 2004; Greene and Haidt 2002). From a functional standpoint, this network suggests the assembly of a number of tasks, including control of behaviour, processing of socially relevant cues, memory and processing of emotional stimuli to produce the overarching work of judging right and wrong (Greene and Haidt 2002).

Some have suggested that consciousness is a kind of workspace within which we can recruit relatively localized and/or specialized mental capacities into more complex, task-linked networks (Baars et al. 1998). This idea can be taken a step further – we can also use culture and externalized knowledge to help prompt choices among the capacities and networks we deploy on a task. For instance, preliminary work suggests that the application of a deductive legal rule to resolve a question of liability may shift our processing on the problem from the classical moral judgment network to brain physiology linked with other kinds of deductive tasks (Schultz et al. 2001; Goodenough and Prehn 2004). In this sense law may provide a kind of hyper-consciousness, with powers of recruitment and direction that span our informational and processing repertoires (Goodenough and Prehn 2004). One critical capacity which the law must both recruit and control is emotion.

Importance of Emotion for Thought, Judgment and Action

Cognitive science is recasting how we think about emotion. The classic emotion/reason divide appears to be crumbling; rather, emotion, paired with other mental capacities, appears an important component in many domains of thought. Furthermore, the more we study emotion, the more we recognize different aspects of the cluster of phenomena which have been grouped under that label. Writing in the context of moral judgment, Goodenough and Prehn (2004) have suggested:

> [P]rogress will be made by separating "emotion," the sensation of arousal that we monitor in ourselves and others, from "emotion," the functional component in mental processes. Its meaning as a sensation state strikes us as being less important to normative judgment than are the functions which the-thing-we-call-emotion-when-we-experience-it is contributing to the processing of normative tasks.

They continue:

> These disparate results suggest that emotion acts as a great emphasizer and highlighter in the brain, an indicator of importance and urgency. Damasio, for instance, has suggested that emotion plays a key role in creating a "somatic marker" which helps guide and prioritize decision making processes (Damasio 1994). In the realm of memory, events that are associated with emotional states are much more likely to be transferred from working memory to long term recollection (Morris and Dolan 2004). In the current brain, emotion drives attention towards its associated objects (Anderson and Phelps 2001). Emotion gets us up and doing. As even Hume recognized, emotion is a great translator of thought to action (Hume 1739; Rolls 1999; Schwartz 2000).

The emotional components of thought also have some degree of physical localization, including major portions of the limbic system. This brain system includes a number of sub-parts often associated with quick, emotion-linked responses and with unconscious processes such as memory formation, hunger and sexual attraction. A key element in emotion is the amygdala, a portion of the limbic brain that sits physically below the outer cortex, but which communicates extensively with cortical areas, particularly those in the adjacent pre-frontal region, behind the forehead. Patients with amygdala injury often show emotional deficits (Anderson and Phelps 2001, 2002; Phelps 2002, 2006), and imaging studies show amygdala activation in emotion-linked thought (e.g., Morris and Dolan 2004).

The limbic involvement and the cognitive intensification we recognize in ourselves as emotion (Dolan 2002) can push a desire or action plan to which it is linked past several inhibition points; we all have done something when we were mad that we would not have done in a moment of cool reflection (Goodenough 2004).

Emotion and Law

Given its importance in thought and action generally, emotion is a key component to be recruited in an effective regime of law (Goodenough and Prehn 2004; see generally Maroney 2006; Bandes 2000). The dry, orderly, normative worlds of Kant, Rawls or Posner may be intellectually attractive, but they seldom lead to human action. It takes someone like Martin Luther King, harnessing emotion and reason together in a united appeal, to move us through our brains to act against injustice.

Like any strong ingredient, however, emotion must be contained by law as well as put to use. Rapid, emotionally charged responses are not always the wisest courses of action. The law's delay, when not excessive, gives time for passions to cool, at least a bit. But excessive control is a problem as well. The law faces a Goldilocks dilemma – it needs cognition that is not too hot, and not too cold, but just right for the task at hand.

Furthermore, it is not just in judging others that emotion is important. It is also a key element in our own moral choices, often empowering our inhibitory functions. Inhibitory checks perform a key role in the chain of processing from sensory impression to resulting action. A hot upwelling of distaste, reluctance or guilt as we contemplate our own actions is a strong element in successfully choosing a rule-abiding path, as is the pleasant feeling accompanying a choice for good. The hypothetical "good person" postulated at the beginning of this essay will be no stranger to these sensations and to the choices of restraint associated with them. Anatomically, inhibition is to some degree localized in the frontal cortex, and damage to this area leads to impulsivity and a lack of control that, when coupled with environmental factors, can lead to increased likelihood of criminal behaviour (Sapolsky 2004).

Law can help redirect our emotion-linked desires and to strengthen our inhibitions. Alexander Hamilton emphasized this need for our institutions to control emotion: "Governments are instituted because the passions of men will not conform to the dictates of reason without restraint" (Clark 1926, at 316). But emotion is also a critical part of control as well, and a personal emotional response is put to use in most legal systems. Because there can never be a police officer on every corner, systems of law must engage the natural self-policing of basically good people. This is particularly true for matters where the breach of the rule is easy to effectuate and not so easy to detect. In such cases, rules must be designed so that people obey out of a strongly felt duty, and not out of fear. It is emotion that drives such duty. The Latin poet Horace put it: "Leges sine moribus vanae," or, as I loosely translate it, "Laws without a moral basis are pointless." Neuroscience suggests we could equally well substitute "emotional" for "moral".

Methodology of Cognitive Jurisprudence

Informed by these principles of neurological study of thought and behaviour, we suggest a five-part methodology for applying a cognitive jurisprudence approach to the study of law and of matters of interest to the law:

1. Identify questions of interest to the law relating to thought and behaviour that are amenable to cognitive study.
2. Examine the strategic context within which the thought and behaviour takes place.

3. Consider the possible cognitive structures and processes that could be involved in the targeted thought and behaviour and form testable hypotheses concerning these processes.
4. Undertake empirical research to test the hypotheses.
5. Bring the results back to inform the formulation of legal doctrine and the factual investigations of courts and other bodies.

The selection of questions is an important first step. Some of the questions of interest to the law will be amenable to cognitive study; others will not. Additionally, some have already been solved adequately as a matter of the naive psychology of law itself or of traditional academic psychology based in behavioural research. Of course, there is always value in a better understanding of our successes. Nonetheless, we suggest that cognitive jurisprudence should particularly aim at problems where there are failures in accepted doctrine to achieve results and where existing legal science is unable to provide good answers for these failures.

We believe that we have such a question in the failures of intellectual property law, particularly copyright, to engage the voluntary compliance of much of humanity, including those in societies that generally respect legal institutions. The remaining portions of the methodology will be explored in the context of how cognitive jurisprudence might help us approach this problem.

A Cognitive Hypothesis about Property

Property is a very productive human institution. It is not simply an assertion as against the world that the possessor of a resource, tool or other item of interest can keep it against potential rivals. Rather, it is at the least a mutually respected understanding to allocate *uncontested* possession to the person who is now the owner. Even stronger, the convention requires others to come to the aid of an owner whose possession is threatened by a third party.

Such a convention reshapes the strategic landscape in extremely important ways. First of all, property avoids rivalrous use disputes (e.g., Stake 2004). The time and energy consumed by fights over resources can be redirected into much more productive paths. John Maynard Smith (1982) famously demonstrated the evolutionary stability of a property-style convention for this reason alone, calling it the "bourgeois strategy".

Property is the source of several other benefits. It often (although not always) provides incentives for conservation and against the overexploitation problems popularly known as the tragedy of the commons (Hardin 1968; Ostrom 1990). It rewards investments in the creation, preservation and improvement of resources. If an asset can be expropriated at will by the meanest and strongest, or by the cleverest and stealthiest, no one else will bother much about investing time or money in it. It enables bargained exchange, making possible the gains of trade (Demsetz 1964), and encourages the internalization of externalities (Demsetz 1967). Finally, as the work of Hernando de Soto (2000) recognizes, an accumulation of property can create the cushion we call capital, which allows us to undertake new creative ventures.

This cascade of multiple strategic gains does have some offsetting costs. The power of property to create further wealth, one of its chief benefits, can shift the opportunity for economic betterment to existing property owners, creating the two-tiered society of haves and have-nots apparent in many parts of the world. A society of serfs and aristocrats is one possible outcome of an unfettered, property-based system. On the whole, however, the productive potential of ownership as a device for redesigning the strategic landscape to permit investment and trade is too powerful to ignore. Property needs to be harnessed and buffered, not rejected.

But property also does not come for free in our cognitive make-up. There are countervailing desires to take and make use of resources. Property in the brain – at least when applied to choices about taking the possessions of others – could be rooted in an inhibitory response, stopping us from appropriating otherwise inviting and useful things. The rules of property need to be powerfully rooted in our emotional reactions if they are to hold us back at the key moment of perceived availability.

Here we move into the realm of informed speculation, or a hypothesis, in the language of science. We believe that our ability to recognize and respect property, at least as it applies to tangible objects such as food, tools, clothing, etc., is connected to one or more cognitive primitives in most human brains. As the fusiform gyrus provides an enhanced, localized capacity for the recognition of faces, so too could the brain have structures that help us to assign the characteristics of property to those things that we recognize as possessions. It should be noted that this theory stands in contrast to a classic explanation, put forward forcibly by proponents such as Thomas Hobbes (1660) and Jeremy Bentham (1843) that property is only a creation of the state, and has no place in a "natural" order of things (see also Stake 2004). As Bentham puts it (1843 at Part 1, Chapter 8):

> Property and law are born and must die together. Before laws, there was no property; take away the laws, all property ceases.

There are a number of pieces of evidence, none as yet conclusive, supporting our hypothesis. To begin with, the Maynard Smith work on the bourgeois strategy, cited above, suggests that a property institution is evolvable as a biological trait. Cross-species comparison shows something looking like a respect for property in a reasonable number of species (Stake 2004). Chimpanzees and bonobos, our nearest cousins, show some respect for possession within their social group, particularly for food (e.g., Stevens 2004; Boesch and Boesch-Achermann 2000; deWaal 1989), and to some degree for tools (e.g., Boesch and Boesch-Achermann 2000). Primates provide a kind of natural laboratory for exploring whether behaviours like property can arise without the support of sophisticated cultural transmission.

Anthropological surveys suggest that some form of the property convention appears in just about every human society (e.g., Brown 1991; Fikentscher 2006) although often interwoven with everyday life in ways different from Western cultural expectations. Property is a major category in the vast ethnographic archive of the Human Relations Area Files,[4] and even most Communist governments recognized private property in personal possessions. This near-ubiquity in culture is not in itself persuasive; a system as potent for benefit as property could be socially created in multiple places, and might well spread rapidly by imitation and adoption once devised (Goodenough 2001b). Nonetheless, this wide distribution is suggestive that recognizing property may well be a capacity, like language, which is supported by particularly suited elements of brain physiology.

Evidence on the failure of property in humans also suggests a brain link. There are a few, still quite limited, studies of patients with injury-induced kleptomania. In one instance the injury was linked to areas that help to provide inhibitory impulse control (Nyffeler and Regard 2001). Other studies suggest a linkage of kleptomania to frontal lobe defects (Grant et al. 2006a), which may also implicate control deficits. Attempts to link more general mental performance to kleptomania are equivocal (Grant et al 2006b), although severity of illness did correlate with executive function deficits. Although very preliminary, these results suggest that the property conclusion may be effectuated through an inhibitory process, like the moment hypothesized in the discussion of decision-making above, when the hungry subject realizes that the food is on someone else's plate, and not on a common serving platter.

Finally, there appears to be a deep emotional component to our property rules as they apply to our physical possessions. The owner of property, fairly naturally, feels a deep violation when such property is taken, and will often defend property vociferously. Even more telling, both third-party enforcement and second-party respect appear to have strongly felt emotional components that, when present, give strength to the convention where it really matters – in the brains of the potential takers and punishers. Traditional property's access to effective, emotion-linked processing is an important element in its relative success as a human institution.

Challenge of Intellectual Property

Intellectual property law, by contrast, faces more serious challenges in promoting voluntary compliance. The problem is not doctrinal. The fields of copyright, patent and trademark have well-developed bodies of law, with clearly established rules, both at the national level and in such international conventions as the Agreement on Trade Related Intellectual Property (TRIPS) and the Berne Union for the Protection of Literary and Artistic Property (Berne Convention). Nonetheless, the rules of intellectual property (IP), and of copyright in particular, are widely disregarded whenever technologically feasible. Moreover, the rules are disregarded by "good" people, and even by people with a deep stake in the effective workings of an IP

4 Available at http://www.yale.edu/hraf/Ocm_xml/newOcm.xml#420.

system. Two anecdotes, not attributable, but shared with us in good faith, help illustrate this point.

The United States military maintains three principal academies for training future officers: the US Military Academy at West Point, the Naval Academy at Annapolis and the Air Force Academy at Colorado Springs. These academies maintain discipline through a strict honour code, widely respected by the students.[5] The West Point version is particularly succinct: "A Cadet will not lie, cheat, steal, or tolerate those who do." Of course there are always unreported infractions, but the codes are generally viewed to be successful. Property crimes among students are particularly rare, we are informed. We have also been informed by someone familiar with one of these academies that records of student Internet usage suggest with near certainty that file-sharing of copyrighted music was very widespread in that institution. For a large group of students in this ultra-law-abiding society, "stealing" intellectual property simply didn't register as theft.

Having a personal stake in the protection of creative production doesn't seem to create better behaviour, either. In conversation about a neurological approach to IP law, the general counsel of a major film production company admitted that many of his co-workers are active in downloading music and, increasingly, movies as well. This is a group for whom the logic of intellectual property rules should be very clear and compelling; and yet it had little impact on their day-to-day behaviour. "What's that about, then?" was this lawyer's puzzled summing up.

What Makes IP Harder? A Further Hypothesis

The approaches of cognitive science suggest a further hypothesis about intellectual property. Starting with a review of its strategic attributes, we see that IP does not map fully onto the full list of advantages of traditional property. While some are strongly present, others are missing. For instance, as is widely recognized, most intellectual property is not subject to rivalrous use disputes (Stake 2004; Landes and Posner 1989). The singing of a song or the use of an invention by one person does not prevent someone else from doing the same thing, although the utility of the song or invention may diminish if it is too widely used. Similarly, overexploitation to depletion is not really a problem. Technological advances may permit the overexploitation of previously abundant physical resources (e.g., ocean fishing stocks in the twentieth century), but with IP the knowledge itself does not go away because many use it.

On the other hand, a property approach to the work of the intellect does create pay-offs for both the effort of creation and for the investment involved in development and dissemination. Providing such an incentive for the creator is the

5 The honour codes can be accessed: Air Force: http://www.usafa.af.mil/34trw/cwc/cwch.cfm?catName=cwc; Army: http://www.usma.edu/Cpme/; Navy: http://www.usna.edu/OfficerDevelopment/honor/honorconcept.html.

rationale set out in Article I, Section 8 of the US Constitution for giving Congress the power:

> To promote the progress of science and useful arts, by securing for limited times to authors and inventors the exclusive right to their respective writings and discoveries.

Beyond creation, the incentives of copyright and patent also extend to the developers and marketers of inventions and artistic works, a critical factor for such intellectual property industries and music, television, computing and pharmaceuticals. IP rights also provide a capital basis that can be used for further research and creativity.

So here we have a category of activity where a property convention can create productive opportunities for creative work and investment, but where it also undercuts the advantages of non-rivalrous sharing. At a strategic level, this partial fit is somewhat ameliorated by such factors as fair use and the idea/expression dichotomy in US copyright law and the disclosure requirements and limited timescale for patent protection. At a cognitive level, however, the limited overlap fits with our historical knowledge that assigning property rights to creative expression and invention is a relative latecomer to human experience. If, as Maynard Smith's "bourgeois strategy" suggests, preventing rivalrous use contests is the initial impulse for the evolution of property, then works of the intellect may not have been part of any historical evolution of property in interaction with the human brain.

We believe that whatever neurological primitives or particularized networks may exist to help us make property-based, emotionally grounded, self-restraining decisions about the control and use of assets, they do not easily recognize creative works as being part of their remit. Viewed from this standpoint, intellectual property could be economically sensible yet cognitively weak. Without a ready connection into the limbic system and highly motivated structures of inhibition, IP can make all the sense in the world as a social policy and still be behaviourally invisible, unable to motivate self-generated observance in hyper-honest cadets and self-interested IP creators alike.

So what, if any, is the emotion-linked processing of IP-related rights in the brain? Evolutionary biology suggests a different set of pathways that may have evolved to reward creativity: pathways related to respect and prestige on the one hand and to secret-keeping on the other.

Acclaim and Secrecy

What Rewards Drive Creativity?

Property is not the only medium within which creativity can be rewarded. Prestige, status, sexual attractiveness, these are all areas where achievement can pay in non-monetary coin. The evolutionary biologist Geoffrey Miller (2000) has argued just such an origin for human creativity and artistic achievement:

> The human mind's most impressive abilities are like the peacock's tail: they are courtship tools, evolved to attract and entertain sexual partners. By shifting our attention from a survival-centered view of evolution to a courtship-centered view, … we can understand more of the richness of human art, morality, language, and creativity (Miller 2000 at 4).

While comfortable living is certainly a goal for many creative personalities, it is often most important as providing the means to continue to be creative. Many also respond to peer and fan recognition – after all, "money can't buy you love". Academics are also players for this coin. This chapter is a case in point. Little, if any, financial compensation will ever be paid to the authors; one of us is tenured and the other is a post-doc; neither will reap any kind of immediate monetary reward. On the other hand, we are aiming to increase our status within the academy by offering what we hope will be seen as a good piece of thinking. There may be long-term rewards attaching to this strategy, but from a financial standpoint a similar amount of time spent on consulting would be a much more lucrative investment. For most scholars, copying, reuse and adoption is the best reward. "Just don't forget to cite me", is the academic's cry. Similar contests for prestige operate in Hollywood (don't forget the credit), in the open source software community, and even among computer hackers.

That is not to say that creative people don't want their share of whatever money may come from their work; they may get cross if they feel they have been used. On the other hand, the legendary inattentiveness to the commercial details of many creators and inventors (although of course not all) is further evidence for a cognitive disassociation between intellectual output and notions of property.

There is a counter-narrative in this story of acclaim, but it is not property – it is secrecy. In a world without intellectual property institutions, that which we want to reserve to ourselves, we keep secret. That which we don't keep secret we trade for acclaim. In a world where IP rules exist, the messages are mixed together. The point becomes to spread it about but to charge a toll. If we are correct in our view of human psychology, however, the act of spreading the works of the intellect sends a deeply understood message to the recipients of the knowledge that runs counter to property, a message that demands respect, but not money.

Fan Psychology

We believe that the psychology of consumers makes better sense when viewed through this alternative story of the motivations and rewards for creativity. If authors and inventors are driven by the hope of respect, or, even better, adulation and acclaim, then consumers are willing to give it. We have a term for such a consumer: a "fan". We take the idea, the song, the story, the technological advance, and we pay for it not with money but with appreciation and social deference. In this context, file-sharing makes perfect sense – what better way to show respect than to pass the subject matter of the acclaim on to others?

Investor and Marketer

Whatever the ambivalence of the creator to finance vs. prestige as a reward system, the developer and marketer of intellectual output by and large has a clear set of financial goals: a handsome return on investment. For this player, the bottom line is indeed the bottom line. In fact, there is a significant opportunity for arbitrage between the psychological motivations of the creator and the audience on the one hand, and the opportunities to demand payment for access and use under copyright and other IP laws, on the other.

The current hit of American television, *American Idol*, provides a perfect example of this (Hedegaard 2006). It is a most exquisite money-making machine wrapped around the desire of the performers for adulation and the willingness of fans to give it. The candidates for stardom (literally the "idol" of the title; it is not called *American Financial Success*) are willing to humiliate themselves in the early rounds for the chance of going to Hollywood for a real opportunity for temporary adulation, including voting by the fans, spiced with the understanding that all but one of the candidates will ultimately be dismissed.

The whole process makes money across a number of levels. First of all, there is the success of the show in grabbing the attention of its viewers, which is then sold to advertisers for a whopping figure. Coca-Cola reportedly pays $15 million a year just to have the judges drink from glasses with the Coke name and logo on them (Sweet 2006).

Secondly, it has been reported that winning singers are often signed up to a recording deal controlled by the programme organizers, such as Taylor Hick's deal with Simon Fuller and 19 Recordings Limited (Reality TV Magazine 2006), so that the financial benefit of the idolatry relationships created through the show can be captured over the future life of stardom. Ironically, the losers from second place on down are apparently free to sign with any record label they can find, and rumour has it some losers end up with more profitable careers than the winners achieve. Season 3 also-ran Jennifer Hudson's win of a 2007 Academy Award for her *Dreamgirls* performance is evidence of the immense recognition value that can flow from participation.

Finally, the show and its on-screen panel are themselves stars, with their own fan base to exploit through merchandizing, spin-offs, etc. (Sweet 2006). In effect, the research and development process of a music business has been turned into something that can be sold – a necessary business expense turned into a profit centre, and most of it made possible because of an intellectual property approach that puts control of the exploitation of the status and adulation-driven psychology of the performers and the fans into the hands of investors and business management acting from financial motivation.

Three Property Hypotheses: Implications for Law and Empirical Research

We have advanced a series of hypotheses about the cognitive aspects of property and intellectual property. To begin with, we suggest that traditional property approaches, and in particular those relating to tangible objects, are supported, at least in part, by functional neurological structures or networks that help recognize property-related choices and to link those choices to emotional, inhibitory processing. Second, we argue that these property-related primitives and/or networks are not readily recruited and mobilized by concepts of intellectual property. Third, and finally, we argue that creative work more naturally stimulates a different set of responses, linked to prestige and respect, rather than to property attributes.

These hypotheses, if correct, suggest that a "more of the same, only harder", approach to the challenges of intellectual property law observance will not produce noticeably better results in terms of compliance. There are, of course arguments by some that our IP rules have become overprotective in their scope, and that better results are not desirable. The pros and cons of such arguments are outside the scope of this chapter. Rather, it presumes that some level of IP protection is beneficial and that it would be best for society, both in terms of optimizing intellectual creation and use and in terms of respect for the rule of law generally, for the rules embodying that protection to be accepted and respected by the majority of the population independent of the technical difficulty of infringement and of any fear of punishment.

From such a starting point, we should seek a legal institution that will recruit the mental structures of its targeted humans so as to engage their emotional responses around the desired choices. This would be aimed both at potential infringers and at those who help enforce the rules in the actions of others. Decades of failure suggest that the rhetoric of property will not provide the necessary emotional content. Perhaps building a law around the idea of respect would be more

In traditional jurisprudence, advancing and arguing for such a model, and seeking to translate it into some kind of public policy and doctrinal approach, would be the end of the story. Thanks to the technological advances of neuroscience, coupled with the methods of traditional psychology, these hypotheses about the cognitive basis for property and intellectual property are no longer just a matter for philosophical speculation; like face recognition or language use, they can be the subject of empirical exploration and testing.

Next Steps: Testing the Hypotheses and Re-examining Intellectual Property Doctrine

If this chapter were a novel, we would be forced to admit that the final chapters can't be written yet. At best, a summary of the expected plot can be sketched in. So far, we have laid out hypotheses about the cognitive basis of the challenges facing any property regime as a means of protecting creative works in a digital age, and we have suggested a methodology for attacking the problem and testing the hypotheses. Designing and implementing an empirical programme of experimentation is clearly the next step in the process. The possibility of confirming – or falsifying – jurisprudential hypotheses through direct testing is one of the advantages of a cognitive approach. It is also one of its challenges. Work on this testing is going forward, but at this writing is still in its preliminary phases.

Targets for the research include a better identification of the physical structures involved in the various cognitive approaches we have discussed: property, respect, secrecy and intellectual property. The emotional engagement of subjects involved in making choices about these kinds of problems will need to be examined. The different positions of a creator of copyrighted material, of its taker and of a third party sitting in judgment will need to be considered. Finally, linkages between the anatomical activity and the behaviour involved will need to be made and tested. Because our understanding of each of these is still in its early stages, there is work that will stretch over some years waiting for us and, we hope, for others who may be inspired to join this effort.

We believe, however, that the work will be worth the investment of time and money, as it can help inform a doctrinal overhaul of the intellectual property field, particularly in copyright. As we discussed at the opening of this chapter, the need for an overhaul is manifest. The current doctrine may have worked well in a technological state that made copying difficult and self-policing by end-users relatively unimportant. The new world of easy replication and dissemination has made the old approaches increasingly untenable (e.g., Slater et al. 2005; Ginsberg 2001) – a development some applaud (e.g., Lessig 2001, 2004).

If we are correct in our hypotheses, then we are likely to need a new model for providing financial support for artistic creators. While simply turning everything loose for free has a kind of anarchic appeal, it would probably lead to a marked diminution of creative output. The new model can involve a move from a pay-for-each-copy approach to one involving payments linked to the technology itself – such as a fee attached to computer sales or to the sales of iPods, burnable CDs and other means of copying. Such an approach has been tried widely in the European Union (e.g., White 2006), which has a history of such technology-tied fees. A subscription approach might also work (e.g., Reese 2001; Slater et al. 2005), similar to the blanket licensing currently used by performance rights societies such as ASCAP and BMI for hard-to-monitor circumstances such as live music in bars and clubs. The role of the record companies and other traditional intermediaries would necessarily change, but it would not necessarily disappear (Slater et al. 2005; Lemley and Reese 2004; Reese 2001).

We should also be able to design new approaches, better linked to human psychology. For instance, if we are correct in targeting respect and acclaim as easily triggered sources of emotional motivation, our legal institutions could be crafted to use this as a basis for rewarding creativity. The moderate success of iTunes as an intermediary (Slater et al. 2005; Gasser et al. 2004) might be further strengthened by tapping the power of self-policing emotions. Some of this is already going on in the private sector. The Motion Picture Association of America, for instance, has run a campaign of commercials called Respect Copyright intended to do just that:

> This commercial packs an emotional punch: it uses patriotic-sounding music in the style of Aaron Copland, and it co-opts a popular movie to remind us how exciting action sequences can be. But most importantly, it recasts copyright infringement, a supposedly victimless crime, as injurious to a likeable, presumably working-class individual. By giving a face to film production, the Respect Copyrights campaign appeals to our sense of fairness (Demers 2006 at 11).

Demers goes on to point out that this image is at least partly a fraud – the movies are owned by studios, and not by these individuals. Furthermore, at this writing (March 2007) the Respect Copyright website has reverted to a message of enforcement and fear. "If you think you can get away with illegally trafficking in movies, think again," its homepage stridently declares.[6]

Notwithstanding the challenges, a respect-based approach needs to be incorporated into the future of intellectual property. If large-scale production is not to go the way of dinosaurs, some kind of inhibiting, emotional contact between the consumers and the creators must be put to work. The law providing a structure of economic support for creative activity needs to engage the sense of ought, and not just provide a technically coherent body of rules (Goodenough 2002). Better knowledge about the psychology of respect and ownership should lead us to better results.

Conclusion

The revolution of cognitive neuroscience is sparking remarkable advances in understanding human thought and behaviour. This new understanding has the potential to help solve a number of classic conundrums of the law, allowing us to create more effective legal regimes. By identifying the functional working of the brain as it tackles particular mental jobs, we can form and test hypotheses about the processing of decision-making on issues of respect for property and the person, moral judgment and punishment. We can call this kind of approach cognitive jurisprudence.

We suggest that law works best when it is able to recruit brain functions strongly linked to attention, motivation and action. Although we often think of the law as cooling emotion, the process is a two-way street; emotion gives law cognitive salience and effectiveness. We examine possible cognitive models for both traditional and intellectual property, particularly copyright, both by way of an example and as a proposed target for further research. We advance three

6 See http://www.respectcopyrights.org/content.html.

hypotheses that can explain why our systems of intellectual property are less successful in recruiting self-enforcement and restraint than are our rules for more traditional forms of ownership.

Finally, we recognize the need to test these hypotheses and sketch a few of the implications which confirmation of the approach would have creating a more effective body of intellectual property law. While the full potential of cognitive jurisprudence awaits the results of empirical programmes such as these, we believe that we are at the early stages of what will be a remarkably productive interaction between law and science.

References

Anderson, A.K. and Phelps, E.A. (2001) Lesions of the human amygdala impair enhanced perception of emotionally salient events. *Nature*, 411: 305–309.

----- (2002) Is the human amygdala critical for the subjective experience of emotion? Evidence of intact dispositional affect in patients with amygdala lesions. *Journal of Cognitive Neuroscience*, **14**: 709–720.

Baars, B.J., Newman, J. and Taylor, J.G. (1998) Neuronal mechanisms of consciousness: A Relational Global Workspace framework. In *Toward a Science of Consciousness II: The second Tucson discussions and debates* (S. Hameroff, A. Kaszniak, and J. Laukes (eds)) pp. 269–278. Cambridge, MA: MIT Press.

Bandes, S. (ed.) (2000) *The Passions of Law,* New York: NYU Press.

Barrett, H.C. and Kurzban, R. (2006) Modularity in cognition: Framing the debate. *Psychological Review*, **113**(3), 628–647.

Bentham, J. (1843) *Principles of the Civil Code*, Bowring edition, available at www.la.utexas.edu/research/poltheory/bentham/pcc/index.html

Binmore, K. (1998) *Just Playing: Game Theory and the Social Contract*, Cambridge, Mass.: MIT Press.

Boesch, C. and Boesch-Achermann, H. (2000) *The Chimpanzees of the Tai Forest: Behavioral Ecology and Evolution*, Oxford: Oxford University Press.

Brown, D.E. (1991) *Human Universals*, Philadelphia, Temple University Press.

Chorvat, T. and McCabe, K. (2004) The brain and the law. *Phil. Trans. R. Soc. Lond.* B, **359**: 1727–1736.

Clark, J. (1926) *Great Sayings by Great Lawyers*. Kansas City, Vernon Law Book Co.

Cooter, R. and Ulen, T. (1988) *Law and Economics.* Glenview, Illinois: Scott, Forsman and Co.

Damasio, A.R. (1994) *Descartes' Error: Emotion, Reason, and the Human Brain.* New York: G.P. Putnam's Sons.

Demers, J. (2006) *Steal This Music: How Intellectual Property Law Affects Musical Creativity*, Athens, GA: University of Georgia Press.

Demsetz, H. (1964) The Exchange and Enforcement of Property Rights. *Journal of Law and Economics*, **7**: 11–26.
----- (1967) Towards a Theory of Property Rights. *The American Economics Review*, **57**: 347–359.
de Soto, H. 2000. *The Mystery of Captial*. New York: Basic Books.
de Waal, F.B.M. (1989) Food-sharing and reciprocal obligations in chimpanzees. *Journal of Human Evolution*, **18**: 433–459.
Dixit, A. and Skeath, S. (2004) *Games of Strategy* (2nd ed.), New York: W.W. Norton.
Dolan, R.J. (1999) On the neurology of morals. *Nature Neuroscience*, **2**: 297–299.
----- (2002) Emotion, cognition, and behavior. *Science*, **298**, 1191–1194.
Ellsworth, P. (2005) Legal Reasoning, in Holyoak, K. and Munson, R. (eds), *The Cambridge Handbook of Thinking and Reasoning*, Cambridge: Cambridge University Press, 685–703.
Fehr, E. and Fischbacher, U. (2004) Third party punishment and social norms. *Evolution and Human Behavior*, **25**, 63–87.
Fikentscher, W. (2006) Intellectual Property and Competition – Human Economic Universals. *The Gruter Institute Working Papers on Law, Economics, and Evolutionary Biology*, **4**(1) article 1, available at www.bepress.com/cgi/viewcontent.cgi?article=1016&contexgt=gwip.
Fisher, W.W. (2004) *Promises to Keep: Technology, Law and the Future of Entertainment*, Palo Alto: Stanford University Press.
Foley, L.A. (1993) *A Psychological View of the Legal System*, Madison, Wisconsin: Brown & Benchmark.
Frackowiak, R.S., Friston, K.J., Frith, C.D., Dolan, R.J., Price, C.J., Zeki, S., Ashburner, J., and Penny, W. (2004) *Human Brain Function*, 2nd ed., San Diego: Academic Press.
Gasser, U., Palfrey, J., Slater, D., Bambauer, D., Bragin, A., Harlow, J., Hoffmann, C. Hwang, R., Jackson, J., Krog, G., Locke, E., Mohr, S., Reidel, I., and Wilson, C.L. (2004) *iTunes: How Copyright, Contract, and Technology Shape the Business of Digital Media – A Case Study*. Berkman Center for Internet & Society, available at http//cyber.law.harvard.edu/media/itunes.
Gazzaniga, M.S., Ivry, R.B. and Mangum, G.R. (2002) *Cognitive Neuroscience: The Biology of the Mind*. New York: W.W. Norton.
Ginsberg, J.C. (2001). Copyright and Control over New Technologies of Dissemination, *Columbia Law Review* 101: 1613–1647.
Gintis, H. (2000) *Game Theory Evolving*, Princeton: Princeton University Press.
Glimcher, P.W. (2003) *Decisions, Uncertainty, and the Brain: The Science of Neuroeconomics*. Cambridge, MA: MIT Press.
Goodenough, O.R. (1997) Retheorizing Privacy and Publicity, *Intellectual Property Quarterly*, **1**: Launch Issue, 37–70.
----- (2001a) Mapping Cortical Areas Associated with Legal Reasoning and with Moral Intuition. *Jurimetrics*, **41**:429–442.

----- (2001b) Law and the Biology of Commitment, in Nesse, R. (ed.), *Evolution and the Capacity for Commitment*, New York: Russell Sage Press.
----- (2002) The Future of Intellectual Property: Broadening the Sense of "Ought". *European Intellectual Property Review*, **24**: 6–8.
----- (2006) Can Cognitive Neuroscience Make Psychology a Foundational Discipline for the Study of Law? in Brooks-Gordon, B. and Freeman, M. (eds), *Law and Psychology, Current Legal Issues Vol. 9*, Oxford: Oxford University Press.
----- (2007) Values, Mechanism Design, and Fairness, forthcoming in Zak, P. (ed.), *Moral Markets: The Critical Role of Values in the Economy*, Princeton: Princeton University Press, available at SSRN Free Enterprise: Values in Action Conference Series, 2005–2006, http://papers.ssrn.com/sol3/papers.cfm?abstract_id=933012.
Goodenough, O.R. and Prehn, K. (2005) A neuroscientifc approach to normative judgment in law and justice. *Phil. Trans. R. Soc. Lond.* B, **359**: 1709–1726.
Grant J.E. and Kim S.W. (2002) Kleptomania: emerging therapies target mood, impulsive behavior. *Current Psychiatry* 2002; **1**(8): 45–49.
Grant, J.E., Correia, S. and Brennan-Krohn (2006a) White matter integrity in kleptomania: A pilot study. *Psychiatry Res.* **147**(2–3): 233–7.
Grant, J.E., Odlaug, B.L. and Wozniak, J.R. (2006b) Neuropsychological functioning in kleptomania. Behav Res Ther. (epub ahead of print)
Greene, J. and Cohen, J. (2004) For the law, neuroscience changes nothing and everything. *Phil. Trans. R. Soc. Lond.* B, **359**: 1775–1785.
Greene, J. and Haidt, J. (2002) How (and where) does moral judgment work? *Trends in Cognitve Sciences,* **6**(12): 517–523.
Halit, H., de Haan, M. and Johnson, M.H. (2003) Cortical specialization for face processing: face sensitive event-relate potential components in 3 and 12 month old infants. *Neuro-Image*, **19**: 1180–1193.
Hardin, G. (1968) The Tragedy of the Commons. *Science,* **162**: 1243–1248.
Hedegaard, E. (2006) The Most Hated and Loved Man on TV. *Rolling Stone*, available at: http://www.rollingstone.com/news/coverstory/american_idol_worship.
Hobbes, T. (1660) *The Leviathan*, variously reprinted, available at http://oregonstate.edu/instruct/phl302/texts/hobbes/leviathan-contents.html.
Hume, D. (1739–40) *A Treatise of Human Nature*. Variously reprinted, available at http://socserv2.mcmaster.ca/~econ/ugcm/3ll3/hume/treat.html.
Johnson, M.H. (2004) Placiticity and functional brain development: the case of face processing, attention and performance, in Kanwisher, N. and Duncan, J. (eds), *Functional Imaging of Visual Cognition,* Oxford: Oxford University Press.
Jones, O. (2001) Time-Shifted Rationality and the Law of Law's Leverage: Behavioral Economics Meets Behavioral Biology. *Northwestern U. Law Rev.*, **95**: 1141–1206.

Kaplow, L. and Shavell, S.M. (2002) *Fairness versus Welfare*, Cambridge MA: Harvard University Press.

Kosfeld, M., Heinrichs, M., Zak, P.J., Fischbacher, U. and Fehr, E. (2005) Oxytocin increases trust in humans. *Nature*, **435**: 673–676.

Kosslyn, S.M. and Andersen, R.A. (eds) (1995) *Frontiers of Cognitive Neuroscience* Cambridge, MA, MIT Press.

Landes W. and Posner R. (1989) An Economic Analysis of Copyright Law, *J. Legal Stud.* **18**: 325–363.

Lemley, M.A. and Reese, R.A. (2004) Reducing Digital Copyright Infringement Without Restricting Innovation. *Stanford L. Rev.*, **56**: 1345–1434.

Lessig, L. (2004) *Free Culture: How Big Media Uses Technology and the Law to Lock Down Culture and Control Creativity*, New York: Penguin Press.

----- (2001) *The Future of Ideas: The Fate of the Commons in a Connected World*, New York: Random House.

Lucentini, J. (2005) Love is Like an Addiction: Looking for correlates in human and animal attraction. *The Scientist*, **19**(3): 20.

Maroney, T. (2006) Law and Emotion: A Proposed Taxonomy of an Emerging Field. *Law and Human Behavior*, **30**(2): 119–142.

Marr, D.C. (1982) *Vision: A Computational Investigation into the Human Representation and Processing of Visual Information*, New York: W.H. Freeman and Co.

Maynard Smith, J. (1982) *Evolution and the Theory of Games*, Oxford: Oxford University Press.

Maynard Smith, J. and Szathmáry, E. (1995) *The Major Transitions in Evolution,* Oxford: Oxford University Press.

Mazur, A. and Booth, A. (1998) Testosterone and dominance in men. *Behavioral & Brain Sciences* **21**: 353–397.

McCandliss, B., Cohen, L. and Dehaene, S. (2003) The visual word form area: expertise for reading in the fusiform gyrus. *Trends in Cognitive Sciences* **7**: 293–299.

Miller, G. (2000) *The Mating Mind: How Sexual Choice Shaped the Evolution of Human Nature*, New York: Doubleday.

Morris, J. and Dolan, R. (2004) Functional Neuroanatomy of Human Emotion. *In Human Brain Function* ((eds) R.S.J. Frackowiak et al.; 2nd ed.), pp. 365–396. San Diego: Academic Press.

Mundale, J. (2002) Concepts of localization: Balkanization in the Brain. *Brain and Mind*, **3**, 313–330.

Nyffeler, T. and Regard, M. (2001) Kleptomania in a patient with a right frontolimbic lesion. *Neuropsychiatry, Neuropsychology, and Behavioral* Neurology, **14**: 73–76.

Ostrom, E. (1990) *Governing the Commons: The Evolution of Institutions for Collective Action*, New York: Cambridge University Press.

Pascalis, O. and Slater, A. (eds) (2003) *Face perception in infancy and early childhood*. Hauppauge NY: Nova Science Publishers.

Phelps, E.A. (2002) The cognitive neuroscience of emotion. In *Cognitive Neuroscience: The Biology of Mind, 2nd ed.* (eds. M.S. Gazzaniga, R.B. Ivry, and G.R. Mangun), pp. 537–536. NewYork: Norton.

----- (2006) Emotion and cognition: Insights from studies of the human amygdala. *Annual Review of Psychology*, **24** (57): 27–53

Posner, R.A. (1998) *Economic Analysis of Law*, New York: Aspen.

Reality TV Magazine (2006) American Idol Winner Taylor Hicks Signs Record Deal. June 1, 2006. Available at www.realitytvmagazine.com/blog/2006/05/31/american-idol-winner-taylor-hicks-signs-record-deal/.

Reese, A.R. (2001) Copyright and Internet Music Transmissions: Existing Law, Major Controversies, Possible Solutions. *U. Miami L. Rev.*, **55**: 237–274.

Ridley, M. (2003) *Nature Via Nurture: Genes, Experience and What Makes Us Human,* New York: HarperCollins.

Rolls, E.T. (1999) *The Brain and Emotion*. Oxford: Oxford University Press.

Sapolsky, R. (2004) The frontal cortex and the criminal justice system. *Phil. Trans. R. Soc. Lond.* **B, 359**: 1787–1796.

Schultz, J., Goodenough, O.R., Frackowiak, R. and Frith, C.D. (2001) Cortical regions associated with the sense of justice and with legal rules, *Neuroimage* **13**: S 473.

Schwarz, N. (2000) Emotion, cognition, and decision making. *Cognition and Emotion*, 14, 433–440.

Skinner, B.F. (1953) *Science and Human Behavior*, New York: Macmillan

Simpson, K. (2001) The Role of Testosterone in Aggression. *McGill Journal of Medicine*, **6**: 32–40.

Skull, A. (2007) Book Review: Mind, brain, law, and culture. *Brain*, **130**: 585–591.

Slater, D., Smith, M., Bambauer, D., Gasser, U. and Palfrey, J. (2005) *Content and Control: Assessing the Impact of Policy Choices on Potential Online Business Models in the Music and Film Industries*, Berkman Center for Internet and Society.

Stake, J. (2004) The property instinct. *Phil. Trans. R. Soc. Lond.* B, **359**: 1763–1774.

Stevens, J.R. (2004) The selfish nature of generosity: harassment and food sharing in primates. *Proceedings R. Soc. of Lond.*, **B 271**: 451–456.

Svoboda, E. (2007) Faces, Faces Everywhere. *New York* Times, February 13, 2007, Section F, page 1.

Sweet, D. (2006) Many can be Counted Among 'Idol' Rich. *MSNBC,* May 24 2006, available at: http://www.msnbc.msn.com/id/12935252/.

White, A. (2006) EU stalls on iPod, disc surcharge reform plan; Electronics manufacturers want governments to end copyright levies. *Associated Press*, Dec. 13, 2006, available at http://www.msnbc.msn.com/id/16189703/.

Winter, S.L. (2001) *A Clearing in the Forrest: Law, Life and Mind*, Chicago, U. of Chicago Press.

Zak, P.J., Kurzban, R. and Matzner, W.T. (2005) Oxytocin is associated with human trustworthiness. *Hormones and Behavior*, **48**: 522–527.

Zeki, S. (1999) *Inner Vision: An Exploration of Art and the Brain,* Oxford: Oxford University Press.

Chapter 16
Cues in the Courtroom: When Do They Improve Jurors' Decisions?[1]

Cheryl Boudreau

> It seems highly unrealistic to assume that a typical juror, who probably has very little scientific or mathematical background, will be able to learn ... subject matter which otherwise requires years of study by a highly select set of full-time students (Fisher 2000–2001, p. 35).

> Jurors ... make decisions based on a sensible set of considerations – the expert's qualifications, reasoning, factual familiarity and impartiality. Our data do not lend support to the critics who paint jurors as gullible, naïve, or thoughtless persons ... (Shuman and Champagne 1997, p. 242).

During criminal and civil trials, jurors must make decisions for which they are not fully informed. Thus, they must often base their decisions upon the statements of others, who they may or may not trust (Lupia and McCubbins 1998; Boudreau 2006). For example, when determining the guilt or innocence of the accused, jurors must rely upon the statements of competing attorneys who try to persuade jurors that their version of the facts is the correct one. Similarly, when assigning punitive damages in civil cases, jurors must often base their decisions upon the statements of expert witnesses and attorneys who try to convey the extent of the damage to jurors.

Given that jurors must rely upon the statements of others, many scholars fear that lawyers, judges and witnesses have ample opportunities to manipulate jurors' decisions and, thus, the outcomes of trials (Fisher 2000–2001; Lilly 2001). Despite these fears, other scholars argue that jurors, despite their lack of legal or scientific sophistication, can learn what they need to know to make informed decisions (Cooper, Bennett and Sukel 1996; Lupia and McCubbins 1998; Vidmar and Diamond 2001). Specifically, many scholars suggest that jurors can use cues

1 This research was funded by the National Science Foundation, Grant #SES-0616904, the Kavli Institute for Brain and Mind, and the Chancellor's Associates Chair VIII at the University of California, San Diego. I thank Mat McCubbins, Scott MacKenzie, Lydia Tiede and participants in the "Law, Brain, and Mind" conference for their helpful comments. I also thank Michael Freeman and Oliver Goodenough for their generous invitation to present this paper at their conference at the University College London.

– such as expert witnesses' credentials (Cooper, Bennett and Sukel 1996) and the number of arguments used to support a particular position (Petty and Cacioppo 1984) – to help them with their decisions. Still others suggest that competition between advocates in a courtroom may lead to the revelation of truthful information that jurors may then use when making their decisions (Milgrom and Roberts 1986; Froeb and Kobayashi 1996; Lupia and McCubbins 1998).

In this chapter, I assess whether and under what conditions characteristics of courtroom settings can substitute for sophistication and enable even unsophisticated jurors to learn what they need to know. Specifically, regardless of jurors' levels of legal or scientific expertise, there are cues embedded in the courtroom that may help jurors to assess the veracity of attorneys' and witnesses' statements and to learn from them. For example, jurors know that witnesses face penalties for perjury if they lie on the stand, and attorneys' cross-examinations (a form of verification) often reveal when witnesses have made false statements.[2] Further, during both direct- and cross-examinations, attorneys typically highlight the interests and incentives of witnesses (for example, a prosecutor might reveal that an expert witness is being paid by the defence). Additionally, during opening statements and closing arguments, attorneys from both sides compete with one another to persuade jurors to find in favour of their client. As I demonstrate in this chapter, when conditions such as these are met, even unsophisticated jurors are able to learn from attorneys' and witnesses' statements and make informed decisions.

Because I cannot manipulate courtroom settings, attorneys' and witnesses' statements or jurors' levels of sophistication during real world trials, I instead conduct a laboratory experiment (extending Lupia and McCubbins's 1998 and Boudreau's 2006 experimental designs) in which I analyse whether and under what conditions even unsophisticated jurors can use cues embedded in the courtroom to help them make informed decisions. To this end, I obtain a pretest measure of subjects' levels of sophistication prior to my experiment. I then randomly assign subjects to either a treatment group or a control group. This enables me to manipulate whether subjects must make their decisions on their own (as they do in the control group) or whether they are exposed to the statements of another individual (who is analogous to an attorney or witness and who may or may not be trustworthy, depending upon the experimental condition) before they make their decisions.

In order to assess the conditions under which the statements of another individual (dubbed "the speaker" throughout this chapter) help both sophisticated and unsophisticated jurors to make informed decisions, I vary whether the speaker has common or conflicting interests with subjects, and I also impose three conditions that have direct analogues in courtroom settings: *penalties for lying, the threat of verification* and *competition*. In the penalties for lying condition, both the speaker and the subjects know that the speaker will incur a penalty if they make a false statement. Similarly, in the verification condition, both the speaker and the subjects know that the experimenter will verify the speaker's statement with some

2 For further discussion of this point, see Lupia and McCubbins (1998, Ch. 10).

probability to make sure that it is truthful. In the competition condition, subjects are exposed to the statements of two competing speakers who have diametrically opposed interests.

The results of my experiments demonstrate that exposure to a speaker who has common interests with subjects, who faces a sufficiently large penalty for lying, or who is verified with a sufficiently high probability enables even unsophisticated subjects to make informed decisions. Contrary to existing literature, however, competition between two speakers (absent any other institutional constraints) does not help subjects to make informed decisions. Based on these results, it appears that, under certain conditions, cues embedded in the courtroom can substitute for sophistication and enable even unsophisticated jurors to make informed decisions during trials.

This chapter proceeds as follows. I begin with a discussion of the literature on juror competence, and I demonstrate that there is much disagreement among legal scholars, social scientists and jurists as to whether jurors are capable of making informed decisions during criminal and civil trials. I then suggest that even though jurors may not possess legal or scientific sophistication, there are substitutes for sophistication embedded in courtroom settings. Next, I describe the experimental design that I use to test this proposition, and I suggest a number of hypotheses regarding subjects' ability to make informed decisions in each of my experimental conditions. I then briefly describe the data source and statistical methods that I use. I next present my experimental results. I conclude with a discussion of the implications that my research has for debates about juror competence and jury reform.

Existing Research: Can Jurors Make Informed Decisions?

Much of the legal and social science literature on juror competence suggests that jurors are not sufficiently sophisticated to process the information and arguments that are presented during trials. For example, many legal scholars lament jurors' lack of knowledge about scientific evidence and legal procedures, while others demonstrate that jurors are easily confused by complicated issues and readily swayed by the way that lawyers frame their arguments (Elwork, Sales and Alfini 1977; Fisher 2000–2001; Lilly 2001).[3] Given the apparent naïveté of the individuals who are charged with determining the guilt or innocence of the accused and deciding the liability and punitive damages of parties in civil suits, many scholars question whether juries should decide the outcomes of trials (Hastie and Viscusi 1998; Mogin 1998; Sunstein, Kahneman and Schkade 1998; Fisher 2000–2001; Lilly 2001; Sunstein et al. 2002a, 2002b; Schkade 2002).[4]

3 For an interesting discussion of the limitations of framing effects, see Druckman (2001).

4 Note that prominent newspapers also suggest that juries should be replaced with judges. Indeed, as Blom-Cooper (2003, p. 10) emphasizes in his article in *The Times*, "The

Indeed, many scholars' doubts about the competence of jurors have led them to advocate various reforms. Specifically, some scholars suggest that, under certain circumstances, we should replace citizen juries with juries composed of experts (otherwise known as "blue ribbon" juries) or with judges (Lempert 1981; Strier 1994, 1997; Mogin 1998; Fisher 2000–2001). According to these scholars, lay jurors are not sufficiently sophisticated to make reasoned choices during trials and they should, therefore, be replaced with other, more competent decision-makers.

In contrast to those who doubt the competence of jurors and question the efficacy of the jury system, many scholars suggest that jurors, despite their lack of legal or scientific sophistication, can nonetheless learn what they need to know during the course of a trial (Kalven and Zeisel 1966; Hastie, Penrod and Pennington 1983; Cecil, Lind and Bermant 1987; Cecil, Hans and Wiggins 1991; Cooper, Bennett and Sukel 1996; Lupia and McCubbins 1998; Boudreau 2006). These scholars (like those discussed above) recognize that jurors may not possess the formal education or training that is needed to process the complex, technical evidence presented during trials. However, rather than condemn the jury system as unworkable, scholars in this camp suggest that jurors are able to use cues to assess the value of particular pieces of evidence and to arrive at reasoned choices (Hovland and Weiss 1951; Chaiken 1980; Hass 1981; Petty and Cacioppo 1984; Cecil, Lind and Bermant 1987; Cooper, Bennett and Sukel 1996; Shuman, Champagne and Whitaker 1996; Lupia and McCubbins 1998; Boudreau 2006).[5]

It is this body of research on how jurors use cues when making their decisions that I build upon in this study. Specifically, I analyse experimentally whether characteristics of modern courtrooms provide jurors with cues, and I assess whether and when these cues can substitute for sophistication and enable even unsophisticated jurors to make informed decisions.

Experimental Design

In order to analyse whether courtroom characteristics enable even unsophisticated jurors to make informed decisions, I design a randomized laboratory experiment. Because such an analysis requires a measure of subjects' sophistication at a particular task and because there does not exist an agreed upon measure of legal or scientific sophistication, I analyse instead subjects' mathematical sophistication, which I argue is analogous to sophistication in general, and to legal and scientific sophistication in particular. The important advantage associated with analysing

jury is the high point of amateurism, potentially a recipe for incompetence and bias. The mood of civilized systems of criminal justice increasingly demands professionalism. I am not contemptuous of the amateur's ability to judge human conduct, only the task of evaluating evidence in the courtroom, which is a job for professionals."

5 For an in-depth discussion of central versus heuristic information processing, see Petty and Cacioppo (1986) and Chaiken (1980).

mathematical sophistication, of course, is that there exists an agreed upon and straightforward measure of it – namely, SAT math scores. For this reason, I obtain a pre-test measure of subjects' sophistication (i.e., their SAT math score) prior to the experiment.

I then randomly assign subjects to treatment and control groups, and I ask them to solve a series of binary choice math problems (i.e., the problems ask subjects to choose whether "a" or "b" is the correct answer). The math problems that I use are drawn from an SAT math test and consist of many different types of problems and several levels of difficulty. I tell subjects in both the treatment and control groups that they have 60 seconds to solve each math problem and that they earn 50 cents for each problem that they answer correctly, lose 50 cents for each problem that they answer incorrectly, and neither earn nor lose 50 cents if they leave a problem blank.

The main difference between the treatment and control groups has to do with the conditions under which subjects solve the math problems. In the control group, subjects solve the math problems one at a time, with 60 seconds allotted for each problem. For each problem that subjects in the control group solve, I pay them according to whether they solve the problem correctly, incorrectly or leave the problem blank.

In the treatment group, subjects solve these very same math problems one at a time with 60 seconds allotted for each problem, and they are also paid according to whether they solve the problem correctly, incorrectly or leave the problem blank. What differs between the treatment and control groups, however, is that before subjects in the treatment group solve any of the math problems, the experimenter randomly selects one subject to act as "the speaker" in the remainder of the experiment. In the competition condition, of course, the experimenter randomly selects two subjects to act as the two competing speakers.

The speaker's role in the experiment is far different from that of the other subjects. That is, unlike the other subjects (whose role in the experiment is to solve the math problems one at a time), the speaker is shown the correct answer to each math problem (that is, the speaker is given knowledge about the correct choice for subjects) and then makes a statement to the other subjects about whether "a" or "b" is the correct answer.[6] After the speaker makes their statement, the other subjects are given 60 seconds to choose whether "a" or "b" is the correct answer to that problem.

The key to this experiment is that both the speaker and subjects know that the speaker must make a statement, but that the speaker can make any statement that

---

6 Note that the speaker makes their statement by putting a checkmark beside the answer that they wish to report. I, as the experimenter, then read that statement out loud to all of the subjects. This prevents the speaker's tone of voice from confounding the experiment. Similarly, throughout the experiment, the speaker sits behind a large partition so that the speaker's gender, race and/or age do not affect the extent to which subjects listen to the speaker's statements. These personal characteristics of the speaker are, of course, interesting factors that I plan to vary in future experiments.

they wish. That is, the speaker can lie about the correct answer to the math problem or tell the truth; it is entirely up to them. The speaker's ability to make whatever statement they wish is constant throughout this experiment and is designed to be an analogy to Crawford and Sobel's (1982) and Lupia and McCubbins's (1998) models.

Although the speaker can lie or tell the truth in all of my experimental conditions, I vary the conditions under which the speaker makes their statement. Specifically, I vary two types of things: the interests between the speaker and subjects, as well as various courtroom characteristics. When varying the interests between the speaker and subjects, I first analyse subjects' ability to solve the math problems when the speaker has *common interests* with them. I then make the speaker and subjects have *conflicting interests*, at which point I impose various courtroom characteristics, such as a *penalty for lying* or the *threat of verification*. In the *competition* condition, I expose subjects to two competing speakers who have diametrically opposed interests (i.e., one person's gain is the other person's loss). Each of these experimental variations (i.e., common interests, penalties for lying, verification and competition) is common knowledge at the outset of each experimental condition.

Because these courtroom characteristics are likely to vary in real world settings, I vary both the size of the penalty for lying and the probability of verification when running my experiments. Specifically, I test the effects that different size penalties (namely, a $15 penalty, a $5 penalty and a $1 penalty) and different probabilities of verification (specifically, a 100%, 90%, 70%, 50% or 30% chance of verification) have on subjects' ability to answer the math problems correctly.

So how do I vary the interests between the speaker and subjects, as well as courtroom characteristics within the confines of my experiments? In short, I vary both interests and courtroom characteristics by manipulating the ways that the speaker and the subjects earn money. For example, in the common interests condition, subjects know that they will be paid 50 cents for each math problem that they answer correctly. Similarly, the speaker knows that they will be paid 50 cents for each subject who answers a particular math problem correctly. So, if 11 subjects answer a math problem correctly, they earn 50 cents each, and the speaker earns $5.50 (i.e., 50 cents for each of the 11 subjects who answer the problem correctly).

For my next experimental variation, I establish conflicting interests between the speaker and subjects, and I then impose a particular courtroom characteristic – namely, a penalty for lying. To induce conflicting interests between the speaker and subjects, I merely alter the way that the speaker earns money. That is, unlike the common interests condition, the speaker in the conflicting interests condition earns 50 cents for each subject who gets the math problem *wrong*. Subjects, on the other hand, still earn 50 cents for solving the math problems correctly. Simultaneously, I also impose a penalty for lying upon the speaker. So, in this experimental condition, the speaker and subjects have conflicting interests with one another, but I announce to both the speaker and subjects that the speaker will incur a penalty (of either $15, $5 or $1, depending on the experimental condition) if they lie about the correct answer to the math problem.

For a different courtroom characteristic – namely, the threat of verification – I again maintain conflicting interests between the speaker and subjects. However, instead of imposing a penalty for lying upon the speaker, this time, I verify the speaker's statement with some probability to make sure that it is a true statement before it is read to subjects. In the 100% chance of verification condition, if the speaker chooses to make a false statement about the correct answer to the math problem, then I charge the speaker $2 and announce the correct answer to subjects. If the speaker chooses to make a true statement, then I simply read the speaker's statement to the subjects. However, in the 90% chance of verification condition, I roll a ten-sided die before the speaker makes their statement. If the die lands on 1, 2, 3, 4, 5, 6, 7, 8 or 9, then I verify the speaker's statement, charge them $2 if they have chosen to make a false statement, and announce the correct answer to the math problem to subjects. If the die lands on a 10, however, then I simply announce the answer that the speaker chooses to report, regardless of whether it is correct or incorrect. The 70%, 50% and 30% chance of verification conditions proceed in a similar manner.

In the competition condition, subjects are exposed to two competing speakers' statements before they make their decisions. Specifically, before each math problem that subjects in this treatment condition solve, speaker 1 first states whether answer "a" or answer "b" is the correct answer to the problem. After speaker 1 makes their statement, then speaker 2 makes a statement about whether answer "a" or answer "b" is the correct answer to the problem.

The key to this treatment condition is twofold: first, speaker 1 knows that they have common interests with subjects (that is, they earn 50 cents for each subject who makes a correct choice), and speaker 2 knows that they have conflicting interests with subjects (that is, they earn 50 cents for each subject who makes an incorrect choice). In this way, the interests of the two competing experts are adversarial, or zero sum. Second, subjects know that one speaker has common interests with them and that one speaker has conflicting interests with them, but they do not know whether it is speaker 1 or speaker 2 who has common interests with them. Stated differently, subjects know that the speakers are adversaries, but as is the case in many courtroom settings, they do not know which speaker's interests are aligned with their own. (For further details about the competition condition, see Boudreau and McCubbins 2007.)

Hypotheses

Many of the experimental conditions described above yield straightforward predictions about subjects' ability to solve the math problems. For example, in the presence of a speaker who has common interests with subjects, I predict that subjects will have an improved ability to answer the math problems correctly, relative to subjects in the control group. This prediction stems directly from Lupia and McCubbins (1998) and Crawford and Sobel's (1982) models, which demonstrate that, in equilibrium, common interests between a speaker and listeners (who in my experiments are the subjects) induce the speaker to tell the truth and the listeners to base their choices upon what the speaker says.

The reasoning behind this common interests prediction is perhaps best understood by considering the nature of my experiments. Recall that in the common interests condition, the speaker earns money each time a subject solves a particular problem correctly. I, therefore, expect the speaker to tell subjects the truth about the correct answer to the math problem, and I also expect subjects to trust the speaker's statement and base their answers to the math problem upon it. Indeed, because each experimental variation is common knowledge at the beginning of the experiment, subjects know that both they and the speaker are better off financially if they solve the problems correctly.

In the $15 penalty for lying condition, I also expect subjects to have an improved ability to solve the math problems correctly. This prediction, again, stems from Lupia and McCubbins's (1998) model, which demonstrates that when a penalty for lying is sufficiently large, then, in equilibrium, the speaker never lies and the listeners trust the speaker's statements.

In my experiments, the $15 penalty for lying is in fact "sufficiently large" – that is, it is large enough to ensure that the speaker always has an incentive to tell the truth. To see why this is the case, consider the way that the speaker earns money under this condition when there are 11 subjects solving the math problems:[7] Given that there are conflicting interests between the speaker and the subjects, the speaker earns $5.50 if each and every subject answers a problem incorrectly. Although at first blush this might seem to give the speaker an incentive to lie, note that the $15 penalty for lying would reduce the speaker's gain of $5.50 down to a loss of $9.50. Further, if the speaker lies and all of the subjects happen to answer the problem correctly (perhaps realizing that the speaker is lying), then the speaker would lose $20.50 (i.e., a $15 loss because of the penalty for lying and a $5.50 loss because 11 subjects answered the problem correctly).

If the speaker tells the truth, however, then the worst they can do is to lose $5.50 (which would happen if each subject answers the problem correctly), and the best that they can do is to earn $5.50 (which would happen if each subject answers the problem incorrectly). As these pay-offs make clear, the speaker is always better off if they tell the truth about the correct answer to the math problem. Thus, I expect that the speaker will make a truthful statement about the correct answer to the math problem, and I also expect subjects to trust and then learn from the speaker's statement.

In the 100% chance of verification condition, I also expect subjects to have an improved ability to answer the math problems correctly. As Lupia and McCubbins

7 The typical number of subjects in each experimental session is 12 (11 subjects who solve the math problems and 1 Speaker who makes a statement to the other subjects).

(1998) note, increasing the probability of verification decreases the probability that the speaker can benefit from making a false statement.[8] Thus, when the speaker is verified with certainty (as is the case in this experimental condition), subjects should trust that the speaker's statement is correct and base their decisions upon it.

Contrary to existing literature, I do not expect subjects to improve their performance on the math problems in the competition condition. Specifically, because subjects do not know whether speaker 1 or speaker 2 is more likely to share common interests with them, they cannot necessarily know which (if any) speaker made a truthful statement about whether answer "a" or answer "b" is the correct choice. For example, if subjects hear the statement "a", followed by the statement "b", they cannot learn anything from these statements because they do not know whether speaker 1 (who signaled "a") or speaker 2 (who signaled "b") has common interests with them. Similarly, if subjects hear the statement "a", followed by the statement "a", they still cannot learn from these statements because they do not know whether both speaker 1 and speaker 2 made truthful statements or whether both speaker 1 and speaker 2 made false statements. Because much research in cognitive science and psychology demonstrates that people ignore stimuli that they do not expect to help them with their decisions (for a survey of this body of literature, see Lupia and McCubbins 1998), I expect subjects to ignore the competing speakers' statements and base their choices upon what they think is the correct answer to the math problem, just like subjects in the control group who must also solve the problem on their own (Boudreau and McCubbins 2007).

As for the other courtroom characteristics that I impose in my experiment (i.e., a \$5 penalty, a \$1 penalty and a 90%, 70%, 50% or 30% chance of verification), I do not have any *ex ante* predictions about how they will affect subjects' ability to solve the math problems. The reason for this lack of predictions is simply that, under each of these conditions, the speaker may earn more money if they lie about the correct answer to the math problem. Knowing this, subjects solving the math problems may or may not trust and then learn from the speaker's statement.

Data and Methodology

In order to test the above hypotheses, I conducted laboratory experiments at a large public university. When recruiting subjects, I posted flyers at various locations on campus (for example, in front of the library, in the cafeterias, in the dormitories and in academic buildings), and I also sent out campus-wide emails to advertise the experiments. A total of 369 adults who were enrolled in undergraduate classes and who were of different genders, ages, races and college majors participated in the experiments.

---

8 Note that Austen-Smith (1994) also models verification, but he focuses on the speaker's inability to verify their lack of knowledge to listeners.

When testing the above hypotheses, I analyse differences among subjects in my various treatment groups and subjects in the control group (recall that subjects in the control group simply solve the problems on their own, i.e., without a speaker). Specifically, I calculate the percentage of math problems that subjects in each condition answer correctly, and I then conduct difference of means tests to examine whether subjects who are exposed to the treatment in each condition perform significantly better on the math problems than do subjects in the control group.[9]

Results

Instances of Successful Cue-taking

My results demonstrate that subjects who are exposed to a speaker who has common interests with them, who faces a $15 penalty for lying or who faces a 100% chance of verification exhibit an improved ability to answer the math problems, relative to subjects in the control group. Specifically, subjects in the control group answer only 40% of the math problems correctly (N = 66), while subjects who are exposed to a speaker who has common interests with them answer 90% of the math problems correctly (N = 62). Subjects who are exposed to a speaker who faces a $15 penalty for lying answer 84% of the math problems correctly (N = 68), while subjects who are exposed to a speaker who faces a 100% chance of verification answer 85% of the math problems correctly (N = 74). Each of these differences between treatment and control group subjects is statistically significant (specifically, $p < 0.01$ for each of these comparisons).

Smaller Penalties, Smaller Improvements in Decision-making

Having confirmed three of my hypotheses, I now examine the effects that smaller penalties for lying have on subjects' ability to solve the math problems. Indeed, because penalties for lying in real world courtrooms may not always be large enough to ensure that witnesses tell the truth, I assess the effects that smaller penalties (which sometimes make the speaker better off if they lie about the correct answer to the math problem) have on subjects' ability to answer the math problems correctly.

As my results reveal, there is a decrease in subjects' ability to answer the math problems correctly when the $15 penalty for lying is reduced to $5 or $1.

9 Note that I also analyse my data using non-parametric Wilcoxon Mann-Whitney tests. Unlike the standard difference of means test, the Wilcoxon Mann-Whitney test does not require the assumption that the differences between two samples are normally distributed. None of the results reported in this chapter change if the Wilcoxon Mann-Whitney test is used instead of a difference of means test.

Specifically, subjects who are exposed to a speaker who faces a \$5 penalty for lying answer only 46% of the math problems correctly (N = 39), while subjects who are exposed to a speaker who faces a \$1 penalty for lying answer 54% of the math problems correctly (N = 141). Both of these percentages are significantly lower than the percentage of problems that subjects answer correctly in the \$15 penalty for lying condition (specifically, $p < 0.01$ when both the \$5 penalty and \$1 penalty conditions are compared with the \$15 penalty condition).

Despite this decrease in the percentage of math problems that subjects answer correctly in the \$5 and \$1 penalty for lying conditions, subjects in one of these conditions still perform significantly better on the math problems than do subjects in the control group. Specifically, a difference of means test reveals that the 54% of problems that subjects answer correctly in the \$1 penalty for lying condition is significantly greater than the 40% of problems that subjects in the control group answer correctly ($p < 0.01$). Thus, it appears that these smaller penalties for lying, though not as effective as a \$15 penalty, may enable subjects to perform better on the math problems.

Smaller Probabilities of Verification, Smaller Improvements in Decision-making

Just as I examine the effects that reducing the size of the penalty for lying has on subjects' ability to solve the math problems, so too do I analyse the effects of reducing the probability of verification. Indeed, given that a 100% chance of verification is unlikely to occur in a courtroom, it seems particularly useful to examine the extent to which subjects are able to learn from the speaker when the probability of verification is reduced. Thus, I assess whether and to what extent 90%, 70%, 50% and 30% chances of verification reduce the percentage of math problems that subjects answer correctly.

As my results demonstrate, there is a decrease in subjects' ability to solve the math problems when the 100% chance of verification is reduced to 90%, 70%, 50% or 30%. Specifically, subjects who are exposed to a speaker who faces a 90% chance of verification answer 70% of the math problems correctly (N = 33), while subjects who are exposed to a speaker who faces a 70% chance of verification answer 58% of the math problems correctly (N = 83). Subjects who solve the math problems in the presence of a speaker who faces a 50% chance of verification answer 60% of the math problems correctly (N = 31), and subjects who are exposed to a speaker who faces a 30% chance of verification answer only 44% of the problems correctly (N = 85). All of these percentages are significantly lower than the percentage of problems that subjects answer correctly in the 100% chance of verification condition ($p < 0.05$ for the 90% verification condition and $p < 0.01$ for the 70%, 50% and 30% verification conditions).

Although there are decreases in subjects' ability to solve the math problems correctly when smaller probabilities of verification are imposed, note that subjects in several of these conditions still perform significantly better on the math problems than do subjects in the control group. Specifically, a difference of means test reveals that the percentages of problems that subjects answer correctly in the 90%, 70% and 50% chance of verification conditions are significantly greater than the 40% of problems that subjects in the control group answer correctly ($p < 0.01$ for all three conditions). Thus, it appears that these smaller probabilities of verification (although not as effective as a 100% chance of verification) still enable subjects to improve their performance on the math problems.

The Effect of Competition

Because subjects do not know whether speaker 1 or speaker 2 has common interests with them, I expect them to ignore the competing experts' statements, make their decisions on their own and, thus, do no better on the math problems than subjects in the control group. This prediction is also confirmed by the data, as subjects in this experimental condition are not able to improve their performance on the math problems, relative to subjects in the control group. Indeed, as Boudreau and McCubbins (2007) demonstrate, the difference in performance between subjects in the competition condition and in the control group is not statistically significant at conventional levels.

How Do Courtroom Cues Affect Sophisticated vs. Unsophisticated Individuals?

Given that one of my central claims is that cues embedded in the courtroom enable even unsophisticated individuals to learn what they need to know, I now compare the effects that various cues have on subjects who are and who are not sophisticated. When classifying subjects as sophisticated or unsophisticated, I rely upon the SAT math scores that subjects provide prior to the experiment, as well as the nationwide SAT math percentile rankings that the Educational Testing Service (ETS) releases each year. Specifically, subjects whose SAT math scores fall in the 97th percentile or higher are considered to be sophisticated, while subjects whose SAT math scores fall in the 27th percentile through the 79th percentile are considered to be unsophisticated. Stated in terms of the scores associated with these percentile rankings, the sophisticated subjects' SAT math scores range from 740 points to 800 points, while the unsophisticated subjects' SAT math scores range from 450 points to 620 points.

I then examine the effects that common interests, a $15 penalty for lying and a 100% chance of verification have on sophisticated and unsophisticated subjects' ability to solve the math problems. As I discussed previously, each of these cues dramatically increases the percentage of math problems that subjects answer correctly, relative to the percentage of math problems that subjects in the control group answer correctly. The question that those results leave open, however, is whether these cues have different effects on subjects who are and who are not sophisticated. For example, it is possible that these cues are more effective for subjects who are sophisticated and who, therefore, already have some idea about how solve particular problems. On the other hand, it is also seems possible that

Table 16.1 The Effects that Common Interests, a $15 Penalty for Lying, and a 100% Chance of Verification have on Sophisticated and Unsophisticated Subjects*

Experimental Condition	Unsophisticated Subjects: Percent Correct	Sophisticated Subjects: Percent Correct
Control Group	27%	58%
Common Interests	**82%** **($p < 0.01$)**	**92%** **($p < 0.01$)**
$15 Penalty for Lying	**80%** **($p < 0.01$)**	**90%** **($p < 0.01$)**
100% Verification	**89%** **($p < 0.01$)**	**90%** **($p < 0.01$)**
Competition	**42%** **($p < 0.05$)**	61% ($p = 0.4$)

* Bold indicates a statistically significant increase, relative to the control group, for each of the two levels of sophistication.

these cues will be more helpful to the unsophisticated, who might be more willing to listen to (and then learn from) the speaker, as opposed to trying to solve the math problems on their own. Given these two conflicting conjectures, I break down my aggregate results to examine the percentage of problems that sophisticated and unsophisticated subjects answer correctly in each experimental condition.

As the results in Table 16.1 reveal, the common interests, $15 penalty for lying and 100% chance of verification conditions enable *both* sophisticated and unsophisticated subjects to improve their performance on the math problems, relative to their sophisticated and unsophisticated counterparts in the control group. Further, in each of these treatment conditions, *there is no statistically significant difference in the percentage of math problems that sophisticated and unsophisticated subjects answer correctly*. Indeed, both sophisticated and unsophisticated subjects answer over 79% of the math problems correctly in each of these three treatment conditions. This result suggests the power of these cues for, regardless of subjects' initial endowments of sophistication, they enable subjects to improve their performance on the math problems significantly.

Note, however, that in the competition condition, sophisticated and unsophisticated subjects do not improve their decisions nearly as much as their sophisticated and unsophisticated counterparts in the other experimental conditions. As shown in Table 16.1, unsophisticated subjects in the competition condition answer only 42% of the math problems correctly. Although this is a statistically significant improvement, relative to unsophisticated subjects in the control group ($p < 0.05$), it is not nearly as large as the improvements that subjects in the common interests, $15 penalty for lying and 100% chance of verification conditions achieve. Further, sophisticated subjects in the competition condition answer only 61% of the math problems correctly, which is not a statistically

Table 16.2 Difference in the Percentage of Problems Answered Correctly Among Sophisticated and Unsophisticated Subjects, Relative to their Sophisticated and Unsophisticated Counterparts in the Control Group

Experimental Condition	Unsophisticated subjects: difference in % correct	Sophisticated subjects: difference in % correct
Control group	–	–
Common interests	55%	34%
$15 penalty for lying	53%	32%
100% verification	62%	32%
Competition	15%	3% (not significant)

significant improvement over the percentage of math problems that sophisticated subjects in the control group answer correctly ($p = 0.4$).

Note, also that there is a statistically significant difference between the performance of sophisticated and unsophisticated subjects in the control group. Specifically, the sophisticated subjects in the control group answer 58% of the problems correctly, while the unsophisticated subjects answer only 27% of the problems correctly ($p < 0.01$). Based on this finding, it appears that particular cues can "level the playing field" between sophisticated and unsophisticated individuals (see Kuklinski et al. 2001 and Rahn, Aldrich and Borgida 1994 for a discussion of how other environmental conditions can level the playing field between sophisticates and novices). Indeed, my results in Table 16.2 show that these cues effect much larger improvements among unsophisticated subjects (relative to their unsophisticated counterparts in the control group) than among sophisticated subjects (relative to their sophisticated counterparts in the control group).

Conclusion

As the results of my experiments demonstrate, courtroom characteristics can provide individuals with cues that help them to make informed decisions. Indeed, in many of the treatment conditions that I impose in this experiment, subjects solve a significantly greater percentage of the math problems correctly than do subjects in the control group. Further, it appears that particular cues enable even unsophisticated individuals to solve the math problems correctly. Taken together, these results demonstrate the powerful, positive effects that courtroom cues (such as common interests, penalties for lying and the threat of verification) can have on otherwise unsophisticated individuals.

Interestingly, subjects were not able to improve their decisions, relative to subjects in the control group, when they were exposed to two competing speakers.

This result is contrary to existing literature, which suggests that competition between lawyers and witnesses in the courtroom leads to the revelation of truthful information and may promote learning among jurors. Although competition has been shown to improve decisions when it is combined with proper institutions (Boudreau and McCubbins 2007), the results reported in this chapter suggest that competition, by itself, is not sufficient to promote learning or improve decision-making.

These results have a number of implications for debates within law and the social sciences. As I noted earlier, within both the legal and social science literatures there has been much debate about whether jurors must possess legal or scientific sophistication to make informed decisions (Frank 1945; Fisher 2000–2001; Elwork, Sales and Alfini 1977) or whether cues are sufficient for jurors to learn what they need to know (Vidmar and Diamond 2001; Lupia and McCubbins 1998; Cooper, Bennett and Sukel 1996). The results of my experiments largely support scholars in the cues camp, for they suggest that jurors can in fact make informed decisions even when they lack sophistication. Specifically, in my experiments, many subjects lack the ability to solve various types of math problems, but even without such ability, they are often able to learn from a knowledgeable and trustworthy speaker's statement and solve the math problems correctly. In this way, otherwise unsophisticated subjects are able to achieve results similar to those that sophisticated subjects achieve.

For this reason, my results suggest that calls for reforming (or doing away with) citizen juries are premature. Indeed, the results of my experiments suggest that it is possible for courtroom characteristics to promote learning even among unsophisticated jurors. Although my experimental results suggest that the efficacy of such characteristics is not absolute (for example, recall the declines in the percentage of math problems that subjects answer correctly in the competition condition and once the penalty for lying or the probability of verification is reduced), they also indicate that, at least under certain conditions, large improvements can be achieved. Thus, sophistication does not appear to be a prerequisite for learning and making informed decisions. For this reason, rather than advocate blue ribbon juries and bench trials as substitutes for citizen juries, scholars should instead seek substitutes for jurors' lack of sophistication in courtroom settings.

References

Austen-Smith, David (1994) "Strategic Transmission of Costly Information," *Econometrica* 62: 955–963.

Blom-Cooper, Louis Sir (2003) "A Judge Can Do the Work of 12 Amateurs, and Better," *The London Times*, 21 October, p. 10.

Boudreau, Cheryl (2006) "Jurors are Competent Cue-Takers: How Institutions Substitute for Legal Sophistication," *International Journal of Law in Context* 2: 293–304.

Boudreau, Cheryl and Mathew D. McCubbins (2007) "From Competition to Competence? Theory and Experiments Regarding Deliberation and Citizen Learning," Working paper, University of California, Davis.

Cecil, Joe S., Valerie P. Hans and Elizabeth C. Wiggins (1991) "Citizen Comprehension of Difficult Issues: Lessons from Civil Jury Trials," *American University Law Review* 40: 727–774.

Cecil, Joe S., E. Allan Lind and Gordon Bermant (1987) *Jury Service in Lengthy Civil Trials*. Washington D.C.: Federal Judicial Center.

Chaiken, Shelly (1980) "Heuristic versus Systematic Information Processing and the Use of Source versus Message Cues in Persuasion," *Journal of Personality and Social Psychology* 39: 752–766.

Cooper, Joel, Elizabeth A. Bennett and Holly L. Sukel (1996) "Complex Scientific Testimony: How Do Jurors Make Decisions?" *Law and Human Behavior* 20: 379–394.

Crawford, Vincent and Joel Sobel (1982) "Strategic Information Transmission," *Econometrica* 50: 1431–1451.

Druckman, James N. (2001) "On the Limits of Framing Effects: Who Can Frame?" *The Journal of Politics* 63: 1041–1066.

Elwork, Amiram, Bruce D. Sales and James J. Alfini (1977) "Juridic Decisions: In Ignorance of the Law or in Light of it?" *Law and Human Behavior* 1: 163–189.

Fisher, Michael A. (2000–2001) "Going for the Blue Ribbon: The Legality of Expert Juries in Patent Litigation," *Columbia Science and Technical Law Review* 2: 1 55.

Frank, Jerome (1945) *Courts on Trial: Myth and Reality in American Justice*. Princeton, NJ: Princeton University Press.

Froeb, Luke M. and Bruce H. Kobayashi (1996) "Naïve, Biased, Yet Bayesian: Can Juries Interpret Selectively Produced Evidence?" *Journal of Law, Economics, and Organization* 12: 257–276.

Hass, R. Glen (1981) "Effects of Source Characteristics on Cognitive Responses and Persuasion" in R.E. Petty, T.M. Ostrom and T.C. Brock (eds) *Cognitive Responses in Persuasion*, Hillsdale: Erlbaum, 141–172.

Hastie, Reid and W. Kip Viscusi (1998) "What Juries Can't Do Well: The Jury's Performance as a Risk Manager," *Arizona Law Review* 40: 901- 921.

Hastie, Reid, Steven D. Penrod and Nancy Pennington (1983) *Inside the Jury*. Cambridge, Mass: Harvard University Press.

Hovland, Carl I. and Walter Weiss (1951) "The Influence of Source Credibility on Communication Effectiveness," *Public Opinion Quarterly* 15: 635–650.

Kalven, Harry, Jr. and Hans Zeisel (1966) *The American Jury*. Boston, Mass: Little, Brown.

Kuklinski, James H., Paul J. Quirk, Jennifer Jerit and Robert F. Rich (2001) "The Political Environment and Citizen Competence," *American Journal of Political Science* 45: 410–424.

Lempert, Richard O. (1981) "Civil Juries and Complex Cases: Let's Not Rush to Judgment," *Michigan Law Review*, 80: 68–132.

Lilly, Graham C. (2001) "The Decline of the American Jury," *University of Colorado Law Review* 72: 53–91.

Lupia, Arthur and Mathew D. McCubbins (1998) *The Democratic Dilemma: Can Citizens Learn What They Need to Know?* Cambridge, UK: Cambridge University Press.

Milgrom, Paul and John Roberts (1986) "Relying on the Information of Interested Parties." *Rand Journal of Economics* 17: 18–31.

Mogin, Paul (1998) "Why Judges, Not Juries, Should Set Punitive Damages." *University of Chicago Law Review* 65: 179–223.

Petty, Richard E. and John T. Cacioppo (1984) "The Effects of Involvement on Responses to Argument Quantity and Quality: Central and Peripheral Routes to Persuasion," *Journal of Personality and Social Psychology* 46: 69–81.

Petty, Richard E. and John T. Cacioppo (1986) *Communication and Persuasion: Central and Peripheral Routes to Attitude Change*. New York, NY: Springer-Verlag.

Rahn, Wendy M., John H. Aldrich and Eugene Borgida (1994) "Individual and Contextual Variations in Political Candidate Appraisal," *American Political Science Review* 88: 193–199.

Schkade, David A. (2002) "Erratic by Design: A Task Analysis of Punitive Damages Assessment," *Harvard Journal on Legislation* 39: 121–137.

Shuman, Daniel W. and Anthony Champagne (1997) "Removing the People from the Legal Process: The Rhetoric and Research on Judicial Selection and Juries," *Psychology, Public Policy, and Law* 3: 242–258.

Shuman, Daniel W., Anthony Champagne and Elizabeth Whitaker (1996) "Assessing the Believability of Expert Witnesses: Science in the Jury Box," *Jurimetrics Journal* 37: 23–34.

Strier, Franklin (1994) *Reconstructing Justice: An Agenda for Trial Reform*. Westport, CT: Quorum Books.

Strier, Franklin (1997) "The Educated Jury: A Proposal for Complex Litigation," *DePaul Law Review* 47: 49–79.

Sunstein, Cass R., Daniel Kahneman and David Schkade (1998) "Assessing Punitive Damages (With Notes on Cognition and Valuation in Law)," *Yale Law Journal* 107: 2071–2152.

Sunstein, Cass R., Reid Hastie, John W. Payne, David A. Schkade and W. Kip Viscusi (2002a) *Punitive Damages: How Juries Decide*. Chicago, IL: University of Chicago Press.

Sunstein, Cass R., Daniel Kahneman, David Schkade and Ilana Ritov (2002b) "Predictably Incoherent Judgments," *Stanford Law Review* 54: 1153–1215.

Vidmar, Neil and Shari Seidman Diamond (2001) "Juries and Expert Evidence," *Brooklyn Law Review* 66: 1121–1180.

Chapter 17
Reflections on Reading: Words and Pictures and Law

Christina Spiesel[1]

The practice of law today is awash with pictures of all kinds – from those that begin conceptually like graphs, diagrams or flow charts to those that originate in perception, like photographs, or those that emerge from the actions of technology, like animations and fMRI. Pictures are used as evidence, demonstratives, and for argument. The legal academy has yet seriously to come to grips with the changes that this infusion of the visual means for legal thinking and rhetoric. This article explores the intellectual implications of picturing in a discipline that has thought of itself as pre-eminently about the use of words and their linear logics. To do this, the author has sought out eye movement research, asking the question: do we read pictures differently from words? If so, what are the implications of this as understood both in cognitive terms and in cultural terms? That is, can the differences in perceptual behaviour be seen as offering clues to differences in cognitive behaviour? Existing knowledge seems to answer these questions in the affirmative, which means that the deeply held cultural bias that maintains that only words containing thought needs revision. This chapter concludes with reflections on some benefits that adjustments to our understanding might give to legal thinkers.

Diego Velazquez, in his masterwork on the dynamics of seeing and representations, *Las Meninas* (1656),[2] paints himself looking both outward and inward at the same time. He, the artist within the painting, has paused in his work and he ostensibly is looking at us, the viewers, implicating us as part of the scene. His gaze betrays an inwardness, however – his eyes are not focused outward – coding for us the scene he sees as internal, his own mental vision, thus making the picture his is painting both in and of the external world and the internal world. He shows us the stimulus of the perception of something out there, 'seeing the picture' and by his implication, the understanding by the mind which we now know happens in the brain.[3] While Velazquez probably had knowledge of technological aids to

1 Yale Law School, Quinnipiac University School of Law, New York Law School.

2 *Las Meninas* hangs in the Prado Museum in Madrid. A reproduction online can be viewed at http:// www.artchive.com.

3 For an extended discussion of this masterwork and its relation to the law, see Spiesel (2006).

representation,[4] he had to have come to his complex understanding of perception and its relation to representation through a close observation and metacognition about his working process and self-awareness about what he was making. The 'double vision' of inside/outside correctly alludes to our current understanding of human cognition of the world 'out there' as arising from perceptual cues assembled and interpreted by the brain. The painter did not have available either modern biological understanding or modern instrumentation for studying human cognition. That had to wait two to three-hundred years.

Why do I begin reflections on reading with this reference to an old painting? As a non-lawyer, and as a non-scientist,[5] I traverse the word/image cultural divide as it comes up in the context of the law and my teaching of law students. There are several parts to this divide. First, there is a strong cultural bias that thinking is accomplished only with words because language is the medium of thought. *Las Meninas* is an answer to that. The painting cannot be understood in any full sense without reference to ideas that we would consider properly in the realm of thought but which are, nevertheless, expressed purely visually. Second, the necessity of translating pictures into words in order to make their meanings socially available involves a loss of information as some issues are highlighted and others ignored. I mentioned above the look in some painted eyes; there is a whole lot more in the painting and if we were standing in front of it, talking, all the rest of the work would still be part of our perception as we discussed those eyes. The painting would continue to 'speak'. Understanding this gap between what we are noticing and what is there is critical if we are going to deploy pictures on behalf of communicative goals, which lawyers are increasingly doing. Third, the digital revolution has changed the relationship between words and pictures in ways that we must understand if lawyers are going to navigate in this new media world.

As someone whose own work alternates between writing and visual production, I experience stress, even visual stress, moving back and forth between these discourses. With the stimulus of the colloquium held at the University College London in February 2006,[6] I decided finally to test my strong intuition that there are differences between reading texts made of words and texts that are pictures by looking at the scientific literature on eye movements in reading because 'eye movement data reflect moment-to-moment cognitive processes in the various tasks examined' (Rayner, 1998, p. 372). Work has been done on reading both words and pictures. This research sits right on the boundary between what is outside and what

4 For a history of the use of visual technologies in art, see Hockney (2001).

5 The author is an artist who has been co-teaching a course, Visual Persuasion in the Law, for the last six years at Quinnipiac University School of Law and New York School. She wishes to thank Neal Feigenson and Sydney Spiesel for their thoughtful reading and commentary. Any problems are strictly of the author's making.

6 Law, Mind and Brain, a colloquium sponsored by the Law Faculty of University College London and the Gruter Institute for Law and Behavioral Research, Vermont University. 13 and 14 February 2006 in the Law Faculty at UCL.

is inside in perception of the kinds of texts I am concerned with. And for an artist, it is particularly interesting because the data are often expressed pictorially in a way that makes them visually richer than just charts of numeric data or graphs. So with the caveat that this cannot be a comprehensive survey, I invite the reader to think with me about the following questions: is there a difference in how we read these two kinds of texts, words and pictures? If so, is it important? And if it is important, how might it be important for the law, which is so deeply connected to the written word?

Reading has been a very attractive site for cognitive science research – experimenters can give subjects conscious tasks[7] that can be measured and monitored; reading uses the visual system about which we actually know quite a bit of the neurobiology. For this discussion, the single most important fact is that what we see in a construct made out of sensory inputs assembled through neural activity in different parts of the brain.[8] There is no analogue film running in our heads even if it feels that way. Further, because the neural impulses carrying visual information are passed through the amygdala prior to cortical processing, what we see acquires emotional valence before we have any conscious awareness of this information about our feeling. In the broadest context, words and pictures as perceptions both represent just dataflow coming in from outside to be understood by the brain and processed for meaning. As kinds of text, though, they are very different from each other.

Perceptual psychologist Rudolph Arnheim addresses the problem directly. A picture is a framed (as in set off, set aside, set out) embodied image expressed in visual terms. 'Images come at any level of abstractness. However, even the most abstract among them must meet one condition. They must be structurally similar (isomorphic) to the pertinent features of the situations for which the thinking shall be valid' (Arnheim, 1971, p. 227). Intuitive cognition, according to Arnheim, 'takes place in a perceptual field of freely interacting forces' (p. 233).[9] Pictures are like that. Words, when set down, are made up of marks that, compared with pictures, have much less sensual appeal[10] with only conventional relationships to the perceptual/conceptual fields to which they refer. They are a vehicle of:

> intellectual thinking [that] strings perceptual concepts in linear succession. Caught in a four-dimensional world of sequence and spatial simultaneity, the mind operates, on the one hand intuitively by apprehending the products of

7 This is not to say that there are no unconscious elements in play, only that participation in the experiments involves subjects in doing tasks chosen by the experimenters.

8 For general description, see Hoffman (1998). For a general description of neurobiology as it underlies vision, see Smith Churchland (2002). For neurobiological debate on mental imagery, see Plyshyn (2006) and Kosslyn (1994).

9 While Arnheim does not make this clear in the passage, presumably intuitive cognition as a mode of thinking independent of perception would have similar features.

10 See Elkins (1999).

> freely interacting field forces; on the other hand, it cuts one-dimensional paths through the spatial landscape intellectually. Intellectual thinking dismantles the simultaneity of spatial structure. It also transforms all linear relations into one-dimensional successions – the sort of event we represent by an arrow (Arnheim, 1971, p. 246).

Are these distinctions of Arnheim's (which describe two kinds of text and two kinds of mental operations that cross each other) echoed in the eye movement research on reading?

Our eyes are continually in motion. Setting aside the small oscillations they make, reading involves two relatively deliberate (because arising from cortical activity) acts: saccade and fixation. When eyes fixate, they align the fovea, the area of clearest focus, highest resolution, on some element in the external world, take in information and move to another site to take in more. The saccade is the movement that occurs when the eye is looking for a new point of fixation. This movement both seeks the next focus and gives more processing time for the data already perceived. Seeing is:

> actually impaired during the saccadic trajectory. The saccade is probably the most rapid somatic movement that any muscle system in the body can produce. For example, a 40 (degree character) human saccade takes about 100 msec to execute whereas a 40 (degree) flexion of the forearm would require more than 300 msec. Unlike an arm movement, however, the saccade is said to be ballistic in nature, so that, once begun, its velocity or goal cannot be modified (Fuchs, 1976, p.39).[11]

These fixations and movements occur in normal visual perception. And they are a necessary part of the visual system:

> By moving the eye so that small parts of a scene can be sensed with greater resolution, body resources can be used efficiently. If an entire scene were viewed in high resolution, the diameter of the optic nerve would need to be larger than the diameter of the eyeball itself. Subsequent processing of such a high-resolution image would require a brain many times larger than its current size.[12]

We do not notice any impairment in our seeing as our eyes move (assuming normal vision); the visual field is uninterrupted by blurring within our visual angle.

---

11 Apparently newer technology has permitted more refined measurements of the velocity: see http://www. Inma.ucl.ac.be/EYELAB/neurophysio/perception_action/saccades.html, accessed 6 February 2006.

12 http://en.wikipedia.org/wiki/Saccades. Note also that this article gives still different numbers for velocity and duration.

The perceptual task in reading either words or pictures involves fixating on some part of the object of perception and moving our fixations around the visual field of the text under examination. If it is a text made up of words, we get a sense of the form of the whole (whether phrase, sentence, entire work) only when we have completed our reading. If the text is a picture, we can grasp the form of the whole but only through time do we discover the relationship of the parts to the whole that we perceived at the start. If it is a verbal text, we find 'space' (its final form as a work) within the time; if it is a picture, we find time (by expending it) in the space. In the case of reading words, we read from word to word or from groups of words to groups of words, even if we are skimming and jumping around. We must keep our fovea (the part of the retina with the highest resolution perceptually speaking) on the words of the text we are reading and move it with a set of rhythms that help us to decode what we are reading. 'Saccades are directed to definite places in the peripheral vision, and are not merely sent off for some excursion whose extent is determined by internal factors, regardless of what awaits the eye at the end of the saccade' (Hochberg, 1976, p. 410). Simply put, the peripheral vision works to orient the eye for the next fixation. 'When readers make two fixations (think when the eye tries again to get useful information) on a word, in the vast majority of cases, an initial fixation on a word is followed by a rightward movement within the word. By far the most frequent pattern is to fixate near the beginning of a word followed by a fixation near the end of the word' (Rayner, 1998, p. 387). That rightward movement that we readers of English (and other Western languages) know so well constitutes a kind of constraint of the visual field that maximizes efficiency as we move forward in the text.

When we look at a picture, 'reading' does not seem to take any particular effort at the level of perception because visual texts, pictures, are just there – because of those isomorphic relationships to the subject of representation, they may seem not to need further decoding, although, in fact, that is far from the case. Pictures are seemingly automatically parsed right along with our visual perception of the world, naturalized. But this can lead us to error because if we simply identify the picture with its subject matter, we will miss a lot of the meaning. Pictures do not have a syntax (in spite of our regular colloquial use of terms like 'the language of art' or 'pictorial grammar') and so they can be entered at any place in the visual field and that sense of constraint in reading verbal text is absent – when we go back for more we don't have to move right. That said, makers of pictures may go to some lengths to make some elements particularly important visually but there is no way to guarantee a sequence of experience. Pictures are in the first instance spatial constructions and therefore we can see a gestalt at the beginning. They take time to read, time to discover all the relationships between pictorial elements, but they do not act like words in a meaningful aggregation which unfolds through time in syntactical sequences.

Order matters in reading words. Think of the difference in meaning when we take the opening words of *Moby Dick* and reorder them. Melville wrote, 'Call me Ishmael. Some years ago – never mind how long precisely …' introducing the storyteller and suggesting a mythic them – signalled by his statements that precise time is unimportant. Changed to 'Never mind how, call me, Ishmael – precisely – some time ago …' makes it all about the storyteller, less about the story. He comes across as a bit peevish and we are not sure we are willing to spend a lot of pages in his company.

The orderly unfolding of language, experienced in concert with the movement of our eyes as they move across a text, seems to match the unfolding of thought, especially reasoned thinking, to which we give special cultural status. Law privileges reasoned thinking. This is how we may believe such thinking works in our brains, just as we can so easily believe that there is a picture in there because we can see images when we close our eyes. We dream with images; we can remember with images. For both words and images, perception works in a different way than our experience of it:

> Reading sentences, the visual system samples different parts of sentences at different times, but the perceiver does not necessarily run the sentence parts together in the mind in correspondence to the order in which they are sampled. To do so, the brain must tag samples with respect to their location, both in pictures and in sentences, mapping temporal order onto structural locations. Hence neither the perception nor the memory of what is perceived can be the result of a straightforward listing or recording of samples (Kolers, 1976, p. 390).

Eye movement research itself shows us the complexity of the problem, both in issues of experimental design and in the content of the data displays in the published reports. What do the pictures from eye movement research tell us? Guy T. Buswell's[13] eye movement research in the 1920s and 1930s used lights, mirrors, cameras and movie film to track viewers' fixations on various kinds of texts. There has, of course, been an enormous change since then in instrumentation for recording and synthesizing eye movement data, but those initial studies are still found to be useful and quoted in more recent work. All we see in Buswell's data reports on reading words are sentences with vertical lines drawn through the line of text, perpendicular to it, almost like marking beats in a musical score. There are small numbers that indicate the length of the fixation expressed in units of thirtieths of a second. That figure matches the speed of the film moving through the camera but does not indicate the length of a single fixation. Saccades are measured by their amplitude and can vary in length. Microsaccades, which might be analogized to the screen saver on your computer monitor, oscillate back and forth at a rate of about 60 per second and 'are completely imperceptible under normal circumstances. They serve to refresh the image being case onto the rod cells and cone cells at the back of the eye. Without microsaccades, staring fixedly at something would cause the vision to cease after a few seconds since rods and cones only respond to

13 Readers interested in seeing this data on reading words visualized can find some of it reproduced in Kolers (1976) and Buswell (1935).

a change in luminance' (Wikipedia). Using the spaces between the fixations and from the size of these intervals we can infer from space an idea of time without even reading the numeric labels, which increases the sense of union between the moving eye and the subject of its gaze.

But there is a gap between this representation and what we know about the cognitive actions happening inside the brain. We cannot infer from these pictures the brain tagging and slotting in elements giving a temporal order to the spatial locations referenced above. The data sets suggest an indexical relationship between mark and fixation so that we can even imagine that we have direct access to the data itself, as if the eyes made the marks which, of course, they did not. This sort of indexical relationship, or seeming to be one, underlies the argumentative power of forensic evidence and eyewitness identifications. These indexical relationships can seem to be unarguable although we know that this is not the case.

One of the most remarkable aspects of these data-set pictures is that we can immediately see, if not understand the reasons for, the comparative ease with which readers of differing skills read written text. Good readers have an evenly spaced 'stroke' of fixation and proceed through the text (as indicated by the vertical lines standing for fixation points) with the regular rhythm of a great swimmer – fixation, saccade, fixation, saccade. Fixations are shorter, saccades are longer. (Remember that the time of the saccade permits the brain to process some of the perceptual image.) In contrast, poor readers go back to resample the stimulus so repeatedly that they have little processing time. Their data sets have thickets of vertical lines, a very fast beat, maybe even an anxious one. If we think common-sensically that bright people have more brain power at their disposal, we might imagine that they put more cells to the task. These pictures show something different than just massive computational power: skill in this context translates into low effort, fewer mental resources required to accomplish the task.

Buswell's research enterprise was to show empirically that reading was a cognitive activity and not just 'implicit speech'. It is noteworthy that he welcomed into his experimental design a lot of cognitive activity that he did not then account for or measure. The exemplar text used in the experiments (see illustrations in Kolers 1976, pp. 376–9) is one that to my reading is loaded with social assumptions:

> Mr. Black was badly hurt. His coloured servant saw that his master has been left to die and carried him to the nearest town. There he hunted until he found a doctor. The young soldier lived. After the war he gave the Negro a little house on his estate. Always on the day of the Battle of King's Mountain a fine dinner was prepared for the old servant. He sat alone at the head of the [the reproduced text ends here].

The caption for the picture reads 'prose of modest difficulty'. In the early twenty-first century this text is hardly neutral prose whether of modest difficulty or not. I wish I had more demographic information on the experimental subject. What social differences were there between the good readers and the poor ones? How did those differences connect with the text in question? Something is left of Buswell's 'picture' – he assumes a simplicity in his experimental system that isn't there based on clear boundaries between the subject, the reader and the text, the object of perception. In fact, we now know that perception itself can be socially mediated and constructed (Berns, 2005). Legal rhetors will need to appreciate how their materials might be socially constructed in entirely different ways depending upon the social context of the finders of fact. Those who view the picture as a simple statement will miss relevant information and be less in control of their messages if not the content of their cases.

Buswell's data maps for pictures are different from those for reading text. They look like the 'join-the-dots' games for children where a figure emerges from a seemingly chaotic field. As in recording his data for reading written words, he places dots for fixations, but with data concerning pictures, he connects the fixations with lines representing saccades and numbers them so that the order of reading the picture can be traced. By numbering the sequence we can follow the reader wandering through the picture and see changes of direction, leaps across space, and so on. These data sets do not reflect rhythms in the same way as the figures for written texts. Because the data is reflected in both dots and lines, and we like to find order in our perceptions, we tend to make figures out of the spaces enclosed by the lines, object-like structures sitting on the field represented by the reproduction on the picture used in testing.[14] Just as our eyes do not shape letters as we read, we do not echo the picture analogically when we read pictures either. Pictures and text may stimulate eye movements but they do not do so analogically, so differences in movements between the kinds of text do not emerge from their visual properties in this way.

What Buswell's research showed is that: (1) there are two patterns of perception of pictures: general scanning and more detailed examination of parts of the picture, and the duration of saccades increases with looking at the picture; (2) there are wide individual differences between subjects as they look (although age is not a significant factor – adults and children are not different as groups); (3) colour and repetitive patterns do not strongly affect patterns of eye movement (colour vision is less a feature of peripheral vision); (4) the directions given 'prior to looking at a picture have a marked influence upon the character of the perception' (Buswell, 1935, pp. 142–44, quote p. 144). (Like all rhetors, lawyers will try to prime their audiences to understand evidence in terms of their case theory. Because pictures are very powerful, they use them increasingly. Buswell's data suggest that lawyers need to be careful, though, to allow enough time for the finders of fact to examine the picture in detail if those details are significant for the case. And even more importantly, the lawyer using pictures needs to remember that what seems obvious to counsel may not seem at all obvious to other viewers and the counsel cannot count on viewers automatically having similar responses. Whether to underscore

14 See Hoffman (1998) for a detailed discussion on how our brains resolve ambiguities in visual perception.

visual meaning verbally or just to allow it to deliver its message directly is a matter of technique; there are benefits to clarifying and there are benefits to allowing the picture to carry meaning that might be difficult to say directly for many reasons. This should be a matter of active choice rather than accidental effect.) Buswell found that he could prime the responses of the experimental subjects by giving them tasks, but this shows up as different patterns of dots and lines. We do not know whether this different reading of the picture entailed different verbal interpretations of the picture as well; Buswell does not seem to have studied or at least reported this. Legal rhetors would do well to give their audiences tasks to prime responses rather than to just tell them an answer.

The 'general scanning' that typified the first encounter with a picture by his experimental subjects did not mean that the fovea passes over all the parts of the picture, as if the eye was like the mechanical scanners we use today. When we look at the mapping of the eye movements for pictures, we can see that the eye did not fixate on all the areas of the picture ever. This shows us that peripheral vision is important as well, otherwise we would see blank spaces of missing data in the picture we are looking at. The mobility of the retinal image occasioned by head 'movements, blinking movements of the eyes, saccades, drift and tremor during fixation on an element of a stationary object ... prevent the formation of an empty field' (Yarbus, 1967). In fact, the brain fills in the missing data.

Yarbus explored further the issue of task and patterns of visual scanning in reading pictures, using an apparatus that attached directly to the eye to keep the retinal image stable. His data sets also record points of fixations and lines representing saccades connecting them recorded on photosensitive paper during the testing session. These recordings look much more art-like, much less formalized in comparison with Buswell's images. Buswell, using film, must have made transcriptions of the data relating the recorded fixations and saccades to the film frame and to the picture that was the challenge text. In carrying out this task, Buswell made his data look very scientific and geometrically neat, measured and ruled. Yarbus's work 30 years later shows data sets that look as if they were made with pen and ink and with an artist's hand. The more an observing subject is interested in something in the picture, the fuzzier and denser the marks become as fixations pile up in the same areas of the picture. Rather than join-the-dots pictures, these look like nets and webs with stuff caught in them. The lines themselves seem to have kinetic energy and occupy the whole picture space in a very different way from Buswell's plots. In fact, they look more like Giacometti drawings than machine prints. When both researchers used pictures that had people in them, whether plotted as fixations and saccades or densities, the faces received much more attention. This should come as no surprise – infants can recognize their own mothers' faces within hours of birth (Eliot, 1999, p. 219; also Sinha, 2005). We must have a propensity to pay attention to faces.

Of the two researchers, Yarbus went more deeply into the question of how patterns of reading pictures altered by task. Taking a famous genre painting by the Russian artist I.E. Repin (1844–1930), *An Unexpected Visitor* (1884), Yarbus tested subjects by first having them freely view the reproduction of the painting, and then gave them various perceptual tasks: from estimating the material circumstances of the family to attributing ages to the persons represented, remembering their clothing, guessing what they were doing earlier in the scene and estimating how long the unexpected visitor had been away from the family. These all could have been loaded questions depending upon the circumstances of the experimental subjects because he is asking about socio-economic status and family relationships. Given his historical period, one of great social unrest, he might have been asking about a visitor who was returning from a forced labour camp. Who knows? But when Yarbus writes about his study, he seems strangely naïve about the issue of meaning when he asserts:

> Records of eye movements shows that the observer's attention is usually held only by certain elements of the picture. As already noted, the study of these elements shows that they give information allowing the meaning of the picture to be obtained. Eye movements reflect the human through processes; so the observer's thought may be followed to some extent from records of eye movements (the thought accompanying the examination of a particular object). It is easy to determine from those records which elements attract the observer's eye (and, consequently, his thought) in what order, and how often (Yarbus, 1967, p. 190)

'The meaning …' Only one? Is it so clear what it might be? How can we know what the observer's *thought* is from this data? Even when we could see the rapid fixations in the crowding lines of Buswell's recordings of poor readers, we certainly could not know the thought of the reader. Do some elements of pictures attract because they are inherently more interesting or because they are harder to parse? Do they attract because they are *visually* interesting or because their content is loaded? We do not know this from the data. Lacking syntax, how would knowing the order of the eye's inspection tell us about the viewer's thoughts? Is Yarbus not insisting on a transparency of consciousness that is unwarranted given what we know about the brain and how many different areas of the brain contribute to any assessment of meaning? (Admittedly, cognitive science has progressed a lot since Yarbus published, but Arnheim was a contemporary of his for all practical purposes.) Some of his naïve realism about the picture might well be attributed to the effects of his experimental situation. Yarbus was, after all, defining the tasks for his experimental subjects, so when he saw the readouts he could legitimately observe close correlations between task and pattern of reading without going further into meaning. Perhaps he fell into this trap, too, because he had so internalized his experimental methodology that it felt completely naturalized and, being visual, 'out there' in the world and less 'in there' in how own conceptions. Buswell was interested in the formal properties of the visual texts he used in studying reading of pictures but did not address the issue of content, so both researchers failed to take into consideration the impact of the uptake of content on the uptake of form.

Buswell was thinking like a formalist and Yarbus more sociologically, but neither fully 'saw' the material they were working with. Likewise, counsel using pictures can fall into this trap of assuming a simple communicative situation and overlook problems of extra content arising from the pictorial nature of visual materials. Before strategy can be deployed using visual materials for either direct evidence or documentation, demonstrative evidence or for argument, the lawyer must start by seeing what is there, including making the effort to imagine how other viewers might see the same materials.

Do these eye movement studies and their data sets in any way confirm Arnheim's proposition about intuitive cognition and intellectual cognition (his terms for the visual and the verbal)? I think that, as representations, they do, in fact, show linear rhythms moving across a line of text (Arnheim's intellectual cognition) and fields of forces explored in complex ways (Arnheim's intuitive cognition) displayed in an empirical system. Further, studying subjects deliberately reading, means that they are engaged in a process that is consciously undertaken, whatever unconscious elements are also present. The researchers may not have been looking at meaning in terms of the subject matter but that does not mean it was not present for the people who participated as subjects.

When Buswell and Yarbus present composite data from multiple test subjects, we can see in their pictures of this data both a statistical person and individual variations, e.g., some readers wandered further around the picture space; more collect key features of the picture. Whether we view the statistical person as providing a baseline for understanding the individual depends, in part, on how we conceptualize individual psychology and the role of outliers, people who do not fall in the centre of the sample. There is intriguing eye movement work done with a class of individuals who as a group are outliers: autistic persons. Instead of giving tasks to subjects, a group of researchers, building on research about face perception in infants and children, were able to show that a group of autistic individuals in the test group demonstrated abnormal patterns of social visual pursuit (Klin et al., 2001). The researchers recorded eye movements while the subjects watched short clips from the film *Who's Afraid of Virginia Woolf?*, a dramatic production with highly charged social interactions among four characters. Autistic viewers focused on the chin and mouth areas while the control group focused on the eyebrows of speakers. Just as social context can influence perception so can individual differences.

Social context; individual difference – these are terms that suggest 'frames of reference' which certainly are relevant. In the two kinds of texts broadly considered – word texts and visual texts/pictures – visual framing needs first to be understood in terms of a different level of analysis. This issue appears in neither Buswell nor Yarbus. Looking at their data sets, it is as if the viewers are plunged into the visual space without any particular cues to the framing edge of the images they are viewing. This may be a result, in part, of the experimental setting, the constraints of the apparatus on the head and eyes, the constraint of the visual field (was anything beyond the picture itself visible to the subject of the test?), the instructions of the experimenter, all those elements of the conditions of the testing situation that Latour would call 'subtle and multiple *trans*formations' in the 'transfers of *in*formation' (Latour, 1999, p. 298). The information gained in these studies is mediated by the experimental system and is part of the data; it is not a neutral player in this game.

The framing edge of the visual representation (and here I make space for sculpture as well as two-dimensional visual text) both marks the boundary between the representation and the real context in which it appears, what is inside the picture and outside it, and it changes all the visual dynamics within. The frame conditions what seems close and what far away, what is large and what is small; it can imply action in the field and whether it feels open or tight, crowded or empty. The frame contributes to the perceptual experience of everything within its field.

Written words, or printed words, are remarkably robust as the conditions of representation change. I could sit and write this text in long hand on a yellow pad and it would look very different. It would also signal things about me that might be interpreted very differently by other people. Yellow pad as 'legal', yellow pad as 'draft', yellow pad as 'professional' but the words themselves, assuming a readable handwriting, would still fall in the same order, still address the sequential flow of thought being represented by me as I write; they would in themselves still essentially add up to the same meaning. I do not mean to diminish the importance of graphic design in signalling all those associated values, but only to observe that the perceptual qualities of words are more stable than the perceptual qualities of pictures. We know from the words themselves where the text stops.

One of the more fascinating studies of reading has to do with reading music (Goolsby, 1994a, 1994b). It was found that musicians read no more than eight notes ahead of their hand and that they often fixated on the blank spaces on the musical score. We experience the silences within the score as meaningful when we hear the music. Reading research has shown that spaces are important to text as well.[15] When spaces are inserted into long compound nouns in German (Inhoff et al., 1996) or when spaces are put between characters in Thai which do not traditionally have spaces between characters, the spaces greatly enhance the speed of reading when they are not semantically meaningful (Kohsom and Gobet, 1997). In pictures, the equivalent to musical silences lies in the spaces between elements but which are shaped by them; we call them negative spaces. Negative spaces are 'real' like negative numbers. They are present and the dialogue between volume and void, shape as full and shape as empty, is crucial to the play of picturing. We use shape cues to distinguish letters, punctuations, etc. but most often the contribution of the empty space between these elements does not contribute to the content in any strong way except in certain art forms.

At the beginning I asked: is there a difference in how we read these two kinds of text, words and pictures? Research answers yes. If so, is it important? Yes, because

15 Readers of poetry will recognize some similarities with reading music. This discussion is about perception and not about the arts *per se*.

it points to different cognitive functions, different aspects of mind. Building a thought piece by piece through words can facilitate reasoned thinking, clarified thought, can enable us to relate elements of our experience to many different kinds of qualities rather like money allows us to relate extremely disparate things on the basis of value. When we 'see' a picture, we can grasp the simultaneous presence of many disparate things within a common frame, harmonized through composition but allowed to retain a visible connection to the things to which they refer. This is the groundwork for the final question: how might it be important for the law which is so deeply connected to the written word?

We regard reading books as an essential skill for navigating effectively in our culture; it represents an achievement. Reading words requires deliberate education. Children do not necessarily learn to read books just because they are lying around, whereas they can tell us about a picture they see. We seem not to have to learn to read pictures, especially photographs (and photography and the optical attitude it represents dominate our exposure to pictures now), and/or culture has not counted this as an achievement if we do. Further, because of the long association of pictures being used as a means to communicate with those who cannot read words, there are without a doubt long-term social class biases as well.

We think of reading (and its partner, writing) as the essential literacy that has made advanced culture possible. The earliest artefacts of human representation go back to marked bones from 35,000–20,000 BCE, believed to represent numbers of some kind; European cave paintings can be dated to 20,000 BCE. It took more than 15,000 years to arrive at Sumerian writing, 3200–3100 BCE (Ifrah, 2001, pp. 9–10). Writing, of course, fixed spoken language in a form that made it transmissible across distance and through time – the reader did not have to be present, or even alive, at the time the writer (as speaker) composed the words. Setting aside the glories of literature and private writing, surviving very early written texts were mostly about bookkeeping and victories in war, treaties and trade. Writing's potential for permanence allowed for the creation of public records of all kinds, which had a number of effects: the growth of bureaucratic means of administration, the possibility of producing historical accounts, uniform communications from leaders to subjects. By separating 'reader and author … [it created] the possibility of greater impersonality and perhaps rationality in human affairs' (Finnegan, 1988, p. 18). In short, the fundamentals were present for the development of law.

Peter Goodrich, in working on a psychoanalytical jurisprudence, sees in the history of the development of English law a conscious wall built against images, essentially shutting itself off from pictures:

> [The] Reformation was concerned overwhelmingly with the status, the power, and the perils, of images. [This was a period when the destruction of both two and three dimensional images, particularly religious images, was a tool of warfare.] Within what was still in practice a dual polity, a civil and an ecclesiastical state, all aspects of public life were affected by the changing definition and role of

> images. In the wake of printing, the text was to replace the image as the principal form of communication of power (Goodrich, 1999, p. 101).

The suppression of imagery that Goodrich is writing about has a kind of logic to it, forcing people, consciously or not, to become readers and writers. Pictures, to become part of a conversation between people, must be translated into words. Words themselves are a different kind of communicative currency because they are directly a medium of social exchange. Following Arnheim's reasoning, words, having conventional and not isomorphic relationships to the things to which they refer, make it possible to stabilize social meanings and therefore the law more easily as well as to create and examine ideas independent of the constraints of perception. The law depends upon the written text for the transmission of its own culture of cases and precedents through time and through the extensive bodies of writing that have developed through the institution of the legal academy. It has been above all the creature of the written word – and the spoken word in legal performance.

As I write, the performance of the law increasingly involves pictures, whether as attachments to legal documents or as evidence and argument presented in negotiations or at trial. Every kind of picture might be in play – from graphic displays of numeric data to photographs of many kinds; flow charts and organizational charts to cartoons; animations to video recreations; virtual reality views to multi-media combinations. Each picture comes with the rhetoric of its genre and materials, and the associations that are attached to those. For instance, in the Soham case in England (the trial of a school caretaker for the murder of two young girls), jurors in England were given a disk containing pictures of the evidence that they could take into their jury room for deliberations; they took a disk that was, through its design conventions, alluding to a video game (Sherwin, 2006). Likewise, participants in the Bloody Sunday Tribunal (Whelan, 2005) have used virtual reality views of the sites of the terrible events so that paths and points of view could be identified through computer-animated reconstructions of the sites. The multi-media disk used in the Michael Skakel prosecution in the US allowed the prosecution's final argument to draw upon sound recordings, their transcripts, and pictorial files in a manner that was one media step short of being a video (Carney and Feigenson, 2004). Finally, courtroom presentation software like Trial Director and Sanction 11[16] present differing kinds of evidence in simultaneous display in multiple windows, like our desktop computer monitors – so that it is possible to play clips from a video deposition while showing the written transcript, among many possibilities. Legal storytelling deploying these resources will refer to cinematic conventions or to the narratives of video games, especially if counsel

---

16 For screen shorts of the capacities of this software see: http://www.indatacorp.com/software/trialdirector.asp? PageID=3; http://www.sanction.com/software/?content=screenshots&title=Screenshots%2oof%20Sanction. The homepage also can direct the reader to demonstrate videos.

chooses to demonstrate a number of logical paths with the aim of showing what they believe to be the true one according to the evidence. The legal rhetor will have to decide what meaning is to be carried by pictures, what by words and be able to move fluidly between them.

These new ways of presenting evidence and legal argument, of constructing legal narratives, are possible because of the digital revolution that has put into the hands of consumers as well as professionals the tools of digital imaging. It is easy to make digital pictures, to disseminate them – not just still pictures but video and audio files as well. Not just the professionals understand how this is done; juries and others involved in the legal decision-making process understand these tools too. Audiences have changed. What is happening in the courtroom and across negotiating tables is a contextually specific instance of a much larger social envelope where political dialogue is carried out as a battle of mass mediated images as well as a matter of barbs and slogans.

Law is now practised on the screens of our televisions and movies in America, so that law stories can be seen almost 24 hours a day.[17] Real lawyers and clients may well wind up on those screens themselves, and the growth of litigation public relations as a profession is testament to the need of lawyers to think about the media frame of their cases as well. Lawyers, like many people, have tended to believe that persuasion involves changing people's beliefs about a question. Recent work in political science shows how framing used by a communication source constructs and defines a social or political issue for its audience. 'Messages may change attitudes by adding information to an individual's stockpile of considerations about the issue (belief change), by making particular considerations temporarily more accessible (priming), or by altering the weight of particular considerations (framing)' (Nelson, Oxley and Clawson, 1997, p. 221). Their study showed that framing issues can activate existing beliefs and cognitions without appearing overtly to persuade. The frames created by media can become absolutely naturalized and therefore invisible to most. The media now are dominantly visual and lawyers are in these pictures.

In this changed media environment, the law as an epistemology dominated by the idea of words as carriers of the most important legal meaning must find a way to integrate and accommodate what is happening – the invasion of the visual. It must integrate the need for some new understanding about the cognitive effects of this change. People expect to be able to act on information, to put it together for themselves. They expect to see the evidence presented in a way that they can understand. I have been ranging widely – from a masterwork of painting to research on eye movements as clues to cognitive function; the history of writing, from old media to new; to the law as a discipline of words. It is a truism to say that the law is reactive. It looks to analogy and distinction to understand new cases in terms of old; it depends upon long chains of decision-making to bind the world

17 See Sherwin (2000).

together through its words. This dramatic shift of the visual[18] in the law represents a moment of change when it is being forcibly challenged to give up some old habits and acquire some new ones.

Deeply embedded in our Western tradition is the metaphor that the person who *sees* is the person who knows. This is a verbal metaphor (the seeing in this sense is happening inside a person's head where a viewer can only find traces in facial expression, if that); it transfers the act of seeing to insight, to actions of the mind (Lakoff and Johnson, 1999, p. 393) and to thought as language. 'Thought has the properties of a language. Thought is external and public. The structure of thought is accurately representable as a linear sequence of written symbols of the sort that constitute a written language. Every thought is expressible in language' (Lakoff and Johnson, 1999, p. 546). Above I discussed the eye movement research carried out by Buswell and Yarbus, both for the insight it provides for those interested in the uptake of pictures, currently of great relevance to legal practitioners, and because it represents also an example of serious scholars being bound by their frames of reference and missing some potentially important questions relevant to their work. To be sure, no one can see everything. At the same time, it is extremely important to try to find the places where framing edges block our views and to ask questions. This is especially true for the law right now. The problems that the law addresses have real world consequences; people's lives are affected and as a civilization of the law, our fundamental social order may be at stake – certainly it is if citizens cease to find the law a credible means of solving conflict.

Pictures, because of their system of reference, have bodies – they are made of materials or, if made of pixels, they still reference other things we can see. By and large we confront the 'person to person' parallel to our eyes. If we think of them as not language and therefore not thinking, we will be blinded to the ways in which they do speak:

> Law (perhaps not unlike other disciplines or practices aspiring to rationality) has tended to identify its rationality (and hence its virtue) with texts as opposed to images, with reading words as opposed to "reading" pictures, to the point that it is often thought that reading words and thinking in words is the only kind of thinking there is – thus creating a real problem when digitization speeds up the transformation of our worlds into increasingly image-dominated ones.[19]

To give a sense of scale for the rapidity of this change:

> Now if a generation is about 20 years, from cave drawings to writing is 1,275 generations; writing to the printing press is 250 generations; from the printing press to photography is 19 generations; from photography to desktop computing

18 See Spiesel, Feigenson and Sherwin (2005). Also, see Sherwin, Feigenson and Spiesel (2006).

19 Neal Feigenson, personal communication, 6 April 2006.

> is 7 generations; and from desktop computing to the Web is less than 1/2 of one generation (Lester, 1996).

It is not surprising that we are just beginning to understand what is happening.

It is ironic that just as we humans managed to build thinking machines that seem to be the ultimate Cartesian expression of mind without body, these same machines have brought us full circle to confront the return of the repressed. The computers that we have built are now changing the world, not just because we can more easily accomplish tasks that would otherwise be impossible due to the vastness of the computations they require, but because we have built a global cultural space of profound implications, a culture of representation – cyberspace – that is itself governed by the rule of images. 'The screen is the site of the image, and the logic of the image dominates the semiotic organization of the screen' (Kress, 2003, p. 65), whether it is showing us words or showing us pictures or playing our music accompanied by visual 'skins' of our choosing. Our encounters with both words and pictures are increasingly happening on the screen and we can no longer claim that words are the only way we speak to one another, the only containers for our ideas, the only generators of real thinking. While the practice of law has always used technologies available to it, the discipline of law has not always paid attention to the implications of their use. This neglect can no longer be tolerated because of the extent and depth of the changes involved.

Just as a frame (thought of as the border and not just the decorative edge of a container for a picture) delimits the perimeter of a visual text, on the computer screen we are reading words and pictures, often together sharing frames. Certainly they share the larger frame of the monitor itself. This presents new reading tasks that involve moving back and forth between words and pictures that qualify and amplify each other. These hybrids are rather like graphic novels, 'demanding and rewarding mental flexibility and nervous stamina. Consuming them – toggling for hours between the incommensurable functions of reading and looking – is taxing' (Schjeldahl, 2005). We know that words and pictures call for different reading behaviours. It has been shown that 'the richer representations of information in pictures require extended encoding durations relative to the encoding of information from text' (Underwood et al., 2004, p. 180) which means, when faced with a multi-media display, there are conflicting demands on our cognitive skills. Multimodality may have its virtues (Kress, 2003) – there are several channels that allow people to use the favoured learning mode – but if not used carefully, legal rhetors may find their audiences becoming confused or less attentive. We have all had the experience of trying to decide whether to listen to a speaker or to read the verbally packed PowerPoint slides, knowing that a choice has to be made or we will not get anything at all out of the presentation. Further, to take full advantage of the powers of multimedia, legal rhetors are going to have to give up full control over their messages by allowing meanings to be filled in by their audiences. If they welcome the participation of their audience they will involve them more powerfully in the meaning-making process but they will have to embrace showing and not just telling. What this means is that they are going to have to get very smart about what is inside the frame of the visual text they are dealing with. The problem is not about recognizing what the picture depicts; it is to see what it says to the lawyer who must then be able to imagine what it might say to people different from themselves. We must not assume a transparency that just is not there, just as we cannot assume that the picture we have in our heads is the movie in our minds. Cognitive science can help by assisting our view inward, which will then affect our view outward.

There is ample evidence that we process unconsciously, associatively, and analogically, as well as consciously solve problems. When we are engaged in thinking about something in a goal-oriented manner, we are bound more closely to the parameters of our window of attention – and therefore apt not to see changes in the field, like missing the card pass in sleight-of-hand magic tricks. Think of the empirical scientists, Buswell and Yarbus, thinking so clearly about how to study fixations and saccades in reading while ignoring other, possibly crucially relevant, elements in the systems they set up. We can be inattentionally blind, and we can be made that way by objects, people, events in the perceptual field that are compelling. Our perceptions can be primed by previous experience (a time-based phenomenon) and anchored in unconscious ways (a spatial metaphor for connection that is more a matter of being?).

From the serial and parallel information processing that must underlie our vision and cognitive capacities inside our heads to the ways we conceive of the world outside (Shanahan and Baars, 2005), time and space are fundamental categories of our experience that are also the basis of one of the fundamental contrasts between the kinds of texts that I have been discussing. We need the resources of both; we need to be able to move between the freely interacting fields of forces and the conceptual linear strings (to use Arnheim's words) defining texts that are picture and those made of words. I am suggesting that the need to communicate and to persuade in this new world can represent an opportunity and a gift and not just a burden. I believe that this is so because in becoming sensitive to a cognitive mode where dissimilar things are brought into relationship within a frame without having to win or lose – what happens in pictures – the discipline of the law may find new ways to look both inward and outward, to see more with wisdom. Understanding pictures requires understanding perception; it means having the double vision on the world reflected in Velasquez's eyes.

References

ARNHEIM, Rudolph (1971) *Visual Thinking*. Berkeley, Los Angeles, London: University of California Press.

BERNS, Gregory S. et al. (2005) 'Neurobiological Correlates of Social Conformity and Independence During Mental Rotation', *Biological Psychiatry* 58: 245–53.

BUSWELL, Guy T. (1935) *How People Look at Pictures.* University of Chicago Press.

CARNEY, Brian and FEIGENSON, Neal (2004) 'Visual Persuasion in the Skakel Trial: Enhancing Advocacy through Interactive Multimedia Presentations', *Criminal Justice* 19(1): 22–35.

ELIOT, Lise (1999) *What's Going On in There? How the Brain and Mind Develop in the First Five Years of Life.* New York: Bantam Books.

ELKINS, James (1999) *The Domain of Images*, Ithaca, NY: Cornell University Press.

FINNEGAN, Ruth H. (1988) *Literacy and Oralit: Studies in the Technology of Communications.* Oxford: Blackwell.

FUCHS, Albert F. (1976) 'The Neurophysiology of Saccades' in Richard A. Monty and John W. Senders (eds) *Eyemovements and Psychological Processes.* Hillsboro, NJ: Lawrence Erlbaum Associates (publishers), New York: John Wiley (distributors).

GOODRICH, Peter (1999) 'The Iconography of Nothing, Blank Spaces and the Representation of Law in Edward VI and the Pipe' in Costas Douzinas and Lynda Nead *Law and the Image.* Chicago, IL: University of Chicago Press, pp. 89–114.

GOOLSBY, T.W. (1994a) 'Eye Movement in Music Reading: Effects of Reading Ability, Notational Complexity, and Encounters', *Music Perception* 12: 77–96.

GOOLSBY, T.W. (1994b) 'Profiles of Processing: Eye Movements During Sight Reading', *Music Perception* 12: 97–123.

HOCHBERG, Julian (1976) 'Toward a Speech-Plan Eye-Movement Model of Reading' in Monty, Richard A. and John W. Senders *Eye Movements and Psychological Processes.* Hillsboro, NJ: Lawrence Erlbaum Associates (publishers), New York: John Wiley (distributors), pp. 397–416.

HOCKNEY, David (2001) *Secret Knowledge, Rediscovering the Lost Techniques of the Old Masters.* New York: Viking Studio.

HOFFMAN, Douglas D. (1998) *Visual Intelligence, How We Create What We See.* New York: W.W. Norton & Company.

http://www.indatacorp.com/software/trialdirector.asp?Page ID=3.

http://www.sanction.com/software/?content=screenshot&title=Screenshot%2oof %Sanction.

http://viscog.beckman.uiuc.edu?djs_lab/demos.htm.

IFRAH, Georges (2001) *The Universal History of Computing from the Abacus to the Quantum Computer.* New York: John Wiley.

INHOFF, A.W., RADACH, R. and HELLER, D. (1996) 'Morphological Processes During Word Recognition', *Abstracts of the Psychonomic Society* I: 54.

KLIN, Ami, et al. (2001) 'Visual Fixation Patterns During viewing of Naturalistic Social Situations as Predictors of Social Competence in Individuals with Autism', *Archives of General Psychiatry* 59: 809–16.

KOLERS, Paul A. (1976) 'Buswell's Discoveries' in Richard A. Monty and John W. Senders *Eye Movements and Psychological Processes*. Hillsboro, NJ: Lawrence Erlbaum Associates (publishers), New York: John Wiley (distributors), pp. 373–95.

KOHSOM, C. and Gobet, E (1997) 'Adding Spaces to Thai and English: Effects on Reading', *Proceedings of the Cognitive Science Society* 19: 388–93.

KOSSLYN, Stephen M. (1994) *Image and Brain: The Resolution of the Imagery Debate*. Cambridge, MA: MIT Press.

KRESS, Gunther (2003) *Literacy in the New Media Age*. London: Routledge.

LAKOFF, George and JOHNSON, Mark (1999) *Philosophy in the Flesh: The Embodied Mind and Its Challenge to Western Thought*. New York: Basic Books.

LATOUR, Bruno (1999) *Pandora's Hope: Essays on the Reality of Science Studies*. Cambridge, MA: London: Harvard University Press.

LESTER, Paul Martin (1996) 'Digital Hegemony: The Clash Between Words and Pictures' at http://commfaculty.fullerton.edu/lester/writings/murspeech.html (last accessed 6 March 2006).

MACK, Arien and ROCK, Irvin (1998) *Inattentional Blindness*. Cambridge MA: MIT Press.

MNOOKIN, Jennifer (1998) 'The Image of Truth: Photographic Evidence and the Power of Analogy', *Yale Journal of Law and the Humanities* 10(1): 17.

MONTY, Richard A. and SENDERS, John W. (1976) *Eye Movements and Psychological Processes*. Hillsboro, New Jersey: Lawrence Erlbaum Associates.

NELSON, Thomas E., OXLEY, Zoe M. and CLAWSON, Rosalee A. (1997) 'Toward A Psychology of Framing Effects', *Political Behavior* 19(3).

PINKER, Steven (2002) *The Blank Slate, The Modern Denial of Human Nature*. New York: Viking Books.

PLYSHYN, Zenon W. (2006) *Seeing and Visualizing, It's Not What You Think*, Cambridge, MA: MIT Press.

RAYNER, Keith (1998) 'Eye Movements in Reading and Information Processing: 20 Years of Research', *Psychological Bulletin* 124: 372–422.

SCHJELDAHL, Peter (2005) 'Words and Pictures, Graphic Novels Come of Age', *The New Yorker*, 17 October 2005, available at http://www.newyorker.com/critics/content/articles/051017crbo_bookslist.

SHERWIN, Richard K. (2000) *When The Law Goes Pop*. Chicago: University of Chicago Press.

SHERWIN, Richard K. (2006) 'Visual Literacy in Action: Law in the Age of Images' in James Elkins *Visual Literacy*. New York: Routledge.

SHERWIN, Richard K., FEIGENSON, Neal and SPIESEL, Christina (2006) 'Law in the Digital Age: How Visual Communication Technologies are Transforming the Practice, Theory, and Teaching of Law', *Boston University Journal of Science and Technology Law* 12.

SINHA, Pawan et al. (2005) 'Face Recognition by Humans: 20 Results all Computer Vision Researchers Should Know About', Department of Brain and Cognitive Sciences Massachusetts Institute of Technology Cambridge, MA, 2005: http://web.mit.edu/bcs/sinha/papers/20Results_2005.pdf (last accessed 6 February 2006).

SMITH CHURCHLAND, Patricia (2002) *Brain-Wise, Studies in Neurophilosophy*. Cambridge, MA: MIT Press.

SPIESEL, Christina (2006) 'A Las Meninas for the Law' in Anne Wagner and William Penzak (eds) *Images in Law*. London: Ashgate.

SPIESEL, Christina, FEIGENSON, Neal and SHERWIN, Richard (2005) 'Law in the Age of Images' in T. Summerfield, F.S.B. Banegas and A. Wagner (eds) *Contemporary Issues of the Semiotics of Law, Cultural and Symbolic Analyses of Law in a Global Context (Onati International Series in Law and Society)*. Portland, OR: Hart Publishing.

UNDERWOOD, Geoffrey et al. (2004) 'Inspecting Pictures for Information To Verify a Sentence: Eye Movements in General Encoding and In Focused Search', *Quarterly Journal of Experimental Psychology* 57A(1), 165–82.

VELAZQUEZ, Diego (1656) *Las Meninas,* Madrid: Museo del Prado.

WHELAN, Darius (2005) 'The Bloody Sunday Tribunal', exhibit at First International Conference on Visual Literacy, Cork, Ireland 14015 April.

www.wikipedia.org.

YARBUS, Alfred L. (1967) 'Eye Movements During Perception of Complex Objects' in L.A. Riggs (ed.) *Eye Movements and Vision*. New York: Plenum Press, ch. VII, pp. 171–96.

Index

FSC
www.fsc.org
MIX
Papier | Fördert
gute Waldnutzung
FSC® C083411

Kolibri 360 GmbH
Ferdinand-Jühlke-Straße 7
99095 Erfurt, Deutschland
produktsicherheit@kolibri360.de